Annotated Bibliography of the Published Writings of W.E.B. Du Bois

Annotated Bibliography of the Published Writings of W.E.B. Du Bois

HERBERT APTHEKER

KRAUS-THOMSON ORGANIZATION LIMITED, MILLWOOD, N.Y.
1973

Copyright, 1973, by Herbert Aptheker
  all rights reserved
First Printing 1973

Introduction copyright, 1973 by Herbert Aptheker

Library of Congress Cataloging in Publication Data

Aptheker, Herbert, 1915–
  Annotated bibliography of the writings of W. E. B.
Du Bois.

  1. Du Bois; William Edward Burghardt, 1868–
1963—Bibliography.   I. Title.
Z8244.9.A65   016.30124'2'0924   73–13805

Printed in the United States of America

TABLE OF CONTENTS

INTRODUCTION

In 1946 the late Dr. William Edward Burghardt Du Bois asked this writer to undertake the editing of his published and unpublished writings, including, in the latter case, his correspondence. With some interruptions, this effort has been going forward ever since that period. The unpublished material is now in process of production through the efforts of the University of Massachusetts Press; the Kraus-Thomson Organization has undertaken to issue in 40 volumes a fully edited compilation of Du Bois' published work.

The present volume, as part of the effort to produce a definitive edition of the Du Bois heritage, is an annotated bibliography of all his published writings. Du Bois lived for 95 years, and he published for 80 of those years. His writings were in print by the time he was fifteen years old, in 1883, and they continued to pour forth until shortly before his death in 1963.

His literary productivity was on a Dickensian scale; not only did he publish and edit books and publish essays in magazines throughout the world, but he also edited for varying periods the following periodicals: *Fisk Herald*; the *Moon*; the *Horizon*; the *Crisis*; the *Brownies' Book;* and *Phylon*. For years, he contributed weekly columns to newspapers, including the *Pittsburgh Courier,* the *Chicago Defender,* and others. He wrote essays for books edited by others and published work in multivolume collections and encyclopedias.

The vast body of Du Bois' published writings is here organized into eight main divisions. These are:

I. Writings, of all kinds, published in periodicals, including newspapers, not edited by himself, with the exception of regular columns he contributed to various newspapers.

II. Writings, signed and unsigned, appearing in magazines edited by himself.

III. Writings appearing as columns in newspapers.

IV. Writings published by various organizational and/or governmental bodies and departments and printed testimony by him before governmental committees.

V. Writings published in books (including encyclopedias) edited by others.

VI. Writings published in books edited by him.

VII. Pamphlets and leaflets by him.

VIII. Books by him.

Within each section, works are listed chronologically.

No effort is made to list all reprintings of either articles or books; but where new editions carry additional material, this is noted.

In addition to name and subject indexes, the reader will find an alphabetical listing, by author, of all books commented upon by Dr. Du Bois.

In all cases the items listed are explicated; at the very least the reader will find an indication of the subject matter that is treated in each of the writings. Biographical and historical data also are provided where these help place the writings in context. Each separate item is numbered; where duplication or repetition occurred, this is noted. Often titles to magazine pieces were provided by people other than Du Bois; these will be apparent to the reader. Not infrequently, Du Bois was interviewed, and printed versions of such instances are listed, but these are not included in the numbering system.

In the years of the preparation of this effort, several young men and women served as research assistants for varying periods. Appreciation is expressed for their help to: Leon Black, Martin E. Dann, Anthony Flood, Jeanne Anne Lunin, Michael D. Merrill, Hugh T. Murray, Jr., and Mindy Thompson.

Special note should be taken of the bibliographical efforts of Paul G. Partington, who, from about 1960, undertook—quite independently and at first without Du Bois' knowledge—the preparation of a listing of his writings. The very considerable labors of Mr. Partington have been placed, with great generosity, at this writer's disposal; Mr. Partington has indeed continued to supply leads and suggestions to the present time. His help is acknowledged with deep appreciation. The encouragement and assistance provided by Shirley Graham Du Bois were an inspiration. As in all this writer's undertakings, the participation of his wife, Fay P. Aptheker, was indispensable.

It is hoped that the result is not altogether unworthy of Dr. Du Bois. Any inadequacies or errors are the fault solely of the undersigned.

January, 1973   Herbert Aptheker

Annotated Bibliography of the Published Writings of W.E.B. Du Bois

CHAPTER I

WRITINGS IN MAGAZINES AND NEWSPAPERS EDITED BY OTHERS

Du Bois' first published writings appeared in the New York *Globe* commencing in the issue dated April 14, 1883, when he was fifteen years old. The *Globe*, an Afro-American weekly newspaper, was edited by Timothy Thomas Fortune (1856–1927), beginning in 1882; its name was changed in 1884 to The *Freeman* and later still to the New York *Age* under which title (with slight variations) it continued to the present era as a highly influential periodical. From the 1880's to the end of the 19th century, T. Thomas Fortune was a leading radical force in Afro-American history; later, however, he permitted himself to become an element in the Tuskegee machine and thereafter lost his influence. Du Bois always recalled with deep appreciation the opportunity that Fortune gave him, in the capacity of Great Barrington, Massachusetts correspondent.

Twenty-seven contributions (Nos. 1–27) by young Du Bois were published in the *Globe* (*Freeman*) from April 14, 1883, to May 16, 1885. They appeared under slightly varying headings —"Great Barrington Notes," "Great Barrington News," "Great Barrington Items," "Great Barrington Briefs," "From the Berkshire Hills". Once the heading was inspired by the story that followed—"Wedding Bells of Berkshire" in the issue of December 6, 1884. The contributions were signed either "W. E. D." or "Du Bois." Where the essay contains something of particular interest, the content is briefly noted in what follows; otherwise, where only the date is given, purely personal items about the coming or going of this or that Black family or individual appear.

1. *April 14, 1883.* Du Bois urges that "some of the colored men" might well join a recently formed "Law and Order society" in Great Barrington, whose object is to "enforce the laws against liquor selling." He adds, "by the way," that he "did not notice many colored men at the town meeting last month; it seems they do not take as much interest in politics as is necessary for the protection of their rights. ... ”

2. *May 5, 1883.*Du Bois notes that two families of Black people and one Black individual have left Great Barrington; he is “sorry to lose so many colored people from our town.” He notes that last week at a meeting of the Sewing Society, a proposal was made to form a Literary Society, but “ ... there was not much interest manifested. It would be the best thing that could be done for the colored people here, if such a society should be formed.”

3. *May 26, 1883.* Black folk in the town have been discussing news—as reported in several issues of the *Globe*—of a projected Negro Convention to be held in Washington, D.C. (one was held in September, 1883, but in Louisville, Ky.); Du Bois states, “The colored people here do not as a whole regard the proposed Colored Convention in a very favorable light.” Du Bois himself offered no opinion.

4. *June 2, 1883.*

5. *June 30, 1883.* A Black man who had “long been an applicant for a pension” finally received it, plus $1,200 in back pay.

6. *September 8, 1883.* Du Bois explains his long absence from the paper by noting that he had made a summer trip and visited New Bedford, Albany, Providence, and other cities. He states that he was “pleased to see the industry and wealth of many of our race. But one thing that struck me was the absence of literary societies, none of which did I see in any of the cities. It seems to me as if this of all things ought not to be neglected.” He adds that there is to be a debate soon at the Sewing Society on the question “should Indians be educated at Hampton [Institute]?” He remarks that Du Bois will argue on the positive side and that “A lively time is expected.”

7. *September 29, 1883.* The debate referred to above (No. 6) was held; it was “contested warmly,” and the affirmative won. Following the debate, the “ladies of Zion Church held their monthly supper.” There follow three paragraphs of about 300 words urging that “colored men of the town should prepare themselves” for the coming local and state elections. He adds that color should not be a bar to any political office and that within the town “the colored people ... hold the balance of power. ... If they will only act in concert they may become a power not to be despised.” Hence, Du Bois urges that “they should meet and decide which way would be most advantageous for them to cast their votes.”

8. *October 20, 1883.* Some consideration is being given to "the holding of a county convention of the colored Republicans"; he adds, "there also seems to be a general regret that among all our people here there are no business men among us, and the desire to remedy this evil is becoming more and more manifest. ... "

9. *December 8, 1883.*

10. *December 29, 1883.* The election of Du Bois as recording secretary of the Great Barrington Sewing Society; he reports that the Christmas exercises at local churches were "very interesting so far, a number of colored children participating."

11. *January 26, 1884.*

12. *February 23, 1884.* "The annual town-meeting draws near and colored voters had best begin to look toward their interests."

13. *April 12, 1884.*

14. *May 17, 1884.* "Those intending to replenish their libraries are advised to consult the *Globe* correspondent, before so doing."

14A. *July 12, 1884.* On the first page of this issue of the *Globe* appears a letter from "Mr. J. Carlisle Dennis from San Francisco" headed "A Globe Agent's Distinction." The letter is headed Great Barrington, July 8, and calls attention to "young Willie Du Bois, who has just graduated with high honors from the High School at Great Barrington." The writer refers to "his hard and untiring efforts to provide for himself ... and the proud distinction he has won, as the first colored graduate from this school." The fact that he is the youngest graduate—at 16—is noted and that his commencement address devoted to Wendell Phillips "was considered by many the best and most original production of the class." The writer remarks that young Du Bois hopes one day to go to Harvard and that "the colored people of Great Barrington are quite proud" of him.

15 *August 2, 1884.* "Mr. J. Carlisle Dennis of San Francisco, Cal., arrived here recently with Mrs. Mark Hopkins.* Your correspondent wishes to return thanks to this gentleman for his flattering remarks ... and hopes that in the future he may continue to merit the high opinion herein entertained. ... "

---

*This was the widow of the railroad tycoon. Mr. Dennis, a rather young Black man, served as her steward and, according to Du Bois, was "in complete charge of Mrs. Hopkins' local business affairs." An English architect, named Searles, soon appeared on the scene and married Mrs. Hopkins; Mr. Dennis committed suicide—Du Bois, *Autobiography* (1968 edition), pp. 103–104.

16. *August 23, 1884.*

17. *September 27, 1884.*

18. *October 18, 1884.* " ... In the political parade held here recently the colored voters marched with the white, and were neither tucked in the rear nor parcelled off by themselves. ... "

19. *November 22, 1884.* Du Bois notes the founding of an African Methodist Episcopal Zion Church in the town.

20. *December 6, 1884.* "Among the most encouraging signs of the advancement of the colored race here was the formation of a club for literary and social improvement to be known as the Sons of Freedom."

21. *December 27, 1884.* The second meeting of the Sons of Freedom was held on December 8 and there was a "good attendance." He notes the election of several officers, including Du Bois as "Secretary-Treasurer" and that "it was decided to take up the history of the United States at the next session [Dec. 22] and pursue it as far as possible."

22. *January 10, 1885.* Du Bois states that the latest meeting of the Sons of Freedom was "especially interesting." Adds, "The study of United States history was profitably continued. ... "

23. *January 31, 1885.* "Your correspondent had the honor of being elected president of the high school lyceum, of which he is the only colored member."

24. *February 28, 1885.* The Sons of Freedom are to hold a debate on the question: "which is of more use to a country, the Warrior, the Statesman or the Poet?" Du Bois is to participate but does not say on which side.

25. *March 14, 1885.* The debate was held and the side arguing for the Statesman was declared the winner.

26. *May 16, 1885.* Du Bois reports that "their lady friends" have presented to the Sons of Freedom a new club room; that at the last meeting a paper on Wendell Phillips was read by James S. Durghardt* of Stockbridge and that all the meetings held by the Sons of Freedom have been "very interesting."

In *Dusk of Dawn,* Du Bois recalled that he had been the Great

*This is a misprint in the paper; the name was James T. Burghardt—a cousin of Du Bois.

Barrington correspondent for the *Daily Republican* of Springfield, Massachusetts. A study of the files of that paper for the years from 1883 through 1885 (he arrived at Fisk University as a student on September 5, 1885) reveals no contribution signed by him; there are two pieces, however, that were probably from his pen. One, entitled "The Housatonic Festival", appears in that paper's issue dated September 26, 1884; the other reports "The Famous $100,000 Leavitt Barn Burned" in Great Barrington and was printed in the issue dated July 8, 1885. Since it is not possible to be certain of Du Bois' authorship in these cases, they are not listed by number in this work.

Entering as a sophomore at Fisk University in Nashville, Tennessee, in the fall of 1885, Du Bois graduated with the class of 1888 in June. From the beginning of his stay at Fisk, Du Bois was connected with the *Fisk Herald;* he is referred to as the editor of its "Exchanges" column in the issue dated November, 1885 and served in this capacity through June, 1886. In the fall of 1886 Du Bois edited the section called "Sharps and Flats" in the *Herald,* and the issue of December, 1886, refers to him as the Literary Editor. From November, 1887, through June, 1888, Du Bois was the editor in chief of the *Fisk Herald.*

As exchange editor, Du Bois would normally fill a column in the *Fisk Herald* with comments upon or outlines of the contents of various other student publications that reached his attention. These appeared as follows (where anything of particular interest appears, it is noted).

27. November, 1885, Vol. III, No. 3, p. 8.

28. December, 1885, Vol. III, No. 4, p. 6. Du Bois observes that "The *College Message* of Greensboro [N.C.] is got up in a bewitching style. The column on woman's work is interesting, and a first rate woman's rights argument."

29. June, 1886, Vol. III, No. 10, p. 11.

During the summer of 1886, Du Bois taught Black children for two months in country districts of Tennessee. He published at the time two accounts of this significant experience.

30. "The Hills of Tenn." A letter dated September 18 and published in the *Fisk Herald,* October, 1886, Vol. IV, No. 4, pp. 6–7. It is written lightly but reflects real difficulties and great pleasure in teaching; he remarks, "I have had to swallow some large lumps of 'sassiness.' "

31. "How I Taught School," *Fisk Herald,* November, 1886, pp. 9–10. " ... Whatever the pupils may have gained, it was little to what I acquired."

The November, 1887, issue of the *Fisk Herald* saw Du Bois as Editor in Chief. In that issue commenced a brief novel. "Tom Brown at Fisk."

32. "Tom Brown at Fisk," *Fisk Herald,* November, 1887, December, 1887, February, 1888. An autobiographical and highly romantic novel, the young teacher in Tennessee appears as a woman and in the first paragraph one reads, "It's hard to be a woman, but a black one—! " All ends happily however.

33. Editorial, *Fisk Herald,* November, 1887, Vol. V, No. 3, pp. 8–9. He wants Fisk to depend not upon Northern philanthropists but upon Black people themselves for finances; he notes the retirement of T. Thomas Fortune from the New York *Freeman* and speaks highly of him; he urges that students help raise the funds for a gymnasium; Du Bois refers to Afro-American music as "the strangest, sweetest" in the world and wants "the Negro race ... to build up an American school of music which shall rival the grandest schools of the past."

34. "Editorial Toothpick," *Fisk Herald,* November, 1887, pp. 9–10. Rather random musings; some about the latest Balkan crisis. He notes that the U. S. flag floated over Jubilee Hall and remarks, "may the nation whose colors we fly protect the rights of those we educate! "

35. Editorial, *Fisk Herald,* December, 1887, Vol. V, No. 4, pp. 8–9. Again, on money for a gymnasium; on money to improve the library; on the need for ambition—"all of us cannot be great we know, but some of us can." And, noting a meeting of the Women's Christian Temperance Union in Nashville, remarks, "the Age of Woman is surely dawning."

36. "Editor's Toothpick," *Fisk Herald,* December, 1887, p. 9. Chit-chat.

37. Editorial, *Fisk Herald,* January, 1888; Vol. V, No. 5, p. 8. He refers with great praise to the work of George W. Williams, "at last we have a historian." Du Bois adds that in being Christians, "we should not forget the practical side of Christianity" in what we do on earth.

38. "Editor's Toothpick," *Fisk Herald,* January, 1888, pp. 8–10. On Christmas at Fisk.

39. Editorial, February, 1888, Vol. V, No. 6, pp. 8–9. Du Bois publishes a letter from a reader (unnamed) who praises his editorship and writing. Du Bois says that "the words of encouragement ... will serve in no little degree as incentives toward a life that shall be an honor to the Race. ... "

40. "Editorial Toothpick," February, 1888, p. 9.

41. Editorial, March, 1888, Vol. V, No. 6, p. 8.

42. Editorial, April, 1888, p. 8. Again a call for support of the drive to build a gymnasium. Praise of the rendition by the school's Mozart Society of the Elijah oratorio: " ... our race, but a quarter of a century removed from slavery, can master the greatest musical compositions."

43. "Editorial Toothpick," April, 1888, pp. 8–9. Du Bois suggests the need for a clear aim in life, and asks, "why isn't there a Fisk student at Leipzig, or a Fisk metaphysician at Berlin?"

44. Editorial, June, 1888, Vol. V, No. 9, p. 8. The end of his stay at Fisk; "We can look back with grateful hearts and forward with renewed zeal to the great work before us."

45. "Editorial Toothpick," June, 1888, p. 9. A farewell paragraph.

In the fall of 1888, Du Bois entered Harvard College as a junior. He received his bachelor's degree in June, 1890, and went on—with fellowships—to graduate study. In history his professors were Edward Channing and Albert Bushnell Hart; with the encouragement of the latter, in particular, he delivered a paper at the December, 1891, meeting of the American Historical Association. It anticipated the theme of his dissertation which was to be published five years later.

46. "The Enforcement of the Slave-Trade Laws," *Annual Report Of The American Historical Association For The Year 1891* (Washington, D.C.: Senate Misc. Doc. 173, 52nd Cong., 1st Sess., 1892), pp. 163–174. The following is from its concluding section. "If slave labor was an economic god, then the slave trade was its strong right arm; and with Southern planters recognizing this and Northern capital unfettered by conscience it was almost like legislating against economic laws to attempt to abolish the slave trade by statutes."

Du Bois in his *Autobiography* (p. 137) states that in the Boston *Courant,* "a type of small colored weekly which was spreading over the nation ... I published many of my Harvard daily themes." This paper was published by Josephine St. Pierre Ruffin but copies of it do not seem to have survived. A damaged clipping of one piece by Du Bois is among his papers; it is signed and states that under the guidance of Mrs. Ruffin "a goodly company of young ladies" went up to Amherst to attend the graduation at that college of George W. Forbes, William T. Jackson and William H. Lewis. Clement Morgan and Du Bois went too and his report of the commencement dwells mostly—insofar as the clipping tells us—on the loveliness of the young ladies who were present, one of whom, "named Fannie Bailey, hailing from Cambridge ... was a symphony in purple." This is signed and appears in:

47. Boston *Courant,* July 9, 1892.

In 1892 Du Bois was awarded a Slater Fund Fellowship which made possible two years of graduate study—mostly in history and economics—at the University of Berlin. He sent long letters in 1892 and 1893 to the *Fisk Herald* and these were published.

48. In the issue of November, 1892, Vol. X, No. 3, pp. 1–4. Devoted to the great opportunities for learning made possible at Harvard and urging that others from Fisk undertake to go there.

49. In the issue of September, 1893 (dated University of Berlin, May, 1893); Vol. XI, No. 1, pp. 5–7. Of the inspiration that European culture and learning may provide, stressing figures such as Goethe, and hoping all this would help in "the rise of the Negro people." Concludes by urging others from Fisk to study in Europe.

Returning—by steerage—from Europe in 1894, young Du Bois applied at once to several Black educational institutions for a position; the first acceptance came from Wilberforce University in Ohio and to that university he reported late in 1894 as a professor of Greek and Latin. On February 20, 1895, Frederick Douglass died; a memorial service for him was held at Wilberforce on March 9, 1895. As the youngest faculty member, Du Bois was among the speakers on that occasion.

50. "Douglass as a Statesman," first published (edited by H. Aptheker) in the *Journal of Negro History*, October, 1964, Vol. XLIX, pp. 264–268.

Receiving a Ph.D. degree in 1895 from Harvard and finding aspects of life, especially religious requirements at Wilberforce University increasingly irksome, Dr. Du Bois and his bride, the former Nina Gomer of Iowa, accepted an invitation from the University of Pennsylvania to undertake a careful investigation of the Black population of Philadelphia. He was given the title of assistant instructor in sociology, but he taught no classes and was not listed in the university's catalogue.

The first published piece by Du Bois, dated University of Pennsylvania, November 8, 1896, was published in:

51. *Conservator* (Chicago), November 28, 1896, under the headline, "Startling Figures." This was reprinted from the New York *Age* and reflects rather strict New England (and Germanic) concepts of morality and duty.

In the *College Settlement News,* published monthly by Julia B. Farrington, there appeared:

52. "A Programme of Social Reform," being a signed "abstract from the lecture of Dr. Du Bois, delivered [at the settlement] on February 14," in the *News* for April, 1897, p. 4. Philosophically, this adopted an idealist position, with emphasis upon the need for "systematic knowledge of society."

In July, 1897, there was held in Norfolk, Virginia, instead of the usual conference of graduates from Hampton Institute, a General Conference of Negroes. Dr. Du Bois delivered the following paper:

53. "The Problem of Amusement," *Southern Workman* (Hampton, Virginia), September, 1897, Vol. XXVI, pp. 181–184. Also published in the *College Settlement News,* October and November, 1897, a fairly long section of the closing portion of this essay in the *Southern Workman,* January, 1899, Vol. XXVIII, pp. 19–20. It urges parents and teachers to assure a childhood for Black children.

The first essay by Du Bois appearing in an influential, nationally circulating magazine was:

54. "Strivings of the Negro People," *Atlantic Monthly,* August, 1897, Vol. LXXX, pp. 194–198. Here appears the famous line," the Negro is a sort of seventh son, born with a veil, and gifted with second-sight ... " and the development of the thought, "One ever feels his two-ness—an American, a Negro ... ." This essay was later included in the classic *The Souls of Black Folk,* first published in 1903.

Concluding his year's work for the University of Pennsylvania, Du Bois accepted an appointment as assistant professor of history and economics at Atlanta University in Georgia. Prior to leaving Philadelphia, he wrote:

55. "The Study of the Negro Problems," *Annals of the American Academy of Political and Social Science,* January, 1898, Vol. XI, pp. 1–23. This was reprinted, together with five pages of a "Résumé of the Discussion on the Negro Problems," participated in by Prof. Samuel McCune Lindsay (who had been mainly responsible for inviting Du Bois to the University of Pennsylvania), John Bach McMaster, Daniel H. Williams, M.D., the Black surgeon, and two ministers, H. L. Phillips and Charles Wood, as *Publications of the American Academy of Political and Social Science,* No. 219, February 22, 1898, 28 pp. This is largely an appeal for a scientific study of the realities of the "Negro problem."

The publication of the two preceding essays marked the beginnings of the flood of publications in periodicals that thereafter was to pour from Du Bois for the next 70 years.

56. "The Problem of Negro Crime Discussed," quoting about 500 words of a speech delivered in Atlanta, Georgia, on January 1, 1899, "at the Emancipation Celebration by the Colored Citizens of Atlanta," clipping in an unnamed and undated newspaper in the Du Bois Papers in custody of the compiler. A rather conservative address, closing with an appeal to white and Black to unite "to found in Georgia a reformatory for juvenile criminals who are now sent to the prison and chain-gang." (No. 59 for later publication this same year on this theme.)

57. "A Negro Schoolmaster in the New South," *Atlantic Monthly,* January, 1899, Vol. LXXXIII, pp. 99–104. This essay was later included by Du Bois in his *Souls of Black Folk.* It is interesting to compare this with his essays (Nos. 30 and 31, above) published 13 years earlier and detailing the same experiences. The essay is filled with Du Bois' love for his people and his sense of identification with them.

58. In March, 1899, Dr. Du Bois delivered a series of three lectures at Hampton Institute in Virginia. Under the title "A History of the Negro Race in America," what was described as an "abstract" of that series was published in the institute's *Southern Workman,* April, 1899, Vol. XXVIII, pp. 149–151. The editor commented (p. 148), "it is doubtful if any visiting lecturer has ever more successfully won the admiration and swayed the thoughts of the students here."

59. "The Negro and Crime," *Independent*, May 18, 1899, Vol. LI, pp. 1355–1357. The first of many pieces by Du Bois to be published in this quite advanced New York weekly; its closest equivalent today would be the *Christian Century*, for which Du Bois later wrote occasionally.

By 1898 the Bureau of Labor of the United States government was commencing to publish special studies made by Du Bois of conditions among Black people in various parts of the South; these are detailed in another section of this work. Occasionally, however, the periodical press reported on Du Bois' findings. Thus.

59a. "Southern Black Belt Studied by Mr. Du Bois," Brooklyn (New York) *Eagle*, July 3, 1899, is a story, signed "A.B.A." with extensive quotations from one such study of communities of Black people located in Alabama and Georgia (No. 1829, 1830).

In the summer of 1899, Du Bois attended conventions then held in Chicago of the National Afro-American Council and of the National Association of Colored Women. He published his impressions in:

60. "Two Negro Conventions," *Independent*, September 7, 1899, Vol. LI, 2425–2427. Republished in large part in H. Aptheker, ed., *A Documentary History of the Negro People in the U.S.* (New York: Citadel Press, 1951), pp. 775–778. Du Bois concluded that the conventions were "an earnest of what we may look for when careful, thoughtful organization among Negroes shall enable them to act for themselves. ... "

As part of the legalization of racism commencing in the late 1880's, there appeared the successful drive to disfranchise the Black men of the South. Du Bois was part of the resistance movement against this. He detailed one aspect of it in.

61. "The Suffrage Fight in Georgia," *Independent*, November 30, 1899,

Vol. LI, pp. 3226–3228. (It is likely that he wrote in whole—certainly in part—*A Memorial to the Legislature of Georgia on the Hardwick Bill*, aimed at disfranchisement and introduced into the Georgia legislature in 1899; it is published in H. Aptheker, ed., *op. cit.*, pp. 784–786.)

One of the results of Du Bois' scientific work for the U.S. government was his effort to induce the census bureau and private groups of scholars to undertake extensive and careful statistical studies of the Black population. Without this, he asked, how could any real beginning be made in determining a proper course to follow? This is the point of:

62. "The Twelfth Census and Negro Problems," *Southern Workman*, January, 1900, Vol. XXIX, pp. 305–309.

In 1900 Du Bois went to England and France. In July he attended, as Secretary, the first Pan-African Conference in London and penned its address (No. 1864 below) and later that summer he went to France, serving with Thomas J. Calloway as organizer of the American Negro Exhibit, which was part of the United States Building at the World's Fair in Paris. The latter experience he described in:

63. "The American Negro at Paris," *American Monthly Review of Reviews*, November, 1900, Vol. XXII, pp. 575–577. A substantial section of this article was reprinted in *Public Opinion* (New York), November 15, 1900.

Reflective of an accumulating sense of estrangement from the status quo—which his every experience, from Pan-African beginnings to Paris and back to Georgia, was reinforcing—was Du Bois' analysis of Black people's religion.

64. "The Religion of the Negro," *New World* (Boston), December, 1900, Vol. IX, pp. 614–625. The essay (which later appeared in his *Souls of Black Folk*) concludes that "the real Negro heart" someday "shall sweep irresistibly toward the Goal ... Liberty, Justice and Right. ... "

The next year, productivity was astonishing even for Du Bois; essays were published in history, in sociology, and in contemporary events, as follows:

65. "The Freedmen's Bureau," *Atlantic Monthly*, March, 1901; Vol. LXXXVII, pp. 354–365. A pioneering piece of historical writing, republished in his *Souls of Black Folk*. (About half this essay was plagiarized by one C. W. Covington in a prize essay—given by the United Daughters of the Confederacy!—published in the *Columbia* (South Carolina) *State*, January 28, 1912.)

66. "The Storm and Stress in the Black World," *Dial* (Chicago), April 16, 1901; Vol. XXX, pp. 262–264. A slashing attack upon the recently published the *American Negro* by Hannibal Thomas, himself a Black man and author of a cynical, viciously hateful assault upon his own people.

67. "The Negro As He Really Is," *World's Work*, June, 1901, Vol. II, pp. 848–866 (republished in his *Souls of Black Folk*).

Responding to his own appeal (No. 62) for the most careful and scientific study of the actual conditions of Black people—and having already, in 1898, developed the Atlanta University annual conferences devoted to this effort, Du Bois published this detailed study of one county in the Georgia Black Belt.

68. "Results of the Ten Tuskegee Conferences," *Harper's Weekly*, June 22, 1901, Vol. XLV, p. 641. A brief and quite positive examination of the results of annual meetings held at Tuskegee.

69. "The Relation of the Negroes to the Whites in the South," *Annals of the American Academy of Political and Social Science*, July, 1901, Vol. XVIII, pp. 121–140. Du Bois commended this very lengthy investigation with the proposition "that the examination of the most serious of the race problems in America is not in the nature of a debate but rather a joint endeavor to seek the truth. ... ."

70. "The Evolution of Negro Leadership," *Dial*, July 1, 1901, Vol. XXXI, pp. 53–55. In this essay, Du Bois, in reviewing Booker T. Washington's *Up From Slavery* (published by Doubleday, Page in 1901) and making clear—for the first time in print—his differences with the Sage of Tuskegee, places Washington within the context of the sweep of Black history.

71. "The Burden of Negro Schooling," *Independent*, July 18, 1901, Vol. LII, pp. 1667–1668. In line with his effort to convey basic data to the nation, Du Bois contributed this detailed—though fairly brief—examination of the economic realities of the dual educational system in the South. He showed its awful inadequacy, demonstrated that much of the money to support it came directly from Black people themselves and that, in his view, financial support from the United States government for education was necessary.

While teaching at Atlanta, lecturing widely, participating in political activity and doing the writing involved in the essays just cited, Du Bois also produced two nearly book length studies. One, of approximately 15,000 words, was entitled "The Problem of Housing the Negro" and was a detailed examination of every aspect of this question, as follows—all published in the *Southern Workman*.

72. "The Elements of the Problem," June, 1901, Vol. XXX, pp. 390–395.

73. "The Homes of the Slaves," September, 1901, Vol. XXX, pp. 486–493.

74. "The Home of the Country Freedmen," October, 1901, Vol. XXX, pp. 535–542.

75. "The Home of the Village Negro," November, 1901, Vol. XXX, pp. 601–604.

76. "The Southern City Negro of the Lower Class," December, 1901, Vol. XXX, pp. 688–693.

77. "The Southern City Negro of the Better Class," February, 1902, Vol. XXXI, pp. 65–672.

As was appropriate for a magazine entitled the *Southern Workman*, the series of articles just cited was confined to the South; at the same general period Du Bois was publishing a series of five articles entitled "The Black North," again coming to some 15,000 words, in the New York *Times Magazine Supplement*. This, too, was detailed, carefully descriptive, and heavily statistical; its tone tended to be more conservative than the series appearing in the Hampton magazine.

78. "New York City" [part 1], November 17, 1901, p. 10.

79. "New York City" [part 2], November 24, 1901, p. 11.

80. "Philadelphia," December 1, 1901, p. 11.

81. "Boston," December 8, 1901, p. 20.

82. "Some Conclusions," December 15, 1901, p. 20.

In this same period of extraordinary creativity, Du Bois published:

83. "The Savings of Black Georgia," *Outlook* (New York), September 14, 1901; Vol. LXIX, pp. 128–130. This emphasized the devastating impact of the depression of the 1890's and the realities of racism; but it noted that the savings (coming to about $14 million) proved hard work and careful thrift.

The horrors of the convict-lease system in the South were so great that a campaign against this practice reached considerable dimensions in the final years of the 19th century and the early years of the 20th century; the writings of George Washington Cable are well known in this connection. Du Bois was also part of this movement; in an influential magazine published by Funk & Wagnalls (in New York and London), Du Bois contributed a major examination:

84. "The Spawn of Slavery. The Convict Lease System in the South," *Missionary Review of the World*, October, 1901; Vol. XIV, pp. 737–745. He closes by referring to "that sort of social protest and revolt which we call crime" and suggests that "we must look for remedy in the same reform of these wrong social conditions, and not in intimidation, savagery, or the legalized slavery of men."

In his ceaseless effort to "get the facts straight," Du Bois contributed still another essay in 1901 refuting the wide-spread idea that the Afro-American was incapable of sustained and effective labor.

85. "The Freedmen and Their Sons," *Independent*, November 14, 1901; Vol. LII, p. 2709.

In the fall of 1901, Du Bois was asked to speak to the young women at Spelman College of Atlanta University; the title of his essay conveys the particular point he emphasized.

86. "The Work of Negro Women in Society," *Spelman Messenger*, February, 1902; Vol. XVIII, p. 1–3.

The first appearance of Du Bois as a contributor to the *Nation* took the form of a letter, entitled by its editors:

87. "The Trust of Girard College," *Nation*, March 20, 1902; Vol. LXXIV, p. 226. Du Bois here attacked the lily-white character of the college, the endowment for which came largely from the profits of the slave trade!

An early instance of the short-story-like quality of some of Du
Bois' reportage appeared in his account of the effort to prevent the
new "public" library in Atlanta from being confined to white
people only.

88. "The Opening of the Library," *Independent*, Apr. 3, 1902; Vol.
LIV, pp. 809–810.

At about the time Du Bois was leading a delegation of Black
citizens to protest the above injustice, he was composing one of his
major essays, the impact of which upon the nation was to be
considerable.

89. "Of the Training of Black Men," *Atlantic Monthly*, September,
1902; Vol. XC, pp. 289–297. Not least in the consequence of such
training, Du Bois suggests, is the fact that they "may give the world
new points of view." This essay appeared in *Souls of Black Folk*. A long
extract from this "eloquent and striking article" was printed in *Literary
Digest*, October 11, 1902.

Du Bois argued that persistence in agitation reflected
hopefulness, not pessimism; he suggested, furthermore, that there
were hopeful signs.

90. "Hopeful Signs for the Negro," *Advance*, October 2, 1902; Vol.
XLIV, pp. 327–328. In this essay appear first the words that the Black
man "never will abate one jot or tittle from his determination to attain
in this land perfect equality before the law with his fellow citizens"
—strikingly similar to the historic Niagara Address of 1906.

The second appearance of Du Bois in the *Nation* also was in the
form of a letter and again was a communication seeking to set the
facts straight; it was entitled by the editors:

91. "Crime and Our Colored Population," *Nation*, December 25, 1902;
Vol. LXXV, p. 499 (the letter itself was dated December 20, 1902).

In November, 1902, Du Bois gave what was called "the college
lecture" at Talladega College in Alabama; a summary of it
appeared as:

92. "Higher Education of the Negro," *Talladega College Record*,
November, 1902; Vol. X, p. 2.

Among the Du Bois Papers is a mounted, printed essay of some 900 words with no date and no source indicated. There is reason to believe that it was published shortly after 1900 and probably in 1902; it suggests that the Afro-American people require both classical and industrial education.

93. "The Two Sorts of Schooling." Du Bois' use of the term "nation" in referring to the Black people—by no means uncommon with him—is especially noteworthy in this brief essay.

In early 1903 Du Bois made the first of his extremely rare appearances in the journal of the American Historical Association. It took the form of a very balanced and properly critical estimate.

94. Review of James C. Ballagh, *A History of Slavery in Virginia* (Johns Hopkins University Press, in 1902), in *American Historical Review*, January, 1903, Vol. VIII, pp. 356–357.

With the work in sociology and economics well advanced at Atlanta University and with its annual conferences firmly established, Du Bois published two accounts of these efforts in 1903, seeking thereby not only to record what was being done but also to urge its further development.

95. "The Laboratory in Sociology at Atlanta University," *Annals of the American Academy of Political and Social Science*, May, 1903; Vol. XXI, pp. 160–163.

96. "The Atlanta University Conferences," *Charities* (New York), May 2, 1903, Vol. X, pp. 435–439.

The level of thinking being what it was in the United States in 1903 (and largely still is), Du Bois labored to bring forward the accomplishments of significant contemporary Afro-Americans. In this connection he published the following article, accompanied with fine illustrations:

97. "Possibilities of the Negro. The Advance Guard of the Race," *Booklover's Magazine* (Philadelphia), July, 1903, Vol. II, pp. 3–15. He treated briefly the careers of ten men: Booker T. Washington; W. L. Taylor (of Richmond, Va., head of a mutual benefit insurance society); the inventor Granville T. Woods; Edward H. Morris, an attorney and

Chicago member of the Illinois legislature; Dr. Daniel H. Williams, surgeon; Kelly Miller, author and professor of mathematics at Howard; the Rev. Francis J. Grimké of Washington; the poet Paul L. Dunbar; the novelist Charles W. Chesnutt; and the painter Henry O. Tanner.

> In one of the most powerful magazines then functioning —Theodore Roosevelt often contributed to it—Du Bois made a ringing appeal.

98. "The Training of Negroes for Social Power," *Outlook* (New York), October 17, 1903, Vol. LXXV, pp. 409–414; Black people, as all people, must promote "the growth of initiative ... the spread of independent thought, the expanding consciousness of manhood. ... ."*

> Very soon after the appearance of *The Souls of Black Folk* early in 1903, it became clear that this was no ordinary book; its impact was almost immediate and continued to mount. One result was an interview with Du Bois, signed by "Raymond," conducted at his office in Atlanta. It was published under the following headline:

98a. "Cultured Negro Model For Race," Chicago *Tribune*, June 18, 1903, p. 1. It quotes Du Bois on some autobiographical memories and his views on education in particular. The interviewer was Clifford Raymond.

> Another of the scholarly journals—this one published by Columbia University—opened its pages (at least, its review pages) to Du Bois in 1903.

99. Review of Joseph A. Tillinghast, *The Negro in Africa and America* (American Economic Association 1902), in *Political Science Quarterly*, December, 1903, Vol. XVIII, pp. 695–697. The book is intensely racist, but Du Bois finds some value in its emphasis upon the significance of Africa in terms of mastering Afro-American history.

> By 1904, the best-known Afro-American other than Booker T. Washington was Dr. Du Bois. By that date, significant European journals had begun to ask for his writings, and his lecture tours

*This article was issued as a pamphlet—*Atlanta University Leaflet*, No. 17 (no date)—of 21 pages of text together with 3 pages detailing "The Work of Atlanta University" and soliciting funds to be sent to President Horace Bumstead of the University. But it is noteworthy that in this reprinted version, the title of the essay was changed to read *The Training of Negroes for Social Reform*—not *Power*, though it is the latter word which Du Bois repeatedly uses in the text and it is as a plea to enhance power that he is writing the essay.

now brought larger and larger audiences—often mainly of white people—and were regularly reported by elements of the white as well as the Black press. Thus, the organ of the prestigious and powerful Society for the Propagation of the Gospel in Foreign Parts published a long essay by Du Bois.

100. "The Future of the Negro Race in America," *East and the West* (London), January, 1904, Vol. II, pp. 4–19. Du Bois thought there were four possibilities for the Black Man: his condition of serfdom to be perpetuated; extinction; migration to foreign land; or "he may become an American citizen." He suggests that positive efforts against racism in Europe—and especially improvement in England's actions in Africa—would be influential in bringing about the fourth possibility.

Again, a letter from Du Bois (with a title supplied by the magazine) appeared in the *Nation* and again it was brief and statistical, representing a correction of widely held misconceptions.

101. "Diminishing Negro Illiteracy," *Nation*, February 25, 1904, Vol. LXXVIII, pp. 147–148. (The letter itself is dated February 20, 1904.)

In 1904, Du Bois' friend J. Max Barber founded a militant Black magazine, the *Voice of the Negro*; Du Bois wrote for it frequently during the few years of its existence. His first contribution was substantially similar to his essay on the work in sociology at Atlanta published in the *Annals* (No. 95 above):

102. "The Atlanta Conferences," *Voice of the Negro* (Atlanta), March, 1904, Vol. I, pp. 85–90.

A basic speech used by Du Bois in his 1904 tour, commencing in February, was one which affirmed that racism in the United States was a form—an especially virulent form—of elitism and class oppression. Delivered first in New York City before the Twentieth Century Club, it was repeated thereafter in every part of the nation and widely printed, in part or in full, as follows:

103. "Caste in America," Boston *Transcript*, February 21, 1904; printed in considerable part in San Antonio (Tex.) *Gazette*, April 17, 1904; Des Moines (Iowa) *Register Leader*, October 19, 1904; Savannaa (Ga.) *News*, October 19, 1904; Helena (Mont.) *Independent*, October 19, 1904; Denver (Colo.) *News*, Oct. 19, 1904; Springfield (Ohio) *Sun*,

October 24, 1904; Washington *Pathfinder*, October 29, 1904; Chicago *Tribune*, December 16, 1904 (a story detailing the intense resentment of the local Daughters of the American Revolution aroused by this speech); Chicago *Examiner*, December 19, 1904; Chicago *Record-Herald*, December 15, 1904.

While Du Bois was on his 1904 tour, newspapers occasionally printed interviews with him; an example was:

103a. "Deplores Act of Vardaman," Milwaukee (Wisconsin) *Sentinel*, March 19, 1904. The Governor of Mississippi had just vetoed an appropriation for a school for Black youngsters, and Du Bois' denunciation of this act is quoted at some length.

Before a considerable Black and white audience at the high school in Springfield, Massachusetts, Du Bois delivered the address "The Development of a People," which was headlined:

104. "Strong Plea for the Negro," Springfield (Massachusetts) *Daily Republican*, March 23, 1904, p. 12. The address urged the need for agitation to achieve equal rights and warned against delay.

One of the earliest of the extremely militant statements from Du Bois appeared in a Hearst magazine under the title:

105. "The Parting of the Ways," *World Today* (Chicago), April, 1904, Vol. VI, pp. 521–523. This is a slashing attack upon the Tuskegee approach, affirming "we refuse to kiss the hands that smite us" and ending, "The way for black men today to make these rights the heritage of their children is to struggle for them unceasingly, and if they fail, die trying."

Developing further his concept of the role of a "Talented Tenth" (see No. 1865 below) Du Bois insisted upon their special role among a people so oppressed and exploited as his own, in,

106. "The Development of a People," *International Journal of Ethics* (Philadelphia), April, 1904, Vol. XIV, pp. 292–311. This was the basis of the speech reported upon earlier (see above, No. 104).

Du Bois hoped by this time that the general press might allow him regular commentary and urged upon the editor of *Collier's* magazine the idea of a department that might be called "Along the Color Line." This was rejected, but one article was solicited and the result was:

107. "To Solve the Negro Problem," *Collier's* (New York), June 18, 1904, Vol. XXXIII, p. 14. In essence: "Justice will cure caste."

Another essay showing the accomplishments—largely through the efforts of Black people themselves—in education and the remaining great needs for further development and for federal aid was:

108. "What Intellectual Training Is Doing for the Negro," *Missionary Review of the World*, August, 1904, Vol. XVII, pp. 578–582.

The single most effective and most widely reproduced essay by Du Bois was this one:

109. "Credo," *Independent*, October 6, 1904, Vol. LVII, p. 787. Reprinted in full in the *Literary Digest*, October 15, 1904; on a card for framing by Ed. L. Simon & Co. in Memphis (soon to be the publisher of Du Bois' first magazine, *The Moon*); in the *Texas* (Austin) *Pythian-Journal*, December, 1904; *British Friend* (London), July, 1905; and thereafter with regularity, as, for example, the *World* (Indianapolis), April [?], 1913. The 500-word essay—a prose poem —invoked peace, justice, equality, endurance and ultimate optimism, and expressed "especially" his pride in his own people.

The editors of the *Independent* invited authors to review and/or comment upon their own books; Du Bois did so, in:

110. "The Souls of Black Folk," *Independent*, November 17, 1904, Vol. LVII, p. 1152. He writes of its subjectivity, perhaps its vagueness, and comments: "in its larger aspects the style is tropical—African."

In a relatively new Black magazine published in Atlanta, Du Bois commenced 1905 with a column that he was to resuscitate and conduct for many years thereafter in the *Crisis*.

111. "Debit and Credit. The American Negro the Year of Grace Nineteen Hundred and Four," *Voice of the Negro*, January, 1905; Vol. II, 677. In the "debit," the spread of Jim Crow, the monstrousness of lynchings, and the use of "hush money" to corrupt the Black press; in the "credit," economic advance and the growth of "an aroused race consciousness" and militancy.

At the request of President Bumstead of Atlanta University, Du Bois spoke in the North, seeking support for the university; on February 8, 1905, he lectured in Boston, and the lecture was published, in large part.

112. "Representative Higher Institutions for Negro Education in the South," Boston *Globe*, February 9, 1905.

Early in 1905, Du Bois wrote: "In four papers on slavery, it is my purpose to lay before you the history of Slavery until the beginning of the Fifteenth Century ... "; these were published as follows:

113. "The Beginning of Slavery," *Voice of the Negro*, February, 1905, Vol. II, pp. 104–106.

114. "Slavery in Greece and Rome," *Voice of the Negro*, May, 1905, Vol. II, pp. 320–323.

115. "The Beginning of Emancipation," *Voice of the Negro*, June, 1905; Vol. II, pp. 397–400.

116. "Serfdom," *Voice of the Negro*, July, 1905, Vol. II, pp. 479–481.

116a. *The Fraternal Union*, organ of the Afro-American Odd Fellows of Arkansas, issued in Fort Smith, Arkansas, February 16, 1905 published an article, from the Boston *Guardian* (n.d.), "Sayings of Dr. W. E. B. Du Bois. A Great Race Champion," which contained excerpts coming to about 1,500 words from various essays urging militant action in the areas of political and social struggle.

117. "The Southerner's Problem," *Dial*, May 1, 1905, Vol. XXXVIII, pp. 315–318. This review examined Thomas Nelson Page, *The Negro. The Southerner's Problem* (New York. Scribner's); William B. Smith, *The Color Line* (New York. McClure, Phillips); and E. A. Johnson, *Light Ahead for the Negro* (New York. Grafton Press). The last was by a Black man and was cast in the form of a seminovel of Utopian vintage; Du Bois thought well of it. The first two were by white men—Page a kind of benevolent racist and Smith a vindictive and brutal one; Du Bois took both of them apart.

Du Bois' increasing concentration upon the socioeconomic roots of the oppression of Black people, the impact of industrialization and urbanization, the differences and yet similarities in the question in North and South and the world-wide implications of racism in the United States are all woven together in:

118. "The Negro South and North," *Bibliotheca Sacra* (Oberlin, Ohio), July, 1905, pp. 500–513. Du Bois here particularly considers Philadelphia and Atlanta. This was reprinted as a pamphlet, with the same title, in 1905, no publisher given.

Another detailed study of Philadelphia, emphasizing the political potential of the growing Black population was:

119. "The Black Vote of Philadelphia," *Charities*, October 7, 1905, Vol. XV, pp. 31–35.

A smashing attack against the racism coming from leading politicians and writers and a ringing affirmation of the Black people's rights in the United States—enriched by their labor and creativity—appeared in:

120. "The Problem of Tillman, Vardaman and Thomas Dixon, Jr.," the *Central Christian Advocate* (Kansas City, Missouri), October 18, 1905, Vol. XLIX, pp. 1324–1325. Du Bois was referring here to Benjamin R. Tillman, senator from South Carolina (1895–1918), to James K. Vardaman, at the time governor and later a senator from Mississippi, and to the author of the best-selling novel *The Clansman* (1905), from which D. W. Griffith made the film *Birth of a Nation* in 1915.

Affirming the special need among Black people for collective effort and explicitly remarking that when he refers to "men" he has in mind a generic term including "women," Du Bois produced:

121. "The Negro Ideals of Life," *Christian Register* (Boston), October 26, 1905, Vol. LXXXIV, pp. 1197–1199.

A declaration of independence from charity and so-called benevolence formed the heart of a brief essay:

122. "Garrison and the Negro," *Independent*, December 7, 1905, Vol. LIX, pp. 1316–1317.

The foregoing essay (No. 122) incorporated quotations from

resolutions adopted by the Niagara Movement, which was founded in 1905 through the efforts and inspiration of Du Bois and William Monroe Trotter, in particular. Two essays directly on that movement were published in this period by Du Bois in *The Voice of the Negro.*

123. "The Niagara Movement," September, 1905, Vol. II, pp. 619–622.

124. "The Growth of the Niagara Movement," January, 1906, Vol. III, pp. 43–45.

An article substantially similar—though more brief and with some data that were new—to No. 100 above appeared under the same title in a New Zealand magazine.

124a. "The Future of the Negro Race in America," *Red Funnel,* February 1, 1906, Vol. XX, pp. 23–28.

One of the earliest, if not the earliest, study of the economy of the Afro-American people emphasizing the fact that different classes existed among them was the 10,000-word essay appearing as:

125. "The Economic Future of the Negro," *Publications of the American Economic Association,* February, 1906, Vol. VII (third series), pp. 219–242.

Not only had Du Bois been abroad, commencing with 1892, but his work was also becoming better and better known throughout the world. One result was the reprinting of his writings (as in No. 109 above) or the publication of essays written at request (as No.100 and 124a. above). In addition, such scholars visiting the United States made a point to see Du Bois. Among them was Max Weber, and as a result of his visit Du Bois contributed a long study to a publication edited by Weber.

126. "Die Negerfrage in den Vereiningten Staaten," *Archiv Für Sozialwissenschaft und Sozialpolitik* (Tübingen), 1906, Vol. XXII, pp. 31–79.

Later that same year, in another distinguished European journal, a long paper of Du Bois' appeared dealing specifically and in great detail with the facts concerning Black workers in America.

127. "L'Ouvrier nègre en Amérique," *Revue Économique Intérnationale* (Brussels), November, 1906, Vol. IV, pp. 298–348.

Characteristic of Du Bois was an article detailing a factual reply to the racist charges emanating from people like James Vardaman.

128. "Vardaman," *Voice of the Negro*, March, 1906, Vol. III, pp. 189–194.

Du Bois again reviewed books by Black and white authors and found the former's work superior, in:

129. "Slavery and Its Aftermath," *Dial*, May 1, 1906, Vol. XL, pp. 294–295, a review of G. S. Merriam, *The Negro and the Nation*, and W. A. Sinclair, *The Aftermath of Slavery*.

At the 1906 Hampton Conference, Du Bois very actively participated; as a result the following two articles appeared.

130. "Negro Mortality," *Hampton Negro Conference, Annual Report* (also listed as the *Hampton Bulletin*), September, 1906, Vol. II, pp. 81–84.

131. "The Minister," *idem*, Vol. II, pp. 91–92.

A major address he delivered at this conference—he was not asked back for many years!—urged the broadest possible concept of education as especially required by the Black people; in this he directly contradicted—explicitly—an address given at this same conference by President Theodore Roosevelt.

132. "The Hampton Idea," *Voice of the Negro*, September, 1906, Vol. III, pp. 632–636.

On June 15, 1906, Du Bois spoke before the graduating classes of the Colored high schools of Washington, D.C. He began by noting that many were talking about the great earthquake and fire that had devastated San Francisco the preceding April and then went on to analyze the life of the saint for whom the city was named:

133. "St. Francis of Assisi," *Voice of the Negro*, October, 1906, Vol. III, pp. 419–426. From that life Du Bois saw as the basic "lesson" this:

"The work of the world is to satisfy the world's great wants"; this meant that service to mankind was the great secret of a full and meaningful life.

A very early argument showing the integral connection between "the color line" and the world system of colonialism and the oppression of the Afro-American as part of that world-wide phenomenon—probably the first presentation of this seminal insight in a generally circulating United States publication—was:

134. "The Color Line Belts the World," *Collier's,* October 20, 1906, Vol. XXVIII, p. 20. Notable here, too, was Du Bois' pointing to Japan's defeat of Czarist Russia in 1905 as signifying the beginning of the end of "white supremacy." Reprinted in the *Public,* October 27, 1906, Vol. IX, pp. 708–709.

One of the worst pogroms against Black people to occur prior to the First World War was that which tore apart Atlanta in September, 1906. A detailed account of the event was:

135. "The Tragedy of Atlanta. From the Point of View of the Negroes," *World Today,* November, 1906, Vol. XI, pp. 1173–1175. Du Bois pointed to the resistance of the Blacks; he noted that the corrupt political system and especially the police force and the enveloping racism were basic causes of the outbreak.

Du Bois was in Alabama conducting a research project for the U.S. Census Bureau at the time of the pogrom in Atlanta—where his family lived. He took the first available train home and while crossing the South and beset with anguish he wrote a great poem.

136. "A Litany of Atlanta," first published in the *Independent,* October 11, 1906, Vol. LXI, pp. 856–858. This was widely reprinted at the time–for example, in *Alexander's Magazine,* November 15, 1906—and has since reappeared in many anthologies. No excerpt can do justice to this inspired cry from the heart.

As a result of racist baiting and brutality, a gun battle involving Black soldiers occurred in August, 1906, in Brownsville, Tex. In November, 1906, all the men of three companies of the Twenty-fifth Infantry were ordered dishonorably discharged by President Roosevelt; this action was fought and finally reversed in 1909. Concerning this Du Bois wrote:

137. "The President and the Soldiers," *Voice of the Negro*, December, 1906, Vol. III, pp. 552–553. Du Bois' general estimate of Theodore Roosevelt was shown here to be rather low; this is one of the roots of the 1912 break-away from the Republican party by a substantial number of Black men.

Speaking under the auspices of the Society for Ethical Culture (its founder, Felix Adler, and Du Bois were friends and coworkers in many causes), Du Bois was at Carnegie Hall the morning of February 17, 1907.

138. "Negro Ideals Described" was the manner in which his address was headlined in the New York *Evening Post*, of February 18, 1907, p. 12. That the newspaper owned by Oswald Garrison Villard would print the speech was indicative of the beginnings of Villard's move away from Tuskegee and toward what was to become the NAACP. The speech filled three columns; an essential point was Du Bois' belief that " ... the contribution of the Negro race, when it comes to its flower, is going to be not a contribution of manual toil nor of business shrewdness, but rather of artistic appreciation and human tenderness."

Having turned, with the Niagara Movement in 1905, to agitation, Du Bois felt impelled to produce the following essay:

139. "The Value of Agitation," *Voice of the Negro*, March, 1907, Vol. IV, pp. 109–110.

Black colleges and high schools had for years been listening to Du Bois; among the very earliest opportunities Du Bois had to speak to a predominantly white audience at a Northern university occurred on February 13, 1907. Du Bois spoke then before the affiliated Social Study Clubs of the University of Chicago. His speech was published as:

140. "Sociology and Industry in Southern Education," *Voice of the Negro*, May, 1907, Vol. IV, pp. 170–175. He noted here the building of what was called "The New South" with its industry and wealth; but, Du Bois asked, what of the distribution of that wealth and what of the creation of really fraternal and human values?

The day before the above address was delivered, Du Bois spoke at Chicago's Hull House—the inspiration of his friend Jane

Addams. In keeping with the date, Du Bois spoke on Lincoln, and his talk was published as:

141. "Abraham Lincoln," *Voice of the Negro*, June, 1907, Vol. IV, pp. 242–247. He urged that while wealth accumulated, soul deteriorated and that without equality for all men and all women of all colors and religions, the celebration of Lincoln's life was a sham. Much of this was reprinted in the *Christian Educator*, February, 1908, pp. 2–3.

Late in August, 1907, the Third Annual Meeting of the Niagara Movement was held in Boston; Du Bois was general secretary. He was interviewed and, while not quoted directly, his views were reported at length, in:

141a. "The Negro Niagara Movement," Springfield (Mass.) *Daily Republican*, August 29, 1907.

A month later, under the auspices of the Brooklyn Institute, Du Bois delivered an address, most of which was published in three newspapers:

142. "The Negro in the Large Cities." A considerable part of the address was published in the Brooklyn (N.Y.) *Standard Union*, on September 29, 1907, and in the Brooklyn *Eagle* of the same date and in fuller detail in the New York *Evening Post*, on September 30, 1907, p. 7. It was also reported, more briefly, in the New York *Herald-Tribune* on September 29, 1907. He directed his remarks especially to New York City and urged the propriety and wisdom of maximum effort by that City to provide really decent education and housing and jobs for the Afro-American people.

Continuing his trip south from Boston, Du Bois spoke before an audience of five hundred Black people on September 30, 1907, at the Shiloh Baptist Church in Washington, D.C., whose pastor, the Rev. J. M. Waldron, was a fellow member of the Niagara Movement. The press headlined the speech as:

143. "Urges Equal Race Rights," Washington *Post*, October 1, 1907. Du Bois urged political effectiveness and said (in 1907!): "It is high time to take steps to show our power."

Much of Du Bois' periodical writing in 1907–1909 was done for his own magazine, the *Horizon*, and this is dealt with in later pages. No doubt as a result of this, only two items by Du Bois appear to have been published in 1908 in other periodicals. These were:

144. A letter headed Atlanta, Ga., February 3, in the Kansas City *Star*, February 7, 1908. This was a reply to an editorial in that newspaper contrasting Booher T. Washington with Du Bois; it hailed the former and denounced the latter as one who was "ashamed" of being Black and therefore demanded an end to discrimination. Du Bois found it "very extraordinary that you should regard the man who stands up for his rights as being ashamed of himself."

145. An untitled paper, a commentary on a paper contributed by a Mississippi planter and author, Alfred H. Stone, to the 1907 annual meeting of the American Sociological Society, a panel of which was called "Race Friction Between White and Black"; the Du Bois essay is in *American Journal of Sociology*, May, 1908, Vol. XIII, 834–838. (Du Bois did not deliver the commentary in person, and it was not read at the meeting itself—it arrived too late, one is told—but it was printed as stated.) It is a serious mistake, Du Bois suggests, to hope for "the survival of such virtues . . . as we expect and cultivate in dogs but not in men." Du Bois asked—in vain—that "this and other learned societies would put themselves on record as favoring a most thorough and unbiased scientific study of the race problem in America."

No American studied the economics of Black people in the United States more carefully and fully than Du Bois. One study among the dozens he produced was:

146. "Georgia Negroes and Their Fifty Millions of Savings," *World's Work* (New York), May, 1909, Vol. XVIII, pp. 11550–11554. This showed that in the face of very great obstacles Black people in Georgia then owned almost one and a half million acres of land (more area than Delaware); it examined the details of how the Afro-American in Georgia made—or tried to make—a living. One of the specific proposals put forth here is for a federal postal-savings system.

Du Bois, who was, of course, a chief founder of the National Association for the Advancement of Colored People (NAACP) wrote an account of the May, 1909, conference held in New York City, which was the immediate propelling event, in:

147. "The National Committee on the Negro," *Survey* (New York),

June 12, 1909, Vol. XXII, pp. 407–409. Du Bois described its "net result" as "the vision of future co-operation, not simply as in the past, between giver and beggar—the older ideal of charity—but a new alliance between experienced social workers and reformers in touch on the one hand with scientific philanthropy and on the other with the great struggling mass of laborers of all kinds, whose condition and needs know no color line."

"Throughout the United States there are numbers of communities of Black folk, segregated, secluded, more or less autonomous, going their quiet way unknown of most of the surrounding world," wrote Du Bois in his study of one such community:

148. "Long in Darke," *Independent*, October 21, 1909, Vol. LXVII, pp. 917–918. This is an examination of the community of Long in Darke County, in southwestern Ohio.

At the year's close, Du Bois was asked to survey the 50 years of Afro-American history and life from the time of John Brown's raid; he did so in:

149. "Fifty Years Among the Black Folk," New York *Times*, December 12, 1909, Sect. VI, p. 4. Du Bois emphasized the growth of self-realization and stated that Black people were "girding themselves to fight in the van of progress" not only for themselves but also for "the emancipation of women, universal peace, democratic government, the socialization of wealth, and human brotherhood." A condensed version of this article appeared in *Missionary Review of the World*, June, 1911, Vol. XXIV (n.s.), pp. 460–461.

The year 1910 witnessed Du Bois' joining the NAACP in New York and his launching of the *Crisis*; most of his writings in that magazine are dealt with in another section of this work. Despite this gigantic effort, Du Bois did publish fairly frequently in other periodicals during the year. In February and March he delivered a paper, "Race Prejudice," before the Free Synagogue and at the Republican Club. As a result there appeared:

150. "As To Race Prejudice", New York *Evening Post*, February 26, 1910, p. 10. It contains about a 400-word summary of the Free Synagogue lecture, where Du Bois insists that a citizen should have the right to "his own individuality," to "public courtesy," "opportunity", "peace," and "truth."

150A. "Race Prejudice," the speech at the Republican Club, was issued in full in pamphlet form by that club and is listed later (No. 1929). Part of it appeared in the Atlanta (Ga.) *Press*, on November 5, 1910.

Beginning around 1904, Du Bois' analysis of the question of racism took on more of an economic, almost Marxian quality. By 1910 he considered himself a socialist and joined the Socialist Party; although his party affiliations varied thereafter, his belief in socialism—the definitions of which changed in his own mind —remained with him to his death. Indicative of this new emphasis was:

151. "The Economic Aspects of Race Prejudice," *Editorial Review* (New York), May, 1910, Vol. II, pp. 488–493. Du Bois noted the use of racism by aspiring politicians and by capitalists (in terms of dividing workers), and he saw its international ramifications, especially in terms of colonies and trade. He closed by urging that support be given to efforts to induce the federal government to financially support the education of Black people.

Du Bois made his second (and last) delivery of a paper to a meeting of the American Historical Association at its 1909 annual meeting, held in New York City in December. It was later published as:

152. "Reconstruction and Its Benefits," *American Historical Review*, July, 1910, Vol. XV, pp. 781–799. Coming in the midst of the Dunning-Fleming school of Bourbon historiography and the Dixon rage in historical fiction, it began the revision in thinking on this subject in the historical profession that was to culminate 25 years later with Du Bois' *magnum opus, Black Reconstruction* (No. 1964).

In his unceasing war on racist stereotypes, Du Bois attacked that of "laziness" (something of which only poor people can be guilty!) with a careful assembly of the facts concerning the accumulation of property by Blacks since about 1890.

153. "Negro Property," *World Today*, August, 1910, Vol. XIX, pp. 905–906.

Having earned international renown with his *Souls of Black*

Folk and his activities and productions in the ensuing years, Du Bois published a study called:

154. "The Souls of White Folk," *Independent*, August 18, 1910, Vol. LXIX, pp. 339–342. Because of racism, he wrote, he saw "the souls of the White Folk daily shriveling and dying in the fierce flame of this new fanaticism." And he asked, over 60 years ago, "Whither has gone America's proud moral leadership of the world?"

Sexual fantasies and scientific illiteracy were and are significant features in racist ideology. Du Bois faced up to these at a time when "the yellow peril" and "the passing of the great race" were very powerful concepts with this essay:

155. "Marrying of Black Folk," *Independent*, October 13, 1910, LXIX, pp. 812–813. He attacked "impudent dictation in the sacredly personal matter" of whom one marries. About 50 years later Du Bois commented on this same question in a magazine also called the *Independent*, as the result of some ideas that Norman Mailer thought he had discovered (see No. 425).

In September, 1910, a devastating forest fire threatened the lives and property of many people in Idaho; important in rescuing scores of women and children were men from the Black Twenty-fifth Infantry Regiment. The press reported the facts but "forgot" to point out that the regiment was made up of Black men—and was the same regiment victimized by President Roosevelt in connection with the Brownsville affair. This brought a letter from Du Bois emphasizing both points.

156. "An Echo of Brownsville," New York *Evening Post*, September 26, 1910, p. 8.

Efforts in Baltimore to legalize ghetto restrictions upon the Black population, and a remark by Samuel Gompers at the St. Louis convention of the American Federation of Labor (AFL) in 1910 to the effect that Black workers "did not understand" the trade-union effort, led Du Bois to write the following letter:

157. "Fair Play for the Negro," New York *Evening Post*, November 25, 1910, p. 8. Du Bois warned that nothing is more necessary to a person than a decent home and a good job and that increasing attacks upon these vital needs must be resisted by anyone who thinks he is "democratic."

In a remarkable, long interview held in New York City, Du Bois insisted that "Negro slavery exists on a large scale in the United States today." He detailed this, in response to questions, in terms of peonage, giving specific instance of resistance thereto. He concluded. "The only way the South can free itself is to do justice to the Negro—to treat him as a political and civil equal." This was published as:

157a. " 'Negro Is Still Slave,' Declares Prof. Du Bois," Cincinnati *Times-Star*, December 5, 1910.

B. Russell Herts, the editor of a New York journal, asked several distinguished figures—Rabbi Stephen S. Wise, Booker T. Washington, the Socialist writer John Spargo, and others, as well as Du Bois—a series of questions concerning racism and whether "miscegenation, deportation, segregation" were solutions. Du Bois' reply rejected all three and suggested instead that the attempt be made "to treat men as men ... ".

158. "A Symposium on Race Prejudice," *International*, July, 1911, Vol. IV, p. 29.

Dr. Du Bois participated in the First Universal Races Congress held in England in July, 1911. While there he granted an extensive interview that was published as:

158a. "Where Black Meets White," *British Congregationalist* (London), July 27, 1911, p. 59. The mood is fairly optimistic but facts are dealt with realistically and the differences with Tuskegee are repeated.

Du Bois published two rather full reports on that Congress; they were:

159. "Coming of the Lesser Folk," New York *Post*, Saturday Supplement, August 19, 1911, pp. 1–2.

160. "The First Universal Races Congress," *Independent*, August 24, 1911, Vol. LXX, pp. 401–403.

Also while in England, Du Bois presented a paper on July 18, 1911, before the British Sociological Society:

161. "The Economics of Negro Emancipation in the United States," *Sociological Review* (Manchester), October, 1911, Vol. IV, pp. 303–313. The paper insisted that emancipation basically must be economic, not political, and concludes that there were three grounds for hope: 1) the objective interests of white workers favored Black emancipation; 2) the Afro-American with his "dogged determination" would not be kept down forever; 3) some outstanding white people—Jane Addams, John Dewey, and others—were participating in a movement to end discrimination. The basic problem is world-wide and is the determination "to reduce human labor to the lowest depth in order to derive the greatest personal profit."

On October 29, 1911, Joseph Pulitzer—owner and publisher of the St. Louis *Post-Dispatch* and of the New York *World*, both relatively enlightened papers—died. Du Bois wrote a poem inspired by this man's life; among other features it conveyed Du Bois' prolonged interest in and almost welcoming attitude toward death.

162. "Joseph Pulitzer," New York *World*, November 1, 1911. p. 10.

Du Bois' joining of the Socialist party by no means lessened his awareness of that party's limitations in terms of combating racism. This formed the basis of a speech he delivered to an audience of 1,000 socialists in New York City on January 20, 1912, reported in considerable part in direct quotation and in summary in:

163. "Socialism Is Too Narrow For Negroes," *Socialist Call*, January 21, 1912.

Du Bois paid close attention also to the rise of a Black bourgeoisie and intelligentsia; he hoped that these elements would be part of forces seeking an end to racism. A prime and, Du Bois felt, splendid example was afforded by:

164. "The Upbuilding of Black Durham," *World's Work*, January, 1912, Vol. XIII, pp. 334–338. He was especially impressed by the wholeness of the Black economy that seemed to prevail in that city.

With the legalization and institutionalizing of Jim Crow in the South and the border states, similar movements developed in the North. Efforts, for example, to introduce legally segregated education in Indianapolis were quite strong before the First World War and were defended by that city's leading newspaper. Du Bois objected in a letter to the paper and again explained his difference with Booker T. Washington.

165. "Dr. Du Bois Explains," Indianapolis *Star*, April 8, 1912. Beneath Du Bois' letter, the editor said that he felt Du Bois' ideas were "false and mischievous" and that Washington "is right."

The New York *Times* on October 30, 1912 published a report on "Negroes Disfranchised" that, in effect, justified this and asserted that it represented the sound determination to keep the United States "a white man's country." Du Bois' fairly lengthy reply was published:

166. "Grandfather Clauses," New York *Times*, November 3, 1912, p. 16. In this letter Du Bois demonstrated that disfranchisement of Black people meant not only the curtailing of their rights but also directly and indirectly the vitiation of the entire democratic process in the United States.

Dr. Du Bois was invited to participate in the joint meeting of the American Economic Association and the American Statistical Association, held in Washington, D.C., in December, 1911. The paper he then delivered was published as:

167. "The Rural South," *Publications of the American Statistical Association* (Boston), March, 1912, Vol. XIII, pp. 80–84. This emphasized the widespread existence of peonage, the almost total disfranchisement of Black people, and the dire impact of this upon the South as a whole.

The year 1913 marked the appearance of the *New Review* in New York City; this was a weekly magazine that stated, in its opening editorial (January 4) that its "primary purpose" was "to enable the Socialists of America to attain to a better knowledge and clearer understanding of the International Socialist Movement." Du Bois was associated with this effort from its beginning (as were his colleagues at the NAACP, William English Walling and Mary White Ovington) and contributed:

168. "A Field for Socialists," *New Review*, January 11, 1913, Vol. I, pp. 54–57. The first sentence gives the theme. "There is a group of ten million persons in the United States toward whom Socialists would better turn serious attention."

In less than a month he returned to this question.

169. "Socialism and the Negro Problem," *New Review*, February 1, 1913, Vol. I, pp. 138–141. He pointed out that one out of five workers in the United States was Black and emphasized, with his extraordinary prophetic sense: "The Negro Problem then is the great test of the American Socialist." To get some idea of what Du Bois had in mind, see the utterly racist contribution in the same magazine (by then a monthly) by the State Secretary of the Socialist Party in Mississippi, December, 1913, Vol. I, pp. 990–991.

The article that Du Bois contributed to The New York *Times* in 1909 (No. 149) was the basis for one contributed in 1913.

169a. "Social Effects of Emancipation," *Survey*, Feb. 1, 1913, Vol. XXIX, pp. 570–573. Some of the data are carried forward a year or two, but the essay is almost exactly the same as the earlier one.

The essay last mentioned was a result of editors observing that 1913 marked 50 years since the issuance in 1863 of the Emancipation Proclamation. Emory R. Johnson, editing the *Annals*, produced in that year an issue entitled "The Negro's Progress in Fifty Years." One of the essays therein was:

170. "The Negro in Literature and Art," *Annals of the American Academy of Political and Social Science*, September, 1913, Vol. XLIX, pp. 233–237. This essay includes a survey of the leading figures, an indication of the great difficulties and obstacles, and a prophecy that given the very rich "mass of material" a veritable renaissance would soon appear (it did, within the decade).

In 1914, in his work for the NAACP, Du Bois prepared the *Memorandum in Support of Proposed Amendment* to what was known as the Lever bill then before Congress dealing with educational questions. The *Memorandum* was a matter of considerable newspaper discussion and at times was extensively quoted, as in a story headlined:

170a. "Square Deal for the Negro," Springfield (Mass.) *Republican,* Mar. 13, 1914.

Someone signing himself "C. L. B." had a letter published in the New York *Times* complaining of some alleged inefficiency on the part of Pullman porters. This provoked a letter headlined:

171. "The Pullman Porter," New York *Times,* Mar. 16, 1914, Vol. VIII, p. 5. Du Bois pointed out that rules of behavior were set by the Company; that the porters were paid $25 a month and were supposed to supplement this from tips. He asked, too, if the public would support efforts at organization and strikes by porters; in less than 10 years A. Philip Randolph would lead the effort to find out.

In 1914 a Boston newspaper conducted a symposium on the question: "Does Race Antipathy Serve Any Good Purpose?" Contributing were Prof. Daniel Evans of Andover Theological Seminary; the distinguished Black critic and poet William Stanley Braithwaite; and Du Bois, who wrote:

172. "Scientific Reasons Against Race Antagonism," Boston *Globe,* July 19, 1914. He noted that "race antipathy is not instinctive, but a matter of careful education" and concluded by suggesting that on its elimination rested the fate of humanity.

In May, 1914, Dr. Du Bois joined the Editorial Board of the *New Review* (see No. 168). Shortly thereafter another contribution by him appeared in that magazine.

173. "Another Study in Black," *New Review,* July, 1914, Vol. II, pp. 410–414. This is a devastating critique of *Democracy and Race Friction* by John M. Mecklin, a professor at the University of Pittsburgh. Du Bois' criticism is directed at Mecklin's theme of placing the blame for the oppression upon Black people themselves.

From about 1890 to about 1920—accompanying the intensified repression of the Afro-American people—there appeared works in history, anatomy, and psychology seeking to give a scientific justification for racist practices. Du Bois reviewed one such:

174. Review of Marion J. Mayo, *The Mental Capacity of the American Negro,* a brief book (70 pp.), in *Journal of Philosophy,* September 24,

1914, Vol. XI, pp. 557–558. The unscientific methods and assumptions of the work are made clear by Du Bois.

With the commencement of the war in Europe in the summer of 1914, Du Bois sharpened further his argument as to the worldwide implications of racism. An example was an address, published as:

175. "The World Problem of the Color Line," Manchester (N.H.) *Leader*, Nov. 16, 1914. The newspaper printed a substantial section of this speech and several of the questions from the audience and Du Bois' replies. Although the weather was bad, there were, according to the newspaper reporter 900 people in the audience. Portions of the speech recall an earlier essay (No. 134) but the insistence that "the present world war is caused by the jealousy among leading European nations over colonial aggrandizement" is new. In his replies Du Bois emphasized evidence of China's awakening and suggested that when it fully takes place, "China will be irresistible."

Three of the publications by Du Bois in 1915 treated aspects of the preceding item in various ways.

176. "What Is Americanism?" *American Journal of Sociology*, January, 1915, Vol. XX, p. 463. Dr. Du Bois, contributing to a symposium in about 100 words made the point that racism denied real democracy and that the United States had become "a hotbed of racial prejudice and of despicable propaganda against the majority of men."

177. "The African Roots of the War," *Atlantic Monthly*, May, 1915, Vol. CXV, pp. 707–714. One of the most influential of Du Bois' essays, emphasizing the colonial and racist roots of the war then being waged in Europe. Programmatically, it is idealist—that is, an appeal for "clean hands and honest hearts." But it points to the "awakening leaders" of lands such as China, India, and Egypt; it suggests, too, that the Afro-American must lead in the awakening of the African continent. Reprinted in 1915 as Mary Dunlop Maclean Memorial Fund Publication No. 3, by the NAACP.*

178. In the spring of 1915 Du Bois visited Jamaica (where he briefly met Marcus Garvey for the first time). At a dinner in his honor attended by the mayor of Kingston and the U.S. Consul, Du Bois

---

*This essay was widely reprinted and commented upon in the contemporary Black and white press; for example: Saginaw (Michigan) *News*, May 5, 1915; Philadelphia *Evening Telegram*, May 3, 1915; Natchez (Mississippi) *Weekly Register*, May 12, 1915.

spoke of the interconnection of the struggles of the colored peoples of the world and the central role of the Black people in the United States. About 1,200 words of this speech were reported in the Jamaica (Kingston) *Times*, May 8, 1915.

Immediately upon his return from Jamaica, Du Bois threw himself back into the work of the NAACP. One of the campaigns then enlisting much of its energy was that opposing the showing of the intensely racist film *Birth of a Nation*. On May 30, 1915, 2,000 people packed a meeting held at Faneuil Hall protesting the showing of that film in Boston. The main speech was made by Du Bois; he contrasted the film, its content and its spirit, with the actualities of the Reconstruction period and the needs in the United States if democracy was to be realized. A considerable portion of this speech was directly quoted, with an added headline:

179. "Charges 'Slavery' Conspiracy Behind 'Birth of a Nation' ", Boston *Traveller and Evening Herald*, May 31, 1915.

Early in February, 1916, Dr. Du Bois addressed the Republican Club in New York City. Prior to his speaking, Ralph C. Ely, chairman of the Republican Committee in New Mexico, urged that the United States not simply intervene in Mexico but go in there and appropriate what he called North Mexico. Du Bois attacked this proposal; he said it typified the lustful purposes behind the war then raging in Europe, and he warned of the waning of democracy and the exacerbation of class differences in the United States. He illustrated this by speaking of conditions among Black people. This address is reported in very brief form and without direct quotation in:

179a. New York *Times*, February 6, 1916, Vol. IV, p. 2.

Victor Robinson, editor of a medical journal, organized a "Symposium on the Medical Profession" to which 66 people —from Eugene Victor Debs to Andrew Carnegie—contributed. Dr. Du Bois was one of those whose opinion was requested and in one paragraph

180. He expressed the view that medicine suffered from a lack of concern with preventive efforts: *Medical Review of Reviews* (New York), January, 1917, Vol. XXIII, p. 9.

Speaking before the Civitas Club in the Brooklyn, N.Y., Women's Clubhouse on March 29, 1916, Du Bois emphasized the colonial roots of the current war. He pointed out that education, mores, and laws produced the policy and practice of racism. He asked these women who were active in the struggle for their own enfranchisement not to confine their ideas to white women; to think of the Black women in their own city and country; and furthermore, "When you settle the problem of the status of women, take into account the women of China, of India, and of Africa." There was a rather full report of his speech:

181. "Dr. Du Bois Talks to Civitas About Recognition for Negro," Brooklyn (N.Y.) *Eagle*, March 30, 1916.

Prior to the entry of the United States into the First World War, Du Bois suggested that if the war resulted in the elimination of militarism it would be worthwhile; this in a letter, which was supplied with a heading:

182. "Bitterness After Peace," New York *Evening Post*, February 10, 1917, p. 8 (the letter was dated New York City, February 1).

In a major article, Du Bois explained why he saw the war then going on in Europe as "the prophecy" of his own soul; that is, he had warned that persistence in racism would so eat away the character of the white peoples of the world that they would descend to mass slaughter even of each other. He developed the thought that if colonialism and racism survived the present war, they would help induce an even greater slaughter in the future; this in:

183. "Of the Culture of White Folk," *Journal of International Relations* (Worcester, Massachusetts), April, 1917, Vol. VII, pp. 434–447. (This publication, issued at Clark University, had been called originally the *Journal of Race Development*.)

Du Bois sought again to explain the humanity of Black people and that given this humanity they would respond to oppression and indignity with many forms of resistance. He warned that this would continue and grow after the present war ended; he noted also "the peculiar inner economic cooperation" that was growing among Black people in South and North. This in an essay strangely titled by the editors:

184. "The Passing of 'Jim Crow,'" *Independent*, July 14, 1917, Vol. XCI, pp. 53–54.

In September, Lajpat Rai, an Indian nationalist leader seeking independence from Britain, and Dr. Du Bois addressed a session on the colonial peoples sponsored by the Intercollegiate Socialist Society and held in Bellport, Long Island (New York). Dr. Du Bois said that he felt the war then raging should be fought in the hope that a result might be the enhancement of the independence of colored peoples; a portion of that speech was published.

185. New York *Evening Post*, September 22, 1917, p. 14.

Du Bois pointed to the silence about Africa's future as ominous in terms of any democratic outcome of the war. He urged that in central Africa a state by and for Africans might be created; he saw also a national upsurge among Afro-Americans and Blacks in the West Indies and wanted this to be furthered after the war:

186. "The Negro's Fatherland," *Survey*, November 10, 1917, Vol. XXXIX, p. 141.

Writing for a socialist readership, Du Bois reiterated that the failure to pay the greatest attention to the so-called Negro question on the part of those who called themselves socialists cast the gravest doubt upon their sincerity and vitiated the possibility of effective action, in:

187. "The Problem of Problems," *Intercollegiate Socialist*, December, 1917-January, 1918, Vol. VI, pp. 5–9. (See, on this, Nos. 168 and 169.)

Of great interest was the quite critical review which Du Bois gave to a book (also critically greeted by Dr. Carter G. Woodson) published in 1918 and thereafter for many years accepted as the authoritative treatment of what it meant to be a slave in the United States.

188. Review of U. B. Phillips, *American Negro Slavery*, in *American Political Science Review*, 1918, Vol. XII, No. 4, p. 722.

An earnest appeal for funds to support the work of the Music School Settlement for Colored People in Harlem—founded by David Mannes and then directed by J. Rosamond Johnson —appears in a fairly long letter:

189. New York *Evening Post*, November 21, 1918 (the letter is headed New York, November 18).

As the First World War drew to a close, Du Bois acted toward assuring an international conference of African and African-derived peoples. Late in 1918, preliminary steps having been taken that eventuated in the 1919 Pan-African Conference held in Paris, Du Bois was sailing to Europe aboard the *Orizaba* with Robert R. Moton—head of Tuskegee and Wilson's emissary to the Black troops—as his room-mate! Aboard, he was interviewed by Arthur D. Call, who edited the organ of the American Peace Society; this interview was published as:

189a. "The Future of Africa," *Advocate of Peace* (Washington, D.C.), January, 1919, Vol. LXXXI, pp. 12–13. The ideas were substantially similar to those expressed in No. 186 above.

From Paris, Du Bois sent back several reports, especially to the *Crisis* (which are noted further on); one of these was a quite detailed report on the background and work of the Pan-African Meeting:

190. "Negro at Paris," Rochester (N.Y.) *Democrat And Chronicle*, May 4, 1919. Reprinted in the *Christian Science Monitor* (Boston), May 16, 1919, p. 3.

Soon after returning from Paris, Du Bois not only published exposures of the racism that was official policy on the part of the United States authorities in France during the war but also spoke about such racism at mass meetings. One such, held at a "filled Tremont Temple" in Boston on April 10, 1919, included "sensational" disclosures, according to the press reports; these reports also quoted Du Bois' remarks that the "power of capital" was now organized "with the armies and navies of the world" to maintain colonialism and racism and "that is the way to prepare future wars".

190a. Boston *Herald*, April 11, 1919.

As part of the general repression that accompanied and followed the war, mass murders of Black people and pogroms repeatedly occurred in the United States in 1919—in Blakely, Ga.; Omaha, Nebr.; Elaine, Ark.; Chicago; Washington; and elsewhere. White newspapers began to treat the subject of Black oppression with a certain degree of seriousness; one devoted several pages to what it headlined as "Leading Negroes Analyze the Color Tragedy." The lead piece was by Du Bois:

191. New York *Sun*, October 12, 1919, pp. 5,7. Du Bois made clear the atrocities against which Black people were protesting and insisted that not Bolsheviks but these conditions evoked militancy and that militancy was justified and would mount if the atrocities persisted.

192. Letter, headed "The Arkansas Riot," New *York World*, November 28, 1919, p. 12. A letter of some 1,200 words in which Du Bois takes issue with an article by Clair Kennmore published in the *World* newspaper on November 16. Du Bois here summarizes the facts and the causes in connection with the so-called Elaine, Ark., "riots" in which scores (perhaps as many as 250) of Black people were slaughtered and hundreds arrested and some executed as part of a drive by plantation overlords to maintain their system of peonage, a system being challenged by efforts at organization by the Black people involved.

The following year marked Du Bois' first appearance in a rather new magazine with which Walter Lippmann was associated. Lippmann had known Du Bois prior to the war and had met with him in Paris in 1919. Du Bois' essay was entitled:

193. "On Being Black," *New Republic*, February 18, 1920, Vol. XXI, pp. 338–341.

Du Bois' appearance as an author in the magazine owned by his NAACP colleague Oswald Garrison Villard also occurred at this time.

194. "The Republicans and the Black Voter," *Nation*, June 5, 1920, Vol CX, pp. 757–758. Du Bois showed that the Black voter held the balance of power in several key states; that local elections meant a great deal to him; and that in these, in particular, he was voting with increasing independence.

Du Bois reviewed seven books—two in French—dealing with aspects of the history of the African continent and in particular with the exploitation of its resources and the awful treatment of its populations by Europeans. He emphasizes that the works under review show the significance of the history of Africa as such, the dimensions of its ravishment, and the relationship of the latter to the wars that rocked human society for the preceding two centuries. He warns that unless the process of enslaving and exploiting Africa is changed, wars will continue to inflame the world.

195. "Eternal Africa," *Nation*, September 25, 1920, Vol. CXI, pp. 350–352. Reviews of Leo Wiener, *Africa and the Discovery of America*; R. C. Maugham, *The Republic of Liberia*; Berthe Georges-Gaulis, *La France au Maroc*; Arthur B. Keith, *The Belgian Congo and the Berlin Act*; E. D. Morel, *The Black Man's Burden*; Leonard Woolf, *Empire and Commerce in Africa*; Joseph Caillaux, *Agadir*.

The next year Du Bois reviewed favorably a biography of E. D. Morel.

196. Review of *E. D. Morel. The Man and His Work*, by F. Seymour Cocks, *Nation*, May 25, 1921, Vol. XCII, p. 749. Morel's best claim to fame was his exposure of the atrocities committed by King Leopold's company in the Belgian Congo.

A Black newspaper conducted an open discussion of the wisdom and usefulness of the Pan-African Movement, and Du Bois was moved to reply in two letters.

197. "Pan-African Congress Defended by Dr. Du Bois," New York *Age*, May 28, 1921.

198. "Dr. Du Bois Replies to Bishop C. S. Smith [of Detroit]," New York *Age*, June 25, 1921. This letter is of particular interest, for in it Du Bois is at pains to distinguish the Pan-African Movement from the effort led by Marcus Garvey.

A quarterly issued by the University of Washington published a Du Bois essay:

199. "The Contribution of the Negro to American Life and Culture," *Pacific Review* (Seattle), June, 1921, Vol. II, pp. 127–132. A general encyclopedic article, somewhat similar to No. 170, but broader and up-to-date.

The Second Pan-African Congress was held in the late summer of 1921 and sat in London, Brussels, and Lisbon. At its London session on August 29, a resolution written by Dr. Du Bois was adopted; this was published widely at the time, for example.

200. "Manifesto to the World," Manchester *Guardian*, August 30, 1921, and *Nation*, September 12, 1921, Vol. CXIII, pp. 357–358. Essentially, this is an affirmation of the right of self-determination for the peoples of Africa.

A characteristically frank delineation of the limits and dimensions of the Second Pan-African Congress, with emphasis upon the disagreements among those representing French Africa and the Afro-Americans appears in this essay.

201. "A Second Journey to Pan-Africa," *New Republic*, December 7, 1921, Vol. XXIX, pp. 39–41.

Again attacking sexual taboos associated with the oppression of Black people (as he had done in 1910 (No. 155), Du Bois contributed a very frank and clear essay to the rather new magazine being edited by Anne Rochester.

202. "Social Equality and Racial Intermarriage," *World Tomorrow* (N.Y.), March, 1922, Vol. V, pp. 83–84.

Du Bois was "dissolved in amazement" at the reality of the Afro-American church as an expression of a people's soul and organizing genius. The facts about this were in a book he reviewed and he praised the author's diligence but lamented that the essence and the real meaning of that church's history were not conveyed. This is:

203. "The Negro Church," a review of *The History of the Negro Church*, by Carter G. Woodson (Washington, D.C. Associated Publishers, 1922), in *The Freeman*, October 4, 1922, Vol. VI, 92–93.

A. Philip Randolph's radical-socialist magazine requested a contribution from Dr. Du Bois (whom it had frequently attacked) to a symposium.

204. Contribution to "Symposium on Garvey," *Messenger*, December, 1922, Vol. IV, p. 551. Du Bois asserted that he did not wish to present his views on this subject this way but would do so and had done so in the *Crisis*.

In a letter, Du Bois remarked on the revealing fact that all the discussion about the appointment of Walter Cohen as Collector of the Port of New Orleans revolved around the single fact that "one of his great-grandfathers was black":

205. Letter, N Y *Times*, December 12, 1922, p. 18.

A pioneering essay in the analysis of U.S. politics was:

206. "The South and a Third Party," *New Republic*, January 3, 1923, Vol. XXXIII, pp. 138–141. The essay showed that the disfranchisement of Black people in the South made a breakaway from the two-party system practically impossible.

The significant shift of the Garvey movement commencing about 1922 from one deeply challenging the system of colonialism to one objectively allying itself with forces of reaction—even the Ku Klux Klan—induced Du Bois to publish increasingly critical estimates of that movement; one such was:

207. "Back to Africa," *Century Magazine*, February, 1923, Vol. CV, pp. 539–548.

In the magazine edited by Henry Mencken, Du Bois contributed a marvelously satirical essay that half-mockingly developed the idea that Black people in the United States really represented:

208. "The Superior Race," *Smart Set* (N.Y.), April, 1923, Vol. LXX, pp. 55–60.

Returning to the hospitable pages of Anna Rochester's magazine, Du Bois analyzed a subject whose importance he was among the first to see and announce, in:

209. "The Segregated Negro World," *World Tomorrow*, May, 1923, Vol. VI, pp. 136–138.

With the migration of Southern Black people to cities and to the North, Du Bois pinpointed the need for a national effort to eradicate racism in the face of the increasing:

210. "Hosts of Black Labor," *Nation*, May 9, 1923, Vol. CXVI, pp. 539–541.

Reflecting the so-called Harlem Renaissance of the 1920's—in which Du Bois was a leading force—was the following essay:

211. "Can the Negro Save the Drama?," *Theatre Magazine* (N.Y.), July, 1923, Vol. XXXVIII, pp. 12, 68. Some historical background is provided and an effort made to convey to the white readers an idea of Afro-American accomplishment in the arts, including the drama; Du Bois is certain that the "wonderfully rich field" of Black life will produce Black Ibsens, Tolstoys, and Molières.

In a magazine published by Funk & Wagnalls and reaching a largely white and religious readership, Du Bois tried to convey something of the basic data of Black life and work and accomplishments.

212. "The Negro as a National Asset," *Homiletic Review*, July, 1923; Vol. LXXXVI, pp. 52–58.

As part of the same impulse which produced everything "new"—from the *New Republic* to the *New Masses* and the "New Negro"—there appeared soon after the First World War a magazine directed to students taking generally a strongly democratic and egalitarian view. Du Bois was asked to contribute to it a kind of editorial; he did, with:

213. "To American Students," *New Student*, December 1, 1923, Vol. III, No. 5, p. 1. In college, Du Bois suggests, one should learn that others—all others—should have "the same preparation for living that you have"; otherwise one has no real "democracy of culture."

In 1923, the editors of the *New York World* asked scholars and public figures to name their ten favorite books.

214. "Ten Books I Enjoyed Most," New York *World*, June 14, 1923. Those selected by Du Bois, with no comment, were: Shakespeare's *Hamlet*; Knight's *History of England**; *The Three Musketeers*; the Old Testament; *The Lady of the Lake; David Copperfield; Uncle Tom's Cabin*; Dunbar's poems; The *Iliad; Faust.*

---

*This refers to Charles Knight, *The Popular History of England; An Illustrated History of Society and Government from the Earliest Period to Our Own Time*. It was published originally in London in eight volumes in the 1860's, but there was an "*Abridged, Revised and Continued*" edition (the continuation by J. H. Beale), in 3 volumes, published in 1883 by W. Gay in New Haven. It is probable that is the edition Du Bois used.

In 1923, after much difficulty, the Third Pan-African Congress was able to hold sessions in London and in Lisbon. The attendance was smaller than two years earlier, but the discussions and resolutions tended to be more militant. Du Bois reported on this in:

215. "The Negro Takes Stock," *New Republic*, Jan. 2, 1924, Vol. XXXVII, pp. 143–145.

Another explosive essay by Du Bois was published in a magazine edited by Henry Mencken (and George Jean Nathan); it dealt with growing segregation in the nation—including the North—and efforts by Black people to meet this development. These efforts did not exclude what was called by some "separation" but which was in fact an effort to achieve fulfillment and dignity. Du Bois warned that bloodshed would be the inevitable result of continued Jim Crow.

216. "The Dilemma of the Negro," *American Mercury*, October, 1924, Vol. III, pp. 179–185.

From his first published writings, back in the 1880's Du Bois expressed profound interest in politics and in Black people engaging in it with an eye to their own advancement. Hence, Du Bois always advocated a sharp independence in politics, and in 1924 he supported the candidacy of La Follette on the Progressive ticket for the Presidency (as did, by the way, both the NAACP and the American Federation of Labor). He issued an appeal to Black voters to support La Follette, and much of it was quoted in a news item.

217. "Negro Aids La Follette," New York *Times*, October 21, 1924, p. 6.

While attending the Third Pan-African Congress in Europe, Du Bois was appointed by President Coolidge to be minister plenipotentiary and envoy extraordinary representing the United States at the inauguration of the President of Liberia. With this opportunity to make his first visit to Africa, Du Bois stayed not only in Liberia but toured much of West Africa. One of his accounts of Africa's great impact upon him appeared as:

218. "The Primitive Black Man," *Nation*, December 17, 1924, Vol. CXIX, pp. 675–676.

Another direct result of the African visit was:

219. "Britain's Negro Problem in Sierra Leone," *Current History* (published by the New York *Times* Company), February, 1925, Vol. XXI, pp. 690–700. Du Bois concluded his survey with this sentence: "Black British West Africa is out for self-rule and in our day is going to get it."

That same month saw the appearance of:

220. "What Is Civilization: Africa's Answer," in *Forum*, February, 1925, Vol. LXXIII, pp. 178–188. Reprinted in Maurice Maeterlinck, *et al.*, *What Is Civilization?* (New York: Duffield, 1926, pp. 41–57.) The theme is similar to the *Nation* essay (No. 218).

From time to time Du Bois resorted to the short-story form to convey his message (as in "The Coming of John" in his *Souls of Black Folk*). An example—using the image of the crucified Christ that recurs in his writings—was:

221. "The Black Man Brings His Gifts," *Survey*, March 1, 1925, Vol. LIII, pp. 655–657, 710.

In a major essay, Du Bois re-examined his 1900 concept that "the problem of the Twentieth Century is the problem of the color line".

222. "Worlds of Color," *Foreign Affairs*, April, 1925, Vol. XX, pp. 423–444. He thought that now the problem "is what we call Labor"; but he added that the oligarchy that owns "England, France, Germany, America, and Heaven" fastens this ownership by its special exploitation of colonial peoples; in this sense, then, he said he still saw the problem of problems as that of "the Color Line." Reprinted, with some revisions and considerable additions, in Alain Locke, ed., *The New Negro* (New York: Boni, 1925), pp. 385–414; and with no alterations in Hamilton Fish Armstrong, ed., *The Foreign Affairs Reader* (New York, 1947), pp. 78–102. The additions in the Locke edition pertain mainly to developing the significance of the failure of labor organizations and parties in Europe to appreciate the significance of the special exploitation of colonial workers.

John Haynes Holmes, a life-long friend of Du Bois', when editing a magazine in Chicago asked Du Bois to contribute an appreciation of Thomas Henry Huxley, who was born in 1825. Du Bois did so, emphasizing Huxley's devotion to the pursuit of truth regardless of consequences, in a tribute published in:

223. *Unity* (Chicago), May 25, 1925, Vol. XCV, p. 214.

Du Bois' "Star of Ethiopia" was an elaborate historical pageant depicting the history of African and African-derived peoples from the discovery of iron in very ancient times to the present century; it was witnessed by tens of thousands in New York City (1913), Washington (1915), and Philadelphia (1916). In 1925 it was produced at the Hollywood Bowl in Los Angeles. An essay by Du Bois telling of the impending production in Los Angeles and —characteristically for him—explaining the significance of the Renaissance in art then flowering among Black people, as a people's form of self-expression and not simply as the reflection of individual talent, was published as:

224. "A Negro Art Renaissance," Los Angeles *Times*, June 14, 1925, part 3, pp. 26–27.

A companion piece to essay No. 219, treating of British colonies in Africa, was:

225. "France's Black Citizens in West Africa," *Current History*, July, 1925, Vol. XXII, pp. 559–564. Du Bois saw real hope for effective African rule, if leadership remained "unseduced by the present economic organization of Europe. ... "

226. Review of Dorothy Scarborough's *On the Trail of Negro Folk Songs*, in *Book Review* (New York), September 25, 1925. Although he was critical of its repetitiousness and its acceptance of "conventional stuff about the South," Du Bois nevertheless highly regarded this work as "an unusual contribution to the Negro folk song."

"A Magazine of the Newer Spirit"—to quote its subtitle—was founded in Baltimore in 1923 by V. F. Calverton. The magazine reflected a kind of Marxian radical orientation, with writers like James Oneal and Harry Potamkin and reprints of the work of G. V. Plekhanov appearing from time to time. To this periodical, Du Bois contributed a brief but incisive essay.

226a. "The Social Origins of American Negro Art," *Modern Quarterly*, October–December, 1925, Vol. III, No. 1, pp. 53–56. Du Bois' essay explicates the point of the title and suggests that to the degree the walls of imprisonment were shattered, to that degree would a great and unique literature enter the culture of the world.

A final essay by Du Bois directly reflecting his experiences while in Africa was:

227. "Liberia and Rubber," *New Republic*, November 18, 1925, Vol. XLIV, pp. 326–29. Du Bois stated that there was "only one power" that might prevent Firestone Rubber from repeating "in Liberia all the hell that white imperialism has perpetrated heretofore in Africa and Asia" and "that is the black American with his vote."

(Note: As part of the struggle against racism in Fisk University, which Du Bois was then leading, the *Fisk Herald* was recreated briefly in 1925; a printed version, Vol. XXXIII, No. 2, was issued and its editor was Du Bois. It contained a brief editorial and some notes by Du Bois and statements by white persons "connected at some time with Fisk University" confirming the racism of the Administration.)

In 1925 the radical and Marxist American Negro Labor Congress was formed; in conservative and bourgeois circles some concern was made public about this. One story concerning this quoted Dr. Du Bois' opinion at some length in a story headlined:

228. "Communists Boring Into Negro Labor," New York *Times*, January 17, 1926, sec. 2, pp. 1–2. Du Bois said that if it was desired to stop Black interest in Communism, racism should be eliminated.

229. Review of volume VII of *The Mythology of All Races*, edited in 13 volumes by John Λ. MacCulloh. Volume II was made up of "Armenian Mythology," by M. H. Amanikian, and "African Mythology," by Alice Werner in the *New York Herald-Tribune*, January 17, 1926, Book Review Section, p. 9. A positive review, analyzing in particular the work of Alice Werner—an English anthropologist and linguist. "The casual reader," Du Bois thought, would find the book "of great and continuing interest" while "the scientist must, of course, read it thoroughly."

One of the platforms consistently open to Du Bois was the Ford Hall Forum in Boston and the *Chronicle* published a very considerable section of a lecture he delivered there in January, 1926.

230. "The Hypocrisy of White Folks," Boston *Chronicle*, January 20, 1926. This lecture emphasized the failure to liberate Black people and women in general and concentrated on the manifestly undemocratic method by which the economy was conducted and its profits distributed.

Student and, to a lesser degree, faculty insurgency in colleges servicing Black people reached rebellious proportions early in the 1920's, and Du Bois and the *Crisis* were in the middle of it. An essay detailing this and also excoriating the rigid anti-Black policies of almost all Northern institutions was:

231. "Negroes in College," *Nation*, Mar. 3, 1926, Vol. CXXII, pp. 228–230.

One of the main tools, after the First World War, in the repression of labor, radicalism, Black efforts towards freedom, and movements such as those for the rights of women was the revitalized Ku Klux Klan (KKK). By the mid-1920's its political and social power was tremendous. Early in 1926 the *North American Review*—a leading magazine of the period—published a defense of the KKK by Imperial Wizard Hiram Evans. It followed this with a symposium on the KKK to which Du Bois contributed.

232. "The Shape of Fear," *North American Review*, June, 1926, Vol. CCXXIII, pp. 291–304. Du Bois here underlined—without using the word—the fascistic character of the KKK. Parts of his comments were noted in the New York *Times*, June 7, 1926, p. 2 (which misspelled his name).

The Seventeenth Annual Conference of the NAACP was held in Chicago in July, 1926. Du Bois spoke there; a newspaper account that carried much of the text headlined it:

233. "Du Bois Asks Freedom and Support for Race Artists," Pittsburgh *Courier*, July 17, 1926. The title summarizes its contents.

Du Bois lived in Harlem in the 1920's; the section then was not yet a fully Black ghetto, and the question of Black-white relations inside the area was an acute one. An interview with Du Bois on this matter was published.

233a. "Dr. Du Bois Tells How Differences Between Harlem Colored and Whites Can Be Solved," *Home News* (New York), Nov. 5, 1926. The solution was for people—and especially for white people—to treat all people of all colors as human beings.

As part of the Harlem Renaissance, Afro-American theaters appeared in the 1920's in several cities; among them was the company called the Krigwa Players, established in 1925 by Du Bois in Harlem; it terminated its lively activity in 1927 and Du Bois wrote of the effort as a whole in:

234. "The Krigwa Players Little Negro Theatre," *Amsterdam News*, Oct. 5, 1927.

The climax of a decade of unrest in the Black colleges came with the student strike in the very citadel of conservatism —Hampton Institute in Virginia. Du Bois wrote of its causes and consequences in:

235. "The Hampton Strike," *Nation*, Nov. 2, 1927, Vol. CXXV, pp. 471–472.

On the fiftieth anniversary of the Chicago publication *Unity*, founded by Jenkin Lloyd Jones and edited at this time by John Haynes Holmes, Du Bois contributed one among several "messages".

236. "Messages from Contemporaries," *Unity*, March 5, 1928, Vol. CI, p. 41.

A brief paragraph appeared in the New York *Times* reflecting Du Bois' thoughts.

237. "Immortality," New York *Times*, Apr. 8, 1928, Sec. 9, p. 1. This was originally written for Sydney Strong and appears in the book edited by him, *We Believe in Immortality* (New York. Coward-McCann, 1929), p. 18. The book's title was a misnomer as far as Du Bois was concerned for he took an agnostic position on the question.

The thought expressed by Du Bois concerning the disfranchisement of Black people and its impact upon third-party efforts (No.

206) was further developed by him in a speech before the ninth convention of the NAACP held in Los Angeles in June, 1928. This was extensively quoted in the press under the headline:

238. "Says Vote in South Equals Ten in North," New York *Times*, June 28, 1928, p. 17.

On the centennial of Leo Tolstoy, Du Bois—along with such other distinguished figures as Theodore Dreiser—was asked to express his thoughts and did so succinctly in:

239. *Unity*, September 10, 1928, Vol. CII, p. 18. Du Bois stressed Tolstoy's courage and his prophetic quality.

A 20-line poem by Du Bois appeared this year.

240. "The Song of America," New York *Herald Tribune*, October 10, 1928. It was a devastating critique of the dominant ethos. (On this, see No. 1975.)

Du Bois returned to the theme of the cost to democracy in general of the disfranchisement of Black people(see Nos.206,238) in an analysis of the then-current presidential election.

241. "Is Al Smith Afraid of the South?," *Nation*, October 17, 1928, Vol. CXXVII, pp. 392–394.

The first massive and scholarly published effort, in English, to examine Africa was the subject of a critical estimate:

242. "Africa," *World Tomorrow*, October, 1928, Vol. XI, pp. 420–421. A review of Raymond L. Buell, *The Native Problem in Africa*. A basic failing, said Du Bois, was in Buell's economics—assuming the perpetuity and propriety of capitalism—and in his ignoring the consequent exploitation of Africans. Further, the author does not understand that "black America is going to have a voice in black America's fate. Black Africa must and will do the same or die trying."

With the idea of the "New Negro" and the fact of the Harlem Renaissance, a few magazines of national circulation began in the 1920's to confront the matter with some seriousness. In an issue devoted to the so-called Negro question, Du Bois contributed an essay.

243. "Race Relations in the United States," *Annals of the American*

Academy of Political and Social Science, November, 1928, Vol. CXL, pp. 6–10. Examining the subject in his usual uncompromising way, Du Bois asked: "What is going to become of a country which allows itself to fall into such an astonishing intellectual and ethical paradox? Nothing but disaster."

On the eleventh anniversary of the Bolshevik Revolution, Du Bois—who had visited the U.S.S.R. for two months in 1926—was asked to contribute to the organ of the International Labor Defense; he did so.

244. An untitled paragraph affirming the new Russia as "a victim of a determined propaganda of lies" and hailing what "it is trying to do" in *Labor Defender* (New York), November, 1928, p. 248.

In the forum on current events then conducted regularly at the socialist Rand School in New York City, Du Bois gave a lecture, on February 2, 1929; significant sections of this talk were quoted in:

245. "Sees Chance in South for Socialist Party," New York *Times*, February 3, 1929, Sec. 1, p. 13. Du Bois emphasized that the struggle for justice and full rights by the Black worker was not a question of charity but rather of mutual necessity for Black and white.

One of the great debates of the 1920's was that between Du Bois and Lothrop Stoddard—author of *The Rising Tide of Color*—held in the Chicago Coliseum before 5,000 people in March, 1929. The texts were published in a pamphlet listed and annotated hereafter (No.1939), but the event was widely reported in the press, and Du Bois' remarks were extensively quoted in the Black press; for example:

245a. Chicago *Defender*, Mar. 23, 1929.

Among the novelists of the Harlem Renaissance period was Jessie R. Fauset, who served as Du Bois' assistant editor on the *Crisis* for some years. One of her books was reviewed by Du Bois.

246. Review of Jessie R. Fauset, *Plum Bun*, in *Book Review*, April, 1929, p. 14. Du Bois was attracted to the book because it treated ordinary features of non-sensational Black life, rather than the exotic, as in Carl Van Vechten and Claude McKay.

Du Bois returned to Hampton Institute—after his 1906 address (No.132)—during its summer sessions; his talk was "The Negro in Literature and Art" and quotations of some significant sections appeared.

247. "Freedom in Art Must Be Fought for Du Bois Says," Norfolk (Va.) *Journal and Guide*, July 30, 1929. Du Bois' main point here was that it was more and more necessary for Black writers and artists to create not for white but rather for Black people.

A debate on the United States occupation of Haiti, under the auspices of the Foreign Policy Association, was held in New York City on December 21, 1929. Defending the occupation was W. W. Cumberland, financial adviser to occupied Haiti from 1924 to 1927; attacking it was Du Bois. The debate was broadcast widely and reported fairly well in the press; in one case, pertinent sections of Du Bois remarks were quoted.

248. "Our Policy on Haiti Scored in Debate," New York *Times*, December 22, 1929, p. 20.. The policy was racist and antidemocratic; the people were kept in peonage in order to bring profits to U.S. corporations.

(Note: There is a fragment of a speech by Du Bois published in the Cleveland *News* sometime in June, 1929; efforts to locate complete copy have failed.)

Du Bois continued debating U. S. policy in Haiti as opportunity appeared. February, 1930, found him debating the question with Captain F. H. Cooke of the U.S. Navy before the Women's Club of Orange, N.J. A few words of Du Bois' analysis were quoted in a news report; he was attacked vehemently by some in the audience. One demanded to know if he were an American citizen; the paper reports that the doctor quietly replied: "I sometimes wonder if I am." The story reporting the debate was:

248a. "Debate on Haiti Rouses Women's Club," New York *Times*, February 21, 1930, p. 10.

Fragments of a speech delivered by Du Bois under the auspices of the Negro Education Club of Teachers College, Columbia University, were reported.

248b. "Du Bois Avers 'Civilized Countries' Settled Human Rights Many Ages Ago," *Amsterdam News*, April 9, 1930.

Knopf published James Weldon Johnson's *Black Manhattan* in 1930, and Du Bois reviewed it in:

249. New York *Evening Post*, July 12, 1930, Sec. 3, p. 5. Du Bois thought very highly of the work, praising especially its section devoted to the history of Black drama as well as aspects of the movement challenging Booker T. Washington.

In another "letter to the Times," Du Bois continued his campaign to expose the deeply antidemocratic character of the voting structure in the United States and to show how the disfranchisement of Black people had disfranchised in fact many white men and women. The letter appeared with a supplied heading:

250. "Remarks on Alabama," New York *Times*, August 31, 1930, Sec. 3, p. 3.

Du Bois reviewed three books, one by a Southern white man and two jointly written.

251. "Concerning the Negro," *Nation*, April 8, 1931, Vol. CXXXII, pp. 385–386 (One page is misdated April 1). The books reviewed were J. L. Hill, *Negro: National Asset or Liability*; L. J. Greene and C. G. Woodson, *The Negro Wage Earner*; and Sterling Spero and Abram L. Harris *The Black Worker*. Du Bois' estimate was positive in all cases; the Spero-Harris book was especially important, he stated, for it dealt with Black people, "not as a group apart, but as a group of millions affecting the economic and social development of America ... to such an extent that no complete picture of America can be made without considering it."

Two speeches by Du Bois were noted in the press at this time.

251a. "Du Bois Scores White Reign at Bryn Mawr," Philadelphia *Tribune*, April 30, 1931. A one-day conference "on the economic status of the Negro" was the scene of a "scathing indictment" of white supremacy and a warning from Du Bois of worldwide violence if that supremacy was continued.

251b. New York *Times*, October 27, 1931. The article quoted part of one sentence from a speech by Du Bois—"We are fighting all over the world today for cheap labor and materials ... "—in its reportage of a "peace mass meeting" sponsored by the *World Tomorrow* magazine in New York City on October 26.

In a very sharp attack upon the record of the dominant white Christian churches in the United States, Du Bois contributed a paper:

252. "Will the Church Remove the Color Line?" *Christian Century*, December 9, 1931, Vol. XLVIII, pp. 1554–1556. Reviewing the record and noting the role of the major churches in maintaining the status quo, Du Bois' reply was in the negative.

A major effort, into which he put a great deal of time, was the Commencement Address delivered by Dr. Du Bois at Howard University in June, 1930. This paper was published in the first number of a quarterly that was to achieve great distinction:

253. "Education and Work," *Journal of Negro Education* (published by Howard University and edited by Charles H. Thompson), April, 1932, Vol. I, pp. 60–74. This essay traces the nature of the Washington–Du Bois controversy; insists that neither college nor industrial school has succeeded; and proposes concentration upon a relevant, dynamic education with special usefulness for the Afro-American population.

The American Birth Control League devoted an issue of its publication to Black people and birth control. Essays were forthcoming from several Black people, including George S. Schuyler, Charles S. Johnson, and Du Bois. Du Bois' was:

254. "Black Folk and Birth Control," *Birth Control Review*, June, 1932; Vol. XVI, pp. 166–167. There is full approval of the idea of birth control and notice of the drive among Black folk to assure survival; the two, Du Bois suggests, are complementary, not contradictory.

An International Conference on African Children was held in Geneva in 1931. It was an occasion for rationalization rather than real investigation and a book of an "official" kind was denounced by Du Bois.

255. Review of Evelyn Sharp, *The African Child*, in *Birth Control Review*, June, 1932, Vol. XVI, p. 181.

In the midst of the devastating depression, an Economic Conference sponsored by the Rosenwald Fund was held in Washington in June, 1933. At its closing session, Du Bois delivered an address reflecting his increasing concern with basic economic questions and his intensifying criticisms of capitalism as such. The address was printed with a supplied headline:

256. "U.S. Will Come to Communism, Du Bois Tells Conference," *Afro-American* (Baltimore), May 20, 1933. Twelve columns were devoted to publication of the speech in full. The headline was not false to the text; Du Bois insisted that production for private profit was wrong and disastrous and that Black people, in particular, should undertake various forms of cooperative and collective efforts, thus helping prepare the way for and preparing themselves to be part of the coming revolution. About 75 words from this speech were quoted in the New York *Times*, on May 14, 1933, p. 25, under the headline "The Nation's Gain in Negro Welfare." The *Times* article featured the speech of Edwin R. Embree, president of the Rosenwald Fund.

In the above address, Du Bois mentioned that he had been studying the role of the Firestone Rubber Company in Liberia as an example of the exploitative essence of monopolistic enterprise. The results of that study appeared in an essay entitled:

257. "Liberia, The League and the United States," *Foreign Affairs*, July, 1933, Vol. XI, pp. 682–695. The essay ends with this question: "Are we starting the United States Army toward Liberia to guarantee the Firestone Company's profits in a falling rubber market or smash another Haiti in the attempt?"

The kind of thinking represented by items numbered 256 and 257 was not that which endeared him to leading forces on the Board of the NAACP. Efforts to curb Du Bois took the form in December, 1933, of moves that would have made the Secretariat of the organization—and especially Walter White—dominant in the control of the *Crisis*. Thus commenced Du Bois' renewed efforts to change the direction of the NAACP. News of this soon was abroad, and friends of Du Bois whose views were to the Left of the Board—like George Frazier Miller, Martha Gruening, and Owen R. Waller—brought this to public notice; in doing so they published, with his permission, a letter dated February 5, 1934, and sent by Du Bois to this group of supporters. The letter was printed in full, with a supplied headline:

258. "See Quick Move to Oust Du Bois as Crisis Editor," Chicago *Defender*, February 24, 1934. Here Du Bois wrote that "the N.A.A.C.P. needs fundamental and complete reorganization from top to bottom. ... "

As of July 1, 1934, Dr. Du Bois resigned and "cease [d] to have any connection whatsoever in any shape or form" with the NAACP. He saw no possibility, he wrote, with the present board of adopting a positive program of action that the crisis demanded. The full statement was widely published,as in:

259. Chicago *Defender*, July 24, 1934.

Du Bois knew, as he wrote, that it was "painfully easy" for one living in a great metropolis to "mistake it for the nation"; he tried to avoid this error by regularly traveling throughout the United States. Thus, in 1934 he visited and lectured in most of the South and in the mid-West. He wrote of his impressions of the latter:

260. "Du Bois Home from Visit to South and the West," *Afro-American*, May 5, 1934. He was impressed with an adult lecture program in Des Moines; a hospital for Black patients and staffed entirely by Black personnel struck him as first-rate in Kansas City; the young faculty at Lincoln University in Missouri seemed to have great promise; and he debated in Chicago against the 49th State separatists, while insisting that where segregation in fact existed one had the duty not only to fight it but also to make whatever institution was in fact segregated into the highest possible quality.

A review of a book by the former secretary of the NAACP, James Weldon Johnson—for whom Du Bois had the highest respect and regard—gave Du Bois again the chance to make clear his concern that so-called integration meant an effort to make of Black people a subordinate part of a nation based on exploitation and class division and profit making; he was opposed to this and urged therefore self-organization of a collective type for the Black population in the United States.

261. Review of James Weldon Johnson, *Negro Americans, What Now?* in New York *Herald Tribune* (Book Section), Nov. 18, 1934.

A rather full explication of Du Bois' views at this time as to the possibilities of independent Black activity was given in:

262. "A Negro Nation Within the Nation," *Current History*, June, 1935, Vol. XLII, pp. 265–270. Du Bois felt that with proper use of political, economic, and brain power, "Negroes can develop in the United States an economic nation within a nation, able to work through inner cooperation ... and at the same time ... keep in helpful touch and cooperate with the mass of the nation." Under the headline "Advocates 'Negro Nation'" some of this is quoted in the New York *Times* May 21, 1935, p. 9.

Facing the reality of racism and advocating a continued struggle against it, Du Bois simultaneously pleaded for the development by Black people of the best of their own institutions, as in:

263. "Does the Negro Need Separate Schools?," *Journal of Negro Education*, July, 1935, Vol. IV, pp. 328–335.

The attack by fascist Italy upon Ethiopia was viewed by Du Bois as a decisive event emphasizing the significance of the color line in world history; he treated this with great candor in:

264. "Inter-Racial Implications of the Ethiopian Crisis. A Negro View," *Foreign Affairs*, October, 1935, Vol. XIV, pp. 82–92. Published in French in *Le Matin* (Port-au-Prince, Haiti), January 7, 1936.

At the National Negro Baptist Convention held in the Bronx, N.Y., and attended by 3,000 people, Du Bois expressed the view that the positive significance of the New Deal lay in the emphasis it gave to the duty of government to provide for the needs of all its citizens; he was quoted briefly to that effect in:

264a. *New York Times*, September 7, 1935, p. 13.

A protest meeting, uniting many diverse groups, against the Italian invasion of Ethiopia was held at Madison Square Garden in New York City on September 25, 1935. Ten thousand Black and white people were present; speakers included James W. Ford, Communist leader; Dr. Harry F. Ward of the League Against War and Fascism; Rabbi Stephen S. Wise; the Rev. John H. Holmes; Walter White; representatives of the U.N.I.A. (Garvey Movement) and of the Brotherhood of Sleeping Car Porters; and Dr. Du Bois. This was reported in:

264b. *Amsterdam News*, Sept. 28, 1935. Du Bois is quoted as asking why world opinion is so aroused today with an event that occurred in the past and hardly gained notice. "Because the World War has taught most of Europe and America that the continuing conquest, exploitation and oppression of colored peoples by white is unreasonable and impossible and if persisted in will overthrow civilization."

Upon the fiftieth anniversary of the publication of the New York *Age*, Du Bois was asked to express appropriate thoughts. He called to mind the positive contributions of the ancestors of the *Age*—the *Globe* and *Freeman*, edited by T. Thomas Fortune —recalled his earlier sharp criticism of the Black press, thought some improvement had occurred but felt much improvement in type of news and in analysis was still needed, in:

265. "W. E. B. Du Bois Discusses the Negro Press," New York *Age*, November 4, 1935, p. 3.

In mid-November Dr. Du Bois lectured on the Ethiopian crisis at Morehouse College in Atlanta; he emphasized the difference in the way the entire world was rendered distraught by the Italian invasion as contrasted with European invasions 30 and 40 years earlier in Asia and Africa; he suggested this as part of the evidence of the waning of colonialism, even while a fresh colonial war was being fought. Considerable quotations from this paper, "The Future of the Darker Races" appeared in:

266. New York *Age*, November 20, 1935, p. 9.

In a major essay examining the various paths to freedom projected by the Afro-American people, Du Bois affirmed his belief in the essential truth of Marxism but his rejection of the program, as he envisioned it, of the Communist Party, U.S.A. For the present he thought that emphasis within the Black community upon cooperative living and working and the overcoming of any sense of inadequacy were fundamental courses to be pursued. This was published as:

267. "Social Planning for the Negro, Past and Present," *Journal of Negro Education*, January, 1936, Vol. V, pp. 110–125.

Writing for a magazine published in Bombay, India, Du Bois developed the theme of the unity of colored peoples in the face of colonialism. He also emphasized, however, that liberation from colonialism must be followed by socialism, else colored peoples would be exploited by colored rather than white people and the leap forward would be very limited; this in:

268. "The Clash of Colour," *Aryan Path*, March, 1936, Vol. VII, pp. 111–115.

In 1936, Dr. Du Bois applied for a grant from the Oberlaender Trust—part of the Carl Schurz Memorial—to study developments in education in Germany. He won this grant and sailed for Germany in June. On this trip Du Bois visited also England, Austria, the Soviet Union, China, and Japan, returning to his teaching position at Atlanta early in 1937. The letter to the trust officials, dated February 7, 1936, and the fact of his receiving the grant were sent out as a news item by the Associated Negro Press and widely published, as in:

269. Pittsburgh *Courier*, March 28, 1936. Du Bois' remarks in this letter concerning Booker T. Washington's plans contain a somewhat different—and less unfavorable—emphasis than in most of his writings.

In a positive review of a book dealing with Africa's ravishment, Du Bois makes the point that so-called scientific history that is passionless and "nonpartisan" is really nonhuman and tends to serve as a prop for an unconscionable status quo.

270. Review of Lamar Middleton, *The Rape of Africa*, in *New Republic*, June 24, 1936, Vol. LXXXVII, p. 210.

Du Bois protested that the pacifism projected by an Indian savant, N. S. Subba Rao, tended to produce acquiescence in the subordination of colored peoples to white ruling classes. He reiterated his idea of the need for a world unity of colored people, not for the purpose of ruling noncolored peoples but for the purpose of ending the overlordship of any group of people over any other group; this in a letter, supplied with a headline:

271. "The Union of Colour," *Aryan Path* (Bombay), October, 1936, Vol. VII, pp. 483–484. (A reply from Subba Rao appears in the same issue.)

Upon his return early in 1937 from his seven-month trip, Dr. Du Bois granted interviews that appeared in:

272. Interview New York *Post*, January 27, 1937, and German *Staatszeitung Herold*, January 29, 1937. In both he stressed the savagery of anti-Jewish persecution. In the *Post*, comment also was offered concerning Japan and China.

Du Bois found illuminating the psychoanalytic approach to the so-called race question that emerged from a study of one county in Mississippi. He thought, however, that too much was claimed on the basis of a few samples and that the lack of socioeconomic data was a severe limitation of the study he reviewed.

273. Review of John Dollard, *Caste and Class in a Southern Town*, in *North Georgia Review*, Winter, 1937–1938, Vol. II, pp. 9–10. The journal was a new one, associated with the efforts of the novelist Lillian Smith.

274. "How Negroes Have Taken Advantage of Educational Opportunities Offered by Friends," *Journal of Negro Education*, April, 1938, Vol. VII, pp. 124–131. This is a historical survey; by "Friends" is meant the Society of Friends, or Quakers. This paper was presented at the Centennial Program of Cheyney State Teachers College, in Pennsylvania, October 16, 1937.

275. In *Birth Control Review*, May, 1938, is reprinted exactly the earlier essay of 1932 (No. 254).

In 1938, marking the fiftieth year of his graduation, Dr. Du Bois received the Fisk University Alumni Award for Distinguished Service. At the Commencement exercises of June 8, 1938, he gave the speech entitled:

276. "The Revelation of Saint Orgne the Damned," *Fisk News*, November–December, 1938, Vol. XI, pp. 3–9 (reprinted, by Du Bois, in 1939, as a 16-page pamphlet). The Saint's name is actually "Negro." Sees the labor movement as "the most promising movement" of the present epoch and insists that Black people "must eventually join it"; adds that Black people must fight more effectively in the national political arena for all democratic and socially useful legislation but that, in addition and as a means toward the general end, Black people must organize themselves and enhance their own capacities and power. Reiterates a persistent theme—namely, the rejection of the money-making values of dominant "industrial monopoly."

Du Bois returned to a central concern of his with this essay:

277. "Black Africa Tomorrow," *Foreign Affairs*, October, 1938, Vol. XVII, pp. 100–110. Modern European interest in Africa has sought conversion of heathens, establishment of colonies, and extraction of profit. Such a condition will not last forever; must it end with blood, the Doctor asks, or can it yield to reasonable and just solution, with the interests of the Africans uppermost? The time for an answer approaches, he warned.

Du Bois made a pioneering examination of contributions from Black scientists in:

278. "The Negro Scientist," *American Scholar*, Summer, 1939, Vol. VIII, pp. 309–320. Du Bois used initials rather than names in describing the significant work of Black chemists, physicians, biologists, and others. He emphasized the discriminations and indignities faced and suggested the cost of racism to scientific progress.

Reiterating his rejection of dominant bourgeois values, insisting that within the mass lay great possibilities of creativity, and calling for the development by Black people of their own best attributes, Du Bois published:

279. "The Position of the Negro in the American Social Order; Where Do We Go From Here?," *Journal of Negro Education*, July, 1939, Vol. VIII, pp. 551–557.

The same town in Mississippi that was studied by Dollard (see No. 272) was examined by the cultural anthropologist Hortense Powdermaker; the resulting book was reviewed positively.

280. Review of Hortense Powdermaker, *After Freedom. A Cultural Study of the Deep South*, in *Social Forces*, October, 1939, Vol. XVIII, pp. 137–139. Du Bois here added a note about "the plight of historical writing" in the United States.

Du Bois greeted as a hopeful sign the beginnings of apparently serious study of Black people undertaken by such Southern white universities as that of North Carolina and, to a lesser degree, Duke. The product of such study, which contained chapters by two Black scholars, was reviewed by him.

281. Review of *Race Relations and the Race Problem*, edited by Edgar T. Thompson, in *Annals of The American Academy of Political and*

Social Science, January, 1940, Vol. CCVII, pp. 255–256. Especially insightful, Du Bois thought, was the chapter by Lewis C. Copeland dealing with the ideology of racism.

Du Bois was deeply impressed with another book.

282. Review of Horace Mann Bond, *Negro Education in Alabama. A Study in Cotton and Steel*, in *American Historical Review*, April, 1940, Vol. XLV, pp. 669–670.

In another review, Du Bois hailed a work now recognized as a classic.

283. Review of *The Negro Family in the United States*, by E. Franklin Frazier, in *Journal of Negro Education*, April, 1940, Vol. IX, pp. 212–213. He called it "an astonishing and revealing study."

Du Bois delivered the Commencement Day address at Wilberforce University in Ohio on June 13, 1940. He surveyed the varied history of the institution—where he had commenced his professorial career—urged its complete secularization, and suggested that it establish productive and consumer cooperatives as models for that economic reorganization toward an end to capitalism that had to come if civilized living were to survive. The address was published as:

284. "The Future of Wilberforce University," *Journal of Negro Education*, October, 1940, Vol. IX, pp. 553–570.

In a paper prepared for the Fifth Annual Meeting of the Southern Sociological Society, held in Knoxville, Tenn., on April 5, 1940, Du Bois stated that the old South of *laissez faire*, of Bourbon domination, had been dealt severe and, he thought, fatal blows by the realities of the depression and the activities of the federal government induced by those realities. He remarked that events of the recent past in the South seemed to him to confirm basic Marxian postulates of social functioning; this in:

285. "Federal Action Programs and Community Action in the South," *Social Forces*, March, 1941, Vol. XIX, pp. 375–380.

Replying to a letter from a Fisk student, Du Bois—writing from Atlanta University on February 3, 1941—urged that Fisk not fall victim to the mounting hysteria for the entry of the United States into the war. He had made a similar mistake in 1917 and regretted it; U. S. hostility to Japan was racist and motivated by our own exploitative desires in China. And to think of the British Empire as a bulwark of democracy was absurd. Hence:

286. "Du Bois Says Stick to Education," *Fisk News*, February, 1941, p. 5.

On the seventy-fifth anniversary of the founding of Lincoln University in Missouri, Du Bois delivered a paper on January 12, 1941, parts of which were reprinted in:

287. "The Future of the Negro State University," *Wilberforce University Quarterly*, April, 1941, Vol. II, pp. 53–60. Du Bois noted that those who dominated society dominated its institutions of higher learning. This in itself made true scientific inquiry at universities most difficult; in the United States the problem was compounded by racism. The Black university should reject dominant values and by doing so could perform a great educational service in matters of economics and fraternal living. Du Bois advanced the idea of Pan-Africanism again —not, as he stated, to be "merely a narrow racial propaganda," but rather as part of the "coming Unities: a unity of the working classes everywhere, a unity of the colored races, a new unity of thinking men." The Afro-American had the historic task of helping lead in the achievement of such a grand Unity. (Printed, in large part, in the Philadelphia *Tribune*, January 23, 1941.)

Du Bois detested Hitlerism, of course; he detected in the fascistic movement, however, what he thought to be the necessary and universal compulsion toward the planning of economic activity, particularly as technical developments reinforced the need for such planning. It is this latter feature of Hitler's social order upon which he concentrated in:

288. "Neuropa. Hitler's New World Order," *Journal of Negro Education*, July, 1941, Vol. X, pp. 380–386.

Under Du Bois' inspiration and from his vantage point again at Atlanta University, the Twenty-fifth Atlanta Conference was held in 1941. Its main purpose was to bring together Black scholars to discuss what the economic future of the Afro-American people was likely to be and what might be done to make that future a happier one than its past. This is described in:

289. "The Twenty-fifth Atlanta Conference," *Unity*, November, 1941, Vol. CXXVII, pp. 145–146. Du Bois stressed here, also, the ambivalence in the Black community toward yet another "war for democracy."

Late in 1941, the Hayes Memorial Foundation of Ohio commenced publication of a vehicle for reviewing books; in its first volume Du Bois contributed two reviews:

290.   Review of Melville J. Herskovits *The Myth of the Negro Past* in *United States, 1865–1900*, September, 1941–August, 1941. Du Bois hailed this work, which "might well prove epoch-making . . . ."

291.   Review of Richard Wright, *Twelve Million Black Voices: a Folk History of the Negro in the United States*, with photographs by Edwin Rosskam, in *United States, 1865–1900*, September, 1941–August, 1942, Vol. I, p. 26. Described as a significant expression of "the voice of the stricken Negro masses. . . . "

Du Bois reviewed a book that "deserves a high place" among works dealing with the South:

292. Review of Allison Davis, Burleigh B. Gardner, and Mary R. Gardner *Deep South* in *Annals of the American Academy of Political and Social Science*, March, 1942, Vol. CCIX, pp. 274–275. Particularly new, Du Bois wrote, was the material on class divisions among the Southern Black people.

293. "Du Bois Was Once a Newsboy," *Afro-American*, March 7, 1942. A somewhat shortened version of a 1935 piece (No. 265) was published with a supplied headline.

In April, 1942, Du Bois lectured at Vassar College in Poughkeepsie, N.Y. His lecture was entitled "The Future of Africa in America." While at Vassar he was interviewed and the interview was published as:

293a. "Du Bois Suggests That Vassar Have 100 Negro Students," *Vassar Miscellany News*, April 22, 1942. Noting that the number of Black women at Vassar was "ridiculously small" Du Bois made the suggestion headlined above. He emphasized that racism constituted a decisive obstacle to the realization of democracy and that removing that obstacle was where "progress for the future must lie."

Rather unusual for Du Bois, he published a second review of a book (see No. 291):

294. Review of Melville J. Herskovits *The Myth of the Negro Past, Annals of the American Academy of Political and Social Science*, July, 1942, Vol. CCXXII, pp. 226–227. This review, however, was substantially longer than the other and favorably compared Herskovits' work with that of Tillinghast, Reuter, Dowd, Weatherford, and others. As to Herskovits' emphasis upon so-called African survivals in Afro-American life and culture, Du Bois felt that while much of this was well taken and needed, "Herskovits probably errs on the side of credence."

A book by a white scholar which treated Haiti with seriousness and Haitians with respect and even affection was reviewed at some length:

295. Review of James G. Leyburn, *The Haitian People*, in *Yale Review*, September, 1942, Vol. XXXII, pp. 188–189. Du Bois thought Professor Leyburn inverted cause and effect when he declared that "caste and class are the cause of economic difficulty." The book underplayed, also, Du Bois thought, "the grasping tentacles of white imperialism."

Imaginatively, the editor of a quarterly asked Du Bois to review two books on anti-Semitism:

296. Review of *Essays on Anti-Semitism*, edited by K. S. Pinson; and *Jews in a Gentile World*, by I. Graeber, S. H. Britt, *et al.* in *Annals of the American Academy of Political and Social Science*, September, 1942, Vol. CCXXIII, pp. 199–200. Summarizing the historical, sociological, and psychological contents, Du Bois went on to suggest that it might be worth considering a viewpoint not taken by the authors: "of regarding the Jews as one among many groups, composed of Chinese, Japanese, East Indians, African Negroes, American Negroes, and American Indians—peoples who form the great majòrity of the inhabitants of the earth and are also excluded from fellowship with the world aristocracy."

In what was called a "Victory Issue" of a Black newspaper during the second World War, Du Bois was asked to contribute; his essay appeared with a supplied headline, as:

297. "We Fight for a Free World ... This or Nothing," Chicago *Defender*, September 26, 1942, Sec. 2, p. 4. As far as we are concerned, wrote Du Bois, "We are fighting race hate; and especially its latest exposition in the case of Adolf Hitler." He concluded, "To uplift the stricken men of all races and colors from the morass into which greed for wealth and power has cast them" must be the outcome of the war.

A quarterly named for a great humorist asked Du Bois to write on:

298. "The Humor of Negroes," *Mark Twain Quarterly*, Fall-Winter, 1942–43, Vol. V, p. 12. Du Bois especially noted "the dry mockery of the pretensions of white folk" and the self-critical humor; "to those who suffer," he added, "God mercifully grants the divine gift of laughter."

Late in 1941 a committee of 40 people, Black and white, from England and the United States, studied the relationship of Africa to the war then raging. The resulting book was reviewed:

299. Review of a study by the Committee on Africa, the War and Peace Aims *The Atlantic Charter and Africa from an American Viewpoint*, in New York *Herald Tribune*, Sunday Book Section, January 10, 1943. A central fact was ignored, Du Bois reported: "the fact that Africa is organized today chiefly for the profit of Europeans." Until that is altered, he added, "Africa will not be free, nor will permanent peace be possible."

The needs of the war forced the feelings and activities of the Black population more fully into the consciousness of dominant white America; as usual the result was a kind of astonishment and alarm. One result was the appearance of articles in such magazines as the *Reader's Digest* and *Virginia Quarterly* "discovering" the existence of the Black press. Du Bois wrote a rather long essay, published in two parts, on this phenomenon, on the role of the Black press, and on areas where improvements were possible. He suggested that since Black people read the white press, perhaps white people might consider reading, once in a while, Black newspapers. This in:

300. "The American Negro Press," Chicago *Defender*, February 20 and 27, 1943 (condensed version printed in *Negro Digest*, April, 1943, Vol. I, pp. 33–36).

Taking off from the failure he noted in his review of No. 299, Du Bois published a long essay:

301. "The Realities in Africa; European Profit or Negro Development?," *Foreign Affairs*, July, 1943, Vol. XXI, pp. 721–732. The theme is reflected in the title; the content demonstrated the fact of exploitation. To assure peace after the war, therefore, this pattern would have to be reversed, Du Bois said, with the result that the land and the resources of Africa would be in the possession of its inhabitants, with political organization reflecting their desires. (Condensed in *Negro Digest*, August, 1943, Vol. I, pp. 75–79.)

One of the rather rare projects that Du Bois did not complete was a history of Black troops in the First World War; but from one of its chapters he published:

302. "The Negro Soldier in Service Abroad During the First World War," *Journal of Negro Education*, Summer, 1943, Vol. XII, pp. 324–334. This is a documentary account of the discrimination faced and of battle contributions by the Black soldiers in Europe.

For a series entitled "If I Were Young Again" Du Bois wrote with characteristic frankness an essay with significant biographical information, entitled:

303. "Reading, Writing, and Real Estate," *Negro Digest*, October, 1943, I, pp. 63–65. The "real estate" referred to a disastrous investment Du Bois had once made; on the whole he expressed satisfaction with his education—except he wished he had spent more time on Spanish, Arabic, and Russian than on Greek and Latin, had studied in France rather than Germany, and had traveled more in countries occupied by colored peoples. He was fiercely critical of his own writing.

In a brief review, Du Bois paid tribute to the editor and the author of a four-volume collection of writings:

304. Review of *Works of Francis James Grimké*, edited by Carter G. Woodson, in *United States, 1865–1900*, January, 1944–December, 1944, Vol. III, pp. 83–85. The Rev. Mr. Grimké was pastor for over 40 years of the Fifteenth Presbyterian Church in Washington and a courageous fighter for justice and equality.

The editors suggested a title but Du Bois began his essay in response to their request by denying the prospect suggested by the title:

305. "Prospect of a World Without Race Conflict," *American Journal of Sociology*, March, 1944, Vol. XLIX, pp. 450–456 (condensed in *Negro Digest*, August, 1944, Vol. II, pp. 45–47). In this essay, Du Bois wrote that the question of the freedom of Asia, as well as Africa, was vital if peace was to follow the war.

Late in March, 1944, Du Bois spoke at an interracial conference held in Chicago, called by Marshall Field, Edwin R. Embree, and Charles S. Johnson. His remarks were reported at some length under varying headlines, in several Black newspapers, such as:

306. "Du Bois Gives Parley Keys to Race Problem," *Chicago Defender*, April 1, 1944, p. 2. The keys were, he thought, overcoming the oppression of Black people by full and good employment—which would require a change in the economic system—and by a campaign of re-education directed at the white population, which the changed economic system would require. Du Bois insisted, too, on the need for Black self-development.

Du Bois was religious but intensely antidenominational; established churches, he believed, had played a reactionary role. Detailing an aspect of this was a "well done and honestly documented" book which he reviewed:

307. Review of *American Catholic Opinion in the Slavery Controversy*, Madeline H. Rice, in *Annals of the American Academy of Political and Social Science*, September, 1944; Vol. CCXXXV, p. 172.

In the summer of 1944, Du Bois was invited to participate in various cultural and scholarly activities in Haiti; he eagerly accepted. Two publications in French resulted.

308. "La Conception de l'èducation," *Cahiers d'Haiti* (Port-au-Prince), September, 1944, Vol. II, pp. 14–19, 22–25, 32, developing in considerable length Du Bois' views as to previous efforts at liberation and the present needs for decisive changes in economic structure and imperial power.

309. "Message du Dr. Du Bois," *Cahiers d'Haiti*, October, 1944, Vol. II (No. 3), p. 28. This was dated September 4 and was addressed to the president of a meeting of the Haitian Philosophical Congress; it expressed regret at his departure from Haiti. It added that a fully satisfactory philosophy reflecting the direction and meaning of human existence had yet to be forged; Du Bois thought it could be found and that the search was edifying.

As the presidential elections of 1944 (with Roosevelt versus Dewey) approached, Du Bois was asked by a Black newspaper to provide some background material and general guidance (he had by this time returned to the NAACP as director of research). His essay was published, under a supplied headline.

310. "Be Intelligently Selfish at Polls, Urges Du Bois," *Defender*, Sept. 30, 1944, p. 3. Du Bois emphasized the significance of economic and antiracist issues and urged that program, not party, be decisive in manner of voting.

Du Bois began contributing a weekly column to the *Amsterdam News* late in 1939; this column ceased in mid-October, 1944. Du Bois stopped writing for the paper because its owner—in the employ of the National Republican Committee—twice excised from his columns in the fall of 1944 statements by Du Bois favoring President Roosevelt in the current campaign. Du Bois, explaining this, sent a signed article:

311. "Reasons for Backing President Roosevelt," *People's Voice* (New York), October 21, 1944, p. 3. Essentially, Du Bois gave a very favorable evaluation of Roosevelt's efforts vis-à-vis Black people and, felt that Roosevelt's social and economic program was far superior to Dewey's.

Under the chairmanship of Edward R. Stettinius—then undersecretary of state—a meeting of representatives from about 80 organizations was held in the State Department in Washington. It was closed to reporters and was meant to provide a means for the State Department to learn citizens' views, especially since the Dumbarton Oaks conference had recently closed. Three Black people attended—Mr. William H. Hastie, Mary McLeod Bethune, and Dr. Du Bois. Du Bois noted with great disappointment that the Dumbarton Oaks Conference had operated on the assumption of the continuation of colonialism; this meant disaster for the postwar world; a significant portion of these views was quoted in an article.

312. "Colonial Question Ignored at Dumbarton Oaks Peace Session," Pittsburgh *Courier*, October 28, 1944, p. 4.

313. "Imperialism, United Nations, Colonial People," in *New Leader* (New York), December 30, 1944, Vol. XXVII, No. 53, p. 5. It warned that colonialism had been an important cause of both world wars and that unless excised it would help induce wars and threats of wars in the period after World War II.

As the Commencement Day speaker at Talladega College in Alabama in June, 1944, Du Bois gave a talk that was reprinted later in the year.

314. "Jacob and Esau," *Talladegan*, November, 1944, Vol. LXII, pp. 1–6. Drawing from the Biblical tale the lesson that exploitation of man by man—no matter what the rationalizations—is wrong and is the cause of awful tribulation and must be replaced by a system of humane living. Both Marx and Henry George were quoted at some length.

Du Bois felt the great power in Richard Wright's prose but he criticized, too, Wright's lack of sympathy for his people and his demeaning of their characteristics; hence "the total picture" was "not convincing" he decided in:

315. Review of Richard Wright, *Black Boy. A Record of Childhood and Youth*, New York *Herald Tribune*, Book Review Section, Mar. 4, 1945, p. 2.

A brief, sharp estimate of the life and work of Franklin Delano Roosevelt was published:

316. "What He Meant to the Negro," *New Masses*, Apr. 24, 1945, Vol. LV, No. 4, p. 9. The estimate was positive but hardly uncritical; it expressed some hope in "an organized white minority in the South" who were showing signs of comprehending the social cost of racism.

Du Bois and Walter White were accredited "consultants" to the United States delegation in San Francisco at the founding of the United Nations; they represented the NAACP. Both men contributed five articles concerning this experience; of these, two were written by Du Bois—the second and the fourth in the series:

*In an extensive interview, Richard Wright discussed, among other matters, Du Bois' estimate of his book, in the *Afro-American* (Baltimore), Mar 24, 1945, p. 5.

317. "750,000,000 Clamoring for Basic Human Rights," New York *Post*, May 9, 1945, p. 8.

318. "Is It Democracy for Whites to Rule Dark Majorities?" New York *Post*, May 15, 1945, p. 14.

In these pieces Du Bois emphasized that colonialism vitiated democracy in general; that those suffering from it were demanding freedom and that it was just and vital that their demand be met.

On his way East at the conclusion of the San Francisco meeting of the United Nations, Dr. Du Bois was interviewed by John Stephenson, and Du Bois emphasized that the colonial question had not been resolved. There was a moral victory in terms of verbal recognition of "human rights" but no way for implementation, he pointed out in:

318a. *Rocky Mountain* (Denver, Colo.) *News*, May 28, 1945.

Du Bois testified on the Charter of the U.N. before the Senate Foreign Relations Committee in July, 1945 (see no. 1836), and again emphasized the failure on the part of the United States and Great Britain to move forward realistically in the necessary effort—if future wars were to be avoided—of liquidating colonialism. A considerable portion of this testimony made front-page news, as in:

318b. Chicago *Defender*, July 21, 1945, pp. 1, 4.

At the conclusion of the Second World War, the Fifth Pan-African Congress was held in Manchester, England; Dr. Du Bois was in the chair and attending were George Padmore, Kwame Nkrumah, Jomo Kenyatta, Nnamdi Azikiwe, and others. In November, prior to returning to the United States, Dr. Du Bois held a press conference attended by representatives from Reuters, TASS, United Press of India, and leading papers of England, Scandinavia, and France. He was extensively quoted in a report by George Padmore.

319. "Du Bois Demands Colonial Liberty at Press Conference," *The Chicago Defender*, Nov. 17, 1945. In addition to the point conveyed by the headline, Du Bois commented upon the hopefulness represented by the achievements of the U.S.S.R. in the national and racial areas.

When he arrived in New York City, Du Bois was questioned by reporters; the result was printed as follows:

320. "Sees Britain 'In Dutch'; Dr. Du Bois Scores Labor Party's Policy Towards Colonies," New York *Times*, Nov. 28, 1945, p. 15. Du Bois warned that "either the British Government will extend self-government in West Africa and the West Indies or face open revolt."

A recently established Afro-American monthly news review published a rather long interview with Du Bois.

321. "Du Bois Peers Into the Future," *Headlines and Pictures* (Chicago), April, 1946, pp. 20–21. Du Bois expressed doubts as to the unselfishness and courage of present Black leaders, thought that in the next decade or so, higher education in the South would not be lily-white, and felt "The really great advance of Negroes has come in the labor movement in the past 15 years."

In a newspaper published in Johannesburg, Union of South Africa, Du Bois reported in some detail on the struggle at the San Francisco founding of the United Nations to get adopted in the original charter the statement "Policy Regarding Non-Self-Governing Territories." A pledge was adopted that the interests of the inhabitants and the effort "to develop self-government" would determine policy. No manner of implementation was provided, Du Bois noted, but the promise was better than nothing.

322. *Trek*, April 5, 1946, p. 12.

Before "a jam-packed Chicago audience" at the Metropolitan Community Church, Du Bois gave a speech entitled "Shall We Fight for Freedom?", insisting that such a fight was necessary and would be successful. He thought India would be independent within ten years, that the struggle to prevent a third world war would succeed, and that planning for the economic and social freedom of masses of people—as symbolized, he said, in the names of Jesus, Gandhi, and Lenin—was vital. Much of this reported in:

323. *Chicago Defender*, April 13, 1946.

In May, 1946, Du Bois was somewhat startled to realize that Mrs. Du Bois and he had been married for 50 years. The agony of the death of their son—some 45 years earlier—still was fresh. He wrote an interpretation of that half century.

324. "My Golden Wedding," *People's Voice* (New York), June 29, 1946.

The guns had barely ceased firing in the Second World War when rumors and more than rumors of impending war between the United States and the Soviet Union began to appear in the press. Du Bois was an original opponent of what became known as the Cold War, as in his essay:

325. "Common Objectives," *Soviet Russia Today*, August, 1946, Vol. XV, No. 4, pp. 13, 32–33. The objectives in common were an end to poverty and to war. The elimination of colonialism and racism was basic to achieving both. Du Bois hailed the U. S. S. R. for its leadership in the effort to eliminate those scourges and wrote that it was, for him, "the most hopeful country on earth."

After an absence of a dozen years, Du Bois' writing reappeared in the magazine he had founded back in 1910, with an essay:

326. "The Future and Function of the Private Negro College," *Crisis*, August, 1946, Vol. LIII, pp. 234–236, 253–254. This was the text of an address delivered at the seventy-first anniversary commencement exercises of Knoxville College (Tenn.), on June 10, 1946. Du Bois stresses the vital consequence of the Black people's own unique experience and culture; the need for small Black colleges; and the propriety of such colleges' being parts of their surrounding communities—especially of the Black communities.

An especially incisive article insisted that the problem of mass impoverishment that still bedevilled most of humankind was *the* question needing resolution. Traditional capitalism had failed; fascism had failed; of the U.S.S.R. it could at least be said that there failure had not occurred despite the suffering of the war. In any case, reason required that this be faced and resolved and its resolution was, Du Bois thought:

327. "Democracy's Opportunity," *Christian Register*, August, 1946, Vol. CXXV, pp. 350–351. Again, Du Bois denounced those who were suggesting the "necessity" of war between the United States and the Soviet Union.

Habits of sobriety and of work were basic to Du Bois' way of life. In a brief essay filled with personal illumination, he attacked the problem posed by alcohol.

328. "Blight of Drunkenness," *Message Magazine* (Nashville, Tenn.), September, 1946, Vol. XII, No. 10, p. 3.

The last white president of Fisk University in Tennessee was Thomas E. Jones (1926-1946). His impending resignation, the demands of the Black population, and the fact that by this time Atlanta University, Howard University, Wilberforce University, and Lincoln University (Pa.) all had Black presidents, presented the white-dominated Board of Trustees with a momentous problem. Du Bois analyzed this in:

329. "A Crisis at Fisk," *Nation*, September 7, 1946, Vol. CLXIII, pp. 269–270. Dr. Charles H. Wesley, then president of Wilberforce and a man of progressive social views, was favored by many of the alumni, including Du Bois as he did not fail to indicate in the above article. (In 1947, Dr. Charles S. Johnson became the first Black president of Fisk.)

Du Bois warned, in a letter dated November 8, 1946, that the continued hostility to determined efforts by Africans to achieve freedom undermined the United Nations and threatened renewed war; he added that the continued special oppression of Black people in the United States demanded a response from the U.N. or else no "new world" could be built:

330. N Y *Times*, Nov. 12, 1946, p. 28.*

Late in 1946 there was consideration of the idea of locating the U.N. center in Philadelphia. Du Bois wrote of the then blatant practice of Jim Crow in the city of "brotherly love" and warned that colored U.N. delegates "would not be comfortable" there, in a letter:

331. New York *Herald Tribune*, December 11, 1946.

An event probably unique in Du Bois' career was the publication of an essay by him, under another person's name, that of Walter White. Prodded by Du Bois, the newspaper that published

---

*This was reprinted in full in the daily English-language paper, *The Sun,* (Montevideo, Uruguay), December 6, 1946, p. 2.

it later carried a correction but the piece appears in the original as written by White.

332. "H. G. Wells—A World Great," Chicago *Defender*, December 21, 1946, p. 15. Du Bois told of his first meeting with Wells in 1911; of other meetings—the last in November, 1945; of his high admiration for Wells' work and courage; and of his agreement with Wells' socialist convictions.

332a. "Georgia: Torment of a State," *New Masses*, September 10 and September 27, 1946. Reprinted from a chapter Du Bois contributed to a book published in 1924 (No. 1872).

333. On October 5, 1946, a conference representing 20 organizations of colored peoples met, under Du Bois' chairmanship, at the Countee Cullen Branch of the New York Public Library in Harlem. Some of its recommendations, drafted by Du Bois, appealing to the UN and denouncing colonialism were published in the New York *Times* October 6, 1946, p. 34.

333a. Sections of a major address Du Bois delivered October 20, 1946, in Columbia, South Carolina, at a meeting organized by the Southern Negro Youth Congress were quoted in the New York *Times*, October 21, 1946. The speech was printed in full as a pamphlet in 1946 by that Congress (No. 1943) and also in full in:

333b. *New Masses*, January 14, 1947, Vol. LXII, pp. 18–20.

333c. "Colonies and Moral Responsibility," a chapter from his book *Color and Democracy* (see No. 1967) appeared in *Journal of Negro Education*, Summer, 1946, Vol. XV, pp. 311–318.

Du Bois emphasized that racism made impossible the achievement of political, social, and economic democracy in the United States. Therefore, the struggle against racism was one that should enlist the support of all who thought of themselves as democrats. This in:

334. "Bound by the Color Line," *New Masses*, February 12, 1946, Vol. LVIII, p. 8.

A Legal Conference on Federal Power to Protect Civil Liberties was sponsored by the National Lawyers' Guild, the National Bar Association, and the National Legal Committee of the NAACP.

The conference met in Washington on January 25, 1947. For this conference Du Bois was asked to prepare the following paper on:

335. "Civil Rights Legislation Before and After the Passage of the 14th Amendment," *Lawyers' Guild Review*, November–December, 1946, Vol. VI, pp. 640–642.

An analysis of the Prime Minister of the Union of South Africa showing him to be "the typical representative of the hypocrisy, double-dealing and coldly calculated cruelty of the modern world" appeared in:

336. "Jan Christian Smuts: Story of a Tyrant," *New Masses*, March 4, 1947, Vol. LXII, No. 10, pp. 7–8.

Responding to the query of an editor, "What will be the status of the Negro 100 years after emancipation?," Du Bois contributed a piece:

337. "Can the Negro Expect Freedom by 1965?," *Negro Digest*, April, 1947, Vol. V, No. 6, pp. 4–9. Du Bois thought there was every possibility of significant advance in political and educational areas but he raised this question: after having gained legal equality—more or less—"Are we going to try to increase the wealth of the richest by climbing on the faces of the poorest among us? Are we going to use our education for enjoyment or for service?" (This essay was reprinted in the *Newsletter* of the League of Coloured Peoples [London], May, 1947, Vol. XVI, pp. 106–111.)

Early in 1947, the Prime Minister of Great Britain conferred with a leader of the Sudan—a descendant of the Mahdi—the Redeemer—against whom Kitchener waged war in the 1890's. Taking off from this occurrence, Du Bois in:

338. "The Black Mahdi," *New Masses*, June 10, 1947; LXIII, No. 11, pp. 20–22, told something of the history of the Sudan, its connection with Egypt, and the role of British imperialism in seeking to maintain the division between the two, the better to undercut the real independence of both.

After a prolonged absence, Du Bois delivered an address before the 1947 Convention of the N.A.A.C.P., held in Washington, in June. In it he pointed to the United Nations as containing the possibility of eliminating war and advancing the liberation of colonies; and he affirmed that socialism was that system which would have to be adopted by Mankind if it were to endure and progress. Sections of this address appeared under the headline:

338a. "Du Bois Declares Socialism A Haven," *N.Y. Times*, June 27, 1947, p. 11.

In October, the N.A.A.C.P. made public a document, later published as a book (No. 1920), which was in the form of a petition to the United Nations seeking redress of grievances on behalf of the Black people in the United States. Du Bois was the Editor and parts of his introductory statement were quoted under the headline:

338b. "Negroes To Bring Cause Before U.N.", *N.Y. Times*, October 12, 1947; p. 52.

Shortly thereafter, Dr. Du Bois and Walter White formally presented this document to then Assistant Secretary General. Du Bois' remarks on this occasion—emphasizing the world significance of racism in the United States—were quoted at some length under the headline:

339. "U.N. Gets Charges of Wide Bias in U.S.," New York *Times*, October 24, 1947, p. 9.

Du Bois' interest in and support of the struggle for independence in India was keen and enduring. He devoted a major historical and analytical essay to the struggle:

340. "The Freeing of India," *The Crisis*, October, 1947, LIV, pp. 301–304, 316–317. Hailing the occasion of the announcement of India's independence (August 15, 1947) as "the greatest historical date of the 19th and twentieth centuries."

Given the existence of widespread racism in the United States, the editor of the organ of the International Workers Order, asked "What Do You Think Should Be Done?" Du Bois gave a brief reply.

341. *Fraternal Outlook*, November, 1947, Vol. IX, p. 5. Du Bois said there were three forms of struggle required: legal, mass agitational, and long-term conscious education.

On the occasion of the 30th anniversary of the Bolshevik Revolution, Du Bois greeted the Soviet Union:

342. "The Most Hopeful State in the World Today," *Soviet Russia Today*, November, 1947, p. 24. "Not," he added, "because its efforts have been perfection or without mistakes, but because it has attacked the fundamental problems of our day. ..." He particularly warned against those who sought war upon the U.S.S.R.

Du Bois was guest speaker at the national convention of the American Education Fellowship, held in Chicago in November, 1947; his paper was published by the Fellowship's organ as:

343. "No Second Class Citizenship," *Progressive Education*, January, 1948, Vol. XXV, pp. 10–14, 21. This is an examination of the actual meaning of democracy and a careful attack upon all elitist theories.

The first essay by Du Bois published in a trade-union paper was entitled:

344. "Only Unity Can Lead Workers to Victory," *Fe News*, January, 1948, Vol. V, 97, p. 9. In the organ of the United Farm Equipment and Metal Workers, C.I.O., Du Bois insisted that racism was a basic cause of organized labor's weakness and that with this overcome, nothing could keep that movement from victory.

A matter of great urgency and controversy then before the United Nations was the creation of Israel; Du Bois wrote of this in:

345. "The Case for the Jews," Chicago *Star*, May 8, 1948.

Still another attack upon elitism and an insistence that the trouble with democracy was that it had not yet been tried made up the essence of a review:

346. "Is Man Free?," a review of Richard M. Weaver, *Ideas Have Consequences* in *Scientific Monthly*, May, 1948, Vol. LXVI, pp. 432–433.

Gandhi was murdered on January 30, 1948; an issue of *Unity* was devoted to him and among those contributing was Du Bois:

347. "The Greatest Man in the World," *Unity*, May–June, 1948, Vol. CXXXIV, pp. 25–26. Despite the title, Du Bois as always avoided mere eulogy and praise; but with all that he criticized he thought Gandhi to have best exemplified the finest morality of any public figure in his time.

In a newly established Left magazine, Du Bois published a favorable estimate.

348. Review of Herbert Aptheker, "Freedom's Partisans," *To Be Free: Studies in Negro History, Masses & Mainstream*, June, 1948, Vol. I, No. 4, pp. 76–79.

In the same magazine he surveyed his political ideas and activities, under a revealing title.

349. "From McKinley to [Henry] Wallace. My Fifty Years as a Political Independent," *Masses & Mainstream*, August, 1948, Vol. I, No. 6, pp. 3–13.

350. In a letter dated August 3, 1948, Du Bois asked if it was "logical" to smear Henry Wallace and. the Progressive Party as being "Communistic" when he and it advocated plans long argued for and in part implemented by people like Norman Thomas and Robert La Follette and by Britain's Labour party. Further, Du Bois insisted that opposition to Truman's foreign policy as manifested in Greece and China was far from "treason." *New York Times*, August 10, 1948, p. 26.

The final contribution by Du Bois to the magazine he had founded in 1910 was:

351. "John Hope. Scholar and Gentleman," *Crisis*, September, 1948, Vol. LV, pp. 270–271. This was an extended review of *The Story of John Hope*, by Ridgely Torrence. Hope, born the same year as Du Bois, was his close friend—perhaps his closest—from the year they met, 1896, to Hope's death in 1936. Du Bois felt the Torrence book was excellent.

Du Bois argued against:

352. "Italy's Return to Eritrea," letter published in the New York *Herald Tribune*, September 18, 1948, p. 12.

At the nineteenth grand boulé conclave of the Sigma Pi Phi fraternity (consisting of 440 families), Du Bois presented a major paper re-examining and significantly amending his 1903 concept of "The Talented Tenth." The heart of the change is in this paragraph. "Very gradually as the philosophy of Karl Marx and many of his successors seeped into my understanding, I tried to apply this doctrine with regard to Negroes. My Talented Tenth must be more than talented, and work not simply as individuals. Its passport to leadership was not alone learning, but expert knowledge of modern economics as it affected American Negroes; and in addition to this and fundamental, would be its willingness to sacrifice and plan for such economic revolution in industry and just distribution of wealth, as would make the rise of our group possible." In a signed essay:

353. "The Talented Tenth Memorial Address," *Boulé Journal* (Wilberforce, Ohio), October, 1948, Vol. XV, No. 1, pp. 3–13. (The address was delivered on August 12, 1948.)

In a letter to a recently established, quite liberal, and short-lived daily newspaper, Du Bois exposed and excoriated the blatant Jim-Crowism practiced in the Panama Canal Zone.

353a. *New York Star*, October 21, 1948.

A careful weighing of developments from the First World War to the beginnings of the period after the Second World War, with emphasis upon the various bodies—all Black and Black-White —that had struggled in the field of racism, formed the backbone of this signed essay:

354. "Race Relations in the United States, 1917–1947," *Phylon*, Vol. IX, No. 3, 1948, pp. 234–247. "Negroes are in a quasi-colonial status" and as such are in the center of "world-wide class strife."

Du Bois' opposition to the Cold War and his outspokenly Left politics assured that a contribution this year to the New York *Times* was the last those editors requested from him:

355. "The Negro Since 1900. A Progress Report," New York *Times Magazine*, November 21, 1948, pp. 24, 54–57. As always with Du Bois, this was not—despite the title—simply a "progress report," though it did not omit advances. Much had been achieved through effort, said Du Bois, but much more still lay ahead if freedom was to be real.

Du Bois offered a positive assessment of the meaning to human progress of the Bolshevik Revolution and of the history of the Soviet Union since then. He noted in particular its multinational and multiethnic character and the basic equality among peoples that he believed existed, in:

356. "Russia. An Interpretation," *Soviet Russia Today,* November, 1948, Vol. XVII, pp. 14–15, 32.

In the first number of the organ of the West African Society Du Bois offered a brief:

357. "Review of African Movements for Freedom," *Africana* (London), December, 1948, Vol. I, pp. 19, 22. He stressed in the modern period the development of industry and the appearance of a trade-union movement.

Du Bois attacked the persistence of discriminatory practices in interstate travel:

358. Letter, *New York Times,* December 11, 1948, p. 14.

358a. *Pittsburgh Courier,* March 20, 1948, p. 2. An article indirectly quoting Dr. Du Bois as insisting that only a planned society would resolve the social problems haunting the nation; it added that he "revealed a preference for Henry Wallace."

358b. *New York Times,* September 9, 1948, p. 27. An article reporting that Du Bois felt that approval of Walter White's appointment by President Truman to represent the United States as a consultant to the U.N. delegation (then off to Paris) was a political act and a bad one. It quoted parts of a memorandum from Du Bois to that effect delivered to the Board of the NAACP.

358c. New York *Times,* September 14, 1948, p. 25. An article reporting that the Board of the NAACP had informed Dr. Du Bois the previous day that as of December 31, 1948 his employment by the NAACP would cease.

For the organ of the newly founded Liberty Book Club, Du Bois did a brief review:

359. Review of *The Poetry of the Negro,* edited by Langston Hughes and Arna Bontemps (New York. Doubleday), in *Liberty Book Club News* (New York), March, 1949. Du Bois felt this was an excellent—"a definitive"—work.

In March, 1949, the Cultural and Scientific Conference for World Peace was held in New York City with figures like Paul Robeson, Olin Downes, Elmer Bernstein, Dmitri Shostakovich, Howard Fast, and Shirley Graham participating. The meeting was subjected to a massive Red-baiting assault in which very nearly the entire New York press participated. Dr. Du Bois was prominent among its participants and delivered a major address at its closing meeting, held in Madison Square Garden on March 27. The full text of that speech was published.

360. "Peace. Freedom's Road for Oppressed Peoples," *Worker,* April 17, 1949, magazine section, p. 8.

A succinct summary of the history of the struggle against slavery and of elements of its impact is offered in:

360a. "The Thirteenth, Fourteenth and Fifteenth Amendments," *Lawyers' Guild Review,* Spring, 1949, Vol. IX, pp. 92–95.

In a New York newspaper that was rather courageous, given the atmosphere of the Cold War, Du Bois summarized his views as to the status and needs of his people.

361. "Dr. Du Bois on Negro America," *Sunday Compass,* July 10, 1949, pp. 4, 6. Du Bois felt that many reports on progress were overly optimistic, though he agreed that some advances had been achieved. Full political and social rights had not been obtained; income was very low and educational facilities were markedly poor. He called for increasing militancy and struggle.

In the midst of further freezing of the Cold War atmosphere, Du Bois contributed an essay:

362. "The Sane Liberal," *Soviet Russia Today,* September, 1949, pp. 7, 26. He insisted that the abolition of war, poverty, disease, and illiteracy was possible and had to have the commitment of any sane person; he warned that "Red baiting" if adopted as a state policy would lead the United States toward "overturning the great landmarks of human liberty which have been raised in the last four centuries."

Du Bois reviewed a massive volume of almost one thousand pages.

363. Review of *Most of the World. The Peoples of Africa, Latin America* *and the East Today,* edited by Ralph Linton (New York. Columbia University Press), in *Science & Society,* Fall, 1949, Vol. XIII, pp. 365–368. He did not think the book successful, noting the total absence of the West Indies and the general downplaying of African and Africa-derived peoples. Only the chapters on Brazil and India seemed successful to him.

A well-beloved friend—of some 50 years—was Wendell Phillips Dabney, publisher of a newspaper, *the Cincinnati Union.* On October 28, 1949, Du Bois wrote a letter to a committee arranging a testimonial dinner in Dabney's honor, regretting his inability to be present, and paying glowing tribute to him. This appeared as:

364. "From the Famous Dr. W. E. B. Du Bois," *Cincinnati Union,* November 5, 1949.

In a periodical published by Lincoln University (Mo.), Du Bois warned that those who radically questioned the social order in the United States faced the danger of being labeled "traitors" (as was to happen to him the next year!).

365. "The Freedom to Learn," *Midwest Journal,* winter, 1949, Vol. II, pp. 9–11. That freedom, he wrote, "is undoubtedly the most fundamental," and he warned against curtailing it.

In 1949, Du Bois made his third visit to the Soviet Union (he had been there in 1926 and 1936). He wrote of that vast land, again with a critical approach but with a fundamental admiration for the sweep of its effort, the grandeur, he thought, of its aim, and the remarkable degree of achievement it had registered despite enormous obstacles and challenges. This in:

366. "Russia. An Interpretation," *Soviet Russia Today,* November, 1949, pp. 14–15, 32.

Two fairly extensive interviews, to mark Negro History Week, were published in 1949.

367. An interview by Abraham Chapman in *Fraternal Outlook,* February, 1949, Vol. XI, pp. 6–7, 22. Du Bois was quoted on his long interest in Africa and its deep connection with questions facing Afro-Americans. He noted, too, a positive change in the attitude of much of the United States toward Black people as compared with that expressed in the 1890's and, on the whole, thought such progress would continue.

368. A somewhat similar interview was published in *Hotel & Club Voice,* but in this discussion with a reporter from the union of hotel workers he stressed the need for greater Black-V/hite unity in the labor movement and, especially, the need for organizing the workers in the South.

Upon his return from the World Congress of Partisans of Peace, held in Paris in May, 1949, Du Bois was quoted under the headline:

368a. "Dr. Du Bois Predicts African 'Awakening,'" *The New York Times* June 2, 1949, p. 10. He was quoted as saying "the Dark World is moving towards its destiny much faster than we in this country now realize."

In August, 1949, Dr. Du Bois testified before the Foreign Affairs Committee of the House of Representatines in Washington. His testimony was published in full in a report by that Committee (No. 1837); considerable portions were published in serial form:

368b. *Daily Compass,* August 11, 12, 1949, pp. 13, 21, in each case.

In the Spring of 1949, Paul Robeson declared in Paris, "The black folk of America will never fight against the Soviet Union." This statement, in the midst of the Cold War, provoked a storm of controversy and led to Mr. Robeson's being refused audiences in the United States. A magazine projected a debate on the question of this statement. Taking the side opposing Mr. Robeson was Walter White, but Du Bois supported him.

369. "Paul Robeson. Right or Wrong?—Right, says W. E. B. Du Bois," *Negro Digest,* March, 1950, Vol. VII, No. 5, pp. 8, 10–14.

Quite briefly Du Bois examined West Africa.

370. "The Role of West Africa," *Crescent* (Organ of Phi Beta Sigma; Published at Atlanta University), Spring, 1950, Vol. XXXIV, p. 10. The essay explores West Africa's role in the developing national-liberation movements of the so-called underdeveloped nations.

To a newly established and unfortunately short-lived journal Du Bois contributed:

371. "Government and Freedom," *Harlem Quarterly*, Spring, 1950, Vol. I, pp. 29–31.

With the appearance of the first two volumes of the Douglass writings, Du Bois published:

372. "A People's Leader," a review of *The Life And Writings of Frederick Douglass* edited by P. S. Foner (volumes I and II, New York. International Publishers, 1950), in *Masses & Mainstream*, May, 1950, Vol. III, pp. 86–89. A substantially similar review appeared in *Science & Society*, Fall, 1951, Vol. XV, pp. 351–354.)

In April, 1950, the pioneer Black historian Dr. Carter G. Woodson died. Du Bois had known him for about 40 years and, while the relationship between the men was not an especially warm one, Du Bois always had the highest regard for the integrity and productivity of Woodson; this comes through in:

373. "A Portrait of Carter G. Woodson," *Masses & Mainstream*, June, 1950, Vol. III, No. 6, pp. 19–25.

In connection with his leadership in the antiwar movement and his candidacy, on the American Labor Party ticket, for United States senator, Du Bois frequently was quoted in the *New York Times* in 1950; thus:

373a. "Dr. Du Bois Calls on Acheson to Promise U.S. Will 'Never Be First To Use Bomb'"—a promise not forthcoming. There was published much of the text of a letter from Du Bois to the Secretary of State evoking the above headline in *New York Times*, July 17, 1950, p. 5.

374. When the Congress passed over President Truman's veto the so-called Subversive Control Act (or McCarran Act), the American Labor Party held a press conference, in Harlem, expressing its opposition to that law. Dr. Du Bois was quoted at some length in denunciation of what he saw as United States trends toward war, in the *New York Times*, September 25, 1950, p. 10.

375. Some quotations from a speech made to about 1,500 people in Harlem were published under the headline "Du Bois Tells Harlem

Only U.S. Wants War," *New York Times*, October 6, 1950, p. 21.

376. In a radio broadcast, as part of his political campaign, Du Bois attacked U.S. foreign policy, said the United States sought to replace Britain as ruler of the globe, and warned that such an effort in the middle of the 20th century was destined to fail. Some of this was quoted under the headline "Du Bois Fears War in Policy of Rivals," *New York Times*, October 10, 1950, p. 36.

377. In another campaign speech, broadcast throughout New York state, Du Bois insisted that neither of the major parties was actively and effectively fighting for real civil rights. Some of his remarks were quoted under the headline "Two Big Parties Assailed. Neither Backs Civil Rights, Says A. L. P. Senatorial Candidate," *New York Times*, October 20, 1950, p. 19.

378. A brief report on another radio broadcast by Du Bois, attacking Senator Lehman for his support of the foreign policy of President Truman, under the headline "Du Bois Says Lehman Yielded to Business," *New York Times*, October 23, 1950, p. 12.

379. Finally, Du Bois' rejection of the red-baiting attack upon the Stockholm Peace Pledge, calling for the outlawing of atomic weaponry, was partially quoted, *New York Times*, October 30, 1950, p. 16.

A very clear statement of Du Bois' views of the major issues and choices in the 1950 campaign—in which he ran on the Progressive Party ticket for the Senate—appeared in German. The central issue of this time, this nation, and this world, he wrote, was peace. As a candidate pledged to the struggle to enhance civil rights and to maintain peace, Du Bois asked for support:

380. "Die Wahl in November für Frieden und Bürgerrechte," [The Choice in November for Peace and Civil Rights], *German-American*, October, 1950, Vol. VIII, No. 7, pp. 8–9.

A significant article prompted by Negro History Week in 1951:

381. "The Negro in America. His Past and His Future," *New York Compass*, February 11, 1951, Magazine Section, pp. 3, 8. Dr. Du Bois suggested that Black historiography had reached the point where the celebration of the past should give way to the elucidation of the present and the projection of a more humane and just future, with emphasis upon the elimination of war.

For the 40th anniversary issue of *The Crisis*, Du Bois was asked (probably around December, 1950) to prepare an article treating of his generation-long association with that magazine. The result was an essay in which Du Bois dealt with his ideas and practices as an editor, the scoops he scored, the people who helped him, and the reasons for his resignation from the magazine and from the NAACP. This issue appeared just as the news of his indictment by the federal government broke; as:

382. "Editing 'The Crisis,'" *Crisis*, March, 1951, Vol. LVIII, pp. 147–151, 213.

In February, 1951, just before his eighty-third birthday, Dr. Du Bois was indicted under the McCormick Act as an "unregistered foreign agent," in connection with his leadership of the Peace Information Center. He issued a statement affirming his innocence and reiterating at some length his critical analysis of U.S. foreign policy, insisting that it was warlike and marked for disaster. All this in:

383. "I Take My Stand," *Masses & Mainstream*, April, 1951, Vol. IV, No. 4, pp. 10–16. This was published in pamphlet form during the same year.

Late in December, 1950, Du Bois participated in a forum devoted to recent U.S. Supreme Court decisions in the area of civil rights, held at the Yale Law School. His remarks were briefly summarized in:

384. *New York Guild Lawyer*, February, 1951, p. 5. Du Bois insisted that the decisions, while welcome, were a "drop in the bucket" and that what they touched was not basically relevant to most Black people since "nine out of every ten American Negroes did not have the means ever in their lives to eat in a railroad diner or receive post-graduate education."

384a. "5 of 'Peace' Group Here Indicted. All Sponsors of Stockholm Plea" was the headline in The New York *Times*, February 10, 1951. Relating to the indictment of that month, as noted above. Du Bois' denial of guilt and his insistence on the righteousness of the fight for peace was quoted briefly in this issue of the *Times*, on page 6.

One of the recurrent themes in Du Bois' writing was the

tremendous symbol of John Brown. He studied Brown when in his twenties, under Albert B. Hart and Edward Channing at Harvard, and continued to publish about him until a few years prior to his death some 70 years later. An especially succinct account of the meaning of John Brown, as Du Bois saw this, was written for a Nigerian newspaper:

385. "John Brown Liveth!," *West African Pilot* (Lagos), November 10, 1951, p. 2.

It was during the period of the indictment that Dr. Du Bois and the writer Shirley Graham were married. After a considerable campaign Dr. Du Bois and his fellow-defendants won a directed acquittal. Dr. and Mrs. Du Bois went on a well-earned vacation to the Virgin Islands. While there, on February 27, 1952, before the St. Thomas Chamber of Commerce, Du Bois delivered a paper published in full:

386. "Address of Dr. W. E. B. Du Bois," *Daily News* (St. Thomas, Virgin Islands), March 1, 1952. The speech emphasized that the West Indies had been used as exploitative bases for capitalism and that this caused their widespread poverty. Such usage had to give way to a decent and planned society where human needs were decisive.

The magazine of The National Institute of Arts and Letters (of which Du Bois was the sole Black member) published a symposium to which the Doctor contributed:

387. "What Leading Literati Think of Television," *Academy Magazine*, June, 1952, p. 11. He thought very poorly of it, said he rarely watched it now, "having given up," and said that the reason for its near-idiocy was its use as an advertising tool for profit.

In a radical Jewish magazine (published in English) Du Bois contributed a passionate excoriation of racism and anti-Semitism; in his peace endeavors he had himself visited the ruins of the Warsaw ghetto and wrote of the impact of this visit in:

388. "The Negro and the Warsaw Ghetto," *Jewish Life*, May, 1952, Vol. VI, pp. 14–15.

Du Bois supported the candidacy of Vincent Hallinan, on the Independent Progressive Party ticket, for president in 1952. I. F.

Stone, the well-known journalist, thought that that candidacy was harmful and argued that support be given to Adlai Stevenson as opposed to General Eisenhower. Du Bois rejected the historical arguments offered by Mr. Stone and insisted that both the Democratic and Republican tickets meant continuation of the Cold War and risk of hot war and that Mr. Hallinan was squarely opposed to both. This appeared as a rather long, signed letter, with an added headline:

389. "Says Stone Misinterprets History in Lincoln Argument," *Daily Compass* (New York), October 8, 1952, pp. 7, 12.

Throughout the McCarthy Era, Du Bois continued his basic critique of U. S. foreign and domestic policy and his call for a turn toward the ways of peace and coexistence; an excellent expression of this outlook is:

390. "America and World Peace," *New World Review*, November, 1952, pp. 49–52.

Du Bois was convinced that the effort to execute the Jewish couple Julius and Ethel Rosenberg for allegedly conspiring to engage in espionage for the U.S.S.R. (during the Second World War) was a frame-up having political and racial motivations not very different from those helping to explain the execution of Sacco and Vanzetti in 1927. At a "Save the Rosenbergs" rally held in New York City under the auspices of the Civil Rights Congress on October 23, 1952, Du Bois presented a carefully argued, extensive examination of this case.

391. "A Negro Leader's Plea to Save the Rosenbergs," *Worker*, (New York), November 16, 1952, magazine Section, pp. 3, 6.

Du Bois published a panoramic view of his own life and times with an emphasis on the need for peace and the possibilities of peaceful social transformation in the present. He emphasized that the Afro-American people had to face up as never before to the question of classes and of socialism versus capitalism; this in:

392. "The American Negro in My Time," *United Asia* (Bombay), March 1953, Vol. V, pp. 155–159.

In a brief letter to the editor of a Jewish magazine, Du Bois expressed doubts as to the veracity of charges of intense anti-Semitism in the U.S.S.R..

393. Letter, *Jewish Life*, March, 1953.

A major essay by Du Bois argued the organic relationship between

394. "Negroes and the Crisis of Capitalism in the United States," *Monthly Review*, April, 1953, Vol. IV, pp. 478–485. He believed that this crisis would drive Black people more and more toward socialism and toward a unity with other colored peoples in the world.

The execution in the spring of 1953 of the Rosenbergs on the trumped-up charge of conspiracy to engage in espionage, and their staunch insistence on their innocence, moved Du Bois deeply. He expressed his feelings in a poem.

395. "The Rosenbergs," *Masses & Mainstream*, July, 1953, Vol. VI, No. 7, pp. 10–12.

A favorable summary of a book by a radical labor leader (a white man) in South Africa appeared in:

396. Review of E. S. Sachs, *The Choice Before Us* in *Science & Society*, Summer, 1953, Vol. XVII, pp. 269–270.

A truce in the fighting in Korea was achieved in August, 1953. To transform this truce into a real and permanent peace and thus to alleviate the threat of a Third World War became a prime desire on Du Bois' part. He wrote of this in the organ of the then existing American Peace Crusade organization (of which Du Bois was an honorary chairman).

397. " 'Insist on Peace. Now, Forever,' " *Peace Reporter* (New York), September–October, 1953, pp. 1–2.

Du Bois published two reviews of books selected by the Liberty Book Club; these were:

398. Review of Lion Feuchtwanger, *'Tis Folly to Be Wise*, in *Liberty Book Club News*, September, 1953. He thought this historical novel concerning the life and ideas of Jean-Jacques Rousseau was quite successful.

399. Review of Benjamin Quarles, *The Negro in the Civil War*, in *Liberty Book Club News*, December, 1953. Highly commended, though Du Bois added. "Perhaps this author is too cautious in trying not to offend the white south."

In the early 1950s, several leaders of the Communist Party, U.S.A., were jailed after conviction under the conspiracy section of the Smith Act—for conspiring to advocate the forcible overthrow of the government. Du Bois was outraged at this political persecution and actively participated in efforts first to prevent its consummation and then to achieve amnesty for the victims. In this connection he wrote of the integrity and effectiveness of Benjamin J. Davis, Jr., one of those jailed.

400. "This Man I Know," *Masses & Mainstream*, February, 1954, Vol. VII, No. 2, p. 43.

Du Bois had earlier sent a letter to the *Daily Worker* in New York City, congratulating that Communist newspaper on having completed 30 years of publication. It had upheld "the right of a human being to believe in Communism" and had helped vindicate the right of an American citizen to disagree publicly and radically with dominant powers—"the foundation stone of all real democracy"; this was published in the letter section.

401. Letter, *Daily Worker*, January 31, 1954.

Du Bois also sent a letter to prominent individuals abroad informing them of the Smith Act prosecutions and asking their assistance in the struggle to release the prisoners; this appeared as:

402. "An Appeal by Dr. W. E. B. Du Bois on Amnesty for the Smith Act Victims," *New World Review*, March, 1954, p. 44.

The economic exploitation of Africa, increasingly by U.S. corporations (data are supplied), and the special oppression of Black workers in Africa and in the United States are pointed to as being of great consequence in preventing the achievement of that which is now possible.

403. "A Decent World for All," *March of Labor* (New York), March, 1954, Vol. VI, No. 2, pp. 20–23.

Another victim of McCarthyite repression was the leader of the Fur Workers' Union; Du Bois wrote of his efforts in that case.

404. "Testifying at Ben Gold's Trial," *Jewish Life*, May, 1954, p. 19.

To assist the 1954 campaign of the Independent Progressive Party in California, Du Bois spoke in Los Angeles on June 3, 1954. A considerable portion of that speech was quoted:

405. "Du Bois Charges Nixon Try to Lead Us to War," *Los Angeles Tribune*, June 4, 1954. The article referred to the Vice-President's suggestion for "sending troops into Indo-China." Du Bois thought the Geneva Conference just concluded gave some hope of peace in Asia, "but there is still grave danger, which lies in the continued insistence that the existence of Socialist and Communist states are in themselves reasons for fear of aggression."

Du Bois' interest in and concern for Asia—especially India and China—were of long standing and intense. He published a calm and reasoned appeal:

406. "Normal U. S.-China Relations," *New World Review*, August, 1954, pp. 13–15. The appeal hailed the Chinese Revolution of 1949 and urged U. S. recognition of the People's Republic of China and urged also its seating in the United Nations.

The death of the distinguished philosopher and literary critic Alain Locke in 1954 led to the production of a collection of essays, to which Du Bois contributed.

407. "The Passing of Alain Locke," *Phylon*, Third Quarter, 1954, Vol. XV, pp. 251–252.

In an Asian magazine, Du Bois published a fairly full accounting of Pan-Africanism.

408. "Pan-Africanism. A Mission in My Life," *United Asia*, March, 1955, Vol. VII, pp. 23–28.

409. "Two Hundred Years of Segregated Schools," *Jewish Life*, February, 1955, No. 4, pp. 15–18, 35 (reprinted in Louis Harap, et al., eds., *"Jewish Life" Anthology*, New York, 1956, pp. 7–9.) A historical overview, with a warning that even with the Brown decision desegregation would not be achieved quickly and that to bring it about would require considerable effort from the Black people.

Du Bois returned to a consideration of United States and Chinese relations and the threat to world peace flowing from their strained condition in:

410. "Formosa and Peace," *Jewish Life*, March, 1955, Vol. IX, p. 20.

In the period after the Second World War, a central commitment on the part of Du Bois was participation in the antiwar movement. He wrote of this in:

411. "The World Peace Movement," *New World Review*, May, 1955, pp. 9–14. An especially useful review of that movement in the late 1940's and early 1950's appears.

Du Bois reiterated his overall positive assessment of the Bolshevik Revolution and of the society it forged in:

412. "Most Hopeful Country in the World," *New World Review*, November, 1955, pp. 10–11, an essay somewhat similar to No. 366.

A prepublication printing of a chapter from his trilogy *The Black Flame* appeared:

412a. "The Ordeal of Mansart," *Masses & Mainstream*, February, 1955, Vol. VIII, No. 2, pp. 21–29.

Late in 1955 Du Bois surveyed the history of the relationship to and attitude toward Africa on the part of Black people in the United States. He summarized and quoted extensively from the history of the Pan-African movement commencing in the twentieth century and noted a persistent resistance on the part of Afro-Americans toward any identification with Africa. As part of the Cold War, a deliberate effort has been undertaken by dominant forces in the United States to "buy off" Black leadership through apparent concessions at home so that that leadership will join in the anti-Communist crusade and in the plans to thwart real African independence. Du Bois doubts that such leadership will last, however; he feels that the real interest of Black people throughout the world will assert itself and force a change in such leadership. He refers to Garvey as "the sincere but uneducated and demagogic West Indian Leader" who "promoted an African movement but it was purely commercial and based on no conception of African history or needs. It was American and not African" (p. 49). This appears in:

413. "Africa and the American Negro Intelligentsia," *Présence Africaine* (Paris), December 1955–January 1956, pp. 34–51. This essay, minus the first seven pages, appears in Adelaide C. Hill and M. Kilson, eds., *Apropos of Africa: Sentiments of Negro American Leaders on Africa from the 1800s to the 1950s* (London: Cass & Co. 1959, pp. 311–321.)

On the occasion of the centennial of the birth of Eugene V. Debs, a memorial meeting was held in New York City on November 28, 1955, under the sponsorship of four Left publications: *The National Guardian, I. F. Stone's Weekly, The American Socialist*, and *The Monthly Review*. Five hundred people attended; Du Bois gave this speech:

414. "If Eugene Debs Returned," *American Socialist*, January, 1956, Vol. III, No. 1, pp. 10–12. The speech was a scorching attack upon the condition of the United States and the domestic and foreign policies of its government.

Analyzing the election campaign of 1956, Du Bois found precious little to choose between the dominant parties and saw no effective third party in operation; he therefore felt that until the latter alternative appeared, abstention by Black people might be best, in:

415. "Negro Voters Face 1956," *American Socialist*, February, 1956, Vol. III, No. 2, pp. 10–11.

In the preceding essay, Du Bois quite incorrectly stated that most Black voters had chosen Eisenhower in 1952; a reader pointed this out. Du Bois acknowledged his error in a letter:

416. "Dr. Du Bois Replies," *American Socialist*, April, 1956, Vol. III, No. 4, p. 31. He added, however, that his main point stood, namely that Republican and Democratic Parties represented "the rule of wealth."

Carrying further the suggestion in No. 415, Du Bois wrote:

417. "I Won't Vote," *Nation*, October 20, 1956, pp. 324–325. Seeing no real choice in a substantive sense, Du Bois decided to abstain. One of the great values of this essay is biographical, for in it Du Bois tells how he had voted in the past and why.

Du Bois offered a passionate defense of the Bolshevik Revolution particularly in terms of its positive impact upon the national subjugation of peoples and the struggle against racism in:

418. "Colonialism and the Russian Revolution," *New World Review*, November, 1956, pp. 18–22.

419. "The Rape of Africa," *American Negro* (Chicago), February, 1956, Vol. I, pp. 6–13. This consists of part of a speech delivered in Chicago on October 28, 1955; it emphasizes that until the question of colonialism and imperialist exploitation is resolved with justice there can not be real peace in the world.

420. "Appraisal of Africa," *Jewish Life*, February, 1956, Vol. X, pp. 15–18, 35. Review of John Gunther, *Inside Africa*. On the whole "an excellent book" packed with data but with two serious weaknesses. Gunther's effort at delimiting "Negro" is "absurd" and his caricaturing of socialism is in tune with the times in the United States but nowhere else in the world and certainly not in Africa.

A very important statement of Du Bois' views on Booker T. Washington may be found in a severely critical appraisal:

421. Review of Samuel R. Spencer, *Booker T. Washington and the Negro's Place in American Life*, in *Science & Society*, Spring, 1956, Vol. XX, pp. 183–185.

As often in the past, when extremely moved—by the Atlanta pogrom of 1906, by the execution of the Rosenbergs in 1953, and later by his visit to China in 1959—Du Bois chose the poetic form for expression. This occurred with the imperialist defeat in 1956 in Egypt and to celebrate it, Du Bois published a poem.

422. "Suez," *Masses & Mainstream*, December, 1956, Vol. IX, No. 11, pp. 42–43.

The exposure of excesses and crimes committed in the U.S.S.R. late in the career of Joseph Stalin, and the outbreak in Hungary in 1956, did not shake Du Bois' partisanship toward either socialism or the Soviet Union—perhaps because he had not been uncritical of either in the past. Expressing this position were two pieces published early in 1957:

423. "The Stalin Era," a review of Anna Louise Strong, *The Stalin Era* (1956), in *Masses & Mainstream*, January, 1957, Vol. X, No. 1, pp. 1–5.

424. "Socialism and Democracy," *American Socialist*, January, 1957, Vol. IV, No. 1, pp. 6–9. This was subtitled by the editors "A Debate," but Du Bois did not cast his piece in that form and stated to the compiler of this volume that he had not been informed that he was contributing to "a debate"; there was a rather lengthy "reply" by the editors in the same issue.

In the magazine edited by Lyle Stuart, the *Independent* (issue No. 49, 1956) Norman Mailer had remarked that the heart of the race question in the United States was in the alleged fact "that the white man fears the sexual potency of the Negro." Mr. Mailer's views stirred some discussion; the editor organized a symposium and invited comment; that by Du Bois, without title, is published in:

425. *Independent*, March, 1957. Du Bois stated that of course sexual oppression was present but that this was reflective of a complete oppression and exploitation of the Black people as such, with questions of state power and economic benefit at the hub.

In a newly commenced magazine Du Bois contributed a fascinating essay.

426. "Gandhi and the American Negroes," *Gandhi Marg* July, 1957, Vol. I, No. 3, pp. 1–4. Important biographical data on the beginnings of color-consciousness are here and the statement that the word "colored" in NAACP was consciously meant to apply to all colored peoples and not only to Afro-Americans. Tribute is paid to Gandhi's influence upon the King movement and hope expressed that such a movement might really lead to "equality and brotherhood in the United States."

An interview with Du Bois was published:

426a. "Portrait of a Scholar," Pittsburgh Courier, Aug. 24, 1957, p. 6. Du Bois is quoted directly as saying of Dr. Martin Luther King, Jr.: "Honest, straightforward, well-trained, and knowing the limits."

Du Bois expressed his belief in the need in Africa for unity if genuine independence were to be achieved. He added that between capitalism and socialism, the latter had to be Africa's choice; he stressed the urgent need in Africa for educators and schools geared toward the needs of the continent; all this in:

427. "The Africans and the Colonialist Tactic," *New Times* (Moscow), February, 1959 (No. 7), pp. 18–19.

On his ninety-first birthday (February 23, 1959) Dr. Du Bois was in the People's Republic of China. On that day he delivered an address broadcast to the world.

428. "China and Africa," *Peking Review*, March 3, 1959, Vol. II, pp. 11–13. This urged that Africa study the path to socialism of China and other socialist countries; it suggested that that path was the best for Africa and warned against entanglement with Western imperialist interests. (Also published in *New World Review*, April, 1959, pp. 28–31.)

With a brief biographical account of himself and his wife, Shirley Graham, Du Bois went on to affirm the need for visits by Americans, in particular, to socialist countries and that for the purpose of learning he was now in China; this in:

429. "Our Visit to China," *China Pictorial*, Mar. 20, 1959, No. 6, pp. 4–5 (with many photographs of the visit and visitors).

Profoundly moved by his extended visit to China, Du Bois turned to poetry to express himself; this poem, dated May Day, 1959, was dedicated to the distinguished writer Kuo Mo-jo:

430. "I Sing to China," *China Reconstructs*, June, 1959, Vol. VIII, p. 6.

In the organ of the Women's Democratic Federation, published in Berlin, Du Bois sent a deeply emotional message:

431. "Greetings to Women," *Women of the Whole World*, No. 7, 1959, p. 24.

On the occasion of the forty-second anniversary of the Great October Socialist Revolution, Du Bois recalled the early efforts to strangle it, the impoverishment he saw on his first visit, and the remarkable advances he believed had been made in the U.S.S.R., which "bears in its hands the hopes of mankind." This in:

432. "The Dream of Socialism," *New World Review*, November, 1959, pp. 14–17.

On the hundredth anniversary of the execution of John Brown, the Doctor contributed an analysis of the meaning of that life in:

433. "The Crucifixion of John Brown," *New Times* (Moscow) December, 1959, No. 49, pp. 26–29. (This was 50 years after the publication of Du Bois' biography of John Brown.)

In an essay dated New York, December 27, 1959, Dr. Du Bois summarized his own relationship to Africa commencing with his college days and going through the Pan-African Movement and the post-Second World War developments. He underscored the relationship of exploitation of Africa and past wars, and that the process of such exploitation and the intent to continue and intensify it boded ill for the possibilities of maintaining peace in the future. This was published in English and French:

434. "The Peoples of Africa and World Peace," *Documents and Texts: Problems of World Peace*, (Vienna, International Institute for Peace), No. 31, February, 1960, pp. 1–8. Appeared in part in the *Bulletin of the World Peace Council*, June, 1960, p. 16.

On February 19, 1960, Du Bois addressed a meeting devoted to Negro History Week, held at Carnegie Hall in New York City and sponsored by the Communist newspaper the *Worker*. This speech was published:

435. "Du Bois Sees Negro Problem in Vital Role in World Freedom Fight," *Worker*, Mar. 6, 1960, pp. 8, 11.

In an essay somewhat repeating the relevant chapter in his *Dusk of Dawn* (No. 1966), Du Bois recalled his Harvard days in:

436. "A Negro Student at Harvard at the End of the 19th Century," *Massachusetts Review*, May, 1960, Vol. I, pp. 439–58.

The Twenty-fifth Conference of the Association of Social Science Teachers was held at Johnson C. Smith University in Charlotte, N.C., early in April, 1960. Then in his ninety-second year, Du Bois delivered on this occasion one of his most vigorous addresses:

437. "Whither Now and Why," *Quarterly Review of Higher Education Among Negroes*, July, 1960, Vol. XXVIII, pp. 135–141. Du Bois expressed his positive convictions about socialism but he called, above all, for Black people to think deeply and without fear and for themselves and to strive as a top priority for peace in the world.

Du Bois offered a highly positive estimate:

438. Review of Herbert Aptheker, *The American Revolution. 1763–1783*, (New York: 1960), in *Political Affairs*, July, 1960, Vol. XXXIX, No. 7, pp. 63–64.

Du Bois contributed a brief piece:

439. "Africa and World Peace," *Bulletin of the World Peace Council* (Vienna), June, 1960, p. 16.

In the first number of a new quarterly, Du Bois contributed an essay treating of the ironic and organic tie between Afro-Americans and the United States.

440. "The Negro People and the United States," *Freedomways*, Spring, 1961, Vol. I, pp. 11–19.

In an essay written for a Soviet publication, Dr. Du Bois traced the history of research on the Afro-American people beginning with his own work in 1896 and detailing the efforts at Atlanta University through 1914, and then efforts that followed the First World War. The great difficulties of raising funds for such study are explained; the opinion is expressed that only with a socialist society will there be provided the means to pursue the fullest scientific study of the great variations in human thought and activity; this in:

441. "Stages in the Study of Negroes in the U.S.A." (in Russian), *Problems of Anthropology* (Moscow), 1961, No. 6, pp. 92–99.

That same year he wrote of the French and Haitian revolutions and their connections with the history of the United States, in:

442. "Africa and the French Revolution," *Freedomways*, Summer, 1961, Vol. I, pp. 136–51 (reprinted as a 20-page pamphlet with the same title, in Lagos, Nigeria, in 1962 by Megida Printers and Publishers).

Du Bois contributed his selections to the annual section called "Outstanding Books" in:

443. *American Scholar*, Fall, 1961, p. 604, Du Bois selected H. Aptheker's *The Colonial Era* (1959) and *The American Revolution* (1960) and suggested his reasons for doing so.

Du Bois briefly described his vision of an Encyclopedia Africana going back to 1909 and the activity concerning this then going forward with the encouragement of President Nkrumah of Ghana. It was in order to take charge of this that Du Bois and his wife went to Ghana in the summer of 1961, this in:

444. "The Encyclopedia Africana," *Baltimore Afro-American Magazine*, Oct. 21, 1961.

An examination of the vital role of Black people in the U. S. Civil War formed the theme of an essay:

445. "The Negro and the Civil War," *Science & Society*, December, 1961, Vol. XXV, pp. 347–352.

Shortly after the U. S. Supreme Court, in the summer of 1961, upheld the constitutionality of the McCarran Act's provisions in relation to Communists and alleged Communists—especially that section making it an offense punishable by 10 years in jail for such a person to request or to use a passport—Dr. Du Bois decided to apply for membership in the Communist Party, U.S.A. On October 1, 1961, he wrote a letter expressing this intention and explaining why; on October 13, the National Board of the party enthusiastically approved the application. Du Bois' letter and the response thereto by Gus Hall, general secretary of the party, are published in full:

446. Letter in *Political Affairs*, October, 1961; Vol. XLII, pp. 31–34. Extracts from Du Bois' letter were printed in the New York *Times*, Nov. 23, 1961.

A photographic essay by Milton Rogovin, illustrating "Store Front Churches" in Buffalo, N. Y. seemed excellent to Dr. Du Bois; he wrote an appreciative foreword to this work, with comments—largely drawn from his *Souls of Black Folk*—on the significance of Black religion, in:

447. *Aperture* (Rochester, New York), 1962; Vol. X, No. 2, pp. 64, 68, 77, 84.

The entire experience of going to Africa as the guest of the head of an independent Ghana and being able there to undertake what he hoped would eventuate in the realization of his half-century-old dream of an Encyclopedia Africana tremendously moved Du Bois; again he turned to the poetic form, with:

448. "Ghana Calls," *Freedomways*, Winter, 1962, Reprinted in the Du Bois Memorial Issue of *Freedomways*, Winter, 1965, Vol. V, pp. 98–101. This poem bore the dedication "To Osagyefo [Redeemer] Kwame Nkrumah."

On August 27, 1963, in his ninety-fifth year, Dr. Du Bois died in Accra, Ghana. At the state funeral, his widow, Shirley Graham Du Bois, read his last testament that he had written in 1957, given to her safekeeping for reading at his burial. This was published, in an essay by the present writer, in:

449. *Political Affairs*, October, 1963, Vol. XLII, No. 10, pp. 40–41. The heart of the message is a warning against cynicism—"the only possible death."

With his assistant, Dr. W. Alphaeus Hunton, Dr. Du Bois had pressed ahead while in Ghana with the organization of the forces to produce the encyclopedia; by the time of his death considerable progress had been made (to be interrupted by the *coup* that overthrew Nkrumah after Du Bois' passing). On December 15, 1962, a conference of participating scholars in the work of the encyclopedia was held at the University of Ghana; Dr. Du Bois' brief address—his last public speech—on that occasion was published in:

450. *Freedomways*, Winter, 1963, Vol. III, pp. 28–30.

From time to time, the compiler of this volume has published material by Dr. Du Bois that had not previously appeared in print. One such—a speech dealing with Frederick Douglass, made in 1895—has been listed earlier (No. 50). In addition, there were the following:

451. "The Joy of Living," a commencement address delivered in 1904, precise date and audience not known, in *Political Affairs*, February, 1965, Vol. XLIV, No. 2, pp. 36–44.

452. "Memorandum to the Labor Party of England on the American Negro," Feb. 21, 1918. Calling for recognition by that party of the realities of colonialism and the relationship between the struggle of metropolitan working classes and colonial liberation efforts, in *Freedomways*, Winter, 1965, Vol. V, pp. 113–115.

453. "Florence Kelley," *Social Work*, October, 1966, Vol. XI, No. 4, pp. 99–100. On March 16, 1932, a memorial service was held at the Friends' House in New York City for Florence Kelley, a founding member of the NAACP, a socialist, a translator of Engels, and a respected friend of Du Bois; his tribute was sharp, challenging—and loving.

In either 1935 or 1936 Du Bois wrote the following essay:

454. "India," *Freedomways*, Winter, 1965, Vol. V, No. 1, pp. 115–117. The essay stresses India's ties to the colored world and Du Bois' hope that when fully free it would so organize its society as to remove exploitation.

There was a public celebration of Du Bois' seventy-fourth birthday; on that occasion—February 23, 1942—Dr. Du Bois prepared a paper:

455. "Comments on My Life," *Freedomways*, Winter, 1965, Vol. V, No. 1, pp. 104–112. He reaffirmed his belief in "the value of a right attitude toward the truth" though he thought, then, that he was less certain than earlier (and later) in "the continuity and inevitableness of progress."

In 1953, at the age of 85, Dr. Du Bois toured the United States and publicly addressed tens of thousands; this was at a low point in the McCarthyite era, and Du Bois was one of the few men of eminence to fearlessly and repeatedly attack the paranoia that characterized the time. One such vigorous polemic was:

456. "On the Future of the American Negro," *Freedomways*, Winter, 1965, Vol. V, No. 1, pp. 117–124. Du Bois insists that the future must lie with working people throughout the world and that: "We should measure the prosperity of a nation not by the number of millionaires but by the absence of poverty, the prevalence of health, the efficiency of the public schools, and the number of people who can and do read worthwhile books."

CHAPTER II

WRITINGS IN MAGAZINES EDITED BY DUBOIS

As a college student, Du Bois edited The *Fisk Herald*, and his contributions therein have been noted earlier in this work. But a significant portion of his life was absorbed in launching magazines and then editing them for many years. This was true of The *Moon: Illustrated Weekly*,* published on Saturdays at the shop of Ed. L. Simon Co., at 358 Beale Street, in Memphis, Tennessee, with Harry H. Pace as manager and Du Bois—then teaching at Atlanta University —as the editor. This commenced in December, 1905, and terminated in July, 1906. Only two issues seem to have survived. The *Moon* was succeeded by The *Horizon: A Journal of the Color Line*, owned, edited, and printed by Dr. Du Bois, Freeman H. M. Murray, and L. M. Hershaw. The print shop was at 609 F St., N.W., in Washington, D.C. Volume I, No. 1, was dated January, 1907. In 1908 the *Horizon* appeared eleven times, since the final number combined the months of November and December. It ceased publication in July, 1910, when it was announced that *Horizon* subscribers would be credited toward a subscription to the organ of the newly established National Association for the Advancement of Colored People, entitled the *Crisis*, whose Volume I, Number 1, is dated November, 1910.

From then until August, 1934, the editor of the *Crisis* was Dr. Du Bois. While Du Bois regularly published material geared to children in the *Crisis*, he acutely felt the need for a magazine "for the children of the sun," as he wrote in the first number of the *Brownies' Book*, which lasted from January, 1920, to December, 1921†.

After leaving the *Crisis*, Du Bois returned to teaching at Atlanta University. While there he launched a quarterly journal, *Phylon* —funded by the University. Volume I, No. 1, appeared early in 1940, and *Phylon* had as its chief editor Dr. Du Bois through Volume V, No.

---

*See Paul G. Parrington's study of the *Moon* in *Journal of Negro History*, (July, 1963), Vol. XLVIII, pp. 206–216.

†See Elinor D. Sinnette's study of the *Brownies' Book* in *Freedomways*, (Winter, 1965), Vol. V, 1st Quarter, pp. 133–142.

2, issued in the second quarter of 1944. After that Du Bois left Atlanta University to return as Director of Special Research for the NAACP.

Du Bois not only edited these publications; he also published his own writings in them and it is the function of this second section of the Bibliography to enumerate these writings and to annotate them briefly but in as complete a manner as available resources make possible.

Only two full issues of the *Moon* are known to survive; both are in the Du Bois Papers, and a copy of the issue dated March 2, 1906, is in the library at Howard University, while a copy of the issue dated June 23, 1906, is in the Library at Fisk University. The issue of June 23, 1906, is listed on the cover as No. 30; there were perhaps three or four additional numbers. This means that out of about 34 numbers, only two survive:

457. *Moon*, March 2, 1906. A memorial issue dedicated to Paul Laurence Dunbar, who died on February 9, 1906. The issue opens with a department entitled "Tidings of the Darker Million." It consumes a page and a half and consists largely of items credited to other papers, such as the London *Mail* and the London *Times* telling of "disturbances" among the Zulu people in South Africa; a letter culled from the New York *Herald* by a white man from Barbados contesting remarks hostile to Black people living there; a news item from a Black newspaper, the Fort Smith (Ark.) *Record*, suggesting that its Afro-American voters will support measures for the improvement of the city as a whole. Four items are not credited to other publications and presumably were written by Du Bois directly on the basis either of reading or, possibly, of correspondence or direct observation. One deals with the views of a Rev. Joseph C. Hartzell, "missionary bishop of Africa for the M.E. Church" holding that there was a good future for Liberia and suggesting that a limited number of Afro-Americans might well consider migrating there; another from Washington tells of the introduction of racist legislation by Representative Heflin of Alabama and reports that "all of the colored schools of the city" during the afternoon of February 14 commemorated the life and work of Frederick Douglass. It added that at one of the high schools, Oswald Garrison Villard and Judge Robert H. Terrell delivered addresses. Several items from Boston appear. One reports the retirement of the department commander of the Massachusetts department of the Grand Army of the Republic, "J. H. Wolff, who is a prominent Negro lawyer"; another notes lectures devoted to "Municipal Ownership" of public utilities and facilities and to Robert Browning, with a reference to his alleged African ancestry.

Several pages are entitled "The Voice of Voices" and consist of appreciations of Paul Laurence Dunbar culled from newspapers throughout the nation. Unsigned, but certainly by Du Bois, is a page entitled "Negro Literature," which commences: "The black man is the central fact in American history" and then goes on to affirm the existence of a literature distinctively his and destined to grow. Appended is a bibliography of the writings of Dunbar, listing 16 titles.

458. *Moon*, June 23, 1906, contains a page entitled "The Man in the Moon." This is unsigned but its author is certainly Du Bois. It contains four items: "Faith" treats of the impact of renegacy (probably referring to the case of T. Thomas Fortune) upon the faith of many people in the possibility of effective struggle, but to lose faith because of this is short-sighted. Another is headed "Council and Ransom" having reference to William H. Council and to Rev. Reverdy C. Ransom and denounces the former for publicly berating the behavior of the latter as "the action of a coward" and hurtful to the cause of the people since both were leading figures behind the Veil. The third is entitled "Wandering," indicating that he is on a lecture tour "again." He remarks on the impact made upon him of the four thousand people in Washington attending commencement exercises of the city's colored high schools—"a scene not to be forgotten." (The address he delivered here is noted earlier, in No. 451.) Finally, half a page is given to the Niagara Movement, reporting in some detail on its work and announcing the 1906 meeting to be held at Harper's Ferry (Storer College). The page ends "Yours for Freedom."

For the first two years of its existence (Volumes 1–4), the *Horizon** was a pocket-size magazine of 28 pages (usually 4 pages of advertisements) $5\frac{1}{2}$ inches by $4\frac{1}{2}$ inches. Through 1907 it was published in Washington; in 1908 in Alexandria, Va.; in 1909 again in Washington. Commencing with Vol. V, No. 1 (November, 1909), its size was increased to 8 inches by 11 inches but its pages numbered 12. Volumes 1–4 consisted of three departments: "The Overlook," by Du Bois; "The Out-Look" by L. M. Hershaw; and (almost always) "The In-Look" by F. H. M. Murray. Volume V carried these features but in addition published, from time to time, contributions from the pens of others —occasionally white people, such as the great anthropologist Franz Boas. Much of Du Bois' writing in the *Horizon* consisted of poetry and short stories.

*Deep appreciation is expressed to the Librarian at Tuskegee Institute who made available, for a prolonged period, the complete sets of volumes I through IV of the magazine—part of the collection maintained by Booker T. Washington himself.

459. *Horizon* (January, 1907), Vol. I, No. 1. "The Over-Look," pp. 2–10. This consists of listings of articles in U.S. magazines of the preceding month dealing either with Black people in the United States or with other colored peoples, such as in Africa and in Asia. The magazines are those produced for the "white world." From time to time here—as in subsequent issues—Du Bois comments briefly on a particular essay as being especially useful or particularly vicious. This number also contains a suggestion that "every Negro American ought to subscribe for a number of good papers." He mentions Trotter's Boston *Guardian* and Barber's *Voice*, by this time issued in Chicago. He then evaluates other papers—thinks highly of the New York *Evening Post* and "above all" the *New York Independent* and denounces the *Outlook* and *Harper's Weekly* as especially racist. He recommends highly the *West African Mail*. This is followed by a brief discussion headed "Books," which calls attention to the recent work of George C. Merriam, George Washington Cable, Owen Wister, and others. A paragraph headed "Congo" briefly summarizes the "shameful" exploitation of the area by Belgium, notes the entry of United States capital—especially Rockefeller's—and warns: "The day of reckoning is coming." Other paragraphs treat of India and the conquest by whites of brown people—all of whom "want freedom" though they differ as to how to get it. Another, headed "Roosevelt," states that Brownsville simply shows that the President "does not like black folk"; a final paragraph notes the demise of the *Moon* because of money problems. Du Bois adds—with pointed reference to the Tuskegee corruption of many Black publications (though, of course, he mentions no names) —"it was a good, honest failure" and, he adds, here he is, in the *Horizon*, trying again.

460. *Horizon*, Vol. I, No. 2, (February, 1907). A listing of relevant articles, including "The Jews" in *Popular Science Monthly*. Du Bois adds that he should have noted in the preceding month the Springfield (Mass.) *Republican* "as a staunch friend of the Negro American in his struggles."

Here appears (pp. 4–6) the poem "The Song of the Smoke" with its affirmation of pride: *I will be black as blackness can—The blacker the mantle, the mightier the man*! A paragraph, "France," suggests "it is civilized," since a balloting was held on the greatest of French people in the 19th century and among the few selected was Dumas, thus showing "absolute indifference to the color-line," and Sarah Bernhardt, thus showing indifference "to the false barrier of sex." This is followed by a paragraph, "Socialist-of-the-Path," which is the way Du Bois then defines himself; he means, he says, one who sees the need for the public ownership of railroads, coalmines and many factories. Then appears "Negro and Socialism," with Du Bois declaring that "in the socialistic trend ... lies the one great hope of the Negro American." He adds he does not agree with the Socialists in everything, "but in trend and ideal they are the salt of this present earth." A page devoted to India follows. It quotes from a militant speech demanding freedom at a meeting of the Indian National Congress, and Du Bois comments: "The dark world awakens to life and articulate speech. Courage, Comrades!" A page headed "Austria" observes that Jews in Austria are raising demands for political rights; once again, Du Bois hails this and adds: "So much for 'gum-shoe'and 'back-door' and 'conciliating' methods!" A final paragraph, "Lagos," reports the continued "exploitation of the native West Africans" by "organized, ruthless and ruling capital backed by greed."

461. *Horizon*, (March, 1907), Vol. I, No. 3, pp. 3–10. Notes the appearance in the preceding month of six books, including one on Africa and one on the peace movement by Jane Addams. In noting relevant articles Du Bois suggests that they "will make the Man of March, 2907 to shriek with laughter." "We shriek now," he adds, "but not wholly with laughter." There follows a listing of some 20 articles, including some dealing with race questions in New Zealand, India, and Africa and with the American Indian. A paragraph, "Hearken, Theodore Roosevelt," urges Roosevelt to undo the injustice of his acts in connection with the Brownsville Affair;another, "Journeying," is significant biographically, touches on a recent tour by him and notes that "shuddering as I always do" he headed back South to Atlanta, "and Peace—and War."

462. *Horizon*, Vol. I, No. 4, (April, 1907), pp. 3–10. Fifteen magazine articles are listed, and a few are commented upon; one deals with the Cuban Negro. A paragraph, "Books," is an appeal to Black people to buy good books and build up their own libraries. Several pages are devoted to Africa, especially South Africa and the Congo. A page, "Unknown," is about the racist ignorance so generally manifested by the White World. A one-page short-short story, "Wittekind," has as its point the denial of the then-widespread idea that Black folk were dying out.

463. *Horizon*, (May, 1907), Vol. I, No. 5, pp. 3–10. Seven magazine articles are noted; one by Ray Stannard Baker in the *American* is praised. Among the articles listed, one deals with the Jewish immigrant and another with immigrants from India. The book section is devoted to *Sex and Society*, by William I. Thomas—"a book to read and ponder." A paragraph, "The Lash," laments (without mentioning a name) the departure of T. Thomas Fortune from his earlier militancy. Two pages describe the celebration in London of the centenary of the abolition of the English slave trade (March 25, 1907). A paragraph, "Dying," denies that the higher death rate among Black people is racial; it is, rather, a reflection of poverty and oppression. He cites the work of "one Rubinow" (I. M. Rubinow) showing that the poor in Russia have a much higher death rate than the rich. (It may be added that Du Bois had been in correspondence with Mr. Rubinow for some years by 1907.) A poem, taking off from a line out of Horace, concludes this section.

464. *Horizon*, Vol. I, No. 6, (June, 1907), pp. 3–10. The section "Magazines" states that "the South is silently boycotting" the *American* because of the Ray Stannard Baker series; it praises an exposé of peonage written by Alexander Irvine, "a Socialist and a Man," and denounces the *Saturday Evening Post* for its consistency in publishing foul racist propaganda. Eight articles are listed; these include three on Africa, one on the American Indian, and one called "The Yellow Man's Burden." A poem follows denouncing the hypocrisy of the "Christianity" preached by the Episcopal Church (of which Du Bois had been a member). Two pages, headed "Africa," are devoted to the work of the Aborigines Protection Society in England, including a list of its publications. Under "Carpenters," admiring note is taken of the efforts at organization among 33 Black carpenters in New York City; this is followed by further discussion of "Brownsville" and by a listing, under "Books," of some that Du Bois thought would make "for serious reading this summer." Sixteen titles were listed—two by Jane Addams, two by the Socialist Jack London, two by the Socialist John Spargo, and one by Henry George—all dealing in one way or another with questions of impoverishment, peace, and the labor movement.

465. *Horizon*, (July, 1907), Vol. II, No. 1, pp. 3–10. Lists, without comment, 12 articles, several dealing with colored peoples other than Afro-Americans. Nine pages are devoted to a short story, "The Case," dealing with a train mystery that is reminiscent of portions of Du Bois' later novel, *Dark Princess* (1928; No. 1962).

466. *Horizon*, August, 1907, Vol. II, No. 2, pp. 3–10. Six articles are noted; one in the Chicago magazine *Tomorrow*, described by Du Bois as "rather unconventional, and socialistic." He adds: "Speaks of 'us' often and is stiffly for us, always." Calls attention to an essay in *Harper's* that "shows how important it is that legal cases involving our rights be carefully watched and adequately defended." Another short story, "The Shaven Lady," again a kind of "mystery" with a train setting and the false accusation of theft against a Black man.

467. *Horizon,* September, 1907, Vol. II, No. 3, pp. 3–10. Notes the appearance of but three articles treating of Black people in the general (White) magazines: "You see there are other 'Niggers' to have their innings—those impudent Japanese in British Columbia and Mexico, and the nasty East Indians, not to mention Jews and Italians and other trash." Several pages are devoted to an accounting of the Niagara Movement and the printing of its "Call" after the Third Annual Convention, held in 1907.

468. *Horizon*, October, 1907, Vol. II, No. 4, pp. 3–10. Eight articles are noted. Several pages are devoted to extracts on racism from books by English and German authors (including H. G. Wells). Correspondence between Du Bois and an official of the Episcopal Church—concerning its racism—is reproduced, as is a letter on a recent lynching in Alabama.

469. *Horizon*, Vol. II, No. 5, November, 1907, pp. 1–8. Eight magazine articles are listed; three treat of Africa and one of Canada. Five books are named, one a novel and four biographical—of Whittier, Dumas, Carl Schurz, and O. O. Howard. Du Bois thinks highly of the novel *Mam 'Linda* (Harper), by W. N. Harben a Southern white man. Two poems are in this issue: "The Burden of Black Women" and a parody of "My Country 'Tis of Thee"; also a very short story, "The Running of the Bishop"—again a satire on a racist "Christianity."

470. *Horizon*, December, 1907, Vol. II, No. 6, pp. 1–8. Ten articles are listed; two deal with Asian peoples and one with Africans. Extracts follow from recent reading by Dr. Du Bois, including pertinent paragraphs from Eaton's just-published *Grant, Lincoln and the Freedmen*. The final page contains a poem, "Death."

471. *Horizon*, January, 1908, Vol. III, No. 1, pp. 1–8. Here appears what was to become a regular feature of Du Bois' journalism —commencing each year with a two-columned page headed "Debit" and "Credit" with major setbacks to Black people and significant victories listed in their respective places. Du Bois also called particular attention to magazine articles by Washington Gladden, Ray Stannard Baker, and H. G. Wells, among others, during the year 1907 and four books: J. Finot's, *Race Prejudice*; S. Oliver's, *White Capital and Coloured Labor*; J. Eaton's, *Grant, Lincoln and Freedmen*; and O. O. Howard's *Autobiography*. For the new year, Du Bois toasted *health, work, more work, love* and *air*—by which he meant getting out and looking at the world and its clouds and trees. Du Bois noted some victories in prosecuting those guilty of peonage—especially where the victims were of Italian or Greek ancestry. A poem appears—"A Day in Africa"—but an actual trip to Africa was still some years in the future for him. There are also some extracts from news items.

472. *Horizon*, Vol. III, No. 2, (February, 1908), pp. 17–24. Three magazine articles are listed. Some advice is offered in "To Black Voters," which is to beat Roosevelt and Taft. The article includes this sentence: "In all cases remember that the only party today which treats Negroes as men, North and South, are the Socialists." A brief essay, "Little Brother of Mine," refers to the taking over of the Chicago paper, the *Conservator*—as earlier of the New York *Age*—by the Tuskegee machine. A poem, "The Song of America," carrying a fierce condemnation of its brutality, follows. The department closes with selections dealing with Africa from British publications.

473. *Horizon*, March, 1908, Vol. III, No. 3, pp. 1–8. As to reading, Du Bois thinks "The magazines are getting silent and suspicious"; he notes only an article in the *American* and an ambitious book by Jerome Dowd "which I have not yet read." A brief poem, "Ave! Maria!," follows and then a biographical sketch of the Black woman Ida Dean Bailey, who had recently died and who was revered by Du Bois as a splendid leader of the Afro-American people. In a paragraph, "Darwinism," Du Bois comments on the distortions making it into Social Darwinism and calls attention to the fact that Alfred Wallace—a cofounder of the theory of evolution—had recently joined such scientists as Franz Boas in denying the validity of racism. Tribute is paid to Augustus Straker, who had recently died. Mr. Straker had been a member of the South Carolina legisture, moved north and served for some years as a judge in Detroit. There is a brief paragraph saying that if the Black voter must choose between Taft and Bryan, Du Bois suggests the latter.

474. *Horizon*, April, 1908, Vol. III, No. 4, pp. 1–8. Eight magazine articles are listed, four of which deal with the Afro-American, one with discrimination against Jews, two with Africa, and one with India. Six books are listed, including *Who's Who in America*, which contains accounts, Du Bois notes, "of nearly thirty Negro Americans whom I know, and there are probably others." Among the books listed one treats of the West Indies, one of Asia and Africa, and a third is *Justice to the Jew*, by Madison Peters (McClure). A poem, "The Prayer of the Bantu," is one imploring victory over the oppressors. A two-page essay, "Taft," argues for political independence on the part of the Black voters for "if we stand, ballot in hand, ready to punish the party that insults and neglects us, it will learn in time to treat us as men and not as dogs." A paragraph praising Charles Cuthbert Hall, who had recently died, follows; this white man, Du Bois says, treated all people as people. Finally, under the heading "The Southern Electorate" Du Bois observes the progress in statesmanship coming from the South with the disfranchisement of Black people—from Blanche K. Bruce to James K. Vardaman, from John R. Lynch to Benjamin Tillman; "the South is redeemed"! Two quotations from The *African Mail* treating of events in Africa close this month's contribution.

475. *Horizon*, May, 1908, Vol. III, No. 5, pp. 1–3. Six articles are listed, one dealing with working people in India. On the basis of a letter from a white "well-wisher" who complains of the "impertinent" and "fresh" Black people who seem too pushy to the "well-wisher," Du Bois goes on to say something about the need for patience and comprehension of the young in general who often appear "bumptious." "Let him grow," pleads Du Bois, "he may be Martin Luther bursting his chrysalis . . . he may foreshadow a mighty people in travail."

476. *Horizon*, June, 1908, III, No. 6, pp. 1–8. Two books are listed. *Southern Agriculture* by F. S. Earle (New York: Macmillan), and *What the White Man May Learn from the Indian*, by George W. James (Chicago: Forbes). Six articles, including one on Brazil, are mentioned. Du Bois has the highest praise for Ray Stannard Baker's article in the June *American*. Two pages are devoted to an exposure of the racist record and words of Taft; Du Bois closes by affirming that his vote goes to Bryan. In a two-page essay headed "Union," Du Bois states that the Niagara Movement, the Afro-American Council, the Negro American Political League, and the Negro Academy represent diverse streams of essentially the same effort; he suggests the propriety and wisdom of their unifying, and concludes: "I hereby pledge myself to accept no office in the gift of the united organizations." A paragraph is devoted to *Twelfth Night*, put on by the seniors of Atlanta University; it was beautifully done, writes Du Bois, attesting to "the tremendous artistic and dramatic power of a suppressed and soul-starved race who despite all bonds must one day be free." A poem by Du Bois, "El Dorado," closes the section.

477. *Horizon*, July, 1908, Vol. IV, No. 1, pp. 1–8. A brief, joyous paragraph, "Free," describes Du Bois on vacation in "the fresh sweet air." Under "Horizon" Du Bois notes that the magazine has grown, that the three men associated with it have received no pay for their labors, that no secret subsidy must be allowed, and that a national magazine of wide circulation is vital. He calls, therefore, for guarantors to put up a yearly sum and thus make certain its expansion and existence. In this issue Du Bois commenced a series of "five heart-to-heart talks with the Negro-American voter"; talk number one affirms that "aside from special considerations of race, the policy of the Democratic party is the best policy for the Nation." This because that party is more favorable to the cause of organized labor, and its cause "is the cause of black laborers"; because it is more hostile to monopolies; because it is opposed to colonialism and imperialism, as manifested in the Philippines and Cuba. The section closes with an excerpt from the *African Mail* dealing with Edward W. Blyden and Casely Hayford.

478. *Horizon*, August, 1908, Vol. IV, No. 2, pp. 1–8. This contains talks number two and three to the Black voter. The second affirms that the proper purpose of the ballot is not to obtain employment for a favored few "but to establish certain great principles of justice and sound policy." The third argues that "the Republican Party has forfeited its claim to the Negro's vote."

479. *Horizon*, September, 1908, Vol. IV, No. 3, pp. 1–8. The statement of the Fourth Annual Meeting, held at Oberlin, Ohio, of the Niagara Movement appears; this is followed by talks number four and five on "The Negro Vote." The former holds "that the Democratic Party deserves a trial at the hands of the Negro"; the latter "that the best thing that can happen in the next election will be a big black Bryan vote."

480. *Horizon*, October, 1908, Vol. IV, No. 4, pp. 1–8. Because of the lapse since June in his listing of relevant articles and books, here one finds those for July, August, September, and October, with a total of 25 articles and six books. Of the books, two dealt with the Philippines, one with Jewish people, and two with American Indians. Three of the books treated Africa, and one India. For the new president, whoever he may be as of November, Du Bois sees three main tasks: "curbing the vicious power of corporate wealth"; terminating lynching; and "securing to Negro Americans their full rights of American citizens lest race prejudice undermine the walls of our nation's liberty."

481. *Horizon*, November–December, 1908, Vol. IV, No. 5 and No. 6, pp. 1–14. Two scenes from a drama, *The Christ of the Andes*, which is a cry against war. A leading statesman in it, explaining the need to continue slaughtering, remarks: "Peace is my dearest dream, but peace with Honor." On politics, Du Bois notes with regret the re-election of Taft and adds: "We did not happen to have the power in the last election of deciding who should be President but we will have the power in certain future elections." A page is devoted to Liberia; the article was evoked by a recent visit of officials from that country seeking United States capital—to offset, Du Bois suggests, the influence of the British. The whole event suggests to him the need for a vast "Pan-African movement" because "the need of Liberia, the cause of Hayti, the cause of South Africa is our cause, and the sooner we realize this the better." On the final page of his section Du Bois announces an enlarged format in 1909 for The *Horizon*; if each subscriber gets two or three new subscribers the magazine will be permanent, he adds, but "otherwise the experiment will be confined simply to the year 1909."

The first number of the enlarged *Horizon* did not appear until November, 1909; it ceased publication in July, 1910. As of this moment, however, only three issues have been found. There is not only a change in size with this number; one is told now that the magazine is "Edited by W. E. Burghardt Du Bois assisted by L. M. Hershaw and F. H. M. Murray."

482. *Horizon*, November, 1909, Vol. V, No. 1, pp. 1–2, 8, 9. "The Over-Look" opens the issue and consists of six paragraphs: "Our Policy," defines the editorial policy describing it as a "radical" one. "Support," asks for subscriptions and financial contributions, for "No periodical that advocates unpopular or partially popular causes, can be a self-supporting proposition." "National Negro Conference," describes the one held in New York City in May, 1909, launching what became the NAACP, as "the most significant event of 1909." "Garrison," pays tribute to William Lloyd Garrison, Jr., who had recently died and who—Du Bois thought—had been worthy of his father.

"Henson" is a paragraph on Josiah Henson, companion and helper of Peary in reaching the North Pole in 1909, which notes the irony in United States history and the great role of Servant (as was Christ) performed by Black people, "in a contemptible age of bull dogs, Big Sticks and Lion slaughterers." Finally, "Schools," calls attention not only to the meager schooling provided Black children in the South but also to the fact that the schooling has been deteriorating during the past decade, as part of an effort by Southern rulers to "stop Negro education" and noting that many among us spend our time "trying to get some worthless politician a new job at Washington."

A page is devoted to books and periodicals; it is signed W. E. B. D. Ten titles are listed; in addition, comment is offered on William P. Pickett's *Emigration of American Negroes to Africa*, which advocates that emigration be assisted. Du Bois wholly disapproves of the book because: "The Negro problem is to be settled in America and settled right. After that we shall be ready and willing to help our brothers in Africa." Seventeen articles are noted in periodicals; several deal with Africa—especially Theodore Roosevelt's hunting trip in that continent —and one treats of Cuba. One page (p. 9) is headed "Along the Color Line"; it is unsigned but is Du Bois' work. It consists of the address adopted by the Fifth Annual Meeting of the Niagara Movement —written by Du Bois. It calls for power—"Political power, Economic power, power of Mind"—and insists that Black people in the United States "must make common cause with the oppressed and down-trodden of all races and peoples ... and with the cause of the working-classes everywhere."

483. Horizon, December, 1909, Vol. V, No. 2, pp. 1–3, 10, 11–12. "The Over-Look" consists of eight pieces. Two are very short stories, "Principles" and "Constructive Work"; the first is a parody on the white "do-gooder" who urges patience upon the Black people; the second is an attack upon the pusillanimous and compromising "race leader." One piece, "John Brown and Christmas," affirms deep parallels in the careers of John Brown and Jesus Christ. (Brown's picture is on the cover of this issue; it is the fiftieth year since his execution. Du Bois' *John Brown* (No. 1957) appeared in 1909). Another, "The Color Line," points to the madness of the concept of the color line as illustrated in recent enactments in South Africa. A paragraph, "Women," hails the developing fight among women, in the United States and Britain, for full rights and notes that some of the most creative minds and courageous fighters then functioning were women.

It derides "the ancient taffy about homes and babies" and relates the movement for the emancipation of women to that for the liberation of Black people. A paragraph pays tribute to the work of General O. O. Howard, who headed the Freedmen's Bureau and who died in 1909; another attacks President Taft for his racist practices; and a final selection, "Consistency," quotes Bernard Shaw's attack upon England's hypocrisy vis-à-vis Egypt and compares that with United States hypocrisy in terms of the Afro-American people. On page 10 Du Bois reprints a letter to him from an (unnamed) white professor in the South; the letter was evoked by *Souls of Black Folk* that the professor had just read. It is a lament of guilt and a cry of hopelessness, placing the reason for racism on the shoulders "of the lower class whites." Du Bois publishes a reply, acknowledges the depth of the feeling in the letter, but insists that those who rule are responsible for the nature of the order they dominate and adds that no one is powerless unless he chooses not to act. Pages 11–12 consist of a summary of the year's magazine and book production with respect to race and Black people. Ninety-eight separate publications treated of these questions; 20 were books, and all are listed. Four were especially important, Du Bois says: A. B. Hart's *Southern South*; E. G. Murphy's *Basis of Ascendancy;* H. P. Douglass' *Christian Reconstruction in the South* (Pilgrim Press); and N. Worth's *Southerner*(New York: Doubleday). Dr. Du Bois reported 63 articles "in the larger national periodicals," ten of which were "signed by Mr. Booker T. Washington." Du Bois selects 5 as the "most notable": W. Archer's, "Black and White in the South," in *McClure* (July); Q. Ewing's, "Heart of the Race Problem," in the *Atlantic* (March); F. Boas's "Race Problems in America," in *Science* (May 28); Kelly Miller's "Ultimate Race Problem," in the *Atlantic* (April); and L. P. Weale's "Conflict of Color," in the *World's Work* (September). All others are then listed by title, author, name, and date of publication.

484. *Horizon*, February, 1910, Vol. V, No. 4, pp. 1–4. This consists of "The Over-Look." It commences with the listing of six magazine articles, including one on the American Indian; it calls attention to "an interesting pamphlet" on plants in Macon County, Alabama, just produced by George Washington Carver. A section entitled "J'Accuse" attacks the dominant white South in specific terms and details the position of Du Bois. A brief short story, "The Optimist," satirizes the Booker T. Washington type of leadership (mentioning no names, of course). A paragraph is devoted to praising Governor Deneen of Illinois for refusing to reappoint a sheriff in that state who had failed to prevent a lynching—the governor was visited by a committee of Black people, led by Mrs. Ida B. Wells-Barnett, which "strengthened his back bone." A note laments the recent death of John F. Cook (whose photo is on the cover), a successful Black businessman and an adherent of the Niagara Movement. A fairly detailed examination of figures on conditions in the Bahamas is offered to show that its administration is far ahead of the United States'. A paragraph, "Slander," denounces the notion then being popularized to the effect that venereal disease was the responsibility of Black people; another, "Black Women," congratulates Ida Tarbell, since in a recent article in the *American Magazine* she had "at last discovered Africa in her history of American women." The discovery was not well presented, said Du Bois, but at any rate Miss Tarbell seemed now to know that not all women were white.

The longest single sustained piece of work by Dr. Du Bois was his editorship of the *Crisis*, organ of the National Association for the Advancement of Colored People; this magazine appeared each month under his editorship from its first number, dated November, 1910, through July, 1934. In the early volumes, very nearly the entire magazine was written by him; later,departments appeared by him —signed and unsigned—as did particular essays often signed by him. This bibliography follows the practice adopted in connection with the *Horizon* and gives a single number to Du Bois' contributions to one issue of the *Crisis*, except where, in addition to his departments, he signs a particular article. Rather typical of the early numbers is the very first; of its 20 pages—outside of advertisements—Du Bois wrote (or edited and gathered where quotations appear) every page except one (p. 13), in which are reprinted extracts from a speech entitled "Athens and Brownsville" by Moorfield Storey, the founding president of the NAACP. The *Crisis* appeared first as "Edited by W. E. Burghardt Du Bois, with the cooperation of Oswald Garrison Villard, J. Max Barber, Charles Edward Russell, Kelly Miller, W. S. Braithwaite and M. D. MacLean." Where changes occurred in this, they are noted.

485. *Crisis*, November, 1910; Vol. I, No. 1, There are six departments or sections to this issue, all by Du Bois: "The Color Line," of four pages, consists of relevant news items in the "political" arena, such as appointments of Black men to office (as J.C. Napier and P. B. S. Pinchback), independent political activity among Black voters, the Socialist Party's appointment of a committee of two (Lena M. Lewis and George A. Goebel) "to investigate the condition of the Negro in

America"; another dealing with education tells of benefactions and tribulations, including a suit by a Black man in Missouri to compel state authorities to transport his children to an adequate school, some six miles from his home (Mr. Sawyer lost the suit); another labeled "The Church" tells of appointments and meetings in this area of life; one called "Social Uplift" calls attention to a forthcoming Universal Races Congress to be held in London in 1911; to the splendid work of the Rhode Island Union of Colored Women; and to a news item in the New York *Sun* telling of the writings of the Frenchman, M. Zeltner concerning highly developed civilizations and states in Africa long before the coming of the European. A section called "Organizations and Meetings" details such by Black people or others relevant to them, such as a conference on the East and Africa recently held at Clark University in Massachusetts, with papers given by Black and white scholars. Still another section, "Economic," carries news of business, real estate, and labor developments; another, "Science," reports findings casting doubts upon concepts of racial inferiority; and a final division, "Art," notes the activities of Black musicians (such as Carl Diton) and—some fifteen years before the "Harlem Renaissance" —calls attention to the fact that "New York is becoming an art center for colored people" with such performers as Bert Williams, Cole and Johnson, Will Marion Cook, and the Clef Club Orchestra of 130 musicians under James Reese Europe.

Three pages are devoted to "Opinion," with quotations from an extraordinary range of sources, reflecting Du Bois' almost unbelievable capacity for work. The "opinions" reflect, of course, varying approaches to race and racism in the United States and elsewhere; the quotations come from newspapers in New York State, Maryland, Georgia, South Carolina, New Jersey, Florida, and Indiana; from magazines in the United States and in England, from state reports (such as the Pennsylvania Bureau of Industrial Statistics), and from books, such as that by William Dean Howells on Mark Twain. An overall impression is that of the universality of the so-called race question and its relationship to every other social and economic and moral question confronting humanity.

Two pages, unsigned, are devoted to "editorial" matter. This commences with a statement of the *Crisis*' policy—"for the rights of men, irrespective of color or race. ... " "Segregation" notes that racial segregation in education is being attempted "quietly" in Chicago, Philadelphia, Atlantic City, Columbus, and elsewhere in the North and Du Bois shows why; "Baltimore" denounces moves in Baltimore to institutionalize residential segregation; another, "Voting," calls for independent and not habitual vote casting; a brief essay on the usefulness of agitation and, finally, a sardonic note to the effect that the protest by the Italian government against the lynching of two Italians had to be rejected by Washington since it was found they were naturalized citizens; there exists, of course, Du Bois writes, "the inalienable right of every free American citizen to be lynched. ... "

A page and a half is given to news of the NAACP; in this case, news of the first and second conferences held in 1909 and 1910, which created the organization, with the names of the members of the General Committee of the association. A page headed "The Burden" was done by Du Bois, though unsigned. It contains four items; two deal with cases of Black men who in self-defense killed their bosses and were now facing death (Steve Green in Arkansas and Pink Franklin in South Carolina); another is a kind of short story grounded on the fact that Black people are forbidden entrance into the "public" park in Charleston, S.C.; the last on a Black schoolchild in Chicago accused —falsely—of theft because of his color. Finally, in this number, a page is given over to "What To Read." The magazine section is divided into two parts: "Africa" and "America" with 11 articles listed under the former and 39 under the latter. Attention is called to the appearance of a new quarterly, *Journal of Race Development*, at Clark University, with Du Bois as a contributing editor. The page closes with the listing of 11 relevant books: 1 on Cuba, 8 on Africa, and 2 biographies, of John Brown (by O. G. Villard) and of William Lloyd Garrison (by Lindsay Swift).

486. December, 1910. Vol. I, No. 2. (This issue is enlarged to 36 pages from the 20 of No. 1: this remains true for the rest of Volume I and also for Volume II commencing with the May, 1911, issue.) "Along the Color Line" runs from page 5 through page 10. Under "Political" Du Bois reported resistance—including physical resistance—by Blacks to efforts in Oklahoma, under the 1910 Constitution, to disfranchise them. In Guthrie representatives from several Black organizations denounced the Republican leadership and urged "the Negroes of the State to support the entire Socialist ticket" and called for the enfranchisement of women. Note is taken of the election for the first time of a Black man (Harry W. Bass of Philadelphia) to the Pennsylvania legislature. Governor-elect Woodrow Wilson of New Jersey is taken to task because no Black student had ever been admitted to Princeton University, including during his tenure as its president. Attention is called to the mounting work in the North and West of the Independent Political League of Colored Voters. Under "Judicial Decisions" Du Bois calls attention to several cases throughout the nation, such as one in Boston where a Black woman won a suit against a cafe that had refused to serve her; where a Court held unconstitutional an effort by the city of Annapolis to disfranchise its Black citizens; and to developing cases, in Alabama, seeking to sustain federal laws prohibiting peonage. Under "Education" Du Bois notes a study by the Slater Fund on inadequacy of schooling for Black children in Georgia; a statement by Edmund J. James, president of the University of Illinois, that the neglect of the education of the Afro-American people was "a national reproach"; and a resolution by the (white) Alabama Educational Association denouncing compulsory education! In a section headed "The Church" Du Bois observed that after much struggle it was finally agreed to permit the body of a Black man to be buried in the churchyard of St. James' Episcopal Church; a Rev. Joseph Dunn, an Episcopal priest of southern Virginia, is quoted as holding "that the emancipation of the Negroes was a dire disaster"; while James H. Dillard, agent of the Jeanes Fund, affirmed that "segregation is not necessarily un-Christian." Under "Economic" Du Bois reports cases of violent and nonviolent resistance to efforts by Black people to break out of the ghetto, in Kansas City, St. Paul, Baltimore, and Atlanta. Remarks by Samuel Gompers of the American Federation of Labor hostile to the overcoming of Jim Crow in trade unions are noted. Under "Crime" Du Bois noted the lynching of two Black men, "for killing a night policeman" and reported "several race riots" in Huntington, W. Va., with a Black man killed and several whites killed and wounded: "There were numerous fights between the whites and the blacks." Under "Foreign" several matters are reported, including the release from confinement of a Zulu Chief named Dinuzulu who had led an uprising against the British; and the results of an investigation by the English Aborigines Society showing the widespread existence of peonage in Mexico. Five pages are given over to "opinion" culled by Du Bois from newspapers in the United States and in Europe. These deal with disfranchisement in Oklahoma; a statement from the New York *Call*, organ of the Socialist Party, hailing the action of Black people in Oklahoma who had resolved in favor of the party; discussion of the Maryland decision prohibiting disfranchisement by Annapolis, including a substantial quotation from a sermon by the Baltimore Rabbi William Rosenau denouncing efforts to curtail the civil rights of Black people. Commentary on Taft's appointment of a Black man, William H. Lewis, as an assistant attorney-general is quoted; also quoted is a London newspaper against Booker T. Washington's speeches while in England to the effect that all was well on the racial front in the United States.

Four pages make up the unsigned "editorial" matter; all of it comes from Du Bois. Seven subjects are discussed: December as the month of Christ and the hope that some day his teachings will be the practices of this nation; an exposition of the purposes of the NAACP and the means to achieve these; fairly extended notice of the forthcoming Universal Races Congress in London in July, 1911, whose "possibilities are tremendous and its plan unique"; hailing the fact that in the 1910 elections more Black voters broke from automatically voting Republican than ever before; a denunciation of the growing ghettoization of the nation and a warning about its great dangers; a contrasting of the anger displayed by a New York *Times* editorial writer over the habit of some passengers on public carriers of usurping more than one seat and the same paper's extreme patience and mildness in the face of the lynching of several thousand Black people; and an insistence that those who excuse social crime by the remark that it is "inevitable" are really rationalizing such crime if not joining in its commission. Two pages are devoted to "The Burden." These present a table detailing the lynching of 2,425 Black people from 1885 to 1910; another description of the Pink Franklin case, mentioned earlier; continued turmoil in Oklahoma resulting from efforts to disfranchise Black men; a report from South Carolina of a Black farmer killing an intruder into his home; of several Black people ordered to leave Warrenton, Georgia, solely because they had managed to accumulate too much property; and a kind of short story—by Du Bois—headed "Precept and Practice," the former being noble and the latter ignoble.

One page devoted to "What To Read" lists 14 magazine articles of which 4 deal with India, 3 with Africa, and 1 with China. Thirteen books (one in French) are listed, 4 of which deal with Africa; interestingly one of the books noted is Gertrude Stein's *Three Lives*. Brief reviews, by Du Bois (unsigned), appear here also; one is of William Archer's *Through Afro-America* and the other is John E. Bruce's *Short Biographical Sketches: Eminent Negro Men and Women* (Yonkers, N.Y.: Gazette Press 1910). The first is by a British visitor who admits to an aversion for Black people; the result is advocacy of a separate all-Black area of residence. The book as a whole and its proposal are denounced. The Bruce book would be useful, Du Bois suggests, "as a supplementary reader in schools," though he thinks the editing could be much improved.

487. January, 1911 Vol. I, No. 3,. "Along the Color Line" consists of five pages; that under "Political" contains follow-up material on the appointment of William Lewis by President Taft and struggles in Oklahoma against disfranchisement. Fairly extensive accounts, under "Colored Colleges" are given of Howard, Lincoln (Pa.), Virginia Union, Wilberforce, Atlanta, Shaw, and Georgia State Industrial College. Governor-elect Cole Blease of South Carolina is quoted as saying "the greatest mistake the white race has ever made was in attempting to educate the free Negro." Data on discrimination in education in Louisiana, taken from official sources, are printed. Reports of vigorous campaigns among the Southern Blacks themselves to further the education of their children appear. Under "The Church," Du Bois noted that there was a total of five Black Roman Catholic priests in the United States. Under "Opinion" Du Bois printed the statement signed by 32 Black leaders in the United States (written by himself) denouncing Booker T. Washington's reports of great progress in race relations in the United States and offering a summary of the actual conditions.*

He goes on to report that the document was translated into German and was commented upon very widely throughout Europe and the United States; he offers a sampling of this comment. Press comments on the Baltimore effort to legalize ghettoes were very frequent, and a large sampling is given by Du Bois. Offering quotations from several newspapers, under the heading "Gompers" Du Bois notes that he "was to some extent misquoted on the Negro problem." A long letter from Horace Bumstead (President of Atlanta University) published in the *Boston Transcript* and denouncing disfranchisement of Black people is published under "Voting"; and under "Negro Soldiers" the remarks made by General Andrew S. Burt (Ret.), who had been commander of the Black battalion involved in the Brownsville incident, at a meeting sponsored by the Boston Literary Association, praising the record of Black soldiers in general in U.S. history, are quoted. A section "In South Africa" quoted a Professor Broon as affirming that in a century—i.e., in 2010—South Africa would be ruled "by the Black man."

Four pages of "editorial" matter appear: "Envy" dismisses the widespread idea that opposition to Booker T. Washington springs not from principled differences with his position and methods but from jealousy; "The Truth" demonstrates the contradictory nature of propaganda from the leading Southern publications, such as, on the

*The names of all signers and the full text will be found in H. Aptheker, ed., *A Documentary History of the Negro People in the United States* (N.Y.: Citadel Press, 1951), pp. 884–886.

one hand, a denial of the disfranchisement of Black men and, on the other, a boasting about the fact that Black men are not allowed to vote! A demonstration, under the title, "Opportunity," is given that racism especially hinders the possibility of economic advancement on the part of Black people, and under "Schools" there is a call for a careful listing of the actual needs in education and some system that will assure good results in the allocation of funds. The details of a typical frameup of a Black man on a murder charge are presented under the title "The Old Story"—this happened in New Jersey and the prosecutor himself finally admitted the fraud. A definition, from the Southern press, is given of the actual content of what is called "social equality"—this being in fact the achievement of full political and economic rights by Black people. There is a little essay, "Ashamed," showing that those who fight for their rights exhibit thereby "race pride" and "it is the man ashamed of his blood who weakly submits and smiles". Under the title "Jesus Christ in Baltimore" Du Bois ironically notes the flight of palatial churches from the "incursion" of Black residents. And, finally, there is a brief note " 'Except Servants'," observing that where Black people are barred an exception is made as to Black servants and the question is asked: "Is this race prejudice inborn antipathy or a social and economic caste?" In a page devoted to "The Burden," the table on lynching is reproduced, the insult to Black women of calling them by first names is excoriated, and other examples of discrimination in employment, education, and property owning are given.

In the two pages devoted to "What To Read," Du Bois lists 8 magazine articles and 12 books, including G. Deutsch's *History of the Jews* (New York: Bloch Publishing, 1910). He calls particular attention to an essay, "The Lady of the Slave States," by Mrs. George Haven Perkins (*Contemporary Review*, December, 1910) since it exposes some of the moonlight-magnolia mythology. He thinks a pamphlet by Melville E. Stone, *Race Prejudice*, just published by the Quill Club of New York City, to be "remarkable" and quotes from it at great length. The quotations constitute indeed a remarkable condemnation of racism and colonialism and a warning that the maintenance of such injustices will not be permitted much longer.

488. "A Winter Pilgrimage," signed W. E. B. D., *Crisis*, Vol. I, No. 3, January, 1911, p. 15. A report by Du Bois on a trip to Ohio—to Toledo, Cleveland, and Oberlin in particular. Each with its different facet of "the race problem"; some showing great advances and in other cities regressive tendencies. For five hours, he talked with the youth at

Oberlin and came away with hope renewed; still the "bonds of medievalism are drawn" and the battle rages.

489. February, 1911 Vol. I, No. 4,. On page 3, under the title "The Crisis: A Business Proposition" Du Bois writes, without signature, of the growth of the magazine which commenced with a printing of 1,000 and in February, 1911, was issued in 4,000 copies. The appeal is for as many as 10,000 subscribers, for contributions, and for criticism. For the first time, in the text of the magazine itself, photographs appear. "Along the Color Line" called attention to memorial meetings—largely organized and attended by Black people—for Senator Charles Sumner held in New York, Boston, and Washington and another for Julia Ward Howe, in Boston. Note was taken, under "Courts," of several hopeful rulings, in particular that by the Supreme Court, in the case of Alonzo Bailey, a Black worker, against Alabama, where peonage was affirmed as illegal and laws upholding it were declared unconstitutional. Details were given concerning efforts by Black people themselves to further the education of their children in Louisiana and South Carolina. Under "Social Uplift" Du Bois called attention to the publication by the American Negro Monographs Company of a new edition of *Nat Turner's Confessions*. He recorded also the formation of "a colored baseball league" in eight cities: Chicago; Louisville; New Orleans; Mobile; St. Louis; Kansas City, Kans.; Kansas City, Mo; and Columbus, Ohio. Under "Vagaries of the Color Line" Du Bois quotes extensively from Southern papers denouncing a newly appointed school superintendent in New Orleans for daring to allow Black and white teachers together to listen to a lecture on penmanship. Under "Opinion" Du Bois quotes a letter to the *New York Post* in which the writer wonders if Mr. Carnegie's gift of ten million dollars to advance the cause of peace might not better have been spent toward assisting in equalizing the education offered Black children. Quotations are offered from several papers on the question whether or not and if so, how far, Dvorak was influenced by Afro-American music in his *American Symphony*. An argument about whether Black people had produced preachers of distinction had consumed some pages in The *Literary Digest*. In the "Editorial" section of four pages, Du Bois exposes the lack of information and the misinformation concerning the realities of discrimination against Black youth as far as education is concerned; he hails the success of the NAACP in bringing about the commutation of the death sentence imposed upon Pink Franklin, in a case previously noted. Du Bois, under "Victory," hails several victories in the courts—to which attention has been called—and thinks these offer "glimmerings of a new dawn." On "Separation" Du Bois states that the point in the opposition to racial separation is not really that separation per se is opposed but rather that when the Southern rulers say "separation" they mean subordination. Du Bois comments in "Southern Papers" that on the race question they are quite insane—or are they really joking all the time? The section marked "The Burden" carries in this issue, at its conclusion, the initials "M.W.O." for Mary White Ovington; perhaps it was assembled in its entirety by her on this occasion. Under "What To Read" one finds eight articles, including Jane Addams' "A Visit to Tolstoy" (*McClure's*), an article on India, and another H. Rosenthal's "The Martyrdom of the Russian Jew" (*Outlook*). Eight books are listed; three deal with Africa.

490. "Along the Color Line" Vol. I, No. 5, March, 1911. (pp. 5–10) begins with a report of a debate between Senators William Borah and Elihu Root concerning direct election of Senators and the question of Afro-American suffrage. Decisions for and against segregation in various state courts are described; note is taken of the incorporation of the Phelps Stokes Fund to assist the education of Black and American Indian students. The formation of a protective "race organization" in New Orleans is described; migration of Black people to Edmonton, B.C., in Canada and to Mexico is reported. Under the heading "Crime" are described violent efforts in Hominy, Oklahoma and in Baxter, Mississippi to drive all Blacks out as a result of "race disturbances." Black men in Stanford, Ky., successfully resisted white mobs. In Wilson, North Carolina, two Black men were held for the murder of a deputy sheriff; Afro-Americans in Cincinnati were banded together to prevent the extradition to Georgia of William Shackelford, a Black man who, in protecting his 12-year-old son, killed a white man.

In the section "Opinion" (pp. 11–14) Du Bois quotes extensively from press comments on the Borah-Root debate in the Senate, noted earlier. Under "The Socialists" he quotes from the New York *Call*, which had editorialized favorably on a speech Du Bois had given before the New York City Socialist Party on the need for a battle against racism among socialists. Letters from readers of The *Call*, pro and con, are quoted. Press and other comment upon efforts at segregation in housing and transportation are assembled. A paragraph denouncing racism in a sermon given by Rabbi Joseph Silverman of Temple Emanuel in New York City is quoted.

In the "Editorial" section (pp. 16–17, 20–21) Du Bois discusses five matters: "The Blair Bill," referring to a bill introduced in 1881 in the Senate by then U.S. Senator (from New Hampshire) Henry W. Blair. It would have provided millions of dollars yearly for ten years to an effort, supervised by the federal government, to eliminate illiteracy. Because of worry in Southern states it was never passed; Du Bois ends with the demand "Revive the Blair Bill!" "The Methodist Church, North" tells the story of the split prior to the Civil War over slavery, of the growing significance of Black membership and the new movement for unity of the Church, North and South, now "embarrassed" by the Black fellow Christians. A brief notice of the remarkable life of the late Abraham Grant, bishop of the A.M.E. Church, follows and then an explanation of the way in which "The White Primary" effectively disfranchises Black people; finally in "Politeness" Du Bois indicates he knows why Black people—and white people—reject courtesy in mutual intercourse and insists "all this is wrong."

In "What To Read" Du Bois lists seven articles which deal with general social problems and questions of evolution; he offers a long extract from "The Discovery of the Fittest" by S. Herbert appearing in The *Westminster Review* (January). Four books are listed; one by Maurice Fishberg is entitled *The Jews: A Study of Race and Environment*. Another, not listed, is reviewed quite favorably; it is Herbert Ward's *A Voice from the Congo*.

491. April, 1911 Vol. I, No. 6. With this number, Du Bois announces a circulation of 10,000; now he writes "we must have 25,000." In this issue, "Along the Color Line" reports some political appointments of Black men; notes that "for the first time" in Texas a jury half white and half Black is sitting in a case involving murder by a white man of another white person; reports a strike by white firemen on a railroad against employment of Black workers; the strike of Black workers in fertilizer mills near Charleston, S.C., broken by police; the University of Missouri cancels a football game because the University of Iowa refuses to oust a Black player; the attack upon Booker T. Washington while in New York City; the acquittal by a white jury of two Black men charged with criminal assault upon a white woman in Murfreesboro, Tenn.; and a pogrom at Forth Worth, Texas. Du Bois also published correspondence from immigration officials in Canada indicating that while no regulation bars Black immigrants, still "since colored people are not considered as a class likely to do well in this country" they are not exactly welcomed! The "Opinion" section (pp. 12–16) publishes correspondence showing that Charles L. Coon, the (white) superintendent of schools in Wilson, N. C., is a civilized human being defending the right and need of Black people for education. Secretary Dickinson of the War Department is quoted at some length denouncing lynching in a public speech delivered at Atlanta; and Rabbi Max Heller of New Orleans, speaking there before a Black audience, is also quoted at length in remarks denouncing race prejudice altogether. Under "Socialism Again" Du Bois commends the New York *Call* because it "keeps hammering manfully against color prejudice." A Pittsburgh (white) newspaper is quoted at some length, for editorially it praises the forthcoming Universal Races Congress. News about political appointments follows; a concluding paragraph discusses the speeches recently delivered before Black audiences in Atlanta by President Taft and Col. Theodore Roosevelt and finds both to have been insulting.

The "Editorial" section (pp. 20–22) is divided into five sections. One, "Easter," is in the form of a parable, and the resurrection is that of the Black people. Under the title "Writers," the death of Frances Watkins Harper (born in 1825) is noted; attention is called to the literary work of this Black woman for a period of over fifty years—"not a great writer, but she wrote much worth reading." Du Bois draws a lesson: "Here is a nation [i.e., the Black people] whose soul is still dumb, yet big with feeling, song and story"; we are not doing enough, as a people, to help bring this song forward. Du Bois promises that if The *Crisis* continues to grow it will undertake to help in "encouraging young writers." Warm tribute is paid to a sincere, modest and heroic white man, George Williams Walker of Augusta, Georgia, whose fraternal regard for Black people was so real "the white South casts him out." In a little essay, "The Truth," Du Bois rejects the idea of reporting only gains for Black people; the fact is, he insists, that there persists the effort "to beat the Black man to his knees" and that truth must be told and that effort must be resisted. The final item is a true story but is written like fiction and is "stranger than fiction"; it is an account of "Smith Jones" and his efforts at writing poetry and his adventures—in and out of jail—until he was accepted at the Boston Latin School. In "What To Read" three books are listed, including Charles A. Eastman's *The Soul of the Indian* (Houghton, Mifflin). Five articles are listed and two articles are abstracted at some length: G. W. Ellis on Liberia in *Journal of Race Development*; L. W. Lyde on climate and skin color in *Contemporary Review*.

492. May, 1911 Vol. II, No. 1, (enlarged now to 44 pages). Of particular interest among the items selected for inclusion in "Along the

Color Line" were evidences of discrimination in housing in Baltimore, Kalamazoo (Michigan), Tacoma (Washington)—and Cornell University. Under "Crime," further developments in the assault case against Booker T. Washington are noted; there have been "several lynchings" in Georgia and Alabama; and members of the mob who slaughtered at least 20 Black people in the summer of 1910 near Palestine, Texas are still not being tried. Under "Economics" there is fairly extensive notice of the development of several all-Black towns in Oklahoma. A new department started in this issue—also conducted by Du Bois—called "Men of the Month" (which frequently included women); it appears on pp. 10–11 and carries brief biographies of Lord Weardale (of England), who is to chair the Universal Races Congress; a businessman named John S. Trower, a dentist of Chicago, Dr. Charles E. Bentley, and a prize-winning student at Columbia University named George W. Scott. Three pages are given to "editorial" matter. It commences with a parable, "Woman," treating of the promise and strength of Black women; there follows a piece, "Prejudice," insisting that the idea that prejudice is something innate is false; this is succeeded by "Humor," which consists of the text of a letter to Du Bois by an unnamed white woman from "one of the most distinguished families in America" describing her own experiences in the face of the madness of racism. Under "Civil Service" Du Bois tells of the case of a civil service vacancy for law clerk. Those finishing one, two, and three in the test were a Black man, a Jewish man, and a Black man, respectively. Faced with this, the office was abolished and a "one hundred percent" American was appointed, under another title to the same task. In an untitled paragraph Du Bois tells a tale which then evokes the observation that the laughter and sweetness characteristic of his people are being muted by the crucifixion they are enduring; he asks: "Will the gain be greater when this people's love and laughter are changed to hatred and bitterness?" In "What To Read" 11 books are listed, together with 10 articles.

493. "Violations of Property Rights," (a signed article) in May, 1911, Vol. II, No. 1, pp. 28–32; Du Bois examines the great obstacles placed before Black people in terms of property accumulation; notes that despite these obstacles, significant advances are being made; and observes that now racism often takes the form of special attacks upon Black people exactly because they have achieved some element of economic independence—the condition which they had been told would eliminate racism!

494. June, 1911. Vol. II, No. 2, (The circulation reaches 12,000; the masthead now reads: Du Bois, Editor, and M. D. MacLean, Managing Editor; Frank M. Turner, Circulation Manager; Albon L. Holsey, Advertising Manager; Contributing Editors: Oswald Garrison Villard; J. Max Barber, Charles Edward Russell, W. S. Braithwaite, and Kelly Miller.) "Along the Color Line" carries items emphasizing evidences of growing Black political strength as exemplified by elections in Chicago and in Baltimore. Under "Economic" appear some data concerning "the largest colony of colored people in the world, in similar limits"—meaning Harlem. "Men of the Month" offers brief accounts of Thomas Wentworth Higginson who died in May and was carried to his grave by six Black soldiers; of Edward D. Green, the only Afro-American member of the Illinois legislature; and of the fiftieth wedding anniversary of a notable Long Island, N.Y., couple, Mr. and Mrs. George E. Wibecan. Editorial writings (pp. 62–65) include "Education," which denies the cliché that education has not solved the race question on the ground that effective education has never been tried. An important expression of differences in outlook with that of Booker T. Washington appears under the title "Starvation and Prejudice." An attack upon the personal aggrandizement drive underlying society in the United States is the point of "Business and Philanthropy." And in "Earning a Living" Du Bois points to the little-known facts about Black inventors who have played basic roles in producing player pianos, telephones, and lubricating devices for trains and in improving the phonograph. Under "What To Read" (p. 80) three books are listed and eight articles, of which two deal with Africa and one with India.

495. July, 1911 Vol. II, No. 3, (circulation now 15,000). Among the matters of interest in the seven pages (pp. 95–101) devoted to "Along the Color Line" is one showing the persistence of peonage despite court orders upholding its prohibition; the raising of a monument to John Brown—paid for by Black people—in Quindaro, Kans.; the celebration of the centenary of Harriet Beecher Stowe in several cities, with the initiative coming from Black women; accounts of anti-Black movements in Berkeley, California, and in Kansas City, Missouri. Under "Crime" is reported the lynching of six Black men in Florida for having killed "a prominent citizen"; of two Black men on different occasions in Georgia and again both had been accused of killing white men—deputy sheriffs; in Oklahoma a woman and her 16-year-old son, charged with killing a sheriff, were both lynched. All this in the month of May. A delegation of Black men called on President Taft on May 31 petitioning him to speak out against lynching; he said he "was powerless" in this case. The "Editorial" section (pp. 112–114) opens with appropriate words on this "powerlessness" and moves on under "Allies" to note that the President had sternly rebuked an Army Colonel for manifesting anti-Semitism and that the *Saturday Evening Post* had spoken highly of the militancy of Mexicans. Du Bois wishes well to Jews—"they are our best friends"—and to "our Indian brother in Mexico," but why does not the president act where Black people are concerned, and why does the magazine praise militancy only outside of the United States? In "Leadership" Du Bois quotes admiringly some recent words by T. Thomas Fortune and goes on to decry an "over-emphasis on leadership." Writing of the coronation of George V, Du Bois observes that most of his subjects are colored and adds that the idea that "the darker millions" in the world can be held "in perpetual subjection is the wildest of dreams." "What To Read" (pp. 124–126) lists seven books; Du Bois quotes part of Franz Boas' foreword to Mary White Ovington's *Half a Man: The Status of the Negro in New York* (Longmans). Fifteen articles are listed; another is excerpted at some length: A. F. Chamberlain's "The Contribution of the Negro to Human Civilization," in *Journal of Race Development* (April).

496. August, 1911 Vol. II, No. 4, The following items of particular interest appear in "Along the Color Line": under "Political," notice that the president of the United States ordered the release of three men—officials of a lumber company in Alabama—who had been jailed for peonage; under "Economic" Du Bois reports that 161 Black union miners were suing because they had been employed, without their prior knowledge, as strike breakers in Iowa. The *International Molders Journal* is quoted as denouncing Jim-Crow unionism; and an account is given of the appointment of the first Black policeman to the force in New York City—28-year-old Samuel J. Battle. An Oklahoma newspaper—the *Wagoner American*—is quoted for the story of two white men named Pony Starr and Joe Davis of Porum, in that state, who denounced members of lynch mobs as cowards, were visited by such a mob, fought them off with rifles, and killed three. Note is made of an address by a Mrs. Isabelle W. Bird in Washington to the effect that if the United States government paid indemnity of ten cents a day to the descendants of slaves who labored without pay during slavery, the sum would come to 11 billion dollars. In "Men of the Month" are sketches

of Joel E. Spingarn, Gilchrist Stewart (head of the vigilance committee
of the New York branch of the NAACP), and of Robert N. Wood
(leader of the movement toward the Democratic Party among Black
people in New York State). The "Editorial" section of three pages (pp.
157–159) is initialed this time W.E.B.D. It deals with three matters;
under the heading "Races" it summarizes the papers given at the
Universal Races Congress—the resulting volume is called "epoch-
making" by Du Bois.*

The basic point is a denial of the validity of racism and an insistence
that overcoming that mythology is vital to world peace. "Lynching" is
an impassioned denunciation of the barbarism of lynching and an
attribution of its source to the cheapness of human life, and Black lives
in particular, that is part of the "getting ahead" attitude so characteristic of the United States. The third section is "London," reflecting
Du Bois' presence there in connection with the Races Congress; he
notes its politeness—even in racial matters—but also its restlessness in
the face of the growing militancy of the "darker world." In this issue
(pp.154–155) under the heading "Dr.Du Bois in England" a portion of
his speech given on June 26 at a Lyceum Club dinner is reproduced; it
is an examination of the racism in the United States and an effort to
connect it with racism as a world-wide phenomenon and as having
class relationships. In the section "What To Read" (pp.168–169) six
books are listed, one dealing with Africa. Fourteen articles are
enumerated. A review follows of the *Life of Harriet Beecher Stowe*, by
Chares E. Stowe and Lyman B. Stowe (Boston: Houghton Mifflin),
which pays tribute to the remarkable woman. A considerable quotation
is offered from the previously listed volume by the Sioux Indian Dr.
Charles A. Eastman, *The Soul of the Indian* (Dr. Eastman participated
in the London Races Congress of 1911). Several paragraphs, undoubtedly from Du Bois' pen, though unsigned, describe recent excavations
in Ethiopia (p. 169) made under the supervision of Professor Garstang
and demonstrating the existence, hundreds of years prior to Christ, of
"a wonderful civilization" in present-day Ethiopia and the Sudan.

497. September, 1911 Vol. II, No. 5. Among the items in the
"Editorial" section (pp. 195–197) is "Triumph," devoted to the recent
torture and lynching in Coatesville, Pa. (Quotations concerning this
from many newspapers are given in the "Opinion" section, on p.188.)
The act was done on Sunday and Du Bois notes that the local press

---

*The volume, *Inter-Racial Problems*, edited by G. Spiller, was published in French and in
English in 1911; a new edition, with an introduction by H. Aptheker, was published in 1970 by
Citadel Press in New York.

stated "the churches were nearly deserted"—the congregations were otherwise engaged. Du Bois' final paragraph reminds the reader of McKay's great poem, "If We Must Die," that appeared eight years later: "But let every black American gird up his loins. The great day is coming. We have crawled and pleaded for justice and we have been cheerfully spat upon and murdered and burned. We will not endure it forever. If we are to die, in God's name let us perish like men and not like bales of hay." "The World in Council" is devoted to the London Races Congress, where for "the first time in the history of mankind ... a world congress dared openly and explicitly to take its stand on the platform of human equality ...." Writing in "Promotion of Prejudice" Du Bois quotes editorials decrying the power of the Black voter appearing in papers in Massachusetts and in Tennessee and observes that they are identical. "Who is paying" for this deviltry? he asks. In "Social Equality" Du Bois refers to a speech by a Black physician, before a white audience in Denver, affirming that social equality was not desired by Black people. Nonsense, writes Du Bois; in the only definition making sense—to be treated decently under all circumstances—of course we Black people demand social equality. If any one among us is too cowardly to want to say this, the least he can do is to "preserve a dignified silence." In "What To Read," two books on Africa are listed and ten articles, one on Africa.

498. "The Races Congress," signed "By Our Own Correspondent" (meaning Du Bois), *Crisis*, September, 1911, Vol. II,No. 5, pp.200–209. A very full account, profusely illustrated, of the Universal Races Congress held in London in July, 1911, with extensive quotations from the papers of several of the participants.

499. October, 1911, Vol. II, No. 6. "Along the Color Line" (pp. 227–233) contains the following items. "A most important political event" was the meeting of the National Independent Political Rights League in Boston; its militant demands are quoted. Appeals for Black-white unity continued to be made publicly by Joseph C. Manning, a white Republican from Alabama. The Socialists in Los Angeles nominated a Black man for the city council. The women's suffrage movement has appointed a Black woman to campaign in California. Some effort is being made, finally, by the American Federation of Labor to unionize Black workers in Pittsburgh. A carpenters' union in Florida compelled the re-employment of two Black men who had been fired. Resistance by Blacks in Indian Springs, Georgia, resulted in the killing of two white men. "A race war" occurred in Pineville, Louisiana; two Black and one white man were killed. In Kansas City, Mexicans and Black men, sitting together, were assaulted by police, and one Mexican was killed. A race war resulted in 1,500 Black people leaving the area of Caddo, Oklahoma; in south Georgia a Black man killed a town marshal—three Black men were then lynched. At Shreveport, La., a Black man who had shot four white men was lynched. "At Louisville, Mississippi, the execution of a murderer was made public. Lemonade and peanuts were on sale. The murderer walked to his death calmly and with a steady step. He probably felt superior to his audience."

In "The Men of the Month" is John E. Milholland, and portions of the paper he gave at the Races Congress in London are quoted. Another person mentioned is the Rev. Dr. R. H. Boyd of Nashville, a leader in the work of the National Baptist Publishing Board. James B. Clarke is introduced to *Crisis* readers as the Black man who recently led in the struggle against racism in Cornell University. Miss Mary Frances Gunner, who led her class at the Suffern High School in up-state New York, is also introduced. Richard R. Wright, Jr., is noted as having received his Ph.D. from the University of Pennsylvania, his dissertation being *The Negro in Pennsylvania*. Finally, Du Bois' close friend, Harry H. Pace, who had just been elected a leader in the Black Elks organization, appears with a brief biography. In the "Editorial" section (pp. 243–245) Du Bois attacks "Mr. Taft," for the president had recently suggested "that the Negro ought to come and is coming more and more under the guardianship of the South." Some guardian, Du Bois points out. A very significant essay here is entitled "Forward Backward"; it demonstrates that "the nemesis of every forward movement in the United States is the Negro question," which is shown again, Du Bois writes, in the racism vitiating the effort to achieve the full emancipation of women—which must mean *all* women. An essay, "Hail, Columbia," warns of the deterioration in moral fiber of the nation; notes that Dr. Du Bois had written recently to "one of the best specimens of American manhood, white and wealthy and philanthropic" suggesting he join the battle against lynching and racism, and the reply came back, no—you do not "turn the other cheek ... you definitely reject this aspect of Christ's teaching ... "! The section ends with "Knowledge," in which the governor of Arkansas is quoted as congratulating a Black audience that suicide is unknown among them as are nervous disorders; Du Bois gives the facts.

In "What to Read" (pp. 256–257) Du Bois lists nine magazine pieces, including two dealing with Africa and one with Black people in

Canada. In "Books" he remarks "a number of volumes" have accumulated on his desk—meaning since he had been in Europe. He reviews two of them: Mary White Ovington's *Half a Man*, which he calls "one of the finest human studies done in America; done by a woman who knew her subject and digested it." More briefly, Du Bois comments upon *Our Race Problems*, by H. F. Suksdorf, which is an affirmation of Anglo-Saxon supremacy—"all of which is nonsense."

500. November, 1911 Vol. III, No. 1. The cover contains a poem, "The Quadroon," which is unsigned but is by Du Bois. It is a hymn of devotion to "Daughter of Twilight."

501. November, 1911 Vol. III, No. 1. "Along the Color Line" (pp. 7–12) notes that Black voters in California helped bring about victory for women's suffrage in the state. At Marietta, Georgia, a Black woman has been charged with murder for shooting the 21-year-old son of a wealthy planter; he had forced his way, unbidden, into her home. Du Bois notes "several strikes are taking place among Southern Negro laborers" and observes such in New Orleans and Memphis. Details about the all-Black town of Boley, Oklahoma are offered. Under "Crime," it is reported that "all the prisoners arrested for the Coatesville [Pa.] lynching have been freed." Du Bois notes that the past month there were reports of 14 Black men being killed in the South and that 10 white men were killed by Blacks in the South during the same month. He calls attention to the repeated occurrence of the killing of Black people by policemen and notes that five policemen have been killed by Black people. He writes of "striking cases of injustice in the courts" and gives examples. This note appears: "One of the most interesting meetings of the month was the first meeting of the American Indian Association at Ohio State University." Among the "men of the month" are two women, Jessie Estelle Muse and Helen E. Hagan; they had won scholarships at the Yale Music School. Attention is called to the important work in medicine being done by Dr. Algernon B. Jackson of Philadelphia. And the first Black man to be elected to state office—as state constable—in Missouri, Charles H. Turpin, is given biographical treatment, as is, finally, the late Bishop James A. Handy of the A.M.E. Church. In the "Editorial" section (pp. 20, 24–26) Du Bois reprints the first editorial from the original *Crisis*; followed by "Thanksgiving," suggesting such a day for particular notice by Black people with emphasis upon an absence from among them of hypocrisy, luxury, and mayhem as cause for their thanksgiving. "The Census" shows a steady increase in the Black population—despite prophecies to the contrary; Du Bois suggests that by 1950 there will be 15 million Black people in the United States, and he expects that to maintain their subordination then will not be easy.* Under " 'Social Equality' " Du Bois takes issue with "a well-disposed" Southern paper which had "accused" him of "desiring social equality." Rejecting social equality means, in fact, accepting domination by others, and the "well-disposed" white people in the South must face up to that fact. In "Christianity Rampant" Du Bois notes Italy's armed conquest of Tripoli, in the face of the declining strength of Turkey, and offers the hope that "the Christian missionaries who go to the Mohammedan lands in the future will go to learn rather than to teach." In a kind of parable, "Ezekielism," Du Bois attacks racist stereotypes that build on the basis of this or that individual absurd generalizations about the "characteristics" of "races." In "What To Read" (p. 35) Du Bois lists 11 books, of which 1 deals with Africa, 1 with India, and 1 with the West Indies. Among the books is his own novel The *Quest of the Silver Fleece* (Chicago. McClurg). Twenty-one articles are listed, four of which deal with Africa, two with India. One is "Some Rights of College Students," in the *Independent*, on September 28.

502. December, 1911 Vol. III, No. 2, (circulation now given as 16,000). "Men of the Month" includes a brief note on the death of "the friend at court"—Justice John M. Harlan. A photograph and brief note are presented about Peter Woods, "an old fighter," the only known survivor of those who in 1851 came to the defense of the fugitive slave William Parker in the so-called Christiana, Pa., "riot." The conferring of the D.D. degree by Victoria College in Toronto, Canada, upon Bishop C. S. Smith of the A.M.E.Z. Church is noted. Finally, a note is offered about Solomon P. Harris, recently elected a city counsellor in Nashville, the first Black man so honored in 25 years (J. C. Napier was the predecessor). Among the pieces in the "Editorial" section is "Christmas," devoted to the care and significance of children as embodying the future; "Christmas Gift" refers to the defeat in Maryland of an effort to disfranchise Black people and to the fact that in the November elections the Socialist Party did quite well in many localities. It "is the only party which openly recognizes Negro manhood .... Is it not time for black voters to carefully consider the claims of this party? " (of which Dr. Du Bois himself had recently become a member). Du Bois adds that all signs point to the likelihood of a close election in 1912 and of the great importance of the Black

---

*The Census for 1950 reported the Afro-American population as coming to 15, 042, 286; as for the remainder of Dr. Du Bois' prophecy, let the reader decide.

man's vote. In "The Sin Against the Holy Ghost" Du Bois defines this sin as lying for reasons of expediency; and in "The Cost of Education" he refutes the common assertion that white people's taxes pay for the Black child's education; on the contrary, Du Dois shows, Black people pay for their own education and contribute to the education of white people.

502a. "Jesus Christ in Georgia," September, 1911 Vol. III, No. 3, pp. 70–74, a short story (unsigned) relating the crucifixion to the practice of lynching. Published as chapter in *Darkwater* (No. 1960)

503. January, 1912 Vol. III, No. 3. "Men of the Month" (pp. 102–103) offers an account of the scientific accomplishments of the Black biologist Dr. Charles H. Turner; the extraordinary scholastic achievements of a new physician, Dr. Lawrence A. Lewis, in Indianapolis; and a brief note on Dr. Edward Wilmot Blyden—"the leading representative of his race in West Africa"—then celebrating his eightieth birthday. Du Bois notes that he "is a firm believer in 'Africa for the Africans.'" In the "Editorial" section (pp. 113–116) Du Bois writes "I Am Resolved" and lists the ends to which he means to devote himself; in "Crime and Lynching" he shows the falsity of the common remark that to stop lynching one must stop crime—on the contrary: "The first step toward stopping crime is to stop lynching. The next step is to treat black men like human beings." Finally, there appears another parable, "A Mild Suggestion," which comes from a Black narrator to a group of white people; the mild suggestion is that white people in the United States arrange for the simultaneous slaughter of all Black people thus solving "the Negro question." (In another form this appeared as part of No. 187.) Under the heading "The Black Folk in America in Account with The Year of Grace, 1911" appear the two columns of the *Horizon* feature of "Debit" and "Credit" (p. 117). Year by year this feature does offer a kind of capsulated version of Black history. Under "What To Read" (pp. 123–124) Du Bois recommends seven books which would "seem to be of permanent value" that appeared in 1911: (1) the Papers of the London Congress of 1911, edited by Spiller;(2) Ovington's *Half a Man*;(3) Franz Boas' *The Mind of Primitive Man*;(4) a pamphlet reprinting the article by A. Chamberlain *The Contribution of the Negro to Human Civilization*; (5) the biography *Harriet Beecher Stowe* (noted earlier); (6) *The College-Bred Negro-American*, edited by Du Bois, (No. 15 of the Publications of Atlanta University); and (7) Du Bois' *The Quest of the Silver Fleece* (noted earlier). Five books—three on Africa—are listed. In addition there is a brief review by Du Bois (unsigned) of B. F. Riley, *The White Man's Burden*(published by the author in Birmingham, Ala., 1911), which is, he writes, "the sincere effort of a Southern white man to be fair." Interestingly, the book concludes that if justice prevailed, there would develop in the South, side by side, two distinct and equal civilizations.

504. Vol. III, No. 4, February, 191. . "Men of the Month" includes an account of the life of Bishop Alexander Walters, described by Du Bois as "a genial, earnest man"; the military career of (then) Captain Charles Young—whose picture is on the cover—is noted, with a list of the ten other Black men commissioned in the U.S. Army (including four on the retired list). Among the "Editorials" (pp. 152–153,156), "Light" observes that the Phelps-Stokes Fund has given $12,500 to the University of Georgia and also to the University of Virginia "to endow a fellowship for the study of the Negro." Du Bois hopes this will lead to such study, for the ignorance at both institutions is appalling. In "The Gall of Bitterness" Du Bois notes that he has heard complaints about the too serious and bitter tone of the *Crisis* but he holds the situation suggests seriousness and leads to bitterness. With "The Durbar," Du Bois points to certain concessions forced, through struggle, by the Indian people even from the might of Great Britain. Under "China" Du Bois notes the developing revolution in that land and the ominous message it carries for those folk "who cannot conceive a world where black, brown and white are free and equal."

504a. March, 1912 Vol. III, No. 5. "Men of the Month" (pp. 190–191) discusses the composer J. Rosamond Johnson who "has developed a new and distinct school of Negro music"; two women teachers, Harriet E. Clifford, a white woman originally from Maine who earned the love of generations of young Black women in her work at Atlanta University (and who had just died), and Bessie B. Bruington, who was seventh among 300 teachers tested in Los Angeles and who had just undertaken her teaching work in that city's system; two religious leaders—the Canadian-born white man Dr. George E. Sale, president of Atlanta Baptist College, and Wesley John Gaines, Bishop of the A.M.E. Church; and Reginald W. Overton, a 16-year-old student at Stuyvesant High School in New York City who had won a city-wide competition in long-distance model-plane building. The "Editorial" section (pp. 197, 200–202) commences with a satirical piece, "Divine Right," and notes the growing challenge to the "right" of white people to treat Black people like dogs; the closing sentences reflect the reaction to the repeated occurrence of lynching and pogrom: "Let black men especially kill lecherous white invaders of their homes and then take their lynching gladly like men. It's worth it!" Writing of "Optimist and Pessimist" Du Bois points out that the former among Black people is really the pessimist, for having no hope in the achievement of freedom and justice, he puts on a smile and tells the white boss what he thinks he wants to hear and pockets the forthcoming money; the pessimist is really the optimist for he believes that through struggle—even with the white people—truth and justice can be made to prevail and so he tells the harsh truth, appears to be pessimistic, but is really an optimist! Writing on "Lee," meaning Robert E. Lee, Du Bois notes the common practice of insisting on his greatness—he just happened to fight for a lost cause. Nonsense, writes Du Bois: "The choice that a man makes is his life," and Lee chose the side of tyranny and slavery. Under the title "Homes" Du Bois notes the atrocious behavior of racists toward Black people seeking decent housing; he comments that the New York *Times*—"which spares few opportunities to treat black folk unjustly"—has recently "explained" that whites act the way they do to protect their property value—and who can argue with *That* motive—in America? The "What To Read" department in this issue notes that it is being conducted by Jessie Fauset.

505. April, 1912 Vol. III, No. 6. Two people are dealt with briefly in "Men of the Month": Dr. Charles V. Roman, a specialist in diseases of the eye, ear, and throat and now editor of "the really admirable" *Journal of the National Medical Association*; and David Mannes, the white man who was director of the New York Music School Settlement, so important to the musical education of Black and white youngsters. Five subjects are dealt with in the editorial pages (pp. 244–247): Under "Easter" Du Bois writes of "the Hope that never dies" that "burned in the breast" of Garrison and Brown; and he writes particularly of "this whole great black and wonderful race (more wonderful perhaps in countless subtle ways than anything this world has seen), whose spirit nothing can break and whose upward rending nothing can stop." In "Unquenchable Thirst" Du Bois notes the remarkable rise of farm holding among Southern Black people "in the midst of outrage, discrimination and lawlessness." Under "Fisk University" Du Bois praises the University's standards, notes that the General Education Board has made unusually harsh conditions for its receipt of a grant, but asks fellow alumni to spite the board and meet the conditions. In "The Servant in the South," Du Bois notes the cry about the difficult problem of "keeping Negro help." To solve the problem, he writes three things are needed: "1)Pay decent wages; 2) Give shorter hours and more definite duties; 3) Treat servants as men and women and not as cattle." In "Modest Me" Du Bois tells and documents the delicious story of how the winner of a prize given by the United Daughters of the Confederacy for the best historical essay had plagiarized wholesale from Du Bois' study of the Freedmen's Bureau (No. 65)!

506. April, 1912, Vol. III, No. 6, p. 235. In this issue appears a poem signed W. E. B. D., "In God's Gardens."

507. May, 1912 Vol. IV, No. 1. In "Men of the Month" a full page (p. 15) is given over to a biography of Abdul Baha, "A Persian Teacher" and the leader of the Bahai movement stressing the brotherhood of man. Abdul Baha was then visiting the United States. Du Bois here also traces the history of this movement, presenting "in many respects a striking parallel with the early growth of Christianity." Note is taken of "the late David H. Ferris" of New Haven, a veteran of the Civil War and father of the author William H. Ferris. The editorials (pp. 24–27) deal critically, though hopefully, with "the Negro Church" and offer a brief history of efforts at collective discussion among Black people while calling attention to "the conference at Chicago," referring to the forthcoming Fourth Annual Meeting of the NAACP. An account of the Fifteenth Annual Conference for Education in the South, held in Nashville in April, is offered. Noting the absence of any Black speakers, Du Bois nevertheless saw improvement insofar as the need for education at all levels for Black people was assumed; he hopes that within fifteen years, at such conferences, Black people will participate and speak for themselves. In "The Bar at the Bar" Du Bois discusses the history of racism in the American Bar Association; the article was occasioned by the extreme difficulty faced by William H. Lewis, Black assistant attorney general of the United States, to be admitted to that association. Finally, "Lynching Again" reports the continued refusal of the Taft Administration to act on the question of lynching. A page is devoted to "What To Read" (p. 41); it is unsigned but is by Du Bois. Two books are briefly reviewed, both with praise: one is a novel that sold well at this time, *The Testing Fire* by Alexander Corkey (New York: H. K. Fly Co.); the other is by a Black man, James F. Morton, *The Curse of Race Prejudice* (published by the author in New York) and is described, by Du Bois "as the last word on the baselessness and silliness of race prejudice." Two magazine pieces are briefly evaluated: a story by Norman Duncan in the April *Harper's* and an essay, "The Negro in Cleveland," by F. U. Quillin in the *Independent* (March 7).

508. May, 1912, Vol. IV, No. 1, pp. 36–37. Under the title "Self-Righteous Europe and the World," Du Bois publishes a correspondence he had with Dr. W. M. Flinders Petrie, professor of Egyptology at the University of London, in which the Englishman commences by praising *Souls of Black Folk* and continues with a manifestation of deep and blatant racism; Du Bois' reply is frank and full and Professor Petrie in his response says he wishes Du Bois well "in the great cause."

509. June, 1912 Vol. IV, No. 2. "Men of the Month" (pp. 67–69) commences with an account of the work in sculpture being done by Mrs. Mary Howard Jackson of Washington, D.C.; this is followed by biography of James Reese Europe, the conductor and composer, who also exhibited a "genius for organization" and so helped bring better income and, above all, dignity, to Black musicians in New York. Another Black composer and musician, William H. Tyers, is the subject of a biographical paragraph; and under "Fifty Years of Service" some note is taken of the work of the Rev. John Thomas Jenifer (who escaped from slavery in 1859) who had just been retired by the Baltimore Conference of the A.M.E. Church. Note is taken of the death of D. J. Lenders, vice-president of the African Political Organization in South Africa and militant fighter "for full political and civil rights to all."

510. Vol. IV, No. 2; June, 1912. Among the editorial subjects one is an appeal for a larger membership in the NAACP; another editorial, "Triumph", notes that the last of those arrested for having participated in the Coatesville lynching had been acquitted. A rather long piece is headed "Education" and is a defense of a speech on education delivered by Du Bois in Indianapolis. Du Bois' point was that education's purpose had to be the development of mature and cultured and really learned men and women and that increasingly the public school system was being employed for the purpose of turning out an efficient and docile working class. This elitism, he adds, "brought the French Revolution." He insists that Black people must seek for their children the best and fullest education to make of them effective *people* and not "hands." Another rather long piece, "Suffering Suffragettes," reiterates that the movement for the rights of women is being gravely undercut because of racism in its leadership. Finally, note is taken, under the title, "Decency" that the German Reichstag had declared that "marriages between Germans and native women in the colonies are legal." This took heavy effort and came about only because of unity among Socialists and Catholics; the absence of such legislation in the

South "denies all protection in law and custom to the helpless black girl before the lust of the white man."

511. July, 1912, Vol. IV, No. 3. In "Men of the Month" is noted the passing of Charles L. Mitchell, who, commencing in 1853, worked with Garrison on the *Liberator*, was severely wounded in the Civil War, and was a member of the Massachusetts state legislature and participated in antiracist struggles throughout his life. Attention is called to the work of Charles Burroughs, who for three years had been a lecturer on Shakespeare for the New York City Board of Education. Two Black men just awarded the Ph.D. are commended by Du Bois and both were already launched on their distinguished careers: George E. Haynes and Carter G. Woodson. The editorials of this month (pp. 129–132) consist of the following essays: "Politics," denouncing the Republican Party for its continued acceptance of Black disfranchisement; "Fraud and Imitation," noting the proliferation of individual fakers and demagogues among Black people who find little difficulty in fooling white folk—ignorant as the latter are; "Organized Labor," which commences with the assertion *"The Crisis* believes in organized labor" but it warns that Jim-Crow unionism is a contradiction in terms and means the death of real working-class organization; and "The Third Battle of Bull Run," which is in the form of a parable and describes the efforts to build a school for Black children in Virginia. This issue of the *Crisis* marks the beginning of what became a yearly feature of the magazine under Du Bois, namely, an "Educational Number." On pages 134–136 appears "The Year in Colored Colleges" followed by portraits of honor students and a defense of higher education for Black people, unsigned but certainly written by Du Bois.

512. "Men of the Month" August, 1912, Vol. IV, No. 4, (pp. 170–173) deals with the following: Joanna P. Moore, born in Pennsylvania in 1832, then living in Chicago and active in support of the NAACP, a white woman who had labored for the education of Black people throughout the South, published a book, *In Christ's Stead* and a paper, *Hope*, commenced in 1885 and still continuing (as of 1912) and ending a letter to Du Bois with "The light has dawned, thank God!" There is a brief note on the new president of Howard University, Stephen M. Newman, and a longer notice of Dr. Ernest E. Just, then professor of biology at Howard, and anticipating the pre-eminent position in that science which Just was to gain. There is some comment on a track star at Harvard, a Black student named Theodore Cable. There is also a biographical summary of the career of the Black physician of Philadelphia Dr. Edwin Clarence Howard who had recently died.

Among the editorials (pp. 180–182) is the significant one, "Politics," in which Du Bois affirms that between the Republican Party and the Democratic Party (with Wilson) he must choose the Democratic; he hopes that Wilson will reflect his learning rather than his background in taking a stance, as president, that will not be overtly racist. He adds that if he could assure the presidency to Eugene Victor Debs he would do so, for of all the candidates "he alone, by word and deed, stands squarely on a platform of human rights regardless of race or class." In a piece headed "Ohio," where voters have the opportunity of enfranchising women, Du Bois urges the Black men to support the proposal, for "Is there a single argument for the right of men to vote, or for the right of black men to vote, that does not apply to the votes for women, and particularly for black women?" In a brief paragraph Du Bois calls attention to the presentment recently made by the Grand Jury of Jefferson County, Ala., showing that officers of the law were victimizing the poor—especially the Black poor—and that this might well lead to "anarchy."

513. September, 1912 Vol. IV, No. 5, (The name of M. D. MacLean no longer appears as Managing Editor; this quite remarkable white woman, Mary Dunlop MacLean, died in July, 1912*). In "Men of the Month" notice is taken of several Black women who were active "Suffrage Workers"; these include Mary Church Terrell, Margaret M. Washington, Ida R. Cummings, and Elizabeth L. Davis. Note is taken of the inventive work of James Marshall of Macon, Ga., who has produced "A Flying Machine"—actually a very early model of what is now called a helicopter. Fairly extended notice is given to Edward W. Crosby, who had just died; Mr. Crosby was an editor of the Buffalo *Times*, and the fact that he was Black was ignored in the obituaries. Du Bois summarizes his career in journalism and notes that he did the publicity work for the Niagara Movement in its earliest days. The editorial pages (pp. 234–236) argue passionately for votes for women; denounce Theodore Roosevelt and his new Progressive Party for its open racism and quote the proposed plank on rights for Black people (written by Du Bois) that was rejected by him and his party; and conclude with a denunciation of Christian Virginia because it has permitted the execution of a 16-year-old Black girl, named Virginia Christian, charged with the murder of the woman for whom she was a

---

*An account of her life, by Mary White Ovington, appears in the *Crisis* (August, 1912), Vol. IV, pp. 184–185.

servant. (The details of this case appear on the ensuing pages, pp. 237–239, of this issue.)

514. October, 1912 Vol. IV, No. 6, (The first issue of the "Children's Number"—an innovation maintained by Du Bois for many years thereafter.) "Men of the Month" includes a sketch of the life of 17-year-old Daudi Chua, who had just become the thirty-seventh king of Uganda, and of the great Black English composer, Samuel Coleridge-Taylor who had recently died and whom Du Bois knew well. Most of the editorial section (pp. 287–291) is devoted to "Of Children." Should Black men and women bring children into a world that torments Black people? asks Du Bois. Yes, he says, for we are in the battle but our children's children will inherit the victory, and if we have no children how shall the victory be enjoyed? He offers suggestions on raising Black children: not to keep the truth from them, not to coddle them, not to lambaste them, but to love them and help them and bring them the truth. This is followed with "The Shifty American Bar," another exposure of the racism in the American Bar Association; and, finally, "Vital Statistics," refuting with facts the repeated assertion that Black people were "dying out" in the United States.

515. November, 1912 Vol. V, No. 1. "Men of the Month" notes the death, at the age of 51, of the Black attorney Frederick L. McGhee, who, since 1889 had practiced in St. Paul, Minnesota. He was, with Du Bois, a founder of the Niagara Movement and throughout a staunch friend and helper. The death of Mrs. Josephine Silone-Yates, who had been a teacher since 1879 and a leading figure in the struggle for equality, is noted. She was the third president of the National Association of Colored Women. Three paragraphs are devoted to the efforts of J. Max Barber, who had founded the *Voice of the Negro* in Atlanta and—after being forced out of that city and refusing to sell himself to the Tuskegee machine while in Chicago—his success in working his way through dental school and starting practice in Philadelphia. The section closes with a biographical note about Henry L. Phillips, recently appointed Archdeacon in the Episcopal Church in Pennsylvania. The Editorial section (pp. 27–29) contains a most important account of Du Bois' efforts at bringing out magazines, from the *Moon* to this issue of the *Crisis* (whose printing was 22,000). It concludes with "The Last Word in Politics," which expresses the hope that perhaps "the Democratic Party dares to be Democratic when it comes to black men" and suggests that "we are willing to risk a trial." In "What To Read" there is a positive review of the anonymously published book (of course, by James Weldon Johnson), *The Auto-biography of an Ex-Colored Man*, and notice of a special issue of the *Outlook* (June 29) devoted to Africa. With this number one finds this at the masthead: "Edited by W. E. Burghardt Du Bois, with the co-operation of Oswald Garrison Villard, W. S. Braithwaite, M. W. Ovington, C. E. Russell and others."

516. "The Colored Magazine in America" (unsigned, but clearly by Du Bois), in November, 1912, Vol. V, No. 1, pp. 33–35, is a brief history of its subject, commencing with the *African Methodist Episcopal Church Magazine* (1841) and concluding with the *Crisis*.

517. December, 1912 Vol. V, No. 2. "Men of the Month" (pp. 66–68) includes a sketch of the work, to that point, of the composer Will Marion Cook and a brief notice of a promising pianist, Hazel Harrison. The appointment of the first Black police lieutenant, William F. Childs, of Chicago, is noted,and a brief account of Mr. Childs' life is given. The death of Alonzo C. McClennan, a Black physician of Charleston, S.C., is the occasion for a biography which includes the fact that he was the first Black cadet appointed to the Naval Academy at Annapolis, from which he was expelled for having fought all comers in protest against the racism there. He founded a hospital and nurses' training school in Charleston and served the Black people of that city for many years. Du Bois commences his editorial pages (pp. 75–78) with an expression of joy that Wilson defeated both Taft and Roosevelt, and partly because about 100,000 Black men voted for him. He hopes this redounds to the benefit of the Black people—and of democracy in general. In "The Truth" Du Bois returns to his insistence that it is the dissemination of the truth, as he sees it, which is the purpose of the *Crisis* and that nothing will keep him from publishing that. He gives examples of the suppression, by the white press, of such truth—when it came to Black people—from the work of Jane Addams, Charles Edward Stowe, and Sir Harry H. Johnston. A brief essay on "The Odd Fellows"—referring to the so-called Negro Elks—tells of its growth and of problems in democratic government that it is now facing. A concluding essay, "The Black Mother," notes a movement to erect a statue, in Washington, "to the black mammy." Du Bois hopes this sentimental figure "has disappeared from American life"; he suggests "let the colored mother of today build her own statue, and let it be the four walls of her own unsullied home."

518. January, 1913 Vol. V, No. 3. "Men of the Month" (pp. 119–120) is devoted to George F. T. Cook, who died in August and was—from

1868 to 1900—in charge of creating and building up schools for Black children in Washington, D.C. This is followed by a biography of William J. White, founder of the Atlanta Baptist College and of the weekly *Georgia Baptist*, commenced in 1880 and then still being edited by him. A brief note is devoted to Joseph L. Jones, a successful Black business man in Cincinnati; and to the newly elected President of Haiti, Tancrède Auguste. The editorials (pp. 127–130) commence with "A Philosophy for 1913" which concludes, in italics: *I shall persistently and unwaveringly seek by every possible method to compel all men to treat me as I treat them.* There follow paragraphs calling for the building of the NAACP as an instrument to free the land of racism, an insistence that through constant reiteration of a refusal to accept subjugation, it can be overcome and a call for 50,000 subscribers to the *Crisis* by 1915.

519. February, 1913 Vol. V, No. 4. Two people are noted in "Men of the Month" (pp. 171–172): the late Mrs. Nellie B. Adams, wife of the dean at Atlanta University, a white woman originally from Maine, whose life was one of devotion—Du Bois writes—to the students at Atlanta; and notice is taken of James Weldon Johnson, formerly consul at Nicaragua and now serving in the Azores. Du Bois remarks on his great poetic and creative capacities. The main editorial deals with Intermarriage (pp. 180–181) because Du Bois notes a proliferation in state legislatures of efforts to enact laws forbidding this in "a determined effort to insult and degrade us." We are opposed to such laws, Du Bois writes, "not because we are anxious to marry white men's sisters, but because we are determined that white men shall let our sisters alone." In two brief notes, Du Bois explains that no one may pay for the insertion of his writings (or photo) in the *Crisis* and also asks "every reader to send us news of the darker races." In response to a reader bothered by the arguments of some as to "blessed discrimination" Du Bois replies at some length. His closing sentences suggest an argument that he is to reiterate with greater emphasis in the depression years of the 1930's. "If in any time and place race hatred is so unreasoning and bitter that separate schools, cars and churches are inevitable, we must accept it, make the best of it and turn even its disadvantages to our advantage. But we must never forget that none of its possible advantages can offset its miserable evils . . . ."

519a. March, 1913 Vol. V, No. 5. In "Men of the Month" (pp. 223–225) the career of a Black artist, William E. Scott, is traced to date; the death of the founding president of Lincoln University (Pa.), Isaac N. Rendall, is noted with the remark that perhaps in the near future that university will find it possible to hire Black teachers. This is followed with an appreciation of the efforts, in YMCA work for Black people, of J. E. Moorland, and a notice of the activities of a Black singer, R. C. Logan, who had gained international esteem. The death of Fanny Jackson Coppin, "one of the most distinguished colored women in the United States", is mentioned and her career traced from purchase out of slavery by an aunt to graduation from Oberlin in 1865 to leadership of the Institute for Colored Youth in Philadelphia (later Cheney State College). Leading off in the editorials of this issue (pp. 236–240) is Du Bois' "Open Letter to Woodrow Wilson," which expresses no regret for his having urged that Black people vote for him, since it was an expression of needed political independence; he ends by urging that Wilson "be not untrue to the highest ideals of American Democracy." A paragraph notes that Black women, led by Mrs. Carrie Clifford of Washington, have so far raised 1,000 dollars to assist art work in the *Crisis*. Another paragraph, "The Proper Way," reiterates the need for constant agitation if progress is to be achieved. A rather long section refutes "the experts"—in particular "Dr. Ulrich B. Phillips of the University of Michigan," as to the realities of conditions in the South and especially among Black people. The rebuttal is valuable in itself but since it is directed against Phillips—who soon became established as the authority on Southern life and not least the past of .Black people as slaves—its significance is enhanced. (See also, for a critique of a later work by Phillips, No. 188)

520. April, 1913 Vol. V, No. 6. In "Men of the Month" (pp. 274–275) note is taken that Beatrice R. Ball, of Seattle, "is the second colored woman to serve as a juror in the State of Washington." This is a result of the enfranchisement of women in that state in 1910; a brief description of Mrs. Ball's career to date is given. Du Bois notes the passing of James Edgar French at the age of 26; too young, Du Bois writes, to fulfill the great literary promise in him. The Editorials (pp. 289–292) consist of "Easter," an affirmation of the unyielding determination to be free; "Hail, Columbia!" a description of the disgusting behavior by white men baiting a women's demonstration in Washington for the suffrage and a quotation from witnesses that Black men among the spectators behaved with respect; a passionate piece, "The Hurt Hound," evoked by a Black man who marveled at the fact that he had met ordinary decency recently from some white people; a rejection of "The 'Jim Crow' Argument" to the effect that those opposing segregation did so because they were "ashamed" of themselves; and

"Resolutions at Cooper Union on Lincoln's Birthday," written by Du Bois, which affirms the Golden Rule as the essence of the actual "solution" to racism. (The circulation of the April issue reached 30,000.)

521. April, 1913, Vol. V, No. 6, pp. 285–288, a poem, "Easter-Emancipation: 1863–1913," unsigned but by Dr. Du Bois and asserting confidence in realization of the dream of freedom.

522. May, 1913 Vol. VI, No. 1. "Men of the Month" (pp. 17–18): A sketch of Gordon David Houston, head of the English Department at Howard University—"a teacher of sympathy and breadth." There follows a brief note on Mrs. Caroline V. Robinson, recently deceased, of Lexington, Ky., promoter of the Colored Orphan Institute in that city. Note is taken of the life and work of Dr. Solomon C. Fuller who received his M.D. from Boston University in 1897. Dr. Fuller did graduate work in New York and Munich and was at that moment on the faculty of Boston University, teaching neurology and was making a name for himself in the scientific world because of his publications in the area of mental afflictions. The section ends with a biographical note on the fabulous Harriet Tubman, who, at the age of 100, died in 1913. Among the editorials (pp. 26–29), one, entitled "Peace" notes that the peace societies in the United States discuss only the question of peace among white dominant nations and ignore the domination, through force, of the colonial peoples—itself a major source of war. Such an approach ensures the ineffectiveness of peace efforts. A long editorial, "The Vigilance Committee: A Call to Arms," notes that "there is scarcely a community in the United States where a group of colored people live that has not its vigilance committee." In an italicized paragraph Du Bois states that *the object of the National Association for the Advancement of Colored People is to offer a central headquarters and a collective force to ensure the greater effectiveness and permanence of such committees.* Under "Woman Suffrage" Du Bois states that racism in that effort has been largely setback; he adds: "Let every black man and woman fight for the new democracy which knows no race or sex." In a few paragraphs called "Personal Journalism" Du Bois decries the personal vendettas that seem to characterize so much of the Black journalism of the day; he urges, "let us fight, not each other, but the common foe." On the masthead for May, 1913, one now reads simply: "Conducted by W. E. Burghardt Du Bois."

523. June, 1913 Vol. VI, No. 2. Four personalities are described in

"Men of the Month" (pp. 72–73): William B. Derrick, Bishop of the A.M.E. Church, had recently died. Du Bois noted he was a veteran of the Navy in the Civil War, had considerable influence with presidents Harrison and McKinley, and was largely responsible for promoting the organization of his church in the West Indies and South America. The death of the 99-year-old Rev. Willis A. Jones of the A.M.E. Church is noted. James F. Bourne, a pharmacist of Atlantic City, New Jersey, had been appointed by the mayor a member of the Board of Education; other members refused to seat him, but a court battle has brought victory to Mr. Bourne. A note on the methods by which a Black engineer, George W. Brown of Baltimore, developed a successful business as the proprietor of a summer resort concludes this section. One of the editorial matters is written by J. E. Spingarn; others, by Dr. Du Bois (pp. 78–79, 81). One, "The Ostrich," concludes that "the complacency of the donkey is annoying, but the cowardice of the ostrich is dangerous." A note on the Democrats states that though that party has been in office for three months no catastrophe has yet befallen Black people. Du Bois adds, however, that ignoring the question of racism—as the adminsitration so far seemed to be doing—will not resolve that pressing matter. In "The Next Step" Du Bois observes that racist measures opposed to intermarriage had been defeated in eight Northern and Western states and in the District of Columbia; he says this came through organization and struggle. The enemy will strike again and both organization and struggle must be continued. Under "Logic" Du Bois insists that the logic of racism is war and murder; to avoid the violence, its source must be eliminated. In "What to Read" (pp. 92–93) Du Bois notes the appearance of "a splendid biography," *The Black Bishop, Samuel A. Crowther*, by Jesse Page, and reviews at some length a novel "making a strong plea for the abolition of capital punishment," *The Upas Tree*, by Robert McCurdy (Chicago. F. J. Schulte). He reviews Benjamin Brawley's *Short History of the American Negro* (New York. Macmillan) at greater length and finds it "a most important and valuable contribution" although he suggests that "he does not always present his case with the emphasis and accuracy which it deserves." Du Bois also comments at some length on the use and origin of the word "Negro."

524. July, 1913 Vol. VI, No. 3. "Men of the Month" (pp. 122–126) commences with an essay on the history of the Fifty-fourth Massachusetts Infantry, whose first engagement in the Civil War occurred on July 16, 1863; this is followed by a sketch of the life of Carl Schurz occasioned because some funds raised in his name had just been donated to the Hampton Institute. The Black woman Jennie Dean, founder of the Manassas (Va.) Industrial School, died in May, and Du Bois briefly sketches her career. The section concludes with remarks about Burt G. Wilder, M.D., who had been a surgeon attached to the Fifty-fourth Massachusetts and who as a professor at Cornell and as a citizen continued to battle for an end to racism. Among the editorials (pp. 130–132) is a tribute to "The Newest South" occasioned by an unprecedented event—Southern white and Black men meeting together in the South (under the auspices of the Southern Sociological Congress) and discussing as equals common problems. Du Bois notes that the dominant Southern press refused to report the event: "The Bourbon South dies hard, but its doom is written in the stars." There is a rather long summary of Du Bois' just completed lecture tour—covering 7,000 miles and bringing him before audiences aggregating 18,000 people. He is struck by the "sheer brute bigness" of the United States and describes vividly areas of the West in particular. The audiences —overwhelmingly Black—impressed him, and he "thanked God" that he had "the privilege of working for them"; especially was he proud that he belonged with Black people.

525. August, 1913 Vol. VI, No. 4. "Men of the Month" (pp. 172–174) includes a sketch of the life and work of Jan Ernest Matzeliger, the inventor of the machine which revolutionized the production of shoes; Du Bois thanks Henry E. Baker, the Black assistant examiner at the Patent Office in Washington for the information. A sketch is offered of the late physician Dr. John R. Francis of Washington, D.C., a member of the Board of Trustees of Howard and the first Black person "to equip and operate a sanitarium for colored patients." Note is taken of the election—after a recount—of R. R. Jackson to the Illinois Assembly and a brief comment is made on the successful pastorate in Los Angeles of the Rev. E. W. Kinchen. The editorials (pp. 181–186) treat of the plans for "a National Emancipation Exposition" in New York in October marking the fiftieth anniversary of the Emancipation Proclamation. They note the increasingly Jim Crow policies of the Post Office Department under Woodrow Wilson. They call for reform in the manner in which the Colored Orphan Asylum in New York City is conducted, denounce the slavery existing in South Africa on the basis of which luxury living is possible in London and New York, and observe that the courts have worn away the last vestiges of the Civil Rights Bill that came from Charles Sumner but add that the Black person "is still a citizen and still has a right under common law, the Constitution and general legislation to appeal against discrimination."

526. September, 1913 Vol. VI, No. 5. (This number's mast head adds "Augustus G. Dill, Business Manager.") "Men of the Month" (pp. 222–223) opens with a sketch of "Our Business Manager," who had served as a professor of sociology at Atlanta University and helped Dr. Du Bois in editing the *Atlanta University Studies*. It is followed by a sketch of a chemist and authority on paving and building materials, Mr. Richard H. Parker of Newark, N.J.—the only Black member of the American Chemical Society. The section closes with an account of J. R. Bourne, formerly of Barbados and now for some years the chief proofreader for the Riverside Press at Cambridge, Mass. The editorials (pp. 232–233, 236) commence with a very strong statement, "The Fruit of the Tree," insisting that "the fruit" of the doctrine of subservience "is disfranchisement, segregation, lynching ... ." He concludes "Is it not time to ... swear by the Eternal God we will NOT be slaves, and that no aider, abetter and teacher of slavery in any shape or guise can longer lead us?" This is followed by "Another Open Letter to Woodrow Wilson", reminding him of the Open Letter sent when he was inaugurated and affirming that the hopes then expressed have been smashed on the reality of Wilson's racist policies. A section headed "Lies" exposes another lie appearing in *Life* magazine over the signature of a Georgia congressman and denying the existence of convict leasing in his state. A concluding paragraph suggests that real opportunities for Black folk exist in the vastness of "The Great Northwest"—and much of this issue is devoted to that region. In "What To Read" (p. 248) Du Bois briefly reviews "a very pretty story ... amateurish ... but sweet" in the novel by Effie Graham, *The Passin'-on Party*, and *Evolution and Life* by Alernon B.Jackson, M.D., which Du Bois thinks is well done and "contrives to reconcile the teachings of science with those of Christianity". Finally, there is fairly extensive notice of a "slim volume" published by the Wesley Church in London, by Rev. J. T. Roberts, *Character Sketch of the Late Rev. J. Claudius May*, first principal of the Wesleyan Boys' High School in Freetown, Sierra Leone; Du Bois found the effort "both attractive and encouraging."

527. October, 1913 Vol. VI, No. 6. "Men of the Month" (pp. 272–273) writes of "a fighting editor," meaning Harry C. Smith of Cleveland, whose newspaper, The Cleveland *Gazette* was celebrating its 30th anniversary. Mr. Smith also served for three terms as a member of the

Ohio legislature and was author of its civil rights law. A letter from "Brigadier-General John W. Appleton" serves as a sketch of his life; he had served as a captain in the fifty-fourth Massachusetts in the Civil War. The editorial section (pp. 285, 288–291) commences with a story, "The Princess of the Hither Isles," again a parable of service and suffering and pain as the essence of divinity. This is followed by some words about and to the philanthropic "Slater Board," hoping that its grants will assist higher as well as vocational education for Black youngsters.Du Bois had attended a recent meeting of "the Business League" of Black people held in Philadelphia, and he thought its emphasis upon thrift was commendable and its note of hopefulness was "excellent." But he heard, too, boasting and lying and evidences of a spirit of aggrandizement which troubled him, for "we do not need to reproduce among ourselves in the twentieth century the lying, stealing and grafting which characterized the white race in the nineteenth century." A particularly powerful editorial, "The Negro and the Church," follows. It points to the revolutionary quality of early Christianity and of Jesus and the Church's hypocrisy in supporting first slavery and now racism; "the real hypocrisy comes, however, when the Negro, eager to take responsibility, cries out for power with which to bear it and is denied such power." Du Bois concludes: "The Negro problem is the test of the church."

528. November, 1913 Vol. VI, No. 7. "Men of the Month" (pp. 325–327) offers sketches of two successful Black businessmen—Peyton M. DeWitt of Bridgewater, Pa., and L. M. Blodgett of Los Angeles —and of George W. Buckner, M.D., recently appointed minister to Liberia by Wilson and of W. W. Sanders, named state librarian of West Virginia. Of particular interest in the editorial (p. 338) is a sketch of "William Dean Howells and Black folk," referring to Howells' novel *Imperative Duty*, his befriending of Paul L. Dunbar, and his being among the original signers of the call that eventuated in the NAACP.

529. "The People of Peoples and Their Gifts to Men," Vol. VI, No. 7, November, 1913, pp. 339–341. The text of a pageant of Afro-American history, written by Dr. Du Bois and produced under the direction of Charles Burroughs and shown as part of the New York Emancipation Exposition on October 23, 28, and 30, 1913.

530. December, 1913 Vol. VII, No. 2.*

*There was no Vol. VII, No. 1. Du Bois ended each volume with No. 6, but an error was made with the preceding number, which was called Vol. VI, No. 7. Hence, Du Bois commenced with Vol. VII, No. 2, and began that volume with page 55.

"Men of the Month" (pp. 65–66) commenced with a brief account of developing Black business enterprise in Ocala, Fla. It went on to note the death of Edward D. Brown, M.D., of Chicago. The career of the Rev. John A. Williams, priest of the Episcopal Church in Omaha, is sketched; he is editor in chief of the organ of the diocese. The editorial pages (pp. 80–82) consist of a parable, appropriate to Christmas, "The Three Wise Men," with emphasis upon the universality of the Christian concept. Several paragraphs are devoted to a scathing attack upon the Episcopal Church for its racism, manifested again in a recent meeting in Atlanta; it is, indeed, Du Bois concludes, "the church of John Pierpont Morgan and not the church of Jesus Christ." In a characteristically prophetic piece, "The Strength of Segregation," Du Bois warns that when this segregation, if persisted in, "finally succeeds in welding 10,000,000 American Negroes into one great self-conscious and self-acting mass," White Americans "will realize their mistake." Finally, Du Bois writes with great praise of the recently concluded New York Exposition, attended by 30,000 people.

531. January, 1914 Vol. VII, No. 3. "Men of the Month" (pp. 120–123) includes sketches of J. R. Archer, a Black Englishman recently elected mayor of Battersea, a city with some 200,000 people; of Byrd Prillerman, born a slave and since 1909 president of West Virginia Colored Institute, then serving some 350 students; of Dora J. Holmes, just appointed a teacher in the public schools of Haverhill, Massachusetts; and of H. Walter Reese, just appointed solicitor-general in Barbados. Editorial matter is largely devoted to arguments and urgings for joining the NAACP—"Join or Die!", writes Du Bois and explains why. The debit and credit for 1913 is published here (p. 135). In "What To Read" Du Bois reviews three volumes: William H. Ferris' *The African Abroad*; Maud Cuney Hare's *Norris Wright Cuney*; and a novel by Mary White Ovington, *Hazel*. Du Bois points to the eccentric character of Ferris and his book but says it "is keen and even brilliant in parts" and "deserves to be in every Negro's library." Mrs. Hare's book "errs," perhaps, Du Bois writes "on the side of overleniency" in writing of her father, but on the whole he finds this account of a leader in politics among Black people from the 1870's through 1896 an excellent work. Miss Ovington's book is "recommended to colored children almost as heartily as to white."

532. February, 1914 Vol. VII, No. 4. In "Men of the Month" (p. 185) an account of young Joseph M. Fareira, who stands at the head of his class at Boys High School in Philadelphia and was elected president of the class, is given. This is followed by some notice of the recently deceased Menelik II, emperor of Abyssinia—who, in 1893, defeated the invading Italians at Adoa. Among the editorials in this issue (pp. 186–190) is one outlining "Work for Black Folk in 1914," with Du Bois emphasizing in particular breaking the ghetto walls, ending discrimination in trade unions, improving education, gaining full political, civil and social rights, including being treated as a gentleman, marrying whomever he wishes and whoever wishes to marry him and in general socializing in terms of mutual desire. Du Bois adds a "P.S.—The above statement was solicited by the *Survey* [magazine] and accepted; then it was returned because the writer refused to omit" the social demands. In "The South and the Saddle" Du Bois asks why Wilson has not kept his promises of fair dealing with the Afro-American people and replies it is largely because of the inordinate political power of the Bourbon South—a power based upon Black disfranchisement. Du Bois in "Migration" rejects this, especially as it is advocated by some in Oklahoma, for it calls for going to Africa and shows no preparation and no understanding of what is required for such an undertaking. "Fight out the battle in Oklahoma," he writes. He adds that a faker is claiming to represent some African chief; further that, contrary to claims, "there is no steamship in New York building for the African trade and owned by Negroes"—a fascinating description of a basic idea and accomplishment of the Garvey movement five years later. (It is not impossible that this statement was read by Garvey—in less than two years to be visiting New York, and Du Bois.) Instead of "What To Read" Du Bois has a heading, "A Little Pile of Books and Pamphlets," in this number (pp. 201–202) under which he comments at length and with some sharp criticism about a booklet published by the Carnegie Institution in Washington and written by Charles B. Davenport, although he notes that it does refute some hoary, but persistent, myths about "throwbacks" and sterility of people with mixed parentage. A pamphlet by W. P. Dabney of Cincinnati, called *The Wolf and the Lamb*, has "some interesting comment." The pamphlet by Archibald H. Grimké, published in Washington by the American Negro Academy, *The Ballotless Victim of One-Party Government*, is praised. The special issue in 1913, by the American Academy of Political and Social Science, *The Negroes' Progress in Fifty Years*, "is on the whole a creditable publication." "The most indefensible thing in the whole volume," Du Bois writes, is that by Howard W. Odum, attempting "to lay a foundation for separate Negro schools in Philadelphia."

533. March, 1914 Vol. VII, No. 5. "Men of the Month" (pp. 224–225) is devoted to William Hayes Ward, who recently retired as editor of the *Independent* and who "stood absolutely square on the Negro problem." Additional information (see No. 531) is offered concerning John Richard Archer, the newly elected mayor of Battersea in England. A lead editorial (pp. 238–239) calls again for a crusade against racism; Du Bois invites all—white and Black—to join. It polemicizes with the Richmond (Virginia) *Times-Dispatch*, which had denounced the *Crisis* as anarchistic and incendiary; it adds: "Ignore the mischievous intimation of venal colored editors that we are 'fighting' Booker T. Washington. We are fighting slavery, caste and cowardice in black men and white; nothing more and nothing less." In "Lynching" Du Bois detects an effort to falsify reports of lynchings and gives evidence of this; he believes lynching has increased, not decreased, in the recent past. "A Little Play" is exactly that—a kind of one-scene play on the absurdity of Jim Crow. In "Some More Books," (pp. 253–254) Du Bois reviews *Facts of Reconstruction*, by J. R. Lynch and finds it to be of immense value; *Gouldtown*, by William Steward and T. G. Steward, he writes, is a fascinating description of the history of an all-Black New Jersey community founded before the Revolution and still (then) functioning; and *Masterpieces of Negro Eloquence*, edited by Alice M. Dunbar, widow of the poet Paul Dunbar, evaluated as a worthwhile addition to the history and thoughts of Black people.

534. April, 1914 Vol. VII, No. 6. "Men of the Month" (pp. 273–275) tells of L. deWitt Simmons, a graduate of Yale who since 1909 has been an electrical engineer employed by General Electric in Schenectady; of the late Earl E. Finch, a dean at Wilberforce who died at the age of 36; John O. Hopkins, a pharmacist, recently elected to the city council in Philadelphia; and of Robert C. Ogden, the millionaire head of Hampton's Board of Trustees and founder of the Southern Education Board, who was a racist. The editorials reiterate the need of Black people to fully organize for struggle; and as though in illustration there follows the report "The Civilization of Mississippi," detailing the burning to death of a Black man in Greenville, named Sam Petty, who had killed a deputy sheriff. In a piece headed "Brazil," Du Bois demonstrates the racist lying of Theodore Roosevelt when writing on that subject for the current issue of *Outlook*. Under "Veiled Insults" Du Bois demands that the word "Negro" be spelled with an upper-case N. Under the title "Song and Story" Du Bois reviews several books. He calls H. E. Krehbiel's *Afro-American Folksongs* "the most important contribution to the literature of Negro art that has been made for several years." *Liberia* by Frederick Starr and *Military Morale of Nations and Races* by Charles Young are reviewed together and both sympathetically. Major Young—a dear friend of Du Bois'—was then in Liberia in his capacity as military adviser. A book by a Black teacher in Washington, A. F. Stafford, is recommended for children; it is *Animal Fables in the Dark Continent.* A novel, *The Strange Case of Eric Marotte,* by J. I. Pearce, is denounced as a racist work.

535. May, 1914 Vol. VIII, No. 1. "Men of the Month" (pp. 13–15) deals with John Hope (Du Bois' closest friend), then president of Morehouse College in Atlanta; Henry A. Rucker, three times appointed collector of internal revenue for Georgia; Alonzo F. Herndon, Atlanta's richest Black man, owner of real estate and president of the Atlanta Mutual Insurance Association; William H. Crogman, for 38 years associated with Clark University in Atlanta and its president (1903–1910); and Charles W. Anderson, for several years internal revenue collector for New York City and an expert, in particular, on income tax law. The editorial section (pp. 23–26) consists of a letter from Charles F. Dole, a white friend who objects to the criticism of Mr. Ogden (No. 534) and urges more restraint, patience, and good-will on the part of Dr. Du Bois. Du Bois replies; he published the letter, for it represents a widely held opinion—"don't antagonize," and so on. Du Bois then lists the realities of the oppression and takes his stand with those "who hate wickedness and oppression with perfect hatred, who will not equivocate, will not excuse, and will be heard" and the *Crisis* "claims no man as friend who dare not stand and cry with it." Under the title "Some Frank Facts" (pp. 40–43) Du Bois reviews very favorably and quotes extensively from *The Human Way: Addresses on Race Problems at the Southern Sociological Congress* (Atlanta, the Congress, 1913), edited by James E. McCulloch. Du Bois called attention to this Congress at the time it met (No. 524) and again he writes that it "is epochmaking" and the message of this book "is tremendous." So, Du Bois notes, the book "has been systematically ignored by the nation" but in it one has younger Southern white men saying what the *Crisis* has been saying for years.

536. June, 1914 Vol. VIII, No. 2. "Men of the Month" (pp. 67–69) mentions the artistic talents of B. E. Fountaine then of Chicago —serving as a janitor in an art gallery. The work of Lewis B. Moore, head of the Teachers College at Howard, is summarized; attention is called to the fact that only two cities had all-Black fire-fighting companies—St. Paul, Minn., and Nashville, Tenn. Among the editorials (pp. 77–79) is one detailing the remarks of U.S. senators who opposed women's suffrage for fear it would add to the numbers of Black voters; another, headed "Mexico," remarked on the racist nature of the subjugation of Cuba and the Philippines and warned of similar possibilities in connection with Mexico (then the subject of Wilsonian intervention). "We may blunder into murder and shame and call it a Mexican war," Du Bois writes. "But it will not be war. It will be crime." Under the heading "History and Facts" (pp. 94–95) Du Bois reviews *The Negro in American History*, by John W. Cromwell; he finds its chapter on the early Black convention movement good but others poor, though he adds that the biographical data are useful. The facts in *Living Conditions Among Negroes in the Ninth Ward* [of New Haven], by Charles W. Burton, are summarized; Du Bois notes that crime in the Black ghetto "is not nearly as prevalent as in the Italian and other foreign districts" and that "Negroes ask for and receive almost no charity." An Occasional Paper (No. 15) published by the Slater Fund, W. T. Williams' *Duplication of Schools for Negro Youth*, is found to be a helpful compilation which might, however, do harm "if it results in reducing the number of private schools and crippling them, with no effort to increase public-school facilities."

537. July, 1914 Vol. VIII, No. 3. In "Men of the Month" (pp. 117–118) Du Bois notes the appointment of Coralie F. Cook as a member of the Board of Education in Washington, D.C. Her role as professor of English at Howard University and as a moving spirit in the NAACP is described. Note is taken of the success in real estate attained by H. M. Burkett in Baltimore. The death of J. A. Henry, for 31 years a beloved teacher in Chattanooga, Tennessee, is reported. In the editorial section (pp. 125–128), Du Bois observes that "The Negro problem is undoubtedly reaching a degree of spiritual complication which makes the onlooker hesitate between tears and hysterical laughter." This is brought on by events at a meeting in Memphis of the National Conference of Charities and Correction, from which Black people were barred and in which their special problems were deliberately not discussed. This contrasting with efforts of the Southern Sociological Congress; here then is a mixture of striving Black folk, some comprehension by younger Southern white radicals, but a cowardly dominant white North and an aggressively racist Southern Bourbon group. "Can one imagine a more mischief-making combination?" On "The Cause of Lynching," Du Bois affirms that the alleged cause and the real cause of lynching are frequently different; he gives examples from Shreveport, Louisiana, where "seven Negroes have been lynched in two years, not counting ordinary murders." Extended notice is given of the work of Samuel Henry Bishop, in whose passing "the American Negro loses a devoted friend." Mr. Bishop headed the American Church Institute for Negroes and occasionally made compromises and adopted policies that Du Bois felt wrong, "but we always loved him personally and honored his unusual singleness of purpose and high ideals." In "College Education," Du Bois urges Black parents to make every sacrifice to see that Black youth get the best possible education, "so that in the day of sundered bonds they can take their place beside their fellows and not be held back then by ignorance as they are now by prejudice." In "Real Estate in New York" Du Bois observes an effort by speculators to force Black people out of properties in Harlem; he urges resistance to this and the building in Harlem of more community-serving efforts, such as churches, Y's, and music schools.

538. August, 1914 Vol. VIII, No. 4. "Men of the Month" (pp. 169–171) contains a sketch of Hallie Quinn Brown of Wilberforce—"of all present forces among colored women she is perhaps the strongest and most far-reaching." Her careers as teacher, author, and, above all, public speaker and interpreter of Black literature, in Europe and the United States, have made her life of great consequence. There is notice of "a busy physician," Dr. Edward A. Carter, who serves the community of Buxton, Iowa—"nearly all colored miners." Brief notice is taken of three Black members of the French Parliament: Gratien Candace and René Boisneuf from Guadeloupe and B. Diagne from Senegal. (Candace and Diagne were to be important associates of Du Bois' in the early building of the Pan-African Movement in 1919.) Two paragraphs are devoted to "a brilliant wife," Waterloo B. Snelson, married to a Methodist minister. She organized the first Black woman's club in Georgia, an orphans' home in San Francisco, a newspaper in New England, from time to time occupied her husband's pulpit, "and brought up a family of four." Du Bois concludes that she is "full of humor, and one of the most beautiful women in America." Several paragraphs are given to the story of Charlotte Searles of Galesburg, Ill., who, though having lost her right hand and foot as a child, was known far and wide as an expert seamstress. Among the editorials (pp. 179–181) is one called "Votes for Women," evoked by elections in eight states that coming fall to decide whether to extend the suffrage to women. Du Bois here argues at some length for women's right to vote and shows its connection to Black emancipation and human advancement as a whole. In " 'Don't Be Bitter' " Du Bois observes how often this advice is offered Black people by "friends"; but it is not bitterness, it is determination and that determination is for full rights—"if this be bitterness, we are bitter." In "The Prize Fighter" Du Bois gives a brief summary of the history of boxing, thinks it is infinitely less brutal than warfare, and offers the opinion that the sudden concern with its "brutality," as expressed by the New York *Times*, arises from the fact that the heavyweight champion of the world is Jack Johnson, a Black man. In two pages headed "Problem Literature" (pp. 195–196) Du Bois evaluates highly the place of Kelly Miller's writing in the body of Black literature but condemns the inexcusable carelessness of the typesetting in *Out of the House of Bondage*. A positive assessment is given to Florence Kelley's *Modern Industry in Relation to the Family, Health, Education and Morality*. Highly significant is the review by Du Bois of William English Walling's *Progressivism and After*. Du Bois notes Walling's two earlier "studies of socialism" (*Socialism as It Is* and *The Larger Aspects of Socialism*) and remarks, "Slowly but surely colored folk are beginning to realize the possible meaning of socialism for them." From Walling's work he shows the racism that has vitiated much of the efforts of socialists (in Europe as well as in the United States). Du Bois adds: "More and more the problem of the modern workingman is merging with the problem of the color line" and then adds—almost quoting Marx,* "So long as black laborers are slaves white laborers cannot be free ... ." A column is devoted to the writings of "a young North Carolina white man," Gilbert T. Stephenson, on race distinctions and the law, commencing with a book† on that subject in 1910 and in 1914 two magazine articles in the *South Atlantic Quarterly* (January and April). The writings "show the dangers of race discrimination in a republic" although the full nature of that danger is missed by Mr. Stephenson.

539. September, 1914 Vol. VII, No. 5. "Men of the Month" (pp. 221–223) commences with a résumé of the outstanding accomplishments of Elnora S. Manson while she attended the Cosmopolitan School of Music and Dramatic Art in Chicago. The death, at age 48, of the anthropologist Alexander F. Chamberlain is reported; tribute is paid to his scientific work, which helped refute racist myths. Nathaniel

---

*Capital, (New York: International Publishers, 1929, Vol. I, p. 309: tr. by Eden and Cedar Paul) "Labour with a white skin cannot emancipate itself where labour with a black skin is branded."

†Race Distinctions in American Law (New York: Appleton, 1910).

B. Dodson, of Brooklyn, New York, long in the employ of the American Press Association, started in 1909 the *Afro-American Page*, a six-column weekly news service for the national Black press, which continues to be useful, Du Bois writes. The death of Clem Page, in Toledo, Ohio, a Civil War veteran—from Mississippi—and esteemed worker, is reported. The editorial (pp. 232–235) takes up the question "Does Race Antagonism Serve Any Good Purpose?" and refutes each of the arguments offered positively. A "marvelously successful moving picture" named *Cabiria* is reported as showing in New York City. It is a tale of the world at the time of the Punic Wars and is made in Italy; hence, Black kings and others of all colors are shown. Had this been U.S.-made all would "have been a dead monotonous white." A parable follows, "The Story of Africa," showing how "a Sorrow was planted and the Sorrow grew." The concluding piece is largely a quotation from an essay by Winston Churchill in the December issue of *Century* affirming the radically challenging role of Christ; Du Bois heads this "Fighting."

540. "National League on Urban Conditions Among Negroes," (unsigned but by Du Bois), September, 1914, Vol. VII, No. 5, pp. 243–246. This is a history and evaluation of what is now familiarly known as the National Urban League, commencing with organizational efforts in 1910 and going through 1914; Du Bois sees its appearance as marking "a new era … in the handling of the city problem as it affected the Negroes."

541. October, 1914, Vol. VIII, No. 6. "Men of the Month" (pp. 274–275) begins with a moving tribute to Charlotte Forten Grimké. who recently died. A teacher in Salem, Massachusetts, and early during Reconstruction in South Carolina, she contributed to many of the leading journals of her time. She was an active force for justice and freedom and the beloved wife of Rev. Francis J. Grimké. The death, in March, of Rev. James Gordon leads to a tribute to "a protector of children" since he had been in charge of the Howard Orphan Asylum in King's Park, Long Island, New York where an average of 250 children were helped each year. The "Editorial" (pp. 289–290) consists of partially autobiographical story, "Of the Children of Peace," treating of the slaughter going forward at that time in what was then called the European War.

542. November, 1914, Vol. IX, No. 1. Mentioned in the "Men of the Month" (pp. 12–13) are John M. Gandy, recently appointed president of Virginia Normal and Industral School; and Mrs. Marie B. Lucas, called "A Woman Physician," who has just been certified to practice in the District of Columbia. The editorial section (pp. 28–30) starts with "World War and the Color Line." Du Bois affirms that to believe that the war is not related to racism is wrong; on the contrary. "The present war in Europe is one of the great disasters due to race and color prejudice and it but foreshadows greater disasters in the future." Du Bois shows no illusions about France and Britain but he holds the German Empire to be more regressive and particularly to exalt and glory in its racism. He concludes: "Let us give then our sympathies to those nations whose triumph will most tend to postpone if not make unnecessary a world war of races." In "Two Books" (pp. 42–44) Du Bois characterizes as an "unusual" book that by L. H. Hammond, *In Black and White: An Interpretation of Southern Life.* Here a Southern white woman writes well and with comprehension of the "race question" in her own land; there is some patronizing in the book, but on the whole its "human breadth stands out splendidly." Secondly, Du Bois writes of a book that is "very well done," for "the author knows his subject." The book is W. A. Crossland's *Industrial Conditions Among Negroes In St. Louis.* Du Bois quotes at length from the author's "more important findings." After this review, Du Bois appends a note about the publication of another scientific paper by Dr. S. C. Fuller; remarks that his standing "is equal to that of Dr. C. H. Turner" and then observes that Prof. J. McKeen Cattell in *Science* had recently announced that no "creditable scientific work" had come from any Afro-American. (In the *Crisis* for, December, 1914, Vol. IX, p. 80, correspondence between Cattell and Du Bois on this is printed.)

543. November, 1914, Vol. IX, No. 1, p. 31. "The Burden of Black Women" (unsigned but by Du Bois) represents one of Du Bois' major poems and—no doubt because of the current slaughter in Europe —contains perhaps the most damning indictment of so-called White civilization ever penned.

544. December, 1914, Vol. IX, No. 2, "Men of the Month" (pp. 65–67) deals with "an essayist," Isaac Fisher, at one time president of Branch Normal College in Arkansas, and at this time editor of the *Negro Farmer*, published at Tuskegee; he has won some 1,500 dollars during the past four years in essay contests conducted by the St. Louis *Post-Dispatch*, the *Manufacturer's Record, Everybody's Magazine,* and others. The death of Major Christian A. Fleetwood, a Medal of Honor winner in the Civil War, is recorded. A résumé of the careers of "two club women" of Pennsylvania follows: Mrs. Evelyn D. Shaw and Mrs. Rebecca Aldridge. Mrs. Sarah E. Tanner, wife of Bishop Tanner of the A.M.E. Church and mother of the renowned artist Henry O. Tanner, died in August. Chaplain O. J. Scott, of the Twenty-fifth Infantry, was just promoted to a captaincy; he had served with the regiment since 1907. Among the editorials is "Christmas," pointing out that it is the fifth Christmas that the *Crisis* has seen and the sixth for the NAACP.Why the work of both has been a positive force for the nation is argued, and all readers are urged to join the association to further that work. Du Bois expresses the hope—only a "possibility," he adds—that the Supreme Court might rule with favor in the near future on cases before it and so end disfranchisement, Jim-Crow transportation, peonage, and legal racism in housing. What a cleansing that would be! Under "Negro" it is reported, on the authority of the manager of the Associated Press, that more and more the capitalizing of that word is becoming the rule; the effort of Lester A. Walton of the New York *Age* in this connection is especially mentioned. "YMCA" calls forth tribute to the fine work by its Black secretaries James Moorland and W. A. Hunton and the philanthropy of Julius Rosenwald but objection to the continued practice of segregation. In "Murder" attention is called to the fact that while the nation is "preening" itself on not participating in the murder going on in Europe, the United States has a record of violence that is not easily outdone elsewhere in the world, and the record sprouts from the "atmosphere of hatred" that is racism. In "The Election" Du Bois notes that the 500,000 Black voters represent more than ever a balance of power; the decline of Progressivism he views "with regret," but "on the greatest human problem of the day it went at the very beginning violently and inexcusably wrong." "William Monroe Trotter" pays high tribute to Trotter's "fearlessness" and "unselfish devotion" to the cause of Black freedom; in the confrontation with President Wilson (then making headlines), where Trotter asked for manhood rights and was rejected, he "voiced the feelings of nine-tenths of the thinking Negroes of this country."

545. "The Christmas Prayers of God," December, 1914, Vol. IX, No. 2, pp.83–84. An unsigned, poem, but by Du Bois, of tremendous force; God calling on Man to help Him.

546. "The Congressmen and the NAACP," unsigned but by Du Bois, December, 1914, Vol. IX, No. 2, pp.85–87. A summary with extensive quotations, of intense interest, of the replies to a questionnaire on attitudes toward Black people from dozens of congressmen and would-be congressmen.

547. January, 1915, Vol. IX, No. 3. "Men of the Month" (pp. 116–118): "A Poet": James D. Corrothers, whose poems have been appearing for many years, especially in *Century* magazine; "Mr. Corrothers ranks with Mr. Braithwaite as the greatest of living American Negro poets." "A Reader": Richard B. Harrison [later "De Lawd" in "Green Pastures"], whose recitals of dramatic works have, since the 1890's, attracted great attention—especially behind the Veil; J. Willis Menard, "The First Negro Congressman," who was unfairly not seated though winning the election in Louisiana in 1868 and who later served in the Florida state legislature and died in 1893; Edward G. Bowden, M.D., serving the community well in Griffin, Ga.; A. Burrell of Carney, Iowa, just re-elected, against a white opponent, as justice of the peace; a farmer and an "honest Negro working man."

The editorials (pp. 132–134) note that in Waterloo, Ky., "police are arresting all unemployed Negroes and putting them in jail"—an interesting solution to the problem of unemployment. In "Bourbons" Du Bois explains that the disfranchisement of Black people has allowed an oligarchy to rule the South and exercise disproportionate power in the country; this system must be "destroyed root and branch" before anything like democratic government in the United States will be possible. Under "Agility" is told the story of Mrs. Belmont, lecturing in the South for women's suffrage, who replied to a question as to whether the movement wanted Black women to vote: "We want the same voting privileges for colored women as are given colored men." Adroit, no doubt, but: "Let the suffrage movement beware! In the turnings of time Mrs. Belmont may not be as adroit as she at present conceives herself." Du Bois appeals in "In Court" for the fullest preparation and the most experienced counsel—whatever their color—when arguing important cases before courts and notes the failure of one such case in Oklahoma that might have turned out differently had the best legal staff being engaged. The section closes with a scathing attack upon Professor Edward A. Ross, who has been contributing articles attacking Black people as well as "Jews, 'dagos' and the unspeakable East." Of course, the magazines print his garbage—"Of such is the kingdom of prejudice!"

548. February, 1915, Vol. IX, No. 4. "Men of the Month" (pp. 169–171): Lafayette R. Mercer, for over twenty years a policeman in Steubenville, Ohio, killed by a drunkard—city offices closed on day of

his funeral; Alexander G. King appointed assistant post-office superintendent at the Wall Street branch in New York; Mrs. Ella E. Ryan,
editor of the *Forum*, a newspaper published in Tacoma and read almost
entirely by the white community but very strong on questions of
segregation and racism, since Mrs. Ryan is a Black woman. Among the
editorials (pp. 181–184) is one, "The President," affirming that Wilson's
racism is now plain and represents "one of the most grievous
disappointments that a disappointed people must bear." "Land Segregation" and "Education" show the impact of Jim Crow; "Suffrage
and Women" again takes to task some in the movement who express
racist views. An essay in *Harper's Weekly* defending segregation in
Washington is torn apart; a positive antiracist directive sent out by the
editor "of a prominent Boston newspaper" is quoted with approval;
tribute is paid to "a lost friend" upon the death of Grace Dodge: "It is
due to her more than to any other person that the Young Women's
Christian Association, while gravely deficient in some respects, still is
so much more Christian and decent than the Young Men's Christian
Association." In two pages (pp. 199–200) Du Bois summarizes and
comments upon "a pile of books" that he thinks are worth reading.
They are W. S. Braithwaite, *Anthology* of *Magazine Verse for 1914*;
Leon Laviaux, *The Ebon Muse* and *Other Poems*, translated from the
French by J. M. O'Hara, T. G. Steward, *The Haytian Revolution,
1791–1804*; G. W. Ellis, *Negro Culture in West Africa*; Charles
Alexander, *Battles and Victories of Allen Allensworth*; C. E. Russell,
Story of Wendell Phillips; J. H. Reed, *Racial Adjustments in the
Methodist Episcopal Church*; A. M. Trawick, ed., *The* New *Voice in
Race Adjustment: Addresses* at *Negro Christian Students' Conference,
Atlanta, 1914*; G. F. Bragg, *Men of Maryland*; M. N. Corbett, *The Harp
of Ethiopia*; S. L. Gulick, *The American-Japanese Problem*.

549. "The Lynching Industry," unsigned but by Du Bois, February,
1915, in Vol. IX, No. 4. A page on lynching, usually only of figures,
often appeared in the *Crisis*; this time there are detailed statistics,
important comments, and proof that the data from Tuskegee and from
the Chicago *Tribune* minimize the realities.

550. March, 1915, Vol. IX, No. 5. "Men of the Month" (pp. 221–224)
reports that one result of the segregationist policy in the post-office
department is the formation of the National Alliance of Postal
Employees, at Chattanooga, Tenn. After describing its purposes, Du
Bois notes that among its leaders are Henry L. Mims of Houston, Tex.,
C. B. Shepperson of Arkansas, R. L. Bailey of Indiana, A. H.

Hendricks of Georgia, and F. A. Carter of St. Louis. The successes in real estate of C. H. Jones of Winston Salem, North Carolina, are described. The work as a dentist of F. A. Bishop, a recent settler from the West Indies, in Pittsburgh, is commented upon, as is the career in insurance of Charles C. Spaulding, founder of the North Carolina Mutual and Provident Association. A description of the significant patents in various aspects of railroading, won by Solomon Harper, forms another section of this feature. It closes with expressions of high hopes for the future artistic career of a young tenor named Roland Hayes.

The editorial section (pp. 235–238) commences with a description of organization achieved among the Jewish people in the United States, then numbering about three million. The *American Jewish Year Book* had been "courteously sent" to Dr. Du Bois, at his request; reading it, he reports that "the organization of the 3,000,000 Jews in America is little less than marvelous." It is then detailed. Du Bois concludes: "This is the great network of organization which makes the Jewish people the tremendous force for good and for uplift they are in this country." A paragraph "To Our Young Poets" describes the nature of poetry, urges that it be read and studied and that then efforts be made by younger people to write poetry. Denunciation of the New York *Tribune* follows, since it is promoting a land-buying scheme which specifically forbids sale to Black people—and this a leading Republican newspaper. Du Bois quotes certain Black "leaders" who have defended Woodrow Wilson against Trotter and otherwise kow towed; they do this out of self-interest and require no reply. A letter from Monticello, Georgia, where a group lynching had recently occurred, gives the actual facts as to its cause; the letter is, naturally, anonymous. "The Battle of New Orleans"—at its centennial—is being celebrated with great fanfare by the U.S. government, the state of Louisiana, and so on. All involved are white; Du Bois calls attention to the important role of Black soldiers in that battle and quotes General Andrew Jackson's letter of appreciation to them. Under the title "The White Christ" Du Bois suggests that one may judge the actualities of "white christianity" by the slaughter going on in Europe and by the exhibitions being put on by the evangelist Billy Sunday.

551. An unsigned essay, "An Old Folks' Home," was probably written by Du Bois; March, 1915, Vol IX, No. 5; pp. 242–243. It concentrates upon the work of the Aged Colored People's Home in Cleveland but has a brief history of such endeavors in Philadelphia, and Springfield and New Bedford, Massachusetts. Remarks on these as characteristic of "the large amount of unrecorded and personal charity that takes place inside race lines."

552. April, 1915, Vol. IX, No. 6. "Men of the Month" (pp. 272–275): Robert Smalls, A Hero of the Civil War has passed away; his exploits in delivering the ship *The Planter* to the Union fleet off South Carolina's coast and then as a leader in Reconstruction in that state and as a congressman are detailed; he had served as collector of the port of Beaufort until ousted by President Wilson. William F. Crockett, who settled in Hawaii in 1901, was recently elected to the territorial legislature. Anna W. Richardson, founder of a fine school in Marshallville, Georgia, has died.

Editorial (pp. 284–285) opens with comment upon the then new Spingarn Award, the many candidates for this honor and its bestowal upon the scientist Ernest Everett Just, professor of physiology at Howard. Letters opposing and praising last month's editorial, "The White Christ," are printed, without comment. Women's suffrage is again defended, the occasion being elections later in 1915 on this question in Massachusetts, New York, New Jersey, and Pennsylvania. The rights of human beings—in this case, of women—are at stake: "The man of Negro blood who hesitates to do them justice is false to his race, his ideals and his country."

553. April, 1915, Vol. IX, No. 6. "Report of the Director of Publications and Research" of the NAACP is published (pp. 296–297) as part of the Fifth Annual Report of the Organization. It is signed by Du Bois. Data concerning the circulation, costs, and income of the *Crisis* are given. The average net circulation for 1914 was 31,450—"more than twice as large as any other Negro publication." It circulates in every state and territory and throughout the world.

554. "The Immediate Program of the American Negro", a signed article in April, 1915, Vol. IX, No. 6, pp. 310–312. The demand is for political, economic, and social equality; what these mean is spelled out. The method of achievement is through struggle on all fronts, a massive educational campaign, enlightened political tactics, national organization, growing Black cultural awareness and not merely the support of organizations like the NAACP by Black people but their control by Black people. In economics, Du Bois stresses avoidance of the self-aggrandizement marking capitalism; for this reason he emphasizes the importance of cooperative economic enterprises.

555. May, 1915, Vol. X, No. 1. "Men of the Month" (pp. 13–15) commences with a biographical account of the life of the English Abolitionist William Wilberforce. Attorney Edward Greene of Ohio appears; he has just been appointed special counsel in the office of the attorney general of the state. A résumé of the life of the Rev. Dr. William H. Sheppard follows; especially noteworthy was his exposure, while he was a missionary for the Southern Presbyterian Church, of the atrocities committed against the inhabitants of the Belgian Congo by the rubber interests.

Editorials appear on pages 27–33; "Peace" notes the persistence of racism in various peace organizations here and in Europe; this makes futile their announced intentions. The complete disfranchisement of the Black component within the Republican Party apparatus has been accomplished but no word of protest has appeared publicly. The explicit provision of the Fourteenth Amendment calling for the reduction in the congressional representation of States disfranchising its citizens is noted (again) by Du Bois, who says he will continue to fight for its enforcement. Another argument for the upper-case rendering of "Negro" appears. Under "Emporia", William Allen White, celebrated editor of the Emporia *Daily Gazette* in John Brown's state of Kansas, is taken to task for defending the Jim-Crow practices of the YMCA. An effort to mislead a visiting and well-known French dramatist, Eugène Brieux, by the white community in Atlanta, Ga., has failed and Du Bois quotes a personal letter from the Frenchman proving the point. Lies appearing in the Southern press about the so-called equality of education provided in that region are (again) exposed. Note is taken of the effective work of the NAACP in the battle against discrimination, but it is added that of course individuals and groups outside that organization also have contributed. It is urged that Black people support—and pay for—lecturers who are really qualified; efforts by such men and women are important parts of the crusade and they deserve to be paid for their work. Something of a history of the vicious film *Birth of a Nation* is given as well as of the vigorous efforts, led by Black people and organizations, to ban the film. Du Bois hopes these efforts will continue and grow; he notes that within the film are some "marvelously good war pictures."

556. June, 1915, Vol. X, No. 2. "Men of the Month" pp. 65–68: included is a brief note on the work of an all-Black fire-engine company in Pittsburgh; on the insurance work of H. E. Perry, president of the Atlanta-based Standard Life Insurance Company; and of the late J. F. Bundy as secretary of the Howard University Law School. A biographical note follows concerning the white social worker Isabel Eaton, who assisted Du Bois in his work on the *Philadelphia Negro*, had worked at Hull House in Chicago, the Ethical Culture Society in New York, had been among the founders of the NAACP and at that moment was in charge of the Robert Gould Shaw Settlement House in Boston. The recent death of F. J. Moultrie, a successful caterer and restaurant operator in Yonkers, New York, is the occasion for an account of his life; similarly for F. A. Robinson, who, since 1894, had been a sergeant in the police department of Cambridge, Mass. The lead piece in the editorial section (pp. 78–81) is by Moorfield Storey, but commencing on page 81, Du Bois' writing appears. First is an account of his recent visit to Jamaica, "An Amazing Island"; he found it hard to discern "the alleged 15,000 white people out of the 900,000 of population." Du Bois concludes that the island is "rich beyond dream; out of it for three centuries and more the white world has reaped its millions." The *Lusitania* ship disaster proves again to Du Bois the failure of European white civilization; he is pleased that he belongs to a race that has been ‘oppressed and not oppressors; "we are not murderers, we are lynched!"

557. July, 1915, Vol. X, No. 3. "Men of the Month" (pp. 118–120) is devoted to "Some Schoolmen" and contains brief sketches of educators J. M. Gregory, W. R. Valentine, G. N. Grisham, and E. C. Williams and notes the appointment, by the United States government, of Lieutenant B. O. Davis, then of the Tenth Cavalry, to Wilberforce University as military instructor. Editorials (pp. 128, 132–133, 136) treat of three senior bishops of the A.M.E. Church—two who have died, Daniel A. Payne and Henry M. Turner, and the new one, Benjamin Lee. In "Education" Du Bois again points out that the denial of effective education for the mass of Black people comes from the design of those who rule—"rich and intelligent people" who often masquerade as our "friends." This is "part of the great modern attack upon democracy." To resist this is to fight effectively for the advancement of our people and of all people.

558. "Our Future Leaders" and "The Colored High School" July, 1915, Vol. X, No. 3, pp. 137–143. are unsigned but undoubtedly by Du Bois. They are grouped together here since they are very much alike, both consist of a factual examination of college and professional school graduates and of high school graduates. Education is regarded as part of the deepest element in the Black people's struggle to endure and to advance toward full freedom.

559. August, 1915, Vol. X, No. 4. "Men of the Month" (169–170) is devoted entirely to women (the issue consists very largely of a symposium on votes for women). They are Anita Patti-Brown, a singer of international distinction; Euretta Bozeman Matthews, a writer and successful real-estate broker (lately deceased); and Musette B. Gregory, a social worker in various efforts in New Jersey and New York.

In the Editorial section (p. 177) under "Votes for Women" Du Bois states that he had planned to contribute an essay himself on the subject but when the results of the symposium came in (printed in that issue) with fine statements from men and women from Tacoma to Boston and from St. Paul to Atlanta, he felt that an essay by himself would be redundant. Under "Frank" Du Bois writes that "this case differs from similar cases" in that the victim was Jewish rather than a Black person. The governor of Georgia has had enough courage to commute the death penalty, but the case throws into question the whole system of "justice"—all this prior to the lynching of Leo Frank, still some weeks off.

560. "Men of the Month" September, 1915, Vol. X, No. 5. (pp. 221–222). The Reverend Dr. J. B. Reeve has retired as pastor of the Lombard Street Central Presbyterian Church in Philadelphia. Dr. Reeve was the first Black graduate (1861) from the Union Theological Seminary in New York and was the organizer of the Theological School of Howard University. The court crier of the U.S. District Court in southern Ohio for 44 years has been George W. Hays; Mr. Hays also served two terms in the Ohio legislature. The death of a Civil War veteran and successful real-estate broker of Danville, Pa., Robert H. Morris, is reported. Fred D. McCracken of Iowa has served for five years as the private secretary of F. C. Stevens, a member of congress from that state; he is believed to have been the first Black person to hold such a position.

The editorials(pp. 230–233) commence with "A Pageant" telling of the plans, under the auspices of the newly founded Hudson Guild, to present a pageant (by Du Bois) in Washington in October celebrating the fiftieth anniversary of the adoption of the Thirteenth Amendment. A note on a "real philanthropist" is devoted to a Chicago Black post-office worker—and the father of three children—who has devoted his time and money to the building of the NAACP and the *Crisis*. The man's name is A. L. Weaver. Note is taken of a recent decision of the U.S. Supreme Court holding unconstitutional the so-called "Grandfather" clauses by which several Southern states had disfranchised Black people. True, the Court took 17 years to do it, but that it did so and reaffirmed the validity of the Fifteenth Amendment giving Black people the vote is very important and "puts us in the shadow of the mightiest advance since 1863." Under "Hayti" an appeal is made to respect that nation and its integrity and sovereignty—in the face of rising evidence of U.S. intervention and domination. In the course of an editorial, "Begging," where Du Bois explains that those associated with the NAACP are not very rich and that certainly he is not rich (and so cannot respond to the many appeals for money that reach him) he pinpoints the assistance offered by the *Crisis* to young Black writers and artists.

Under the title "A Little Bushel of Books" (pp. 251–252) there are unsigned reviews, certainly by Du Bois, of C. G. Woodson's *The Education of the Negro Prior to 1861*, William H. Holtzclaw's *The Black Man's Burden*; Thomas P. Bailey's *Race Orthodoxy in the South*; and a pamphlet issued by the American Negro Academy in Washington, the annual address of its president, Archibald H. Grimké, *The Ultimate Criminal*. Woodson's is held to be a "most significant book"; Du Bois hopes that this volume represents "the beginning of a worthy career in the writing of Negro history." Holtzclaw's book has important material in its first section telling truthfully of the struggles of the author as a Black man growing up in the South. The chapters on Tuskegee display a "frank and beautiful worship" of Booker T. Washington, while that on Utica Institute in Mississippi headed by the Author is of value but less than fully frank.The Bailey book—"a southern white man who wants to be just"—is really not a book but a calamity.

561. Two essays, unsigned, but by Du Bois, "Colored Chicago" and "Some Chicagoans of Note," September, 1915, Vol. X, No. 5, pp. 234–242. The essays treat of its history and of some of its major Black personalities; among the latter are Dr. C. E. Bentley, Oscar De Priest, Dr. Daniel Williams, Mrs. Ida B. Wells-Barnett and Edward H. Wright.

562. "Men of the Month" October, 1915, Vol. X, No. 6, (pp. 274–275) records the death of Mifflin W. Gibbs, a lawyer of Little Rock, Ark., where he had served as city judge; President McKinley appointed him U.S. consul in Madagascar. The death of Samuel B. Allen, a well-known businessman of Ohio, calls to mind that he had been elected mayor of Rendville in that state, serving from 1891 to 1893. The uniting of two Black Baptist groups was achieved recently under the leadership of the Rev. M. W. Reddick, who also serves as president of the Georgia Association of Teachers in Colored Schools. In addition to a lead editorial by A. H. Grimké, Du Bois' editorial (p. 291) deals with "Hayti" and condemns United States military intervention. In "What To Read" (pp. 302–303) Du Bois recommends highly Rose Strunsky's *Abraham Lincoln*, and a satirical novel by T. Shirby Hodge, *The White Man's Burden.*

563. "Men of the Month" November, 1915, Vol. XI, No. 1, pp. 13–16 considers the following men: Wade H. Hammond, bandmaster of the Ninth Cavalry; the late Harris Barrett, who was the founder, in 1885, of one of the oldest organized efforts to encourage loan and home-buying among Black people, the People's Building Loan Association of Hampton, Va. W. C. Handy of Memphis is introduced as one who has, Du Bois writes, "contributed an entirely new style of music composition—the Blues." It is remarked with approval that Mr. Handy has joined H. H. Pace in creating an all-Black music-publishing firm of Pace & Handy, "which boasts of being the only colored music publishing house in existence today." Note is taken of the award of the Carnegie Medal for heroism to William Dyke, principal of the Goode Public School in Bedford County, Virginia, for having risked his life to save a white child caught in a fire. Ulysses G. Dailey, M.D., has just been elected president of the National Medical Association; he serves as associate surgeon at Provident Hospital in Chicago. The inauguration of Fisk's fourth president the preceding month is announced. He is Dr. Fayette A. McKenzie whose work in the past had been in Indian education in the West. Dr. Du Bois wishes this man success—a bit of historical irony, for Dr. McKenzie is the man Du Bois did so much to drive from office, as a racist, 19 years later. The editorials, by Du Bois (pp. 25–30), are devoted largely to several paragraphs on the growth of The *Crisis* (from 1,000 circulation in 1910 to 35,000 as of that moment) and to its role and its relationship with the NAACP. In "Woman Suffrage" Du Bois reminds his readers that this month decides that question in several states; he hopes Black men will vote for it. He adds that he has printed in this issue an argument against it by Prof. Kelly Miller, which he urges his readers to examine; but he remains convinced of the need for women's suffrage.

564. "Men of the Month" December, 1915, Vol. XI, No. 2, pp. 67–68 in this issue contains simply one-paragraph notices of a rather large number of people, among them J. T. Settle, a well-known attorney in Memphis, who just died; George Powers of Xenia, Ohio, whose inventions for automobiles and airplanes are attracting attention; Leslie L. Pollard, was an all-American football player (Dartmouth), who died in New York City and whose early death was a great loss. Among the editorials (pp. 79–82), "The Elections" notes that where the women's suffrage movement took the Black voter seriously—as in Pennsylvania—his vote was decisive in carrying the proposition; where the movement did not—as in New Jersey—his vote helped beat it. Also it is observed that when the Republican party tried through gerrymandering to refuse Black men seats in the state assembly, Black people put up independent candidates which threw the election to Democrats. Fine, says Du Bois; he hopes this teaches the Republicans a needed lesson. Under "Benson" Du Bois notes the early death of a dear friend, Will Benson. Du Bois writes of him: "All the long years the voices of little black children shall make his silence sweet." Again Du Bois takes up U.S. intervention in "Hayti" and denounces it and calls for its termination. "The Douglass Home" supports an effort then going forward to raise funds to assure that Frederick Douglass' home in the District of Columbia be made into a memorial. Finally, a page is devoted to Booker T. Washington, who had just passed away. In characteristic Du Boisian fashion, the eulogy is ungrudging. It is not simply an encomium, however, but is a critical analysis of the man's career.*

565. "The Star of Ethiopia," signed by Du Bois, December, 1915 Vol. XI, No. 2, pp. 91–93. Tells of Du Bois' concept of pageantry, the background for his particular pageant given in Washington, D.C., and seen in three nights by tens of thousands and hailed by the entire press as highly successful. Du Bois notes of himself that he "was always pushing out into some frontier of wilderness endeavoring to do the impossible." After the splendid first night performance "I walked home alone and knew the joys of God."

566. "Men of the Month" January, 1916, Vol. XI, No. 3, pp. 118–121 includes brief sketches of a Haitian pianist, Justin Elie, soon to visit the United States; of the life of the great U.S.-born Black actor Ira Aldridge; of Bessie Glenn, the first Black woman to be appointed a teacher in any of Ohio's public schools; the work of the Black artist, William E. Scot, whose murals adorn the Indianapolis City Hospital.

*This editorial note on Booker T. Washington was reproduced and commented upon, quite critically, especially by the white press; examples are Chicago *Evening Post*, December 13, 1915, Sioux City (Iowa) *Journal*, December 7, 1915. Several Black newspapers, friendly to Washington, also attacked Du Bois, but a spirited and lengthy defense of his estimate, by Rev. William A. Byrd of Rochester, N.Y., entitled "Be Just to the Living," appeared in the Cleveland *Gazette*, February 19, 1916.

The editorials (pp. 132–135) begin with "The New Year"—a call for rededication to the hard struggle: "*A New Year*: A clean, white sheet of Life, the rugged swell of endless earth, the great, swift curve of sky; and all within the unshaken Will to be, the unfaltering Dream to do—what more shall we ask, Comrades, what more was ever asked by men?" "Lazy Labor" takes to task a recent piece of racist madness pointing to Black people as lazy—and doing all the work! "The Latest Craze" is a denunciation of another attempted swindle upon Black people in Oklahoma (after that of "Chief Sam" and migration to Africa) namely, an insistence that there is a fund in the treasury to compensate Black people for unpaid labor during slavery and a suggestion that Black people pay "the attorney of record" for his "help" in getting some of this allegedly appropriated money—alas, not appropriated at all. A quotation and translation from the French of an editorial from a Haitian newspaper denouncing United States intervention is published. Du Bois in "A Suggestion" thinks it would be quite appropriate if the fund being raised to make the Douglass Home a memorial might be known as a "Booker T. Washington Memorial Fund".

567. "Men of the Month" February, 1916, Vol. XI, No. 4, pp. 169–171 is devoted to leaders of the Black community in New Orleans, including Rev. Robert E. Jones, editor of the *Southwestern Christian Advocate*, Walter L. Cohen, for 12 years Registrar of the Land Office, the outstanding attorney, James M. Vance, J. E. Mullen, M.D., and Frances Joseph-Gaudet, founder and head of the Colored Industrial Home and School.

In the editorials (pp. 184–187) Du Bois again explains the propriety of capitalizing "Negro"; he details the facts confirming the undemocratic nature of elections in the South; of the Slater Fund, Du Bois notes the good its contributions to Black schools no doubt accomplishes but he also observes that its annual reports always refer to unexpended funds. Might not these be used to subsidize a regularly conducted scientific inquiry into the realities of Black life? On "Germany" Du Bois returns to a point he had made earlier namely, that all the states have a bad colonial record but that that of Germany in Africa is the worst. Under "Library" Du Bois asks for contributions to a library on "the treatment and progress of the Negro race, together with books by Negroes," being set up in London. In "Lies Agreed Upon" Du Bois again attacks dominant historiography for its racism —another example has come recently from the pen of E. S. Cox.

568. "Men of the Month," March, 1916, Vol. XI, No. 5. (pp. 224–227) treats the civil service career, in Dayton, Ohio, of T. W. Wheeler and of Fred F. Smith of Boston. The death at the age of 22 of Eleane S. Dickson, of Seattle, who had edited a magazine called *Progessive Westerner* and who showed enormous promise, is reported. The attorney, George H. Woodson, of Iowa, who also served as a judge of the Sixth Judicial District of that state, is brought to the attention of the *Crisis* readers. The section concludes with some of the latest exploits of the world's fastest sprinter, Howard P. Drew.

The editorials (pp. 240–244) begin with an account of the struggle of the Black community (assisted by some white people) in St. Louis to beat back efforts to institute legalized segregation. Extended notice is given to the career of Major Charles Young since he is the second Spingarn Medallist. Under "preparedness" Du Bois chides Woodrow Wilson for paying attention only to the "need" for a greater navy and ignoring the appeals from white Southern professors, organized in the University Commission on Southern Race Problems, calling upon the federal government to wipe out lynching. A note headed "Stone" refers to Alfred Holt Stone, of Mississippi, who a decade ago suavely predicted the demise of the Afro-American. Since the 1910 census, no word has come from the learned Mr. Stone; where is he? Du Bois strongly favors the nomination of Louis D. Brandeis to the Supreme Court. As a Jew we may expect him to know what it is to be of the despised, but "especially as a friend and advocate of laboring men he knows what the curse of poverty means and what its abolition involves." The progress of the NAACP and of *The Crisis* whose circulation had now reached 43,000 is pointed to with pride by Du Bois. The section concludes with a condemnation of the widespread tendency to consider public schools for Black children as training grounds for menials.

569. "Men of the Month" April, 1916, Vol. XI, No. 6, pp. 290–292 include the following: the late Rev. J. B. Massiah, originally of the Barbadoes, a graduate of the General Theological Seminary in New York city, for many years in charge of St. Thomas' Church in Chicago; the death of W. N. Page, who as editor of the *Pittsburgh Courier* had made that paper widely respected, is reported; the death of J. C. Duke, editor of the Pine Bluff Arkansas, *Herald,* is reported. Mr. Duke had earlier been driven out of Montgomery, Alabama, where he had edited a newspaper, because of his "fearlessness." Note is taken of the promotion to the position of superintendent of colored schools in Memphis of G. P. Hamilton, who has been a teacher in that city for many years. Another veteran teacher passed away, H. Cordelia Ray, daughter of Charles Ray of Abolitionist fame. Versed in Greek, French and German she had taught for years in the public schools of New York City.

The editorials (pp. 302–306) begin with an essay on "The Church"; it notes that the white church is far indeed from Christ and the Black church is infinitely nearer the teachings of "Jesus, the Jew." But it is torn by internal dissensions which must be overcome and the Black churches must again lead in social struggles. "Will the church do so? In the long run and after much travail of soul we believe it will." A rather long editorial on "Peonage" is evoked by the latest lynching horror in Lee County, Georgia, where five Black men were hanged. Du Bois shows that lynching is essentially a devise of terrorism for the purpose of maintaining the special exploitation of the Black masses held, as most of them are, in peonage. There follows warm acknowledgment of a gift of $100 to the NAACP from "the wonderful blind girl, herself born in Alabama," Helen Keller. Her beautiful and strong letter is fully quoted. On "Intermarriage" Du Bois again argues against laws forbidding this. He offers a recent case to show why—that of a white man in Indiana, near the Kentucky line, who had sought to adopt his daughter, a light-colored girl of 17. He was forbidden from doing so by a court which held that if he adopted the girl this would "have the same results as permitting the intermarriage of races." "Therefore," concludes Du Bois, "let us piously ruin the life of an innocent girl!"

570. April, 1916, Vol. XI, No. 6, pp. 312–313, 314–316. Two brief unsigned pieces, by Du Bois are "Three Churches" and "The Baptist Controversy". The first tells the story of the Dixwell Avenue Congregational Church in New Haven, Connecticut; St. John's A.M.E. Church in Norfolk, Virginia; and St. Mark's M.E. Church in New York City. The second analyzes the factions and splits which have appeared in the National Baptist Convention and concludes that "something of right and something of wrong" appears on the sides involved, while "the interests of three millions hang in the balance."

571. In "Along the Color Line" May, 1916, Vol. XII, No. 1, appears the first mention of Marcus Garvey in the *Crisis* (p. 9). It announces his presence in the United States and that he will be giving a series of lectures "in an effort to raise funds for the establishment of an industrial and educational institution for Negroes in Jamaica." Among "Men of the Month" (pp. 16–18): William H. Hunt, U.S. Consul, since 1906, at St. Etienne, France; a white priest, Father Jannigan of

Richmond, Virginia, "fearless" friend; the late Sir Thomas F. Buxton, of the British abolitionist family and president of the Anti-Slavery and Aborigines Protection Society; Mildred Bryant, in charge of musical education for the Black children in Louisville, Kentucky; the Rev. G. W. Moore, a former slave, in charge of Negro Church work for the American Missionary Association; Dr. Roger S. Tracy, connected with the New York City Board of Health, is revealed as the author, "T. Shirby Hodge" of "that interesting book," *White Man's Burden* (see No. 562) Young men coming "forward to preserve and rescue the good that is in the Negro Church": H. P. Anderson of Atlantic City, New Jersey; Ira T. Bryant of Nashville, Tennessee; Dr. R. R. Wright, Jr., editor of the *Christian Recorder*.

The editorials (pp. 28–32) contain a quotation from George Bernard Shaw on the South's obsession with the exploitation of Black people; a critical note on the racism displayed by the conductor, John Philip Sousa; a report that Du Bois' "Pageant" is to be given in Philadelphia in May to celebrate the convening of the Centennial Conference of the A.M.E. Church; the motto on the Liberty Bell—"Proclaim Liberty throughout the Land and to the inhabitants thereof"—comes from Moses' father–in–law, Jethro, a priest of Midian and an Ethiopian; decries the paucity of grants for "The Negro College" from the General Education Board—"it does not believe in the higher education of Negroes"; in "Florida" an effort is being made to drive Black workers out of the cigar–making trade—it would be well if schools teaching that craft for Black youngsters were supported in that State; in "Social Equality" Du Bois again refutes the argument—this time from the editor of *Outlook*—that so-called social equality is rejected by "right-minded" Black people, and he shows that Booker T. Washington himself *in his actions* did not reject it either; in "The Baptists" Du Bois reiterates his hope that the factionalism hurting the National Baptist Convention be overcome and quotes a letter from Nannie H. Burroughs supporting his stand; "To The Rescue" notes that Black Men—some under Major Charles Young—are fighting Wilson's war in Mexico, "a foolish venture." So, in America, in Europe, and in Africa, Black men are fighting in wars representing the interests of some of the whites. "One of these bright mornings," Du Bois suggests, "Black men are going to learn how to fight for themselves"; in "Salutations" Du Bois congratulates a young Black lad, Hubert Eaves of Des Moines, Iowa, who has refused to salute the American flag during pledge of allegiance ceremonies; in "Public School" Du Bois notes that a Southern paper has "accused" him of wishing to have the public schools employed as means of breaking down social distinctions. Of course he does, writes Du Bois, and that is the purpose of the public schools. The Southern paper opposes democracy: "I favor it," he declares.

572. "Men of the Month" June, 1916, Vol. XII, No. 2, (pp. 67). Edward J. Davis has been a physician for a dozen years to the Zuni Indians and he is a fellow of the American Geographical Society; Thomas W. Fleming, an attorney, has been elected city councilman in Cleveland, Ohio, in a ward whose voters are overwhelmingly white; a minister "of ability and character" is Edward H. Hunter, serving people well in Norfolk, Virginia; the retirement of George D. Powell, a regular army sergeant, after 30 years with the 24th Infantry, is announced; the retirement of Major Walter H. Loving, the conductor of the Constabulary Band in the Philippines for 14 years is announced; the excellent work of R. G. Jackson as a music teacher of Western University in Quindaro, Kansas, is noted.

Editorials (pp. 79–83) begin , with a true story illustrating the subtleties of racism, especially as they seek to deny initiative to Black people; "Consolation" notes that Black people may realize that it is not always they against whom discrimination is manifested and Du Bois tells of the indignities suffered by a white woman, the oldest woman physician in the United States, Dr. Anna M. Comfort, while she attended the Bellevue Medical School in New York in 1865 and all "for the unforgivable crime of being female"; under "Protection" the editor of the *Morning Telegraph* of New York is chided for his blindness in insisting that the idea of oppression of Black people is a myth; in "The Crisis and Schools" Du Bois observes that a few schools for Black students seek to bar the *Crisis* and that some professors in such schools advise against social involvement—"here is the real inner Negro problem"—do we "really want our rights . . . do we dare stand and fight . . .?" In "Tenements" Du Bois demands that so–called friendly individuals and organizations must not use announced schemes for housing projects to line their pockets and to intensify segregation; under "Deception" Du Bois notes the effort by the Bourbon press to convey the notion that racism is as pervasive and blatant in the North as in the South—"this is false," he declares; under "Boomerang" Du Bois shows "how the Southern white people suffer from their own prejudice." The example he uses is the state of education for white children in Mississippi; under "Little Letters from the Heathen" Du Bois reports the continuing effort to force the capitalization of

"Negro"; a letter from the Rev. F. J. Grimké of Washington is quoted which praises Du Bois most recent book, *The Negro*; a note tells readers that a previous editorial (No. 571) attributing the motto on the Liberty Bell to Jethro is an error.

573. July, 1916, Vol. XII, No. 3;. Editorials (pp. 135–137) greet "Our Graduates" numbering over 350 Black men and women who have received bachelor's degrees and "large numbers" who have earned professional degrees. All this shows that Black people have in practice rejected the advice of being content to be hewers of wood and drawers of water for others; pretensions of the United States to any kind of moral leadership are rendered absurd in the face of "Lynching" as the horror just committed at Waco, Texas; a plank, written by Du Bois, condemning all forms of Jim Crow and affirming the right to democracy and justice of the Black people in the United States has been prepared for insertion in both the Republican and Progressive Party platforms (neither adopted it); "An Open Letter to Robert Russa Moton," successor to Booker T. Washington at Tuskegee, hopes to see that institution carrying forward the best of its work but also that Tuskegee agrees with Charles Sumner "that 'Equality of rights is the first of rights' "; Du Bois finds the results of conferences of the A.M.E. and A.M.E.Z. churches "on the whole encouraging." He observes that "The Methodists" are seeking to unite their Northern and Southern branches at the expense of the Black people—"Thus white Methodism leads us toward the Brotherhood of Man!".

574. August, 1916, Vol. XII, No. 4. In Editorials (pp. 163–167) "Two Letters" are printed in adjacent columns; one is the actual letter sent by the United States Secretary of State to the Secretary of Foreign Relations of Mexico complaining of "disorders" there, while another is penned by Du Bois, signed by President Wilson and addressed to the Governor of Georgia, complaining of the barbarism rife in that state. Under "Civilization," Du Bois shows, from official data, that the South is backward in all areas of social welfare. The battle of "Carrizal" in Mexico, wherein Black men from the United States fought and died, was "a fool's errand." The National Education Association is denounced for its racist policies; under "Health" Du Bois notes that the U.S. Public Health Service has recently confirmed findings reported earlier by the Atlanta University Conferences that the death rate among Black people was falling and that with equality of socioeconomic conditions, Black and White death rates should reach similar levels. On "Ireland" Du Bois explains the sources of Irish—Black hostility in the past but maintains "all this is past". Now Black people in the United States should sympathize with the rebellious Irish for their suffering under British rule is like our suffering. Du Bois concludes, "The recent Irish revolt may have been foolish, but would to God some of us had sense enough to be fools!"

"Men of the Month" (pp. 190–191) mentions "Three Musicians": R. Nathaniel Dett, in charge of vocal music at Hampton, is "a promising composer"; Harry A. Williams, formerly in charge of the Vocal Department of the Washington Conservatory, is now teaching in New York City; Ford T. Dabney is "the first colored man to lead an orchestra on Broadway" and is now furnishing the music for a Ziegfield production; Dr. St. Elmo Brady, head of the science division at Tuskegee, has contributed several articles in the field of chemistry to leading journals, including *Science*; attention is called to the artistic work of Lorenzo Harris of Philadelphia and to the medical work of Dr. J. E. Dribble, of Kansas City, Missouri.

575. "The Drama Among Black Folk," signed article in August, 1916, Vol. XII, No. 4, pp. 169–173. "The Negro is essentially dramatic," writes Du Bois. He offers a brief history of the theater and of acting among Black people, sees the beginnings of a new flowering in this area, and concludes with an account of his own efforts in pageantry from 1911 to 1916.

576. September, 1916, Vol. XII, No. 5. Editorials (pp. 215–218) begin with an appeal for continued support to "The Anti–Lynching Fund" of the NAACP; a strong statement on "Sir Roger Casement—Patriot, Martyr" follows. This deals with the recent execution for treason of the Irishman who had sought to assist in the liberation of his own country; from "The Battle of Europe" that continues Du Bois suggests that it demonstrates the bankruptcy of so-called Western civilization and that it points out the need for full democracy. "Out of it," he suggests, "it takes no prophet to presage the advent of many things—notably the greater emancipation of European women, the downfall of monarchies, the gradual but certain dissolution of caste and the advance of true Socialism."

"Men of the Month" (pp. 239–241): Major Allen W. Washington assumes the post of Commandant at Hampton; the work in architecture of W. S. Pittman is detailed; the music of Henry T. Burleigh is described as composer and as baritone soloist at both St. George's Church and Temple Emanuel in New York City; the Rev. Dr. Harvey Johnson of Baltimore has been pastor for 43 years at the Union Baptist

Church and has also been an effective fighter for the rights of Black people; I. M. Terrell, for many years principal of the Fort Worth High School, has been appointed Principal of Prairie View State Normal and Industrial College in Texas; John S. Brown, Jr., a graduate of Brown and of Columbia Universities, has been a successful teacher for several years at a Manhattan public school.

577. October, 1916, Vol. XII, No. 6. Editorials (pp. 267–271) begins with "The Immortal Children" since this is the annual Children's Number. Some day, he writes, Black people will read the pages of this magazine and wonder, "Can these things be true?" In the hands of our dark children lies the fate of the dark world—and therefore of the world. As to "The Presidential Campaign," without enthusiasm, Du Bois suggests Hughes rather than the insufferable Wilson; would that the Socialists had a chance to win, but they do not. As for the Black electorate, Du Bois sees the need for "The Negro Party," that is, "The American Negro must either vote as a unit or continue to be politically emasculated as at present." This idea was outlined "with singular clearness" by Inez Milholland "on the lines of the recently formed Woman's Party" and she was right. To make real the above suggestion there should be undertaken nationally the systematic education of Black people in "Lessons in Government." In "Discipline" Du Bois attacks the rigid rules governing conduct which exist in "colored private schools and colleges in the South." A school must not "break" students; on the contrary, a real school wishes to produce in students "self-reliance, self-respect and initiative." Schools will forestall trouble if they would eliminate "mediaeval rules and look upon their students as embryonic men and women rather than babes or imbeciles." In "Migration" Du Bois says Blacks should come North for the same reason that Jews flee Russia and peasants leave Austria—to get away from oppression and to seek wider opportunities. The North often does offer both possibilities and they should be grasped and Black people in the North should help their brothers and sisters eagerly. In "Cowardice" Du Bois castigates Black men in Gainesville, Florida for yielding to lynchers and in one case even assisting them. He closes: "In the last analysis lynching of Negroes is going to stop in the South when the cowardly mob is faced by effective guns in the hands of the people determined to sell their souls dearly."

"Men of the Month" (pp. 278–281) tells how Lt. Col. Charles Young managed to get his two children out of Belgium and back to the United States; a bust, "Mother and Child" by Mary Howard Jackson evokes a story by Du Bois explaining the purposes of the artist, for the woman looks "white" and the child is clearly Black; the career of Alexander P. Camphor, recently elected Bishop to Africa at the General Conference of the M.E. Church, is detailed; notice is taken of a youngster in her second year at high school, in Philadelphia, whose voice has attracted attention and whose career is being helped by donations from Black friends, but who is one of four children and her father is dead. Writing of Marian Anderson, "Will she be able to continue her studies?" Du Bois wonders.

578. November, 1916, Vol. XIII, No. 1. Editorials include almost a page devoted to very brief observations on "The World Last Month." Du Bois expects—he was correct—that the United States would soon acquire the Danish West Indies, "then we shall welcome some 40,000 more colored comrades to help us in the fight for freedom." The strikes of workers in the United States are eminently justified, and he adds that more Black workers should be among them. Happily, Du Bois adds, "our sister, Mexico" seems free at the moment of further war by the United States. "The Great War totters to a close" and Du Bois expects Germany will be defeated. He recommends Helen Marot's *American Labor Unions* and Louis Boudin's *Socialism and War*. Du Bois excoriates the Y.M.C.A. and Hampton Institute for projecting the movie, "Birth of a Nation." The death of Josiah Royce, with whom Du Bois had studied at Harvard, is noted with keen regret and his book, *Race Questions and Other American Problems* (1908), is highly recommended. A physician Dr. Woods Hutchinson who may know something of medicine, has pontificated in Hearst's New York *Journal* about "the Negro question". He knows nothing about it and makes a fool of himself. We are assured that Charles E. Hughes, the Republican candidate for President, is "all right" on the Negro question, but he has not taken the trouble to speak up himself in public. This will not do, Du Bois says; no Black person can vote for Wilson. He can vote Socialist, for Allan L. Benson, or he can stay home. Among the "Men of the Month" (pp. 19–21) is noted the death of S.D. Ferguson, Bishop of the Episcopal Church in Liberia for thirty-five years and the only Black member of the House of Bishops of that Church. The deaths of "Three White Friends" are reported: William Hayes Ward, of the *Independent* (noted in the March, 1914 *Crisis*); Seth Low, a former New York City mayor and a friend only in a patronizing sense; and Martha Schofield, who died in South Carolina in February, 1916, and was one of those selfless white teachers who went South after the Civil War to bring literacy to the Black people. A brief biography to date is offered of John Henry Murphy, editor and publisher of the influential Baltimore newspaper, the *Afro-American*.

579. December, 1916, Vol. XIII, No. 2. The editorials again begin with brief allusions to "The World Last Month" and remarks about the "distracting and unsatisfactory campaign" held in November. British repression in Ireland and U.S. tyranny in Haiti are denounced. The views of Rabindranath Tagore, the Indian poet and Nobel Prize winner, are summarized. He is a colored man and denounces racism in vigorous language. Handsome tribute is paid to Dr. Carter G. Woodson and his *Journal of Negro History* on the completion of its first year of publication. Surely it merits more than its 1,000 subscribers. Du Bois insists that lynching can be eliminated and affirms again that only through effective agitation, education, and organization can it be done. The "damnable impertinence" of racists is illustrated by Jim Crow regulations in the library at Springfield, Missouri, and the arming, with rifles, of police in Georgia in order to prevent the movement northward of Black people. Under "The Artful Dodger" Du Bois reports that the new president of Vassar College, Dr. H. N. McCracken, has written that that college had no policy of exclusion; Du Bois asks him if this means that Vassar will finally admit Black young women. His secretary replies, "that the question to which you refer has not arisen during his administration!" A young Black woman writes to take issue with Du Bois when he wrote that the Black people might well be able to use some of the "foolishness" displayed by Irish rebels. She urges only "culture, refinement, service and love." Du Bois says "terrible as it may be, the awful fact faces the colored races in this world: That no human group has ever achieved freedom without being compelled to murder thousands of members of other groups who were determined that they should be slaves." He hopes this may not be necessary "in the case of colored folk" but, he adds, *"it may be necessary."* He concludes, "War is Hell, but there are things worse than Hell, as every Negro knows." "Men of the Month" (pp. 75–77) include the physician and social activist of Durham, North Carolina, Dr. Aaron M. Moore; a Black woman, "one of the few colored teachers in the schools of Boston," Harriette L. Smith, has recently died; a white woman, May Hallowell Loud, of Boston, staunch battler against Jim Crow and a member of the Board of the NAACP; and Mrs. N. F. Mossell, an author and very active in assisting the work of Dr. Mossell, who founded the Douglass Memorial Hospital in Philadelphia.

580. January, 1917, Vol. XIII, No. 3. In the editorial section, "The World Last Month," includes "The sweeping of Prohibition over the country is, undoubtedly, getting at a great evil in a wrong way"; another suggests that in one way or another it is likely the Great War will result in Poland's independence and this means, hopefully, that "another suppressed race will have a chance for self-development after a high noon of despair." In "Schools" Du Bois denounces institutions such as the General Education Board which kill initiative with philanthropy geared to one set of principles for the education of our youth. Du Bois calls for Black people to "rally to the defense of our schools." Under "Lynching" Du Bois tells the facts—based on correspondence from the scenes—of lynchings in Thomasville, Georgia and in Leary, Georgia; both arose because of resistance by Black people to indignities and violence—in the second case the victim was a woman. The migration of Black people from the South—faced by such conditions—is proper; but Du Bois repeats the need for fraternal care to be given them by our people in the North and cites a fine example of such care by the New Haven Black community. Moving tribute is paid to "Two Friends" who had recently died, the white young woman, Inez Milholland and the Black Y.M.C.A. leader, William A. Hunton. (Page 119, unsigned and devoted to Mr. Hunton was probably written by Du Bois.)

581. February, 1917, Vol. XIII, No. 4. In December, 1916, and early January, 1917, Du Bois underwent two operations resulting in the removal of a kidney; as a result the editorials are written by J. E. Spingarn (a tribute to Du Bois) and by Augustus Dill and Mary W. Ovington. Half a page is by Du Bois. "The Curtains of Pain" is a description of the New York hospital where he is recovering.

582. March, 1917, Vol. XIII, No. 5. "The World Last Month" saw the occurrence of the February Revolution in Russia "makes us wonder whether the German menace is to be followed by a Russian menace or not." Du Bois notes the acquisition of the Danish West Indies and more "citizens" without rights, as well as the apparent approach of the United States entry into the war. Du Bois again exposes the boasted "Civilization in the South" as predominantly barbaric because of its special oppression of Black people. An exposure of the sensationalist press—in this case the *Chicago Record–Herald*—and its falsification of reality in "Haiti" follows. The "Contradiction" in dominant Southern propaganda about Black people and their feelings is exposed in adjacent columns of news from various newspapers. The remarkable advance of the *Crisis* is detailed so that in 1916 the magazine was self-supporting and out of debt. Du Bois hopes that the year 1917 will see its circulation up to 50,000. An exposure of the racism characterizing the practice of the British empire follows with examples of Australia, Canada, and the African colonies. The section concludes with a denunciation of resolutions recently adopted at a Tuskegee conference because "any system of Negro leadership that today devotes ten times as much space to the advantage of living in the South as it gives to lynching and lawlessness is inexcusably blind." In "Heroes of Death" (pp. 223–224) two people are discussed, Alexander Walters and Caroline Putnam, but the material on the latter is signed by F.J. Grimké. It is probable the brief notice about Alexander Walters is by Du Bois. Walters died in February, 1917; he was senior bishop of the A.M.E.Z. Church and a sketch of his life is offered. Of interest is the remark that Walters' autobiography, *My Life and Work*, "was not begun until he was too sickly really to finish it properly." "Men of the Month" (pp. 227–231) include notice of the death of Mrs. Andrew F. Hilyer of Washington, D. C., a teacher of music in the public schools and an organizer of book and music clubs which added to the enjoyment of the Black community for over a score of years. The career to date of Albertus Brown an attorney in Toledo, Ohio, is sketched; he had been a clerk for Senator Mark Hanna and served briefly as Police Judge in Toledo. The death of Baswell H. Stillyard, born a slave and self–educated to the point of being a physician in Wheeling, West Virginia, is reported. Dr. Stillyard had also served as a member of Wheeling's City Council. The death of John E. Bush of Little Rock, Arkansas, induces a sketch of his life as organizer of Black postal workers and a founder of the industrial insurance society, Mosaic Templars, which functioned for 35 years. The early death of an active fighter for full rights is noted with regret; this is Joshua A. Crawford of Boston. The first Black woman admitted to practice before the Supreme Court in the District of Columbia achieved that distinction very recently, Caroline E. Hall, a native of Peoria, Illinois. The mayor of New York City has recently appointed to the Board of Education a Black physician, Dr. E.P. Roberts; the first Black police woman, Georgia A. Robinson, who has been active in the women's rights movement and was an organizer of the NAACP, has been appointed in Los Angeles.

583. April, 1917, Vol. XIII, No. 6. Du Bois shares the editorial department with Moorfield Storey; the sections written by Du Bois deal with "This World," a bleak picture of the corruption and greed marking U.S. civilization, "and yet, withall, our country and the land of our dreams." "The South" is a brief description of a swiftly growing region still bound by its obsession with race; "Atlanta" is a word picture of the vast distinction between its rich and poor sections and a hopeful comment on the rising Black youth of the city; tribute is paid to John Hope and to Morehouse College, which he heads and to "a lone, little black woman," Lucy Laney, who, despite great obstacles has made her school in Augusta, Georgia a first–rate institution. Du Bois tells of his visit to Charleston and its Black community and churches, of the "souls of fathers and grandfathers who knew Cato of Stono and Denmark Vesey" [leaders of slave rebellions in 1739 and 1822]. In one of the churches, Du Bois "could not forget that God in the stained–glass window was all too evidently a bearded white man." Charleston "is guilty of the meanest act toward colored folks" because it insists on having white teachers in the Black public schools. Let the Black community end "this abomination" by striking and keeping their children at home if necessary. In "The Perpetual Dilemma" Du Bois defines it as a constant choice "between insult and injury; no schools or separate schools; no travel or 'Jim Crow' travel." Here it is again, in terms of the possibility of Black officers in the army—either a separate training camp for them or no officers who are Black and "strengthening the present custom of putting no Black men in positions of authority." Faced with this, "our choice is as clear as noonday. Give us the camp." If war comes, conscription will follow; are those who object to the separate camp for training Black officers prepared to advocate rebellion as a policy for Black people should this nation go to war? "Men of the Month" (pp. 281–283) begins with a sketch of the career to date of Maria F. Baldwin, a teacher in Cambridge, Massachusetts, and for 25 years principal of the Agassiz School in that city. She was recently appointed master of the rebuilt Agassiz School and is one of two women holding such a position. Miss Baldwin directs a school with 12 white teachers and 410 pupils, all of whom are white and many of whom are the children of the Harvard faculty. The death of Dr. R. S. Lovinggood, president of Samuel Houston College in Austin, Texas, occurred recently; Colonel Edward House, President Wilson's confidant and a native of Austin, paid tribute to Dr. Lovinggood. Dr. David A. Ferguson, the first Black man to practice dentistry in Virginia, has been actively combatting "Jim Crow" railroads in that state.

584. May, 1917. Vol. XIV, No. 1. Reflecting the entry into war by the United States, the Editorial department (pp. 7–10) opens with "A Call to Counsel," sponsored by the NAACP, of all Black leaders to be held in New York on May 17 to May 19, 1917. In "The World Last Month" Du Bois hails the revolutionary advances in Russia, the enfranchisement of women in England, and urges that Black men fight fiercely in the present war, not forgetting their grievances but hoping that out of the war a better world will come—for Black people, too. The charges against the "Loyalty" of Black people come from Southern Bourbons whose ancestors were the really disloyal ones. To the best in the United States tradition no one is more loyal than Black people. "Back of the German mask is the grinning skeleton of the Southern slave driver." Du Bois urges that "The Migration" towards the North continue for "trained, honest colored laborers are welcome in the North." The United States is attacked when it "takes possession of foreign territory" by sending naval officers to govern as in Nicaragua, Haiti, Dominican Republic, and the Virgin Islands. What do men trained as naval officers know about the art of equitable human government? Du Bois projects the need of a legal battle against the white primary; meanwhile, he urges his fellows to "Register and Vote." Again, "The White Church" is excoriated for its racism. "Is there not," Du Bois asks, "a spirit of moral leadership in this powerful aggregation of men that can touch with mighty hands our real problems of modern life and lead us?" "Men of the Month" (pp. 31–33) include Dr. Arthur S. Gray, linguist, statistician, private secretary to the Chief of the Bureau of Statistics of the government and recently deceased; Mr. C.M. Battey, a leading Black photographer, formerly in charge of the Bradley Studio on Fifth Avenue in New York, his work published in many of the leading magazines including the *Crisis* and now teaching photography at Tuskegee; two of the supervising architects working for the United States Superintendent of Construction are Black men —Lowell W. Baker and William W. Cook; brief description of Franklin B. Sanborn, "A Friend of John Brown" appears in view of his recent death.

585. June, 1917, Vol. XIV, No. 2. pp. 59–62 The editorial department begins with the "Resolutions of the Washington Conference" to which reference was made earlier (No. 584); they were written by Du Bois, pointed to racism as basic to the sources of the current war, expressed a lack of illusions in the Allies—including the United States—but preference for them over Germany, called for Black service in the war but insisted that this should not reduce the demands for full equality. On "Officers" Du Bois reiterates his argument in favor of a camp solely for training Black men as officers rather than having no such officers; he announces that this demand has finally been acceded to. In "We Should Worry," Du Bois suggests that if Black men fight in France, they'll come back with intensified militancy; if they are forbidden to fight, only white men will die, and meanwhile, Black men will move North and into industry. Let the Bourbon choose—"we should worry." And as to the movement North, Du Bois devotes a signed essay to it in this issue.

586. "The Migration of Negroes," June, 1917, Vol. XIV, No. 2, pp. 63–66. Latest data are presented; reasons for the movement culled from the Black press are offered and the prophecy made that the migration will persist. In "Men of the Month" (pp. 82–84) comment is offered concerning C. H. Payne, United States Consul at St. Thomas, now the Virgin Islands; Paul R. Williams, a young architect in Los Angeles, who shows great promise; the effective social work of Mrs. Robert T. Brooks, then in Columbia, South Carolina.

587. July, 1917, Vol. XIV, No. 3. The editorial department begins with "The World Last Month" in which particular attention is paid to revolutionary developments in Russia and Ireland and the enfranchisement of the women of England. This is followed by a brief comment upon a recent lecture trip through the mid-West and "Justice" in which is described the visit of two gentlemen from the Justice Department, to the offices of the *Crisis* looking, they said, for two German employees and then offering Du Bois a lecture on "loyalty". Du Bois denounces the Department of "Justice", (he adds the quotation marks), which has been able to ignore such episodes as the lynching of thousands of Black citizens. In "Promoting Race Prejudice" Du Bois offers examples of racism from so varied a group as the New York Community Chorus, Theodore Roosevelt, the official bulletin issued by the Information Service of the United States government, and the printed draft circular which spells Caucasian, Indian, Mongolian, Malayan, Indian with upper-case but Negro with the lower-case. A denunciation of racism in trade unions follows as well as Southern efforts to forcibly prevent Black migration.

588. August, 1917, Vol. XIV, No. 4. pp. 163–166 In the editorial department, Du Bois writes of "The World Last Month" and is encouraged by the hundreds of Black college graduates and the thousands graduating from high schools. He notes that the United States seems set on trying to take over Asia but he doubts it will succeed. Further on, he praises Theodore Roosevelt for his condemnation of the pogrom in East St. Louis while Woodrow Wilson remains silent. Du Bois warns that the World War means a new world is in birth and new questions face the Black people. A great need is for unity of the Black people—"team work" it is called here; in the first place such unity in politics. In terms of earning a living Black people must not imitate the economic conduct dominant among whites but must move in the direction of cooperation. Among the "Men of the Month" (pp. 189–191) are James S. Russell, archdeacon of Southern Virginia and principal of St. Paul's School in Lawrenceville; Elias T. Jones, an alumnus of Oberlin College, class of 1859, died in that town in May; the death of a surgeon in Springfield, Illinois, Dr. N.B. Ford, is recorded; the successful medical practice in Bowling Green, Kentucky, of Dr. O. D. Porter is noted.

589. September, 1917, Vol. XIV, No. 5. The editorial department (pp. 215–218) asks whether Kerensky's "blood and iron methods" will work in Russia and condemns the slaughter of Black people in East St. Louis largely by white men in uniform. Du Bois notes that 10,000 Black people showed their unity in the Silent Protest Parade against Lynching in New York City; such unity should manifest itself in economics, too. "In every large city where 10,000 or more Negroes live, the business of buying groceries, food, clothing and fuel can, by a single determined effort, be put into the hands of colored people." He closes, "White people are not in business for their health. We should be in business for our health and for the health of the world." Commenting on the recent pogroms in Chester, Pennsylvania, Youngstown, Ohio, and East St. Louis, Du Bois says they are "the pools of blood through which we must march, but march we will" despite the racism of the nation and of Gompers' unions. An impassioned call, "Awake America," ends, "No land that loves to lynch 'niggers' can lead the hosts of Almighty God." The "Men of the Month" (pp. 256–257) are: the white poet and playwright, Ridgely Torrence, who helped found a pioneer "Negro Players" theater and whose three plays on themes of Black life have recently been published (*Granny Maumee*, Macmillan Co.). The plays and the efforts of Mr. Torrence are highly praised by Du Bois. "No one has done as much as he in opening up to them [Black people] a new field of art, and none ever approached the people of another race in a more generous spirit." The educational work of the Rev. A. J. Bray is summarized as first Black president of Lane College in Tennessee, president of Miles Memorial College in Birmingham, Alabama, and recently elected General Secretary of Education of the C.M.E. Church. Mary E. Cromwell is the first Black woman to receive a master's degree from the University of Pennsylvania; she is a social worker and especially active in building the NAACP; the attorney of Chicago, Louis B. Anderson, who had served as assistant corporation counsel for Chicago, has just been elected an alderman, the second Black person to achieve this position in that city.

590. "The Massacre of East St. Louis" September, 1917, Vol. XIV, No. 5, pp. 219–238 is a report done jointly by Martha Gruening and by Du Bois on behalf of the NAACP. It dramatically tells the story of the pogrom from the lips of survivors and is profusely illustrated.

591. October, 1917, Vol. XIV, No. 6. There are two essays by Du Bois in the Editorial department (pp. 284–285). One, "Consecration," continues his appeal for a new type of business devoted to a people's benefit rather than to individual profit; the other, "Houston," deals with the resistance to baiting and police brutality that led to the killing of several whites in Houston, Texas, by Black soldiers of the twenty-fourth Infantry. No doubt, he adds, what they did requires punishment, but "is not the ink within the very wells crimsoned with the blood of black martyrs" "Our lips tremble to rise and exult, our lips to cry" but he warns, we must not do this. "Men of the Month" (pp. 295–297) tells of "Three Dead Workers": Hollis B. Frissell, the white principal of Hampton from 1893 to his death in 1917; Philip A. Payton, the Black real-estate man who pioneered in providing housing in Harlem for Black people; Col. F. C. Antoine, a leader of the Black community in New Orleans. Under "Five Public Servants" readers are told of the distinguished career in the United States Navy of J. C. Jordan; of R. J. Tams, the first and only Black member of the fire department of Dayton, Ohio; of the late S. H. Johnson, who had once served as a deputy sheriff in St. Louis and prior to his death was captain of an engine company in Denver's fire department; of Ashby Johnson, the only Black man in the fire department of Wheeling, West Virginia; and of the late Robert H. Holmes, the second Black man on the New York police force, recently killed in line of duty.

592. November, 1917, Vol. XV, No. 1. The editorial department begins with "The Oath of the Negro Voter" which pledges independence, honesty, concern for all humanity, and in particular, for the needs of Black people, a desire to remake the socioeconomic structure so that "Land and Capital ought to belong to the Many and not to the Few." "Votes for Women" follows and is directed to the 75,000 Black voters in the state of New York where the question is to be decided upon that month and favors such enfranchisement. "Co-Operation" again treats Du Bois' idea that cooperation marks the path towards enhancing the economic independence and well-being of Black people; a long letter defining its nature, from Dr. James P. Warbasse, a leader of the movement, is published. In the form of correspondence—on the occasion of Dr. Frissell's death—Du Bois explains the source of his opposition to the "Hampton Idea" and his vision of how the institute might become a more creative educational organization by and for Black people. A denunciation of the 24th Infantry Regiment, in view of the Houston outbreak that came from the Black Lieutenant Henry O. Flipper is quoted and judged as slanderous. The Editorial department concludes by quoting from "A Resolution" adopted in October by the National American Woman Suffrage Association denouncing discrimination based upon sex, race, or national origin, attacking lynching and insisting on the need of equal rights for all. "Men of the Month" (p. 22) treats five persons: Dean Kelly Miller of Howard University, an author of distinction whose recent pamphlets urging an end to racism have had wide impact; Dr. Conwell Blanton, a physician, who was recently elected to the Board of Education in Wilmington, Delaware; William H. White, a headwaiter at a Baltimore hotel, who has "shown himself a public-spirited citizen"; James A. Jackson, who was recently appointed librarian to the Supreme Court of West Virginia; Harry S. Cummings, an attorney, who for thirteen years has been a member on the city council of Baltimore, prior to his death in September.

593. December, 1917, Vol. XV, No. 2. Appropriate to the season, the editorial department opens with "The Second Coming" a parable, set in Georgia, concerning the birth of Christ—in this case, the Child is Black. The "Victory" scored by the NAACP in *Buchanan* vs. *Wiley*, where a unanimous Supreme Court overruled the Kentucky law requiring residential racial separation (November 5), is hailed and the role of William Ashbie Hawkins, the Black attorney of Baltimore, who first started the proceedings against such laws seventeen years earlier, is especially commended. Tribute is paid to Newton D. Baker, Wilson's War Secretary, who, Du Bois states, has done better than expected on the question of Black troops and officers, considering that he is in Wilson's Cabinet. Du Bois urges pressure upon him to assure a second camp for the training of Black officers. As to "The Elections" in New York, Du Bois is delighted that the woman suffrage provision is passed. that Black people elected their first Black representative to the assembly in the person of an attorney, Edward A. Johnson, and the first representative on the Board of Aldermen in New York City is another attorney, J. C. Thomas, Jr. "Men of the Month" (p. 74) include Eva D. Bowles in charge of YWCA war work for Black soldiers; the Rev. Dr. G. M. King, died in October, "a tried and true friend" of Black people and for many years president of Virginia Union University; Cleveland Buchanan, recently appointed Criminal Investigator in the office of the District Attorney in Los Angeles; Travis J. Johnson, a physician in New York City, who showed much promise in research but who died at the age of 34; Wendell P. Dabney, teacher, musician, Assistant Paymaster of Cincinnati, editor of the newspaper, The *Union*, and "genuine, unafraid, and strikingly original."

594. January, 1918, Vol. XV, No. 3. The editorial department opens with the debits and credits for the year 1917. A tribute is paid to Major Joel E. Spingarn, recovering from a serious operation, "For who can replace the few white friends who are willing to work WITH us and not merely FOR us?". Other sections of the editorial department are written by F. J. Grimké and John Haynes Holmes; then quite brief paragraphs by Du Bois. "Thirteen" denounces the quick execution by order of the President of thirteen men of the 24th Infantry in connection with the Houston outbreak: "Above all we raise our clenched hands against the hundreds of thousands of white murderers, rapists, and scoundrels who have oppressed, killed, ruined, robbed, and debased their black fellow men and fellow women, and yet, today, walk scot-free, unwhipped of justice, uncondemned by millions of their white fellow citizens, and unrebuked by the President of the United States." Du Bois projects as "The Future of Africa", to come out of the War, an independent Negro Central African State, under international control and guarantees, comprising at least the Belgian Congo and the German colonies and, if possible, Uganda, French Equatorial Africa, and the Portuguese colonies. In the Lansing-Ishii Agreement, the United States has acknowledged that "Asia is primarily for the Asiatics." "A Prayer" follows, calling for justice and peace. "The Rochdale Pioneers" tells the story of that effort at cooperation and insists that "we Negroes of the United States could parallel this success." A spirited defense of the effectiveness of the NAACP "in its comparatively brief career" closes the section. "Men of the Month" (pp. 128; 133) include Richard L. Brown who died at the age of 24 and who showed great talent as an artist. Du Bois blames himself and "perhaps all of us" for not seeing to it that so talented a person was better cared for; the death of Prof. L. L. Jordan of Straight University in New Orleans is noted—"a man of great force of character"; Mrs. Ellen Craft Crum, daughter of the famous William and Ellen Craft, who together fled slavery and created an international sensation, has died; Mrs. Florence Randolph, a minister of the A.M.E.Z. Church, has been elected president of the New Jersey Federation of Colored Women's Clubs; the 24-year-old Francis W. Wand has been appointed an inspector of meat by the United States government in Chicago; Dr. Charles C. Johnson is a well-loved physician serving the Black community in Aiken, South Carolina; the work in sculpture of Meta Vaux W. Fuller, who lives with her husband, Dr. Solomon Fuller in Framingham, Massachusetts, is commented upon with high praise.

595. February, 1918. Vol. XV, No. 4. The editorial department (pp. 163–165) starts with a note about the editor, Dr. Du Bois, who reaches his 50th year this month; another stating that the circulation of the magazine in December was 54,000—the goal is 100,000 by 1919. A call for unselfish political work is made which could result—on the basis of population trends—in Black Congressmen from New York, Illinois, Pennsylvania, Ohio, and New Jersey (now there are none). "Here lies our line of march, comrades!" Tribute is paid to the NAACP Conference, its seventh, and to Mary Talbert for her fine work in assuring the Douglass Home in Washington. On "Youth," Du Bois calls to mind the death of Richard L. Brown (No. 594), though he mention's no name, and concludes, "We have got to organize more carefully and thoughtfully for the support and encouragement of talented youth." The dominant white group does not wish to support such talent—it wants us to be servants only. "No Negro genius must die from neglect or lack of appreciation." The taking over of the railroads by the government as a war measure is a good move and Black people should fight for continued government retention after the war. This may make easier the breaking of Jim Crow. "'The Negro Theater" notes the success in New York of the London-born musical "Chu Chin Chow"; it has "dozens of colored folk in the cast, and some of them are treated as recognized artists." He particularly mentions Matty Thomas. The play, "The Servant in the House," recently shown at the Lafayette Theater, in New York, was well done; however, Black actors are generally underpaid and productions poorly staged and this must be overcome. The Editorial department ends with questions to the Adjutant General of the army about the fact that the move to force the retirement of Col. Charles Young is racist and motivated by a desire to see that he is kept from active duty and, possibly, from promotion to Brigadier-General.

596. "The Shadow of Years," signed, February, 1918, Vol. XV, No. 4, pp. 167–171. It is the first fairly extended autobiographical effort, with many details about his parents and grandparents, on high school, Fisk University, Europe, and Atlanta from which "I emerged a man, scarred, partially disillusioned, and yet, grim with determination."

597. "Negro Education," signed, February, 1918. Vol. XV, No. 4. pp. 173–178. A review-essay on the two-volume work published by the United States Bureau of Education in 1917; Thomas J. Jones (of the Phelps-Stokes Fund) *Negro Education: a Study of the Private and Higher Schools for Colored People in the United States*. Valuable for data but harmful analytically and directed towards making "the higher training of Negroes practically difficult, if not impossible."

598. March, 1918, Vol. XV, No. 5. The editorial department rejects the "Advice" offered by The *Outlook* to Hampton Institute—which would intensify the worst features of that school. Under "Crime" the effort of the two regional branches of the Methodist Church to unite at the expense of Black Methodists is again discussed. "Our President" notes that Mr. Wilson's heart bleeds for Poland, Armenia, and Palestine, but as for the twelve million Black Americans, "Silence!" Hence, apparently, "distance from Washington certainly lends enchantment to Democracy!" A long section is devoted to "The Black Man and the Unions" and excoriates the A.F. of L. for its persistent racism. Other paragraphs disclose plans in the District of Columbia to reduce appropriations for the education of Black youth, take up, again, the efforts to retire Colonel Young, commend the Rand School in New York City where subjects are taught from a socialist viewpoint and where "above all" a cordial welcome is extended to Black men and women, denounces the continued racism displayed by the Civil Service in Washington despite a letter—here published—from the president of the Civil Service Commission, that it "has never knowingly been guilty of discriminating against colored citizens." "Men of the Month" (pp. 229–31): the death of Mrs. A. V. Andrews, an effective social worker of Sumter, South Carolina; the death of a young dentist, Dr. T. R. Mozee of Chicago; a fairly long account of the scholarly and athletic prowess of the 19–year–old Paul Le Roy Robeson of Rutgers University, who also "is a baritone soloist"; Dr. I. Garland Penn, author and leader in affairs of the M. E. Church. A page, unsigned, but by Du Bois, is headed "The New Philanthropy" (p. 232) and treats of four white people: Emilie B. Hapgood, R. E. Jones, J. C. Freund and R. J. Coady. The first two persons were helpful with the Negro players drama group in New York City; Mr. Freund, as editor of *Musical America*, "has always given prompt and generous recognition to Negro music" and Mr. R. J. Coady has assisted young Black painters. These people do not function on "the usual assumption that Negroes are inadequate and inefficient and need 'help'", but rather because they "have been especially stirred by the artistic possibilities of the Negro race."

599. April, 1918, Vol. XV, No. 6. Editorials commence with an attack upon the Department of Labor for actively seeking to dissuade Black people from migrating North; cordial thanks are given readers since this issue has been printed in 100,000 copies; note is taken that the one hundred sixty-seventh Field Artillery Brigade of the 92nd Division will be the first artillery unit in combat manned by Black troops; the racism of the Republican Party as exhibited in its insults to Perry Howard of Mississippi and Reverdy C. Johnson of New York is complete. A page is devoted to "Houston and East St. Louis" with two columns contrasting the fatalities suffered by whites and Blacks in each and the punishment meted out to the two peoples as a result. A photo is published showing the entrance to the "public" park in Houston with a sign reading "Negroes Keep Out." "Men of the Month" (p. 279): Charles J. Ryder, for 25 years has served the American Missionary Association; Judith C. Horton, a teacher and social worker and organizer of the first library for Black people in Guthrie, Oklahoma and of the first Black women's club in that State in 1904; Charles L. Rice, an attorney who served as City Attorney in Mound City, Illinois, for eight years and recently twice elected to its Board of Education; Lucius S. Hicks, a graduate of the Boston University Law School, was recently appointed Assistant Corporation Counsel of Boston.

600. May, 1918. Vol. XVI, No. 1. Editorial paragraphs by Du Bois document specific instances of racism on the part of the U.S. government and demand that these cease. Under "The Unit Plan" attention is called to a community governing proposal being implemented by the Black people in Cincinnati with its purpose to provide better health conditions and fuller employment, with the local people themselves running things. Quoted with distinct approval is its expressed aim, "To hasten the coming of a democracy both genuine and efficient by building up on a basis of geographical units an organization through which the people can get a clear idea of their common needs and can utilize the technical knowledge of skilled groups in formulating and carrying out programs to meet those needs." Once again, in an open letter, the blatant racism of *The Outlook* is exposed and attacked. "Men of the Month" (p. 15): Dr. S. Maria Steward, a physician for many years in New York City, "when it was a rare career for a woman," and lately, until her recent death, resident physician at Wilberforce University; Dr. J. H. Lowery is a physician in Donaldsonville, Louisiana, and is a fighter against Jim-Crow conditions; Major G. W. Prioleau had served as Chaplain with the Ninth and Tenth Cavalry and is now assigned to the Twenty-Fifth Infantry; James E. Gregg, originally of Hartford, has been appointed the new principal of Hampton Institute; Channing H. Tobias' work as Secretary of the International Committee of the YMCA is noted.

601. June, 1918, Vol. XVI, No. 2. In the editorial department, tribute is paid to "The Black Soldier" of the United States and the "dark men" of Africa and India, and of the French and British Colonies who in hundreds of thousands are fighting "for the world, and you and your people are a part of the world." "Out of this war will rise, soon or late," Du Bois writes, "an independent China, a self-governing India, and Egypt with representative institutions, an Africa for the Africans, and not merely for business exploitation." Also, there will come "an American Negro, with the right to vote and the right to work and the right to live without insult." The Black Assemblyman and the Governor of New York are congratulated on the passage of a good civil rights law, and it is urged that such laws be passed "throughout the civilized parts of the country." The Department of Labor is congratulated for appointing as an expert "on Negro Economics," Dr. George E. Haynes. The efforts for good in the South by a "gentle Catholic priest [Father Vernimont] in Texas" are noted and the barbarous racism of R. P. Robbins, editor of the Little Rock, Arkansas *Daily News*, is attacked.

602. July, 1918, Vol. XVI, No. 3. The Editorial department contains the much commented upon "Close Ranks" where the war is viewed as determining whether the world was to be dominated by "the menace of German militarism" or was to witness the building of "the United States of the World." Here Du Bois wrote the sentence he was later to regret more keenly, perhaps, than any of the tens of thousands sentences from his pen: "Let us, while this war lasts, forget our special grievances and close our ranks shoulder to shoulder with our own white fellow citizens and the allied nations that are fighting for democracy." (In fact, of course, Du Bois never did "forget.") Thus, this very editorial insists that public schools for all children, for Black as well as white children, must be compulsory for eight years and must concentrate upon reading, writing, counting, and learning how to think and to communicate; that national aid must be provided for such education and that Black people must "have a voice in their own education." The editorials continue by prophesying that the era of philanthropic support for higher education among Black people is closing and that "Negro universities and schools of higher training have got to be supported by Negroes or, for the most part, they will not be supported at all."

603. August, 1918, Vol. XVI, No. 4. In the editorial department is the text, written by Du Bois, of the petition to the United States government adopted at a June meeting in Washington and signed by 31 editors of Black newspapers and magazines. It affirms dedication to the nation in war but also insists that the elimination of racism is necessary for the best conduct of the war and for the sake of the nation itself. Noting the death of Senator Benjamin R. Tillman of South Carolina—Populist turned fiercely racist Democrat—Du Bois suggests that the time must come when leaders of white workers and small farmers in the South will understand the need for unity with the Black people. "Men of the Month" (pp. 183–184) begins with notes on three women: Mrs. A. B. Thoms, acting superintendent of nurses at Lincoln Hospital in New York; the late Celia Parker Woolley, a white woman of Chicago who since 1904 had directed the Frederick Douglass Center; Mrs. S. E. Phillips, an effective church worker of Philadelphia. Among the men are Dr. J. W. E. Bowen, for 25 years a teacher at Gammon Theological Seminary in Atlanta; Dr. J. Stanley Durkee, newly selected as president of Howard University.

604. September, 1918 Vol. XVI, No. 5. The editorial department announces a forthcoming meeting at the office of the *Crisis* of experts in cooperative economics. "A Momentous Proposal" tells of the suggestion, which fell through, to make a special "effort to satisfy the pressing grievances of colored Americans," in the army to be headed by Du Bois, who was to be offered a captaincy. Objections to the "Close Our Ranks" editorial have been numerous; Du Bois repeats its theme, "the *Crisis* says, *first* your Country, *then* your Rights!" In "The

Reward" Du Bois attempts to show that as a result of participation in past wars—as the Revolutionary War and the Civil War—gains were made by Black people and that similar gains have been made during this war. "Men of the Month" (pp. 235–236) include: Blanche A. Perkins of New Orleans, and Frances R. Elliot of Tennessee are doing effective war work; the latter is the first Black nurse enrolled under the American Red Cross. The deaths of two friends and successful Black businessmen are recorded: B. F. Powell of Georgia and David C. Fisher of Lorain, Ohio. "Two Fighters," then still in the midst of the struggle, the Rev. George Frazier Miller, of Brooklyn, "frank fighter, radical Socialist," and John Robert Clifford of Martinsburg, West Virginia, an attorney who empaneled the "first colored jury in West Virginia, and incidentally, was knocked down three times during the process . . . at the time he was pulled off of his would-be assassin even the judge had left."

605. October, 1918, Vol. XVI, No. 6. The editorial department calls for Black parents, despite all difficulties, to fight to preserve the lives of their children and to keep them in school for "our rise is founded on the rock of knowledge." A Negro cooperative guild was formed at a meeting held at the *Crisis* in August. Du Bois hopes for its growth. The selection of John Hope, president of Morehouse College in Atlanta, to inspect YMCA work in France insofar as it touches Black men, is a wise move. "Men of the Month" (pp. 283–284) include: Edna C. Robinson, D.D.S., the only Black woman dentist in New England (in Cambridge, Massachusetts); William Warley, founder and editor of the Louisville, Kentucky *News* and plaintiff in the famous case of *Buchanan* v *Warley*.

606. November, 1918, Vol. XVII, No. 1. Instead of "Editorial" the issue opens with "Opinion" and is signed by Du Bois. It notes a "tremendous speech" delivered in New York City in September by President Wilson. Surely, Du Bois writes, when he spoke of the right of self-rule and the immorality of tyranny and denial of rights, he could not have meant only Germany and not Mississippi, only Serbia and not Africa? If that is so—if he meant all humanity—then this speech was very great indeed. An effort to enforce Jim-Crow regulations within the Student's Army Training Corps, even in schools where segregation had not ordinarily been practiced, brought prompt protest from the NAACP and the abandonment of such effort. Black soldiers are performing well in France and are being commended by French officials. A call on "The Colored Voter" to take local elections seriously and to defeat racists—for example, Rep. Charles P. Caldwell, of New York. Again, Du Bois emphasizes the cooperative movement which is spreading in Europe and which, he repeats, holds much promise for Black people in the United States. Du Bois affirms his "Patriotism" in his sense of a love of that promise which, he thinks, America may yet fulfill. "Men of the Month" (pp. 28–30) pays tribute to an 18-year-old lad named Kenneth Lewis of Washington, D. C., killed in action in Europe; to Jenkin Lloyd Jones, the effective social worker of Illinois, who had died; and to Dr. Ernest Lyon, formerly U.S. Minister to Liberia, now a pastor in Baltimore.

607. December, 1918, Vol. XVII, No. 2. "Opinion" starts with a salute to "Peace"—"The nightmare is over." A parable on "The Flight into Egypt" follows. It is announced that the NAACP "has appropriated funds and commissioned" Du Bois to be in charge of the preparation of a "War History" and Du Bois asks for help. In "The Ballot" Du Bois demands, now that the fighting is over—in which 350,000 Black men participated—a vote for every literate adult and *"schools where every American child must learn to read and write."* "Steve" tells the story of Du Bois' love for the dog of that name and his recent death.

608. January, 1919, Vol. XVII, No. 3. The editorial, "Old Desires," is about the demands hitherto raised and still to be realized—"on then, Black Americans, and remember the pass word—*Organization and Cooperation!*" Four paragraphs on "The Peace Conference," may not have been written by Du Bois; they tell of his departure for France, on December 1, with three purposes: representing the *Crisis* at the Peace Conference; to further his research for a "History of the American Negro in the Great War"; representing the NAACP at the Peace Conference and advancing the interests "of the colored peoples of the United States and of the world." The intention of convoking a Pan-African Congress is announced. In a brief essay, "Jim Crow," Du Bois notes a rising dilemma to oppose segregation and fight the realities of segregation through forging greater and greater Black unity. "Not every builder of racial co-operation and solidarity is a 'Jim-Crow' advocate, a hater of white folk. Not every Negro who fights prejudice and segregation is ashamed of his race." In "After the War" attention is called to programs being formulated by "labor and radical bodies." The Social Democratic League announces "many excellent points" but nowhere mentions Black people; however, the congressional program of the Socialist Party does strongly condemn the awful oppression and intensive exploitation of Black people and demands "full benefits of citizenship" for them and the enforcement of the fourteenth Amendment. Du Bois comments, "It is unfortunate that the attitude of the Socialist Party during the war goes far to nullify this rather late espousal of the Negroes' cause." A page is devoted, again, to explaining "Consumers' Co-Operation" and recommending it to the Black people. In "Men of the Month" (p. 123) the careers of two Black men elected to the West Virginia legislature are sketched: T. G. Nutter and H. J. Capehart. The retirement, after almost fifty years as a teacher in the New York public schools, of Maritcha R. Lyons is announced.

609. February, 1919, Vol. XVII, No. 4. The editorial department opens with a fulsome eulogy of Theodore Roosevelt, who has died; it is not clear that Du Bois, who is away in Europe, wrote the article because its style is somewhat florid. It continues with "Letters from Dr. Du Bois," dated December 8, at sea, and December 14, Paris. These letters deal mainly with the need to move Africa away from European domination and towards control by Africans which would open the possibility of considerable migration by Black Americans to Africa. On the whole, Du Bois writes, "this is not a 'separatist' movement"; in any case, no one is more American than we Black people and it is "absurd" to talk of a return-to-Africa movement. But, he adds, "The African movement means to us what the Zionist movement must mean to the Jews, the centralization of race effort and the recognition of a racial fount."

610. March, 1919, Vol. XVII, No. 5. The editorial begins with "Vive La France!" an exclamation evoked because of France's public celebration of the role of African and Asian soldiers in preventing her defeat. The French themselves had almost believed the propaganda about the superiority of the Germans, but they held at the Marne and at Verdun. Do we Blacks need a Verdun, asks Du Bois. No, we have the pride of not oppressing others, of not lynching others. "Honest pride will help its possessor to 'carry on' when faith is a failure and optimism is dead. Believe it." Among the "Men of the Month" (pp. 233–234): D. C. Suggs appointed president of Livingstone College in North Carolina; Eslanda C. Goode has been placed in charge of the surgical pathological laboratory at the Presbyterian Hospital in New York City and shows great promise in chemistry; Dr. J. B. Ford is the first Black surgeon to practice in the ambulance service of Bellevue Hospital in New York City.

611. "The Black Man in the Revolution of 1914–1918," March, 1919,

Vol. XVII, No. 5, (pp. 218–223) signed. The essay is described as "a preliminary and tentative foreword to the history I hope to write." It outlines the basic contributions of the colored peoples of the world to the defeat of the Central Powers; it emphasizes the racism manifested by white Americans against Black and the relative friendship shown Black troops by the French people and the French army—a friendship that will not be forgotten, Du Bois thinks. He ends, "And the black officer and private? They return at once bitter and exalted! They will not submit to American caste and they will ever love France!"

612. "Memorandum to M. Diagne and Others on a Pan-African Congress to be held in Paris on February, 1919," in French and English, signed, March, 1919, Vol. XVII, No. 5, pp. 224–225. This Memorandum is dated Paris, January 1, 1919 and projects the plans for a Congress and proposes its objectives—"inaugurating gradually an Africa for the Africans,"—developing Black art and culture, developing "sympathetic co-operation" of Black, Yellow and White peoples, bringing pressure for these ends upon the Peace Conference and the League of Nations, assuring the integrity of the existing independent Black states, and inquiring about the Mandate system of the League for the former German colonies in Africa.

613. April, 1919, Vol. XVII, No. 6. In the editorial department (pp. 267–270) the Easter season is described as especially appropriate with peace present once again. The policy of supporting the war was wise, Du Bois argues, for it places Black people now in a sound strategic and tactical position to insist upon realization of their demands.* He notes that in Europe he found himself thankful—for what? "God! It was simply human decency" that he encountered in meeting other people, unlike white people in his own country. "The Fields of Battle" in France are described. Meeting with Black Africans, Du Bois is led to emphasize the importance for Afro-Americans of mastering French and Spanish in order to be able to communicate more easily with African brothers. "Men of the Month" (pp. 286–287): George H. White has died. He was an attorney, and in the early 1880's solicitor for the Second District of North Carolina, a member of the State House and Senate and, since 1896, elected twice to the congress from North Carolina, and thereafter moved to Philadelphia, where he had served as Assistant City Solicitor; Noble M. Johnson, the first prominent Black actor in Hollywood appearing both as an Indian and a Black man and at present the producer and director of the Lincoln Film Company.

*In "Opinion" for June, 1919 Du Bois states that the comments on Easter were "written during the Editor's absence."

614. "The Pan-African Congress," signed, April, 1917, Vol. XVII, No. 6, pp. 271–274. A factual statement, held in Paris, from February 1921, to February attended by 57 delegates from 15 countries. It includes the names and résumés of the speakers, the texts of the resolutions adopted, which demanded an enhancement of the rights of the African peoples, and looked towards achieving self-government.

615. May, 1919, Vol. XVIII, No. 1. "Opinion" opens the issue (pp. 7–14). It explains "My Mission" which he did not talk about prior to its accomplishment because "the American Secret Service" was "at my heels." However, the Pan-African Congress was held and "the world fight for black rights is on." Du Bois adds, "We plan an international quarterly, *Black Review*, to be issued in English, French and possibly in Spanish and Portuguese." Du Bois expresses keen disappointment in the performance of Robert R. Moton—President Wilson's appointee —"to see and talk to Negro troops." Thomas Jesse Jones was always on his heels; his speeches were poor; he did not appear at the Pan-African Congress; he missed numerous opportunities for service to the Cause. And "To Emmett Scott," the assistant to the Secretary of War as an advisor on "Negro Affairs," Du Bois states that what he learned of the bestial treatment of Black troops in Europe shocked him. Did you know of this? If not, why not and if yes, *"what did you do about it?"** Du Bois thinks the "League of Nations" may be very helpful, for, he says, while apparently we cannot reach the conscience of White America, it should be possible to influence the conscience of the rest of the world. Du Bois announces plans for a three-volume "History" of Black people in the war and regrets that he has not been able to achieve a unified effort for such a result, mentioning in particular Carter G. Woodson's refusal to join with him. Under "Rape" Du Bois refutes this charge against his people—again—and shows that in Europe Afro-American troops were less often convicted of this crime than others, but that, nevertheless, a systematic campaign charging "rape tendencies" was organized. The editorial ends with another very widely quoted and discussed piece of Du Bois' writing, "Returning Soldiers." The United States, despite its best dreams, remains a land which lynches, disfranchises, steals, insults, and encourages ignorance. "Under similar circumstances, we would fight again. But by the God of Heaven, we are cowards and jackasses if now that the war is over, we do not marshal every ounce of our brain and brawn to fight a sterner, longer, more unbending battle against the forces of hell in our own land."

*Mr. Scott's reply—a rather *ad hominem* attack on Du Bois and the plea that "I could not do everything"—was widely reported. See, for example, the Nashville (Tennessee) *Globe*, May 30, 1919.

616. "Documents of the War," collected by Du Bois, May, 1919, Vol. XVIII, No. 1, pp. 16–21. Military orders and directives proving the policy of blatant racism; Du Bois writes that he "has absolute proof of their authenticity"—and later scholarship has confirmed this.

617. June, 1919, Vol. XVIII, No. 2. In "Opinion" (pp. 59–62), a call to attend the annual meeting of the NAACP to be held in Cleveland at the end of June. "We have waited fifty years. The Negro must and shall be free and the NAACP must do it." "Lynching" reports on the developing movement to wipe out this stench. "The History of the Great War" announces publication of a volume in October (it did not eventuate). Under "I.W.W." a letter from F. H. M. Murray of Washington takes exception to the editorial, headed "Easter" in the April issue and commends the I.W.W., noting the leadership therein of the Black man, Benjamin Fletcher. Du Bois states that the editorial was written in his absence, and that he respects the I.W.W. "as one of the social and political movements in modern times that draws no color line." He adds that he has high regard for socialists like Eugene Debs who remained true to their antiwar principles, but he reiterates that he thinks the tactics of the I.W.W. and of Debs were wrong in terms of this particular war. "Descent Into Hell" calls attention to amendments aimed at enfranchising women but worded in such a way as to encourage disfranchisement of all Black people. On the Versailles Treaty Du Bois calls it "a hard, bitter penalty ... to fit a hard, cruel crime." He greets the appearance of Poland, the Slav States, Armenia, "the half-redeemed colonies of Africa," and Arabia "where our blood mingles." Noting armed uprisings in India and Egypt, Du Bois expresses sympathy for the fighters. For us in the United States, he writes, peaceful methods must be used because "War, Force, Revolution are impossible, unthinkable." The "Tercentenary" commemoration of the 1619 landing of Black people at Jamestown commencing on August 1 will take the form of a national day of fasting and prayer, a pageant of history and local meetings.

618. "An Essay Toward a History of the Black Man in the Great War," signed, June, 1919, Vol. XVIII, No. 2, pp. 63–87. Probably the longest essay ever published in one number of the *Crisis*. "A first attempt," Du Bois explains, with notes on Black men from Africa, but most of the material detailing the work of labor battalions, field artillery units, and the 92nd and 93rd Divisions and the racism that enveloped the whole effort.

619. July, 1919, Vol. XVIII, No. 3, In "Opinion" (pp. 127–131), the meeting at Cleveland reaffirms his conviction that "there is Strength in Unity, but in Knowledge there is Freedom." In "Our Success and Failure" Du Bois reiterates his criticism of Mr. Scott and states that in France he "was utterly amazed and dumbfounded at the revelations [of racist persecution] poured upon him." He reveals secret orders that he be followed, and repeats the three questions he had earlier put to Emmett J. Scott. Under the title, "Reconstruction," Du Bois suggests a program for Black people now that the war is over: in organization of Black parents to see that good *education* is provided for their children at the public schools; in *religion*, the use of Black church organizations as bases for social service and for developing economic cooperative institutions; in *business*, train for manufacturing, get skills, pool resources—"we raise the cotton—why not spin and weave it"; in *politics*, particularly now that our women are to vote, purify it, make it really independent, activate ourselves and then vote. "A Great Woman" brings tribute to the late Madame C. J. Walker, of beauty products fame.

620. August, 1919, Vol. XVIII, No. 4. In "Opinion" (pp. 179–183), "To Your Tents, O Israel!" records the fact—through quotations of several delegates at the Cleveland NAACP Meeting—that a new sense of militancy characterizes the Black people, and he adds that we must "FIGHT, FIGHT, FIGHT for Freedom!" As to the "Three Hundred Years," since 1619, we must remember each drop of blood and sweat and each insult—not for purposes of hate and vengeance but for purposes of undoing wrong and because if evil is forgotten, it returns. "The Fourth Century dawns and through it, God guide our thrilling hands." "Men of the Month" (p. 200): Robert B. Barcus, recently appointed Special Counsellor in the office of Ohio's Attorney General; William H. Gilbert has retired after thirty years service in the army and navy; U. Conrad Vincent, M.D., is the first Black physician to be appointed an interne at a "white" hospital—in this case Bellevue in New York; Charles R. Humbert, M.D., is the first Black physician to be hired by the Rockefeller Institute in New York for purposes of research.

621. September, 1919, Vol. XVIII, No. 5. In "Opinion" (pp. 231–235), "Let Us Reason Together" is a call for the use of self-defense so that "when the armed lynchers gather, we too must gather armed." Du Bois continues, "We must defend ourselves ... but we must carefully and scrupulously avoid on our own part bitter and unjustifiable aggression against anybody." (All this is to be placed within the context of the pogroms and lynchings which made the Summer of 1919 known to contemporaries as "The Red Summer.") In "Labor Omnia Vincit" —labor conquers all,—Du Bois poses the question of the unity of Black and white workers for the achievement of industrial justice as the question of questions, "transcending the problem of Labor and Capital, of Democracy, of the Equality of Women—for it is the problem of the Equality of Humanity in the world as against white domination of black and brown and yellow serfs." Under the title, "The Black Majority," it is noted that Du Bois and the *Crisis* have been discussed several times in Congress by such savants as Senator James Reed of Missouri and Senator Kenneth McKellar of Tennessee who are anxious to retain white supremacy, but "can the dark majority of mankind always be ruled by the white minority." Furthermore, Du Bois suggests, that "the white world will be so busy fighting and hating itself during the next century that it will have scant leisure to keep black folk in their place." "The American Legion" is denounced for its racism; Du Bois encourages the ongoing creation of all-Black veterans' groups but urges that at the same time Black men fight to end the racism in the Legion. Faint indications of some reason are discerned and described in "Signs from the South." In "Forward" Du Bois observes a certain provincialism in the thinking of his people, tending to ignore questions like the public ownership of utilities or questions arising in Ireland, India, and Russia. We should favor liberation struggles there as everywhere. And " . . . the one new Idea of the World War—the idea which may well stand in future years as the one thing that made the slaughter worth while—is an Idea which we are like to fail to know because it is today hidden under the maledictions hurled at Bolshevism . . . it is the vision of great dreamers that *only those who work shall vote and rule.*" Preparatory to an increase in price (and size) of the *Crisis*—to come with the November, 1919 issue—Du Bois recounts the growth of the magazine from an average of 9,000 copies in 1911 to a sale of 104,000 copies in June, 1919.

622. October, 1919, Vol. XVIII, No. 6. "Opinion" (pp. 283–287) begins with an attack upon the officials and rulers of Texas for the brutal physical attack upon the white Secretary of the NAACP, John R. Shillady—"the answer of the Coward and the Brute to Reason and Prayer." Under "Byrnes," Du Bois rebuts the remarks in Congress made by James F. Byrnes of South Carolina [the future Senator, Secretary of State and Supreme Court Justice] attacking him and the *Crisis* as Bolshevik agents and demanding that the Attorney General investigate the man and the magazine. But it is Byrnes who sits in Congress illegally and who—along with his kind—have been responsible for the crucifixion of a people and the vitiation of democracy. Du Bois attended four large social dances given by various Black organizations and was again struck with the graciousness, politeness and beauty of his people, "there is nothing in white Europe or America that can measure up to" all this. The forthcoming magazine for children is announced—the *Brownies' Book*—to be edited by Du Bois, to see the beauty of their color, to familiarize them with Black history, to inspire and instruct them and to help them. A report follows on the progress of publishing the history of Black people in the War; it is seen now as two volumes—one, narrative and one, documentary.

623. November, 1919, Vol. XIX, No. 1, added to the masthead the name of Jessie R. Fauset as Literary Editor; however, the promised enlargement of the magazine did not occur until the December issue. "Opinion" (pp. 335–337) commences with an apology for the above mentioned delay and then prints "A Statement" affirming that the cause of the pogroms and so-called race riots lay in Jim Crow and in oppression and not in the advice of "outsiders"; it adds the right to self-defense is inviolate. Du Bois asks readers to support a resolution before Congress for a Federal investigation into the riots in Washington and elsewhere. A cordial welcome is given to the statement recently issued by the Federal Council of Churches of Christ in America calling for justice to Black people; but a statement emanating from a meeting of Governors affirming that the first necessity in preventing lynching is to "enlist Negroes themselves in preventing crimes that provoke mob violence" is denounced as a fraud. Paragraphs express Du Bois' support of "The Plumb Plan" for the nationalization of the railroads and for "The League of Nations." On "Honesty" Du Bois insists that its propriety is self-evident; he notes that out of 99 dental students in Nebraska who had access to advance copies of an examination, only one remained honest and he was a Black man, John Singleton, who "bore on his shoulders, not simply his personal honor, but the honor of a great race." Again, Du Bois exposes the demagogic and racist use of "Social Equality" to thwart efforts at Black freedom. Tribute is paid to the "Heroes"—the mass of Southern Black people—who do not yield their dignity in the face of torment —"in God's good time such martyrdom must and shall win." "Men of the Month" (pp. 341–342): C. D. B. King, the President of Liberia is on a state visit; Jessie R. Fauset, newly appointed to the staff of the *Crisis*, is introduced as a frequent contributor to its pages. She is a Phi Beta Kappa from Cornell and had pursued graduate studies in France and at the University of Pennsylvania and had taught French and Latin in high school. The death of John Merrick, founder and head of the North Carolina Mutual Life Insurance Company in Durham, is announced.

624. December, 1919, Vol. XIX, No. 2. "Opinion" (pp. 41–46) opens with a story, "The Gospel According to Mary Brown" in which her Black son, Joshua, is lynched even as Jesus was crucified. "Votes" speaks of these as the vehicle toward achieving power and with power can come freedom; hence, build up the voting habits and use them wisely and see to it that Black people are sent to Congress. "Again, Ophelia" tells the story of the remarkable response of offers of a home to a Black child, Ophelia, whose motherless plight was noted in an earlier issue—there were offers from 449 homes and Du Bois suggests, "Let us organize to place our orphans in our best homes." "The Negro Soldier" excoriates *Harvey's Weekly* for its scurrilous attacks upon the honor of Black men in the late war; Du Bois details a refutation. Under "Radicals" Du Bois condemns racists in Congress and in the Attorney General's office (A. M. Palmer) for their attacks upon so-called radical magazines coming from Black people—such as the *Messenger* (edited by A. Philip Randolph) and the *Negro World* (edited by Marcus Garvey). The *Crisis* may differ from these but it defends the right of a free press; Du Bois names and refers to a score of Southern racist newspapers which publish filth and insults with no protest from any government or official. On page 48 and page 50 there appears an account—undoubtedly by Du Bois—of cooperative stores in Memphis run by Black people and doing well. "Men of the Month" (pp. 63–65) notes the appointment of John W. Davis as president of West Virginia Collegiate Institute; the tragically early death of a young teacher at Atlanta University, Annadel C. King, is recorded; William W. Sanders has been appointed Supervisor of Colored Schools for the state of West Virginia; Louis T. Wright, M.D., has been appointed Physician to the Out-Patient Department of Harlem Hospital; Edward E. Brown, Deputy Collector of Boston, died; William S. Quinland, M.D., has been awarded the first of the new Rosenwald medical scholarships—he will do graduate work at Harvard Medical School.

625. January, 1920, Vol. XIX, No. 3. "Opinion" (pp. 105–110) opens with a call, "Brothers, Come North"—"Not in a rush—not as aimless wanderers, but after quiet investigation and careful location." Attorney General Palmer is attacked for reporting any effort to legalize intermarriage as some kind of subversive opposition on the part of Black people; the blindness of white southerners who think of " 'Our' South" as constituted simply of white people is noted; in "Race Pride" Du Bois says that those who maintain white supremacy will have to choose between leaving the black and yellow world alone and getting out of Asia and Africa and "giving us our states and sections and let us rule undisturbed" or establishing mutual respect and real equality and democracy. Home rule must come for all the colonies and peoples; otherwise, an awful world war against a tyranny worse than the Kaiser's will ensue. Du Bois appeals for a continued struggle to eliminate the racism within the American Legion. Under "the Macon *Telegraph*" Du Bois quotes at length the characteristic racist slanders especially directed against him appearing in that Georgia newspaper and then patiently rebuts each one. "Men of the Month" (pp. 126–127): Horace Bumstead, past president of Atlanta University, close friend of Du Bois and of the Black people, has died; J. D. Kirksey is the 22-year-old mayor of an all-Black town, Hobson City, Alabama; he recently received some threatening letters, "but he merely purchased a pistol" and is unperturbed. This is one of approximately 60 all-Black towns and cities in the country from Allensworth, California to Brooklyn, Illinois, to Boley, Oklahoma. Wiley Hinds, bought out of slavery by his father, has died; he had accumulated a large fortune, mostly in real estate in and around Berkeley and Oakland, California; Joseph S. Cotter, Jr., has died at the age of 23 but he left important books of plays and poetry; Charles S. Scott has retired after 50 years of work as a railroader; the Tremont Trust Company of Boston "is directed by the type of white men who sense merit beyond the color line." Dr. C. N. Garland has been elected a member of its Board of Directors and several of its clerks and tellers are Black men and women.

626. February, 1920, Vol. XIX, No. 4. "Opinion" (pp. 169–173) opens with "Danger" in censorship bills before Congress aimed at curbing radical publications; Du Bois calls upon the *Crisis* readers to oppose these bills. "The Unfortunate South," obsessed with its racism, produces "no literature or art, except that based on the Negro." In "Arkansas" life insurance is being denied to Black people on the grounds that they advocate equality! "A Matter of Manners" points out that for a Black man to display courtesy to a white woman may go against his grain for no respect is shown him; moreover, should he display courtesy he may be accused of being "uppity" and then suffer

some dire penalty. "The House of Jacob" lists the known evils of the
South and asks where the voices of protest are from whites in that area?
An effort to create "A New Party" is going forward under the auspices
of a Committee of Forty-Eight; Du Bois quotes its program and
suggests that it merits support. Again, Du Bois writes of the cooperative
program and commends it; in "Crime" Du Bois affirms its existence
among Black people as among all people, points to the difference
between accusation and guilt given the racist character of U.S.
"justice" and to the special social roots of crime among Black people.
"Leadership" comments on England's support, together with Wilson,
of the League of Nations; with such "leadership" of course it failed, yet
the idea of the League must succeed "for civilization needs it."

627. March, 1920, Vol. XIX, No. 5. "Opinion" (pp. 233–238) starts
with a call for the defense of Edgar Caldwell, a Black soldier, under
sentence of death in Alabama "for defending himself against the crew
of a street car and killing one of them." Congratulations are offered to
William T. Andrews who has maintained for two years a daily Black
newspaper, Baltimore's *Daily Herald.* Du Bois expects that by the next
Presidential election three million Black women will have the right to
vote; let them study politics now and be prepared: "They may beat and
bribe our men, but the political hope of the Negro rests on its
intelligent and incorruptible womanhood." "Just Like Folks!" when
something goes wrong among us we say "just like colored folks!" But
look at the mess the world has been in and still is in and it is not
"colored folks" who are in charge! In an effort to extradite from
Kansas Robert L. Hill, a leader in the effort of Black farmers to
organize at Elaine, Arkansas, which led to massacre of Blacks and the
hanging of 12 men, the Arkansas sheriff has presented the Kansas
Governor with a petition favoring such extradition signed by Bishop J.
M. Connor of the A. M. E. Church, J. M. Cox, president of Philander
Smith College, and J. A. Booker, president of Arkansas Baptist College.
Du Bois gives these men one month to answer: "*Did you sign that
petition? If you did—why did you?*" Noting the use of Black workers to
help break the recent steel strike, Du Bois knows very well why Black
men took such work and he still does not commend it. "The deeper,
bloodier, guilt lies with those Masters of Industry, who today,
yesterday, and tomorrow, plan to make the petty, human jealousies,
hatreds, rivalries, and starvations of workingmen, the foundation of
their colossal fortunes." "Again, Social Equality" this time rebutted
through the use of a brief satire. In "England, Again," Du Bois notes

that many readers have objected to his earlier attack on England and that he had not taken note of the contribution by Englishmen to the antislavery movement, nor had he given weight to the traditional hostility shown by the Irish in the United States to Black people. Du Bois replies that he knows of both but they are irrelevant to his argument: the realities of the racism and colonialism of the British Empire and the justice of the cause of Irish national liberation. "Men of the Month" (pp. 272–274): Mary L. Gaines, an effective social leader in Atlanta, has died; A. A. Watkins, formerly Assistant Corporation Counsel of Chicago, has been appointed Assistant United States Attorney in Chicago; R. L. Brokenburr has been named Deputy Prosecuting Attorney for the nineteenth Judicial Circuit Court in Indianapolis; the deaths of Bishop Alexander P. Camphor, most recently pastor of St. John's M.E. Church in Orange, N.J., and of David V. Scott, M.D., of Montgomery, Alabama, and of George W. Ellis, the historian, former Secretary of the United States Legation in Liberia, Assistant Corporation Counsel in Chicago, and author of important works on life and culture in West Africa, are all reported.

628. "Unrest," a poem, initialed, March, 1920, Vol. XIX, No. 5, p. 274.

629. April, 1920, Vol. XIX, No. 6. In "Opinion" (pp. 297–301), "Every Four Years" the Republican Party goes through the farce of excluding Black men from the South in its National Convention; "Remember," he writes, that the present excessive power of the Bourbon is built on sand, an awakening will yet come—"suppose the 'dirty foreigners' and the disfranchised Socialists and the disfranchised Blacks should get together and vote together at the next election!"; "Haiti" has been invaded by the United States and today a bloody and illegal war is being waged there: "The greatest single question before the parties at the next election is the Freedom of Haiti"; "Hyde Park" real-estate agents are trying to keep Black people out of that part of Chicago —resist and demand your rights, Du Bois advises; "The Second Battle of Lexington"—five men died in 1775 at the first Battle and the shots had great historic impact. Five men have been killed in the latest outbreak in Lexington, Kentucky. What impact will that have? "Universal Military Training" was voted down by Southerners who feared Black men with arms; "To General Leonard Wood"—some people are suggesting him as the next President; however, the Black people have evidence of his racism—please answer to the charges. "Negro Writers" and artists have been encouraged and discovered by the *Crisis* and this is fine; the charge to the contrary by Claude McKay is "arrogant nonsense." "A renaissance of American Negro literature is due." "Southern Representatives" argues for the enforcement of the Fourteenth Amendment, which would sweep out of Congress most of the Southern Representatives and this would help the country. The department closes with a short short story, "Of Giving Work" which ends, "The white man blustered: 'That's Bolshevism!' he shouted. And then church broke up." "Men of the Month" (pp. 334–336): Charles H. Garvin, M.D., the first Black physician commissioned in the U.S. Medical Corps has now been appointed clinician in Lakeside Hospital in Cleveland—the first appointment of a Black physician in that city's hospitals; the life and work and struggles of Millie J. Henderson—born a slave—who raised and educated four children two of whom are school principals, one is a public school teacher, and the other is a physician in Dallas; Toronto, Canada, has placed a portrait of a Black man, W. P. Hubbard, in its City Hall in recognition of his 20 years of service as Comptroller and Alderman; the appointment of William Pickens, formerly vice president of Morgan College, as Associate Field Secretary of the NAACP, is announced; Eugene K. Jones, Executive Secretary of the National Urban League, is brought to the attention of the *Crisis* readers.

630. May, 1920, Vol. XX, No. 1. In "Opinion" (pp. 5–8), "Atlanta" is to be the site of the next Annual Meeting of the NAACP because it is at the center of the 11 million of us and because we insist on our full rights in the South and everywhere else. "Extradition Cases" notes that in 1917 and in 1920 the governors of Massachusetts and Kansas refused Southern requests for extradition of Black men on the grounds of manifest injustice; now the governor of Michigan has returned a Black man, Grant Smith, to Kentucky and within 24 hours he was lynched! Woman Suffrage will be achieved this year; "Get Ready" by planning now to see to it that Black women who qualify under the law do vote. Du Bois heard Roland Hayes at a concert—"an hour to live for and remember." Two pages are devoted to "White Co-Workers"; these deal with a charge made openly and covertly against the NAACP—that it "is not a Negro association, but is conducted by white people and that, therefore, it cannot effectively serve the cause of Negro freedom." The alleged facts are wrong because of the 90,000 members, 80,000 are Black and "colored persons predominate on the Board of Directors, on the Committee of Executives, and among the executive officers. ... The policy of the NAACP has from the beginning been the policy proposed and advocated by the colored members of the Board." All this mutual regard and work "is a sample of what we aim to accomplish in the nation and the world." "Do we want to become American citizens or not? Do we want to share in a world state or not?" Otherwise, the logic is for "separate cities, colonies and states and eventually, a separate nation. This is a possible aim. It is an aim which we may be driven by race prejudice sometime to adopt. But it is not our present aim and we cannot consistently or effectively at the same time pursue *both* these aims." The aim now is:

> in voluntary unions, to develop a new Negro ethos—a music, a literature, a school of art and thought; but they will do this as freemen in a free democracy, joining wholeheartedly with their fellows of all colors whenever that freedom is menaced. Not narrow, excluding, other-hating particularisms, but broad, sympathetic, all-embracing nationalism is our aim and spirit.

The "Men of the Month" (pp. 36–38) include Clarence C. White, of Boston, internationally known violinist; Elizabeth Piper-Ensley, a teacher at Howard University in Washington and Alcorn College in Mississippi, treasurer of the Colorado Equal Suffrage Association, sponsor of a movement that resulted in building a monument to Paul Cuffee which was dedicated in 1913 in Westport, Massachusetts. Mrs. Piper-Ensley has died in Denver which was her home for the past 39 years. The death of Rev. B. W. Paxton of St. Andrew's church in Cleveland, Ohio, is reported; Edmund T. Jenkins of Charleston, South Carolina, has made a mark as a composer and conductor.

631. June, 1920, Vol. XX, No. 2. In "Opinion" (pp. 69–72), seventeen men mentioned as likely "Presidential Candidates" were sent questionnaires as to racism and Haiti. Three only responded: Senator Miles Poindexter favors equality of opportunity for all; Senator Warren Harding stands on the Republican Party's platform; General Leonard Wood denies that he expressed prejudice against Black officers. Fourteen said nothing, "We will forget these gentlemen neither in our prayers nor in our votes." Two pages are devoted to "Mississippi" which has just passed a law illegalizing the publishing or circulating of material "favoring social equality or marriage between the white and Negro races." An agent of the *Crisis* in Mississippi, Rev. E. R. Franklin of Jackson, was almost killed by a mob for letting others see copies of the magazine. He was arrested and sentenced to a fine of $400 and four months on the chain gang. Efforts by the NAACP to help him have resulted in a lynch mob terrorizing an attorney and the Governor and Lt. Governor of Mississippi sent threatening telegrams to the NAACP.

Bail of $1,000 was raised, Mr. Franklin is to face an appeal in the fall. Under "Arkansas" Du Bois summarizes the reply from the three Black men who had urged the extradition of Robert L. Hill from Kansas for trial and who had been asked by Du Bois to explain their actions. The replies come down to serving the Governor—we are among "his closest advisers." Du Bois rejects the explanation and details the reasons therefor. The "Resignation" of John R. Shillady, who had served for two years as NAACP Secretary, is announced and his letter published. "Men of the Month" (pp. 90–93): Bishop C. S. Smith of the A.M.E. Church, a doctor and former member of the State Legislature of Alabama, continues after 50 years as "an outspoken defender of the rights of the Negro." Charles S. Gilpin's career as an actor, to date, is sketched; he is currently appearing on Broadway in John Drinkwater's "Abraham Lincoln." George W. Cabaness, a practicing physician in Washington for thirty years, has died; Robert G. Fitzgerald, a wounded veteran of the Civil War, has died at his home in Hillsboro, North Carolina; the death some time ago of Mrs. J. H. Long brings a note concerning the career of the late Jefferson H. Long, the only Black Congressman ever to represent Georgia.

632. July, 1920, Vol. XX, No. 3. In "Opinion" (pp. 117–120), "In Georgia" concerns the meeting in Atlanta of the Eleventh Annual Conference of the NAACP—epoch-making, for a "radical Negro organization" has gathered publicly in the South and demanded an end to racism. "Two Methods" tells of the work of a vigilance committee in Des Moines, Iowa, led by Mrs. L. B. Smith, which undertakes to unite the Black parents and help their children attending the city's public schools (in the manner suggested earlier by Du Bois)—and in Indianapolis, the Black community holds meetings with each Black graduate from the public schools urging that the student go to high school. Du Bois reports, also, the "Go To High School, Go To College" drive being conducted by Alpha Phi Alpha Fraternity. "Race Intelligence" is an exposure of the unscientific nature of the efforts —from brain weight to bone structure and now so-called intellgence tests—to establish the inferiority of Black people. The latest fraud is a Professor M. R. Trabue of Columbia University and Du Bois shows his deception. "A Question" exposes blatant racism at recent conventions of the YWCA in Cleveland and the National Conference of Social Work in New Orleans. The question is put to "pale friends". Shall such episodes be exposed and denounced or shall they be passed over in silence, as is done by the White press? "Soldiers" calls attention to an article by the Secretary of War Baker in that issue of the *Crisis* (p. 137) and says it is poor, which means second class service by Black men in the military forces. "Latin" tells of an unnamed Black teacher who has tried to insist on teaching Latin in his high school and has finally been overruled. What is the point? That Blacks are enamored of a dead language? Of course not. But leading colleges require Latin for entrance and therefore forbidding its teaching in Black high schools means prohibiting their graduates from entry into leading colleges.

633. August, 1920, Vol. XX, No. 4. In "Opinion" (pp. 165–166), "The Task" refers to Shillady's resignation as NAACP Secretary (No. 589) and his remark that he is "less confident than heretofore" of the "speedy" overcoming of racism. Of course, Black people never expected this to be done "speedily" for the racism reflects an institutional structure to which those who rule are deeply committed. But the case of Shillady is instructive:

> We called to our aid one of the best of America's social workers. The haters of black folk beat him and maltreated him and scarred him like a dog because he tried to talk quiet reason to Texas. Here is the problem and what will white men do about it?

The Methodist Episcopal Church is congratulated for after "a fight of 25 years" it recently elected as bishops two Black men. "There are still white Christians in Zion." A paragraph on "Pettiness" derides this when it takes subjective form and divides us one from another. A brief short story recounts a conversation of white ladies in the South and ends with one of the women speaking some shocking truths. "Men of the Month" (p. 182) briefly describes "The Nine New Bishops"—two being the Black men elected by the Methodist Episcopal Church —Robert E. Jones, editor of the *Southwestern Christian Advocate* and Matthew W. Clair who for seven years was District Superintendent for the Church in Washington. Five bishops were elected at the St. Louis meeting of the A.M.E. Church: Archibald J. Carey; William A. Fountain; William D. Johnson; William T. Vernon and W. S. Brooks. The A.M.E.Z. church meeting in Knoxville elected two bishops: Thomas W. Wallace and J. W. Wood.

634. "The Political Conventions" unsigned, August, 1920, Vol. XX, No. 4, pp. 174–176. The article details events at the Democratic convention where James Cox was nominated and the Republican convention where Warren Harding was selected; the first completely ignored Black people while the second did its best to ignore Black people though it did not fully succeed. The Democratic platform said nothing and the Republican platform has "a half-hearted remark on lynching." Hence, "we are, therefore, under no obligations. We are free of entangling alliances."

635. "Wilberforce," signed, August, 1920, Vol. XX, No. 4, pp. 176–178. A history of Wilberforce University and of the Normal and Industrial Department at the university, explaining the complications arising from A.M.E. Church control of the former and the state support of the latter. The forced resignation of William A. Joiner, effective head of the department, is due to the machinations of Bishop Joshua A. Jones. Du Bois mentions a recent strike by 700 Wilberforce students and urges the modernization of the university and the continued independence of the department.

636. September , 1920, Vol. XX, No. 5. "Opinion" (pp. 213–215): "Forward" notes the repression since the war and the tendency this induces to bring on despair or cynicism. Resist this, he advises, the road to liberation lies through "grim, determined, everyday struggle." It "must be ordered and continuous and carefully considered—the campaign of an army and not the tactics of picturesque but ineffective guerrillas." Du Bois adds that we in the NAACP have an effective army and now with a new secretary, James Weldon Johnson, the battle must continue. "How Shall We Vote?" it cannot be for either the Republicans or the Democrats—both despise or ignore us. Neither the Farmer-Labor nor the Socialist Parties, which "speak out bravely in our behalf" has a chance; but we should carefully cast our ballots in the Congressional campaigns and *"vote for friends of our race and defeat our enemies."* In "The Rise of the West Indian" attention is called to the fact that while there were some 20,000 Black West Indians in the United States in 1900, there now were, probably, some 100,000. Du Bois writes that we easily forget that our 12 million Black folk are but one-half the number in the Western hemisphere. Approaches differ; in much of South America there has been amalgamation, but not in most of the West Indies. And in a place like Jamaica, rule is by a small number of whites with light-colored people as assistants and the great mass of the Blacks are heavily exploited peasants. "It is this mass of peasants, uplifted by war and migration, that is today beginning to assert itself at home and abroad, and their new cry of 'Africa for the Africans' strikes with a startling surprise upon America's darker millions." The movement is "as yet inchoate and indefinite" but its real possibilities are great; indeed, "it is not beyond possibilities that this new Ethiopia of the Isles may yet stretch out hands of helpfulness to the 12 million black men of America." In "Murder Will Out" Du Bois quotes at length from T. W. O'Connor, president of the International Longshoremen's Association, who has denounced the South as utterly reactionary and hostile to working people. Of course, says Du Bois, and the rulers of the South have used racism the better to keep labor down; "To entrenched Privilege the underpaid day's work of black and white all looks alike, and entrenched Privilege finds the South its finest, freest dwelling place."

637. "The History of Haiti," unsigned, September, 1920, Vol. XX, No. 5, pp. 216–217. This is a brief summary serving as an introduction to the report of the investigation of the United States intervention and occupation in Haiti conducted for the NAACP by James Weldon Johnson, in this issue, under the title, "The Truth About Haiti" (pp. 217–224).

638. October, 1920, Vol. XX, No. 6. In "Opinion" (pp. 261–263; 266), "Triumph" welcomes the passage of the Woman Suffrage Amendment, notes that opposition to it came from nine states—all of them Southern—and closes, "A civilization that required nineteen centuries to recognize the Rights of Women can confidently be expected some day to abolish the Color Line." "Haiti" notes that the NAACP means to help free Haiti from its "seizure by the National City Bank of Wall Street." The "impudent assertion" of President Wilson's Assistant Secretary of the Navy, Franklin Delano Roosevelt, of his part in dominating Haiti is quoted—and this line comes from Du Bois on the eve of the Presidential election—" ... may Haiti find New Freedom when the impossible Wilson and his lackeys disappear." In "Steal" Du Bois calls attention to the attacks upon the Interchurch Movement since its exposure of the nefarious conduct of the steel corporations during the 1919 strike, "Christianity again was crucified." "Persecution" decries the feud within the Black community of Washington, D.C. directed against Roscoe C. Bruce, "the colored Superintendent of Public Schools." Du Bois points out he has disagreed with Mr. Bruce quite often and has said so, but the attacks upon him in the past few months have been vindictive and despicable and all have gone unproven. Let this persecution stop and let Black Washington spend its energies in united efforts against the real foe, he advises. "In Black" Du Bois' attends a lecture in Chicago by John Haynes Holmes who had remarked on the beauty of two children, "one as fair as the dawn, the other as beautiful as the night." The audience was predominantly Black and at his remark it "guffawed in wild merriment." Why, Du Bois asks and answers, "because the world had taught them to be ashamed of their color." The shame is of the caricature and not of ourselves. "Off with these thought-chains and inchoate soul-shrinkings, and let us train ourselves to see beauty in black." From North Carolina's white press Du Bois shows the state's intention to continue the illegal disfranchisement of its Black citizens; from Texas he culls the news that all the officials involved in the assaults upon John R. Shillady have been defeated in recent elections. In "Men of the Month" (p. 286) the remarkable inventive genius of Elijah McCoy of Detroit—with over sixty inventions largely in the field of automatic lubrication of machinery—is reported, and it is noted that Mr. McCoy was the child of runaway slaves who had reached Canada. Obituaries of four men are published: Edward Seabrook of Savannah, mortician and banker, director of the Wage Earners' Savings Bank; Richard W. Thompson, editor of the *Washington Colored American* and founder of Thompson's News Bureau which sent a weekly letter to the Black press that was widely used; Charles B. Dunbar, a graduate of Lincoln University (Pennsylvania), a Senator in Liberia and her representative at the Peace Conference in 1919; J. H. Shepperd, M.D., the first Black physician in Peoria, Illinois, and one who served "both colored and white people."

639. November, 1920, Vol. XXI, No. 1. In "Opinion" (pp. 5–9), "Progress" states that during the last five years it has been "astounding"; specific advances have been made in education, but "above all comes the New Spirit: from a bewildered, almost listless sense of impotence and despair have come a new vigor, hopefulness, and feeling of power. We are no longer depending upon our friends; we are depending upon ourselves. If mobs attack us we are prepared to defend ourselves." With all this, he adds, is there yet full recognition among us of "the Industrial Revolution that is sweeping the earth?" In "Reason in School and Business" it is again affirmed. "Efficiency and devotion do not lie in color or race, and we should be the last of any men to let our resentment lead us into a silly cry of self-segregation or a scream of 'Up Black and Down White!'" It is right and proper, he writes, for us and natural, too, to favor our own people, but not to the neglect of efficiency and not in an invidious manner. A note of anguish comes through in "Pity the Poor Author" where Du Bois explains to those who ask him to give away his books, that he must pay for them. On "Suffrage" the argument used to be that Black people were not to vote because they were illiterate; now the argument is that they should not vote because they know too much! Force is the threat behind all this; what will be the result? An appeal follows for all Black men and women to be certain they register and vote. In "Men of the Month" (p. 32) Edwina Kruse, for many years Principal of Howard High School in Wilmington, Delaware, has retired; Hallie Q. Brown, a professor at Wilberforce University, was elected president of the National Association of Colored Women's Clubs. The deaths of the following persons are recorded: Mrs. John J. Castner of Belt, Montana, manager of a hotel in that frontier town for 30 years; Ethel L. Richardson, a concert pianist of promise at the age of 28; Jacob H. Schiff, the banker who put off from helping Du Bois establish a magazine in 1905 because he was told it was "radical" but since the appearance of The *Crisis*, a devoted friend of its efforts, thus giving "evidence of that great bond which exists between two oppressed races."

640. "The Social Equality of Whites and Blacks," signed, November, 1920, Vol. XXI, No. 1, pp. 16–17. The demagogy associated with this concept has been harmful for too long; "social equality means moral, mental and physical fitness to associate with one's fellowmen." The *Crisis* is for this and always has been and will be. The right of two adults to marry each other if they wish is sacred and brings no harmful results from a physical point of view. Its social difficulties are manifest and certainly if any iota of condescension is present, intermarriage is to be rejected. Moreover, there is a proper determination "to build a great black race tradition of which the Negro and the world will be as proud in the future as it has been in the ancient world." For these reasons, only, The *Crisis* "advises strongly against interracial marriage in the United States today."

641. December, 1920, Vol. XXI, No. 2. In "Opinion" (pp. 53–57), "Pontius Pilate" recounts a parable with lynching as crucifixion; "The Unreal Campaign" of 1920 was an abomination. No issues were presented; the idea of Harding's "taint" in terms of possible African ancestry, "taint, forsooth! what *could* taint America?" Many Black candidates were defeated, "but more were elected than ever before." The Farmer-Labor and the Socialist parties ran poor campaigns; Du Bois commends the "great" British Labour Party and the "right wing Socialists of Italy" both "are hewing, waveringly but stubbornly, a real path, leaving on the one side intransigent communism and on the other, organized and reactionary theft." "The A.M.E. Church" is commended for the fact that it has raised, in the preceding four years, over one million dollars for general expenses. "And Now Liberia" refers to President Wilson's plans for a loan which in fact would have made Washington absolute ruler of Liberia; this has been fought off up to now by President King. The growth of "Cooperation" as a movement leads Du Bois to ask "Shall American Negroes lag behind!" "MacSwiney" pays tribute to Terence James MacSwiney, mayor of Dublin, Sinn Fein, patriot and martyr, who died in prison, October 25, 1920, after a hunger strike lasting two months. "No cause with such martyrs," writes Du Bois, "can ever die." "Martyrs" refers to the hanging of the 13 Black soldiers on the morning of December 11, 1917, in connection with the Houston outbreak; 56 more prisoners are suffering life terms and five men have terms of 15 years; "This shameful injustice is a trumpet call to every American Negro and we should never rest until these men are pardoned and freed." "Men of the Month" (pp. 75–76) records the retirement of Rev. Doctor E. M. Brawley, pastor of a Baptist church in Durham, North Carolina, formerly president of Selma University and founder, in 1908, of Morris College in South Carolina—he is the father of the historian, Benjamin Brawley; the appointment of Emanuel M. Lazare as the first Black member of the Legislative Council in Trinidad, is reported; notice is given to the work of the musical team of J. Turner Layton and Henry S. Creamer who did the musical score for a recent Broadway production and wrote songs for such performers as Eddie Cantor, Eva Tanguay, Al Jolson, Bert Williams, Eddie Leonard and Belle Baker. J. J. Jones, Jr., has just had a volume of poetry, *The Heart of the World*, issued by Stratford Company, in Boston—"a book of elegant style, noble thought and deep sentiment." Mr. Jones, a graduate of Brown University, was sports editor and later labor editor for the Providence *News*, city editor of the Boston *Daily Advertiser*, and founder of the *Union Advocate*, "a weekly publication devoted to union news."

642. "Marcus Garvey," a two-part article, signed, December, 1920 and January, 1921, Vol. XXI, No. 2 and No. 3, pp. 58–60; 112–115. Part one summarizes the life of Garvey, from his birth in Jamaica "about 1885" [actually 1887], to date. It is factual up to the meetings held in late 1920. The movement strikes Du Bois as expressive especially of the desires of the exploited Black peasantry of the West Indies; Garvey has been charged with dishonesty, but Du Bois knows of no evidence of this and thinks he is "an honest and sincere man with a tremendous vision, great dynamic force, stubborn determination and unselfish desire to serve." He notes also what he sees as "very serious defects of temperament and training: he is dictatorial, domineering, inordinately vain and very suspicious." Du Bois records the extraordinary turnover since 1914 in officers associated with his effort. But "the great difficulty with him is that he has absolutely no business sense, no *flair* for real organization and his general objects are so shot through with bombast and exaggeration that it is difficult to pin them down for careful examination." He is, however, "an extraordinary leader of men. ... He has become to thousands of people a sort of religion. He allows and encourages all sorts of personal adulation." Du Bois gives an example of Garvey's "curious credulity and suspicions"—his statements made in March, 1919, of Du Bois' work in Paris which were completely without foundation.

643. In part II of this essay, Du Bois expresses more doubt about "Mr. Garvey's industrial and commercial enterprises" than about his character. He has "never published a complete statement" of the income and expenditures of the Negro Improvement Association nor of the Black Star Line or of any other of his enterprises. "A courteous letter of inquiry, sent him on July 22, 1920, asking for such financial data as he was willing for the public to know, remains to this day unacknowledged and unanswered." Du Bois then presents what data he has been able to discover; they all point to extreme financial problems. All this has "threatened him continually with disaster and legal complication." "On the other hand, full credit must be given Garvey for a bold effort and some success. At least he has put vessels manned and owned by black men on the seas and they have carried passengers and cargoes. The difficulty is that he does not know the shipping business, he does not understand the investment of capital, and he has few trained and staunch assistants." The "main lines" of the effort "are perfectly feasible" and not new with Garvey. "What he is trying to say and do is this: American Negroes can, by accumulating and ministering their own capital, organize industry, join the black centers of the south Atlantic by commercial enterprise and in this way ultimately redeem Africa as a fit and free home for black men. This is true." But to realize it requires time and effort of "the whole Negro race"; but Garvey has popularized it and that "is a great, human service" but his exaggerations, his talk of "conquest" of Africa, are dangerous bombast. If he changes his style and methods and "is willing to be a co-worker and not a czar," in time "some of his schemes" may be started towards accomplishment. "But unless he does these things and does them quickly he cannot escape failure"; above all, "do not let him foolishly overwhelm with bankruptcy and disaster one of the most interesting spiritual movements of the modern Negro world." "Marcus Garvey," January, 1921, Vol. XXI, No. 3, pp. 112–115.

644. January, 1921, Vol. XXI, No. 3. "Opinion," pp. 101–104 begins with the following sentence (in italics), "*It's better to be Right than White.*" The forthcoming Second Pan-African Congress, scheduled to meet in Paris in the fall of 1921, is announced. The NAACP financed the first congress and will underwrite "the call for the second"; its official connection will cease thereafter and it is hoped that the Pan-African Congress then will become "a permanent, self-supporting body." Moved by a letter from a teacher in Texas, "Thrift" calls for the exercise of this by Black people, for the accumulation of capital is a necessity since "there are white banks in Texas, in Atlanta and in black Harlem that with millions of Negro money would sooner lend to the devil than to a Negro business enterprise." Du Bois expresses doubts about the intent of the official Inter-Racial Commission appointed by the governor of Illinois to investigate the 1919 Chicago outbreak and explains why he has these misgivings. A rejection of the application for entrance of a Black youngster to a school in Massachusetts, conducted by William R. Moody, the son of the evangelist, Dwight L. Moody, on the grounds that he would deprive a "poor white boy" of an opportunity for education, while there are many "rich" schools in the South maintained for Black youngsters, results in some caustic words from Du Bois on the ingenuity of the racist mind. In "Votes for Negroes" Du Bois warns that disaster faces the nation if the present line of Bourbon intransigence continues, for the Black people will not tolerate it. In "Political Rebirth and the Office Seeker" Du Bois remarks that slowly but steadily "the American Negro is returning to political power." How shall we use this power now and in the future, he asks. Not to gain lucrative offices for a few; for we want "*not offices but deeds.*" We want the following: an end to lynching; an end to Jim-Crow transportation; an end to peonage; the enforcement of the Fourteenth Amendment; the liberation of Haiti; an effective and honest ballot throughout the United States.

645. February, 1921, Vol. XXI, No. 4. In "Opinion" pp. 149–152, the section begins with a quotation from the Irish martyr, Terence MacSwiney (No. 641), (in italics), "*Not those who inflict most, but those who suffer most are the conquerors.*" Two pages are given to arguing in favor of "Reduced Representation in Congress" in accordance with the Fourteenth Amendment for those states in the South which disfranchise citizens on the basis of race. "A Question of Facts" reiterates and brings forward further data proving racist discrimination suffered by the Black women Mary B. Talbert and Dr. Mary F. Waring—who attended the International Council of Women; this occurred at the hands of white U.S. women present. In "Phonograph Records" Du Bois details the gross racism characterizing the recording business and concludes by noting that the only solution is a Black owned effort; he is "pleased to learn that such a company is now forming."* "Men of the Month" (pp. 171–172): Charles S. Gilpin has scored a great triumph in Eugene O'Neill's "The Emperor Jones"; a sketch of his life is offered; the great success in real estate achieved by John W. Lewis of Morrissville, Pennsylvania, is reported as is the fact that he is a director of the city's Chamber of Commerce; the appointment of John H. Lewis, formerly a high school principal in Springfield, Missouri, as president of Morris Brown University in Atlanta is announced.

646. "The Election and Democracy," signed, February, 1921, Vol. XXI, No. 4, pp. 156–160. The coincidence of a census and a Presidential election in 1920 makes possible a careful analysis of the political features of the United States. These are shown—with tables and maps—to be significantly undemocratic, largely because of the disfranchisement of millions of Black people in the South and the overrepresentation of that region in Congress in violation of the Fourteenth Amendment.

647. March, 1921, Vol. XXI, No. 5. "Opinion" (pp. 197–200) begins with an appeal to make of the NAACP an organization having 250,000 members; there follows "An Open Letter to Warren Gamaliel Harding" stating that "*the first and fundamental and inescapable problem of American democracy is Justice to the American Negro*" and urging the newly elected President to press for its resolution; a two-page essay on "Pan-Africa" summarizes the history of this effort and calls attention to the forthcoming 1921 meeting; "The League of Nations" has come into being; it is a forward step and the United States cannot forever remain aloof. But the League is dominated today by "the imperial, military and industrial dictators of the world." Without a really free world of all—"black, brown, yellow and white"—no League can be effective for human advance. "Bleeding Ireland" comments on the similarity of Britain's oppression of Ireland and that of the white rulers

---

*This was the Pace Phonograph Corporation, issuing Black Swan Records. Its president was Harry H. Pace; its offices were in Harlem. Du Bois was one of those who invested in this effort. It lasted several years and released dozens of recordings but with the coming of the radio it went out of business. The first full page ad of the company appeared in The *Crisis*, May, 1921, Vol. XXII, p. 44.

towards Black people in the United States. May Irish freedom soon come. The Irish in the United States often have led in attacking Blacks but this does not make less our desire for Irish freedom; it shows how "it is the Oppressed who have continually been used to cow and kill the Oppressed in the interest of the Universal Oppressor." Du Bois congratulates "The Woman Voter" and notes that Black women despite special obstacles voted in large numbers. One Black man, James B. Dudley of the state school in Greensboro, did write an article opposing suffrage of Black women and was praised by the white press but this time (unlike fifteen years ago) he was alone in such advise, so "it is to be hoped that James B. Dudley is the last of a pitiable group." "Men of the Month" (pp. 215–217) records the death of Charles R. Douglass, son of Frederick Douglass, a veteran of the Civil War, an active member of the NAACP in Washington, formerly United States Consul in Santo Domingo and a secretary of the Board of Education in the District of Columbia; Alonzo Herndon, born a slave, is a leading businessman of Atlanta and an active participant in all efforts to advance Black people; the death of John C. Dancy, who had been elected to several offices in Edgecombe County, North Carolina, and Recorder of Deeds in Washington from 1901 to 1910; the successful work of the newly appointed principal, Leslie P. Hill, of the Cheyney Training School for Teachers in Pennsylvania, is commended; Harry S. Blackiston, now an instructor in German at West Virginia Collegiate Institute, was awarded a Ph. D. by the University of Pennsylvania in 1920 when he was 23 years old—the "youngest in the history" of that university.

647a. "A Correction" signed, March, 1921, Vol. XXI, No. 5, p. 213 a brief paragraph correcting a statement made in a previous article on Marcus Garvey (No. 642) to the effect that the "*Yarmouth*" is wooden since it is in fact a steel vessel. "We have naturally no intention to embarrass this [Black Star] corporation in its business or operations."

648. April, 1921, Vol. XXI, No. 6. In "Opinion" (pp. 245–248) the first page is signed by Robert W. Bagnall, the organizational secretary of the NAACP; "A Letter" from Du Bois to Mrs. Paul G. Darrot of the National Board of the YWCA again refers to the significance of the affront suffered by Black women at the hands of the YWCA at the international meeting in Europe (No. 602); "The Liberal South" quotes several statements and letters from so-called liberals in the South protesting the "bitterness" of Du Bois and insisting that his "dem-agogy" is harmful. Du Bois suggests a simple way to put all the demagogs out of business—let those having the power end Jim-Crow, democratize Southern politics and provide really democratic education in that area, and terminate lynching. "Men of the Month" (p. 264) include Clement T. Branch, M.D., who has been appointed to the Board of Education of Camden, New Jersey; James F. Rickards, a leading Mason, has just retired after 40 years of service with the post office in Detroit; some details of the life of Rev. William H. Brooks, pastor of St. Marks M.E. Church in New York since 1897, is recorded; C. Bethany Powell, M.D., is recently appointed to the radiotherapy department of Bellevue Hospital in New York; at the age of 24, M. Russell Nelson earned his M.D. in 1920 from the University of Pennsylvania; he has now been placed in charge of the Tuberculosis Division at Bellevue Hospital.

649. May, 1921, Vol. XXII, No. 1. In "Opinion" (pp. 5–9) "Atlantis" calls attention to the monumental work on African history and art of Leo Frobenius of Germany and that it should be translated into English.He again calls attention to the Second Pan-African Congress to be held later that year. Notes his lecture tour of 7,000 miles from Massachusetts to Minnesota, Oklahoma, Louisiana, and New York, speaking before 20,000 people. "Slavery" exists in fact—in peonage—in much of the South and the "distinguished" leaders of the South know it and profit from it. Occasionally there come rays of hope, some of which are here recorded; "Inter-Racial Comity" greets the proliferation of interracial committees in the South and sees them largely as the result of the agitation led by the NAACP, but to be effective, they must have on them upright and militant Black people and not those who fawn and they must not simply talk but must bring about actual changes. Du Bois sees some reassurance in statements on lynching from President Harding and hopes that the Black political leadership will not settle for a few offices but will insist on deeds. "The Drive" calls for 250,000 members in the NAACP. Since great advances are being made and the enemy is on the run, hence, all sorts of hare-brained schemes are now getting great public notice from the white press. "They are encouraging and advertising any and all crazy schemes, to cut and run from the hard and bloody battle here, to Africa and the South Seas." Du Bois thinks, "Twenty-five years more of the intelligent fighting that the NAACP has led will make the black man in the United States free and equal." "Anti-Lynching Legislation" records the struggle against lynching led by the NAACP and the successes hitherto scored; he asks why, therefore—except for purposes of political preferment—Perry Howard [a leading Black Republican politician] is now calling for the formation of another anti-lynching organization. "Men of the Month" (p. 22) include Malachi D. Cornish who has retired after 41 years service as a teacher and a principal of the high schools in New Jersey; Mrs. Cornish, after 28 years of similar activities, has also retired; Joseph H. E. Scotland was elected Justice of the Peace in Newark, New Jersey in 1905, and in 1920 he had been elected to a similar position, in Irvington, New Jersey, for five years. An extended notice is given to the work to date of the West African patriot, attorney, and author, Casely Hayford who, in conjunction with Dr. Akiwandi Savage of Nigeria, was a leader in creating the National Congress of British West Africa. The death of Mrs. Martha E. Tucker, for 50 years a beloved teacher and principal and social worker in Washington, D.C., is recorded.

650. June, 1921, Vol. XXII, No. 2. "Opinion" pp. 53–57 begins with "An Open Letter from the President of Liberia" signed by C. D.B. King and aimed, in fact, against the Garvey movement, although that movement is not mentioned; "The Rising Truth" calls attention to the publication by Governor Dorsey of Georgia of findings which document the rule by fraud, terror, murder, and racism in Georgia, all of which the *Crisis* has been denouncing—actually with moderation—for years. Now perhaps these findings will be believed in the nation but will they lead to real remedial action or simply more words? "Negro Art" condemns the tendency widely present among Black people to demand only glorification from their own writers; that is not art and we need not be afraid of the truth because it is only in the creative presentation of the truth that our art will flourish. "Crime" exists but not so-called Negro crime for all people have criminals and in any case what basically causes crime, "Every school boy knows: poverty, ignorance, ill-health, unjust courts, unintelligent sentences, unspeakable jails." "Men of the Month" (pp. 72; 87) Zaad Zaghlul Pasha's career as a leader in the national freedom movement of Egypt is sketched; Eugene A. Clark is the newly appointed principal of the Myrtilla Miner School in Washington, D.C.; Walthall M. Moore, the newly elected Black member of the House in Missouri, is responsible for an appropriation of $850,000 for higher education in that state —largely to transform Lincoln Institute into a university. Kathleen P. Howard has been appointed Supervisor of Music in the Black schools in Birmingham; the scientific, professional and political leadership careers of the Chicago dentist, Dr. Charles E. Bentley of Chicago, a member of the Niagara Movement and a founder of the NAACP, are sketched.

651. "Colored Teachers in Charleston Schools," unsigned, June, 1921, Vol. XXII, No. 2, pp. 57–60, tells the story of the difficult and prolonged struggle which finally has succeeded in seeing to it that the all-white teaching staff maintained by Charleston for Black schools is changed and Black teachers are to be employed (No. 583).

652. July, 1921, Vol. XXII, No. 3. In "Opinion" (pp. 201–204), "Amity" greets a convention of Black and white people held in May in Washington, D.C., calling for good will among all peoples. The record so far of "Mr. Harding" is shown to be quite inadequate. "The Libelous Film" reports the renewed showing of "The Birth of a Nation" and the success of the effort in Boston to ban it. Pickets of the Capitol Theater in New York City have been arrested and later insulted by the judge who found them guilty. The case is on appeal; Du Bois prints the names of "these public servants": Mrs. Helen Curtis, Mrs. Laura J. Rollock, Miss Katherine Johnson, Llewelyn Rollock, E. Franklin Frazier. "The Negro and Radical Thought" publishes a letter to Du Bois from Claude McKay who questions why he seems to neglect or sneer at the Russian Revolution and why he pays insufficient attention to the program of socialism and the role of the working class. Du Bois replies by asserting that he does not wish to sneer at the Russian Revolution but "Russia is incredibly vast," and while he thinks there is much good in Russia, he also has been "hearing of other things which frighten us." He was delighted with a recent declaration by the Third International (quoted at some length) which denounced the Second International for, in fact, being concerned only with white people and declaring the need for the unity of working people of all colors. Du Bois thinks of himself as a socialist, he declares, but he rejects German state socialism and the "dictatorship of the proletariat," and "he is not prepared to dogmatize with Marx or Lenin." He is worried about whether or not the working class can overcome its racism; however, he agrees that one must be aware of "the great programs of social reform" that are being put forward. He adds that there is an immediate program at the NAACP so we must not give this up in order to go to Africa or to join a revolution "which we do not at present understand." At the same time, "as Mr. McKay says, it would be just as foolish for us to sneer or even seem to sneer at the blood-entwined writhing of hundreds of millions of our whiter human brothers."

653. "The Second Pan-African Congress," unsigned, July, 1921, Vol. XXII, No. 3, pp. 119–120. It includes a brief factual report of its background, an appeal for support, and some idea of its program.

654. August, 1921, Vol. XXII, No. 4. In "Opinion" (pp. 149–152) "Pan-Africa" is another brief appeal for support; "A Telegram" includes a message to President Harding from a Young People's Conference under the auspices of the Fellowship of Reconciliation calling for an end to United States occupation of Haiti; "Lynchings and Mobs" points to the complicity of police and courts in the system of terrorization; "Of Problems" declares that only Black people are "accused" of wanting social equality; only they should give up the vote; only they should not exercise the right of self-defense; only they should be meek and wait—"for all others: Equality, Votes, Fight for Right! Such is the Negro Problem." "Mixed Schools" tells of the rising demand in Indianapolis for Jim-Crowing the public schools and notes that the separation of people can only mean an end to democracy. "The Class Struggle" reiterates the argument offered to Claude McKay (see No. 652) adding two thoughts: 1) that class divisions have just begun among Black people so we have no significant class divisions as yet; 2) we need capital accumulation to effectively fight racism as we find it in the U.S. in the present period, but we must try to guide such accumulation along cooperative lines and away from those paths trod by the white world. "Men of the Month" (p. 166) include William L. Houston, an attorney in Washington, D.C., recently appointed to the Board of Education; it is noted that "a son, Charles H. Houston, is a student of law at Harvard." George W. Carver, born a slave, educated at Iowa State College, has been at Tuskegee Institute for 21 years and has made significant scientific discoveries. The death of Marietta L. Chiles, for 35 years a teacher in Richmond, Virginia, is recorded. Mr. and Mrs. Edgar R. Beckley have celebrated their 62nd wedding anniversary; Mr. Beckley was General Grant's orderly during the Civil War and later served for 55 years in various capacities for the United States government.

655. "Hopkinsville, Chicago and Idlewild", signed, August, 1921, Vol. XXII, No. 4, pp. 158–160. The first and last cities are all-Black communities and the second "scares me" but the Black people are militant and moving ahead. The descriptions of the all-Black communities are especially filled with Du Bois' sense of love for his people; though the form is prose, the content is really poetry.

656. September, 1921, Vol. XXII, No. 5. In "Opinion" (197–201), "Of Boards" tells of the presentation of gifts to Mary White Ovington and James Weldon Johnson by branches of the NAACP. Special tribute is paid to Miss Ovington who, though white, works with a sense of equality and inspires respect and cordiality from her Black co-workers, and who, though a woman, demands and gets equality from men. Mr. Johnson's work in Haiti "stands as one of the greatest single achievements done in colored America." "About Pugilists" notes the release of the former heavyweight champion, Jack Johnson from Leavenworth. He was jailed on a technicality because he was Black and now the newspapers are denouncing him while they are praising Jack Dempsey. Why—except because of color? "The Spread of Socialism" is what is really occurring in the world, while the daily press falsely gives the opposite impression. Insofar as socialism means the democratization of industry, it must come, else civilization will fail. An attack is launched against the railroad unions for their despicable policy of barring Italians, Jews, and Black workers. "Of Cold Feet" Du Bois chides big talkers and small doers, for instance, the falling away when people were asked to picket "Birth of a Nation." In "Girls," at a conference under the YWCA auspices in Germantown, Pennsylvania, Du Bois was happy to see so many Black youngsters, not only because of their loveliness but also because they were noisy, happy, and unfettered. So often Black girls, especially in the Southern schools, are made to be so prim and proper that it is quite unnatural. There are growing "Investments" by Black people with capital, often in efforts helpful to all but with this comes a growing army of swindlers so Du Bois offers some principles to watch for in investing one's money.* "Men of the Month" (p. 216) include Charles H. Dodge's career as librarian in charge of the United States Circuit Court of Appeals library in St. Louis; the death of Christopher J. Perry, founder and editor for 36 years of the *Philadelphia Tribune*, is reported; Mrs. Elizabeth Mitchell, a musician, has pioneered in travelogue moving pictures with lectures of Europe and Africa; the retirement of William H. Crogman after 45 years as professor of Latin and Greek and as president of Clark University in Atlanta is observed. He is, writes Du Bois, "one of the finest specimens of upright and staunch Negro manhood."

657. October, 1921, Vol. XXII, No. 6. "Opinion" (pp. 245–248) returns to "Socialism and the Negro" by way of printing long extracts from a

---

*It may be appropriate to add that Du Bois' own investments at various times—in publishing, in recording, in modest real-estate efforts—all turned out rather badly although he took the above cited rules seriously.

letter to him by John H. Owens of Washington, arguing for the position taken by Claude McKay and against that offered by Du Bois. Du Bois repeats that he finds much to agree with in the argument of Mr. Owens; he adds that while white workers in imperialist powers are not as guilty as those who rule such nations, they "cannot escape responsibility" altogether because they are part of a system of "subjugation of over half the world." "Haiti" reports that a Senate Committee is to investigate conditions there; Du Bois urges his readers to write to the members, who are named. "Tulsa" hails the Blacks in that city for their armed resistance against the mobs that finally leveled the ghetto (with the aid of air bombings!) and hails their efforts to rebuild their part of the city. "The Young Idea" reports a fantastically falsified report about the conditions in the South in a textbook, "A Short Course in American Civics" which is widely used. Du Bois writes the author and points out the error and is happy to state that the author has written him, agrees, apologizes, and affirms that future editions will be changed. "The Single Tax" summarizes Henry George's *Progress and Poverty*, suggests it contains much truth, and urges that it be read among Black people. A short note on the work of Alexandre Dumas appears, remarking on his "French and Negro blood." "Men of the Month" (pp. 264–266) includes the late James D. Carr, for 16 years Assistant Corporation Counsel of the City of New York, and a graduate of Rutgers and Columbia Law School; the late John Brown of Montgomery, Alabama, who started in 1855 with nothing, and had built up a major fruit-farming and trucking business in his native city prior to his death; H. Ray Wooten has been appointed principal of the Howard High School in Wilmington, Delaware; Rev. Robert F. Wheeler, a Congregational preacher who commenced in 1878 and continued his services in many states for over 40 years, has died; Dorothy Canfield Fisher, a Ph. D. from Columbia, is known to *Crisis* readers for a long story in the issues of April and May, 1920; she is the author of well-known novels (*The Bent Twig, The Brimming Cup*) and her writing shows an "inflexible determination not to leave the Negro as he is out of her pictures of American life"; Mrs. Charlotte Hawkins Brown, founder and principal of the Palmer Memorial Institute in North Carolina, was recently appointed as "the first colored member of the National Board of the Young Women's Christian Association."

658. "Thomas Jesse Jones," signed, October, 1921, Vol. XXII, No. 6, pp. 252–256. Du Bois earlier had reviewed a two-volume work on *Negro Education* by Jones (No. 597). In this essay Du Bois traces the career of this white man who had been a teacher at Hampton, worked for the United States Census Bureau, and at present is the Director of the Phelps-Stokes Fund. In case after case—the YWCA, the YMCA, missionary work in Africa, questions of Afro-American education —Mr. Jones has become the "expert" and the Spokesman for Black people as selected by other white people. His actions have been hostile to our interests, but in any case, the time is past when a leader selected by white people—and a white person, at that—was to be accepted as the spokesman for Black America, for "we propose to speak for ourselves and to be represented by spokesmen whom we elect."

659. November, 1921, Vol. XXIII, No. 1. "Opinion" (pp. 5–11) begins with the full text of "To the World," the Manifesto of the Second Pan-African Congress (No. 197); "Robert T. Kerlin" pays tribute to the white Southern professor of English at Virginia Military Institute who in 1919 had published The *Voice of the Negro* and later had published a pamphlet on *Contemporary Negro Poetry*. Mr. Kerlin could not remain silent in face of the projected executions of the Black men who had resisted peonage in Arkansas and addressed an open letter to Governor McRae of that State appealing for justice. As a result he has been dismissed by the trustees of Virginia Military Institute removing "from its force a man displaying the finest courage the Institute is ever likely to see." Without self-criticism neither a person nor an area can progress; forcing out Kerlin is an action that helps explain the backwardness of the South. The *World* newspaper in New York is congratulated for its exposure of the racket known as the "Ku Klux Klan," an exposure in which the NAACP participated. Somewhat prematurely Du Bois suggests that as a result "their power is ended." Black people are participating in the planning and presentation of a pageant, "America's Making" under the supervision of the State Board of Education of New York; it is to be presented in October and November and Black people are represented by James Weldon Johnson and Eugene K. Jones. "Men of the Month" (pp. 26–28) includes Charles F. M. Browne, a Washington attorney, who earlier had served the British government for 33 years; he has been awarded the Order of the British Empire—the first Black man so honored; Samuel J. Ross, M.D., was president of the College of West Africa in Liberia until his recent death; Mrs. Musette B. Gregory, a prominent social worker and NAACP leader in New York and New Jersey, has died; Aurelio E. Bermudez has been appointed Captain of the Investigation Department of the Republic of Panama; David J.

Phillips, M.D., has had a distinguished scientific career in England, did similar useful work when he lived in Philadelphia, and recently in his native Jamaica was elected to the City Council of Kingston; four Black physicians have their careers briefly sketched. They are: Dr. Darrington Weaver of St. Louis; Dr. Harvey A. Murray, on the Board of Health in Wilmington, Delaware; Dr. T. E. Stevens, recently elected to Cleveland's Board of Aldermen; Dr. D. B. Johnson, a founder of a hospital in his native Petersburg, Virginia, and now on the staff of the Harlem Hospital.

660. "Manifesto to the League of Nations," signed (Geneva, September 15, 1921), November, 1921, Vol. XXIII, No. 1, p. 18. As Secretary of the Second Pan-African Congress, Du Bois submits to the League "three earnest requests": 1) that the needs of Black workers be made the concern of a special section of the International Bureau of Labor; 2) that a Black person be appointed a member of the Mandates Commission; 3) that the League itself "take a firm stand on the absolute equality of races and that it suggest to the Colonial powers connected with the League of Nations the forming of an International Institute for the Study of the Negro Problems, and for the Evolution and Protection of the Negro Race." (A long letter of appreciation for this message from Albert Thomas, the Director of the Bureau of Labor, is printed in the *Crisis*, December, 1921, Vol. XXIII, pp. 69–70.)

661. December, 1921, Vol. XXIII, No. 2. "Opinion" (pp. 53–59): "President Harding and Social Equality" refers to a speech by the President at Birmingham containing these sentences: "racial amalgamation there cannot be" and "men of both races may well stand uncompromisingly against every suggestion of Social Equality." This is denounced as insulting, reflecting ignorance and racism, denying reality, and attempting to perpetuate the domination of the colored world by the white. Added here is the exposure of President Harding's contradiction where in one part of his speech he denounces the playing of one group against another and seeks no such separation while in another part of the speech he urges that the Black people have "a pride of race" out of which "will come natural segregations." No white man need teach us what is called "pride of race" for "our pride is our business and not theirs." It is a thing they do not understand adds Du Bois, and had better not invoke, "for the day that Black men love Black men simply because they are Black, is the day they will hate White men simply because they are White. And then, God help us all!" There follow two pieces of prose poetry: a hymn to the beauty of Mont Blanc in Switzerland and another Christmas parable, "The Sermon in the Cradle." "Men of the Month" (pp. 77–78) include the late Robert A. Caldwell, born a slave in Georgia, rose to prominence as a farmer in Texas and a power in Republican politics in that State; Henry M. Minton, M.D., recently made Superintendent of Mercy Hospital in Philadelphia; a Civil War veteran, Loyal F. Friman of Springfield, Massachusetts, has died; Cal F. Johnson, a successful businessman and active member of the NAACP in Knoxville, Tennessee, has just seen a park and playground named after him by the City Commission; the late Gustavus W. Wickliffe was the first Black man to practice as an attorney in California; Frank A. Byron, an attorney, is the first Black man to be appointed clerk of the Committee on Naval Affairs of the House of Representatives in Washington.

662. January, 1922, Vol. XXIII, No. 3. In "Opinion" (pp. 103–107), "The World and Us" treats the economic depression and the unemployment especially afflicting Black people and the relationship thereto of wars and armaments, emphasizing the central importance of racism to both. It notes the mounting strikes among workers and remarks, "... the union organization is still here and the colored laborer must learn to use it." On "Ireland and India" Du Bois wishes well to the liberation struggles in both lands; he adds, "The real question of Ireland today is how much of the island is going to be allowed to govern itself and how much of it the industrial interests of Ulster are going to be able to keep as part of England, and as a center of English power." A paragraph expresses Du Bois' wonder that some method might not be found by the Black people to meet "distinguished" visitors from abroad and bring them into contact with the Black community; an appeal is made for fuller support and the rapid growth of the NAACP; "The Harding Political Plan" of a lily-white Republican Party is denounced and again the Black people are called upon for political alertness and independence; a letter from "Mr. [Perry] Howard" is partially quoted and Du Bois, in effect, admits error in underestimating the significance of his political appointment in Washington but he insists that Mr. Howard should do the work of his office rather than also serving as a messenger for the Republican National Committee; the developing national recognition of "Negro Art" is noted with pride; and, finally, it is emphasized that despite some failures, "Cooperation" in economic affairs remains a promising field for the Afro-American people. (With this issue Du Bois suspends his "Men of the Month" feature; its content is incorporated in "The Horizon Department" conducted by Madeline G. Allison.)

663. February, 1922, Vol. XXIII, No. 4. In "Opinion" (pp. 151–155), "The World and Us" sees movements elsewhere for enhanced land distribution but the opposite is true in the United States, which in this and much else, bids "fair to lead the world—backwards." The Disarmament Conference accomplished little and the color line—especially towards China—has been tightened; Ireland probably should accept half a loaf but it must keep before its eyes, the real goal, namely, entire unity; two great men have been in the news—Eugene V. Debs, "free of chains which should never have bound him" and Abdul Baha, of the antiracist Bahia movement has died and is free of Life. A debit and credit listing for 1921 is offered. A demand for the passage of the Dyer Anti-Lynching Bill is made; either lynching will be stopped or it will "end these United States." "Vicious Provisions of a Great Bill" calls attention to the Smith-Towner Education Bill [actually the Sterling-Towner Bill] in Congress which would have the federal government, at last, appropriate money to help end illiteracy but would have the money appropriated to the states and so would perpetuate racial injustice. In "Politics and Power" the connection between the two is documented through citations from a letter which S. D. Redmond of Jackson, Mississippi, sent to the Southern press but which was not printed. In "Africa for Africans" Du Bois denounces lies about his attitude towards the question put in Associated Press despatches from Paris and sets the record straight; he reiterates that Africa should be for Africans and by Africans and that migration to Africa by Black people would have to be selective as to where one goes—and would require considerable sacrifice and hard work, even if one goes to places that would more or less welcome them. When he says Africa for Africans, he does not mean "that Africa should be administered by West Indians or American Negroes." A very moving tribute is paid to his friend the late Col. Charles Young, "one of the few men I know who literally turned the other cheek with Jesus Christ." He was in fact killed by the army which feared him and sent him back to Liberia to die.

664. "The Link Between," unsigned, February, 1922, Vol. XXIII, No. 4, pp. 170–171, is a tribute to the pioneering work of compiling and annotating the music of the American Indian, Afro-American, and African people done by the late Natalie Curtis Burlin, a white woman whose creative work "gives us hope" in the eventual building of a humane society.

665. March, 1922, Vol. XXIII, No. 5. "Opinion" (pp. 199–202) begins with the story of a 19-year-old lad named "Boddy" convicted of murder in New York City and sentenced to die. Du Bois writes that the fault is hardly his because of the ghetto in which he was raised, because of the racist violence that fills the land, and because of the brutality of the police. An article by Norman Angell in the *Freeman* expresses horror at French indifference to color; the horror in all its impact appears in Mr. Angell's special reaction to sexual relations between white and Black in France. Du Bois writes, "To the ordinary American or Englishmen, we have always realized, the race question is at bottom simply a matter of the ownership of women; white men want the right to own and use all women, colored and white, and they resent any intrusion of colored men into this domain." (see No. 425). In "Homicides" Du Bois notes repeated statements and articles—one by Frederick L. Hoffman, for example—affirming that where Black people are numerous the homicide rate is high. The inference is that Black people tend to be murderers, but actually the figures are derived from the fact that it is Black people who are murdered in large numbers by white people! A letter from Du Bois to Hoffman confirms this; yet Hoffman allows his statement with its vicious ambiguity to go out to the world. "The Woman's National Foundation" is really an exercise in vanity; it is of some interest that while it bans Black women it does not have the courage to say this openly, which may reflect ironically the progress of our efforts.

666. "Gandhi and India," unsigned, March, 1922, Vol. XXIII, No. 5, pp. 203–207. A fairly full account of the career of Gandhi from England and South Africa to his leadership in the national liberation movement of India: " ... a man who from sheer impeccability of character, and extraordinary personality, and from loftiness and originality of doctrine and ideas, takes rank at once among the great men of the world. ... "

667. "The Ruling Passion," unsigned, March, 1922, Vol. XXIII, No. 6, pp. 224–225. Subtitled "An Estimate of Joseph C. Price" (1854–1893), who was born a slave, and was founder, when 28 years old, of Livingstone College in Salisbury, North Carolina, and for 25 years was its head and inspiration. A militant leader during his lifetime and one who rejected many "important" positions to build this school and build it he did. His great characteristic was "the quality of grit." The biography is of interest in itself and has distinct autobiographical overtones—possibly not fully known to the author himself.

668. April, 1922, Vol. XXIII, No. 6. In "Opinion" (pp. 247–252), "The

World and Us" begins with the estimate that at the recent Washington Naval Conference, Japan was the victor and that Japan and China will yet unite and "present an unbroken front to the aggressions of the whites." Advances towards freedom and autonomy of the dark colonies of Britain are going forward, against the will of the British rulers, but going forward nevertheless. The capitalists in the United States seek to put the full burden of the depression upon the working class; that class, because of the AFL leadership, is not able to respond with sufficient vigor and organization. "Russia is the most amazing and most hopeful phenomenon of the post-war period." Despite all that has been done to thwart her, she goes on and develops her effort at "industrial reconstruction." In Rome sits a new Pope—Piux XI—and "the question that concerns us is whether or not he is going to continue catering the Holy See to the wealth of American Catholics; will he continue to allow the American hierarchy, despite some of its nobler souls, to refuse to train and ordain Negro priests?" "The Dyer Bill" against lynching can be passed if the Republican Party really wants it to pass; if it doesn't, let Black voters respond accordingly. Again an attack upon "The Sterling-Towner Bill" with a correction of the error in naming it in the February, 1922 issue of the *Crisis*; the death of the great Black teacher of Massachusetts, Maria Baldwin—whom Du Bois first met in 1885—is recorded. "The Case of Samuel Moore" is brought into prominence by Eugene V. Debs and Martha Gruening and concerns a Black prisoner who in his 48 years has spent only eleven years out of prison and this prison sentence was imposed for the unintentional killing of a man when he was 17 years old, (the man was in the process of attacking him with a shovel). He has been treated with great cruelty in prison, parole has been repeatedly denied while "President Harding and Attorney General Daugherty are playing golf in Florida." "The Spanish Fandango" is a short story which describes a wonderful evening of fellowship with Charles Dabney and his stories and his banjo and Charles Gilpin and *his* stories and ends with a train ride where Du Bois has triumphantly overcome Jim Crow and "The thoughtful porter brought me a pillow." "Show Us, Missouri" hails the accomplishment of the Black people in that state in forcing the legislature to move towards the creation of a real state university for Black youngsters. God speed in your work and "you have the pick of a black nation to choose from" for your faculty. In "Again, Africa" Du Bois argues against the position of the Garvey movement although he mentions no names; we have no armies and navies but we have justice on our side and a large part of world public opinion. We must continue to organize ourselves, to demand advances in the rights of Africans, to meet periodically for counsel; "to promote industry, commerce and credit among black groups" but this "does not mean yelling and lying and ranting about gigantic projects that never existed." In "The Demagog" Du Bois warns that such personalities will increase; that they feed on class distinctions and gulfs separating us. We must attain and maintain "a feeling of group responsibility" else these demagogs "will be doubly strong because they can count on the applause and backing of the sinister whites."

669. "The Negro Bank," unsigned, April, 1922, Vol. XXIII, No. 6, pp. 253–254. A brief history is followed by data concerning 49 banks owned by and run by Black people; Du Bois thinks there are a total of perhaps 60 in the country.

670. May, 1922, Vol. XXIV, No. 1. In "Opinion" (pp. 7–11), "The World and Us" describes a strike in South Africa which was unsuccessful because Blacks are kept out of unions; Gandhi is in prison and English Christianity is in shame; a King has been crowned in Egypt but the ruler remains Britain; in the Near East trouble brews, and "beneath lie the miserable millions of the Balkans, crushed and raped for a thousand years"; Du Bois feels a bonus for soldiers robs Peter to pay Paul, but of course the politicians promise anything when they feel it is helpful; Black members of the Methodist church are opposing a change in its code that rules out dancing and theater-going as wrong, and that is nonsense. Again, Du Bois takes up "Social Equality", "of course, we want social equality and we know that we will never be real men until we get it." In "Art for Nothing" Du Bois again protests against the practice of refusing to pay or paying very poorly Black artists, writers, lecturers, and musicians. This kills creativity. "Publicity" is a call for such in terms of income and especially corporate income; "The Negro Farmer" offers data culled from the latest reports of the Census Bureau and notes the South's desire "to keep Negro farmers ignorant, to hold them in peonage, and to refuse them their share of Federal funds." In "Kicking Us Out" Du Bois repeats the story of the Black people's political efforts and records the result: neither of the major Parties wants us. Very well, those Parties are also rejecting just social demands on all fronts and so a movement towards a new, radical, and independent politics is growing. We must be part of it, "may God put us down as asses if ever again we are found putting our trust in either the Republican or the Democratic Parties."

671. "Some Fraternal Orders," unsigned, May, 1922, Vol. XXIV, No. 1, pp. 20–21. "Next to the church among us come the secret and fraternal orders." A brief history of these orders is given and some accounting of their present condition.

672. June, 1922, Vol. XXIV, No. 2. In "Opinion" (pp. 55–60), "The World and Us"tells of: a call for the liberation of Haiti and of the Philippines, Hawaii, and Puerto Rico. The assaults upon Britain from Ireland, India and Egypt, mount. The great coal and iron and steel monopolies are raping West Virginia and only its miners are protesting and "we still send missionaries to China!" China is writhing in pain "seeking to give birth to a great modern free state ... and yet where there is Pain there is Life." The Russians handled themselves very well at the Genoa Conference; they "may be dreamers, but they are not fools." We are a poor people and no doubt many among us still require charity but is it really charity, in terms of what has been taken from us in 300 years of slavery and 50 years of serfdom? It might be wise for White America if they considered some scheme to pay all this back. "The Taboo of Methuselah" observes that the commercial press has carefully refrained from even reporting that in one act of George Bernard Shaw's play an England in 2170 A.D. is depicted ruled by Chinese and Black people. Similarly, Mary Hoyt Wiborg's "great play 'Taboo'" also spoke to deaf hearts in New York because of its theme and because its cast was Black and white. Du Bois makes an appeal for the establishment of "An Institute of Negro Literature and Art" and describes some of its possible functions. "Sidney" refers to Sidney De La Rue, a white man to whom a minor political debt was owed but who seemed unusually incompetent—he's been assigned to Liberia, of course! Next November 33 Senators are to be elected; nail them to the one issue of lynching and vote accordingly. "Haiti" is still an island ruled by the United States but a renewed campaign gives some hope of justice and liberation soon; "Self-Help" states that Jews in the United States had been asked to raise $14,000,000 to help starving co-religionists in Europe. They raised $18,000,000 in seven months and most of it in cash and much of it coming from the poor and the workers among the Jews. "This is self-help. This is a lesson and a vivid lesson to black folk."

673. July, 1922, Vol. XXIV, No. 3. In "Opinion" (pp. 103–107), "The World and Us" notes that a high tariff raises prices and workers pay for it and that is why bosses favor it; a paragraph in praise of Lincoln as a big man with many faults and many inconsistencies, but brave and one who pushed humanity forward; both Virginia and Mississippi are analyzed in terms of their expenditure of funds for education and the analysis shows that the Sterling-Towner Bill must not be passed; Hampton Institute is becoming a college; this is shown in its latest catalogue. Along with Lincoln University (Pennsylvania), she must do one more thing "and that is put colored teachers and officers in real places of power and influence upon her faculty." This, because, "the time has gone when the colored people of the United States are going to have the world interpreted to them solely by white people ... they want men and women of the best trained mind and heart to guide them, and in the choosing of these leaders they will brook no color line." The purposes and requirements for a "Rhodes Scholarship" are detailed. Under "Haiti" and "The Army" Du Bois records the mimicking of Democratic Party practices by the Harding Administration. In "Evil" Du Bois calls attention to the suffering and hunger and injustice afflicting peoples other than Black throughout the world and not least in the United States; he mentions in particular the case of Sacco and Vanzetti. In "First Blood" Du Bois refers to the effective use by Black voters of their power in several recent elections. In "Ten Phrases" he cites those which constitute all the wisdom needed especially by "white students in Southern colleges" commencing with "The Southerner is the Negro's Best Friend" and concluding with "Lynching is the defense of Southern womanhood."

674. August, 1922, Vol. XXIV, No. 4. In "Opinion" (pp. 151–155), the census figures declare that illiteracy among Black people fell from 33% in 1910 to 26% in 1920 but we know that census figures on illiteracy "are not worth the paper upon which they are written." "The United States is one of the most ignorant of modern civilized countries." Data on the growth of "Higher Training of Negroes" are offered. There also has been a general growth in higher education and Du Bois notes a fear that "we are over-educating 'the masses' "—especially workers, Jews, and Black people. Du Bois denounces the rising anti-Semitism in the United States, with Harvard, Yale, and Columbia universities taking the lead, apparently afraid of the brains and the keen social consciousness that so often—for good historical reasons—mark the best among the Jews. We Blacks have long known this and as we advance there seems to develop a partnership between elements in North and South to fasten our chains. New England means to maintain an Anglo-Saxon domination in the United States and such forces fight against democracy in general and people like Blacks and Jews in particular. But "the great alliance then between the darker people the world over, between disadvantaged groups like the Irish and the Jew and between the working classes everywhere is the one alliance that is going to keep down privilege as represented by New England and old England." And even in "New England" there always appear people like Roger Williams, William Lloyd Garrison, Wendell Phillips, Moorfield Storey. "New England has learned, albeit hardly, to let these prophets and rebels speak. And this is the glory and hope of New England and of America."

675. September, 1922, Vol. XXIV, No. 5. In "Opinion" (pp. 199–202) there is again a call for the passage of the Dyer anti-lynching bill; a note on Lincoln whose imperfections when mentioned earlier troubled readers, but they were part of his greatness; praise is given to the fine musical, "Shuffle Along," with the Black comedian team of Miller and Lyles, and music and lyrics by Sissle and Blake. It was a great success in New York but the monopolists of the stage refuse to allow it to be booked elsewhere. Again, continued United States domination of Santo Domingo and Haiti is denounced.

676. "The Black Star Line," signed; September, 1922, Vol. XXIV, No. 5, pp. 210–214. This was "the main economic venture of Marcus Garvey" and its creation was "a brilliant suggestion and Garvey's only original contribution to the race problem."* Though he now blames "jealous" opponents, spies from the NAACP, the work of "Bolsheviks" and dishonest associates, the responsibility for the failure of the Black Star Line is basically Garvey's as he was in charge. The essay consists largely of quotations from Garvey's newspaper, the *Negro World*, and testimony at several court hearings.

*Du Bois may have forgotten that he projected something along these lines 6 years before (No. 532).

677. October, 1922, Vol. XXIV, No. 6. In "Opinion," (pp. 247–253) there is an extended essay accompanying "The Children's Number" of the magazine, on marriage, birth, infancy, childhood, and education. It concludes: "But with children brought with thought and foresight into intelligent family circles and trained by parents, teachers, friends and society, we have Eternal Progress and Eternal Life. Against these, no barriers stand; to them no Problem is insoluble."

678. November, 1922, Vol. XXV, No. 1. In "Opinion" (pp. 7–11). "Truth and Beauty" Du Bois notes that the *Crisis* commenced in November, 1910. It has tried to adhere to truth and will do so in the future; it wishes, however, in particular to bring forward beauty for "the great mission of the Negro to America and the modern world is the development of Art and the appreciation of the Beautiful." Let not our souls be stifled by an "over-emphasis to ethics to meet the Puritans round about" because we must affirm ourselves—"our song ... our love of life, the wild and beautiful desire of our women and men for each other. ... " Support is urged for the noble renewed crusade against lynching under the leadership of Mrs. Mary B. Talbert. With the coming to the fore of the Black pugilist, Siki, Du Bois says he expects that prize fighting will again fall into disrepute. Du Bois details the court cases involving 12 remaining defendants from the 1919 Elaine, Arkansas, "conspiracy" and asks for continued financial support. A subscription from the KKK has been received; hence, Du Bois sends that organization a message. It is ridiculous; it is cowardly; it is powerful; and the United States must destroy it or its existence as a Republic is over.

679. "Leroy Bundy", signed, November, 1922, Vol. XXV, No. 1, pp. 16–21. In August, 1922, Dr. Bundy was made a "Knight Commander of the Distinguished Service Order of Ethiopia" by Marcus Garvey and also appointed his "First Assistant." Upon announcing this, the *Negro World*, lauded Dr. Bundy "of East St. Louis riot fame" and accused the NAACP of dishonesty in the use of $50,000 allegedly collected in his defense. Du Bois replies to the attack with the details of Dr. Bundy's betrayal of the defense during the East St. Louis cases; his "confession," without the knowledge of the NAACP attorneys, that he was part of the corrupt political gang running East St. Louis, and of his effort to turn his "defense" into a personal racket for the raising of money. All moneys collected for the defendants in the case were carefully accounted for in audited records and Du Bois prints them. Since Dr. Bundy now feels it proper to attack us, concludes Du Bois, and only for this reason, do "we publish the facts."*

680. December, 1922, Vol. XXV, No. 2. In "Opinion" (pp. 55–57), "slowly, remorselessly, the Federal Administration, representing and backed by huge financial interests, is crushing Haiti." Under "The Problem of Sacrifice" is told the story of the death, at the age of 40, of Rufus Meroney, "YMCA secretary for the colored Brooklyn, New York branch." He devoted himself without restraint to the welfare of

---

*In a section called "The Looking Glass," in this issue (pp. 34–35), there is additional material from the court testimony of Marcus Garvey of the bankrupt condition of his enterprises and his distortion of the news concerning the activities in Europe. Much of the material in the section was culled by Du Bois and many of its comments came from him.

"colored boys and young men" and drove himself to an early grave. And how he was insulted in this land! But "if a man has a life, who shall call him crazy if he spend it in a decade rather than dribble it to a century?"

681. "The Great Surgeon," unsigned December, 1922, Vol. XXV, No. 2, pp. 58–60. A Christmas fable of the Jewish Surgeon and the Rich Patient.

682. January, 1923, Vol. XXV, No. 3. In "Opinion" (pp. 103–107), much of the editorial is devoted to the nearly successful effort to gain passage of the Dyer Anti-Lynching Bill which actually passed the House of Representatives only to be filibustered to death—or lynched —in the Senate by Bourbons with the covert blessing of powerful Republicans. But it does show the possibilities of "the power of the black man in America when he learns the mere rudiments of using it" for a historic victory was almost achieved. And this was achieved despite the traitors among us, like "Perry Howard, the lickspittle politician." And we Black people are not the only ones to whom the two major parties spell death. "The trend toward a Third Party is irresistible. It may take years but it must come. The fight against lynching is just begun." We must continue and intensify the efforts —not least the widest kind of an advertising campaign to reach the white population by the tens of millions.

683. "The U. N. I. A.," signed, January, 1923, Vol. XXV, No. 3, (pp. 120–122). This article presents "the facts concerning the membership and finances of the Universal Negro Improvement Association under the leadership of Marcus Garvey" insofar as Du Bois has been able to obtain them. The conclusion is "that the U.N.I.A. has at present less than 18,000 active members."

684. February, 1923, Vol. XXV, No. 4. In "Opinion" (pp. 151–154), the debit and credit for 1922 is discussed. There is an explanation and defense of the anti-lynching advertisements placed in various leading white newspapers throughout the country; they reached some five million readers and were reproduced throughout Europe. A letter from Dantes Bellegarde, Haitian Minister to France and a Member of the Assembly of the League of Nations, is published showing "at last the truth" concerning baseless claims for credit made by the U.N.I.A. as to certain developments at the League of Nations. "The West Indies" affirms that "England has never given political freedom to any but white men." Agitation in the West Indies, under the leaderhip of T.

Albert Marryshow of Grenada, has recently forced some slight steps towards at least England's thinking of the right of West Indians to have their own government. A debate proposal by Perry Howard to James Weldon Johnson and Du Bois is declined and the refusal is explained for "we are perfectly willing to leave the recital of Mr. Howard's eminent services to his race and country to the gentleman himself, unhampered by any pessimistic remarks of our own."

685. March, 1923, Vol. XXV, No. 5. In "Opinion" (pp. 199–203) there is a call on the "brothers and sisters" to "sit tight." The white world has gone crazy and in a fight for coal and steel in the Ruhr and oil in the Middle East they are displaying their madness. "Evil dies because it is Death. Right triumphs in the end because it is Life." "Harvard" tells of the university's shame in having sought to Jim Crow a Black student, the son of Roscoe C. Bruce. "Imagine, my masters, six decades after emancipation, a slave's grandson teaching the ABC of democracy to the Puritan head of Harvard!" A report is made of some progress in the fight to liberate "The Houston Martyrs." It is reported that the effort begun in 1921 by the Pan-African congress to have a special commission established by the International Bureau of Labor to concern itself with questions of Black workers in Africa has borne fruit and an official with this duty is to be appointed. "Correspondence" is published on the question of "social equality"—again—between Du Bois and a person from Waco, Texas. Du Bois notes that his reply to the Texan evoked a front-page editorial in a Dallas newspaper, demanding that Du Bois, "the arrogant ebony-head, thick-lipped, kinky-haired Negro 'educator' must be put in his place and made to stay there." Du Bois has attended a dance and social evening of many Black people; he knows he "could not find in all the world a group of human beings more beautiful, more filled with the joy of living and sweetness of spirit" than that group. He concludes, "The exasperating thought is how beautiful and interesting most human beings could be if some fools like [Lothrop] Stoddard and Madison Grant did not spend their lives hindering and hating them, and other selfish scoundrels not steal more food and clothes than they can use, and so upturn the balance of human satisfaction."

686. "The Negro and the Northern Public Schools," unsigned, a two-part article March and April, 1923, Vol. XXV, No. 5 and No. 6, pp. 205–208; 262–265. In some mixed schools there is no doubt that Black children suffer but on the whole separation creates more evils than it overcomes. But "it will not do simply to rail against the advocates for separate schools" and there must be careful and expert work to make mixed schools really work well for the children in them. In New York City some progress has been made along these lines because of the active interest of some Black parents and the work of certain teachers, in particular the remarkable work of a Black woman, Mrs. Elise Johnson McDougald. Her work and that of her staff is described and the conclusion is this: Let the school system by all means remain open to all, democratic and without discrimination and with the one idea of developing the child and not simply of feeding industry as it is . . . above all by just treatment keep up the ambition and courage of the colored child in the years of his life when these are most likely to lag.

687. April, 1923, Vol. XXV, No. 6. In "Opinion" (pp. 247–251), "As To Pugilism" Du Bois admits he does not think very highly of it but he does think the fighters are infinitely to be preferred to soldiers. In any case the discrimination being shown in Paris against Siki and in the United States against Jack Johnson and Harry Wills "is beneath contempt." An exchange between Du Bois and George H. Lorimer of the *Saturday Evening Post* is published, the point being the magazine's notoriously anti-Black bias and the correspondence does nothing to resolve it. In a two-page essay on "The Negro and Labor," Du Bois finds that the dark world was on the verge of rebellion prior to the First World War and that after the war, it has rebelled.

The greatest post-war problem is whether white laborers are going to recognize the demand of these dark laborers for equal consideration, or whether white capitalists and employers are going to continue to play off black and white labor against each other and thus seek to exploit and develop Asia and Africa, simply for the benefit of the privileged classes of the white world.

Du Bois calls attention, favorably, to the program of the British Labour Party which calls for Egyptian independence, self-government for India, the recognition of the Irish Republic, progressive taxation, the nationalization of mines and railways, government supported housing, and increased old-age pensions. Sherwood Eddy "is a missionary" and is worried about the Indians in Asia but when he spoke at Atlanta before an audience made up of several hundred white people and 100 Black people and when he was asked by the white audience if his demands for change did not also apply to Black people in the South, he hemmed and stammered and continued this while more Southern whites repeated the question. "His cowardice had separated him from the anxious forward-striving South and ranged him with Watson, Vardaman and the Ku Klux Klan; and he *knew* it." A letter is published from Raymond O'Neil, the Black actor and director, reporting the success of a Black theater recently established in Chicago. "We shall do all we can to encourage colored and white writers in the creation of a Negro dramatic literature ... " and Du Bois wishes the effort godspeed.

688. May, 1923, Vol. XXVI, No. 6. In "Opinion" (pp. 7–11), an extended description of another Du Bois' lecture tour, written after 7,500 miles had been travelled and the same yet to go. He has spoken to 11,550 people, Black and white, and he has listened and looked, with stops in Toledo, Zanesville, Chicago, Indianapolis, Denver, Portland, Eugene, Sacramento, San Francisco, Oakland, Los Angeles and San Diego and more to come. He has spoken at high schools and colleges and felt a "deep thoughtfulness"; he notices a new quality, also, among the white audiences in general. "They knew I was stating and not overstating the truth. And they wanted the truth."

689. June, 1923, Vol. XXVI, No. 2. In "Opinion" (pp. 55–57), "A University Course in Lynching" refers to the mob murder—largely by students at the University of Missouri (with women participating)—of James T. Scott. It is noted that the students at the University of Georgia staged a lynching a few years before "but this was at night and the girls did not have a fair chance to see it." The Doctor concludes, "We are expecting great results from this course of study at one of the most eminent of our State Universities." "The Fear of Efficiency" observes that in the past Black people faced discrimination on the grounds that they were incapable; now this is less often heard and what gnaws at the vitals of the racists is "the fear of efficiency." But Du Bois thought this would not apply in the area of art; however, he has found discrimination from the National Academy of Design, the Architectural League, the Beaux Arts Institute, etc., in the case of Augusta Savage, the sculptor (whose name is not mentioned here). At Tuskegee, where a hospital is to be built for Black veterans, the white rulers are demanding that physicians and nurses all be white—on the ground that Black people are not efficient! Du Bois hears that though the KKK has demanded that Dr. Moton sign a statement in support of this, he has refused and has invited them "to take vengeance on him if they must." A short story "On Being Crazy" concludes the editorial, the point being that between Black and white, the discovery of the mad one is not as easy as racism assumes.

690. July, 1923, Vol. XXVI, No. 3. In "Opinion" (pp. 103–107), a mass meeting was held in Mississippi by Black people to protest their treatment; the leader was S. D. Redmond and Du Bois bows to his courage. The coming together of the third Pan-African Congress in the fall is announced. "The Ethiopian Art Theatre," under Raymond O'Neil, has performed *Salomé* on Broadway; "financially the experiment was a failure, but dramatically and spiritually it was one of the great successes that the country has seen." Evelyn Preer in the title role was especially fine. The white press ignored the production and Theodore Dreiser—in a letter here quoted—observes the boycott but remarks that of all the productions of *Salomé* he has seen, "none" was the peer of this one. The funeral of Colonel Charles Young at Arlington Cemetery was attended by thousands; Du Bois reiterates in detail the racist treatment he met throughout his army career commencing with West Point. The efforts of Alabama authorities to keep white control over the hospital for veterans being built at Tuskegee are detailed leading to the exclamation, "human hatred, meanness and cupidity gone stark mad!" Du Bois thinks the best way to proceed is to terminate the building program in Alabama and put up the hospital somewhere "within the confines of civilization."

691. "Political Straws," unsigned, acknowledges information from Morris Lewis of Chicago and R. McCants Andrews of Durham, North Carolina, July, 1923, Vol. XXVI, No. 3, (pp. 124–126). The Black vote in the North in 1924 will probably come to nearly one million; hence, its importance mounts. In local elections—Du Bois examines Chicago, Baltimore, and New York City in some detail—Black voters showed great care and independence and voted not in accordance with the party but in terms of how candidates had responded to their special needs. Du Bois adds that it is most "unfortunate" that both the Farmer-Labor and the Socialist Parties have done nothing or very little on this subject.

692. August, 1923, Vol. XXVI, No. 4. In "Opinion" (pp. 151–154) note is taken of a victory in the Elaine, Arkansas, case for the courts have been forced, finally, to free six of the remaining twelve prisoners and Du Bois thinks it likely the last six prisoners will be freed soon. "It pays to fight and it costs to fight." The Spingarn Medal award to George Washington Carver, to be presented in August, is announced. When Jack Johnson knocked out Jeffries, a federal law was passed barring interstate transportation of the films of the fight; now when Jack Dempsey—having avoided a contest with Harry Wills—knocks out a stool pigeon in a Montana gambling joint, the films are sent "quickly and secretly" throughout the country and will be shown everywhere. "Aren't we the Greatest Hypocrites on Earth?" Details of the discrimination practiced against Augusta Savage (No. 689) are given, complete with relevant correspondence. "The Woman's Medical College" tells the story of the refusal of the Philadelphia college to give an internship to one of its leading graduates, Dr. Lillian A. Moore. Again the relevant correspondence is published. "there is no doubt about it, colored Americans have got to quit having brains; it's putting our white friends in all sorts of embarrassing positions."

693. "The Tragedy of 'Jim Crow'", signed, August, 1923, Vol. XXVI, No. 4, pp. 169–172. The text of a speech delivered before 3,000 people (largely Black) in Philadelphia defending the record and performance of Leslie P. Hill, in charge of Cheyney State Normal School in Pennsylvania, a school for training of Black teachers. It is not a defense of segregation, which is an evil, but a defense of a man who—faced with a fact and not a theory—is proceeding to make Cheyney into an excellent school. There is something worse than segregation and that is ignorance. The real fight should be along these lines: to stop the increase in segregation; to insist on the appointment of Black teachers in white schools; to support all efforts to improve schools presently segregated; to make Cheyney an excellent school and to "encourage the entry of white students"; to see to it that "colored pupils are kept in every other normal school of the state"; and "to make the colored teacher feel that no calling is so fine and valuable as his and that the Negro race and the world knows it."

694. September, 1923, Vol. XXVI, No. 5. In "Opinion" (pp. 199–202), the department opens with a gentle piece on "The President" for Harding has died; there is a renewed appeal for support of the NAACP and the *Crisis*; a good exposition was held in New York City under the auspices of the Association of Trade and Commerce, a Black organization—but all the National Business League does is "talk and talk and talk." Senator Oscar Underwood of Alabama (hon., LL. D., Harvard) has announced his candidacy for the presidency; Du Bois spells out his past record and that of his state and remarks ironically he would make a splendid candidate for president of the United States. The Black community in Springfield, Ohio, after a two-year-struggle against plans for a segregated school has won and has also won the appointment of Black teachers. They met, talked, planned, paraded, picketed, boycotted, "and some of the more headstrong" turned to arson. The latter was wrong, but in general, the method of struggle was splendid—and successful. From Florida comes a letter asking how one can get to Liberia and what are the prospects. Du Bois replies that Liberia, "wants men with capital, skill, education and health." Such men if they combined courage and hard work, may succeed—"no others can." In six months the Black women, led by Mary B. Talbert, and working entirely as volunteers have contributed over $13,000 in cash to the anti-lynching effort of the NAACP. The Lausanne Treaty with Turkey was a failure on the part of European imperialists; it marks indeed "the greatest triumph of Asia over European aggression since the Russo-Japanese War." Under "Publicity" it is noted that appeals for help in several cases when published in the *Crisis* have been successful. Another appeal for help is now published for the Pushkin family who, in Soviet Russia, are having a difficult time making ends meet. This is printed, writes Du Bois, in recognition of the part-African ancestry of the great Pushkin. Under "Exodus" Du Bois notes the continued migration of Black folk out of the South and ridicules the Southern white press, whose comments on this are manifestly contra-dictory and absurd. From an official report on education in Arkansas, Du Bois shows the fantastic degree of discrimination against Black children and argues again against the Sterling-Towner Bill.*

695. October, 1923, Vol. XXVI, No. 6. In "Opinion" (pp. 247–250). This month is the children's number and Du Bois apologizes to the parents of the 150 children (out of 300) whose photographs space forbade him to reproduce. A friend has complained to him that there is not enough "Joy" in the *Crisis*. Du Bois remarks that "few have more joy in life than I." He lists some of his joys in life, ranging from "the patter of rain at night" to "the love of dancing" and adds that it had not occurred to him that most people may "not find life supremely beautiful and interesting." He says, "I dare to look Hell in the face because I love Heaven." And ends, "But which is more dangerous: the joy that knows no evil, or the joy that faces it fully and lives?" Various forces have delayed the holding of the Third Pan-African Congress but it will meet. The appointment of Bascom Slemp as secretary to President Coolidge is a disaster for there is no more blatant racist in the United States. A Bok Peace Prize of $100,000 has been offered by the American Peace Award society; actually ending war is not too difficult, Du Bois suggests. It now pays to make war, "to 'develop' the tropics; it pays to kill 'niggers.'" "Reverence for humanity is the end of war."

*A detailed critique of this bill, by Florence Kelley, is in *The Crisis*, October, 1923; Vol. XXVI, pp. 252–255.

Killing and mob assaults upon white people are increasing in the United States; this is a deep matter and related to the 400 years of murdering of Black folk. Du Bois confesses to a certain satisfaction at this blood letting. Under "Photography" Du Bois wonders why more Black people do not enter that profession for "the average white photographer does not know how to deal with colored skins and having neither sense of their delicate beauty of tone nor will to learn, he makes a horrible botch of portraying them." Two letters "From Our White Friends" in the South are published without signature; one from an attorney in Florida, the other from a woman in Texas and both in effect hail Du Bois' work.

696. November, 1923, Vol. XXVII, No. 1. In "Opinion," (pp. 7–10), Despite the insistence in the U.S. press on the failure of the League of Nations, Du Bois thinks it "is still the most hopeful international movement in the world today"; it has just admitted Ethiopia and seats Liberia and "stolen Haiti," and despite England's influence, is a positive force. November 11 is Houston Martyr Day and it is urged that a petition with 100,000 signatures then reach the President demanding the release of those men still in jail. The head of the hospital at Tuskegee must be a Black man; on this no compromise should be made. A good civil rights bill has been achieved in San Diego through the efforts of the NAACP branch there. In the Virgin Islands, held by the United States, Marines spend their time insulting the Black inhabitants. Professor Crogman, after 41 years service at Clark University in Atlanta, is being asked to vacate his rent-free cottage; he is 80 years old and this is "a piece of ingratitude which we did not expect from the Methodist Episcopal Church." W. P. Dabney, Paymaster of Cincinnati, has resigned because the city refused him a salary commensurate with his position because he was Black. In resigning, Dabney "did what we call a very fine piece of work." Du Bois again sets forth the facts on how the disfranchisement of Black people adds to the political strength of the Bourbon South and again he demands the enforcement of the Fourteenth Amendment. The Committee on Peace and Foreign Relations of the National Association of Colored Women has asked Du Bois to represent it at the forthcoming Third Pan-African Congress. He is grateful and it is a mark of the growing appreciation of the connection between all areas of the Dark World. In "Page Mr. Gompers" Du Bois calls attention to an open shop—a foundry in Muncie, Indiana,—which alone in that industry in that city employs skilled Black workers, who are forbidden entry into the racist

Union of Molders. That Union now demands the shop fire its Black workers and unionize; Du Bois asks for Mr. Gompers' advice.

697. December, 1923, Vol. XXVII, No. 2. In "Opinion" (pp. 55–59), a parable for Christmas is based on "And Martha Served." A tribute to Mary Burnett Talbert, who has died, having worked herself to death. She saved the Frederick Douglass Home; she helped build the National Association of Colored Women; she fought for liberty in her city of Buffalo; she led the latest and fiercest crusade against lynching—"hers was a triumphant life." The story of how difficult it was to actually hold the Third Pan-African Congress is told and what was accomplished? "We have kept an idea alive; we have held to a great ideal, we have established a continuity and some day when unity and co-operation come, the importance of these early steps will be recognized." A call for building the NAACP and for continued struggle on behalf of the 54 Houston martyrs still in prison.

698. January, 1924, Vol. XXVII, No. 3. "Opinion" (pp. 103–106) opens with a contribution by Mary White Ovington. It continues with Du Bois on "Negro Colleges" taking off from a report issued by the Slater Fund; some progress is evident, but "the endowment is lamentably and dangerously small." There is a greeting to "Mr. B. Weevil"—that is the boll weevil whose work has helped cause thousands of Black families to leave the South. "Mr. [H.L.] Remmel" Arkansas' National Republican Committeeman has seen President Coolidge and has asked for a law to prevent the migration of Black people from the South; Du Bois agrees and therefore urges passage of the Dyer Anti-Lynching Bill. "Propaganda" quotes the same, with antiracist intent, from a typical British paper, the *Daily Mail*. It is done to convince readers that the only proper thing for white men to do in Africa is to "stand on the necks" of its inhabitants and extract millions in profits from the labor and resources of the continent. Correspondence is published showing the lashing of women by U.S. employees of American firms in the Belgian Congo; apparently the United States "is 'doing' Africa as badly as ever Belgium did." A "Crisis Book Club" is projected, asking that people pledge to buy a certain number of books each year, thus helping "to preserve the thought and experiences of the world and of my own people."

699. "The Black Man and the Wounded World," Subtitled, "A History of the Negro Race in the World War and After," January, 1924, Vol. XXVII, No. 3, (pp. 110–114). This is the first chapter of a work which Du Bois never completed. It is called "Interpretations" and posits the class divisions characterizing history in the past and present with those dominating in wealth also dominating in knowledge and propaganda. In the last half of the nineteenth century the development of imperialism and the special exploitation of the dark people intensified antidemocratic and pro-elitist tendencies. But the World War—arising largely out of competition for colonial mastery—has created a deep crisis in the White Supremacist world and it is not possible that the masters of that world can forever persuade the white working class that it does not have any interest in combining with the exploited colored majority in the world. In reality they do have a common interest. The essay shows a marked change in Du Bois' earlier thoughts on the sources of the war (as expressed in 1917, not in 1915) for now he distinctly affirms that the cause does not lie primarily with Germany but rather with all of the imperial and colonial powers; he adds that the guilt is individual, however, and that men created the deviltry of World War.

700. February, 1924, Vol. XXVII, No. 4. In "Opinion" (pp. 151–154), note is taken of Du Bois' appointment by President Coolidge as Special Envoy to represent the United States at the inauguration of President King of Liberia in January, 1924. "Summer Military Camps" are discriminating against Black men; nevertheless, Black men should apply and attend for "*unless we American Negroes go into these camps and get this training when war comes our boys are going to be the dumb driven cattle of white officers.*" In "Kenya" the British, combining British East Africa with German East Africa, are trying to establish an altogether unjust system of white supremacy: "It will never succeed but it will cause endless bloodshed and misery before it falls." Appeals from Black people in Oklahoma are published having as their object the establishment of schools for their children. Representatives from Haiti and Santo Domingo did a fine job at the Fifth Pan-American Conference lately held in Chile in exposing the activities of the United States.

701. "The Younger Literary Movement", signed jointly by Du Bois and Alain Locke, February, 1924, Vol. XXVII, No. 4; pp. 161–163. Two books are mainly dealt with, Jean Toomer's *Cane* (Boni & Liveright) and Jessie Fauset's *There is Confusion* (Boni & Liveright); the second is reviewed by Locke. Du Bois thinks the two books "will mark an epoch" and besides these books he notes five poets: Langston Hughes, Countee Cullen, Georgia Johnson, Gwendolyn Bennett, and

Claude McKay and two essayists and critics, Eric Walrond and Walter White. Toomer is a writer "who first dared to emancipate the colored world from the conventions of sex." He knows human beings—better than Georgia Johnson—his writing is true, impressionistic, but true. Often it is excessively puzzling but "(the whole world is a puzzle)" and in any case "Toomer strikes me as a man who has written a powerful book but who is still seeking for the fullness of his powers. ... "

702. "Pan-Africa in Portugal," signed, February, 1924, Vol. XXVII, No. 4, p. 170. Details are given of the second session of the Third Congress held in Lisbon, from December 1 to December 2, 1923.

703. March, 1924, Vol. XXVII, No. 5. "Opinion" (pp. 199–202), Du Bois devotes almost entirely to reiterating the opposition to the Sterling-Towner Education Bill and showing in great detail how under its provisions the racist and discriminatory nature of education in the South would be strengthened. "In response to many requests" Du Bois publishes the notification of his appointment as Special Envoy to Liberia and the text of the telegram to President King from President Coolidge about it. A note is added, "The appointment of Dr. Du Bois carried with it no salary."

704. "Sketches From Abroad: Le Grand Voyage," signed, March, 1924, Vol. XXVII, No. 5, pp. 203–205. These sketches are impressions of his trip, and this piece is confined to its European portion; in Spain, "my brown face attracts no attention. I am darker than my neighbors but they are dark. I become, quite to my surprise, simply a man ... I feel relieved."

705. April, 1924, Vol. XXVII, No. 6. In "Opinion" pp. 247–251, Du Bois has just returned from a 15,000 mile journey and has seen four African islands and five African colonies. A diary of the trip, with "when shall I forget the night I first set foot on African soil—I, the sixth generation in descent from my stolen forefathers." The address made by Du Bois in presenting his papers to President King is quoted in full; the relationship of Du Bois' appointment to the question of Liberian sovereignty runs throughout it and throughout Du Bois' other remarks in this issue of "Opinion."

706. "Little Portraits of Africa," signed; April, 1924, Vol. XXVII, No. 6, pp. 273–274. A prose-poem, it is filled with enthusiasm and delight and the promise of a new kind of life—when Africa is free—where "women will be happy."

707. May, 1924, Vol. XXVIII, No. 1. "Opinion" (pp. 7–12), thinks nothing came out of the "Sanhedrin" called and headed by Kelly Miller; the pronouncement of "the so-called Negro Press Association" denouncing trade unions and "economic radicalism" was "most pitiful." "Union labor has given the modern workman, white and black, whatever he has of decent wages and hours and conditions of work." And exactly in so-called economic radicalism "lies the only hope of the black folk." Two pages are devoted to "A Lunatic or a Traitor" which is a fierce attack upon the activity, statements, and positions of Marcus Garvey, now that he has become "an open ally of the Ku Klux Klan"; it comes in response to repeated personal attacks by Garvey on Du Bois and his ideas and his "unremitting repetition of falsehood after falsehood" (See No. 207) In "Sensitive Liberia" Du Bois writes that England and France want Liberia and explains how inspite of the pressures from Washington, Monrovia has sought and to a point has been able to maintain her sovereignty. Du Bois adds that many American Black people go to Liberia to give advice but what they advise has already been thought of by the Liberians who are not fools.* In "Stealing" Du Bois places the current "Teapot Dome" scandal rocking Washington in perspective: the whole system and society is based on stealing. A tribute is paid to Harry Burleigh, who for thirty years has been soloist at a leading New York City church; he is today "the greatest American composer of songs." Under "Tanner" Du Bois records that the artist, Henry Tanner, once remarked to him in Paris that no Black person ever had bought one of his paintings. Now two have and Du Bois suggests that every Black church adorn its interior with a Tanner painting and the works of other Black artists.

708. "The Black Man and the Wounded World," Chapter 2: The Story of the War, May, 1924, Vol. XXVIII, No. 1, (pp. 36–38), commences with the hopes of the 1911 Universal Races Congress and goes on to repeat a sketch of the war's causes and then to briefly summarize the military highlights of 1914 and of 1915 (No. 699).

709. June, 1924, Vol. XXVIII, No. 2. "Opinion" pp. 55–60 points to the coming Meeting of the NAACP, to be held this year in Philadelphia, and calls for greater dedication in the fight for freedom. "On Being Dined" refers to the dinner in his honor recently given and attended by 500 friends. He was especially pleased that speakers

---

*In this issue of the *Crisis*, a full-page map is devoted to illustrating Du Bois' trip; the text carries very brief comments about its highlights. The trip began on October 28, 1923, when he left New York City; he returned on March 19, 1924.

affirmed that in working for the freedom of Black people one works for the realization of democracy for all and that in using the pen for propaganda, where the cause is just, one does not demean art but rather ennobles it. Writing on "The Negro and the American Stage," Du Bois observes that the traditional role of clown or fool must give way for "the most dramatic group of people in the history of the United States is the American Negro." Indeed, he adds, "It would be very easy for a great artist so to interpret the history of our country as to make the plot turn entirely upon the black man." He emphasizes the "tremendously sensitive" nature of the Black world and this often leads to a fear of true art, but it must come. In this connection, Du Bois commends the efforts of Eugene O'Neill. Du Bois repeats advice given earlier "On Migrating to Africa" and adds that he observed there in particular the splendid manners displayed by all and suggests that it would be well if Africans could come as missionaries to the United States for the purpose of teaching good manners. A page is turned over to the young E. Franklin Frazier whose essay on "The Negro and NonResistance" (March, 1924) had created quite a stir for Frazier had insisted on that right for Black people as for all people. Frazier here reiterates his position with Du Bois' approval since it "seems to us so eminently clear and sound." Tribute is paid Bishop W. S. Brooks of the A.M.E. Church who has spent over three fruitful and arduous years of work in Africa.

710. July, 1924, Vol. XXVIII, No. 3. In "Opinion" pp. 103–106, "Unity" is discussed as vital but diversity also is consequential and unity can be formed only where something exists in common. In "Vote" Du Bois again calls for Black conscious voting and not voting by party labels and again emphasizes the importance of local and Congressional elections. "If I Had You Down South" tells of a young Black man who accidentally stepped on the toe of a white man in the subway, he was then pushed by the white man, and when he struck back a scream came from the white man; Du Bois explains its illuminating meaning. "To Your Tents, O Nordics!" for Wills has beaten Madden in a fight—the Black besting the white again—other examples are offered and Du Bois is willing to bet that "intelligence" tests will soon be announced, again, "proving" whites superior to Blacks. An essay on "Alhambra" draws the thought that "Spain has suffered nothing that her treatment of brown Moor and Black-a-Moor and Jew did not let her deserve." "Helping Africa" rejects the paternalism of outsiders telling Africans how to conduct themselves

—"Africa belongs to Africans" and "they have not the slightest intention of giving it up to foreigners, white or black."

711. August, 1924, Vol. XXVIII, No. 4. In "Opinion" (pp. 151–155), there is a brief description of the NAACP Meeting in Philadelphia; there is the text of its public statement (written by Du Bois) and that of its address to the AFL (also by Du Bois) calling upon it to terminate its racist policies and so make itself an effective force for the rights of the working class. The platform of the La Follette party is an excellent one but La Follette personally persists in avoiding direct reference to Black people. Printed in this department is the text of a statement from Ernest Lyon, the Liberian Consul-General in the United States, dated July 10, 1924, declaring (in italics) that *"no person or persons leaving the United States under the auspices of the Garvey movement in the United States, will be allowed to land in the Republic of Liberia."*

712. September, 1924, Vol. XXVIII, No. 5. In "Opinion" (pp. 199–203), the NAACP "does not attempt to tell its members or anyone else how to vote" but it and the *Crisis* do urge independent voting by Black people, voting which sees politics not as a game or a matter of a certain office but as a vehicle for the advancement of the welfare of Black people—and all people. Praise is bestowed upon the Maud Cuney Hare exhibit, illustrating "the rise and development of Negro music" which was displayed at Wanamaker's department store in Philadelphia in connection with the recent NAACP meeting. Du Bois' gives unstinted praise to "Tuskegee and Moton" on the momentous victory of its hospital which was achieved in the face of great difficulty and despite the KKK and all the Bourbonry. Finally some notes are added on a recent trip by Du Bois through the South—and his success despite the KKK. Of Fisk University he will write again "for it was to me a place of sorrow, of infinite regret; a place where the dreams of great souls lay dusty and forgotten."

713. "Array of Books," signed reviews, September, 1924, Vol. XXVIII, No. 5, p. 219. of the several books reviewed in this issue, four were commented upon by Du Bois; W. D. Weatherford, *The Negro from Africa to America*; J. A. Rogers, *From 'Superman' to Man*; Ronald Firbank, *Prancing Nigger*; N. I. White and H. C. Jackson, editors, *An Anthology of Verse by American Negroes*. The Weatherford book is "too much on mushy sentimentalism and not enough on stern justice and right" but it does represent a white southerner who is trying; the Rogers book is highly recommended; the Firbank book, despite its title, is worth reading and its West Indian setting adds to its importance; the White-Jackson anthology is praised highly as a "sincere bit of work" by Southern white men.

714. October, 1924, Vol. XXVIII, No. 6. In "Opinion" (pp. 247–252) Du Bois writes that we will cast perhaps two and a quarter million votes in November, so let's cast them with forethought and care. In "An Interview" Du Bois reports about a meeting he had with a ten-year-old boy and that the education of parents is not easy —perhaps it should not be left entirely in the hands of children. Two pages follow on "Fisk" elucidating No. 712. The university had failed in providing education for black people—to respect them, to seek to give them the best and the most needful, to develop their self-knowledge and self-pride—and had, in fact, insulted them and curried favor with the racists.

714a. November, 1924, Vol. XXIX, No. 1. In "Opinion" (pp. 7–11), Du Bois hears a report that the white Northern Methodist Episcopal Church on the eve of its union with its Southern break off has made official overtures to the A.M.E. for the transfer to the latter of Black members in the Northern church. If this is true, does the Northern church have "the present address of Jesus of Nazareth?" "The Fight" describes Wills' outpointing Firpo; but he didn't kill him and therefore it was "à poor fight." "Can you beat these white folks?" A Supreme Court decision has ruled that laws forbidding the teaching or use of foreign languages in schools are unconstitutional and violate the fourteenth Amendment; how about laws prohibiting marriage on grounds of race, Du Bois wonders. In "Education" Du Bois records that from 1917 to the present time the Black population in Atlanta has been fighting for better education; in 1924 the city "capitulated and promised five new schools" and now it is completing the first high school for Black youngsters: "Does it pay to agitate?" A map of South Carolina is published, showing its counties and the respective salaries paid white and Black teachers. Comment follows on the splendid work in education being done in Africa by Mrs. Adelaide Hayford and the impact upon Afro-Americans of meetings with Africans of such stature. The work of the Hubbard Industrial Mission in Liberia is praised. Du Bois happily notes that now both *the Crisis* and the newly founded organ of the National Urban League, *Opportunity,* are both offering prizes "To Encourage Negro Art."

714b. "How Shall We Vote? A Symposium," November, 1924, Vol.

XXIX, No. 1; p. 13. Eleven Black people reply to this question, including the editor, Du Bois. He will vote for the Progressive candidates, Robert M. La Follette and Burton K. Wheeler. He wishes La Follette had said something on the question of Black oppression, but he has condemned the KKK and has promised "to free Haiti" and the remainder of his program is infinitely better than that of the major parties.

714c. "Fall Books," signed, November, 1924, Vol. XXIX, No. 1, pp. 25–26. Three books are reviewed: Walter White, *The Fire in the Flint*; William H. Skaggs, *The Southern Oligarchy* and E. M. Forster, *A Passage to India*. The important point is that publishers will now publish the kind of novel White has written about the South. Mr. White "succumbs too easily to the common mistake of piling the blame of southern wickedness on the 'poor whites' and absolving the aristocrats and former slaveholders" and with one exception, the "characters do not live and breathe and compel our sympathy" but the story does move. Skaggs' book "is the most important volume that has come out of the white south since the Civil War." A defense of the poorer white in essence and at the same time "an astonishing vindication of our cause." Forster's book is "a tremendous epic of racial clash held down to earth by honesty and subtle insight such as few novelists ever used."

714d. "The Political Power of the South," unsigned, November, 1924, Vol. XXIX, No. 1, (pp. 27–28). A detailed study of the data on disfranchisement, complete with map, showing that government of the people and by the people simply does not exist.

715. December, 1924, Vol. XXIX, No. 2. In "Opinion" (pp. 55–57), "The Election" saw about 2 million Black people cast ballots; probably 1 million votes for Coolidge, half a million votes each for the Democrats and for La Follette. It is a splendid showing of independence. In Illinois a Black municipal judge and state senator were elected and two Black men running for Congress in New York (as Republicans) and in Chicago (as a Progressive) piled up big votes, although they did not win; in Texas it was the Black vote that defeated the KKK candidate for Governor; on the other hand, the KKK won important victories in Indiana, Kansas, Oklahoma and Colorado. An appeal is made for support of the *Crisis* in order to push its influence further. In "West Indian Immigration" Du Bois comments that the racists "put one over on us in the recent immigration bill" which, in fact, bars further immigration of Black people from the West Indies.

716. "The Temptation in the Wilderness", unsigned, December, 1924, Vol. XXIX, No. 2, p. 58. A parable for Christmas and a fierce denunciation of established churches, "the devil was a priest in robe and mitre chanting long prayers."

717. January, 1925, Vol. XXIX, No. 3. In "Opinion" (pp. 103–106), "Debit and Credit for 1924" is discussed; "The Politician's Price" affirms the political independence of the NAACP with its purpose not to sell votes "for petty political jobs" but rather to use the vote "for the freedom of the Negro race." Uncomplimentary remarks are made about certain Black figures who lean to the two major parties for since the election they seem to be expecting favors; those named are: Benjamin Davis of Georgia, Perry Howard, Henry L. Johnson, and Robert Vann of the *Pittsburgh Courier*. It is not job appointments that are wanted but an end to racism. Dr. Charles Roberts, a Black Republican candidate for Congress from New York City, would have been elected, but he was knifed by white bosses. Another paragraph on Texas shows the need to defeat the Sterling-Towner education bill.

718. February, 1925, Vol. XXIX, No. 4. In "Opinion" (pp. 151–156), greetings are extended to the Black fraternities and sororities for their fine work in encouraging the education of their brothers and sisters; Du Bois welcomes gifts from wealthy whites and from white dominated foundations to help Black education, but it is a scandal that such gifts are needed and they are needed because of the robbery of the Black people as a whole and they lead to less than full freedom among us. "We thank the givers for priceless gifts but we eternally damn the system that makes education depend upon charity." "Sudan" tells of the rape of this land and of Egypt by England, but, "Africa lived before England was born and the pyramids of Egypt will yet look on a land free of British task masters." In "Who Checked Lynching" Du Bois observes that commencing in 1920 when the figure stood at 65 the number of victims has been steadily declining and was at 16 in 1924. Many participated in the struggle to bring this about, but none was so important as the NAACP. But the 16 is too large a figure and anything above zero is too much; hence, fight for a federal anti-lynching law. In "The White Primary" Du Bois comments that while tests of its constitutionality have hitherto been defeated, the Supreme Court has indicated in some of its language that a properly prepared case would lead to the illegalizing of the white primary—let's get such a case and present it.

719. March, 1925, Vol. XXIX, No. 5. In "Opinion" (pp. 199–202) a description of the island of Goree appears, off Africa's coast near Dakar. "Radicals and the Negro" is a two-page essay on the fact that radical white organizations and individuals function very often without even being aware of the special and awful oppression of over 12 million Black people. Du Bois adds that they not only do not see those millions but they do not understand that because of it their own programs are stymied. Du Bois illustrates this in several areas and adds, "it is absolutely certain that the future of liberal and radical thought in the United States is going to be made easy or impossible by the way in which American democracy treats American Negroes." Du Bois then gives examples of the kinds of statements and demands that would unite the radical and the Black liberation movements—even "A simple statement" calling for "the political, social and economic emancipation of the Negro would meet the issue." That this is not done seems to Du Bois "astonishing." The work of a conference held at Vassar College in June seems to Du Bois worth reporting for it advocated not tolerance but appreciation and called upon white women and their organizations to actively invite the participation of Black women and their organizations.

720. April, 1925, Vol. XXIX, No. 6. In "Opinion" (pp. 247–252) four pages are devoted to events at Fisk, including the sources of the students' strike, the nature of the racism and tyranny prevailing there and the need to force changes looking towards democracy and real education. Du Bois hails the appearance of militancy among the Black students and ends, in italics: *"Men and women of Black America: Let no decent Negro send his child to Fisk until Fayette McKenzie* [the President] *goes."* "Inter-Marriage" refers to bills illegalizing the same supported by the KKK and getting serious support in Ohio, Iowa and Michigan. Such measures really are "to encourage prostitution and degrade women of Negro descent." "Shame on a race and a people that must stoop to such measures in order to maintain their vaunted supremacy." The failures of two important Black businesses, Standard Life Insurance in Atlanta and Brown and Stevens Bank in Philadelphia, are not the fault of the men involved in any criminal or moral sense. But our businessmen must be especially careful, knowing that decisive control of the economy is in the hands of white men.

721. May, 1925, Vol. XXX, No. 1. In "Opinion" (pp. 7–11), a glowing tribute is offered to Moorfield Storey, president of the NAACP, on his 80th birthday; under "The New Crisis" appears a presentation of its direction for the future: stressing economic development; political independence; the encouragement of education and talent; of art; material on peace and international understanding; on the Black church; more self-criticism among ourselves; continued criticism of racism. A letter from Wilson M. Powell, attorney, president of the Swarthmore College corporation, banker, treasurer of the New York yearly meeting of the Society of Friends, has cancelled his subscription to the *Crisis* because while in London he found that it "washed the dirty linen" of the United States—especially lynching—abroad. Du Bois replies: " ... damned be Wilson Powell and all other lynchers of Thoughts and Men!" Again material in opposition to the Sterling-Towner education bill is presented—this from Clark County, Alabama. At an entertainment offered at Hampton, if whites wish to attend they are seated wherever seats are available in the audience; the White press demands that Hampton repudiate "amalgamation" and principal James Gregg is writing whining letters and is being asked pointed questions by the Virginia white newspapers.

722. "The Browsing Reader," May, 1925, Vol. XXX, No. 1, (pp. 26–27). The department commences with a review by Robert W. Bagnall, but much of it is by Du Bois. He reviews: Ernest Gruening, (ed.), *These United States; Problems of Citizenship*, by H. Baker-Crothers and R. Hudnut; *Races, Nation and Classes*, by H. A. Miller; *Population Problems*, by E. B. Reuter. In the Gruening book, Du Bois' essay on Georgia appears; he also notes that the essays on Mississippi and on Alabama (by B. A. Ratliff and Clement Wood) deal "frankly" with Black people. Especially weak, he finds, is Ludwig Lewisohn's piece on South Carolina. The textbook by Herbert Miller is rated highly by Du Bois, especially in view of "the shameful propaganda of lies" in most of the current texts and "the idiotic article on the Negro in the current *Encyclopaedia Britannica*." Reuter's book is fairly good, Du Bois writes, and is better than his earlier *Mulatto*. The Crother and Hudnut volume "is a fairminded compendium." Du Bois goes on to welcome the special number of the *Survey* evoked by the Harlem Renaissance and edited by Alain Locke with splendid illustrations by Winold Reiss. The contributions by Rudolph Fisher, William Domingo, and Melville Herskovits are especially commended. Du Bois comments, too, on recent developments in the New York theatre which he finds excellent. "All God's Chillun" and "Emperor Jones" and the revived "Othello" with Walter Hampden are especially praised.

723. June, 1925, Vol. XXX, No. 2. In "Opinion" (pp. 59–63), announcement of KRIGWA—a Black theater for Harlem in which Du Bois is deeply involved; replies to the Virginia press for Principal James Gregg of Hampton are supplied gratis, but "to be perfectly frank" we doubt he will use them. Under "Germany" Du Bois suggests that the setbacks represented by the coming to power of Hindenburg in Germany, Mussolini in Italy, Baldwin in England, and Coolidge in the United States are not permanent and that the replacement of production for private profit by a system of socialism will come about by different ways in different places and at different times—probably "sad, long years of effort." In "Disfranchisement" Du Bois spells out in detail the various devices used for this purpose; he explains the special significance of the NAACP suit against the White Primary in Texas.

724. July, 1925, Vol. XXX. No. 3. In "Opinion" (pp. 111–115), Kelly Miller has written a tribute to the work of the NAACP, which is especially welcome because of his distinction and because in the past he has tended to ignore the association. An effort is underway by political hacks in Missouri to remove the new Black president, Nathan B. Young, of Lincoln University; Du Bois calls for resistance. A Black man, Tom Lee, saved thirty white men from drowning in the Mississippi River at Memphis; he has been hailed by President Coolidge and there is some irony in that. Indians have demanded, and to a degree attained, civil service positions in their own country; this tends to reduce the number of Englishmen willing to serve there and thus hastens the day of full Indian independence—in this case "God bless race hatred!" Tribute is paid to Mary Bethune and Hallie Q. Brown who cleared a Black chorus representing Hampton from a stage in Washington because of Jim Crow seating arrangements—and every Black person walked out of the theater.

725. "Ferdinand Q. Morton", unsigned, July, 1925, Vol. XXX, No. 3, (pp. 115–116). This Black Civil Service Commissioner of New York City is leader of Tammany Hall in Harlem and a real power in city and state politics. He was a protégé of Robert N. Wood, the first effective Black Tammany leader. Today there are about 50 Black policemen in the city and hundreds more as clerks, stenographers, court attendants, etc. The Morton-Wood method of developing effective Black political leadership is not that recommended by the *Crisis* but it does work. Morton is "strong, skillful" and no doubt "cynical" but basically "honest and sound; and he deserves respect."

726. "The Catholic Church and Negroes: A Correspondence," Vol.

XXX, No. 3, July, 1925, pp. 120–121. This consists of an exchange of four letters between a Roman Catholic priest, Joseph B. Glenn of Richmond, Virginia and Du Bois (written in February and March, 1925) concerning the realities of that church's activities vis-à-vis Black people. Du Bois' closing remarks, "Because Catholicism has so much that is splendid in its past and fine in its present, it is the greater shame that 'nigger' haters clothed in its episcopal robes should do to black Americans in exclusion, segregation and exclusion from opportunity all that the Ku Klux Klan ever asked."

727. August, 1925, Vol. XXX, No. 4. In "Opinion" (pp. 163–165), (part of this department was written by R. W. Bagnall). Du Bois notes the report of the dismissal of Kelly Miller from Howard University by President J. S. Durkee and denounces it—with a postscript that news has just come that the dismissal has been withdrawn—"which is in our opinion exceedingly lucky—for Mr. Durkee. But it does not end the matter." A prose poem follows, "Georgia," painting a picture of its corruption and misery—and promise. "The Virgin Islands" tells of the dictatorial and racist policies being pursued there under the aegis of the Navy; the Black journalist, Rothschild Francis, is fighting this, at great personal peril, and deserves the support of all lovers of democracy.

728. September, 1925, Vol. XXX, No. 5. "Opinion" (pp. 215–220) notes that through James Weldon Johnson, it is announced that the American Fund for Public Service has provided the funds for two scholarships for Black persons to attend the Brookwood Labor College in Katonah, New York—set up to train union organizers. The death of John E. Milholland is announced; a devoted friend of Du Bois, a founder of the Constitution League which was one of the streams creating the river of the NAACP in 1909–1910. Du Bois notes an advance in "Education" with about 800 Black graduates of colleges in 1925. But this is far from enough—to keep abreast we must graduate at least 3,200. Why cannot each of our churches support at least one Black youngster through college? If this occurred we would have 50,000 students in colleges instead of 7,000 as at present. George W. Cook, a dean at Howard University, was to be fired but a howl was raised and his tenure is to endure for another year. What are the Howard alumni going to do about situations of this nature? A description of the mounting of Du Bois' historical pageant before thousands at the Hollywood Bowl is described. The white press is laughing at the Scopes trial in Tennessee but it is not a reason for laughter. It reflects the commitment to ignorance and hypocrisy which characterizes so much of White America; "It is menace and warning. It is a challenge to Religion, Science and Democracy"—this effort to punish a teacher for presenting elementary scientific truths about Man's evolution. General Robert Lee Bullard, the Alabama white man in command of the ninety-second Division in the World War, has attacked the courage of Black soldiers; of course such a "bully" would lie and we expect this of him—he spent more time fighting his own Black soldiers than he did the Germans.

729. "Missouri Shows Us," unsigned, September, 1925, Vol. XXX, No. 5, (pp. 226–227). Through a veritable "uprising" of the Black people of Missouri the position of President Young at Lincoln University has been confirmed and we now have the chance of seeing a first-class State university for Black youth actually function.

730. October, 1925, Vol. XXX, No. 6. In "Opinion," (pp. 267–272), an appeal on the fifteenth anniversary for renewed support of the *Crisis*; tribute to the excellent work, for 12 years, of the magazine's business manager, Augustus Granville Dill; an exposure of some of the sources of the hostility between President Durkee of Howard university and Dean Miller, dating back to 1919. In "Louisville, Kentucky" it is reported that so-called intelligence tests given Black and white youngsters turned out "wrong" and so a deep silence is permeating the white world about this matter! The play, *White Cargo*, by Leon Gordon showing on Broadway is praised—depicting "a beautiful, ignorant, mulatto bastard and harlot whom the degenerate white men engaged in uplifting Africa have made their toy"—because "it's fine for white folk and splendidly true. They need it."

731. November, 1925, Vol. XXXI, No. 1. In "Opinion" (pp. 7–11), it is announced that the American Fund for Public Service (also known as the Garland Fund) has granted $5,000 to the *Crisis* to conduct research "in the social condition of American Negroes." Almost five pages are devoted to "The Challenge of Detroit" giving the facts and the background relative to the case of Dr. Ossian Sweet, the Black physician who—together with his family—defended his home with force of arms from attack by a white mob intent on forcing him to abandon it since it was outside the ghetto. In defense one of the mob was shot and killed. The Sweets are now being held and charged with murder. "Dear God! Must we not live? And if we live may we not live somewhere?" "The YMCA" notes the separation of a white and a Black "Y." The development is due to racism; given the condition,

Black men have tried to make their "Y" as good as possible and have more and more succeeded in running it themselves. "What is our goal? For long years we have said: It is to be an integral part of this nation," but with this kind of development must we not ask, "whither? whither?" Henry L. Johnson, one of the last of the "old-time" politicians and from Georgia has died. "At times he gained for us, at other times he yielded and lost. But always he was the big, genial, fearless man, fighting in the jungles of Georgia. God rest his restless soul."

732. "Our Book Shelf," November, 1925, Vol. XXXI, No. 1, (pp. 31–32). Two books are reviewed by Du Bois, *The Book of American Negro Spirituals*, by James Weldon Johnson, J. Rosamond Johnson and Lawrence Brown (Viking); and *The Basis of Racial Adjustment*, by Thomas J. Woofter, Jr. (Ginn & Co.). The first is hailed as "authoritative"; the Woofter book also is highly praised, "I know of no book by a Southern white man with which I so thoroughly and heartily agree."

733. December, 1925, Vol. XXXI, No. 2. In "Opinion" (pp. 59–62), "The Sermon on the Tower"—for the Christmas issue—Jesus speaks from the tower of the Woolworth Building in New York City, "and the people were dumbfounded." "Now or Never"—the need for $50,000 to fight three cases: against restrictive covenants in the District of Columbia; against the White Primary in Texas; in defense of the Sweet family on trial for their lives for defending their home in Detroit. The American Fund for Public Service has given $20,000; now let's have the remaining $30,000. "The Black Man and Labor" hails efforts to organize the Pullman porters and a meeting of Black communists in Chicago—the American Negro Labor Congress—as healthy. As for the latter, "it is unjust of white men and idiotic of colored men to criticize the attempt." "We should stand before the astounding effort of Soviet Russia to reorganize the industrial world with open mind and listening ears." "The Terrible Dilemma" reports that after Columbia University barred Black girls from its dormitories, the girls were later accepted and now the Black and white young women are friends; at the University of Wisconsin a similar result ensued when the young women were simply permitted to behave as civilized human beings. They did and it worked. "Philippine Mulattoes" tells of an appeal for funds, delicately phrased and signed by such as Chief Justice William Howard Taft of the Supreme Court, to assist children in the Philippines. "What is all this about? In plain, cold English, the American people in bringing Peace and Civilization to the Philippines have left 18,000 bastards in the islands! ... Can you not see how Americans hate Social Equality with brown women?" Let the money be sent and let the protests, too, be sent to the Washington leaders "who permit the holding of the Philippines as a house of prostitution for American white men under the glorious stars and stripes." Du Bois' suggestion about Black churches providing scholarships for students to attend colleges is being acted upon; and why should not the fraternities and sororities enter into programs for the building of housing? Du Bois notes that the porters at Grand Central Station in New York are supporting a student at Howard University. "The Firing Line" for the Black people of the world today is not in Africa, nor in the West Indies but rather here in the United States and Du Bois explains why.

734. January, 1926, Vol. XXXI, No. 3. "Opinion" (pp. 111–115), Debit and Credit for 1925; "No Room in the Inn" a parable for Christmas; a play by Garland Anderson, "Appearances" is termed "excellent" and Du Bois urges its support; the "case" of the alleged "discovery" of Black ancestry in the bride of a scion of the Rhinelander family has all New York excited; if he had kept the woman as a mistress, not a peep would be heard—"magnificent Nordic morality!" Du Bois again defends the organizational efforts of "The Pullman Porters" and denounces in particular the role of the federal government in paying for spies to destroy the union; he adds that since Mark Sullivan and the Southern white press oppose the union, "thinking Negroes" will favor it. Thomas Jesse Jones and the Phelps Stokes Fund are denounced for the audacity in having selected a white man from Alabama "to take charge of missionary education and social uplift work" in Liberia. It is announced that "The First Battle of Detroit" has been something of a victory for the defense won a mistrial and the defendants are now out on bail. The next task is to gain an acquittal. The work of Clarence Darrow is praised as one of the attorneys in the case.* Note is taken of efforts in the South to browbeat Black people into becoming policemen and turning over alleged Black criminals to the forces of "law and order"—or else lynchings will occur. "We doubt if modern history can parallel this" duplicity, arrogance, stupidity, and cruelty.

735. "Our Book Shelf," a signed review of Alain Locke, ed., *The New Négre*, January, 1926, Vol. XXXI, No. 3, pp. 140–141. This book "In many ways marks an epoch ... a singularly satisfying and inspiring

*Full reportage on "The Sweet Trial," by Walter White is in this issue of the *Crisis*, pp. 125–129.

thing." With only one point made by Mr. Locke Du Bois disagrees and this is Locke's idea that "Beauty rather than Propaganda should be the object of Negro literature and art ... if Mr. Locke's thesis is insisted upon too much it is going to turn the Negro renaissance into decadence."

736. February, 1926, Vol. XXXI, No. 4. In "Opinion," (pp. 163–166), black people have contributed over $71,000 to the defense fund—not $30,000 as asked earlier and this is fine. Actually with our needs we ought to raise one million dollars each year. "The Newer South" notes signs of actual change inside the white South on the question of racism; examples are given. It is only a beginning but it is a beginning, Du Bois says. "A Questionnaire" gives the text, drafted by Du Bois and sent to several authors, putting this subject for discussion: "When the artist, black or white, portrays Negro characters is he under any obligations or limitations to the sort of character he will portray?"

737. A signed review of Norman Leys, *Kenya: A Study of English East Africa*, February, 1926, Vol. XXXI, No. 4, pp. 188–191. This "is perhaps the most important revelation of the shame of white imperialism in Africa published in the last decade." Its content is summarized, including its critical comments upon the Phelps Stokes Fund and Thomas Jesse Jones.

738. "Our Book Shelf" reviews ten books, all initialed as a group, February, 1926, Vol. XXXI, No. 4, pp. 191–193: *The Negro and His Songs,* by Howard W. Odum and G. B. Johnson; *Social Progress: A Handbook of the Liberal Movement* [no editor, *The Arbitrator*]; *Everyman's Genius,* by Mary Austin; *Negro Orators and Their Orations,* ed. by Carter G. Woodson; *The Education of Negro Ministers,* by W. A. Daniel; *Between Black and White,* by H. H. Proctor; *The Anthology of Magazine Verse for 1925,* ed. by W. S. Braithwaite; *White and Black in East Africa,* by H. Norden; *Free Negro Heads of Families in the United States in 1830* and *Free Negro Owners of Slaves in the United States in 1830,* both by C. G. Woodson. Largely brief summaries of the books and no major criticisms; those by Braithwaite and Woodson are highly recommended.

739. March, 1926, Vol. XXXI, No. 5. In "Opinion" (pp. 215–218), "peace on Earth" requires as a first step agreement to outlaw war; as a second, to agree on modes of arbitration; as a third, disarmament. Now with the Locarno agreements some progress has been made, but there will be no peace until the realities of racism, colonialism and imperialism are faced and overcome for these are basic sources of war. Du Bois congratulates Tuskegee and Hampton on new endowments totalling $5,000,000; use that new wealth to achieve a new freedom. The death of the Washington judge and genial companion, Robert H. Terrell, is observed. An anonymous letter is published showing the racism of James L. Sibley and then Du Bois asks why this man is appointed to advise on education in Liberia by the Phelps-Stokes Fund. Dr. Elizabeth Leonard of Broken Bow, Nebraska, president of a woman's club which has spent two weeks studying *The Souls of Black Folk*, asks for Du Bois' views on intermarriage and on race assimilation. Du Bois replies that no race is permanent; that probably marriage within one's own group has the best chance of success; that marriage outside it is a matter for the people themselves to decide and no one else's business; that where a people are treated as inferiors it is a matter of self-respect, usually, for them to marry within their own group; and that the basic point is not "to insult or degrade other groups or deny them the same rights."

740. April, 1926, Vol. XXXI, No. 6. In "Opinion" (pp. 267–271), four pages are devoted to his "annual pilgrimage"—his lecture and learning tour of Youngstown, Fort Wayne, Detroit, Toledo, Tulsa, Kansas, and Chicago. Two arrogant white youngsters who have all the answers; a Black master of ceremonies, fearful of Du Bois' radicalism, who seeks to answer the audience's questions for him (and fails), a long talk "with a group of Jews" where we found much in common and "had a gorgeous evening," the conductor who was himself ashamed of the Jim Crow car, the great courage of the Black people in Tulsa who had fought "the beasts" in the 1921 outbreak and now stood up and looked every man in the eye, and of Chicago—"I always feel like a lost stranger in Chicago." The hope of the white South to get control of the hospital in Tuskegee is not yet dead but it will be killed. Praise is heaped upon the Black Pullman porters for their remarkable record of public service—to white and Black alike under most difficult conditions. Their effort at unionization is being balked at every turn and the company wants to keep them as slaves or dismiss all of them. No job is worth slavery, so, if the effort at unionization cannot succeed, let the company have the job and get itself slaves instead of men.

741. "Dantes Bellegarde: International Spokesman of Black Folk," unsigned, April, 1926, Vol. XXXI, No. 6, pp. 295–296—the public career of the Haitian statesman and fighter against imperialism is sketched, Du Bois closing, "More shame to America in Haiti!"

742. May, 1926, Vol. XXXII, No. 1. In "Opinion" (pp. 7–11), it is noted that Jessie R. Fauset, after seven years as Literary Editor, is now a Contributing Editor. "For the first time" Du Bois approves of something done by the Phelps-Stokes Fund—it has granted $5,000 to help finance a resurvey of Negro colleges and this money to be used by the Association of Colleges for Negro Youth. Changes are developing at "Howard and Lincoln" and they reflect the mounting insistence of Black people to have a decisive role in their own affairs; Dr. Durkee has resigned from Howard university and that is good and now a Black man should become its President. "Disfranchisement" again it is explained how the South accomplishes this, despite renewed lying by Southern Governors affirming that their states do not practice disfranchisement of Black people. Under "Crime" Du Bois summarizes the contents of a pamphlet treating so-called Negro criminality being distributed in thousands of copies by the KKK and shows in detail its lying character. He then attacks the really criminal nature of racism in the United States. A call is repeated for the passage of an anti-lynching bill; the crime occurs less frequently but this is no reason for failing to enact the needed law; a delegation of Black Republicans visited President Coolidge and they asked him to reaffirm his opposition to lynching and to make clear that he will keep a Black man as U.S. Minister to Haiti; he did both. A section titled "By the Way" appears with a sentence or two of crisp comment upon items in the news, ranging from racism at Columbia's Teachers College, to a note that Britain has executed 450 Black men in Nigeria for murder in recent years and that "none of these were allowed the advantage of being defended by counsel," to a report that in Brooklyn, New York, Black women picketed police headquarters demanding an end to police brutality.

743. "John Work: Martyr and Singer", unsigned, May, 1926, Vol. XXXII, No. 1, pp. 32–34. An account of the life of John Wesley Work (1873-1926), who despite terrible difficulties and obstacles and opposition, did more than any other single person "to resurrect and make eternal the Negro spiritual." Du Bois writes: "On the foundation labors of John Work all of the modern flowering of Negro music has taken place."

744. June, 1926, Vol. XXXII, No. 2. In "Opinion" pp. 59–64, the growth of the *Krigwa* movement is heralded; appreciation is expressed to the American Fund for Public Service (established by Charles Garland with a gift of over $900,000) not only for the significance of its grants but also because on its Board of Directors sits a Black man, James Weldon Johnson. The suspension of *The World Tomorrow*, [edited by Anna Rochester] after eight years of publication as a monthly magazine is a tragedy; it was an honest publication and that the United States could not support it reflects upon this country. As Black people assert more and more control over the higher education of their offspring, white philanthropists are going to stop their donations. We must face this and do more ourselves and plan for the future and insist upon increasing government support of higher education; what we will not do is go back to alms-taking and white domination. In "Italy and Abyssinia," Du Bois reports signs that Mussolini intends to take Abyssinia by war and that so far the only "open objection to this high-handed program of theft, lying and slavery is Soviet Russia." The "By the Way" section contains a tribute to the British workers in their general strike effort; it is part of the revolution proceeding in the world and this will mean not only a reduction of ruling class power in England "but in the world."

745. A signed review of *Education in Africa: Recommendations of the African Education Committee*, chaired by Thomas Jesse Jones (Phelps-Stokes Fund: 2 vols., 1922–1925,), June, 1926, Vol. XXXII, No. 2, pp. 86–89. A detailed examination of the report of a committee which made two visits to Africa in 1921 and 1924 and one which finds it prejudiced, uninformed, and highly detrimental to the best interests of the Black African population. "Small wonder that British officialdom is rhapsodic over Jones. ... "

746. July, 1926, Vol. XXXII, No. 3. In "Opinion" (pp. 111–116), "Insanity" is a commentary on the census reports which in the past showed little insanity among Black people and now shows a substantial amount; both reports were used—somehow—to "prove" inferiority! The Women's International League for Peace and Freedom is hailed as really having an effective program for unlike some earlier peace organizations this one faces up to racism and colonialism and has as a real part of its staff and work Black women as well as white. The Rev. G. W. King, of a white Presbyterian church at West 115th Street, New York, has resigned. He said, "This section is now almost completely taken by Jews, Catholics and Negro people, so there is no possibility for the accomplishment of any real Christian work." The Reverend's honesty is marvelous and we love him for it, though God will certainly keep him out of Heaven, nonetheless. Du Bois remarks on the extraordinary rate of homicide in the United States; our history and our racism have produced "a nation of murderers." A call is made for the Black colleges to teach modern European languages, especially French and Spanish; this will help Black world unity. The acquittal by an all-white jury in Detroit in the Sweet case is a remarkable achievement and came from struggle, from Black unity and from the splendid talents of Clarence Darrow, the attorney. With great admiration, the story is told of Mrs. Nannie J. Myers of Chicago who, after months of labor, forced some slight change in a racist textbook used in the Chicago public schools. In "The Month's News" Du Bois points to: the general strike in Britain and its lessons (as in the previous month); the case of Sacco and Vanzetti again is mentioned; that they should be condemned to die "seems to us a miserable miscarriage of justice."

747. "Krigwa Players Little Negro Theatre," unsigned, July, 1926, Vol. XXXII, No. 3, pp. 134–136. Black drama must be by, for, and before Black people in order to fulfill itself; that is the purpose of the *Krigwa* movement begun in Harlem in 1925; the plays are to be about us, by us, for us, and near us. The story of the origins and fruition of the effort is here told.

748. W. P. Dabney, *Cincinnati's Colored Citizens*, initialed review, July, 1926, Vol. XXXII, No. 3, p. 142. The book is encyclopedic and therefore not possible to summarize, but splendid and causing comment and "ought to be widely read."

749. August, 1926, Vol. XXXII, No. 4. In "Opinion" (pp. 163–166), there is a new demand for college training and it must be met; the election of John A. Gregg as president of Howard university is momentous; for the first time a predominantly white board of trustees has selected a Black man to head a great organization. But Gregg has declined and now Mordecai Johnson has been selected and "may he succeed." Will W. Alexander of Atlanta is reflective of the New South among white people; he is not radical but he has honesty and he does criticize, and though attacked, he has held his ground—it is from such people that the white South may yet gain salvation. Senator William Edgar Borah has promised, at Du Bois' urging, to explain his attitude on the right of Black people to vote. Du Bois notes the Senator's reply "with interest."

750. September, 1926, Vol. XXXII, No. 5. In "Opinion" (pp. 215–218), The Fontainebleau School of Music in France is maintained by a committee of distinguished Americans—all of whom are named and include Mr and Mrs. Walter Damrosch and Mrs. H. H. Flagler. In its application blank it makes clear that only white students are admitted. Du Bois has written to all the members on the committee; no one has replied. The racism of the Catholic Church in the United States continues despite admonitions from the Pope. it is noted that Du Bois has left for Europe, travelling in Germany and Switzerland for a few weeks, and that in his absence, Mr. Dill and a young Mr. John P. Davis, a Fellow in Journalism at Harvard university, are in charge.

751. October, 1926, Vol. XXXII, No. 6. "Opinion" (pp. 283–288), announces that the Fourth Pan-African Congress will be held in New York City in August, 1927, largely because of the initiative of the Black women making up the Circle of Peace and Foreign Relations under the leadership of Mrs. A. W. Hunton. The retirement of Albert Bushnell Hart, after 40 years as professor of history at Harvard University, has been announced. He, together with William James and Josiah Royce, made deep impressions upon Du Bois as a student; what he most remembers is that all three made him a friend and made him welcome in their homes—"How singular a commentary" on the United States that this above all remains with me from Harvard! Mrs. Coralie C. Cook has retired after 12 years service as a member of the Board of Education of the District of Columbia; she "brought dignity and intelligence to bear in a nest of intrigue and graft" and "protected Negro womanhood from white skunks in Congress and out, Northern and Southern." Under "Crime" Du Bois publishes data on the fantastic cruelty regularly practiced against Black men and women held in prisons in the South. He notes that on the passenger list during his recent voyage he was listed as "Col. W. E. B. Du Bois." How did that happen? Perhaps someone had written his name and then after it had placed, "Col." to warn those who made arrangements for accommodations and then some innocent soul had assumed this meant rank and not color? In any case, Du Bois remarks that he did not take advantage of his high military rank.

752. "Criteria of Negro Art," signed, October, 1926, Vol. XXXII, No. 6, pp. 290–297. Text of a speech delivered earlier that year at the Annual Meeting of the NAACP in Chicago. Art as part of the struggle for freedom is affirmed. And it has been said we wish the rights of other citizens of the United States and we do, but does this mean that we wish to accept the standards and values of White America? No, and our different values reflect our different psychologies, outlooks, feelings and a different vision perhaps of Beauty. Some people assert that the Negro Renaissance and the achievements of a Cullen or a Hughes mean we are free. Nonsense, the discrimination is fierce and the oppression is heavy and not least for our artists (Du Bois gives examples). The art we produce must be ours and to achieve this will require a mighty struggle. As for the worry about propaganda, Du Bois insists that "all Art is propaganda and ever must be ... I do not care a damn for any art that is not used for propaganda." The absence of real freedom in art afflicts whites and Blacks, but the latter in a special and most onerous way, given the racist society in which we function. But "we can afford the Truth" while the dominant whites, being oppressive, cannot. And "we must come to the place where the work of art when it appears is reviewed and acclaimed by our own free and unfettered judgment."

753. November, 1926, Vol. XXXIII, No. 1. "Opinion" (pp. 7–8), "Building New Churches," suggests, on the basis of a letter from Henry W. Wheeler of St. Louis, that too much money is being spent too loosely on this kind of effort. "Russia, 1926" is written while there. Alone and unaccompanied he has walked through half a dozen of the larger cities; he has tried to look and understand in two months and he concludes, "I stand in astonishment and wonder at the revelation of Russia that has come to me. I may be partially deceived and half-informed. But if what I have seen with my eyes and heard with my ears in Russia is Bolshevism, I am a Bolshevik."

754. December, 1926, Vol. XXXIII, No. 2. In "Opinion" (pp. 59–65), "Peace" is a prose poem. "NAACP Funds," is a detailed answer to various charges recently given publicity as to alleged misuse of moneys. There is a description of his recent trip commencing with Antwerp, "to see Rubens," and then Cologne, Frankfurt, and Berlin, but "always the center" of the experience was Soviet Russia. Commenting on the celebration of the sesquicentennial of United States independence, Du Bois noted a lack of enthusiasm, perhaps because so few in this country are truly free. The great event was the Dempsey-Tunney fight. The country acclaims a Queen Marie of Romania—"the ruling monarch of one of the most disgustingly reactionary lands in the world"—and lets "Eugene Debs die in moral exile." Tribute is paid to Debs, who "knew that no real emancipation of laboring classes in the United States can come as long as black laborers are in partial serfdom."

755. January, 1927, Vol. XXXIII, No. 3. In "Opinion" (pp. 127–131), "Assets and Liabilities" of the preceding year; "The War Amendments" is offered as a lesson to Senator Borah, whose answer to Du

Bois' invitation to express his views on Afro-American voting appears in this issue and reflects profound ignorance of history and of the present; "Pickens" announces that William Lloyd Pickens, on the staff of the NAACP, recently sailed for Europe to lecture in England and to attend the International Congress of the Oppressed Nations in Belgium. A person named Lawton affirms in a recent issue of the *Independent* that the NAACP advocates intermarriage. It does not and Du Bois again explains the position; he concludes, "Despite everything we still maintain that English dukes should have the right to marry Americans. But we do not 'advocate' it. We have too much respect for Americans." The singing of Roland Hayes is again hailed and the point is made of its impact upon the thousands of whites who hear him. The November elections show vividly how true it is "that the rulership of wealth in the United States is more and more open and direct." Attacks upon the leadership of the NAACP as being above the real battle are rejected; it is pointed out that Walter White covers lynchings at risk of his life; that the editor of the *Crisis* has travelled repeatedly through every southern state and has spoken publicly there exactly as he does elsewhere and that all its officers are continually in the field. Three efforts recently undertaken by the League of Nations especially concern the Afro-American: the Mandates system but it does not really fight colonialism; the anti-slavery treaty but this seems aimed mainly at household workers in Ethiopia rather than real slavery in the colonies in Africa; and efforts by the International Labor Office to draft minimum standards for workers but colored labor has not been called into council on this question. We should have permanent representation in Geneva. "Unions" notes that the process of Blacks joining unions is slowly going forward; mentioned are the Pullman porters, the strike of Paper Box industry workers in New York City and of a strike of Black women in Chicago which has been helped by white workers. Attention is called to the rise in the number of lynchings—18 in 1925 but 31 in 1926.

756. "Five Books," signed reviews, January, 1927, Vol. XXXIII, No. 3, pp. 152–153: Eric Walrond, *Tropic Death*; Leo Weiner, *Mayan and Mexican Origins*; Rossa B. Cooley, *Homes of the Freed*; J. W. Johnson and J. R. Johnson, eds., *Second Book of Negro* Spirituals; and W. S. Braithwaite, ed., *Anthology of Magazine Verse*, 14th edition. The Walrond collection of ten stories "is a distinct contribution to Negro American literature"; it shows "with singular vividness the life of black laborers of the West Indies." Leo Wiener again shows the heavy

African influence in early Latin-American civilizations; Rossa Cooley, a principal of a school for Black youngsters in South Carolina, has written "interestingly" of "three generations of Negro women"; the book by the Johnsons is a beautiful one; and Mr. Braithwaite's anthology maintains the high level of his earlier efforts.

757. February, 1927, Vol. XXXIII, No. 4. "Opinion," (pp. 179–183) " 'Science' " derides and rebuts the findings of a Dr. N. M. Hirsh allegedly showing the inferior intelligence of Portuguese and Black children in New England. There is danger of U.S. war upon Mexico, just as it is intervening in Nicaragua: "Let us face death, jail and poverty before war with Mexico on any pretext." Corruption has been discovered in Georgia and when it is proposed to investigate the disfranchisement of Black people "the bourbon New York *Times* is aghast." The increase in the number of lynchings in 1926 (actually 34 men and not 31, as stated in No. 755) is due to the collapse of the effort to pass an anti-lynching bill. A bronze bust of the late John E. Milholland is pictured and Du Bois appeals for funds to place a replica in the national office of the NAACP for "unless we remember, young eager folk will lightly assume in 2010 that it was an easy, costless thing in 1910 to defend Negro suffrage and propose a paid, permanent office staff for the radical Negro Conference" which Milholland did and then so acted as to help carry these things forward. Congratulations are offered two Black newspapers, the *New York Age* and the *Philadelphia Bulletin* each of which has past its fortieth birthday. "Optimism" is called for, Du Bois believes, in the signs of advance on the part of Black people, in their organization of legal defense, in their growing self-assertiveness, in their heightened artistic achievements, in their educational progress and "finally, in the dull brain of white America" some realization is growing of the potential of Afro-Americans.

758. "Judging Russia," signed, February, 1927, Vol. XXXIII, No. 4, pp. 189–190. "Russia is trying to make the workingman the main object of industry." Organized capital in the United States and in Western Europe "has used every modern weapon to crush Russia" and this impedes the loosening of controls in Russia. "The real Russian question is: Can you make the worker and not the millionaire the center of modern power and culture? If you can, the Russian Revolution will sweep the world."

759. March, 1927, Vol. XXXIV, No. 1. A change occurs here; Jessie R. Fauset is no longer mentioned; Aaron Douglas is listed as "Art

Critic." The department, "Opinion," is dropped; instead there is "The Wide Wide World," (p. 3) and a department called "Postscript." These two departments will hereafter be treated and numbered separately. "The Wide Wide World" declares a push to the Right in Germany is discernible but resistance, especially by "Socialistic Labor," is still strong. Fascism in Italy becomes more and more repressive and imperial England is able to resist the force of labor at home because it "holds in its hand millions of voiceless darker people." China "has awakened and is going to be Free." U.S. investments in Latin America may yet cause further bloody intervention. A fundamental problem in the United States is monopoly. "Poverty and Wealth will gird themselves for a new battle in this land during the 21st Century."

760. "What to Read," unsigned, March, 1927, Vol. XXXIV, No. 1, pp. 20, 32. Reviewed are Langston Hughes, *Fine Clothes to the Jew*; William A. Banks, *Beyond the Rockies*; Carter G. Woodson, ed., *The Mind of the Negro as Reflected in Letters Written During the Crisis, 1800–1860*; W. J. King, *The Negro in American Life*. The poems of Banks are "not strong or striking" but not without merit. The Hughes book is described as splendid and readers are urged to buy it as they are the immensely useful collection edited by Dr. Woodson. King's small book "seems thorough and well done." Notes about relevant articles in current magazines appear with special attention to essays by Patric Duncam in *Foreign Affairs* for January, Franz Boas in *Current History* for February and a story by Rudolph Fisher in the *Atlantic Monthly* for January.

761. March, 1927, Vol. XXXIV, No. 1. In "Postscript," (pp. 33–34), Black people are urged to support the work of the Children's Bureau in the U.S. Department of Labor; William Pickens' journey in England, Germany, the U.S.S.R. and Belgium is affirmed a great success; conditions at Lincoln, Pennsylvania, Fisk and Howard Universities are improved. A speech by Edwin Mims of Vanderbilt University reflects the mounting disenchantment of younger Southern whites with Bourbon domination. Du Bois comments, "I have always believed that when the definite open split between liberal and Bourbon came in the South, the day of real emancipation for black and white slaves would dawn." When Black bishops decided not to participate in any way in the "National Citizens Committee of One Thousand for Law Enforcement" because they were asked to come to its business meetings but not its dinner, they did themselves and all of us proud. Concessions to Firestone in Liberia certainly are a cause for concern, but if the

Black voters of the United States exercise their power with care this need not mean disaster. What an appalling spectacle it is that in Aiken, South Carolina, several Black people are lynched and their killers are known and yet they walk the streets freely and it is said that the United States can do nothing!

762. "The Wide Wide World," April, 1927, Vol. XXXIV, No. 2, p. 39. Portugal, Mexico, Poland writhe under landed aristocracies with the first dominated by England and the second by the United States. The third has the added characteristic of intensive anti-Semitism and also serving "as Europe's cat's paw against Russia." Germany's Right tendencies intensify. The effort to divide and rule in China may yet fail. President Coolidge calls for disarmament but with the holding of colonies and with inter-imperialist rivalries there will be no disarmament.

763. May, 1927, Vol. XXXIV, No. 2. In "Postscript" (pp. 69–70), a projection is made of what it would mean if the poorer and middle farmers of the West and the laboring people of the nation and the Black people were to unite in opposition to wealth. He recently faced two audiences of several hundreds—mostly white—in Philadelphia and in Denver; in the one he was merely a symbol and the audience sensed mood not fact but in the latter there was keen interest because the KKK is strong and the struggle is intense. In "Boys and Girls" Du Bois reports the tendency among Black folk of giving more education to the girls than to the boys—unlike other people. This is wrong and "the remedy is not less education for the girls but more for the boys." He finds what he calls "the higher friction" in relations between white and Black people in the United States; he thinks the key areas were: 1860, physical freedom; 1870, crime and poverty; 1880, the right to hold property; 1890, reading and writing; 1900, voting; 1910, lynching; 1920, homes. "The founding stones still waver, far from fast, but the trembling walls reach up to higher friction." In "Criteria of Negro Art," Du Bois reiterates his belief "that the Negro as a race has always exhibited peculiar artistic ability." To flourish, this requires freedom for the artist to perform and create and the artist must be supported by an audience so that he may and will produce. The theme of the Black experience provides for artists, given those conditions, "an astonishingly fertile field."

764. May, 1927, Vol. XXXIV, No. 3. In "The Wide Wide World" (p. 75), intrigue and slaughter continue in China and it is Russia alone which assists that nation's true interests; the lying of the State department is extraordinary—this time the occasion is Mexico; Italy has its eyes on Albania and Abyssinia but a divided Europe cannot prevent the realization of that dream. Henry Ford in defending himself in court insists that a race cannot be libeled (in this case Jewish people). "We Negroes could give the courts some information on that matter. Our history here from 1619 to 1927 has been one long vicious libel, mis-called the *Negro Problem*."

765. "The Browsing Reader," unsigned, May, 1927, Vol. XXXIV, No. 3, pp. 92–102. Attention is called to a series, "Economic Classic," being published by the Vanguard Press New York, including works by Ruskin, Tolstoy, Wells, and Lenin. The same press recently issued Harry Laidler and Norman Thomas, *The New Tactics in Social Conflict* and "the excellent study" by Charles H. Wesley, *Negro Labor in the United States*. Du Bois states he will review that in the future along with Julia Peterkin's *Black April*. On the whole, he finds more to praise than to blame in the English edition of André Siegfried's *American Comes of Age*. Scanning the magazines, Du Bois summarizes articles of value on Africa by Lord Olivier in the *Contemporary Review* (February); Evans Lewis in *Foreign Affairs* (April) and an editorial in the *New Statesman* (March 5). All show an awareness "that at bottom, the race problem is in truth an economic problem." James Weldon Johnson's "beautiful poem," "Go Down, Death," appears in the *American Mercury* (April) and Rayford Logan contributes an illuminating study of Haiti today in the *Nation* (March 16).

766. May, 1927, Vol. XXXIV, No. 3. In "Postscript" (pp. 105–106), the few Afro-Americans employed in the foreign service of the United States are treated with contempt; the meeting devoted to Africa and held at Le Zoute in Belgium last summer marked a renewed attempt by whites to run affairs in Africa and to dominate so-called reform efforts there. Data on so-called Negro Crime is offered from the census. Black people form 10 percent of the population and 23 percent of those in jail. This is the result of racism and of the social conditions produced by racism and should induce renewed efforts on our part. The NAACP has won significant victories in the courts in the 17 years of its existence: 1915 against the "Grandfather Clause"; in 1917, against residential segregation; in 1923, that a fair trial meant one without mob intimidation; and in 1927, so far, two more: against the White Primary and declaring the New Orleans segregation ordinance unconstitutional. "It means," writes Du Bois, "that the battle of the color line need never be a battle of blood and blows. It can be a battle of laws and justice."

767. June, 1927, Vol. XXXIV, No. 4. Here begins the editorial section called "As the Crow Flies" rather than "The Wide Wide World" (p. 111). The civilized world seems to despise truth, as illustrated by the lies peddled about what the United States is doing—and why—in Haiti, Nicaragua, and Mexico. And Massachusetts is to execute Sacco and Vanzetti "without really knowing whether they are guilty of murder or not." Efforts to curb the right to strike—in England, Italy and the United States—are regressive. Japan's serious economic troubles may yet force her to side "with the colored race where she belongs" rather than being, as she is, among China's main oppressors. The effort of man to fly across the Atlantic ocean is thrilling but it is marred by the military uses to which aviation is put. A disaster such as the recent Mississippi flood is for us an awful calamity for in its valley live millions of our people and 80 percent of the flood's victims are Black.

768. "The Browsing Reader", signed with initials, June, 1927, Vol. XXXIV, No. 4, pp. 129, 139. In Honoré W. Morrow's novel, *Forever Free* appears the character of Elizabeth Keckley, the headseamstress of the White House in Lincoln's day; Du Bois recalls that he knew her when he taught at Wilberforce university and she was the teacher of sewing. He goes on to commend the novel as, generally, a valid depiction of the circumstances leading to the Emancipation Proclamation. Hallie Q. Brown's *Homespun Heroines* contains biographies of 54 Black women and provides information "hitherto difficult to find." Julia Peterkin's novel, *Black April* does not possess "that fine sympathy with poor black folk" that made her earlier *Green Thursday* "an excellent book." It wallows in dirt and "unspeakable stuff"; persons "who enjoy diving in mud" will enjoy this book. Margaret L. Thomas has produced "a readable children's book of travel," *George Washington Lincoln Goes around the World*. Articles of consequence in current magazines include a discussion of the economic foundations of racism by Abram L. Harris in *Social Forces* (March), a discussion about segregation by Kelly Miller and H. J. Seligmann in *Current History* (March) and a group of poems from West Africa by Aquah Laluah in the *Atlantic* (April) which "is a relief from the hectic efforts of the modernists." "That Marcus Garvey is still in the mind of America," is shown, Du Bois adds, by references to him in "magazines of both races": Benjamin Brawley in *Southern Workman* (April) "attributes to Garvey the feeling of race consciousness which has come since the World War" and Kelly Miller in *Contemporary Review* (April) says the same thing, adding, as phrased by Du Bois, "Other movements which have been sponsored by the intelligentsia have made no impression upon the laboring classes."

769. "Postscript," June, 1927, Vol. XXXIV, No. 4, pp. 131–132. The late election in Chicago was "a serious misfortune." The Democratic candidate for mayor had made "overtures" to our people and the Republican incumbent, William Thompson, "is a well-known demagogue who represents open house to gamblers, bootleggers and prostitutes." However, in the campaign, the Democrats produced some of the vilest racist propaganda in history and so the Black population felt it had to vote for Thompson and he won. "For bull-headed asininity, commend us to the Democratic party." Du Bois adds, however, that Tammany functions with a "glimmering of common sense." Published is an exchange of letters with an unnamed editor who has asked for Du Bois' help in finding a white Southerner "who would vigorously ask for civil rights for the Negro in the South" but neither he nor Du Bois have found one. A report is made documenting U.S. influence upon Mexico and Brazil to "keep Negroes from migrating, especially to Mexico and South America." An impressionist picture is painted of the "Near East"—Turkey and Greece—as a result of Du Bois' recent trip.

770. July, 1927, Vol. XXXIV, No. 5. "As the Crow Flies" (p. 147), The Supreme Court took "a backward step" in upholding the conviction of Anita Whitney under California's sedition act—"thus do we try to dam the waters of progress." The torment of Sacco-Vanzetti continues. The U.S. government taxes the poor much more heavily than the rich and spends much too little on health, education and social purposes. U.S. interference in other nations' affairs continues as exemplified recently in China and Nicaragua. Lynching can be stopped and will be when Black people stand and fight. England provokes disputes with the Soviet Union and Christendom quietly applauds the killing of Soviet diplomats in Poland and Switzerland.

771. "George Forbes of Boston: A Servant of Jew and Gentile," unsigned, July, 1927, Vol. XXXIV, No. 5, (pp. 151–152). George W. Forbes had served the Boston Public Library branch in the West End for thirty-two years; that part of Boston had been a center of Black folk but for many years its heaviest population was Jewish. Upon his death fine tribute was paid to him in the *Jewish Daily Forward* in an essay by

M. Bender and it is published in this issue. This is introduced by Du Bois with a chronicle of Forbes' life, especially his key role, with Trotter, on the Boston *Guardian* in fighting the influence of the Tuskegee Machine; Du Bois adds, "Time has mellowed some of his judgments. We look upon Washington now as a necessary phenomenon—as a sort of stepping sideways before Almighty Prejudice; but with all that, the work of Forbes was just as necessary and just as inevitable."

772. "The Browsing Reader," initialed; July, 1927, Vol. XXXIV, No. 5; pp. 159–160. Mentioned are: Leon Whipple, *The Story of Civil Liberty in the United States*; Scott Nearing, *Where is Civilization Going*, and Robert Blatchford, *Not Guilty*, all published by Vanguard Press in New York. Reviewed are: James Weldon Johnson, *God's Trombones: Seven Negro Sermons in Verse* which "blazes a new path toward the preservation of the Negro idiom in art"; Charles H. Wesley's *Negro Labor in the United States* is called a book "thoroughly and competently done" with "an excellent bibliography"; James E. Amos, *Theodore Roosevelt: Hero to his Valet* has some illuminating comments on the famous dinner Roosevelt had with Booker T. Washington; Samuel Schmalhausen, *Humanizing Education* "is a fearless appeal for reason in modern education" and so will probably not get a wide circulation in the United States. Du Bois notes the receipt of a brief work edited by Alain Locke, *Four Negro Poets* containing poems by Toomer, McKay, Hughes, and Cullen. Among the pieces in magazines to which Du Bois calls particular attention are: L. Singhor, a Black man from Africa, who condemns colonialism in the *Living Age* (May 15); the same issue publishes labor songs from China—Du Bois adds: "China and Russia are becoming the beacons of all oppressed peoples." Thomas A. Dabney's essay on "Class or Race" is in the *Socialist Review* (January) and "it outlines clearly the story of the rapid rise and fall of the racial movement led by Marcus Garvey and the beginning of the Negro Socialist movement." E. Franklin Frazier has a useful essay, "The Pathology of Race Prejudice" in the *Forum* (June); and Granville Hicks publishes "an entertaining interview" with the Black novelist, Wallace Thurman, in *The Churchman* (April 30).

773. July, 1927, Vol. XXXIV, No. 5. In "Postscript" (pp. 167–168), two white high school girls are raped in Coffeeville, Kansas, and claim Black men were guilty. The ghetto is attacked; Blacks fight back—led by men named Anderson and Ford—and check the mob, though some are wounded. Three Black men are arrested for "rape" and two are released quickly as no evidence against them exists. The other later is released and now it is confirmed that white men were involved; one is in jail and one of the girls also has been jailed as "accessory." Mrs. Thelma E. Williams, head of the Domestic Science Department at Howard High School in Wilmington, Delaware, has been refused permission to study "advanced cookery" in a school—in Boston! The United States Public Health Service is funding the giving of so-called intelligence tests in some Southern cities and its purpose is racist. "There is no scientific test of native intelligence and that every honest person knows." Why is the United States government spending money in this area? The death of Alice Work, teacher of music (as well as her husband John) at Fisk university is noted; the two of them led sacrificial and beautiful lives. Rose Ward Hunt, who, as a girl was sold at a mock auction at Beecher's church in Brooklyn, New York, returned to that church recently. This is a reminder "that the bulk of the Christian Church, together with the wisest and richest of the people of the United States, defended this system for 250 years; and there are some still defending it." Condemned is the damnably racist treatment meted out to the Black survivors of the Mississippi flood, at the hands of President Coolidge and his cabinet member, Herbert Hoover.

774. August, 1927, Vol. XXXIV, No. 6. In "As the Crow Flies" (p. 183), the means being tried to crush revolution in Russia are exactly the means used by Austria, England and Czarist Russia against France. "China is slowly and relentlessly kicking Europe into the sea." "Henry Ford has apologized to the Jews! The Negroes are now expecting to hear from [Senator] Cole Blease."

775. August, 1927, Vol. XXXIV, No. 6. In "Postscript" (pp. 203–204), several Afro-Americans have been burned alive in Louisville, Mississippi; the reason, according to the Southern press," ... widespread indignation at the refusal of the Negroes traveling in slow, second-hand Fords to give road to faster cars." And U.S. "statesmen" try to persuade the world that this is a civilized country! Every once in a while, the New York *Herald-Tribune* announces the discovery of bolshevism among us Black people. In the lynchings and discrimination practiced, there might well be reason for more such among us, in fact. The forthcoming Fourth Pan-African Congress is announced. W. A. Robinson, Supervisor of Colored High Schools for North Carolina, has just issued a study showing that in any one of the Southern states there are more high schools for white children than there are such schools for Black Children in all the Southern states combined! "Mob

Tactics" in the United States have reached institutionalized forms —accusation, lynchings, looting, police participation, victimization, and no whites punished. "The only solution to this kind of problem is not only to permit but to encourage Negroes to keep and use arms in defense against lynchers and mobs."

776. September, 1927, Vol. XXXIV, No. 7. In "As the Crow Flies" (p. 219), a little boy now rules Romania, where "Jew-baiting and stealing land from Russia are popular industries." The Roman Catholic hierarchy has found something in the United States of which to complain: prize fighting and lecherous movies; "we laugh."

777. "The Browsing Reader, September, 1927, Vol. XXXIV, No. 7, p. 227. Initialled reviews are of *Congaree Sketches* by E. C. Adams, with an introduction by Paul Green (Chapel Hill: The University of North Carolina Press); E. B. Reuter, *The American Race Problem* (New York: Crowell-Collier); T. E. Lawrence, *Revolt in the Desert*; O. A. Scott, *Home Buyer's Guide and Calculator* (Kansas City, privately printed). In the first book, Green's introduction is "a fine essay"; for "like everything that Green writes about the Negro it is at bottom full of the spirit of human brotherhood." The collection is worth reading, but it is very one-sided for "the author has carefully cut out from all this folk stuff every reference to Negro ambition, education, aspiration to better earthly things. ... " Reuter's is a textbook collecting all accepted wisdom, which is to say there is little in it. "The writer is not a human being and is not acquainted with human beings. He is studying books and statistics with the usual result." Lawrence's best seller is interesting "to colored folk chiefly for the light which it throws on the methods of English imperialists." Scott's little book will help those who are buying on installment. Du Bois also notes the appearance of the *Home Mission College Review*, edited by Benjamin Brawley and issued by the ten colleges supported by the American Baptist Home Mission Society. He thinks the first number is a good one.

778. September, 1927, Vol. XXXIV, No. 7. In "Postscript" (pp. 239–240), the NAACP as of July, 1927 achieved full triumph in the defense of the Sweet family because Detroit gave up all attempt to prosecute its members; to achieve this cost almost $40,000 and months of work. "It is possible to get justice in the United States but one has to be able and ready to pay a fortune for it." Du Bois comments on the revolution in the education of Black people; he refers especially to higher education, for in 1927 there were "in Negro colleges alone *ten* *thousand students of full college grade!*" He contrasts this, and the acceptance of the need for higher education for Black people, with conditions just 25 years ago when to advocate higher education was to be "driven from jobs and to be ridiculed in the public press." It is necessary to end the practice at Lincoln University (Pennsylvania) which alone of the schools teaching our young people "refuses to have a Negro professor." Tribute is paid to Alonzo F. Herndon, of Georgia, born a slave, who has managed to be among the most successful business men in his state, despite all obstacles. Du Bois remarks that Herndon's first wife, Adrienne McNeil, "a woman of extraordinary dramatic ability" was once offered the leading role in "The Klansman" by Thomas Dixon, "in blissful ignorance of her Negro descent!" The principles of legal aid undertaken by the NAACP are explained; they concern only cases "involving discrimination and injustice because of race and color" and cases which "will serve to establish a precedent that will favorably affect the rights of colored people as a whole." Writing of "Harlem" Du Bois notes "it is not chiefly cabarets, it is chiefly homes; it is not all color, song and dance, it is work, thrift and sacrifice." If it is to be "bribed and bought by white wastrels, distorted by unfair novelists and lied about by sensationalists, it will lose sight of its own soul and wander bewildered in a scoffing world."

779. October, 1927, Vol. XXXIV, No. 8. In "As the Crow Flies" (p. 255), Judge Gary, of United States Steel, is dead; as a fierce foe of organized labor, his life shows that to fight such men successfully takes organization, brains, and money. Herbert Hoover is again denounced for his racism as manifested in the handling of flood relief. Du Bois rejoices at the news of uprisings among the Indians in Bolivia; they have been suppressed, but other uprisings will occur and victory will yet come. It is time to call back all the occupation troops in Germany.

780. "The Pan-African Congresses," unsigned, October, 1927, Vol. XXXIV, No. 8, pp. 263–264. A bare—almost statistical—summary of the first three Congresses and a fuller report on the fourth, held in New York City in August, attended by a total of 5,000 people with 208 paid delegates from 22 states and the District of Columbia, the West Indies, South America, much of West Africa, Germany, and India. The Resolutions are published in full with demands for the enhancement of the right of Africans and African-derived peoples as central. Added is the wish for the freedom and "real national independence" of Egypt, China, and India, and the termination of U.S. interference in the affairs of Central and South America. The U.S.S.R. is "thanked" "for its liberal attitude toward the colored races and for the help which it has extended to them from time to time." "White workers" are urged "to realize that no program of labor uplift can be successfully carried through in Europe or America so long as colored labor is exploited and enslaved and deprived of all political power."

781. "The Browsing Reader," unsigned, October, 1927, Vol. XXXIV, No. 8, pp. 266; 283: Two books are reviewed at some length: Emily Greene Balch, editor, *Occupied Haiti* (New York: Writers' Publishing Company,) and Lord Olivier's *Anatomy of African Misery* (London: Hogarth). The first is the report by the committee created by the Women's International League for Peace and Freedom which consisted of two Afro-American women—Charlotte Atwood and Addie W. Hunton—with Emily G. Balch, Zonia Baber, and Paul H. Douglas, of the University of Chicago, the sole male member. Its damning indictment of the occupation is persuasive; this is indeed "the book for which we all have long been waiting." Olivier's book is "by long odds the best book which has appeared on the race problem in South Africa."

782. October, 1927, Vol. XXXIV, No. 8, In "Postscript" (pp. 275–276) "Children" (this is the magazine's 16th Annual children's number), Du Bois agrees with scientists who are now stressing the significance of environment in molding people; this contrasts with a prior insistence upon heredity as being all-decisive. He also observes, citing an article by L. I. Dublin (in the September *American Mercury*), that there has been a very substantial reduction in the death rate among Black people—by 50 percent in the past 40 years. The annual meeting of the "colored Elks" in Harlem was wonderful; 50,000 people came and Harlem was lit up and friendly and all went well but the white press—except the *World* "as usual"—simply did not report it because the news was too good and the sight too lovely. The death of Sir H. H. Johnston of England brings forth a high evaluation of his scholarship on Africa and an expression of warmth for his friendship. The 75th birthday of the banker, George Foster Peabody, should not pass unremarked in the Black press. He has not seen eye to eye with me, writes Du Bois, and many others among us, but as a white Southerner he has been generous and decent and far ahead of "most Southerners." In August of this year, a white woman has confessed that in 1919 she—having blackened her face and donned male attire—had killed a white woman. For years the NAACP had fought to save the life of Maurice Mays who was accused of that murder but the community wanted to lynch him—he was "uppity"—and though his story was air-tight Tennessee did execute him in 1922. An article by Henry Mencken in his *American Mercury* (September), insisting that Black people as artists had produced only second-rate work, has aroused much comment. As to Mencken, his attitude towards us "is calmly and judiciously fair" for he "neither loves nor hates us"—he just is ignorant, that is all, and alas, it is to be expected. Du Bois states some facts and concludes, "On the whole, then, we Negroes are quite well satisfied with our Renaissance. And we have not yet finished."

783. November, 1927, Vol. XXXIV, No. 9. "As the Crow Flies" (p. 293), notes that "Katherine Mayo, white American, declares that brown India is sexually immoral. Thus the pot calls the kettle black." "This month Russia celebrates ten years of freedom from the tyranny of the Czars. Congratulations." Corruption in Pennsylvania and Indiana has reached new lows—"white civilization is blossoming."

784. "The Browsing Reader, initialled, November, 1927, Vol. XXXIV, No. 9, p. 308. Brief commentary upon the reissuance of James Weldon Johnson's *Autobiography of an Ex-Colored Man* with an introduction by Carl Van Vechten; Ralph W. Bullock, *In Spite of Handicaps* offers brief biographies of certain Black personalities like Roland Hayes, Countee Cullen, John Hope, which "should be popular in homes and schools"; W. P. Dabney has published through his own company in Cincinnati a brief *Life of Maggie L. Walker* which "should have wide reading"; Countee Cullen's *Copper Sun* "is full of exquisite poetry and adds to his rapidly growing reputation"; "three studies on Negro life" are all "encouraging" and their data are briefly summarized: Abram L. Harris, *Negro Population in Minneapolis*; Niles Carpenter, *Nationality, Color and Economic Opportunity in Buffalo* and T. Edward* Hill, *Report of the West Virginia Bureau of Negro Welfare and Statistics for 1925-26*. Occasional Papers of the Slater Fund, Nos. 23, 24 are worth reading: James Weldon Johnson, *Five Letters of the University Commission on Southern Race Questions* and *Native African Races and Culture*. The latter is an "excellent compilation."

785. November, 1927, Vol. XXXIV, No. 9, pp. 311–312;322. Herbert Hoover has appointed a committee with Black members on it to investigate charges of peonage growing out of the Mississippi flood, but Du Bois fears its report will be a whitewash. A letter is quoted from a white woman, Helen D. Pecu of Washington State, who is a regular

---

*This should be Arnold.

reader of the *Crisis* and thinks it "excellent" but who is troubled by Du Bois' "violently prejudiced" feelings towards white people; she asks him to "withhold your private political and prejudiced rancor." Du Bois replies that he is "one of the greatest sinners" in being "prejudiced against white people." This comes from "long experience." But it is true that "the worst fruit of prejudice is retaliatory prejudice" and this may appear even against "those white people who are not prejudiced, or who earnestly desire not to be." But Mrs. Pecu must learn that "no Negro born in America can be expected to be sweet-tempered, charitable and broadminded toward white people." Still, writes Du Bois, "he should nevertheless try to achieve such an attitude." But, "If he fails ... lay it to the last lynching, or to the last time he was insulted in the theatre, or to the last time he went hungry because all available hotels and restaurants were closed against him." The nomination of Alfred E. Smith by the Democrats delights him, for the South will have to take him—though he is a Catholic and a "wet" and far from an "aristocrat." A true story is told by Du Bois, involving the treatment by a Black physician in an emergency of the Southern wife of a Senator aboard a train; he pulls her through and refuses payment and this presents the problem of his assuming to be a social equal! A law to ban intermarriage has Georgia worried; it does not bother Black people, but white people have to prove they are white! There is much criticism of Liberia and there are things to criticize about it, but Liberia exists and is "stronger in its independence than it has been for a half century" and for this "all Negroes should be proud."

786. December, 1927, Vol. XXXIV, No. 10. In "As the Crow Flies" (p. 327), the deaths of two surpassingly beautiful artists, Isadora Duncan and Florence Mills, are recorded. Vicksburg has erected a statue to Jefferson Davis, "the great Apostle of Freedom." In the Soviet Union, a jury has acquitted the killer of the White Guard pogromist, Petlura. "Suppose some American Negro should slap the Grand Dragon!" We dark people are not saints, it is true, but what with people like Albert Fall and Harry Sinclair and others of the Teapot Dome scandal, "we are distinctly uplifted and hopeful."

787. "The Browsing Reader," unsigned Vol. XXXIV, No. 10, December, 1927, p. 338. Mary White Ovington's *Portraits in Color* "is an honest and moving piece of work"; J. H. Nankivell, has edited *The History of the Twenty-Fifth Regiment United States Infantry* (he is a Captain) and it is a "deserving tribute," but "colored readers will hunt in vain for any reference to the late Colonel Young or any of the colored officers who from time to time served with the regiment." John J. Niles, a white man, has produced *Singing Soldiers*; it is "made up of Negro songs, of all sorts and kinds." "Most of the illustrations are but caricatures, but the book as a whole is finely and sympathetically done."

788. December, 1927, Vol. XXXIV, No. 10, pp. 347–348. The strike of students at Hampton Institute is greeted as a positive sign of the appearance of independence and militancy among our youth. It has been known for a long time that the authorities there did not have feelings "acceptable to self-respecting black men." Distressing was the attitude of some alumni and parents who turned against the youth. Students "are far better judges" of the school than parents or alumni; what shall students do if not protest when they know their school is going wrong? "Students are not sent to school to learn to obey. They are sent there to learn to do, to think, to execute, to be men and women." The Durham, North Carolina, Conference on Race Relations, to meet this month, should be worthwhile for its purpose is to discover the actual state of affairs among our people, what best ought to be done, and then agree how to do it. Such gatherings are needed. The tenth anniversary of the Bolshevik Revolution is hailed. The Czarist government was a stench, but all high society wanted to be presented at its court and even liberals rarely spoke out against it. In 1905 Western Europe rushed to save the Czar. Since the revolution the western press has damned the new society, yet it is one that should have congratulations and not condemnation. Despite everything, "the Union of Soviet Socialist Republics is celebrating today its Tenth Anniversary, and here's hoping that this is but the first decade towards its hundred years." A concluding section pays tribute to the Pullman porters and their brave efforts at organization; these have not yet fully succeeded, but with effort they will and the effort is worthwhile.

789. January, 1928, Vol. XXXV, No. 1. "As The Crow Flies" (p. 3)—there is general talk of peace but few signs of it. Soviet Russia's actual advocacy of disarmament brings her under suspicion. Writhing in Egypt and China and India. ...

790. "The Browsing Reader," January, 1928, Vol. XXXV, No. 1. Initialled review of Countee Cullen, editor, *Caroling Dusk* is "delicately and discreetly done"; it is the fourth anthology of Black verse within past six years, but there is very little duplication, testifying "to a virility and new birth of Negro literature." The book edited by Alain Locke and Montgomery Gregory, *Plays of Negro Life* "supplies a wide demand." This is "a new province in our national literature." The splendid artistry of Aaron Douglas adorns both volumes. Attention is called to the fourth edition of Carter G. Woodson's *The Negro in our History*—"it has become the best handy encyclopedia of the Negro in America that one could buy." Walter Fleming's *Freedmen's Savings Bank* "is a story of philanthropy and fraud." The author is "no friend of Negroes" but he exposes "with dispassionate impartiality this disgraceful episode." *North Carolina Chain Gang* by Jesse F. Steiner and Roy M. Brown is "excellent" and "ought to form a basis of intelligent reform." William English Walling's *The Mexican Question*, attacking intervention by the United States in Mexico, contains "a true thesis."

791. "Postscript," January, 1928, Vol. XXXV, No. 1, pp. 23–24; 34. Assets and Debits of 1927; an attack upon anti-Semitism in education as formerly practiced in Czarist Russia, and now in Hungary—and in Harvard, Columbia and Butler Universities; he calls attention to British-Ethiopian-United States conflicts and tangles centering on control of the Nile; a depiction, from official statistics, of the gross racist discrimination practiced by South Carolina in education; a tribute to a Black young man in Louisville, Kentucky, William Warley, who has been fighting a battle with his newspaper for independence in politics and for anti-lynching legislation. His press was destroyed by a mob of Black men, obviously in the employ of hostile gangsters and political hacks. What are we doing to see to it that Black men are raised in such a way that none would participate in such an undertaking and what are we doing to encourage the Warleys among us? An exchange of letters between a Bernice E. Brand of San Diego and the Doctor is published. Typical racist clichés come from the reader and Du Bois explains and clarifies—yet again—in detail and with calm. Finally, Lincoln University (Pennsylvania) has elected its first Black trustee —Dr. E. P. Roberts—and this is the result of the battle put up by the alumni, led by Dr. W. G. Alexander.

792. February, 1928, Vol. XXV, No. 2. "As the Crow Flies" (p. 39), Attacks upon Hearst, Chiang and U.S. intervention in Nicaragua; able to subsidize manufacturers of woolen clothes, but not the cost of a subway ride in New York City; Sandino, George Washington, Maceo, Toussaint were all bandits once, "a *bandit* fights for a lost cause. A *Patriot* fights the cause that wins."

793. "Marcus Garvey and the NAACP," unsigned; February, 1928, Vol. XXXV, No. 2, p. 51. Written as a summary of the past writings about Garvey appearing in the *Crisis* which, until September, 1922, tended to be favorable and then changed as he did; the occasion for this summary is Garvey's release from prison and his deportation, Du Bois affirms he had no connection in any way either with his imprisonment or with his deportation. We wish him well and "will be the first to applaud any success that he may have."

794. February, 1928, Vol. XXXV, No. 2, p. 58. "The Browsing Reader," initialled reviews: Paxton Hibben, *Henry Ward Beecher*, is praised for its realism which does not detract, writes Du Bois, from Beecher's important contribution to the movement for emancipation. He notes that Hibben finds it "astounding" for that day "or any day" to conceive of a woman running for President and a Black person for Vice President of the United States; Du Bois asks, "why so 'astounding' and in *any* 'other day'"? William H. Jones, *Recreation and Amusement Among Negroes* in Washington, D.C. "is valuable chiefly in opening a field for unprejudiced and informing inquiry." Its protest against discrimination in the capital's theaters and public institutions is well taken. Alice Werner of the University of London has produced a *First Swahili Reader*, which "shows the extraordinary ingenuity and flexibility of the African languages."

795. "Postscript," February, 1928, Vol. XXXV, No. 2, pp. 61–62. Tremendous excitement exists in England concerning the wording and use of a prayer book, and "that same England is unmoved by starving miners, child-slavery in South Africa" the enslavement of India—and "they call this White Civilization!" In Cullen's *Caroling Dusk*, the editor was deceived by the plagiarism of Albert Rice; a dastardly act and we "should drive the young thief out from the congregation of the decent." A prose poem recalling his view of Seville, Spain, follows. Considerable excerpts from his debate recently with Lothrop Stoddard, "protagonist of the Ku Klux Klan," are offered and it is noted that Stoddard "made two astonishing admissions": Black people are not inferior, but "different" and if courtesy were extended Black people according to their merit it would encourage intermarriage among the masses. Both admissions prove, Du Bois writes, "what we have always said"—that it is not the "morons and criminals" in the lynch mob who are truly guilty of lynching but rather "the educated and thoughtful Christians ... who refuse to attack race prejudice" though they know it rests on falsehood.

796. March, 1928, Vol. XXXV, No. 3. "As the Crow Flies," (p. 75) an innocent Mooney remains imprisoned; Sandino, a patriot of Nicaragua, is hailed; a U.S. delegation paying its respects to the monument in Cuba to "the mulatto Maceo" no doubt made him turn in his grave and smile.

797. "The Browsing Reader," initialled reviews, March, 1928, Vol. XXXV, No. 3, p. 86. Blaise Cendras, *The African Saga*, translated from the French by Margery Bianco (New York: Payson & Clarke) says "many lovely and interesting things"; W. S. Braithwaite, *Anthology of Magazine Verse*, 15th annual edition (Boston: Brimmer,)—"no praise is too great for the compiler of this work of love and erudition." *Black and White*, edited by J. C. Byars, Jr. (Washington: Crane Press, 1927.) is an anthology of Washington verse, "noteworthy because it represents four Negro and thirteen white authors" and "it has much worth reading." Dr. H. N. Green, of the National Medical Association, on *Pellagra*, "ought to be of interest to medical men and others."

798. "Postscript," March, 1928, Vol. XXXV, No. 3, pp. 96–98. "With deep regret" the resignation of Augustus G. Dill as business manager —after 15 years—is announced. A letter from Roland A. Barton, attending high school in South Bend, Indiana, objects to the word, "Negro" as being insulting and a white man's invention. Du Bois suggests that one must not mistake names for things. And names are difficult to change. The point is not to seek to change names but to seek to change conditions which make this or that name have invidious connotations. The effort to canonize Robert E. Lee—in which "Copperheads like the New York *Times*" take the lead—are despicable. He fought for slavery and therefore "was a traitor and a rebel—not indeed to his country, but to humanity and humanity's God." Devastating, long quotations of blatant racism are offered from the widely used text of Henry R. Burch and Samuel H. Patterson, *American Social Problems* (New York: 1923, Macmillan,). The great stumbling block before both "Black and White Workers" is racism and the resulting prejudices which divide members of a class mutually exploited. Data show that only one out of every three eligible voters did vote in 1926; racism is closely connected with this corrosion of so basic a tool of democracy as the suffrage.

799. April, 1928, Vol. XXXV, No. 4. In "As the Crow Flies," (p. 111), England's announcement of Egypt's "absolute independence" is farcical; U.S. domination of Latin America is a fact; public transportation in city after city costs too much and this is because "the people are paying interest and profits [to bankers] on capital consumed twenty-five years ago."

800. "The Browsing Reader," initialled reviews, April, 1928, Vol. XXXV, No. 4, p. 123 of William J. Robertson, *The Changing South* is "funny and pathetic" insofar as it presents the view of a Southern white man who tries to be human; George E. Stevens, *History of the Central Baptist Church of St. Louis* tells of a church which started at the initiative of George B. Meachum, a carpenter, who purchased the freedom of over 20 slaves, including his own wife and children.

801. "Postscript," April, 1928, Vol. XXXV, No. 4, pp. 133–134. "Of Things Contemptible" tells of the refusal of the entire white press of Philadelphia to print the photo of a Black child who was lost—"they said it was against their policy to print pictures of colored folk!" The publications of the United States Bureau of Education tend to hide the reality concerning Jim-Crow education. The autobiographical essay, "The House of the Black Burghardts," describes his great joy when he learns that friends, for his birthday, have bought the house on Egremont Plain that was so dear to his childhood.

802. May, 1928, Vol. XXXV, No. 5. In "As the Crow Flies" (p. 149), Russian insistence upon its willingness to disarm is embarrassing; U.S.-created torment in Nicaragua and Haiti continues; the instability of world currency and the growth of unemployment—including in the United States—are observed as threatening phenomena.

803. "Black Banks and White in Memphis," signed, May, 1928, Vol. XXXV, No. 5, pp. 154; 173–174. A history of two Black banks—the Solvent Savings and the Fraternal Savings, which had merged to form the Solvent and Fraternal Bank. Its recent failure was the result of vengeance by the KKK-dominated administration to punish the political independence and militancy of the Black community in Memphis; however, leaders among the Black people insist they are not beaten and will move to establish a bank under national rather than state supervision.

804. "The Browsing Reader," initialled reviews, May, 1928, Vol. XXXV, No. 5, p. 165. Sherwood Eddy, *Religion and Social Justice* and Kirby Page, *Dollars and World Peace* "are earnest students" but both fail to "realize the role that race prejudice plays in war and social insult." C. S. Johnson, editor, *Ebony and Topaz* (New York: National

Urban League) "is a sort of big scrap book"—some good and some poor. *Stalin's Interview with the First American Trade Union Delegation to Soviet Russia* is a pamphlet which "has some clean, straight questions and answers" and some are quoted.

805. "Postscript," May, 1928, Vol. XXXV, No. 5, pp. 168–170. "The Negro Politician" poses the dilemma that corrupt machines pay off with some jobs and some benefits while the "reformers" usually offer the Black community absolutely nothing. In the face of this, naturally Black voters support such as the Thompson machine in Chicago or Tammany in New York City. Bishop Wilbur P. Thirkield, of the M.E. Church, was a true and firm friend of our people, though most of his labors were in the South. Du Bois finds himself among the people condemned by the Daughters of the American Revolution; since this places him with those having "either brains or backbone" he thanks the Daughters. He describes in detail his "Spring Pilgrimage"—that is to say, his annual lecture tour of nearly 5,000 miles and with an audience of 9,200 persons, of whom about 5,500 were white—mostly in the mid-West, and adds, "altogether the message spelled Hope."

806. "Postscript," Vol. XXXV, No. 5, May, 1928, pp. 168–170: Of great consequence is "Our Economic Future" where Du Bois spells out the impact of economic decline, monopolization, chainstores, the failure of so-called vocational education and the continued racism among employers, bankers, and unions. To assure our survival we must form cooperatives among ourselves in both production and distribution and in credit systems, developing our own "economic independence" and also "carefully articulated co-operation with the West Indies and South America, with West Africa and South Africa."

807. June, 1928, Vol. XXXV, No. 6. "As the Crow Flies," (p. 185). Egyptian subjection to Britain continues; United States bombing of Nicaragua also continues. A prediction that the Democrats will nominate Alfred E. Smith and the Republicans, Herbert Hoover; if neither of these come true, "something equally dangerous will."

808. "So the Girl Marries," initialled, June, 1928, Vol. XXXV, No. 6, pp. 192–193; 207–209. The marriage of their daughter, Yolande, to Countee Cullen; especially significant is the biographical data as to Du Bois' feelings towards his daughter as child and adult.

809. "The Browsing Reader," June, 1928, Vol. XXXV, No. 6, pp. 202; 211. Reviews of Nella Larsen, *Quicksand* and Claude McKay, *Home to*

Harlem. The Larsen book is "a fine, thoughtful and courageous piece of work"; the McKay book, "on the other hand, nauseates me." Not wholly bad and at times great writing, but overall caters "for that prurient demand on the part of white folk" and so one has the display of "every art and emphasis to paint drunkenness, fighting, lascivious sexual promiscuity ... as a picture of Harlem life or of Negro life anywhere, it is, of course, nonsense." Hailed is the brief, "epoch-making" work of the young Melville J. Herskovits in *The American Negro*.

810. "Postscript," June, 1928, Vol. XXXV, No. 6, pp. 203–204: The Black ministers of Washington who have closed their churches to a projected lecture by Clarence Darrow, because of his agnosticism, have done a shameful act. Such witch-hunting would have barred Lincoln and Garrison and Douglass; and "the greatest of religious rebels" was—Christ! In "Sunny Florida" the details of the police-killing of a Black man and the connivance in the "cover-up" of the authorities are exposed.

811. July, 1928, Vol. XXXV, No. 7 [misnumbered 6]; "As the Crow Flies," p. 221. A hope that the farmers' protest movement grows; of the federal budget coming to 4\frac{1}{2}$ billions almost $3 billions are for war.

812. "The Browsing Reader," July, 1928, Vol. XXXV, No. 7, pp. 230–231, reviews: Leslie P. Hill, *Toussaint L'Ouverture*, is "the longest serious poem of sustained literary quality that the American Negro has produced." John W. Vandercook, *Black Majesty: The Life of Christophe, King of Haiti*, "is a gorgeous book—gorgeous in its physical finish and much more so in its splendid message ... written with truth and yet with sympathy." Arthur Garfield Hayes, *Let Freedom Ring*, tells well the story "of the extraordinary way in which freedom, even in its ordinary limited sense, has been withdrawn from white Americans since the World War." Louis I. Dublin, *Health and Wealth* is truthful and generous in its estimate of our people, unlike "the malevolence of F. L. Hoffmann, the Negro-hating statistician of the Prudential Life Insurance Company." Frank H. Hankins, *The Racial Basis of Civilization* is a strangely contradictory book which affirms and denies the inferiority of Black people. Notice is taken of the appearance (January, 1928) of the journal *Africa*, an organ of the International Institute of African Languages and Cultures in London. An article on "African Negro Music" and on the Mandingan Theatre in the French Sudan are praised but both the Journal and the Institute are condemned for being devoid of Black people as participants and being headed by Lord Lugard "who himself has probably murdered more Africans than any living Englishman, which is saying a great deal."

813. July, 1928, Vol. XXXV, No. 7. In "Postscript" (pp. 239–240), Du Bois intends to focus on the presidential campaign and thinks "that the Negro has at last become of political age." He notes the problem of "Visitors" from out of town who "drop in" and whom he cannot always see promptly. The case of "Ben Bess" of South Carolina is told; he had a white mistress with the consent of her husband, who later charged "rape" and he was given 30 years. He has served 14 years and now the woman, near death, swears to his innocence. There are hundreds of such cases, Du Bois affirms. Again, Du Bois pushes "Co-Operation" noting he has urged this for many years.

814. August, 1928, Vol. XXXV, No. 8. In "As the Crow Flies" (p. 257), both parties are corrupt; their campaigns are frauds; their bosses are the combined resources of Big Business. "Moral: Vote for Norman Thomas."

815. "Postscript," August, 1928, Vol. XXXV, No. 8, pp. 275–276. An analysis of "The Negro Voter," showing its significance in every non-Southern state. The Fourteenth Spingarn Medal was given to Charles W. Chesnutt, and the medal "has seldom, if ever, been more fittingly awarded." Tribute is paid to Joseph C. Manning, now very ill. A white man, he fought for an enlightened, antiracist South with the Populists in Arkansas, Alabama, and Texas; it is suggested that his book, *The Fade-Out of Popularism* be read. In "Propaganda in the Public Schools" Du Bois tells of the denunciation of John Brown in one; of the assertion by a teacher in another that no Black men fought in the Civil War; and in a third, the teacher had never heard of Frederick Douglass. All were New York public schools.

816. September, 1928, Vol. XXXV, No. 9. This issue announces Pierce M. Thompson as Business Manager. "As The Crow Flies," (p. 293) condemns the idiocy and demagogy characterizing the election campaign and calls attention to the Kellogg-Briand Peace Treaty—"the chief fighters of the world are signing gayly" and affirming that they will not fight "unless they want to."

817. "The Possibility of Democracy in America," a two-part article, September and October, 1928, Vol. XXXV, Nos. 9 and 10, pp. 295–296; 314–15; 336; 353–355. Originally prepared for a Durham Conference on December, 1927, it was delivered again at the June, 1928 NAACP Meeting in Los Angeles. It demonstrates the vitiation of democracy —in the sense of "the policies of government [being] controlled by the vote of its citizens." It emphasizes, also, that the disfranchisement of Black people has been a basic force in this corroding of democracy. The data are profuse.

818. "The Browsing Reader," September, 1928, Vol. XXXV, No. 9, p. 301, reviews: Monroe N. Work, (ed.), *A Bibliography of the Negro in Africa and America* is "monumental" and "the most complete bibliography" in its area ever published. Some "minor" mistakes are noted. Of booklets being published "by young Negro writers" in various cities, Du Bois recommends in particular *The Saturday Evening Quill*, published in Boston in June, 1928.

819. "Postscript," September, 1928, Vol. XXXV, No. 9, pp. 311–312. A long and positive appraisal of the NAACP Conference in Los Angeles is followed by a description and denunciation of the proceedings at both the Democratic and Republican Party Conventions. Again, Black voters are urged to give more attention to the congressional rather than the presidential campaign. Word has come to Du Bois of a lynching of an unidentified man—shown hanging, with wrists manacled—in Florida in late February or early March of 1928—and hitherto unreported.

820. October, 1928, Vol. XXXV, No. 10. In "As the Crow Flies" p. 329, the new era is marked by "the Talkies, sight by radio, and color movies, meantime, Russia grows." "The first modern Christian," was Leo Tolstoy; this on his centenary.

821. "The Browsing Reader," October, 1928, Vol. XXXV, No. 10, p. 340. Review, initialled, of Arthur Huff Fauset, *For Freedom: A Biographical Story of the American Negro* "an excellent book" giving biographies of many Black people and written so that children will enjoy and understand them. (Most of this section in this issue is devoted to a review of Du Bois' *Dark Princess* by Allison Davis.)

822. "Postscript," October, 1928, Vol. XXXV, No. 10. Hoover and Smith are saying nothing at great length; the Black voter could and should vote for a Third Party. It cannot win, but it is a manifestation of moral protest. A statue to the Black Soldier is being erected in Chicago; why?—because of the Black people's power in that city. Rumors of corruption in the A.M.E. Church must be overcome and that can be done by truth and honesty. "Protest" calls for this kind of action if there is to be human advancement. He adds that the tendency to consider judges as immune to criticism is wrong and harmful.

823. November, 1928, Vol. XXXV, No. 11. In "As the Crow Flies" (p. 365), now that the United States has recognized the Kingdom of Albania, perhaps it will recognize the U.S.S.R. New York's crisis might be dealt with were it not that its great wealth, "concealed in stocks and bonds," escapes effective taxation.

824. "The Browsing Reader," initialled reviews, November, 1928, Vol. XXXV, No. 11, pp. 374; 390–391 of: Rudolph Fisher, *The Walls of Jerico*—"a step upward from Van Vechten and McKay—a strong, long, interesting step." Mary Moseley, *The Bahamas Handbook* and *The Early Settlers of the Bahamas Islands* ignore the color line, but if the reader does not he will find much useful information in these books. H. P. Davis, *Black Democracy: The Story of Haiti* is "a curious work" from "an open or secret agent of the American government in Haiti"—with some sympathy for the country but with manifest limitations.

825. "Postscript," November, 1928, Vol. XXXV, No. 11, pp. 381–382. "On the Fence" argues that as between Hoover and Smith the choice is nonexistent. In "A Third Party" Du Bois shows the Solid South, based on racism, as a basic obstacle to the appearance of strong, organized, and national dissenting political parties. In writing of the newly organized "Dunbar National Bank," in Harlem, with assets of over $1,000,000 and with Black and white directors though the latter predominate, Du Bois suggests one sees an epochal event. Those possessing capital have power, and in the present, it is the White World which controls that capital. Is it possible for the Black people to be taken into that world and so achieve freedom? That was the belief of Booker T. Washington, "most of the leaders of West Africa, and some of the leaders of India" but "others, including the editor of the *Crisis*, believe that industrial reform must be far more radical than this." Du Bois hopes that this bank venture—which includes the Rockefellers —means more than simply making money and helping induce class divisions among the Black people. "If it takes a real step toward an industrial democracy which includes the darker races, we shall hail it as one of the great steps of the 20th Century."

826. December, 1928, Vol. XXXV, No. 12. In "As the Crow Flies" (p. 401), those who executed Sacco and Vanzetti were "murderers"; again a note on the absurdity of the non–recognition of the U.S.S.R. and an observation on how favorable most of the U.S. press is towards

Mussolini unlike its previous behavior towards Lenin. Germany was no more guilty of causing the World War than England, France, and the United States.

827. December, 1928, Vol. XXXV, No. 12, p. 417. "The Prodigal Son," a parable, points to the actual meaning of life—"you can't work for yourself unless you work for others."

828. "Postscript," December, 1928, Vol. XXXV, No. 12, pp. 418–428. "The Campaign of 1928" was "the most humiliating" ever experienced by the Black people who were openly and deliberately ignored by both parties; hence, they must prepare to throw their entire weight towards a third party but only if that party agrees to support their basic demands. Some success has been achieved through struggle in the effort to eliminate racist segregation and discrimination in Washington by the Government itself, but much remains to be done. Hoover's victory was a victory of Wall Street and the KKK. The only positive result was the election to congress of the Black man, Oscar De Priest of Chicago; he represents "a vicious political machine, but he cannot be nearly as bad as the white men who run that machine."

829. January, 1929, Vol. XXXVI, No. 1. In "As the Crow Flies" (p. 5), emphasis is given to U.S. domination of Latin America; the death of the Indian liberation fighter, Lajpat Rai, at the hands of "English violence" is something that should arouse all "of the 800,000,000 darker peoples of the world."

830. "Postscript, January, 1929, Vol. XXXVI, No. 1, pp. 21–22. Debit and Credit for the past year; questions concerning Black schools and education change constantly, therefore, one must go into the field and listen and look. He did and went 3,000 miles into 10 states where about 5,000,000 Black people live. The death of young Eugene Corbie, a Black man whose early work showed great promise, is a deep tragedy. Tribute is paid Charlotte Manye, "a Basuto from South Africa" who was a student when Du Bois was teaching in Wilberforce University. She is a great force for progress in South Africa; she is fearless and honest yet the support given her by the A.M.E. Church is far from adequate. Basic to "Social Reform" is factual information; we do not have it now and must plan to get it. Two Black men received degrees from Princeton University, Dr. Leonard Z. Johnson and Rev. George S. Starks. On "Legal Defense" Du Bois estimates that in the past 16 years, the NAACP has expended approximately $125,000. A letter has reached him from Yugoslavia; a woman wishes to wed "a coloured man" who can provide her with "a hearty and careless life." Will now letters pour into the *Crisis'* office for her address? He doubts it.

831. "As the Crow Flies," February, 1929, Vol. XXXVI, No. 2, p. 41. The United States "refuses to make Porto Rico either slave or free"; "President-elect Hoover took a trip to South America to see if there was anything lying around loose"; speculation on Wall Street "reaches its highest figure ... Russia celebrates ten years of reform. ... "

832. "A Pilgrimage to the Negro Schools," signed, February, 1929, Vol. XXXVI, No. 2, pp. 43–44; 65–69. "Impressions" are offered of several schools he recently visited: Palmer Institute at Sedalia, North Carolina; Virginia Normal at Petersburg, Florida; Shaw in Raleigh, State Normal at Fayetteville, and Johnson C. Smith in Charlotte all in North Carolina; Allen in South Carolina and Bethune-Cookman in Florida; Edward Waters College in Jacksonville, Florida; Avery High School in Charleston. Friends arranged his transportation with great tact; he often moved about almost secretly, going either by Pullman or drawing room in many cases. Of course, he was often obliged to ride the Jim Crow cars and found most of them bad but not as bad as ten years ago. The automobile helps in contesting Jim Crow railroads. In Georgia he spoke at the Haines Institute in Augusta, with Lucy Laney in charge but "lonesome"; Atlanta is "taller and fiercer and richer ... no culture, no humanity, American in the crassest sense." One hundred students at college level at Tuskegee—which he revisits after 25 years. Still too much regimentation there; the National Veterans Hospital "is a miracle." Fisk university is considerably improved and the freedom of the students is greater but it needs new buildings. Only Fisk and Talladega dare choose from among Du Bois' list of lecture topics, "The Russian Revolution." At Fisk a few teachers and students of adjacent white universities attended as did people from abroad.

833. "The Browsing Reader," February, 1929, Vol. XXXVI, No. 2, p. 48. Reviews of Raymond L. Buell, *The Native Problem in Africa*, on the whole positive and for its data, "indispensable" (a fuller review by Du Bois of this book is noted in No. 241); Donald Young, editor, *the American Negro*, being volume 140 of the *Annals of the American Academy of Political and Social Science*—"one of the best compendiums on the American Negro ever published"; Elizabeth L. Green, *The Negro in Contemporary American Literature*, " ... only thing of the kind that exists ... done with admirable poise ... ought to have wide circulation"; *The Fastest Bicycle Rider in the World*, an autobiography of

Major W. Taylor; " . . . an interesting human document." Noted also
are the publications of C. G. Woodson's *Negro Makers of History* and
African Myths, both issued by the Associated Publishers in Washington; and Kirby Page (ed.), *Recent Gains in American Civilization*
with special attention to the essay therein by Charles S. Johnson. Jessie
Fauset's second novel, *Plum Bun*, has just been published in London
and will be issued in New York by Frederick Stokes.

834. "Postscript," February, 1929, Vol. XXXVI, No. 2, pp. 57–58.
Margaret DeLand, a well-known white writer, urges that Du Bois
"repudiate" Oscar De Priest because of his machine connections; Du
Bois explains why this is not possible and what the actual alternatives
facing Black people are in terms of local and city politics. In "Third
Party" Du Bois again shows that without a principled attack upon
racism, especially as this leads to political domination in the South, no
third party movement can—or should—succeed. He notes some
progress in comprehending this on the part of the Socialists in the 1928
election.

835. "The National Interracial Conference," initialled, February,
1929, Vol. XXXVI, No. 2, pp. 47; 69–70. A factual report of the
conference held in Washington, December 16–19, 1928, sponsored by
16 organizations and attended by 151 delegates, examining "what do
we know about Negro life and relations"; what "significance has this
knowledge" in terms of improving conditions; "what gaps in knowledge are revealed?" The essay summarizes answers offered in each of
the fields examined, as education, industry and agriculture, race
relations, etc. Du Bois hopes that the labor that went into this
conference is not lost; that, on the contrary, it can be the groundwork
for yearly meetings devoted to particular subjects, as was done by the
Atlanta University Conferences.

836. March, 1929, Vol. XXXVI, No. 3. In "As the Crow Flies" p. 77,
"nothing in modern history is so touching as the sudden interest of the
New York *Times* in Leon Trotsky." A refuge for birds has been opened
in Florida; "no refuge for Negroes has been planned as yet."

837. "The Browsing Reader," March, 1929, Vol. XXXVI, No. 3, pp.
87; 98. E. C. L. Adams, *Nigger to Nigger* "the material published here is
serious and often beautiful philosophy of the peasant Negro and the
outlook upon life is everything that a black man could wish." Anna
Nussbaum (ed), *Afrika Singt: Eine Auslese Neuer Afro-Amerikanischer
Lyrik [Africa Sings: An Anthology of the Newer Afro-American Poets]* is

described as an excellent work and the first of its kind. Notice is taken of the reappearance of the annual, *Black Opals*, published by young Black authors in Philadelphia. This issue contains three drawings and twenty poems; that by Marjorie Marshall is especially fine.

838. "Postscript," March, 1929, Vol. XXXVI, No. 3, pp. 93–94. An attack upon Hoover's appointment of William Doak as Secretary of Labor since the man has been notoriously anti-Black for years.

839. April, 1929, Vol. XXXVI, No. 4. In "As the Crow Flies," (p. 115), Du Bois is delighted that Doak has been rejected for his cabinet post—"the *Crisis* did not eliminate him but we helped." Seventy-five percent of the Afro-American people have incomes below "health and decency" standards according to the U.S. government.

840. "The Browsing Reader," unsigned, March, 1929, Vol. XXXVI, No. 3, pp. 125;138. In "Our Monthly Sermon" Du Bois suggests that the increase in published works by Black authors is not "a fad"; he asks, however, that Black people themselves foster the habit of buying books. *Survey of Negro Colleges and Universities* (Bulletin No. 7, 1928, Bureau of Education, United States Department of the Interior)* is quite a contrast from the two volumes by Thomas Jesse Jones 12 years ago. "Today, the whole program of industrial education as worked out in the Nineties, is a confessed failure ... Negro education is going to follow the same lines as all education of human beings." He rejoices that Charles W. Chesnutt's *Conjure Woman* has been republished with a fine foreword by Joel Spingarn. *Mamba's Daughters* by Du Bose Heywood "is an excellent book and worth reading, but I do not like it." In nine cases out of ten I know that the white person cannot write perceptively about us; this is an exception but the Black people he writes about are "so strange to me" and "I do not like its subject." He does like Jessie Fauset's *Plum Bun* for it "talks about the kind of American Negroes that I know." The book "will not attract those looking simply for the filth in Negro life, but it will attract and hold those looking for the truth." The "Periodicals" section was normally done by Marvel Jackson but in this issue it is unsigned (pp. 138–139) and is clearly by Du Bois. He reports a magazine published in Holland, edited by Noto Soeroto, *Oedaya*, which "deals most interestingly with the race problems of the Dutch, particularly the Javanese and the Guianians." *Africa* continues to put forth the idea of Africa run by and for Europeans. "It is singular how we tend to forget the obviously good

*A summary of this work appears in The *Crisis* for August, 1929, Vol. XXXVI, pp. 261ff.

and indispensable"—by which Du Bois means the *Journal of Negro History*, now entering its 14th year.

841. "Postscript," April, 1929, Vol. XXXVI, No. 4, pp. 131–132. He publishes "without comment and for the edification of the civilized portion of mankind" the text of a segregation ordinance just passed by Richmond, Virginia. In "Mr. Hoover and the South" all plans for remaking the South, as it is called, will fail if the fact of disfranchisement of Black people is not faced frontally and overcome. The "next step" of the NAACP must be a "crusade" directed towards gaining equality in educational opportunities for the Black children in the United States.

842. May, 1929, Vol. XXXVI, No.5. In "A the Crow Flies" p. 151, a handful of rich people really govern most of the earth; someday this will be changed. "The time for the complete collapse of the Russian Soviet Government has again been indefinitely postponed."

843. "The Negro Citizen," signed, May, 1929, Vol. XXXVI, No. 5, pp. 154–156; 171–173. Text of the paper delivered at the Washington Conference, December 19, 1928 (No. 835). Full citizenship, full political power is now basic for the achievement of Black freedom; the history of this effort, its obstacles, present requirements, and probable future are discussed.

844. "The Browsing Reader," unsigned, May, 1929, Vol. XXXVI, No. 5, pp. 161; 175–176. It begins with "Our Monthly Sermon" and makes the point that if more Black people bought books more publishers would have to pay attention to what they publish in the Black market. In "Current Books," *The Magic Island*, by W. C. Seabrook is reviewed favorably, though held to be much too long. As a "story of Haitian life and religion," however, it is well done. *Thirteen Days*, by Jeannette Marks tells the story of the period from August 9 to August 22, 1927 and "the desperate efforts" made by "liberal America to save Massachusetts from murdering Sacco and Vanzetti." Sydney Strong, (ed.), *We Believe in Immortality* contains remarks by 90 Americans (5 are Black) on this matter; L. G. Jones, an Englishman has issued a pamphlet, *Negro Schools in the Southern States* (Oxford, Clarendon Press) which is "curiously distorted." Highly recommended is Savel Zimand's *Living India*. The Indian martyr's book, *Unhappy India* by Lajpat Rai "is teeming with facts and unanswerable arguments." A Black South African—rather conservative and a religious leader—D. D. Jabavu, has authored an important study, *The Segregation Fallacy* *and Other Papers.* Roark Bradford's *This Side of Jordan* "is pure rot."

845. "Postscript," May, 1929, Vol. XXXVI, No. 5, pp. 167–168. President Hoover's effort to create a White Republican Party in the South may yet have results he does not contemplate for it might lead to a breakdown of white supremacy in that part of the nation. Du Bois discusses the debate between Lothrop Stoddard and himself in Chicago, attended by 4,000 people, of whom one-fourth were white. Stoddard's arguments are weak now for the data have destroyed the props of white supremacy and he knows it; further, his doctrine really is an assault on democratic theory and he knows that, too. Du Bois notes a disinclination on the part of Christian missionary societies to send Afro-American missionaries to Africa and sees the root in embarrassment and fear. "Optimism" is what the developments in the struggle during the past generation bring to Du Bois. He is especially encouraged by the sense of "self-assertion" that he feels showing itself in the demand by Black people to run their own institutions—especially schools and to "undertake their own self-interpretation." Among some whites, too, he senses a suspicion "that the most virile future force in this land, certainly in art, probably in economics and possibly in science is the Negro."

846. June, 1929. Vol. XXXVI, No. 6; "As the Crow Flies" (p. 187). Du Bois explains that this column is not meant to be sugar and molasses, but rather to report the truth, bitter though it be and as that truth is perceived by Black people.

847. "The Browsing Reader," unsigned, June, 1929, Vol. XXXVI, No. 6. Three books are reviewed: *What the Negro Thinks*, by Robert R. Moton; *Rope and Faggot: A Biography of Judge Lynch* by Walter White; *Black America*, by Scott Nearing. All are of "intense and vivid interest." The Moton book is greeted for its firmness. "It is extraordinary that a book like this can come out of Tuskegee, Alabama, even in 1929." White's book is "exhaustive and thorough-going"; Nearing's work is of enormous importance, calling as it does for working class solidarity across color lines.

848. "Postscript," June, 1929, Vol. XXXVI, No. 6, pp. 203–204; 212. A great opportunity has come with the announced merging of Spelman and Morehouse into a greater Atlanta University. Especially needed is the fullest development of graduate instruction for Black people so that they may produce work in history, languages, and the sciences. Atlanta may lead in this, especially with the leadership of John Hope, who is particularly well-suited to push such an effort forward. Langston Hughes, a senior at Lincoln University in Pennsylvania, distributed a questionnaire to the seniors and juniors. One hundred and twenty-seven answered and of these 81 stated they *"were opposed to having colored professors!"* This is the result of a system wherein only white teachers were employed; the students lose faith in themselves and their own people. "Is it not time that the graduates of Lincoln aroused themselves and took firm hold of this threatening situation?" Deep tribute is paid to the recently deceased Paul Kennaday, one of the white founders of the NAACP.

849. July, 1929, Vol. XXXVI, No. 7. (In this number Du Bois drops the title of business manager and carries only editor). In "As the Crow Flies" (p. 223), the Labour Party victory in the English elections is notable for that party has condemned racism. Chiang Kai-shek is denounced as a "traitor" and the agreement between the Pope and Mussolini heralds "expansion in Africa."

850. "Captain Floyd and Cuba Libre," unsigned, July, 1929, Vol. XXXVI, No. 7, pp. 230–231; 247. The story of the exploits of a Black man, James W. Floyd of Jacksonville, Florida, who was captain of the "Dauntless" which made repeated trips to Cuba bringing arms to the rebels fighting the Spaniards prior to the Spanish-American War. Mr. Floyd was honored by Cuba with a medal for his services in 1927.

851. "The Browsing Reader," July, 1929, Vol. XXXVI, No. 7, pp. 234, 238. Three books are reviewed, and signed with initials: *Banjo*, by Claude McKay; *Passing*, by Nella Larsen, and *The Blacker the Berry* by Wallace Thurman. McKay's book is "better" than his *Home to Harlem* and "as a book of racial philosophy is most inspiring." *Passing* "is one of the finest novels of the year." Thurman's book shows, Du Bois feels, a certain failing on the part of the author to really love his own people; still it "may be promise and pledge of something better."

852. "The Color Problem of Summer," unsigned but probably by Du Bois, July, 1929, Vol. XXXVI, No. 7, pp. 235; 250. Travel is difficult but especially for one who is Black. The essay spells out the places and forms of travel, especially in the United States, that offer the least difficulties arising from racism.

853. "Postscript," July, 1929, Vol. XXXVI, No. 7, pp. 242–245: An exposé and attack appear in connection with J. P. Frey's recent "awkward and insincere defense of the color line in the A. F. of L." Du

Bois knows that in the United States one has "government by graft" but cannot the younger Black men and women break out of this and introduce the needed honesty and sincerity into politics? The music critic of the New York *World* "got quite fussed up" because at a Carnegie Hall concert Roland Hayes waited for the audience to become quiet before singing. Of course he was right and "I hope that Roland Hayes will continue to teach Americans manners." On "Negro Journalism" Du Bois, taking off from a letter from a young writer, warns of its hard work, of the temptations towards corruption for a Black writer, and the ultimate temptation of trying to write for a white audience, when "the chief reason for his writing" is "the revelation in his own soul, and the picturing of his own problems and his own people."

854. August, 1929, Vol. XXXVI, No. 8, (this issue announces Thomas J. Calloway as business manager). In "As the Crow Flies" (p. 257), Black boxers again "threaten" the sport of boxing; we persecute Margaret Sanger while Texas Guinan flourishes. "Again, the collapse of Russia has been indefintely postponed." The South fights white workers who seek organization; if white and Black workers ever united, "the Solid South will crumble." Again, attention is called to the extraordinary amount of speculation on Wall Street.

855. "Postscript," Vol. XXXVI, No. 8; August, 1929, pp. 277–278;284–285: An enthusiastic account of the Cleveland Meeting of the NAACP is offered. The third white Principal—James Gregg—has resigned from Hampton Institute; "The next step is to appoint a colored Principal." That leads to two questions, Will he be able to retain "that proportion of white teachers so necessary to normal racial adjustment?" And will white trustees trust a Black man to administer an endowment of $8,000,000? A reason the United States refuses to join the League of Nations is that it permits oppressed minorities to appeal to it for redress—as the Jews in Romania and the Greeks in Turkey have done. "One of the things we really fear in joining the League is giving twelve million black folk a chance to appeal to the world with legal and moral right." Only 69 percent of those entitled to vote, did so in 1928; the New York *Times* suddenly has discovered that this may be due to lack of real choice; and the latter stems in large part from the "Solid South" which itself rests on Black disfranchisement, but the *Times* did not say this. Denunciation of the immigration quotas—largely racist—is made. Tribute is paid to Clement G. Morgan, his dear friend and Harvard classmate, who has died, "he was one of the cleanest men I ever knew, without, and within."

856. September, 1929, Vol. XXXVI, No. 9. In "As the Crow Flies" (p. 293), the USSR refuses to fight China and "the world that loves peace is infinitely indebted" to it; Fiorello La Guardia, the Republican candidate for mayor of New York, sneers at Black Haiti, and James J. Walker, the Democratic candidate, "objects to Negroes in ball rooms; and there you are." "After a time the revolt of tens of thousands of convicts all over the country may bring the attention of philanthropists to the slavery, degradation and exquisite cruelty of the thing we call punishment for crime." The textile strike in Gastonia, North Carolina, may teach Southern white workers who their real enemies are: the owners of those mills.

857. "Mrs. DePriest Drinks Tea," unsigned, September, 1929, Vol. XXXVI, No. 9. pp. 298–299; 317–320. "For the sake of historical accuracy, and to the astonishment of our descendants, we are publishing the following article"—which culls from the press of the United States and England comments when Mrs. Herbert Hoover included the wife of Representative DePriest of Illinois in her invitations to tea and Mrs. DePriest attended.

858. "Postscript,'' September, 1929, Vol. XXXVI, No. 9, pp. 313–314; 317. "Pechstein and Pecksniff" states the findings in favor of segregated education made by a Dr. L. A. Pechstein of the University of Cincinnati and then exposes his methodology and his deep racism. Du Bois adds, "the success of some separate Negro schools is a crushing indictment of hatred and prejudice and not a demand for further segregation." Segregation has meant in fact reduced standards for the Black students; furthermore, wrote Du Bois, in italics, *"The logical end of racial segregation is Caste, Hate and War."*

859. October, 1929, Vol. XXXVI, No. 10. In "As the Crow Flies" (p. 329), England traditionally has governed by the "divide-and-rule" principle and this is showing itself again in Palestine in Arab-Jewish hostility. "The bursting of the Wall Street speculation bubble seems about due. ... And still barbarous, Bolshevik and irreligious Russia is showing a world sick to death of war how not to fight."

860. "Postscript," October, 1929, Vol. XXXVI, No. 10. pp. 349–350; 357. Government by intelligent public opinion—the ideal of democracy—is not working in the United States, basically, "because we are ruled by organized wealth." A Charleston newspaper denounces James

Weldon Johnson's "Lift Every Voice and Sing" because it still bemoans slavery—an institution which actually made the Blacks deeply indebted to the benevolent whites! Du Bois writes, "The larger part of the debt which we owe to the South consists of ignorance, poverty and bastards." Using the end of 1929 as a vantage point what may one say as to the fundamental changes in the 20th century? In the 19th century it was assumed that the world belonged to and always would belong to the superior peoples of white Europe and America; no longer is this true and the changes came with the World War, the Bolshevik Revolution, the struggle for independence in India, and the great changes in Japan and in China. The fight for independence intensifies in Africa—North, East and West. In the van of this fight are the Afro-American millions, "they may eventually succeed in placing America again in the procession of liberalism instead of in the forefront of imperial oppression and reaction."

861. November, 1929, Vol. XXXVI, No. 11. In "As the Crow Flies" (p. 365), "Russia sold last year 90 million dollars more than she bought which is impossible because every capitalistic country in the world said it could not be done. ... Of all modern traitors to the cause of sweating humanity commend us to Matthew Woll. He is a white labor leader who has sold out body and soul to the Rich. ... "

862. "Business as Public Service," signed, November, 1929, Vol. XXXVI, No. 11, pp. 374–375; 392. If one enters the field of music, religion, medicine, or education it is not assumed that he has done so to make money; but if one enters business, to make money is commonly offered as the reason for the choice. Business should be as much a public service as any other effort. It isn't and this is wrong. Business is being challenged in many places especially in the U.S.S.R. The latter direction is the one that the world will increasingly follow. Now what shall our path be? Shall we, in moving into business, copy the practices of White America, or should we understand the tendencies in the world and plan accordingly and build up among ourselves the ideal of business as public service? If the latter—and Du Bois urges it—then serious consideration must be given to cooperative economic endeavors.

863. "The Negro in Literature: May to September, 1929, " unsigned, November, 1929, Vol. XXXVI, No. 11, pp. 376–377; 392. (In a note, Du Bois remarks that recent books by Walter White, Scott Nearing, Claude McKay, Robert Moton and Nella Larson have been reviewed earlier) A new and revised edition of Sidney Olivier's *White Capital and Colored Labor* (originally issued in 1906; in this edition, Hogarth Press, London) is "indispensable to students of Negro problems." Harry Dean's*The Pedro Gorino* (Boston: Houghton Mifflin), written with the assistance of Sterling North, "records the adventures of a Negro sea captain in Africa and on the Seven Seas in his attempts to found an Ethiopian Empire." Du Bois recalls meeting Captain Dean in London in 1900 when "he wanted to lead a black army across the straits of Gibraltar. I saw his point of view, but I did not think the scheme was practical." Paul Morand's *Black Magic* (New York: Viking) "is mainly nonsense." The "indefatigable University of North Carolina Press" has recently produced three books that are relevant: *Black Roadways* by Martha W. Beckwith, *John Henry* by Guy B. Johnson, and *The Tree Named John* by John B. Sale. Useful and interesting but, as usual with this press, "the Negroes in these books are never human." "Quite in contrast" with this is André Gide's *Travels in the Congo* (New York: Knopf), a translation of two books in French published in 1927 and 1928 and "done with sympathy and beauty." Recommended are two books by Bruno Lasker, *Race Attitudes in Children* (New York: Holt) and *Community Conflict* (New York: The Inquiry). Edwin L. Clarke's *The Art of Straight Thinking* (New York: Appleton, 1929) is first rate. Recommended is Marcus Graham, editor, *The Anthology of Revolutionary Poetry* which includes selections from several Black poets. Two books by Dantés Bellegarde have reached him, *L'Occupation Américaine D'Haiti, Ses Conséquences Morales et Economiques* and *Pour Une Haiti Heureuse* [For a Happy Haiti] (1929, Port-au-Prince: Cheraquit); they are "powerful briefs against American injustice." The North Carolina State Board of Charities and Public Welfare, in its *Special Bulletin* No. 10, shows that "capital punishment is chiefly a method of intimidating Negroes." Many articles are cited by Du Bois; in particular essays by Oswald Garrison Villard, George S. Schuyler, H. L. Mencken and James Weldon Johnson.

863a. "Postscript, November, 1929, Vol. XXXVI, No. 11, pp. 386–388: The issue marks the commencement of the *Crisis'* twentieth year; it will continue the battle as long as the need for that battle continues; the world moves and some instances of this, in terms of growing appreciation of the realities of the color line, are offered. Warm tribute is paid to the late distinguished attorney, Louis Marshall, who often gave his invaluable services to the NAACP. He is one of the indispensable white partners in the common effort to end racism; in

this "American Jews [as Mr. Marshall] have been especially prominent." The retirement of Myron Adams, the fourth white President of
Atlanta University, is noted and his unselfish work is lauded. Apologies
offered to Dr. Du Bois and to James Weldon Johnson by Robert L.
Vann of the *Pittsburgh Courier*, for an article published in 1926
questioning the honesty of those two men, have been published in that
newspaper and the apologies are accepted. "The Negro in Politics"
must consult first of all his own special needs and this means that he
will vote for the candidate who has delivered the most or has offended
the least. Some racist remarks and acts of Rev. Blackshear of a church
in Brooklyn, New York, bring to Du Bois' mind the story of the Black
man who explained to the minister of a church that he did not really
mean to join for Jesus had told him in a dream that He had been trying
to get in and could not do it.

864. December, 1929, Vol. XXXVI, No. 12. In "As the Crow Flies,"
(p. 401). Southern chivalry shows itself again in the murder of the white
worker-picketer in Gastonia, North Carolina, Ella Mae Wiggins; and
the jailing of seven Communists there makes it clear now "that the
world is safe for democracy. ... "

865. Untitled and unsigned tribute to the late Moorfield Storey by Du
Bois appears beneath a photograph of him, December, 1929, Vol.
XXXVI, No. 12, p. 404.

866. "Elizabeth Prophet," unsigned; December, 1929, Vol. XXXVI,
No. 12, pp. 407; 427–429. Glowing tribute to and appreciation of the
art of this "brown woman born in Providence, Rhode Island" and now,
finally, making a name for herself as an artist, though she "has starved
herself and gone almost without proper clothing."

867. "The Browsing Reader," unsigned, December, 1929, Vol.
XXXVI, No. 12, p. 414. Countee Cullen, *The Black Christ and Other
Poems* is highly evaluated; Adah B. Thoms, *Pathfinders: The Progress of
Colored Graduate Nurses*, with an introduction by Lillian Wald, "is an
excellent and inspiring record". William H. Jones, *The Housing of
Negroes in Washington, D.C.* "is a painstaking and thorough piece of
work." Dorothy G. Bolton, a Georgia white woman, has written the
words of Afro-American hymns from her own area and these have
been arranged by Harry T. Burleigh in *Old Songs Hymnal* making a
volume "worthy of wide use." The white Captain Chester D. Heywood
has published *The Story of the 371st Regiment* and it is not illuminating
because it leaves out much but it does have useful documents and

maps. Blaise Cendrara, *Little Black Stories For Little White Children*, translated from the French by Margery Bianco has produced a book that "all children will find beautiful." Evans Wall's novel, *The No Nation Girl* is the "usual white Southerner's idea of the mulatto's going 'native' "—everybody commits suicide. *The Negro as a Business Man* by J. J. Harmon, A. G. Lindsay and C. G. Woodson "is an excellent and accurate compendium."

868. "Postscript," December, 1929, Vol. XXXVI, No. 12; pp. 423–424. Tribute is paid to the late Dr. Charles E. Bentley, a leading dentist of Chicago, a member of the Niagara Movement and of the NAACP board and outstanding in his profession, overcoming in the latter the tremendous obstacles of racism. "The time will come when the Negro race will look upon men like Charles Edward Bentley as their real emancipators." Plans for holding the Fifth Pan-African Congress have not matured; one reason is "that the importance of these meetings is not yet realized by educated and thinking Negroes." "The unfortunate words and career of Marcus Garvey" have "dampened" interest. "Nevertheless, the idea back of the Pan-African Congress is sound and important, and in less than a hundred years, it is going to be realized." In celebrating the work of Thomas Edison, no attention is paid to that of his Black colleague, Lewis E. Latimer, whose work on the telephone and incandescent lighting was very important. Similarly, in a recent commemoration of the Battle of Savannah in the American Revolution in which Pulaski was killed, the presence of Black men from Haiti among the French troops was ignored.

869. January, 1930, Vol. XXXVII, No. 1. In "As the Crow Flies" (p. 5). "Our idea of the best joke of the season is the New York *Times* explaining how the stock crash was evidence of the essential soundness of American business. ... "

870. "Postscript," January, 1930, Vol. XXXVII, No. 1, pp. 27–30. "About Marrying" carries a long letter from a white man asking for advice. He is in love with a Black young woman and she with him; should they marry? The advice: yes; it will be difficult but if the two of you want it that way, go ahead and do it. The Wall Street crash is not to be lightly dismissed as the New York *Times* and President Hoover tend to do; "it was above all, a shaking of the faith of Americans in American industrial organization and in all private capitalistic enterprise." Exposed is "the fundamental weakness of our system."

871. February, 1930, Vol. XXXVII, No. 2. In "As the Crow Flies" (p.

41), developments in India, Egypt, China, and Ethiopia show that "the myth of the divine overlordship of *Europe* over the *Colored world* is beginning to fade. ... "

872. "The Negro in Literature, 1929," unsigned, February, 1930, Vol. XXXVII, No. 2, p. 51. A list is made of the most significant books and magazine articles by and about the Afro-American people.

873. "Postscript," February, 1930, Vol. XXXVII, No. 2, pp. 63–66. Du Bois urges increased work among the branches of the NAACP—out in the field. Jan Smuts, former Prime Minister of the Union of South Africa, is now visiting the United States and being hailed as a great statesman, but in his country 90percent of the population has no rights at all and it is justified by the barbarism of racism. George Jean Nathan recently suggested in the *American Mercury* that he was tired of "wails from Negroes"—what with all the progress they have made. Du Bois notes the progress made through bitter struggle, but so much remains to be done that with or without Mr. Nathan's permission, "we are not going to change our wailing to grinning just yet." Basic to what Congress could do is to provide funds for the education of Black people; for example, in 1926–1927 South Carolina with a majority of Black people, spent almost $15,000,000 for white schools and less than $2,000,000 for Black schools!

874. March, 1930, Vol. XXXVII, No. 3, (only the name of Dr. Du Bois appears on the masthead now). In "As the Crow Flies" (p. 77), millionaires rule the United States and not the people; India will yet be free; "Sigmund Freud, the great psycho-analyst, greatly doubts the value of civilization." Looking at it, it is clear "he has some grounds for his argument." The U.S.S.R., which is supposed to fail, doesn't.

875. "Postscript," March, 1930, Vol. XXXVII, No. 3, pp. 100–102. Mr. Smuts lectured at Town Hall in New York City and six "Negro leaders sat upon the platform." Among them only Dr. Moton had the courage to publicly dissent from his racist and insulting remarks. But why were any Black people on that platform? We do not sufficiently understand the common exploitation which African and African-derived peoples endure. Pan-Africanism is the answer; this does not project inter-ference by one people into the affairs of another but only mutual assistance in the face of common problems. In "Our Economic Peril" Du Bois points out that neither trade unions nor philanthropists are assisting us in the face of the economic crisis; hence, we must develop among ourselves—if we are to survive—economic cooperation. More and more newspapers and magazines have adopted the upper case "N" in Negro; hence, those that refuse are being deliberately insulting; they include the New York *Times*, the New York *Sun*, the U.S. Government Printing Office, the *Encyclopedia Britannica*, and the *Dictionary of American Biography*. Along with cooperative economic methods, Black people should use the boycotting of racist enterprises where possible to forward their struggle for survival and betterment.

876. April, 1930, Vol. XXXVII, No. 4. In "As the Crow Flies"(p. 113), a suggestion appears as to the reactionary character of the church in Czarist Russia; unemployment in the United States was not going to happen, did not happen, has begun to recede, etc., but it continues to be present and to grow and it is the Black worker who is hit first and hardest. Hailed is the civil disobedience campaign in India led by Gandhi and Nehru.

877. "The Browsing Reader," unsigned, April, 1930, Vol. XXXVII, No. 4. Kathleen Simon, *Slavery*, is "unfortunate" for it ignores the slavery that exists in the British Empire, in the French and Belgian Congo, and the peonage in the United States. Taylor Gordon, *Born To Be* is written by a white woman, Muriel Draper; the book is sordid and one-sided and untrue; it is illustrated by Covarrubias and Du Bois does not like his work. Charles H. Wesley's *The History of the Alpha Phi Alpha* is "most valuable as a book of reference." R. C. Samuelson, *Long Long Ago*, "is too largely missionary twaddle" but has some "interesting facts" concerning the Zulus. A *Health Inventory of New York City* by M. M. Davis and Mary Jarrett was done by an all white committee which illustrates "the attitude of professional social reformers toward American Negroes."

878. "Postscript, April, 1930, Vol. XXXVII, No. 4, pp. 137–138. The program of the American Negro Labor Congress, "a Communistic organization" is placed in a column by the side of the program of the NAACP. Striking similarity is found, though the first places major emphasis upon labor organization and criticizes the NAACP "as the potential leader of a class of small capitalists." Some of us in the NAACP "have warned against an attempt to solve the American Negro problem simply by the capitalistic program of accumulating wealth." The NAACP has not favored "the landlord and the employer against the laborer." But the chief difference between the two organizations "is that we do not believe that similar reform [like Russia has achieved] in the United States need entail violence. It will call for sacrifice, patience, clear thinking, determined agitation and intelligent voting. But if civilization is not a failure, it will call for nothing more than this. And on this platform the NAACP puts its feet." Disapproval is expressed as to President Hoover's proceedings in reference to the United States occupation in Haiti. Rev. A. M. Pierce is the author of a pamphlet, *Christian Obligation to the Negro* published recently by the Commission on Inter-Racial Co-Operation in Atlanta. It is thorough and excellent; had it been published 15 years ago, its author would have been driven out of the city. In response to a priest's request for information on his church and Black people, Du Bois provides an account of the record and says it means "that the hierarchy of the American Catholic Church does not desire black communicants." Every so often the white South calls for Black people to go back to the farm; what nonsense. Let the South assure security, the vote, real help to Black farmers, freedom from insult and there would be no need for such hypocritical invitations. The recent death of Edward C. Williams, the librarian at Howard university, is noticed with deep regret.

879. May, 1930, Vol. XXXVII, No. 5. In "As the Crow Flies" (p. 149), "the Haitian fiasco cost $25,000,000. The total endowment of all Negro colleges in the United States amounts to $21,000,000."

880. "Dramatis Personae", unsigned, May, 1930, Vol. XXXVII, No. 5, pp. 162–177. A review of the play "Green Pastures" by Marc Connelly begins with thoughts on the special difficulties in the United States of presenting in dramatic form aspects of the truth concerning Black life. "Green Pastures" is "an extraordinarily appealing and beautiful play based on the folk religion of Negroes. ... It is the beginning of a new era, not simply in Negro art but in the art of America."

881. "Postscript," May, 1930, Vol. XXXVII, No. 5, pp. 172–174. Sardonic fun is poked at the state of Virginia which seeks by law to define who is and who is not "tainted"! A drive is going forward to force out several hundred young Black men from the position of taxi-cab driver and to make it a monopoly of the Yellow Taxicab Company as in Chicago. A strong campaign, led recently by Roscoe C. Bruce, has induced most publications now, even the New York *Times*, to capitalize the word Negro. The *Forum* magazine and the U.S. Government Printing Office still refuse. President Hoover, having gotten rid of Black Republicans in the South on the charge of "corruption," now finds scandal after scandal emanating from the greed of his lily white Southern Republicans. Again, and in terms similar to the argument in No. 878, why Black people are not about to "go back to the farm" is explained. Sir Michael Sadler, an English educator, is arguing for an elitist education for the elite; but who are the latter? Talent and genius often come from the masses and therefore the opportunity for the best possible education must be open to all. The report of the Hoover Commission is "muddled and not nearly as clear and straightforward as it ought to have been." In "Our Program" Du Bois again suggests that radicals do not pay enough attention to the realities and the persisting quality of racism. The "first job" of a Black organization is "to fight color discrimination as such."

882. June, 1930, Vol. XXXVII, No. 6. In "As the Crow Flies" (p. 185), "Why is it," Du Bois wonders, "that May 1st is a day when all the world except Russia gets scared to death, mobilizes the police and keeps its soldiers ready in barracks?" "The real trouble with any Anglo-Saxon entente is that no country in the world would believe Great Britain and America on oath. ... Statisticians are still trying to figure out a decrease in the number of unemployed. The unemployed are trying to figure out enough to buy breakfast. ..."

883. "Postscript," June, 1930, Vol. XXXVII, No. 6, pp. 209–210. An effort to expose the racism of the Beaux-Arts Institute of Design continues. Neval Thomas, late President of the NAACP in Washington, D.C., was a principled and militant fighter for freedom. Under "Eurasia," Du Bois writes of the millions in Asia whose parentage is both European and Asian. They have faced racism as we have and increasingly they are standing up to it, uniting against it and "are determined to solve it." The work of Cedric Dover in this field is noted.

884. "As the Crow Flies," July, 1930, Vol. XXXVII, No. 7, p. 221. Du Bois is not surprised that some white folk are frightened by "the naked manhood of Paul Robeson." Another Red hunt is disgracing the country. "Jew-baiting in Romania has risen to the dimensions of a major sport."

885. "The Defeat of Judge Parker," signed, July, 1930, Vol. XXXVII, No. 7, pp. 225–227; 248. John J. Parker of North Carolina was nominated for the U.S. Supreme Court; the nomination was opposed by the AFL, and the NAACP and was turned down by the Senate on May 7. A detailed account of this struggle, with copious quotations from newspapers, is here offered.

886. "The Browsing Reader," July, 1930, Vol. XXXVII, p. 234.

Harriett G. Marshall's *The Story of Haiti* is "clear, concise and unbiased." Sidney De La Rue's *The Land of The Pepper Bird: Liberia* is by the U.S. financial adviser to Haiti who had been in Liberia for some years in a similar capacity. It reflects "a close acquaintance" with Liberia and a belief in that country. In the magazines Du Bois calls special attention to an article by Carl Jung in the *Forum* and by J. A. Rogers in the *American Mercury*.

887. "Postscript," July, 1930, Vol. XXXVII, No. 7, pp. 243–246. Du Bois has lectured at three schools for Black youngsters, Cheyney and Downington in Pennsylvania and Bordentown, in New Jersey. All impressed him, especially the second, with its informality and rapport between faculty and students. They all are high schools and Du Bois wonders, "if our educational attention is not shifting and ought not to shift from the college to the high school." Hints on travel to Europe for Black folk are offered by Du Bois including suggestions not to attempt to visit too many places, and to expect to see different things—which is one reason for the voyage. "The Parker Fight" against his confirmation as Justice in the Supreme Court was guided by Walter White and led by the NAACP; the details of its success are spelled out. The particular help of Heywood Broun is acknowledged. It helped expose the pretensions of President Hoover. Senators like Robert Wagner of New York, Robert La Follette of Wisconsin, and George Norris of Nebraska held firm. The Commission on Inter-Racial Co-Operation, headed by Will W. Alexander, seeks a fund of nearly $1,500,000 to help develop "a sane approach to the race problem." Many of its members have not been known, in the past, for advocacy of such an approach and Du Bois spells out what this now requires—an end to Jim Crow and racism in the laws and practices of the South. Du Bois quotes in full a penetrating column by Heywood Broun analyzing and denouncing a recent lynching in Sherman, Texas, accompanied by the burning of a large part of the ghetto; Broun was moved to write this article because the action was defended by the Atlanta *Constitution*. The Travel Institute of Bible Research in New York City insists on Jim-Crow travel arrangements to the Holy Land and within the Holy Land! "Consecrated Hypocrites" is Du Bois' description. The death of Bishop John Hurst, of the A.M.E. Church is reported. Bishop Hurst also served as a Member of the Board of the NAACP. Black people in the United States should look upon India's struggle to be free "with reverence, hope and applause." That effort, together with the Russian Revolution, "are the greatest events of the modern world." The death of Thomas J. Calloway, business manager of the *Fisk Herald*, 1886-1888, and of the *Crisis* in 1930 is announced.

888. August, 1930, Vol. XXXVII, No. 8. In "As the Crow Flies" (p. 257), there is much ferment in China; it is fighting to rid itself of home grown exploiters and foreign leeches. Cuba is under a murderous tyranny but since it does not interfere with United States investments, Washington says not a word.

889. "Postscript," August, 1930, Vol. XXXVII, No. 8, pp. 280–282: The NAACP convention in Springfield, Massachusetts, was a great success; special thanks are offered to Rev. G. R. Waller who first extended the invitation. The theme of the commencement address by Du Bois on "Education and Work" delivered this past June at Howard is summarized by him; "the real objective" of education should be "to place in American life a black man of culture and learning fitted to earn a living according to present economic conditions." "Freedom of Speech" is defined, with emphasis upon its importance in terms of noninterference with opinions *not* widely approved. Du Bois denounces efforts to curb the rights of Communists and points especially to Georgia's revival of old slave statutes to serve as pretext for the arrests of Communists. [This refers to what became world famous as the Angelo Herndon Case]. Again, Du Bois hails the heroic struggle of the Indian people for national independence. The public services—telephone, electricity, gas, food distribution—increasingly are monopolized and are privately controlled for profit. This is wrong; and to intensify the evil these utilities and monopolies are always fiercely racist employing no Black people or very few at the poorest paying jobs. Black people should fight this by all and every means and not least by joining in the effort to nationalize such industries and businesses. The Association of Colleges and Secondary Schools of Southern States, since 1895, has been all white and all powerful. That must be changed. A college library has asked him to donate a copy of his latest book; he will not do it; the college pays for everything else; why should it build its library by begging and at the cost of authors? A letter from Ida B. Wells-Barnett condemning police murder and brutality in Chicago is published. The effort of the League for Independent Political Action —seeking to create in the United States something approximating Britain's Labour Party—has a good program and it is here spelled out.

890. September, 1930, Vol. XXXVII, No. 9. In "As the Crow Flies" (p. 293), revolution moves ahead in India; "only an upheaval from below, not a compromise from above, will save and restore China."

891. "The Browsing Reader," unsigned, September, 1930, Vol. XXXVII, No. 9, pp. 313; 321. Eslande Robeson's *Biography of Paul Robeson* is excellent, though somewhat uncritical. But something "unusual these days when everything black in literature has to come from the slums, wallow in Harlem, and go to Hell." James Weldon Johnson's *Black Manhattan* is highly recommended and Du Bois quotes from his review in the New York *Evening Post* (No. 249). Charles S. Johnson's *Negro in American Civilization* is not reviewed by Du Bois but he quotes at length from a review by Benjamin Stolberg in the New York *Herald Tribune* where the volume is described as an almanac and not really a book at all. C. G. Woodson's *Rural Negro* "brings together much interesting material." Praised as thorough is Lorenzo D. Turner's *Anti-Slavery Sentiment in American Literature Prior to 1865.* A Jesuit priest, José J. Williams, is the author of *Hebrewisms in West Africa* which tends to emphasize outside influences but does contain important data. Charlotte R. Wright, editor, *The Poems of Phillis Wheatley* is thorough. Langston Hughes' first novel, *Not Without Laughter* is "realistic and close to human beings ... not very strongly knit together ... touches dirt but is not dirty ... ends with the upward note ... is well written."

892. "Postscript," September, 1930, Vol. XXXVII, No. 9; pp. 316–318: The returns of the 1930 census mean that the South will lose eight Representatives in Congress—a good sign. A Black newspaper in Kansas urges that the NAACP not seek to defeat Senator Henry J. Allen of that state, despite the fact that he voted to confirm Justice Parker; the paper fears this may cast a "radical" aura about the Association. Nonsense, says Du Bois, labels mean nothing. Black voters must react when politicians do not favor their interests and this is such a case. "Segregation" again discusses the question; what it comes down to, Du Bois writes, is this, "voluntary grouping of people according to their personal likes and dislikes is defensible and to be encouraged. Involuntary compulsion, either from the group itself or by reason of outside pressure, may lead to every sort of material and physical evil." "The Bourbon South" has exposed its thinking again in a recent editorial in the Charleston, South Carolina, *News and Courier.* It is racism mixed with fear of and contempt for democratic theory and practice; such thinking threatens civilization and must be extirpated. The Union of South Africa is so barbarous that it has rejected an offer of $325,000 from the Carnegie Fund towards building a hospital for its Black population. The development of intercollegiate debating between

Black and white colleges is welcome. The 1928 election campaign should have taught the Catholic hierarchy in the United States that attempts to forge unity with the Bourbon South will not work. It can operate effectively among the Black millions but this requires that the church shed its racism. Will it do it?

893. October, 1930, Vol. XXXVII, No. 10. In "As the Crow Flies," (p. 329): William Green and Matthew Woll denounced—again—as "leaders of Labor and followers of millionaires." Among those who rule the United States are no artists, no laborers, no scientists, no servants, "and *no women*. And yet we think we are civilized!" Europe and the United States are not intervening in China, because "yellow Asia and Red Russia forbid it. Which is another lesson in race superiority."

894. "The Browsing Reader," unsigned, October, 1930, Vol. XXXVII, No. 10, pp. 341; 358. A listing of magazine articles by and about Afro-Americans of the past six months is offered. Attention is called to Richard B. Gregg's *Gandhiji's Satyagraha or Non-Violent Resistance* with a letter from its author; a detailed analysis and estimate of the third number of the *Saturday Evening Quill*, published annually in Boston and edited as before by Eugene Gordon, is given. "Perhaps in the catholicity of its interests and freedom of its conclusions lies the chief charm" of the publication. A pamphlet giving the proceedings of the first annual session of the Conference on Education for Negroes in Texas has been published by the Prairie View State College. It contains useful information, here summarized.

895. "Postscript," October, 1930, Vol. XXXVII, No. 10, pp. 352–354. "The City Child" among us is being neglected terribly and in part because of the needs of the parents to work to make ends meet; but there is appearing a truculence and a lack of courtesy among such children which is alarming and if not dealt with collectively will create serious problems in the future. In "Protest" there is a tendency to approve of it only if it is felt that it may really succeed. This is ridiculous; protest has an effect upon your opponent and it also has an effect upon you—and the latter is as important as the former. With protest you keep your own self-respect. Taking off from a letter published in the *New York Times* Du Bois again shows how widespread "rotten boroughs" are in the South due to Black disfranchisement. Two Black men were lynched, in August, in Marion, Indiana; again filthy lies about the men are told and with these lies the entire Black people are besmirched. Meanwhile, though names are known, the murderers walk about undisturbed. (There is a photograph of the lynching with faces of the mob clearly recognizable on p. 348 of this issue.) A pamphlet on *Unemployment* by Henry R. Mussey, issued by the League for Independent Political Action, shows that unemployment is not the fault of the unemployed especially among Black people. The government should stop lying about this and there should be an accurate count of the numbers out of work—it will certainly reach five millions. What is needed is shorter hours at the same pay; unemployment insurance; a great public works program; and control over employers in terms of what they may do as this effects the employment of people. "A colored sorority" won highest scholarship averages at Colorado Teachers' College; therefore, the award for such an accomplishment has been abolished! Hardly believable, but Du Bois quotes from so-called mass pamphlets circulating in the South and West which are frankly racist; one calls for explicitly denying citizenship and all rights of citizenship to all people "not of the White Race." Praise is offered to a speech on "Education in Kenya" in the British Parliament by Josiah C. Wedgewood, a Member of the Cabinet; it is quoted at some length and its point is that it is proper and necessary that the African rule himself.

896. November, 1930, Vol. XXXVII, No. 11, (This issue announces Irene C. Malven as Business Manager. It also announces that the magazine is conducted by an editorial board with Dr. Du Bois as Editor-in-Chief and James Weldon Johnson, Walter White, and Herbert J. Seligmann as board members). In "As the Crow Flies" (p. 368), "South America is blowing up." The overt battle is among different property owners, "beneath are the still inarticulate Indians and mulattoes." Here in the United States, plenty of goods, plenty of workers and plenty of hunger and homelessness, "Yet we cannot buy, sell nor eat."

897. "The Browsing Reader," initialled, November, 1930, Vol. XXXVII, No. 11, pp. 378, 393. Thomas J. Woofter, Jr., *Black Yeomanry: Life on St. Helena Island* is a typical product of "recent school of white southern investigation." Well-printed, heavily funded (almost $17,000 from the Social Science Research Council) "yet on the main subject of what life means to these black folk, of the real difficulties of their economic and social development, of the way in which emancipation has developed into the modern color line, there is not a single word of really illuminating information." Du Bois concludes, "Why is it that Negro scholars, like Woodson, Frazier, Ira

Reid, men who when they see obvious conclusions have the common honesty to express them, can seldom get funds for work?" Illustrating the last remark is the fine study done by Ira De A. Reid, published by the National Urban League, *Negro Membership in the American Labor Unions*, which presents the facts without frills and draws the necessary conclusions from those facts; what "he has done is of unusual and lasting value."

898. "Postscript," November, 1930, Vol. XXXVII, No. 11, pp. 389–390. Attention is called to the decline in income of the NAACP and an even steeper decline in that of *the Crisis*. This is due to the depression but in such a period the Association and the magazine are more needed than ever. Under "Ohio" Black voters are urged to support the Democratic candidate for the Senate; there are really two Democratic parties and the one in the North tends towards a liberal position. The effort of the United States to prevail upon Latin-American countries to make travel there difficult for Afro-Americans, especially emigration there most difficult, reflects a need of our labor and a fear that we will help stir political unrest in the South. In the present economic crisis Du Bois rejoices in the spread of the boycott and picketing movement among Black people—as in Chicago. He hopes that the depression will force a much needed rethinking about the nature of capitalism and the economic needs of our people. The coronation of Haile Selassie to the Ethiopian throne is the occasion for Du Bois to wish the monarchy well as one embodying the hopes of colored peoples for a really independent Black government promising "a rebirth of culture" in Africa. The Delaware press has deliberately lied concerning Du Bois' views in his recent speech in Wilmington; the record is set straight.

899. December, 1930, Vol. XXXVII, No. 12. "As the Crow Flies" (p. 404), ridicules various promises of a returning prosperity or Charles Schwab's opinion that there is no depression; business has merely paused. The projected naval base in Singapore is intended to keep colored people out of Australia and force white people into China. At first we were told the Russian Revolution was bound to fail and the Russians would starve to death. Now we are told the Russians are dumping products in the rest of the world and threatening it with starvation. "Somehow the Russians are not able to suit us." China has had enough troubles, but now that it is reported that Chiang Kai-shek has embraced Christianity "we can confidently expect anything."

900. "Postscript," Vol. XXXVII, No. 12, December, 1930, pp. 425–

426: Generally speaking the November elections turned out fairly well for us; the reelection of De Priest, though he broke from the machine in Illinois, and the defeat of several of the men who had voted for Judge Parker were noteworthy. The failure of several Black banks—in Chicago, Savannah, Memphis—has shaken our people. They could have been saved but the masters of financial monopolies did not want to save them; they were troubled by the possibility of Black control of significant sources of credit and so deliberately let those banks crash. Speeches made by Du Bois in Boston, on the Puritans, and in Philadelphia, on the Quakers, have aroused hostile criticism. The latter is based on misunderstanding and the sensationalized press reports. What I tried to do was to tell the truth, get across the facts, refute the idealizations that pass for history and in this way actually emphasize the real possibilities that have and do exist for social advances if struggle and effort appear. President Hoover has insisted that the economy is sound and that, therefore, "any economic depression was bound to be temporary." He is wrong; the source of the depression lies in the irrational and antihuman character of capitalism, with its lack of planning and its profit purpose.

901. January, 1931, Vol. XXXVIII, No. 1, In "As the Crow Flies" (p. 8), questions have been raised as to whether or not Abyssinians are Negroes; "If Abyssinians are not Negroes there is scarcely a Negro in the United States."

902. "The Browsing Reader," January, 1931, Vol. XXXVIII, No. 1, p. 16. An initialled review of *A History of Atlanta University* by Myron W. Adams, a former president of the university who sets down in "concise" form its history. A rather long paragraph is devoted to the writings of George S. Schuyler, a young radical who has, "so far," Du Bois writes, stuck to his radicalism and writes things that must be read and a recent essay in the *American Mercury* (December, 1930) is especially recommended. Du Bois adds a note of praise for the Blue Book series published by Haldeman Julius in Kansas.

903. "Postscript," January, 1931, Vol. XXXVIII, No. 1, pp. 29–30. A critical comment is offered on a recent speech by President Hoover, delivered in the South and commending the American system where all people begin as equals in the race of life! Du Bois rejoices that Senator Cole Blease of South Carolina is retired and that James Vardaman and Benjamin Tillman are dead, but the sources creating such demagogues have not been eliminated. He condemns the widespread attitude of relatively affluent Black people towards their own people who are imprisoned: "that the Negro who is arrested is guilty of crime and deserving of no sympathy from his more fortunate fellows." Du Bois affirms: "The truth is quite different ... we know perfectly well how often that they are the victims of police discrimination and judicial unfairness and that their poverty and ignorance make them the scapegoats of our present criminal law." A paragraph is devoted to the continued struggles in India: "Magnificent India, to reveal to the world the inner rottenness of European imperialism. Such a country not only deserves to be free, it will be free." Noted "with interest" is the establishment of the New School for Social Research in New York City; it may be "new" but it is thoroughly American and old-fashioned insofar as its catalogue shows nothing touching upon the Black people in the United States nor African peoples in general. Data are offered on the enormous profits extracted from the cocoa crop produced in the Gold Coast colony of Great Britain.

904. February, 1931, Vol. XXXVIII, No. 2.* In "As the Crow Flies" (p. 44), Machado's war upon the Cuban people is awful but is backed by U.S. investors. A railroad may request government aid and that is all right; but if a starving man does, that is the "dole." "The world is flooded with deleterious drugs, not because Turkey and Asia raise them but because England and America sell them and make good profit thereby." To fight the depression two things need doing: cancel war debts and reparations and recognize the U.S.S.R.

905. "Postscript," February, 1931, Vol. XXXVIII, No. 2, pp. 65–66. Du Bois hails the work of William Lloyd Garrison on the centenary of the *Liberator*. Biographical notes on the recently elected officers of the NAACP, Joel E. Spingarn as president; James Weldon Johnson as vice-president; Walter White as secretary. The British refusal to permit Africans in their colonies to learn English is motivated by a desire to keep them subordinate by keeping from them a common language. A formerly white school house has been turned over to the Black community in Atlanta; that city has built only one new building for the education of Black children since the Civil War! Dr. Robert Moton is congratulated for having produced a frankly critical report of the educational work in Haiti during U.S. occupation. Debits and credits for 1930.

---

*A mistake in this number labels it as Vol. 39; an error in the volume number continues until July, 1932, when the correction is made. We ignore the mistake and give the volume number in proper sequence.

906. March, 1931, Vol. XXXVIII, No. 3. In "As the Crow Flies" (p. 80). The economic depression is fine testimony to "the supreme genius of the white race for organizing industry. ... "

907. "Woofterism," signed, March, 1931, Vol. XXXVIII, No. 3; pp. 81–83. An attack upon a report by T. J. Woofter on *The Economic Status of the Negro* done with a grant from the Julius Rosenwald Fund. It is "neither candid, scientific nor conclusive ... I regard it as a distinctly dangerous symptom ... when a Southern white man comes to the study of the race problem apparently with the idea of leaving out all 'controversial' matter, and nevertheless calls the results scientific, then something is not only wrong but vicious. ... Above all, there is an attempt not so much to say as to assume as for granted, the dictum that color prejudice, disfranchisement and poor schools, have nothing to do with the problem of the industrial colored employment in the United States."

908. "The Browsing Reader," initialled, March, 1931, Vol. XXXVIII, No. 3, p. 100. Lists most important books by and about the Afro-American people in 1930; James Weldon Johnson's *Saint Peter Relates an Incident of the Resurrection Day* (New York: Viking, 1931) "is a serious satire of the loftier sort." George Schuyler's *Black no More* (New York: Macauley, 1931) "is extremely significant in American Negro literature ... a rollicking, keen, good-natured criticism of the Negro problem in the United States." A summary is offered of the main works by and on Black people in the magazines of 1930; essays by Carl Jung in *Forum*, Eugene Gordon in *Scribner's* and George Schuyler in the *American Mercury* are called "most striking."

909. "Postscript," March, 1931, Vol. XXXVIII, No. 3, pp. 101–102. Six new schools for Black youngsters had been built in Atlanta since the Civil War, not one, as he had earlier written; Du Bois apologizes for his mistake. The Spingarn Medal Award to Richard Berry Harrison, the distinguished actor, is an especially appropriate one.

910. "Postscript," Vol. XXXVIII, No. 3; March, 1931, pp. 101–102. The fiftieth birthday of William Pickens, Field Secretary of the NAACP, brings forth a summary and appreciation of his remarkable career, commencing as a peon in Arkansas. A Christian Conference in Detroit protested against Jim Crow hotel arrangements, but only 25 percent of those present actually withdrew from the conference, including Dr. Reinhold Niebuhr, Sherwood Eddy, and Charles W. Gilkey, dean at the University of Chicago. The U.S. Secretary of State recently delivered himself of a scathing attack upon slavery in Liberia; Du Bois does not defend it but places Liberia in the context of its time and place and suggests that for the United States to protest against anything is ironic. A Philadelphia man has asked for a list of books that might be purchased with a very modest budget; Du Bois provides such a list, with 60 volumes which cost in all about $150.

911. No. 4, April, 1931, Vol. XXXVIII,. In "As the Crow Flies" (p. 116), Du Bois suggests that "Socialism, Hitlerism, Fascism and Bolshevism" have in common "one world effort to substitute reason for competition in the economic world." He hopes the stirrings in South America herald real freedom "for several million of brown peons."

912. "Postscript," April, 1931, Vol. XXXVIII, No. 4, pp. 137–138: The Du Bois Literary Prize of $1,000, is announced in this issue; the money comes from Mrs. E. R. Mathews and Du Bois tells of their meeting some five years before when he was aboard a steamer returning from Europe. He hopes the award will turn our writers away from the Van Vechten and the later McKay school towards "a more human and truthful portraiture of the American Negro in the 20th Century ... writers frank and unafraid ... thinking last of all of the wealth which books and poems seldom bring." Du Bois has spoken to a white audience in a New York suburb; with him was a Japanese and an Indian. The latter two were servile and played upon every racist prejudice of the audience. He himself attacked racism and made clear his contempt for the other colored speakers, "but it did give me a jolt to realize that even out of those oppressed lands can come nonsense and servile flattery quite equal to our own from those who have not yet learned to stand up as men." He quotes without comment from KKK literature denouncing the NAACP—and other organizations—as pawns of an international Red conspiracy. In the name of "Drouth Relief" Du Bois shows that the U.S. government actually is subsidizing peonage farm operators. The Southern Commission on Lynching, with six white and five Black members, is a fine effort; he hopes they will have the courage to say truthfully that the causes lie in ignorance, economic exploitation, disfranchisement, religious bigotry, and sex prejudice.

913. May, 1931, Vol. XXXVIII, No. 5. "As the Crow Flies" (p. 152), recalls that in 1905 French banks staved off revolution in Russia but they lost their investments in 1917; U.S. banks are now staving off revolution in Spain—will they collect on their investments?

914. "Beside the Still Waters," signed, May, 1931, Vol. XXXVIII, No. 5, pp. 168–169. Du Bois' speech at Spingarn Medal Award to Richard B. Harrison giving a history of the stage and Black people and the turning point achieved in the masterful performance of Mr. Harrison in "The Green Pastures," then beginning its second year on Broadway.

915. "Postscript, May, 1931, Vol. XXXVIII, No. 5, pp. 171–172: An argument among racists in South Carolina—the governor and the *News and Courier* of Charleston—exposes the fact that it has been their policy to expend on the education of Black children "as little as we can and at the same time avoid the accusation of ignoring them altogether in defiance of law" as quoted from the newspaper. A scathing attack, under the title, "Misrepresentation," is delivered against Benjamin F. Hubert, president of the State Industrial College for Negroes in Savannah, Georgia, for the fawning and false speech, which he delivered at Columbia University. A no less scathing attack is made upon many corrupt "Colored Politicians" who should "be driven out in the open and called by the plain name which they deserve."

916. June, 1931, Vol. XXXVIII, No. 6. In "As the Crow Flies" (p. 188), a prize for stupidity should go to the *Cleveland Press*; it blames the high homicide rate in the South upon Black folk, since of the 150 people murdered in 1930, in Memphis 122 were Black! He would like to live to see the nation's geography textbooks picture representatives of the three great branches of humanity with photographs of Paul Robeson, Sun Yat-sen and—Calvin Coolidge.

917. "Postscript," June, 1931, Vol. XXXVIII, No. 6, pp. 207–208; 212. Commenting on the two articles about religion and the Black church in this issue by Clarence Darrow and Bishop R. E. Jones, Du Bois notes that there is underlying agreement that the greatness of that church lies in its social commitment and functioning; to the degree that this is expanded to that extent will the church grow in power and greatness. Dr. Mordecai Johnson of Howard University has succeeded in an effort to prevent the politicalization of the university and is congratulated. The death of Ida B. Wells-Barnett brings a tribute to this great pioneer who "began the awakening of the conscience of the nation." In "Fifty Years of Tuskegee" Du Bois makes the point that most of its graduates have not become artisans and farmers—as was supposed to be the objective—but teachers, professionals, small businessmen; this no fault of the school but of the conditions surrounding it. The debits and credits of President Hoover as far as Black people are concerned are spelled out at some length with the debits far outweighing the credits. The U.S. government gives over $6,000,000 to land-grant colleges in 17 southern states. Black people form 25percent of the population of those states, but land-grant funds for Black people amount to 5.5percent of the total. It is fitting that on the centenary of the birth of Abbé Henri Grégoire celebrations are to be held among Black people in New York and in Haiti, for he was among the first Europeans to challenge racism, early in the 19th century.

918. July, 1931, Vol. XXXVIII, No. 7. In "As the Crow Flies" (p. 224), "Otto Spengler still insists that the white world made the mistake of its life when it brought machines and technique to colored folk."

919. "Postscript," July, 1931, Vol. XXXVIII, No. 7, pp. 241–242. The facts of the Scottsboro case must be kept in mind—a frame-up of eight "Negroes scarcely more than children" by a state notorious for its brutality and racism. Only united mass effort will save their lives and "toward this end and toward no other the NAACP is bending every energy." "The Negro's Industrial Plight" in the depression suggests examination of possible ways out. Two books will help: *The Coming of Industry to the South,* edited by W. J. Carson and *Racial Factors in American Industry,* by Herman Feldman (New York; Harper, 1931). The first shows the "tremendous" industrial revolution which has come to the South and the second examines its results, especially in terms of the obstacles confronting effective working class organization. All this means for us, Du Bois suggests, sober facing of the facts; group effort to "retain present employment, enter new fields of industrial technique, expand retail trade" and "definite and far-reaching effort to organize our consuming power." And the creation among us of an "economic General Staff" to develop our own economy to the greatest possible degree. A Conference on African Children is being held in Geneva but it is one not devoted to their interest but to the interest of those who exploit them. The specific tax bill of a Black citizen of Charleston, South Carolina, is detailed and it is shown how he suffers from "Taxation without Representation." Note is taken of the dinner given James Weldon Johnson on his Sixtieth birthday and in honor of his NAACP work.

920. August, 1931, Vol. XXXVIII, No. 8. In "As the Crow Flies" (p. 260), Du Bois writes, "Pity the poor railroads, down and out and begging for a few per cents. Remember what the dear things have done for us in the past."

921. "The Twenty-Second Annual Conference, NAACP," August, 1931, Vol. XXXVIII, No. 8, p. 271, initialled. A factual summary of the conference held in Pittsburgh.

922. "Postscript," August, 1931, Vol. XXXVIII, No. 8, pp. 278–279. Du Bois affirms that Black people, more than most, make every possible effort to educate their children; he hopes they retain this passion. Benjamin Davis in his Atlanta newspaper has suggested that the NAACP has received funds from the Democratic Party. This is a lie. Lincoln University (Pennsylvania) is congratulated on having finally appointed its first Black professor, Joseph N. Hill. Du Bois describes a recent lecture tour through much of the South as "The Perfect Vacation" and this is only half facetious. He remarks, "And above all, and over the South, there is still the custom of murder." In Charleston Du Bois visits the tree from which Denmark Vesey was hung.

923. September, 1931, Vol. XXXVIII, No. 9. In "As the Crow Flies" p. 296, "Chicago has paid its gangsters but still owes its teachers." "Franklin Roosevelt, who tore up the Haitian Constitution and wrote one of his own in its stead, is about to buy the Democratic nomination."

924. "The Browsing Reader," September, 1931, Vol. XXXVIII, No. 9, p. 304, initialled. Maurice Delafosse, *The Negroes of Africa* (Washington, Associated Publishers, 1931) Excellent translations of two works in French written in 1921 and 1925. James Weldon Johnson, editor, *The Book of American Negro Poetry*, revised edition (New York: Harcourt, Brace 1931) is issued ten years after the first edition, contains a hundred additional pages and remains excellent. Edward A. Johnson, *Adam Against the Ape-Man and Ethiopia* (New York: 1931 published by the author) is useful especially for its material on Ethiopia. Arna Bontemps, *God Sends Sunday* (New York: Harcourt, Brace 1931) is his first effort at fiction and "is to me a profound disappointment." Nearly all "is sordid crime, drinking, gambling, whore-mongering and murder."

925. "Postscript," September, 1931, Vol. XXXVIII, No. 9, pp. 313–315, 318–320. The entire editorial is actually an essay on "The Negro and Communism" evoked by the Scottsboro Case and the role of the Communist Party in that struggle. Du Bois finds himself in disagreement with what he takes to be the tactics of the party. He writes, "American Negroes do not propose to be the shock troops of the

Communist Revolution, driven out in front to death, cruelty and humiliation in order to win victories for white workers. They are picking no chestnuts from the fire, neither for capital nor white labor." Black people know "that the real interests of the white worker are identical with the interests of the black worker; but until the white worker recognizes this, the black worker is compelled in sheer self-defense to refuse to be made the sacrificial goat." The essay concludes:

> *Present organization of industry for private profit and control of government by concentrated wealth is doomed to disaster. It must change and fall if civilization survives. The foundation of its present world-wide power is the slavery and semi-slavery of the colored world, including the American Negroes. Until the colored man, yellow, red, brown and black, becomes free, articulate, intelligent and the receiver of a decent income, white capital will use the profit derived from his degradation to keep white labor in chains.*

926. October , 1931, Vol. XXXVIII, No. 10. In "As the Crow Flies" (p. 332), "Gandhi in a loin cloth with a quart of rice starts out to conquer Europe."

927. "Postscript," October, 1931, Vol. XXXVIII, No. 10, 350–351. "Education" offers additional examples—from the Canal Zone, New Orleans, Oklahoma—of gross discrimination against Black children's education. "Something must be done to remedy a situation which seeks to fasten slavery permanently upon the colored people of the United States by denying their children decent education." A Black young man asks if he should pursue engineering—given the depression and racism. Du Bois says, "yes—go on and prepare yourself and fight for a job." The 1930 census shows a considerable growth of the Black population—over 13percent in the past ten years. It gives the lie to those who had said that because of inferiority Black people could not survive without slavery. Two books published in France show a high awareness of the realities facing us in the United States. These are Georges Duhamel, *Scènes de la vie future* (Paris, 1930) and especially Magdeleine Paz, *Black Brother*; the latter in particular "is a splendidly written book with fine insight and ideals."

928. November, 1931, Vol. XXXVIII, No. 11. In "As the Crow Flies" (p. 370), The New York *Times* has a new "funny" column on the editorial page consisting of comments on Gandhi. This replaces its former "merry quips about Russian women and the fall of the Bolsheviks."

929. "Postscript," November, 1931, Vol. XXXVIII, No. 10, p. 393 (two preceding pages consist of selections from past issues of the *Crisis* commencing with Vol. I, No. 1 in November, 1910). "Buying and Selling" touches on "the paramount problem in the minds of black folk:Jobs for Negroes." Through boycotting, cooperative buying, cooperative producing, the Black people—"We Negro Americans are a nation larger than Belgium or Holland, Greece or Hungary"—could achieve economic sufficiency if this problem was really tackled.

930. December, 1931, Vol. XXXVIII, No. 12. "As the Crow Flies" (p. 412), "The United States (which stole a large part of Mexico, invaded Nicaragua and Santo Domingo and raped Haiti, annexed the Philippines and Porto Rico and dominates Cuba . . .) is now explaining the Golden Rule to Japan."

931. "The Browsing Reader, unsigned, Vol. XXXVIII, No. 12, December, 1931, p. 430. *Brown America* by Edwin R. Embree (New York: Viking 1931) is a good book by a white Southerner with Abolitionist background. Frederic Bancroft, *Slave-Trading in the Old South* (Baltimore: Furst Co., 1931) is trail blazing; as in the case of W. H. Skaggs' *The Southern Oligarchy* (No. 717) not published by a leading house and it too will probably "be ignored by those who are interested in distorting history and making Negro slavery in the United States a benevolent institution." *Zeke*, by Mary White Ovington (New York: Harcourt, Brace 1931) "is a clean, interesting, fine piece of work" that somewhat older Black children will especially find delightful.

932. "Postscript," December, 1931, Vol. XXXVIII, No. 12, pp. 431–432, 438. Again Du Bois concentrates upon "Jobs for Negroes" and announces that The *Crisis* plans to emphasize this basic question and help bring about a condition which will "complete the emancipation begun in 1863, and allow the Negro to walk the world like a free man." Proud note is taken of the fact that David Baird, Jr. was defeated in his effort to become Governor of New Jersey. As a Senator he had voted to confirm Judge Parker, and the Black people in New Jersey did not forget and helped defeat him now. Latest developments in Haiti have shown brutal and overt U.S. interference there. Allyn & Bacon, a well-known textbook publishing house, finally has yielded and will hereafter capitalize "Negro."

933. January, 1932, Vol. XXXIX, No. 1. In "As the Crow Flies" (p. 448), "Long live the Revolution in Spain! They have attacked Religion, Marriage and Land monopoly. We dare not even discuss them."

934. "Postscript," January, 1932, Vol. XXXIX, No. 1, Again a Christmas parable with a pregnant Black woman talking to God; appropriate remarks come from Du Bois relative to the dedication of a tablet at Harpers Ferry erected by the United Daughters of the Confederacy! Du Bois is not happy about the appointment of Will W. Alexander as president of Dillard University in New Orleans; he was doing well as head of Atlanta's Inter-Racial Committee. As a result of the initiative of Helen Bryan of the Friends Race Relations Committee, a dinner in celebration of 21 years of The *Crisis* was given in Philadelphia. The details of this are given. The three Black members of President Hoover's National Advisory Committee on Education (first appointed in 1929) have issued a slashing and courageous minority report appended to the majority report and it is one that tells the truth about Jim-Crow education. President Robert Moton of Tuskegee Institute, President Mordecai Johnson of Howard University and President John W. Davis of West Virginia State College did a noble thing; their report is summarized.

935. February, 1932, Vol. XXXIX, No. 2, "As the Crow Flies" (p. 44), attacks the Democratic nomination of Franklin D. Roosevelt—the man who helped rape Haiti. "Churches are saying that Employment and not Wage Cuts is the Cure for Unemployment. Sounds logical, but there must be a catch in it somewhere."

936. "Postscript," February, 1932, Vol. XXXIX, No. 2, pp. 58–59. Tribute is paid to Julius Rosenwald upon his death. "As a Jew, Julius Rosenwald did not have to be initiated into the methods of race prejudice, and his philanthropic work was a crushing arraignment of the American white Christians." "Blunders" is an attack upon the social order that can produce a tragedy as monumental as that which passes by the name "Scottsboro." Tuskegee Institute reports 13 lynchings in 1931; it generally under-reports and perhaps there were 18 lynchings in that year. A courageous study of the reported lynchings for the year is made in a pamphlet, *Lynchings and What They Mean*, issued by the Southern Commission on the Study of Lynching. It shows that the charge of rape was involved only twice; that white men disguised themselves with blacking and committed crimes; that lynchers were known and not arrested; and that of those lynched it is certain that some were guilty of nothing at all. The report "bravely" puts the source of lynching at the door of the social nature of the South. In December a "Non-Partisan Negro Conference" called by Congressman De Priest was held in Washington. Most of the resolutions were good, but that on economics was poor and it is there—on the question of making a living—that we can least afford soft-headedness and clichés. In "Christmas Festivities" Du Bois urges that Black sororities and fraternities concentrate on social activities assisting the masses and not permit themselves to become snobbish and elitist groups.

937. "The Browsing Reader," February, 1932, Vol. XXXIX, No. 2, pp. 67–69, unsigned. Otelia Cromwell, L. D. Turner, Eva B. Dykes, editors, *Readings from Negro Authors for Schools and Colleges with a Bibliography of Negro Literature* "is exactly what has long been needed." Benjamin Brawley, A *Short History of the American Negro* is better than Woodson's for it is shorter and "is written in clear and beautiful English." Vernon Loggins, *The Negro Author: His Development in America* shows "sympathetic understanding and knowledge." George Schuyler's *Slaves Today* (New York: Brewer, Warren & Putnam, 1931) is not good because Schuyler does not know Africa and did not learn much about it in the quick trip which is the basis for his journalistic effort. Monroe N. Work, editor, *The Negro Year Book, 1931–1932*, published by Tuskegee Institute, appears again after a lapse of six years. It is invaluable, though it tends to minimize the work of the NAACP.

938. March, 1932, Vol. XXXIX, No. 3, In "As the Crow Flies" (p. 80), "China is eternal. She was civilized when Englishmen wore tails. She cannot be killed. She cannot be enslaved. She cannot be conquered. Before Civilization was, China is."

939. "Reclus and Miscegenation," unsigned (*probably* by Du Bois), March, 1932, Vol. XXXIX, No. 3, pp. 83, 104. Comments on the life of Jean Jacques Elisee Reclus (1830–1905), the great geographer and author of the 20-volume *New Universal Geography*. He was exiled because of his support of the Paris Commune and had lived in Louisiana as a teacher. He left Louisiana because of his antipathy toward slavery. He married a woman in France whose father was white and mother a Black Senegalese. He published attacks on slavery and a defense of John Brown. The quotations from Reclus books sound like mottoes of Du Bois' life.

940. "Dalton, Georgia," signed, March, 1932, Vol. XXXIX, No. 3, pp. 85–87. Juliette Derricotte, Black dean at Fisk University—formerly a leader in the world student and Y.W.C.A. movements—died on November, 1931, as a result of an automobile accident and the refusal of the city hospital in Dalton, Georgia, to tend to her.

941. "Postscript," March, 1932, Vol. XXXIX, No. 3, pp. 93–94, 101. The Disarmament Conference in Geneva is of great consequence to "every colored citizen of the world. The moment that Europe begins to disarm, that moment the development of the darker nations begins in earnest ... this is the reason that the only nation at the disarmament conference which comes with clean hands and a real desire for peace is Russia, led by [Maxim] Litvinoff." Japan's assault upon China is not simply naked aggression because there looms upon China the rapacity of the white imperialist nations. The case involving the alleged rape of the wife of a U.S. Navy lieutenant in Hawaii, Mrs. Massey, leads Du Bois to review the island's past and to highlight its domination by five main groups of capitalists. A call is repeated for the economic salvation of the Black people—Du Bois adds those of the West Indies as well as of the United States or a total of about 22 million—through a self-development program. Let the Black colleges help train the cadre for this and then let the group do it because "to the ideal of poverty we must add that of service." Such "a racial economy is possible" Du Bois insists; it "is an economic program for times of depression." Some advance has been made in the past two years in the recognition of the academic standing of Black colleges but the latter still are not permitted to be part of the association which determines such standings; this must be fought for. Du Bois publishes an eyewitness report of the struggles and sufferings of miners—many on strike—in Kentucky and Pennsylvania and they are Black as well as white. Du Bois adds, "They have been starved, beaten and killed; yet they have stood up staunchly for a living wage, for freedom of speech, for the abolition of feudalism."

942. "The Browsing Reader," initialled, March, 1932, Vol. XXXIX, No. 3, pp. 102–103. *The Black Worker*, by Sterling D. Spero and Abram L. Harris was reviewed by him, he notes, in the *Nation* (No. 251) but he wishes again to call attention to it. It represents a "re-orientation which avoids the previous provincialism of our point of view" as in Du Bois' Atlanta University studies and his *The Philadelphia Negro*, wherein the problems were examined "from the point of view of religion, humanity and sentiment." The book is highly recommended particularly for those "who do not yet realize that the Negro problem is primarily the problem of the Negro workingman." E. Franklin Frazier, *The Negro Family in Chicago* is a "distinctive contribution." It is "a most painstaking and illuminating piece of work."

943. April, 1932, Vol. XXXIX, No. 4, In "As the Crow Flies " (p. 116), to see England, France and the United States attacking Japan for its actions in China is "the Hypocrisy of Hypocrisies." As to Japan, those powers "forced [her] to choose between militarism or suicide."

944. "George Washington and Black Folk," signed, Vol. XXXIX, No. 4, April, 1932, pp. 121–124. This is a pageant for the bicentenary of Washington's birth with most of the material directly quoted from authentic texts of the period.

945. "Postscript," April, 1932, Vol. XXXIX, No. 4; pp. 131–332. A Brooklyn, New York, newspaper has advocated "meekness" as the best tactic for Black people; this, on the contrary, "would be just about the worst possible attitude, not only for Negroes themselves, but for its effect on their white neighbors." Howard University must have real control over its own budget, and its board must be purged of "certain white elements whom the highest officials of the District of Columbia know to be untrustworthy and dishonest." As a "platform for radicals" Du Bois suggests beginning with publicity about property ownership and income and no tax exemptions for any kind of property. Tribute is paid to the late Florence Kelley, "save Jane Addams, there is not another social worker in the United States who has had either her insight or her daring, so far as the American Negro is concerned." The U.S. Bureau of the Public Health Service openly and brazenly and illegally refuses to employ Black physicians and says so in writing —here quoted. Again, Du Bois takes up the matter of Black prisoners. "It is to the disgrace of the American Negro, and particularly of his religious and philanthropic organizations, that they continually and systematically neglect Negroes who have been arrested, or who are accused of crime, or who have been convicted and incarcerated. Only in sporadic cases do we visit the jails and hear the tales of the damned ... this attitude toward Negro crime is the most damning accusation yet made." The failure of Ramsay MacDonald and the Labour Party in Britain is a failure of reformistic socialism and is a severe blow to those who preferred a moderate program of social action. It is a "failure for liberal, peaceful reform throughout the world."

946. "The Browsing Reader, April, 1932, Vol. XXXIX, No. 4, pp. 138–139, initialled. Jessie Fauset, *The Chinaberry Tree* marks an advance over her two earlier novels and continues to describe the existing but little known world of middle class Black America. Victor Daly, *Not Only War* is a brief novel dealing with Black people and the

World War—"racey and interesting." Walter H. Mazyck, *George Washington and the Negro* "is most timely and extremely interesting ... authentic and carefully compiled. ... ." Devere Allen, editor, *Adventurous Americans* treats people like John Dewey, Scott Nearing, Norman Thomas and "the Editor of the *Crisis.*" Du Bois mentions a pamphlet by J. A. Rogers about the lives of outstanding Black people of African descent; a bibliography on the education of Black people in the United States issued by the U.S. Office of Education and edited by Ambrose Caliver, which "differs from most bibliographies in showing that the compiler has read and digested everything that he has set down"; booklets of poems and of dramatic readings by Langston Hughes have recently been issued.* The Rockefeller Foundation, in collaboration with the journal, *Africa,* is endowing research, but the people in charge of that magazine "cannot be made to conceive of any scientific help from African sources or of an African as a human being, in any sense, except as a thing to be studied."

947. May, 1932, Vol. XXXIX, No. 5, In "As the Crow Flies" (p. 150),† "It has been a full year now since the New York *Times* has set a date for the fall of the Soviet Government. ... What's happened to the Corner around which Prosperity is hiding? Let the veterans have the Bonus, they earned it."

948. "Postscript, "Vol. XXXIX, No. 5," May, 1932, pp. 158–159. An effort to recall Mayor Key of Atlanta was defeated; the effort sprang from the worst racist elements and the defeat of the effort was due to the determined backing of the mayor by the Black electorate. Mayor Key was important in helping get funds for a new high school for Black youngsters and for the employment of Black workers in the building of Atlanta's airport. A movement has been called for—as by Mark Sullivan in the New York *Herald Tribune*—to get Black people in the cities "back to the land." The movement would succeed at once if lynching stopped, if peonage was ended, if racism was terminated. Surprising that Mr. Sullivan fails to mention these little things! There has been some protest, from Black friends, over the awarding of the Spingarn Medal to Dr. Moton, as the latter allegedly supports

---

*J. A. Rogers, *World's Greatest Men of African Descent*; Ambrose Caliver, comp., *Bibliography on Education of the Negro ... from January, 1928 to December, 1930*; Langston Hughes, *Dear Lovely Death; The Dream Keeper and Other Poems; Scottsboro Limited: Four Poems And a Play in Verse.*
†This issue drops Walter White and adds Roy Wilkins to those assisting the editor.

segregation. Du Bois quotes from Dr. Moton's book, *What the Negro Thinks*, to show how false this idea is.

949. "Books", unsigned, May, 1932, Vol. XXXIX, No. 5, p. 166. Very brief notice of several books. Those "recommended" are: Sterling A. Brown, *Southern Road*; Clarence Darrow, *The Story of my Life*; Mark deWolfe Howe, *Portrait of an Independent: Life and Letters of Moorfield Storey*; Paul K. Edwards, *The Southern Urban Negro as a Consumer*.

950. June, 1932, Vol. XXXIX, No. 6, In "As the Crow Flies" (p. 182), "the Presbyterians have swatted birth control in order to prove 100 years hence that the church leads all really great reforms. . . . If war can be arranged between Russia and Japan, you can depend on every effort of these United States to bring it to pass. It would be killing two birds with one stone, say We."

951. "Postscript, June, 1932, Vol. XXXIX, No. 6, pp. 190–191. The late Julia Lathrop, friend of Jane Addams, first head of the Federal Children's Bureau, was "a woman without race prejudice" who labored for Black as well as white children. Tribute is paid to attorneys Arthur B. Spingarn and James Marshall for their able fight against the White Primary. Du Bois comments upon the series the *Crisis* has been publishing on Communism and Black People. He urges a careful study of the questions involved and recommends the reading of Karl Marx, *Capital*, and books by Norman Thomas, Harry Laidler, Herbert A. Miller, Henry George and Scott Nearing. [Of some interest is his failure to mention Lenin's work.]

952. July, 1932, Vol. XXXIX, No. 7, In "As the Crow Flies" (p. 214), "the nations are at last happy. France, America and Company have forced Germany from Socialism to Fascism ... now for Hitler, Repudiation and War." Several digs are directed against Franklin Delano Roosevelt.

953. Excerpts from speech by Du Bois, May 18, 1932, delivered in Washington, D.C. at the Twenty-third Conference of the NAACP July, 1932, Vol. XXXIX, No. 7, p. 218. Quoted is the section which offers "four criticisms of the NAACP" These are: 1) in the main it has worked for the Black masses but not with them; "the interests of the masses are the interests of this Association, and the masses have got to voice themselves through it," 2) there must be decentralization in the Association's organization; 3) it must "have a positive program rather then mere negative attempt to avoid segregation and discrimination."

This must concentrate upon "economic guidance" and "a program which recognizes the color and race problems of the world as part of our problem here in America;" finally, 4) we must get the strengh for this "readjustment of our objects by attracting and assisting and welcoming Youth."

954. "Postscript," July, 1932, Vol. XXXIX, No. 7, pp. 234–235. Special attention is called to two of the resolutions adopted at the Washington meeting of the NAACP: denunciations of the White Primary and Lily-White Movement as being a class movement and political as well as racial in motivation; and the favoring of world disarmament, the freeing of Haiti and Nicaragua, and noninterference with Liberia. In building the British Embassy in Washington, the AFL appealed for use only of union labor. That meant, actually, only white workers since Blacks are barred. The recent general conference of the A.M.E. church was memorable insofar as it cleansed the church of many fakers and frauds at its top. The failure of the Douglass National Bank in Chicago was not only racial, it also reflected the monopolization of credit. It points again to the need of remaking the socioeconomic order; and credit and consumer and producers' cooperatives must replace that order else there is no peaceful way to a reasonable world. In certain respects race relations have improved; notable illustration is the fact that increasingly national organizations are refusing to meet in cities where Jim-Crow arrangements are required. The antics and injustices connected with the Massie case in Hawaii and the Lindbergh baby case lead to the question, "where did we get this complex of crime, publicity and murder?" Du Bois replies, "We got it from killing 'niggers'; from lynching innocent people whom we hate."

955. August, 1932, Vol. XXXIX, No. 8. In "As the Crow Flies," (p. 246), "Mr. Roosevelt's record on the Negro problem is clear. He hasn't any. Mr. Hoover's record on the Negro problem is not clear and in that respect it resembles his record on everything else."

956. "Books," unsigned, August, 1932, Vol. XXXIX, No. 8, pp. 264–265. Brief commentary on B. A. Botkin, editor, *Folk-Say: A Regional Miscellany* selections "ably selected" especially praised is a piece by Sterling A. Brown; J. J. Williams, *The Black Irish of Jamaica* is a good study of the forced migration of Catholic Irish in the 17th century to Jamaica; J. H. Hofmeyr, *South Africa* takes a moderately advanced view on the rights of the Black people in the Union of South Africa.

957. "Postscript, August, 1932, Vol. XXXIX, No. 8, pp. 266–268. Vassar remains the "only first grade woman's college in the North which still refuses to admit Negroes." Mount Holyoke and Bryn Mawr held out for a long time but finally yielded, although the latter "still keeps its dormitories 'lily-white'." The death of Albert Thomas, Director-General of the International Labor Office, is a great loss; unlike many philanthropists and socialists, he included colored workers among the working classes of the world. Theodore Roosevelt, governor of the Philippines (and a member of the Spingarn Award Committee) has ordered that the Manila Central High School reduce its fees and open its doors to all children regardless of color. A Peary Memorial was recently erected in Greenland; the United States saw to it that all involved in Peary's trip to the North Pole were present—except the one man, Matthew Henson—who was with him at the Pole and this because Mr. Henson was Black! Frances Wayne, writing in the Denver *Post*, insists that the honor of white women is sacred and that the rule is white women for white men only. Strange, says Du Bois, that white prostitutes exist in every land in the world; and that the rule in general seems to be "colored women for white men." The Rev. George Frazier Miller, of Brooklyn, is all for the social gospel but he does not want this to replace the religion of the Atonement and of Easter. Du Bois thinks there is "no meeting place" for these two aspects of religion. A rather long commentary is offered on Charles Edward Russell's *Blaine of Maine* (New York: Cosmopolitan Book Co., 1931) which combats "the morass of propaganda which has been trying for fifty years to lie about slavery and the Civil War." In this commentary Du Bois summarizes the theme of his *Black Reconstruction* which he was then writing. Du Bois describes, in a strictly factual way, the first three meetings of the Negro Encyclopedia effort, from November, 1931 to March, 1932. He observes that neither he, Alain Locke, nor Carter G. Woodson had been invited to the first meeting. At the next two meetings Locke and he were present but Woodson has rejected all invitations.

958. September, 1932, Vol. XXXIX, No. 9. In "As the Crow Flies" (p. 278), referring to the rout of the veterans, in connection with demands for a bonus "against inconceivable odds, the United States Army have killed, routed, wounded, and chased men, women, children, rags, and bedbugs out of Washington. ... In the attic of the White House, he [President Hoover] directed the action from under a bed at great risk. O Say Can You See?"

959. "Postscript," September, 1932, Vol. XXXIX, No. 9, pp. 298–299.

"Young Voters" among us should be encouraged especially in the South. We need a concerted and militant effort to register, to vote, and to overcome inhibitions and regulations against our voting. Du Bois notes the striking growth in Black college students; in 1912 there were 991 students while in 1932 there were about 21,000. Charles H. Wesley was wise in rejecting the offer of the presidency of Wilberforce University because of its structural complications—part state and part church. Richard R. Wright of Philadelphia has accepted and it is hoped that he will show the necessary courage to make of Wilberforce a first-rate institution for Black youth. Our educational institutions still follow slavishly patterns of the dominant white institutions. But we must educate the young for service to our people and we are not yet doing that.

960. October, 1932, Vol. XXXIX, No. 10. In "As the Crow Flies" (p. 310), "honest to God, if Herbert Hoover don't quit stopping the crisis, he's going to put [William Z.] Foster and [James W.] Ford in the White House next March."

961. "Books," unsigned, Vol. XXXIX, No. 10, October, 1932, p. 326. Guy B. Johnson, *Folk Culture on St. Helena Island* "represents much work but would hardly be read as pastime." J. A. Jarvis, *Fruits in Passing* "a little book of poems"; J. F. Moore, *Will America Become Catholic?* calls attention to two chapters which deal especially with the church and Black people; *The Mob Murder of S. S. Mincey*, published by the Southern Commission on the Study of Lynching, (headed by George F. Milton of Chattanooga), tells of murder "for political reasons" in Georgia in 1930—the commission "is keeping up its most excellent work"; Evelyn Sharp, *The African Child* details a conference on the subject held in Geneva in 1931 (No. 255); Jacques Romaine has published two novelettes: *Les Fantoches* and *La Montagne Ensorcelee;* Sam Kemp, *Black Frontiers: Adventures in Africa* consists of memoirs of service with Cecil Rhodes in 1889–1892 which "make fascinating reading."

962. "Postscript," October, 1932, Vol. XXXIX, No. 10, pp. 331–332. Data on Haiti's finances and trade are offered; efforts to stampede the Black population of Newark, New Jersey, into "returning" to the South were stopped by protests and mass meetings; a description of a new series of dinners to Black authors has been instituted by the *Crisis* and one was held with great success recently in Harlem; the U.S. War Department carries on engineering work in the South and its employment practices are as racist as can be found in that area; in the coming presidential election the main issue ought to be the manner of organizing economic activity in the nation but it appears that the question of alcoholic beverages will be the preferred question. On that question, an attempt to solve it by force and law is characteristically American and futile "and thus we add illegal liquor to our usual program of lawlessness and inefficiency."

963. Vol. XXXIX, No. 11 November, 1932,. "As the Crow Flies" (p. 342), discusses Einstein's arrival to the United States and his post at Princeton's Institute for Advanced Study. "Welcome to Einstein, but Dear God!"—Could there not have been found "some place beside Princeton for real higher education in the United States? Some place beside a school still dominated by Nigger-hating, slave-driving, money-grubbing psychology?"

964. "If I had A Million Dollars," initialled, November, 1932, Vol. XXXIX, No. 11; p. 347. An accounting of how the Phelps-Stokes Fund had expended almost $1,000,000 from 1911 through 1931. No doubt some good has been done but in its support of Hampton-Tuskegee it supported that which "has not been successful and has been given up, while the essential soundness of the Atlanta, Fisk and Howard program of general and higher education and teacher training has with all its omissions proved the salvation of the Negro race." Du Bois thinks that the greatest accomplishment of the fund is that its members now hopefully realize "that Negro leadership is indispensable for the uplift of the Negro race and that race relations are only of real value as they bring together equals to strive for mutual advancement."

965. "Books," unsigned, November, 1932, Vol. XXXIX, No. 11; p. 359. Welbourne Kelley, *Inchin' Along* is a novel with a Black theme by a Southern white man; it "stands out from its fellows for the simple reason that it is not defeatist." Evelyn Waugh, *Black Mischief*, a novel with a fictional kingdom that is probably Ethiopia which is "vivid and more than half believable." *Selected Writings of James H. Dillard*, "are worth reading, especially the short and pithy criticisms of modern education."

966. "Postscript," November, 1932, Vol. XXXIX, No. 11; pp. 362–363. Most of this is devoted to "Herbert Hoover" and the indictment "which Americans of Negro descent have against him is long, and to my mind, unanswerable." This is then spelled out. Du Bois recounts questions asked him by audiences during a recent lecture tour; they dealt with economic power, literature, class distinctions, education, "methods of uplift," the U.S.S.R., and methods of political action.

967. Vol. XXXIX, No. 12, December, 1932. In "As the Crow Flies" (p. 372), "One thing characterizes our day. You can have vast marches of hungry, ragged human beings in the greatest capitals of the world concerning whose awful plight there is no dispute, and yet the world holds great stores of wheat and corn and cotton that are rotting for want of use. This isn't merely an incident; it isn't simply a problem; it is the suicide of civilization."

968. "Books," unsigned, December, 1932, Vol. XXXIX, No. 12, p. 385–386: Carolyn B. Day, *A Study of Some Negro-White Families in the United States,* "is one of the most intelligent studies of the Negro yet made." Arna Bontemps and Langston Hughes, *Popo and Fifina* "is a delightful little book for children." C. V. Kiser, *Sea Island to City* is found not to be an honest study which "minimizes and distorts". Alma Herbst, *The Negro in the Slaughtering and Meat-Packing Industry* is "an exhaustive study." Charles A. Battle, *Negroes on the Island of Rhode Island,* "a most interesting story"; Alpheus Butler, *Make Way for Happiness,* "pleasant, readable" poems "touching race difficulties only lightly, here and there."

969. "Postscript," December, 1932, Vol. XXXIX, No. 12, pp. 387–388. Appropriate particularly for Christmas, a little essay on the travail and glory of parenthood. "From a Traveller" is a tale of the insolence and brutality of whites which Du Bois witnessed when he was in the Gold Coast; he cites this to indicate that stories of corruption so widely told in the United States about Liberia may be true but the real and fullest guilt lies with those who dominate the dark peoples of the world and ruthlessly exploit them. There is the foe and not those holding titles in Liberia.

970. January, 1933 Vol. XL, No. 1; (this issue mentions only Du Bois as editor and manager; no other name appears). In "As the Crow Flies" (p. 5), "keep your eyes on this one truth: the central problem today is so to distribute present income as to prevent a few from getting much too much and keep the mass from starving body and soul. ... What joy it is to 'investigate' the Negro. We don't dare study Wealth or Politics or the morals of Peachtree street; but 'niggers'—Lord! any fool can make a doctor's thesis on them full of lies that universities love to publish."

971. "Postscript ," Vol. XL, No. 1, January, 1933, pp. 20–22. A warm appreciation and estimate of the late Charles Waddell Chesnutt, "dean of Negro literature." A call to Japan and China to cease their warfare and to unite; they, with India, would then be able to drive the white exploiters from all Asia. Du Bois wishes to make clear that in what he has written of the difficulties at Howard University he did not mean to impugn in any way the motives or honor of its secretary, Emmett J. Scott. Du Bois believes that the NAACP has not faced "the present problems of the Negro." with sufficient clarity and force. Therefore, he means to employ the *Crisis* to help develop 12 themes: the physical survival of ourselves; improvement of our health; problems of home and neighborhood; problems of jobs and occupations; problems of education; problems of income; what should be our attitude toward discrimination and the struggle around it; our attitudes towards government and laws; towards "race pride"; towards religion; social contacts, standards and class behavior; recreation.

972. February, 1933, Vol. XL, No. 2. In "As the Crow Flies" (p. 29), "the Inter-Collegiate Socialists have not only repudiated Socialism but want to change the name of their magazine 'Revolt.' Why not call it 'The Kiss'!"

973. "The Health of Black Folk," unsigned, February, 1933, Vol. XL, No. 2, p. 31. The pessimism of "experts" in the past as to the possibility of the survival of Black people in the United States has faded away. Death rate among us is not accurately known because statistics are poor, but it is certainly substantially higher tham among white people. Tuberculosis is our most serious disease; our death rate among children is "distressing."

974. "Books," unsigned, February, 1933, Vol. XL, No. 2, p. 43. Donald Young, *American Minority Peoples*—no comment but a substantial quotation is offered; Leonard Ehrlich, *God's Angry Man*, this novel on John Brown is called "a tremendous biography." *Prize Sermons*, Edited by E. A. Mcalpin, et al. 25 sermons; one by the Black Rev. W. O. Carrington of Hartford. It suggests Christianity as "the hope of a confused and tottering world." Du Bois, "We wonder!"

975. "Postscript, February, 1933, Vol. XL, No. 2, pp. 44–46. A statistical study of "Our Rate of Increase" and then advice as to how to better "Our Health" with social change as basic. A spirited defense is offered of the role and work of Dr. Louis T. Wright at the Harlem Hospital. There follows a detailed prospectus of the *Crisis* for the year's remainder, as outlined in No. 971. In writing of the birth of a girl to a reader, Du Bois states, "the ancient idea that boys are intrinsically and naturally better than girls is a relic of barbarism that dies a hard death ... be glad it's a girl and make life wider and safer and more equal in burden for all girls because of this one." Comment on the struggles of the sharecroppers in and around Camp Hill, Alabama—which have been met by murderous violence from the state and landlords—has been concerned largely with warning Black people to avoid militancy and to beware of Communists. All this is "dodging the issue" and that issue is "how long is the sheriff's posse, recruited from the white mob, going to be permitted to be the willing and pliant tool of Southern Capital, Credit, Extortion and Graft?" As for violence, "I believe in Peace. I shudder at Revolution. But when in 1906 the Atlanta mob began killing Negroes wholesale, I went and bought a repeating shot-gun and loaded it with buckshot. I have got it yet."

976. March, 1933, Vol. XL, No. 3. In "As the Crow Flies" (p. 53), "The Cotton seed oil and Sugar Trusts have handed independence, with strings, to the Philippines. Take it, brown cousins. Liberty even from thieves is sweet."

977. "Karl Marx and the Negro," unsigned, March, 1933, Vol. XL, No. 3; pp. 55–56. "Without doubt the greatest figure in the science of modern industry is Karl Marx." Essay summarizes some of Marx's comments and activities during the U.S. Civil War and just after. Unfortunately his "extraordinary insight" did not continue into the later period and he had not studied first-hand the "peculiar" problems connected with our condition in the United States. We must, however, study him and his ideas, if we are to see our way "clearly in the future."

978. "Color Caste in the United States," unsigned, Vol. XL, No. 3; March, 1933, pp. 59–60. The impression is inculcated that "the main lines of the American Negro problem are settled. ... This is not true," and the essay spells out the realities of racism in the United States.

979. "Postscript" March, 1933, Vol. XL, No. 3; pp. 68–70. Du Bois favors enactment of the proposed law extending democratic rights in the Virgin Islands. The Black person in the United States —overwhelmingly a worker—favors any kind of reasonable, planned economy which will see to it that he has employment and compensation enough to sustain reasonable needs. The injustice and lawlessness—exemplified in the frame-up of young Angelo Herndon in Georgia and the attacks upon sharecroppers in Alabama—"call increasingly for national rebuke." Eight years ago, under the presidency of Professor Thomas W. Turner, of Hampton, there was formed the Federated Colored Catholics of the United States, which sought to struggle within the church against racism. This has been attacked by the church and its technique is to try to capture the organization and impose white leadership upon it. So far this effort seems to have been successfully resisted. Ira Reid, conducting a survey of conditions among Afro-American people in New Jersey, has done a fine job; his recommendations for improvement are sensible and practical and would help not only New Jersey but every part of the nation.

980. April, 1933, Vol. XL, No. 4. In "As the Crow Flies" (p. 77), "so far the net result of putting the race question out of Southern politics has been Tillman, Vardaman, Blease, Heflin, Huey Long, Lynching and Fundamentalism. The South should pray earnestly for a little honest old Reconstruction."

981. "Hubbard of Liberia," signed, April, 1933, Vol. XL, No. 4, p. 87. A sketch of the life of selfless service rendered by Edmund D. Hubbard as a missionary in West Africa, where he now lies buried, together with "a host of other Negro Americans who felt the call of the fatherland and gave their lives for it."

982. "Postscript," April, 1933, Vol. XL, No. 4, pp. 93–94. Devoted largely to a major essay, "The Right to Work." The present economic system is not static; everywhere it is in crisis and socialism grows, whether in the U.S.S.R. or in Denmark or in housing for workers in Vienna—the forms vary but the present system of monopoly capitalism is doomed. Liberal and radical movements in the United States all have failed up to now; we cannot wait and cannot depend upon them. "We must have power; we must learn the secret of economic organization." The road of cooperatives is the road for us. It must be done by us and controlled by us and used by us. This road is not easy but it is possible and with it we will inspire our brothers in Latin America and Africa. We then will be able to "stretch hands of strength and sinew and understanding to India and China, and all Asia. We become in truth, free." Raymond Pace Alexander, the Philadelphia Black attorney, has won a new trial for Willie Brown, admittedly the victim of torture by the police and of an openly racist trial judge.

983. Vol. XL, No. 5; May, 1933, In "As the Crow Flies" (p. 101), "the spectacle of Great Britain and France defending China against Japan reminds us of two fat tabbies taking charge of the interests of mice." . . .

"It is not so much what Roosevelt has done as it is that he is doing something and is eager to admit that something must be done. Four years of stolid inertia in the White House has prepared us to welcome even an energetic game of tag."

984. "Marxism and the Negro Problem," signed, May, 1933, Vol. XL, No. 5, pp. 103–104, 118. "We see in Karl Marx a colossal genius of infinite sacrifice and monumental industry, and with a mind of extraordinary logical keenness and grasp." Many of his basic propositions clearly hold, but "as it seems to me, the Marxian philosophy is a true diagnosis of the situation in Europe in the middle of the 19th Century. ... " The specific questions of our people are not resolved in this outlook—certainly not in terms of now and here, whatever may be true in a large historic sense. Hence, our need is "internal organization" as described in earlier essays. [Once again, there is no reference to Lenin.]

985. "Postscript," May, 1933, Vol. XL, No. 5, pp. 116–117. Most of this department is signed by others. Du Bois writes on three subjects: an attack upon the ideas of William A. Sutton, Georgia's Superintendent of Public Schools, who thinks that Black people are the beneficiaries of the generosity of white people, who employ them! From our labor, as slaves and peons and underpaid workers, has come much of the wealth of Georgia—and we should thank them! Scottsboro proves the basic rottenness of the system of racism; it is a fundamental indictment of the civilization resting upon that poison. The full implementation of the political rights of Black people alone will make possible the elimination of such barbarism as is denoted in the word, "Scottsboro." Writing on "The Jews," Du Bois condemns the anti-Semitism rampant in Germany. "One has only to think of a hundred names like Mendelssohn, Heine, and Einstein, to remember but partially what the Jew has done for German civilization ... race prejudice ... is an ugly, dirty thing. It feeds on envy and hate."

986. June, 1933, Vol. XL, No. 6. "As the Crow Flies" (p. 125), "any Alabama Negro accused of anything is guilty, even if proven innocent. Which shows that Reconstruction was all wrong."

987. "A History of the Negro Vote," unsigned, Vol. XL, No. 6; June, 1933, pp. 128–129. As the title suggests, commencing with colonial era, together with a fairly extensive treatment of the Reconstruction era, quoting from his own article on the subject in *The American Historical Review* (No. 152). He concludes, "The problem, therefore, is how democratic government is going to be restored in the South through Negro votes, and how the votes of white and black workers are to be used for the advancement and development of the nation."

988. "The McGhee's of St. Paul," unsigned, June, 1933, Vol. XL, No. 6, p. 130. A brief and loving account of the l.fe of the Minneapolis Black attorney, Frederick L. McGhee (1861–1912) who was a co-founder of The Niagara Movement. The occasion is the recent death of his widow, Mattie B. McGhee.

989. "The Slater Fund," unsigned, June, 1933, Vol. XL, No. 6, pp. 131–132. Its 50th Anniversary was celebrated at Hampton in April. Its purpose was "uplifting the lately emancipated population of the Southern states and their posterity. ... Seldom has a foundation been more consistent and effective in carrying out the wishes of the donor." In time and "above all, it has recognized that in matters concerning the Negro, the Negro must have a voice."

990. "Postscript," June, 1933, Vol. XL, No. 6, pp. 140–142. This is devoted to "The Strategy of the Negro Vote." "Keeping his eye upon ideals, and measures which make for the uplift of mankind, and particularly for the establishment of a state ruled by the working classes for the benefit of all the workers, his object is so to use his vote as to accomplish any and all reforms leading toward the great goal, so long as he is able, simultaneosly and in some degree to break down color caste. ... He will tell both Socialists and Communists that their first job is to make the American working classes free from color prejudice."

991. July, 1933, Vol. XL, No. 7. "As the Crow Flies" (p. 149), "Liberty, Equality, Fraternity! Some one suggests these are all old stuff and suggests Determination, Law and Authority! We propose Theft, Lies and Force."

992. "The Rosenwald Conference," unsigned, July, 1933, Vol. XL, No. 7, pp. 156–157. A positive evaluation of a conference on the status of Black people—with white and Black participants—recently held in Washington. The various papers are summarized and quoted.

993. "Postscript, July, 1933, Vol. XL, No. 7, pp. 164–165. "Our Class Struggle" is of a peculiar kind for we hardly have a significant bourgeoisie among us. We do, however, have a numerous group of so-called prisoners and delinquents, labelled so by a racist society. And it is a fact that those among us who are relatively secure tend to look down upon these our brothers and sisters who then suffer "not only ostracism but lack of sympathy." On May 11, Congresswoman Edith N. Rogers of Massachusetts delivered an address condemning the racist acts of Hitler in Germany. Side by side with quotations from her speech is a speech in almost identical words that Hitler might have delivered but did not, arraigning the United States for its treatment of Black people. In "Our Music" Du Bois takes exception to the common criticism—he quotes Olin Downes of the New York *Times* as an example—that when Black people sing the "old-time" songs there is something special and that is what they should really sing. Nonsense, says Du Bois, Black people should sing whatever they want to sing, just as other people. "It is to be trusted that our leaders in music, holding on to the beautiful heritage of the past, will not on that account, either be coerced or frightened from taking all music for their province and showing the world how to sing." (A letter from Olin Downes is in the *Crisis*, September, 1933, Vol. XL, No. 9, pp. 212–213.)

994. August, 1933, Vol. XL, No. 8. In "As the Crow Flies" (p. 173), "if any colored groups met as often and talked as much and accomplished as little as the white folks in the last ten years, it would be a sure sign of racial inferiority. ... Let's see—it began in 1917, and six times since it was due to collapse. Now just when *is* Russia going to recall the Czar, re-establish Mumbo-Jumbo in its lovely churches and admit to Lombard and Wall Streets, 'We have sinned'?"

994a. "The Negro College," signed, August, 1933, Vol. XL, No. 8; pp. 175–177. This is an abridged version of Du Bois Fisk Commencement address issued in pamphlet form.

995. "Postscript," August, 1933, Vol. XL, No. 8, pp. 188–189. The Baltimore *Afro-American* of July 1 has interpreted his Fisk speech as meaning that Black colleges should give B.S. degrees in plumbing. If there is anything I did not mean that is it, says Du Bois. We must have *our* Colleges teach all truths and science and culture, but *our* colleges must teach *our* youth how to face and to deal with *our* world as we find it and as we want it to become. The lack of ethics among the lawyers of the United States is shocking. Serving the rich and making money is the goal, but the fact that the poor are victimized and the colored poor doubly victimized by a "justice" system—as everyone knows—arouses not a word from that profession nor from many liberals and socialists. We have not yet really learned the secrets of "Organization." By success many of us mean escape; what kind of leadership is this? We must combine and we must organize for ourselves and among ourselves and in self-service and this can be done; when it is done our power will surprise us.

996. September, 1933, Vol. XL, No. 9; In "As the Crow Flies" (p. 197), "Frances Perkins, Secretary of Labor, has common sense. She demands a wage for Negroes equal to that of whites as the best thing for whites. ... Nothing has filled us with such unholy glee as Hitler and the Nordics. When the only 'inferior' peoples were 'niggers' it was hard to get the attention of the New York *Times* for little matters of race, lynching, and mobs. But now that the damned include the owner of the *Times*, moral indignation is perking up."

997. "On Being Ashamed of Oneself: An Essay on Race Pride," signed, September, 1933, Vol. XL, No. 9, pp. 199–200. This is another among Du Bois' several seminal essays. At first the objective seemed to be assimilation—not so much biologically as socially and politically. This still dominates and carries with it the fight for full citizenship rights. But there was often in this, explicitly or implicitly, an under-estimation of ourselves, a sense of shame. Success has tended to be defined in the dominant sense and has carried with it withdrawal from the mass of our people. "What are we really aiming at? The building of a new nation or the integration of a new group into an old nation?" The time has come when "a new plan must be built up. It cannot be the mere rhodomontade and fatuous propaganda on which Garveyism was based. ... Our advance in the last quarter century has been in segregated, racially integrated institutions and efforts and not in effective entrance into American national life." Then, in italics:

> *The next step, then, is certainly one on the part of the Negro and it involves group action. It involves the organization of intelligent and earnest people of Negro descent for their preservation and advance-ment in America, in the West Indies and in Africa; and no sentimental distaste for racial or national unity can be allowed to hold them back from a step which sheer necessity demands.*

There must be "deliberate propaganda for race pride. ... We can refuse deliberately to lie about our history" but we must encourage "belief in our own ability by organized economic and social action."

998. "Postscript," Vol. XL, No. 9; September, 1933, pp. 212–214. An analysis of the meaning of the National Industrial Recovery Act (NIRA) of the F.D.R. administration showing it will have very little positive impact for Black people, that it will probably "be administered from the point of view of the great employer" and that the control of industry would be "primarily in the interest of capitalism." The passing of Henry Hugh Proctor—a classmate at Fisk—brings an appreciation of his character and work. Data from official census figures show the deliberate effort to curb the education of our children.

999. October, 1933, Vol. XL, No. 10. In "As the Crow Flies" (p. 221), "Mr. [H. G.] Wells puts the next World War in 1940, which relieves us of some personal anxiety. ... Wouldn't it be fine to invite Hitler to lecture at a few white Southern colleges? They might not understand his German but his race nonsense would fit beautifully. ... When a revolution merely changes officials we pat it on the back. When it changes ideas, we send warships."

1000. "Youth and Age at Amenia," unsigned, October, 1933, Vol. XL, No. 10, pp. 226–227. Du Bois recalls the first Amenia Conference held in 1916 at Joel Spingarn's home in upstate New York and details the developments at the second, recently held at the same site and seeking some agreement and comprehension among older and younger workers in the struggle.

1001. "Postscript," October, 1933, Vol. XL, No. 10, pp. 236–237. Extreme pressure is being brought to destroy the sovereignty of Liberia. Black America should help it resist. In "The Church and Religion" Du Bois distinguishes between the two, largely in terms of the priestly and the prophetic. The youth who question dogma are to be encouraged; they are "the salt of the earth and the hope of the future." Religion in the sense "of a striving for the infinite, the ultimate and the best" is necessary. Mr. Ickes is the best person perhaps in F.D.R.'s Cabinet and was an officer of the NAACP; he has appointed an estimable young man in Clark Foreman, of Atlanta's Inter-Racial Commission, as his assistant to advise him on affairs concerning Black people. But Mr. Foreman is white, "and it is an outrage that we again, through the efforts of some of our best friends, should be compelled to have our wants and aspirations interpreted by one who does not know them and our ideals and ambitions expressed by a person who cannot understand them." The death of Harry Potamkin, in a charity ward in New York, is recorded. He was a Communist; he knew more about the cinema than anybody else in the United States but because of his views and his refusal to either hide them or change them, he was starving. His essays on film-making "will remain the finest contribution to that branch of art criticism yet made. And yet our art critics must believe in the present organization of society or die. There is no adequate comment to be made upon this."

1002. November, 1933, Vol. XL, No. 11. In "As the Crow Flies" (p. 245), "have you noticed how polite the American press is to Russia these days? No women for sale; no real famines; no revolution around the corner; what's up? Are we all going red?" (This issue announces George W. Streator as Acting Business Manager.)

1003. "Pan-Africa and New Racial Philosophy," signed, November, 1933, Vol. XL, No. 11, pp. 247; 262. "There are still large numbers of American Negroes who in all essential particulars conceive themselves as belonging to the white race. ... This, of course, is quite natural ... if this young, black American [however] is going to survive and live a life, he must calmly face the fact that however much he is an American there are interests which draw him nearer to the dark people outside of America than to his white fellow citizens." Hence, as a matter of common sense, facing a common oppression, these people must join together. "Pan-Africa means intellectual understanding and co-operation among all groups of Negro descent in order to bring about at the earliest possible time the industrial and spiritual emancipation of the Negro peoples."

1004. "Postscript," November, 1933, Vol. XL, No. 11; pp. 260–261. The centenary of William Wilberforce induces a brief biography. A call is made for the continued support of the NAACP and the *Crisis*—and the defense of Liberia.

1005. December, 1933, Vol. XL, No. 12. In "As the Crow Flies" (p. 269), "the Nazis made a mistake in beginning their propaganda in New York. They should have started in Richmond or New Orleans. Their whole philosophy of race hate has been so evolved in our own South that Hitler himself could learn a beautiful technique by visiting us. ... We wouldn't want to think that the United States is about to achieve peace and friendship with Russia with the hope that Russia may fight Japan and relieve her of the task. After all, Russia isn't nearly as dumb as she sometimes looks."

1006. "The Son of God," initialled, December, 1933, Vol. XL, No. 12, pp. 276–277. A Christmas story about Joe and Mary and his wonder as to who is the father of her Child.

1007. "Tshekedi," unsigned, December, 1933, Vol. XL, No. 12, pp. 277–278. Du Bois tells the story of Tshekedi Kahma, Acting Chief of the Bamangwato, in Bechuanaland, who had ordered the whipping of an Englishman, Phineas Macintosh, for the lustful dealings of that man with Black women. He was deposed for the "crime" (British marines were on hand) but after taking his case to London, he was reinstated. Du Bois says, "After reading the facts in this case, what we are wondering is: Who is civilized in South Africa and who is not?"

1008. "James Weldon Johnson", unsigned, December, 1933, Vol. XL, No. 12; p. 279. A brief account of his life on the occasion of the publication of his autobiography, *Along This Way*, with quotations from the book.

1009. "Too Rich To Be A Nigger", unsigned, December, 1933, Vol. XL, No. 12, pp. 282–283. The true story of the lynching of a young Black man in Clinton, South Carolina. His crime was as stated in the title, taken from a letter written to his family by one of the murderers.

1010. "Books", unsigned, December, 1933, Vol. XL, No. 12, pp. 290–291: notice of the autobiography of Charles Edward Russell, *Bare Hands and Stone Walls* (New York: Scribners 1933) with extensive quotations from sections dealing with his NAACP work.

1011. "Postscript," December, 1933, Vol. XL, No. 12, pp. 292–294: The N.R.A. has reinforced the AFL "a most sinister power"—racist and elitist. "Some time there is coming a great wave of demand from the mass of exploited laborers for an organization which represents their injuries and their wishes. And that new organization is going to sweep the AFL off the face of the earth." In "A Matter of Manners" Du Bois notes that Black people have been more polite than white but he fears this may be passing. "Some how and in some way our younger generation must learn that courtesy and manners are not solely for the benefit of the other person; they are tributes to our own self-respect." Blanton Winship, a Georgia-born Army officer, is in charge of U.S. relations with Liberia per Hoover's appointment. Is it not time F.D.R. undid this? Du Bois welcomes a report of closer relations between Japan and Ethiopia. Once there is unification and reasonable oneness of purpose between Japan and China, then between these great nations and India, and finally between yellow Asia and black Africa, "a new era will open in the world and the impossible domination of one mad race will end." War again threatens and it feeds on racism and on militarism. Huey Long is being investigated for corruption in Louisiana but top bosses there fear he may yet turn to the enfranchisement of Black people to save his position.

1012. January, 1934, Vol. XLI, No. 1. In "As the Crow Flies" (p. 5), "it has taken just 157 years for a President of the United States to say in plain English that lynching is 'a vile form of collective murder.' ... We may yet be able to date the fall of Hitler in Germany at the disfranchisement of German women. ... Every statesman who yells about Children, Church and Kitchen, ought to be made to bear twins, to listen to as many sermons as we have, and to wash dishes and diapers for at least ten years."

1013. January, 1934, Vol. XLI, No. 1, p. 9. "A Sign," unsigned play *probably* by Du Bois; a take-off on Governor Rolph's hailing of the lynching of two white men in San Jose, California, recently.

1014. "Postscript," January, 1934, Vol. XLI, No. 1, pp. 20–21. "Segregation" is not something that should stampede us. "The opposition to segregation is an opposition to discrimination." In the United States these have usually gone together, but they need not and segregation merits opposition only when it does mean an invidious distinction. "The great step ahead today is for the American Negro to accomplish his economic emancipation through voluntary determined co-operative effort." In F.D.R.'s behavior towards Haiti and his declaration on lynching one finds cause for hope. Rolph and Hitler teach us the need for improving methods of knowing public figures before they hold places of power. The French are praised as "the most civilized people in the Western world." A fierce denunciation of the dominant culture of the South, evoked by Scottsboro, closes this section.

1015. February, 1934, Vol. XLI, No. 2. In "As the Crow Flies" (p. 31), "when the United States fights a colored nation there are 12 million colored Americans who will do a little fighting for themselves; and don't let that slip your mind for a minute."

1016. "The Big House Interprets the Cabin," unsigned review of *Roll, Jordan, Roll,* by Julia Peterkin and Doris Ullman, February, 1934, Vol. XLI, No. 2; pp. 37–38. The photographs by Doris Ullman of Southern Black life are excellent; Julia Peterkin, however, brings conventional upper-class Southern white biases and misconceptions to her text. The material does have value in terms of Black and white folklore and "for the revelations of the interpreter and the class she represents."

1017. "Postscript," February, 1934, Vol. XLI, No. 2, pp. 52–53. These pages are devoted to a discussion of segregation and an invitation to readers to send in their views, since the *Crisis* has always been a "Free Forum." There follows a rather detailed history of the NAACP and its position on segregation, commencing with the 1909 founding. As to nuances and variations Du Bois touches on the fight for a Black Officers' Training Camp during the World War, the Harlem Hospital fight and the struggle for the hospital at Tuskegee. The NAACP "has never officially opposed separate Negro organizations—such as churches, schools and business and cultural organizations." Let us have an open and full discussion of all aspects of this question of segregation. [Thereafter for months articles with varying viewpoints on this subject were published in the *Crisis*.]

1018. March, 1934, Vol. XLI, No. 3. (This issue carries Du Bois as Editor in Chief, with George W. Streator and Roy Wilkins as Managing Editors.) In "As the Crow Flies" (p. 61), "the current economic philosophy is to buy off revolution by national charity. What kind of men will this breed, and will the results be worth the price? Dollars to doughnuts that Hitler wangles up a war in Europe before 1940."

1019. "Postscript," March, 1934, Vol. XLI, No. 3, pp. 85–86. "Subsistence Homestead Colonies" projected as part of the New Deal are welcome; but like everything else in the United States, they raise the question of racism. It would be idiotic for Black people to refuse such Colonies on the grounds of segregation, which would mean none for us and we need them surely more than any other group. This is an example of the "paradox" of race segregation given the conditions here. A central paragraph reads:

> Let the NAACP and every upstanding Negro pound at the closed gates of opportunity and denounce caste and segregation; but let us not punish our own children under the curious impression that we are punishing our white oppressors. Let us not affront our own self-respect by accepting a proffered equality which is not equality, or submitting to discrimination simply because it does not involve actual and open segregation; and above all, let us not sit down and do nothing for self-defense and self-organization just because we are too stupid or too distrustful of ourselves to take vigorous and decisive action.

"Internal self-organization" is vital no matter how one views the paradox of segregation. Briefly noted is the President's foundation for polio victims in Georgia." ... The President in his gracious acceptance of the national gift toward this endowment, never mentioned and probably never thought of this intolerable and cruel discrimination against half the child cripples of the South."

1020. April, 1934, Vol. XLI, No. 4. In "As the Crow Flies" (p. 93), fascism's rule is temporary, and so is England's domination over India. We have heard nothing from all those distinguished Black people connected with the New Deal. "For God's sake, say something!"

1021. "A Journey to Texas and New Orleans," signed, April, 1934, Vol. XLI, No. 4, pp. 97–98. In the Black colleges the economics being taught is reactionary. Religious fundamentalism struck him as "puzzling." He notes a triple color line in Texas—Black, Brown (Mexican) and white. Often the Black teachers are selected by white Boards but in Texas there was some political power in the hands of Blacks and so the teachers were not altogether dependent. He was impressed by the students in Houston, Beaumont, and Marshall due to "their vigor and brightness." He never says anywhere what he does not believe and he follows this rule in the South, too. He notes that audiences there tend to ask very few questions.

1022. "Postscript," April, 1934, Vol. XLI, No. 4, pp. 115–117: "Segregation in the North" is a fact and, indeed, Du Bois thinks has grown worse in many instances in the past generation. The objections by Walter White to his articles on segregation do not impress him for "in the first place, Walter White is white. He has more white companions and friends than colored ... It is fantastic to assume that this has anything to do with the color problem in the United States." We have won some legal victories "but beyond that we have not made the slightest impress on the determination of the overwhelming mass of white Americans not to treat Negroes as men." Therefore? "Organize our strength as consumers; learn to co-operate and use machines and power as producers; train ourselves in methods of democratic control within our own group. Run and support our own institutions." Of course, we want an end to all racial and economic distinctions connoting inferiority and oppression; one way to get that, in time, given the world as it is, is through our own organization and the upbuilding of our own strength.

1023. May, 1934, Vol. XLI, No. 5. In "As the Crow Flies" (p. 125), Du Bois warns that Mussolini is eyeing Ethiopia; observing Huey Long's antics in the Senate persuades Du Bois of the beneficial results of Black disfranchisement and of "the superiority of the white race."

1024. "William Monroe Trotter," initialled, May, 1934, Vol. XLI, No. 5, p. 134, occasioned by his death—probably by his own hand. "Curiously aloof" when at Harvard. All his life an "intense hatred of all racial discrimination and segregation"; nothing "ever quite equalled" his Boston *Guardian*, though it was "often as unfair as it was inspired." At first he doubted Trotter but in time he revered him. His association with the Niagara Movement is noted, "but Trotter was not an organization man." Du Bois notes that discrimination is more intense now in Boston than 30 years ago. Trotter was not a failure for he devoted his life to what he believed in and his belief is basically correct—that of human equality. Many lives will be taken in this great struggle and not the least among these was that of Trotter's. His life teaches, also, that organization is needed; a freelancer and a "loner" will not do. "We have got to unite to save ourselves," and insofar as the unbending character of Trotter's attack upon anything purely our own was opposed to this, it was wrong. "Let no trump of doom disturb him from his perfect and eternal rest."

1025. "Postscript." May, 1934, Vol. XLI, No. 5; pp. 147–149. Again on "segregation" repeating former arguments and showing the need to take what one can get while keeping in mind and striving for full freedom. Du Bois notes that the "barbarians" Jim Crow the restaurants in the capital which serve the congressmen and their friends and commends De Priest and the students at Howard University for fighting this. He considers whether or not Black people should resort to force as a strategy for liberation; he hears suggestions along this line, especially from young people more and more often. No, says Du Bois and this is because we could not win. The situations in Haiti and in the American colonies were altogether different. If there were enough white allies to support a violent Black effort, then the effort would be clearly unnecessary, but since there are not enough supporters, such a policy would be suicidal. "It is, therefore, our clear policy not to appeal to force until clearly and evidently, there is no other way." Du Bois chronicles a trip to the mid-West—Indiana, Iowa, Missouri, Illinois. He insists "that the Negro should *not* seek a separate culture in the United States." He rejects the separatist "49th State" idea. "Segregation was evil, and should be systematically fought" while, at the same time, living in a segregated society, people must also "make the best of their life ... and that was our present job." His proposal and the proposal of the Board of the NAACP on segregation are printed here and Du Bois challenges the Board to say whether or not it believes "in the Negro spirituals" or "in Negro history, Negro literature and Negro art" or "in 200 Negro newspapers which spread NAACP news and propaganda?"

1026. June, 1934, Vol. XLI, No. 6. In "As the Crow Flies" (p. 157), "it's always the same: stop crime by longer sentences, more policemen, bigger guns and more hideous threats; instead of stopping crime by cutting down the manufacture of criminals."

1027. June, 1934, Vol. XLI, No. 6, p. 174. A reply to Rev. F. J. Grimké, pastor of the all-Black 15th Street Presbyterian Church in Washington, who in this issue opposes Du Bois' position on segregation. "In fine, we can only regret that Dr. Grimké sees in the 15th Street Presbyterian Church only the insult that caused its founding, and has no word for the magnificence of the opportunity which he has had in leading and developing it."

1028. "Postscript," June, 1934, Vol. XLI, No. 6, pp. 182–184. Du Bois' position on segregation has been described as a counsel of despair. "We can't win, therefore, give up and accept the inevitable. Never, and nonsense. Our business in this world is to fight and fight again, and never to yield. But after all, one must fight with his brains, if he has any." The essential arguments already offered are repeated. Protest alone will not do; it is vital, but to it must be added a positive program. We must condemn racism forever and as bitterly as possible. At the same time, and not in contradiction to this, we fight for Black jobs and Black controlled businesses and the best possible schools for Black children even if we are forced to have schools *only* for our children. We will make our churches the best there are, and so forth. Du Bois quotes from the consciousness of self and race that filled his 1897 pamphlet, *The Conservation of Races* (No. 1921) and says, "on the whole, I am rather pleased to find myself still so much in sympathy with myself." The real struggle for liberation requires thought and study, long training, "the inculcation of racial and national ideals. It is not a publicity stunt. It is a life." He hails the picketing in Washington and Chicago in the ghettoes for jobs—"this is fighting segregation with segregation." Transmute segregation "into power." "Power that some day will smash all race separation." "Nothing illustrates better our current philosophy and practice in segregation, than the rise and development of Negro fraternities in colleges." They are splendid and one result has been not less Black students in so-called white fraternities, but more. The July, 1934 issue of the *Crisis* is the last to carry Du Bois' name as editor; it does not contain, however, either his departments or any other contribution from his pen.

1029. "Dr. Du Bois Resigns," August, 1934, Vol. XLI, No. 8, pp. 245–246, prints the full text of his letter, dated June 26, 1934, to the board of the NAACP. Du Bois affirms that the matter of "segregation" was the occasion but not the cause of his resignation. Important was the fact that "the Board peremptorily forbade all criticism of the officers and policies [of the Board] in the *Crisis*." The NAACP does not now have a positive program to deal with the tremendous problems faced by the Black people. Since the depression in particular I have labored, he writes, for such a program and for "economic readjustment" and for necessary changes in personnel but all this has been ignored. If I do not act, he adds, I would seem to be consenting and I cannot do that; hence, my resignation and severance of all connection with the Association and with the *Crisis*. Perhaps his departure will help stimulate "a great and gifted race" to rescue the Association "with a re-birth of that fine idealism and devotion" that founded it. In leaving, "I do not, however, cease to wish it well, to follow it with personal and palpitating interest, and to applaud it when it is able to rescue itself from its present impossible position and reorganize itself according to the demands of the present crisis." (The board's acceptance is published immediately thereafter and is completely gracious and complimentary.)

* * *

For 24 months, from January, 1920, through December, 1921, Du Bois edited *The Brownies' Book*, a monthly magazine published in New York City and aimed at Afro-American children. In each issue he contributed a department, "As The Crow Flies" (in June, 1927, as we have seen, this became a feature in the *Crisis*.*)

1030. January, 1920, Vol. I, No. 1, pp. 23–25. "The Crow is black and O so beautiful. ... " And he talks with and to "the Little Boy with the Big Voice." He talks of the war in 1918 and the peace through 1919—the year of peace and "the 300th year since our black fathers settled in America." How the peace conference remade the world is to be seen on your atlas; other results of the conference—as the League of

---

**The Brownies Book* was published by a company formed by Du Bois and Augustus Dill. An excellent account of this effort, by Elinor D. Sinnette, is in *Freedomways*, Winter, 1965, Vol. V, pp. 133–142.

Nations—are explained. The monstrous character of war is sketched. Conditions in Ireland, India, Russia, Poland—"thousands of Jews have been killed there"—Mexico ("we ought to leave her alone")—are touched upon, as well as in the United States with appropriate emphasis on the doings of Black folk.

1031. February, 1920, Vol. I, No. 2; pp. 63–64: The Crow asks what did he see flying about the world in December and January? Terrible hunger. "We must do all we can to avoid another war." Special note of the "Soviet government—that is, the government of the working people" and of India and Egypt where brown and black people fight for independence. Then, again, news of happenings in the United States.

1032. March, 1920, Vol. I, No. 3, pp. 76–77. Du Bois notes the rebellion of the "colored people of Haiti ... against the tyranny of the United States ... Congress is trying to frame a bill to keep people from advocating violence and riot. So far, the bills proposed would stop folks from thinking." Du Bois rejoices that soon women will be able to vote and "the greatest discrimination against them" will end. The effort of the New York Legislature to expel five members because they are Socialists "is dangerous and un-American."

1033. April, 1920, Vol. I, No. 4, pp. 118–119. Again an overview of main world events. Strikes are noticed and explained—in Cuba, Italy, and France. The lust for oil is driving the United States towards greater and greater intervention in Mexico; Mexico resists and "Mexico is right."

1034. May, 1920, Vol. I, No. 5, pp. 159–160. Fear of the new government in Russia is widespread; nevertheless, peace is returning there. People arrested during the war because they spoke out against it or refused to fight in it should now be released.

1035. June, 1920, Vol. I, No. 6, pp. 183–184. Sinn Fein is explained; revolutions in Mexico and Guatemala. Details of the political process in the United States are given. The death of William Dean Howells —"perhaps the most distinguished of American authors"—is recorded. His relationship with Dunbar is recalled.

1036. July, 1920, Vol. I, No. 7, pp. 211–212. Strikes have occurred in New Bedford, Massachusetts, among lumber workers in Wisconsin and Michigan and railroad workers in Buffalo.

1037. August, 1920, Vol. I, No. 8; pp. 234–235. The attack by Poland upon Soviet Russia has been beaten back. "There is a new general in the world who is doing great things and you must know about him. His name is 'General Strike.'" What he is and does is explained. The Zionists, whose purposes are explained, have been meeting in Paris.

1038. September, 1920, Vol. I, No. 9, pp. 272–274. Wars are being fought in many parts of the world; they are pinpointed; 70,000 American soldiers lie in French graves, among them are 1,000 Black men. Japanese, who number 80,000 in California, are "the best farmers." Whites are trying to prevent them from buying land. "Their excuse is that the Japanese want to marry the whites, which is, of course, untrue." Eugene V. Debs, the socialist candidate for president, is in prison because he opposed the war. "He is a brave man of fine character." To keep other hundreds of conscientious objectors in prison, especially now that the war is over "is nothing less than idiotic barbarity."

1039. October, 1920, Vol. I, No. 10, pp. 318; 320. Socialism and communism are explained, as is the Third International. The granting of partial independence to Egypt by Great Britain "is a great triumph for colored men. Central American countries are forming a Central American Union. Most of the people are colored. Three thousand Negroes, chiefly West Indians and led by Marcus Garvey, have held a month's convention in New York City and made a demand for 'Africa for the Africans!'."

1040. November, 1920, Vol. I, No. 11, pp. 332–323. Anti-Jewish laws have been passed in Hungary. Figures on income distribution in the United States are given, as "18 million families get less than $2,000 a year ... and 90 families get $750,000 a year or more."

1041. December, 1920, Vol. I, No. 12, pp. 378–379. Again, a call for the release of Eugene Debs from prison. The NAACP has sent people to investigate U.S. intervention in Haiti.

1042. January, 1921, Vol. II, No. 1; pp. 16–17. "Rainer Maria Rilke, who was born in Prague in 1875, is one of the most original of modern poets." ... "Some good people who want to make folks better by law have started a movement to close the movies on Sunday and otherwise keep people from enjoying themselves on the Sabbath."

1043. February, 1921, Vol. II, No. 2; pp. 52–53. The Crow says, "There are things I do not understand as I fly among men. There is food—they eat not; there are clothes—they freeze; there is joy—they cry. Why—why—why? ... There were 65 persons lynched without trial in the United States during the year 1920. No other civilized country in the world has such a record." The KKK is explained and its recent revival noted.

1044. March, 1921, Vol. II, No. 3; pp. 82–83. The widespread character of economic depression—from the United States to Austria —is observed.

1045. April, 1921, Vol. II, No. 4; 114–115. Charles Gilpin, the great Black actor, has conducted himself with manliness and dignity when some grossly prejudiced people sought to bar him from being among the honored guests at a dinner of the Dramatic League in New York City.

1046. May, 1921, Vol. II, No. 5; pp. 158–159. The Crow asks children if they read books, for once only kings and priests could learn but now all persons may do so if they read. Investigations of peonage —explained—is going forward in the South. John Williams of Jasper County in Georgia killed 11 of his peons for fear of exposure—he has been convicted of murder. Einstein's theory of relativity is explained.

1047. June, 1921, Vol. II, No. 6; pp. 184–185. A statue to Bolivar, the liberator of South America, is unveiled in New York. "When Bolivar was a fugitive and in danger of his life he found refuge and help in Haiti."

1048. July, 1921, Vol. II, No. 7; pp. 206–207. There has been race rioting in Tulsa, Oklahoma, with many Black and white people killed, "but the Negroes prevented the threatened lynching which started the riot." The Haitians are demanding that the U. S. occupation end.

1049. August, 1921, Vol. II, No. 8, pp. 225–226. The Second Pan-African Congress is to meet. "Representatives from groups of colored peoples all over the world will be present to discuss their problems."

1050. September, 1921, Vol. II, No. 9, pp. 271–272. It has been suggested that the United States not enter any war until a referendum on the question has been submitted to and approved by the nation's voters.

1051. October, 1921, Vol. II, No. 10. Revolutionary activity has appeared in parts of India. Again, reference to the revival of the KKK.

1052. November, 1921, Vol. II, No. 11, pp. 322–323. "The rebellion in India against English rule is still going on." The Crow talks, "I saw a curious sight yesterday in London and Brussels and Paris; hundreds of folk, black like me, were sitting together and talking earnestly. Finally, in Paris, they placed a wreath on a grave and on the ribbons of the wreath was written, 'Pan-Africa to the Unknown Soldier.' I wonder what it all meant."

1053. December, 1921, Vol. II, No. 12, pp. 345–346: The desires of Ireland and Egypt and India vis-à-vis England are explained. So is the case of Sacco-Vanzetti. Black people set up their own political parties in Louisville, Kentucky, and in Virginia. In Virginia the Black candidate for governor received 20,000 votes. The people of Porto Rico—"many of whom are colored"—and the people of the Philippines are dissatisfied with U.S. rulers.

1054. "Honey," signed, with the note (rewritten after Maeterlink), a story, *The Brownies' Book*, August, 1920, Vol. I, No. 8, pp. 227–232. The work of bees and the importance of work—"work is Love. Love is Life"—says Mother, "with bees and with men."

1055. "Taboo," signed, *The Brownies' Book*, May, 1921, Vol. II, No. 5, pp. 142–143. The word is defined and explained as to source and use. Today the attempt is made to have reason function in place of taboo, but some people wish to return to taboo and abandon reason; this however, is a remedy which is worse than any possible illness.

* * *

Having resigned from the *Crisis* and from the NAACP Board, Du Bois accepted an invitation from John Hope, president of Atlanta University, to join its faculty, which he did in 1934. Very soon thereafter, he conceived of a scholarly journal to come from that university and serve, in a way, as a continuation of the Atlanta University Studies issued from 1897 to 1914. From the conception of the magazine to its actual launching took about five years—questions of finance and control were stumbling blocks. Beginning, however, with 1940, such a journal, called *Phylon* (from the Greek meaning race) did appear and through the Second Quarter of 1944 (at which time Du Bois, under pressure, resigned from Atlanta University) the Doctor was its Editor in Chief. The original editorial board also included, Ira De A. Reid, Managing Editor, William S. Braithwaite, Mercer Cook, Rushton Coulborn, William H. Dean, Jr., Oran W. Eagleson, and Rufus E. Clement (who was the university's president). At the founding there were three contributing editors: Horace M. Bond, president of Fort Valley State College; Rayford W. Logan, professor at Howard University; and Allison Davis, professor of anthropology at Dillard University. Du Bois' contributions to *Phylon*, while he edited it, follow.

1056. "Apology," *Phylon*, Vol. I, No. 1, 1940, pp. 3–5. "We seem to see today a new orientation and duty which will call not simply for the internal study of race groups as such, but for a general view of that progress of human beings which takes place through the instrumentality and activity of group culture ... we shall usually proceed from the point of view and the experience of the black folk where we live and work, to the wider world."

1057. "A Chronicle of Race Relations, 1939," unsigned, Vol. I, No. 1, (1940), pp. 90–97. "Japan is convinced that European influence in China will make her very existence insecure unless she herself dominates China." In India "a stalemate has been reached." Promises of democracy made by Britain have not been implemented and Indian troops have been employed—contrary to promises—outside India in the present war. The British promise that an independent Palestine will have a Jewish population not in excess of one-third its total inhabitants. Attention is paid to the racism of Hitler with extensive quotations from his writings. The agreement between Nazi Germany and the USSR results from the latter's merited suspicions of the Allies. News from Africa is sparse due to censorship. Continued labor strife in the West Indies throughout 1939. News of the United States, in terms of race questions, is summarized, with attention to the Marian Anderson concert at the Lincoln Memorial, the Baptist's World Alliance meeting in Atlanta and its striving to curb Jim Crow arrangements; in the arts, attention is called to the work of William Grant Still, Ethel Waters, Dorothy Maynor, Richmond Barthé, Augusta Savage, Sargent Johnson, and Cab Calloway. Chronicled are "conspicuous appointments of colored persons to positions which involve contact with white colleagues and in many cases authority over them."

The work of Ales Hrdlicka, of the Smithsonian Institution, in refuting the "contention that criminals bear a physical stamp which betrays them" is observed. The deaths of Kelly Miller, Benjamin Brawley, and Joel E. Spingarn are reported. Of the latter, Du Bois writes, "Mr. Spingarn was of Jewish descent and an unselfish and inspired fighter for desperate causes and universal justice. With this he combined deep sensibilities and a keen, critical temperament."

1058. "Books and Race, 1939," unsigned, Vol. I, No. 1, (1940), pp. 98–100. Books are listed and a few are commented upon very briefly. Among those held to be of high quality are E. A. Hooten, *Twilight of Man;* E. R. Embree, *Indians of the Americas*; Jacques Barzun, *Of Human Freedom*; Otto Neurath, *Modern Man in the Making* and, in particular, Robert S. Lynd, *Knowledge For What?*. A section on "Race in Periodicals, 1939" calls special attention to Gould Beech, "Schools for Minorities" in *Survey Graphic* (October) and Manuel Gottlieb's article on the land question in Georgia during Reconstruction in the summer issue of *Science & Society*.

1059. "A Chronicle of Race Relations," unsigned, Vol. I, No. 2, 1940, pp. 175–192: Du Bois notes the widespread use of "colored people" among the British and French soldiers, in Europe and in the Near East. In Britain a hint of yielding on racism is shown since the first Black man has entered officer's training school in England. A report of eight years of work by the International Institute of African Languages and Cultures of London is the occasion for an estimate of its work. The latter has some value, especially in "relatively innocuous matters" but it treats Africa and Africans as subjects to be studied—*by Europeans* —and is generally an instrument for the maintenance of an iniquitous *status quo*. Its work has especially "been seriously handicapped by making anthropological science the servant of present methods of administration." The denial of civil rights for Black Africans, as decided by the Privy Council in the case of Wallace Johnson, a Black trade-union leader of Sierra Leone, is described. Forms of racist oppression in South Africa are detailed. An analysis is made of "the underlying reasons for the present war between Japan and China." Great attention is given to the continuing struggle in India for independence. Unrest in the West Indies intensifies; movements looking towards a federation and greater autonomy are growing. Documentation is given of "the extraordinary racial philosophy current in Germany." The antiracist statement adopted by the recent convention of the American Anthropological Association is quoted. Examining the recent proposals for a peaceful world from the Pope and the

New York *Times*, Du Bois notes that they tend to ignore colonies and colored peoples. The former Kaiser has suggested a unity of the Western nations for a crusade against Bolshevism but presumably it is not a serious peace proposal. Leonard Barnes, of the University of Liverpool, on the other hand, is quoted at length for his insight into the connections between colonialism and racism, and war. Katherine Dunham's work in the dance is discussed. It is noted that the *Washington News*, running a contest to discover the man bearing the closest resemblance to Abraham Lincoln, was disconcerted when the winner turned out not to be a white man; the prize was given but not publicly! The existence of sharp class stratification and monopoly domination in the United States is documented and its connection with "race propaganda cannot be ignored." Commendation is given to the work of Rachel Davis Du Bois [no relation] in developing techniques for intercultural and interracial education. Attention is called to the "heartening" work of the Southern Conference for Human Welfare.

1060. "Pushkin," signed, Vol. I, No. 3, (1940) pp. 265–269. A factual account notes that Pushkin described himself as a "descendant of Negroes." In a "postscript" Du Bois comments that this is the kind of article that is to appear in a projected four-volume encyclopaedia of the Negro and that Pushkin must be included therein, just as Alexandre Dumas, John Hope, P. B. S. Pinchback, and John Mercer Langston would have to be included.

1061. "A Chronicle of Race Relations," Vol. I, No. 3, (1940), pp. 270–288. Du Bois posits a victory by Germany in the war and discusses possible results; notes that Jules Verne's novel, *The Five Hundred Millions of the Begum*, has as its hero, Herr Schulze, someone "who closely resembles Hitler." Black Africans are being used as fighters by France and Britain in Europe as in the First World War. He quotes at length the remarks made by Dr. William H. Kilpatrick, accepting a position with the Service Bureau for InterCultural Education. Du Bois reports on a recent Inter-American Congress in Mexico dealing with the question of the liberation of the Indian peoples of Latin America. The decrease in illiteracy in the U.S.S.R.—51 percent in 1926 and 20.8 percent in 1939—is "an astonishing accomplishment." The result of the refusal by Britain and France to support Ethiopia when ravished by Italy is now apparent. Again an expression of Du Bois' tendency to sympathize with Japan in the present world scene is made manifest in his writings about the Dutch East Indies. The position of the Indian National Congress towards "minorities" in India is summarized and recent speeches by Gandhi are quoted at length. Forcible repression of workers in Africa—as in Northern Rhodesia—is reported. Conditions for workers in the Canal Zone and in all Panama are "a crying shame." Data released in advance from the 1940 census, in regard to Black people, are summarized. The Catholic Church, through its social action department, has issued a fine pamphlet by Rev. F. J. Gilligan on *Negro Workers in Free America.* "There is increasing evidence in the South of growing awareness of social and economic problems including the race problem." The meetings of the Council of Young Southerners and of the Southern Conference for Human Welfare are noted; speeches made at the conference by Ragni Patel, of India, Frank P. Graham, John B. Thompson, Barry Bingham as well as Maury Maverick are quoted at some length, especially that by the last named, the Mayor of San Antonio, whose speech is called "sensational." The "Citizens Fact-Finding Movement" in Georgia, which started in 1937 and includes no Black groups, nevertheless does face up to the race question in its reports and often takes bold positions. But, of course, the Bourbon South remains powerful; thus it forced the cancellation of a scheduled lecture by the Black Congressman from Illinois, Arthur W. Mitchell, to be given at a white Baptist school, Howard College, in Alabama. Don West, of Georgia, writing in the *Southern News Almanac,* exposes something of the truth about peonage in his own state. The essence of the proceedings of the third meeting of the National Negro Congress in Washington is offered.

1062. "Youth," a review of Ira De A. Reid, *In a Minor Key* (Washington: American Council on Education, 1940) initialled, Vol. I, No. 3, (1940), p. 293. Praised as something of "lasting value"; it is for "those who want accurate information [concerning Black youth] in readable form."

1063. "Moton of Hampton and Tuskegee," signed, Vol. I, No. 4, (1940), pp. 344–351. The Postscript makes clear that this, as the essay on Pushkin, (No. 1060), is meant for the projected *Encyclopedia of the Negro.* In that postscript, Du Bois writes revealingly of Moton and of their personal relationship. He concludes, "I do not think in my judgment of him I had been wrong, although I had not seen the whole picture. I do think that my criticism and that of other Negroes helped him to find a stronger and more tenable platform. But in any case Robert Moton was a great and good man who suffered for a noble cause."

1064. "A Chronicle of Race Relations," Vol. I, No. 4, (1940), pp. 368–389. Du Bois quotes at length from an article, "On the Meaning of Race," by Alexander Lesser which appeared in the "one and only issue" in 1935 of the magazine *Race*, which "deserved a longer life." At a recent meeting of the American Psychological Association "Dr. David Wechsler emphasized that existing intelligence tests in general could not forecast intelligent behavior." The text of a German pamphlet distributed in Poland is quoted for it shows striking similarity to Bourbon racist propaganda in the United States. Harold Callender's series in the New York *Times*, reporting on his travels in the colonial areas of the world, concludes that the people there "desire British and particularly European leadership rather than Asiatic autonomy." Du Bois thinks this "is wishful thinking." In the United States "the greatest inter-racial event is the draft." Despite all the talk "there is not the slightest doubt but what Negro units will be separated from all other Americans." "In many respects," Du Bois writes, "the crucial center of the modern race problem lies in India." And that is based to a large degree upon the enormous wealth of India and its exploitation by Europe. Efforts by Britain to divide India in terms of Muslim and Hindu are spelled out and statements opposing this coming from the All-India Azad (Independent) Muslim Conference of the past April are quoted to show this. The spread of the anti-Jewish activities from Germany into Roumania and Hungary is detailed. Du Bois observes evidences of "a new spirit looking toward Arabian unity and independence" which is now having increasing influence even in Egypt, "which earlier had stood apart from Arabian movements." Data on exploitation and discrimination in South Africa are offered. Student exchange between Atlanta University and Haiti has been established. A long and documented attack is made upon U.S. policy towards Mexico. Du Bois notes that the statement concerning Black people in the Democratic platform adopted in July is the strongest ever to come from that party, while that in the Republican party is probably weaker than hitherto for that party. Extracts are printed from a speech made in September by Thomas C. Hennings, Jr. (D., Missouri); it is called "one of the most striking speeches in Congress on race discrimination." The testimony before a Senate Committee, offered by Professor Rayford W. Logan, in April, 1940, demonstrating the racism within the defense establishment, is quoted at length. A ballad by Katherine Garrison Chapin, with music by William Grant Still, has been performed with great success; it is entitled, "And They Lynched Him on a Tree." The work in drama of Shirley Graham—in the past "Tom Tom" and

"Swing Mikado" and most recently an adaptation of the "Pirates of Penzance" moving the locale from England to Cuba—is commended. So, too, is the work of the painter and sculptor, Henry Bannarn.

1065. "The Saga of L'Amistad", unsigned, Vol. II, No. 1, (1941), pp. 2–4. A stirring historical introduction to the reproduction of the three panels on the theme of the *Amistad* mutiny done by Hale Woodruff for the library at Talladega College.

1066. "A Chronicle of Race Relations," unsigned, Vol. II, No. 1, (1941), pp. 76–90. It commences with a rather full analysis of the recent elections: only 23 percent of the press supported the winner (F.D.R.). Of the 80,000,000 potential voters only 50,000,000 voted. The greater disfranchisement of the South persists—though to a lesser degree than in the past—and its enlarged direct and indirect political power is documented (as in Congressional committees). He spells out elections of Black candidates in various states. An accurate attack upon the antidemocratic political system in Georgia was made in a pamphlet issued in May by that state's Citizens Fact-Finding Movement; it is entitled *Political System* and Du Bois quotes from it at some length. The work in psychology—on so-called race differences—by O. W. Eagleson of Spelman College is commended and summarized. Hamilton Basso has written an illuminating essay on racism in the *New Republic* in November, 1939; extensive quotations are offered. Du Bois corrects himself on the journal *Race*, previously mentioned (No. 1064) of which there were two issues and not one; from the second he quotes Mark Graubard on biological and cultural differences. An essay by Ashley-Montague in the June, 1940, issue of *Scientific Monthly* is called "notable" and quoted. He observes that a recent speech by Hitler attacking the colonialism and elitism of the Allies was hardly reported in the United States. Of course, Hitler means no improvement, "but that does not keep the man in the street, particularly if he is colored, from asking the Anglo-Saxon frankly, 'suppose you do overcome Hitler and obtain power, where do we come in?'" The war aims that should motivate the Allies are best expressed by H. G. Wells in a recent issue of *The Nation,* extensively quoted. A summary done by Rufus E. Clement on how far the states have complied with the 1938 Supreme Court decision in *Gaines* v. *Missouri* (where separate schools are provided, racially, they must indeed be equal) is published. "The most serious condition that faces American Negroes today is the merging of the race problem into a problem of economic class as determined by racial prejudices." Examples follow. The AFL continues to kill proposals put before it to end racial discrimination. Unions which deny Black people membership are listed. A conference on "The Participation of the Negro in National Defense" was held in November at Hampton. It sent President Roosevelt a bill of particulars. Many organizations and some news agencies have met and decided on a central organization for the definition and the counting of lynchings. Some of the nuances and idiocies of "The Etiquette of Race Relations" are illustrated from recent news items.

1067. "A Chronicle of Race Relations," (it is stated here, arranged by W. E. B. Du Bois), Vol. II, No. 2, (1941), pp. 172–193. A summary is offered of Hans Habe's essay, "Nazi Plans for Negroes," appearing in the *Nation*, March 1. President Roosevelt's speech of March 16 mentioned China but omitted India; it was, also, notably deficient in terms of racism in the United States. This "continuing failure" is a "matter of distress." Du Bois sees a mounting pressure for the United States to enter the war, but quotes from Norman Thomas and from Joseph P. Kennedy on the dangers and costs of such entry. Du Bois thinks that "perhaps the finest single word in the war controversy has been uttered by Anne Morrow Lindbergh" in her *The Wave of the Future* (N.Y: Harcourt, Brace, 1940) where she calls for making our own civilization better and urges "reform at home rather than crusade abroad." He notes the racism in the practice of the Census Bureau as counting "whites" and "non-whites" the latter lumping together Negroes, Chinese, Indians, Japanese, and others. "Anti-Semitism may be an injury to the Semite, but it is a disease for the anti-Semite." Du Bois suggests that this entire theme of racism and its devastating impact upon the racists is one that should produce in time great epochal works of literature. Vice-President Henry Wallace is quoted and commended since he "is thinking more clearly on the subject of race and economic emancipation than most members of the present administration." A call for brotherhood and one denouncing racism has been issued recently—and is quoted—from the English League of Colored Peoples. Historical data are offered on the Maoris of New Zealand; also on Japan now allied with Hitler. More material is offered on African participation in the Second World War. The Indian struggle against British domination is described again with comments on Nehru's work and writings. The artistry of Marian Anderson and the dramatic writing of Shirley Graham are described. Tribute is paid to Franz Boas on his 83rd birthday; he "has done more to clear away the myth of inherent race differences than any living scientist." Extended note is taken of the fact that for the first time the Charles Eliot Norton Professorship of Poetry at Harvard is held by a "Latin-American scholar of Negro descent"—Pedron Henríques Ureña, of the Dominican Republic.

1068. "Books and Race", several volumes reviewed by him, initialled, Vol. II, No. 2, (1941), pp. 191–192. Effie Lee Newsome, *Gladiola Garden* (Washington, Associated Publishers, 1940), consists of poems for children; "one need not add that Mrs. Newsome's poems are always delicately done and bits of beauty which all children appreciate." *The Negro in Virginia*, compiled by Writers Program, W. P. A., in Virginia, and sponsored by the Hampton Institute (New York: Hastings House, 1940); the work was directed by Roscoe E. Lewis. It is excellent. Alain Locke, editor, *The Negro in Art* (Washington: Associates in Negro Folk Education, 1940), represents "a most interesting collection of reproductions of painting and sculpture by Negroes and something of the Negro as portrayed by white artists. It is an heartening and singularly interesting collection and emphasizes as nothing else could do the essential beauty of the darker peoples."

1069. "A Chronicle of Race Relations," arranged by Du Bois, Vol. II, No. 3 (1941), pp. 272–79. An extended notice is taken of David Livingstone on the centenary of his activity in Africa; this is based largely on an essay by A. V. Murray appearing in the journal, *Race Relations.* The death of C. G. Seligman is reported with details concerning his significant anthropological work in Africa; he was author of *Races of Africa* (1930). Material relative to current conditions in the Union of South Africa is given as well as in British colonies in Africa; in the latter case particular attention is called to statements and activities coming from the African peoples themselves. The liberation of Ethiopia and Emperor Selassie's insistence that Italian prisoners should not be harmed is a lesson in civilized behavior. The settling of numerous refugee Jews in the Dominican Republic is described. In the United States attention is called to the fact that Black workers are "systematically demanding employment especially in war industries." A statement by Max Yergan, president of the National Negro Congress, is quoted. Other organizations, such as the NAACP and the National Urban League, have been bringing pressure to bear for the opening of jobs to Black people. All this culminated in the March on Washington Movement and in Roosevelt's executive order affirming the policy of the United States Government as "that there shall be no discrimination in the employment of workers in defense industries or government because of race, creed, color or national origin. ... " The present movement has similarities to developments during the First World War, but it "is much more fundamental as it is aimed at the economic exclusion of Negroes from industry." Harold Laski's essay in a recent *Nation* affirming that the present war is "a declaration of bankruptcy on the part of capitalist civilization" is quoted at length. Attention is called to the new constitution adopted by the International Long-shoremen and Warehousemen's Union, CIO, headed by Harry Bridges, barring racism. Du Bois quotes from the Boston *Transcript* showing that racist practices in Boston in the field of medicine are much sharper than they were 30 years earlier. Dr. Walter D. Cocking, an Iowan and Dean of the School of Education at the University of Georgia, has come under severe attack because of proposals that its students be assigned to teach an experimental school attended by both Black and white children.

1070. "A Chronicle of Race Relations", arranged by Du Bois, Vol. II, No. 4, (1941), pp. 388–406. The exhibit on Man in the Smithsonian Institution is "a vast and striking improvement on the usual illus-trations in school geographies" for it does not show the White Man in any superior guise to those who are colored. Peace plans hitherto published suffer from a "most serious omission ... the failure to give any serious consideration to the position of the colored world after the war." This failure is illustrated by examples ranging from the Pope to the American Friends Service Committee to various statements from Churchill and Roosevelt. The change in the nature of the Second World War with Hitler's attack in June upon the U.S.S.R. is analyzed. The racist and exploitative character of the British Empire is empha-sized; articles documenting this, by Norman Thomas (in the *Nation*) and by Albert Viton (*the New Republic*) are quoted. Five columns are devoted to "The Jews" with the theme that "the fundamental tragedy of this second World War is the treatment of the Jews ... murder, degradation, theft on an extraordinary scale and personal humiliation." Du Bois notes the widespread existence of anti-Semitism in the United States; quotes an article with this characteristic by Albert J. Nock in a recent issue of the *Atlantic Monthly*. He writes, "There has been effort in the United States to combat anti-Semitism but it has suffered on the one hand from the 'hush-hush' methods of certain Jews and from a clear lack of enthusiasm on the part of a surprising number of Gentiles." Norman Leys, long an anti-imperialist among Englishmen (who participated in the 1921 Pan-African Congress), has written another excellent book exposing imperialism, *The Colour Bar in East*

Africa, from which data are quoted. Du Bois offers reasons for fearing British designs on the independence of a restored Ethiopia. Labor difficulties in South Africa are reported. Lewis Hanke's contribution in *The Journal of Negro Education* (July) on "the problem of Negroes and Indians in South America" is characterized by "unusual clarity." In the same journal, there are important contributions from Gilbert Freyre and Arthur Ramos. Du Bois finds "the growing insistence of the American liberal press on war with Japan" to be "disquieting." Examples are offered and a defense of the Japanese position from Tokyo is quoted. Struggles for independence in India, Burma, and the Dutch East Indies are described. The blatant racism in the Panama Canal Zone, dominated by the United States, is exposed. President Charles Seymour of Yale in a recent address painted an idyllic picture of the character of society in the United States; as usual he "forgot" us and Jim Crow. Du Bois offers examples of the persistence of racism in sports; he notes that this is strongest in baseball and tennis. But, of course, it is the Churches which are the most discriminatory of all institutions! Attention is called to the appearance in July of the first number of the *National Bar Journal*, an organ of the Association of Black Attorneys, formed because of the racism of the A.B.A.

1071. "A Chronicle of Race Relations," arranged by Du Bois, Vol. III, No. 1, (1942), pp. 66–86. The Second World War—even more than the first—carries with it racial overtones, as illustrated in Hitlerism and now with the war between Japan and the United States. Hence, "even before there is any outlook for peace we should bestir ourselves for a worldwide fight against race hatred and racial propaganda in the days of peace which may sometime come." The international meeting of intellectuals held in Cuba in November "was an inspiring and promising" one though it had serious drawbacks in management and though the U.S. delegation was rather weak. Under the leadership of Freda Kirchwey, "they were wild for war." Joseph Wood Krutch "especially voiced in word and mien a fine and traditional disdain for Latins." Du Bois quotes from his own remarks; the point of which was his hope that "this conference both in its written word and unwritten conviction will not forget that the overwhelming majority of the people of this earth belong to the colored races; and their interest, their wishes, their cultural freedom, must be considered in any Peace Plan for the world—else there can be no peace." The English Fabian Society Publication, *Research Series* (No. 44), is a good overview of "the general economic condition of the West Indies"; generous quotations are offered. The remarks of Dantes Bellegarde at the Cuban November conference, concerning the nature of Haitian culture, are quoted. Summaries of late developments in the Dutch East Indies and in India follow. In the United States "there has been renewed discussion of the general inter-racial conditions"; quotations on this from the American Missionary Association and from Pearl Buck are given. With Jim Crow arrangements, the National Council of Teachers of English met in November in Atlanta. Black people therefore did not attend. Meetings were held with discussions of books for children, on intercultural relations. Professor John Erskine spoke on "My America" and other national dignitaries participated in other aspects of this "American" gathering. A Committee of Negro Teachers of English wrote to the President of the Council in protest and pointed out that completely inter-racial meetings had been held by the American Chemical Society (1930), the Association of American Colleges (1935), the Baptist World Alliance (1939), the National Physical Education Association (1939) and the Southern Conference for Human Welfare (1939) in the city of Atlanta. Since the meeting the National Council of Teachers of English has resolved that it "will accept invitations to hold its annual conventions only in cities which can provide equality of participation." The Southern Historical Association held its meeting in Atlanta in November; it was inter-racial, though some objections were voiced. Governor Talmadge of Georgia has dismissed Dean Cocking of the College of Education at the University of Georgia; the latter had demanded an end to lily-white higher education in the state (No. 1069). Twenty-three textbooks have been banned in the Georgia high schools because they "opposed Southern views on the Negro question and favored evolution." Du Bois lists them. Attention is called to an article on "Permanent Minorities" in the current *Antioch Review*, by Albert Viton with full quotations.

1072. "Books and Race," Vol. III, No. 1, (1942), pp. 93–95. Initialled reviews of three books: Alrutheus A. Taylor, *The Negro in Tennessee, 1865–1880* is "notable for the same careful scholarship" that has characterized the author's earlier studies of South Carolina and of Virginia in the Reconstruction period. This one, however, "is written with a broader and more confident grasp of the subject." Frederick A. McGinnis, *History and Interpretation of Wilberforce University* is by a man who has taught there for over 25 years. It "puts in available form the records of this interesting institution" but this is done "in rather a didactic and uninteresting way." Though the author is still in the university's employ it is an "unusually frank" book and very "valuable." George W. Brown, *The Economic History of Liberia* is carelessly produced but it contains very helpful information and is superior in interpretation to books on Liberia by H. H. Johnston, Frederick Starr, and George Schuyler.

1073. "The Cultural Missions of Atlanta University," signed, Vol. III, No. 2, (1942), pp. 105–115. "The aim of a university is so to change the culture of its day and group as gradually to raise the level of civilization." The "missions" of Atlanta University were, first, higher education, then racial equality, third, academic freedom and now, its mission is "democracy and social power." None has been achieved but all must be and to a degree have been and are being striven for, despite ordinary obstacles and extraordinary obstacles—such as being in Georgia! "The abolition of poverty, the scientific distribution of work, the just allocation of income, the protection of health and a wider and more thorough education of human beings from birth to death are the first objects to which this world must attend in its reconstruction of life after the present series of struggles ... It is the next cultural mission of Atlanta University to put the American Negro in a position where he will be able, not simply to follow, but to lead in this universal reconstruction."

1074. "Postscript: Looking Seventy-Five Years Backward," Vol. III, No. 2, (1942); pp. 238–248. Presented as "a sort of will and testament." A history in autobiographical form of Georgia and of Atlanta University putting all within the framework of an overview of world developments. Of some interest is a fairly positive evaluation of Theodore Roosevelt—"in the main a friend of the American Negro." But with Taft a reversion set in. Du Bois speaks of his "love" for John Hope. "Lifting my head I look the South full in the face." He decides, "all life is death; all progress dying; nothing lasts forever—yet nothing lives in vain; ceaseless, eternal change is the story of the world."

1075. "A Chronicle of Race Relations," signed, Vol. III, No. 3, (1942), pp. 320–334. Du Bois observes that recently "there have come increasingly clear expressions of the thought that this war in essence is a war for racial equality." Examples are culled from an editorial in the *Atlanta Constitution*, remarks of Sumner Welles, Harry Laidler, Vera Micheles Dean, Wendell Willkie, Anne O'Hare McCormick in the New York *Times*, Dorothy Thompson, Eleanor Roosevelt, and—"strongest and clearest"—from Pearl Buck. Du Bois observes, however, as J. F.

Brown writes in the *New Republic*, that "there are those in dark corners who are whispering that we must first bring Hitler to his knees and then unite with him to turn on Russia and the Orient." And there is the *Fortune-Time-Life* program, as enunciated by Clarence Streit for example (*Union Now*), which envisages "the present war as a chance for America to supplant England as the greatest nation on earth and to see the domination of the world after the war by an American-British police force on sea, land and in the air." He cites a telling criticism of the Streit book by Rosika Schwimmer who says that Mr. Streit's "democracies" are vitiated by racism and male supremacy. Du Bois notes that Streit "utterly ignores India, China, South America and Russia". The Henry Luce program is "even more crass" and "economic exploitation is foremost in the minds of these prophets." Quotations are offered to demonstrate this. Du Bois spells out the complications and contradictions in the world and concludes "there has got to be increased clarity of thought and strengthening of conviction before our war aims become clear." The persisting and indeed growing problem of poverty is emphasized by Du Bois; he cites an essay by T. Swann Harding which offers relevant data. H. F. Artucio and J. S. Herzog have published studies on poverty in Latin America, while African sources and George Padmore are quoted on the question in Africa. Meanwhile, of course, distribution of wealth in Europe and the United States is grossly unjust—data are brought forward. The labor movement's growth and the development of industrial democracy are the way out. The offer of "independence" to India from Churchill has been rejected by Gandhi because he cannot accept from a person with the record of a Churchill "post-dated" promises. Du Bois recurs—citing especially an article by R. G. Woolbert in *Foreign Affairs*—to Ethiopia, now freed of Italian military occupation but still threatened with British "protection." A seminar on racism in the United States, sponsored by the American Missionary Association, was held in New York in January. It was favored with a "straight-forward discussion" from E. R. Embree, Buell Gallagher, Oswald Garrison Villard, Bronislaw Malinowski, Mrs. J. D. Ames and Ambrose Caliver. The war has brought to the fore the racism of the United States, manifested towards Chinese and Filipinos resident in this country. Ted Poston tells of "The Revolt of the Evil Fairies" in the *New Republic*. The essay, treating of an incident in Kentucky, is important for it—like Richard Wright's *Native Son*—"is a case of frank self-criticism within the Negro group." The death of Bronislaw Malinowski brings a tribute to this Pole, who worked in the United States and in England, and "who had

had wide contacts in the South Sea and Africa, and who brought to his study of the science of man, a clear unbiased set of attitudes and sympathetic understanding of cultural patterns."

1076. "A Chronicle of Race Relations," signed, Vol. III, No. 4, 1942, pp. 417–434. The ideals of the war are "wavering"; some—like Henry Wallace and Pearl Buck—still emphasize its antiracist and democratic essence, but others like *Fortune* magazine and former Ambassador Joseph Grew, speak in terms of United States domination of the future world order. Fear of and hostility towards the U.S.S.R. is present and this is reflected in the failure to provide a second front. Certainly Churchill does not consider either China or the U.S.S.R. as "real colleagues" and the "tragedy of India" emphasizes the dubious nature of dominant war aims. Extended treatment of this Indian question follows. Quite apart from India, Britain is hardly a "democratic" power; the writings of Fenner Brockway, the Laborite, are quoted. Liberals now tend to damn socialism and sneer at communism, which is most unfortunate. "The new movements in accordance with the best Marxian philosophy are concentrating themselves and must concentrate themselves upon the economic foundation of society." Attention is called to literature on "economic reform" as Jennie Lee's *This Great Journey* and the work of Stuart Chase and Harry E. Barnes. Particularly for our own people economic questions are basic. Du Bois touches on Roosevelt's executive order No. 8802 which came after the March-on-Washington threat and its limited real execution with the persistence of racism in unions. A Black reporter is quoted saying that Marshall Field would do more good for the Negroes if he saw to it that 50 Black women got good jobs in his store than all the fine editorials in his newspapers, like the Chicago *Sun* and the New York *PM*; the same applies to the "Sears, Roebuck of Donald Nelson, who is managing all the war industries in which the President says there must be no discrimination." The recent election in Georgia was especially crude and while it is true that Ellis Arnall defeated Eugene Talmadge as Governor, and that he "is to be preferred to Talmadge," still that "is surely a new low in compliments." Denunciations of racism by the American Association of Physical Anthropologists are quoted. Under "Art and Race" Du Bois notes that the Daughters of the American Revolution "has capitulated and invited Miss [Marian] Anderson to sing in Constitution Hall." On the other hand, Roland Hayes was physically assaulted in Georgia and to date no one has been arrested for this outrage. His life is appearing serially in the *Atlantic Monthly*.

Paul Robeson appeared in "Othello" in the little theater, Brattle Hall, in Cambridge, Massachusetts—the"first time since Ira Aldridge that the character of Othello was played by a Negro, which, despite critics, was undoubtedly the type that Shakespeare had in mind." *The Saturday Review of Literature*, edited by Henry S. Canby, in its issue dated September 19, entitled "Deep South" gives "the Negro a curious slap in the face" for it omits the Black people. Du Bois records demands for greater political power coming from Black people in West Africa and the West Indies.

1077. "A Chronicle of Race Relations," signed, Vol. IV, No. 1, (1943), pp. 73–84. Pearl Buck has recently said that "the war has ceased to be a fight for freedom ... but only a war to save European civilization." E. R. Embree says something similar in reviewing the work of the Julius Rosenwald Fund. Du Bois quotes from his book, *Darkwater* (1920) and from speeches by people as unlike as Franco in Spain and Vice-President Henry Wallace to emphasize that the fundamental question of the world is that of poverty and racism and both are related; this must be faced in the future. He points to the writings of Robert S. Lynd in a recent *New Republic* and to the book, *Business as a System of Power*, by Robert A. Brady, as elucidating "the real meaning of the current economic revolution in terms of politics." Du Bois notes reports of movements to the Right and manifestations of this in mounting anti-Semitism in the United States. A summary of developments in the army and in industry affecting the Afro-American for the past six months is then offered. He also notes that Black workers are entering trade unions, especially of the CIO, in considerable numbers. Developments inside Britain in relationship to race and within its empire, especially in Africa, are recorded.

1078. "Books and Race," Vol. IV, No. 2, (1943), pp. 89–91, initialled review of *Toward Freedom: The Autobiography of Jawaharlal Nehru*. "One of the most significant books" of our time for it illuminates "the paradox and contradiction of the present world situation." Few books have "held me so enthralled." The book shows that "the so-called race problems of the modern world are essentially one: primarily they are matters of economic exploitation, of racial arrogance and the utter failure to recognize in people of different color, appearance and ways of life, the essential humanity of all mankind."

1079. "A Chronicle of Race Relations," signed, Vol. IV, No. 2, (1943), pp. 164–80. There are plans, as announced by Roosevelt and as the

Beveridge Plan in England, for overcoming poverty; perhaps they will work but they are defective insofar as such plans are meant to apply only to the imperial powers and not to the darker world. Madame Chiang Kai-shek in speeches while visiting the United States dealt only in generalities but the reality of China's suffering and exploitation at the hands of imperialism must be faced and undone. Proposals for the devastation of Japan—as those of Nathaniel Peffer in *Basis for Peace in the Far East**—are wrong and will not work. Extensive quotations from writings held to be enlightening concerning India are offered—especially those of Herbert L. Matthews in the New York *Times*. Movements for unity in the Arabic world are reported. Again, Du Bois reverts to the question of Ethiopia and ways of assuring its viability and true independence after the war. The effective work of Black soldiers fighting in Africa against the Italians and Germans is described. Writings of Oliver La Farge and John Collier on the needs and rights of American Indians are summarized. Aspects of the New Deal as they affect Black people are examined; Thomas Sancton reports in the *New Republic* that the Black population "has passed from the defensive to the offensive" and this is being met more and more by "brute force." He thinks "the New Deal in the South is dead" and that the spirit of militancy among the Black people is the real thing and will last. Du Bois himself feels that "some extraordinary things are taking place within the Negro group"; he calls attention to recent writings by Roi Ottley and V. V. Oak.

1080. "Books and Race," initialed reviews, Vol. IV, No. 2, (1943), pp. 181–182; 187–191. Charles S. Johnson, *Patterns of Negro Segregation*, is the second of the monographs inaugurated by the Myrdal survey. "It is difficult to see how any person reading this book can fail to be amazed that the United States is able to keep a straight face in contemplating its program for fighting a war for democracy!" The book represents an "improvement" over earlier writings by the author "in that it is clear and definite in its statements." Du Bois comments that the book is based on samples and draws general conclusions therefrom. In the future, social science "must more and more expand and intensify its study so as to approach nearer to complete coverage of the whole field" and then such studies must be repeated so that "a continuous dynamic change in social relations is recorded over wide stretches of time." Of course, this asks much, "but it is the ideal toward which a real science of human action must strive." *Angel Mo' and Her Son, Roland Hayes*;

---

*This refers to *Prerequistes for Peace in the Far East*.

the collaboration here is splendid and necessary, since Hayes had only a fifth grade formal education. "The main point which intrigues us in this life is the shattering realization of what the suppression of a whole race means: how much of genius and ability, of friendship and social charm is being daily killed in little black boys and girls not simply in the South but in the North, in the West Indies and in Africa." Merze Tate's *The Disarmament Illusion* "is one of the best examples of thorough painstaking study of historical documents." It is published under the auspices of Harvard University and shows "infinite care" in its study of the period from 1870 to 1907. But while noting the repeated failure of efforts at disarmament, the author never really tackles the problem of why these efforts failed and this is because she omits the economic foundations of armaments and wars. "To leave out this economic basis of the destructive wars in recent European history is to leave out Hamlet from his tragedy. Harvard University ignores the epoch-making philosophy of Karl Marx."

Via radio station WGST, in Atlanta, four broadcasts, sponsored by the People's College of Atlanta University * on the theme, "Freedom in the Modern World" were given in November and December, 1942. One was:

1081. "Africa and World Freedom", Supplement, Vol. IV, No. 2, pp. 8–12, with Dr. Reid asking Du Bois questions and the latter responding with facts concerning African history and with emphasis upon the resistance to conquest marking African history and its connection with Europe and world history.

1081a. "Reconstruction, Seventy-Five Years After," signed, Vol. IV, No. 3, (1943), pp. 205–212. Du Bois states in summary form the thesis of his magnum opus, *Black Reconstruction* (1935). The crushing of Reconstruction did not, of course, "settle" the so-called Negro question; it vitiated the republic and remains today in the South and in the nation on the agenda for democratic solution. That which is true for the South "faces the nation in this Second World War." The fact is that "the thrust to the front is but an interpretation of what America and Europe have practiced against the colored peoples of the world. No matter who wins this war, it is going to end with the question of the equal humanity of black, brown, yellow, and white people, thrust firmly to the front. ... The problem of the reconstruction of the United

*This was an adult education program, largely inspired by Du Bois, conducted by Atlanta University in cooperation with other agencies in the city where subjects from reading to arts to philosophy were taught in the evenings by university faculty members; its Director was Ira Reid; tuition was ten cents; the faculty was unpaid.

States, 1876, is the problem of the reconstruction of the world in 1943."

1082. "A Chronicle of Race Relations," signed, Vol. IV, No. 3, (1943), pp. 270–289. At a meeting with the president of Mexico in that country in April, President Roosevelt said, "we know that the day of the exploitation of the resources and the people of one country for the benefit of any group in another country is definitely over." Du Bois, "we can only hope that President Roosevelt thought of Asia and Africa as well as Mexico." Vice-President Wallace has "a complete grasp of the racial and economic implications of this war ... his frank statements have made his accession to the presidency practically impossible but they have made him an historic figure." He is quoted at some length. Pearl Buck has also shown great "courage and clarity"; she is also quoted at length. But Winston Churchill continues to strike an opposite note and he, too, is quoted. Du Bois notes that the Office of War Information (OWI) and the Associated Press "have said very little about the participation of black soldiers in this war"; Du Bois gives some data and relevant quotations. Great attention is given to various points of view on the future of Africa and of Japan. In connection with the latter, Du Bois summarizes and denounces the movement of Japanese-Americans in California to what amounts to concentration camps. Reportage continues on the monstrous anti-Jewish slaughters carried out by the Nazis in Europe. The merging of the question of economics and racism is emphasized; Du Bois notes this in terms of problems in French Canada. Du Bois is pleased at the fine courtesies extended to President Barclay of Liberia on his recent visit to the United States. He also welcomes Roosevelt's order of May re-establishing the F.E.P.C. and hopes good will come of the appointment as its chairman of Monsignor F. J. Haas. Racism in the United States "is coming in for more careful and detailed discussion." Examples are culled from a speech by Broadus Mitchell—who calls himself 'a refugee from the south'—at the University of Richmond in Virginia; resolutions adopted by the NAACP; a spirited essay by Saunders Redding in the *Atlantic Monthly*, and the experiences described by I. F. Stone in the *Nation* which led him to resign from the National Press Club because it refused to serve his guest Judge William H. Hastie at a luncheon (being addressed by Elmer Davis of the OWI).

1083. "A Chronicle of Race Relations," signed, Vol. IV, No. 4, (1943), pp. 362–387: The *Scientific Monthly* (August and September) publishes two good articles on the mythology of racism by W. M. Krogman and Robert Redfield of the University of Chicago; they are summarized and quoted. S. J. Hayakawa is also quoted. Nevertheless, "despite the increasing unanimity of science on the subject of race," racism in practice continues. The indictment made in July by the March-on-Washington Movement substantiates this. Quotations are offered from a pamphlet, *The Struggle for Negro Equality*, published by the Socialist Workers Party saying that there is nothing innate to racism and pointing to the organization of Black and white workers in the CIO which shows what may be accomplished to overcome it. Robert O'Brien has produced a study on the Afro-American in the Northwest (*Research Studies*, Vol. X, No. 1, State College of Washington) showing a deterioration in conditions faced today as compared with 1910.

Probing essays on the race situation in the South have come from Thomas Stokes (*Common Sense*) and from Lillian Smith (*South Today*). In the *Emancipator*, Harold Preece writes of the peonage in Oglethorpe County, Georgia, and Royal W. France relates some truths about Florida. James Boyd, described by Du Bois as "a Southern 'Liberal' " tells in the *Nation* "what Negroes should do about the race problem —or rather what they should not do." They should not fight for their rights is the sum total of the advice. It is not too much unlike the gratuitous advice from John Temple Graves and Mark Ethridge. Du Bois summarizes and quotes from various studies of the pogroms and riots that occurred recently in Detroit and in Harlem. He notes, too, that now that Earl Browder, the Communist leader, has been released from jail, he "has had a rare chance to talk to the nation." Du Bois quotes from Browder to the effect that racism serves Hitlerism and that to attack racism is to serve the war effort against fascism. The outrageous frame-up of Festus Coleman to a term of 65 years in jail in California is denounced by Du Bois. He quotes from a letter by Madame Litvinov, wife of the U.S.S.R. Foreign Minister, and from the writer Alexey Tolstoy denouncing racism in the United States and affirming the release of formerly subject peoples in their homeland. Du Bois quotes from "the much discussed manifesto issued by the Free German Committee in Moscow" which promises that a new Germany must be cleansed of all racist laws and practices. Herbert Matthews, Louis Fischer, Agnes Smedley and others are quoted in terms of the problem of racism and the Allied war conduct in India and China. The fighting in Africa is described.

1084. "Phylon: Science or Propaganda," signed, Vol. V, No. 1, (1944), pp. 5–9. A professor at the University of Chicago has asked, "when is *Phylon* going to make up its mind to be either an organ of science or of propaganda?" Du Bois then summarizes the contents of the journal now that it has completed four volumes. Social science "must begin with the near and known as a starting point; and then despite temptation set goals of dispassionate and ruthless adherence to truth. It can no longer find refuge in detachment from its subject matter; nor just as surely, none in refusal to regard its own personal problems as subjects of scientific investigation." When the Black people, or problems associated with them, are treated in the general run of journals, they are treated as separate and apart from human history and social development. "Scientists may study democracy, labor, woman and education, without the slightest reference to 13 million Negroes, and yet none note the omission." *Phylon* "would not fall into the opposite error and see the Negro Problems as the content of all American life."

1085. "A Chronicle of Race Relations," signed, Vol. V, No. 1, (1944), pp. 68–89. Long extracts are published from Allison Davis' article on "Personality and Race" in the *Science Monthly*. Oswald Spengler's analysis of what he called the "Coloured World" in *The Hour of Decision* (1933) is reproduced. Various plans for peace are reprinted, from the statements of the Moscow Conference of October, 1943, through the Cairo and Teheran Conferences to statements from private groups and individuals such as E. Sylvia Pankhurst. "For the first time in history" the U.S. State Department has made a statement (August 13, 1943) on United States relations with Africa; it has come from Henry Villard who is a grandson of the great Abolitionist and serves in the Division of Near Eastern Affairs. It is reproduced and sharply criticized. The growing literature on colonialism is described and some of it quoted; in this connection, George Padmore, writing in England, is quoted at length. A national survey of higher education among the Afro-American has been made by Dr. Ambrose Caliver of the U.S. Office of Education. It is able but it does not face up to economic questions and therefore provides no real answers. The debate between Malcolm Ross, chairman of the F.E.P.C., and the owners of U.S. railroads, who resist the commission's directives, is published. Extensive material is published concerning the Arab and Jewish peoples and Palestine; Du Bois sees "the power-politics now being pushed in Great Britain and America" as "a discouraging combination with Hitler's anti-Semitic program." Recent race outbreaks in New York, Michigan and elsewhere have produced an outpouring of suggestions for their prevention in the future; Du Bois summarizes and quotes many. Some effort has been made at a meeting in Mexico City in October, 1943, toward setting up an inter-continental center for the study of African-derived peoples in the New World. Dr. Fernando Ortiz of Cuba is a leading figure in this enterprise.

1086. "A Chronicle of Race Relations," signed, Vol. V, No. 2, (1944), pp. 165–188. On the 70th anniversary of the passage of the Fifteenth Amendment, Du Bois publishes the history of the Amendment as given in his *Black Reconstruction*. Attention is called to the decision of the U.S. Supreme Court, in April, denying the constitutionality of the White Primary—"this is an extraordinary victory, not only for black America but for white democracy in the United States and in the world." Much attention is devoted to the Brazzaville Conference of Free France, which met in January and February, 1944, with documents and speeches reprinted. Recent literature touching on the relationship between the colonies and future peace is summarized and analyzed. A full history of the Chicago Conference, called by Marshall Field, E. R. Embree and Charles S. Johnson to study questions of racism and held in March, 1944, is provided. Dr. Du Bois read a statement before the conference, which is printed in full; it stresses the need for increasing the income of Black people, of a new crusade for education, of socialized medicine, and a recognition of the need among Afro-Americans to "organize among themselves for self-defense and inner development." Work must intensify for the achievement of "full equality, in law and custom." Extracts are offered from an essay by Louis Wirth of the University of Chicago in the *Scientific Monthly* (April). Lucille D. Milner has written "a significant article" on Jim Crow in the U.S. Army; it appears in the *New Republic* (March 13). Much of it is here quoted. A quotation appears from a recommended pamphlet by Edward Holton James, *I Am a Yankee*, which attacks racism frontally. Du Bois observes the relative absence of racism in the acting profession as reflected in the Actors Equity Association. A demand is growing for making the F.E.P.C. permanent; details are reported. An article on the early history of writing in Africa is recommended by Du Bois; it is by O. F. Raum and appears in *African Studies* for December, 1943; the magazine is published by Witwatersrand University in South Africa. Evidence continues to grow of high-level desires to dismember Ethiopia; it is here presented.

1087. "Books and Race," Vol. V, No. 2, (1944), pp. 189–190, initialled review. Mercer Cook's *Five French Negro Authors* has displayed a "modest and painstaking" scholarship especially in calling attention "to the role which Negroes have played in other languages and other cultures." The authors here dealt with are: Julien Raimond, Charles Bisette, Alexandre Dumas, Auguste Lacaussade and René Maran.

CHAPTER III

NEWSPAPER COLUMNS

Important in the body of Du Bois' writings were the columns he wrote for various periodicals edited by people other than himself. Most were done for the Afro-American press where finances often were precarious, and so at times, the effort abruptly ceased. Some columns, on the other hand, continued for many months; if these alone had constituted Du Bois' entire output it would have been noteworthy but since they were done in the midst of his other publishing, editing, writing, teaching, lecturing, and organizing activities, their regular production is nearly incredible.

In the Summer of 1927 Du Bois began a regular book review column in the *Amsterdam* (New York) *News* which lasted a short time. In the Spring of 1931, through an Afro-American-owned Eastern Features Syndicate, Du Bois contributed columns to the *Amsterdam News*, which ended in December, 1931. He contributed very briefly early in 1932 to a venture edited by George Schuyler, in New York City, called the *National News*.

A column by Du Bois appeared each week from February, 1936, through January, 1938, in the *Pittsburgh Courier* and then in the *Amsterdam News* from October, 1939, through October, 1944. He wrote on "Pan-Africa" each week beginning in March, 1947, and ending at the end of February, 1948, in Adam Clayton Powell's Harlem newspaper, *People's Voice*. Meanwhile his "Winds of Time" column, begun in the *Chicago Defender* in January, 1945, appeared regularly until the end of May, 1948. The Council on African Affairs published a newsletter called *New Africa*; Du Bois wrote regularly for it, especially throughout 1949 and 1950. When the radical anti-cold war weekly, *The National Guardian* appeared—edited by Cedric Belfrage and James Aronson—it requested regular contributions from Dr. Du Bois; they began in December, 1948, and ended in May, 1961. A brief venture, the *Chicago Globe*, printed columns from him during 1950. At about the same time Paul Robeson sponsored a newspaper in Harlem, largely edited by Louis E. Burnham, called *Freedom*; Du Bois appeared in its introductory number in November, 1950, and thereafter irregularly until August, 1954. Indication of the contents of these columns follows.

AMSTERDAM NEWS 1927

1088. "Books I Have Read Recently," August 22, 1927, p. 4. A review of Lord Olivier's the *Anatomy of American Misery* is called "by far the most interesting recent book on Africa" and the analysis of the Union of South Africa by a white Britisher who had formerly been governor of Jamaica is extensively quoted. (No. 781)

1089. August 24, 1927, p. 20, hails Emily Greene Balch, editor, *Occupied Haiti* as a book that "at last ... tells the truth"; quotations from it are fairly full. (No. 781). Attention is called, very favorably, to the books being published, at low cost, by Vanguard Press in New York; especially recommended is Charles H. Wesley's *Negro Labor in the United States*. (No. 772) Lenin's *Imperialism* is mentioned.

1090. E. C. L. Adams' *Congaree Sketches* is by a Southern white man, but one of the chapters in this book "is the funniest Negro story written in years." The introduction by Paul Green is commended. (No. 777). To "make your Negro music library fairly complete" Du Bois suggests: W.A.Fisher, *Seventy Negro Spirituals*; E. A. Jessye, *My Spirituals*; a "new Hampton collection," by Nathaniel Dett, called *Religious Folk Songs of the Negro*; two editions (1926, 1929) of the *Book of American Negro Spirituals* by James Weldon Johnson and his brother J. Rosamond Johnson; and W. C. Handy's *Blues*.

AMSTERDAM NEWS*

1091. July 29, 1931. "The Menace of the United States," stresses its enormous wealth and resources and world-wide investments; these, with its racism and aggressiveness and profit-motive, make the nation a "menace" but if the best traditions and promises of the country came to the fore, the country would be a great blessing. We Black people can help bring about that change. He concludes by urging the reading of

---

*Du Bois' "The Wide, Wide World" column was released by the Eastern Features Syndicate and therefore appeared in some newspapers in addition to the *Amsterdam News* at slightly different dates; this was notably true of the *Philadelphia Tribune* and the *Louisiana Weekly*.

National Defense by Kirby Page and *The Fight For Peace* by Devere Allen.

1091a. August 5, 1931. "The Eleko of Lagos" tells the story of the hereditary ruler in Nigeria who, through persistent struggle, has scored a significant legal victory in England over those who wished to divest him of proper perquisites.

1092. August 12, 19, and 26, 1931. Three columns offer a summary view of Russian history from the early 19th century– through the 1905 and 1917 events– to the Intervention and to the present.

1093. September 9, 1931, "The Story of Cocoa" makes the point that that crop illustrates well a central feature of modern world-wide capitalist organization: it is so arranged "as to employ raw materials from colored countries and colored labor for the raising of these materials. The low wages of these laborers and the high selling price of manufactured articles represent the immense profit which modern civilization is making at the expense of colored folk."

1094. September 16, 1931, "The Five Year Plan". While in the past the dominant press in the United States discussed the U.S.S.R. in terms of "new marriage laws ... and the punishment of the rich," suddenly one hears of a Five Year Plan. Du Bois explains it. Distinguished gentry in this country say it cannot work; "we shall see," says Du Bois. He urges the readers to examine Ilin's *New Russia's Primer*.

1095. September 23, 1931, "The League of Nations". Du Bois observes that not enough attention is paid to this important effort in the United States, no doubt because the United States is not a member. Du Bois proceeds to give a brief history of past ideas of such a league and of the organization of the present body.

1096. September 30, 1931, "Gold and Trade". Trade should be a natural enterprise among those who have what others need and need what others have, but with profit as motive and nationalism as deceiver, the trade patterns of the world are quite illogical. "Moral: Where did we get the impression that white folks had brains?"

1097. October 7, 1931, "India". A brief history and description of India, its growing independence movement, and the meaning thereof.

1098. October 14, 1931, "Europe in India". A survey of the relationship of Europe and India since the sixteenth century and an affirmation of its importance for the Afro-American people, since the colored peoples of the world are really one in oppression and suffering.

1099. October 21, 1931, "China and Japan". Japan is fighting Europe in the war it wages in China; however, Japanese militarism is a menace and should it conquer China this would be a calamity for civilization.

1100. October 28, 1931, "Mahatma Gandhi". Mahatma Gandhi's background, ideas, and history are sketched. A poor man representing hundreds of millions of the poor and doing it with complete identification, brilliance, and effectiveness.

1101. November 4, 1931, "The English Election". The sweeping defeat of the Labor government is "a calamity," but it was brought on by the defection and blundering of MacDonald himself.

1102. November 11, 1931, "Wealth and Power". Wealth is in fact power and it is socially created; its production and distribution should be socially controlled.

1103. November 18, 1931, "The Program of Peace in Manchuria". The League cannot stop Japan in China for its members have bloody hands. Europe fears the U.S.S.R. in China; so does Japan and the latter fights to keep China out of Europe's hands as well as to get it into her own.

1104. November 31, 1931, "Muddle". The political and economic condition of the capitalist world reflects that word, "muddle." Certainly it speaks ill of the vaunted brain power of white men and it points to the need for straight thinking, planning and talking.

THE NATIONAL NEWS (New York City)

In this short-lived paper two columns under the title, "The Wide Wide World," signed, appeared.

1105. February 25, 1932, "The Place of Force". Because of the continual appearance in history of force, more and more of our younger people insist that only through the use of force can progress come. War-making today requires vast resources; moreover, because of the nature of modern war, does anyone "win"? For us Afro-Americans the path of violence as a strategy of revolution will not work; we must depend upon our reason, our case, our cooperation, and our willingness to struggle and sacrifice. Through this must come real "revolutionary change." In any case, if there is any chance of success along these lines, should it not be tried "rather than to descend into the Hell and Hate of the slaughter house?"

1106. March 10, 1932, "Again Japan". This is a survey of Japanese history, especially in terms of China and Europe, from the end of the Sino-Japanese War of 1894 to the end of the Russo-Japanese War of 1905, with emphasis upon Japan's effort to resist European domination of Asia as well as a review of the defeat of the Czar in 1905 and the appearance of the revolution in Russia 12 years later.

THE PITTSBURGH COURIER

The column was entitled "A Forum of Fact and Opinion"; it was preceded by the following quotation: "This column represents the personal opinion of Dr. Du Bois and in no way reflects the editorial opinion of the Pittsburgh Courier—the Editor."

1936

1107. February 8, 1936. A history of Ethiopia and its present position vis-à-vis Italy, France, and Great Britain.

1108. February 15, 1936. A history of the suffrage as exercised by Black people in the United States. In 1936 the Republican party once again will try to purchase victory and the Democratic party continues to function "with a radical head and a reactionary rump." Meanwhile, the other parties "still refuse to attack disfranchisement in the South as the key to democracy" and thus lose effectiveness.

1109. February 22, 1936. The essence is in the first paragraph: "when the next war comes, where will Negroes fight and why? Last time we fought to end war and didn't. Time before last, we fought to be free, and aren't. Next time, we might try not fighting at all. We could hardly lose." Emphasis is given to the significance of the anti-Jewish atrocities in Germany, "no such affront to the human conscience and to modern reason has happened in our day." It helps universalize the so-called problem of racism.

1110. February 29, 1936. A section entitled "No Chance" contains capsules of thought: he wonders if there are not Black people with "guts" enough to try living and working in the U.S.S.R., which would welcome them. A polarization of politics based upon real issues would be very helpful. Crime's sources are basically social; hence, more punishment solves nothing. A letter is quoted from an African on the Italian attack upon Ethiopia. Japan is choosing via imperialism to bar Europe and the U.S.A. from Asia. "In the meantime, the thing that must impress us as colored people is that the chances for economic reform [in China] under Japanese imperialism are infinitely greater than any chances which colored people would have under the most advanced white leaders of Western reform, except in Russia."

1111. March 7, 1936. Again, some brief comments on sundry subjects, as the artistry of Marian Anderson, the splendid efforts of the Knights of Labor and the I.W.W., and a hope that industrial unionism really goes forward now. A résumé is offered of Du Bois' efforts in the area of consumer cooperatives, commencing in 1914; he still thinks they hold much promise, especially for Black people in the United States. Colonialism is attacked; the conclusion, "We must begin organized work to rescue the colored races from a situation where they are looked upon as a source of private profit and not human beings, capable of contributing to human culture. This is the larger socialism. This is a program of communism that far out-strides anything that even Russia has attempted. This is a program of religion which will make or break the so-called followers of Christ."

1112. March 14, 1936. Du Bois notes that Mary R. Beard is attacking historians for omitting women; well and good, but Mary R. Beard omits Black people. He recommends Sinclair Lewis' *It Can't Happen Here*. A summary is offered of the "six phases" of the relationship of the Republican party and Black people. Goebbels, in Nazi Germany, has demanded colonies in Africa; this is a development of great portentousness.

1113. March 21, 1936. Du Bois recommends a study of James P. Warbasse's *What is Cooperation?* Cooperation is "the one way out" for the Afro-American people. The New Deal "has done nothing for the tenant-farmer and sharecropper." He quotes at length from the work of Maurice Delafosse on African artistry.

1114. March 28, 1936. Du Bois recommends study of Marquis Childs' *Sweden: The Middle Way*, and quotes from it. He adds, "I still believe that the end of economic reform is socialism, or as some call it, 'collectivism,' but I also just as firmly believe that the next step toward

this is consumers' co-operation and that for the American Negro it is
the only step." Glowing tribute is paid to his friend, John Hope, who
has recently died. The National Negro Congress meeting in Chicago
moves him to say that at some point there will have to be created an
actual congress of the Black people based upon careful voting and real
representation.

1115. April 4, 1936. Only industrial unionism is worthy of respect. All
Republicans being mentioned as possible candidates are poor—this
includes Borah, Landon, and Knox. He recommends reading a book
by Edwin Embree, Margaret Simon, and B. Mumford dealing with the
Dutch East Indies, *Island India Goes to School*, and summarizes its
data. The death of Maud Cuney Hare brings a long and keen appraisal
of this remarkable woman long loved by Du Bois. Again, a long
explanation of and plea for cooperatives are offered.

1116. April 11, 1936. Briefly expressed thoughts, among which, "not
by the development of upper classes to exploit the workers, nor by the
escape of individual genius into the white world, can we effect the
salvation of our group in America. And the salvation of this group
carries with it the emancipation, not only of the darker races of men
who make the vast majority of mankind, but of all men of all races."
An analysis of the Populist movement is offered, stressing its genuinely
radical character and its degree of Black-white unity; in the election of
1896 wealth literally purchased the presidency and killed that movement. Tribute is paid to the greatness of African art; an appeal is made
for greater understanding between the Afro-American and the people
of India.

1117. April 18, 1936. The purpose of the Townsend Plan—to provide
for the aged—is excellent, but its method—mere "ballyhoo"—will not
do. Mussolini rules in Italy but certainly not in behalf of those who
work or those who "dare to think." The role of Black soldiers in the
battle of Savannah during the American Revolution has been forgotten. The beauty and flexibility of certain African languages are
described. Both medicine and the practice of law must be socialized;
why is explained. In connection with the latter, denunciation is offered
against "the wretched jails and penitentiaries where innocent Negroes
are today confined by the thousands." Among us as a people not many
are of the bourgeoisie, but many among us think in terms of getting
rich as an end of life.

1118. April 25, 1936. An especially significant column treating the attitude of Afro-Americans towards Africa which is often one of ignorance mixed with shame. Du Bois feels it is wrong and very harmful. The question of anticolonialism is part of antiracism and these are really one question. This is behind his Pan-Africanism and this was opposed by many members on the board of the NAAACP. It is opposed today by many Afro-Americans who believe that their problem is only the question of their rights in the United States without seeing the denial of those rights as part of an international phenomenon and system. All this was induced by the visit of a delegation of colored and white people from Africa to the South under the guidance of Prof. C. T. Loram of Yale (originally from South Africa).

1119. May 2, 1936. Ethiopia has been conquered by Italy but it does not mean the disappearance of Ethiopian people because they will one day be independent again as will all Africa. The ridicule of the Townsend Plan is not just; its ideas are simplistic but its aim is righteous and should be accomplished. Maurice Delafosse is quoted again on the history of African literature. Attention is called to efforts to encourage credit unions and the work of the Black man, Henry A. Hunt, is described.

1120. May 9, 1936. So-called farm relief in the United States has benefitted not the small but the large farmer, just as the tariff benefits not the worker but the boss. A comment: "the great American housing movement for the poor has had unparalleled success in everything except housing for the poor." A parable, "About Leadership," is offered which is plainly autobiographical and suggests that leaders cannot simply advance without considering obstacles and opposition. Again a note in favor of cooperatives.

1121. May 16, 1936. There must be—Italy's rape of Ethiopia has made clear—some kind of international armed force "to compel peace." A rapid and incisive summary is offered of "white writers" and their depiction of Black people in literature from the 17th century. The column closes, "consumers' organizations, democratically directed by intelligent men, can re-organize, re-arrange and revolutionize our present stupid methods of production."

1122. May 23, 1936. The crime of Mussolini in Ethiopia is colossal. Du Bois recommends *The African Saga* by Blaise Cendrars (New York: 1927 Payson Clark,) and quotes from its foreword by Arthur Spingarn. A call is issued to end "defeatism" among ourselves and to end the idea "that everything White is Right." "When we think of the sort of experience through which we colored people have come and yet have kept our souls when everything around was calculated to make for despair, it is a matter of infinite hope for all oppressed men." Humanism is magnificent and has in fact achieved great successes; "the finest and broadest education" requires contact with all kinds of human beings.

1123. May 30, 1936. He has not yet seen Langston Hughes' play, "Mulatto" but is happy it is still running on Broadway; he feels it cannot be bad since "Joseph Wood Krutch" of Tennessee, who is the professional liberal that writes for the *Nation*, and "has never yet seen anything decent in 'niggers'" does not like it. Du Bois prints a letter from a white pacifist—Rev. Ashton B. Jones—who was forcibly driven out of La Grange, Georgia, with the connivance of the police. No newspaper in Georgia will print Mr. Jones' story even though he is a native of Atlanta. "The Christian religion has suffered a great many setbacks in this world, but nothing recently comparable to the crucifixion of Haile Selassie with the Pope in the background upholding Mussolini's hands." There is a unity in the struggles in India and the struggles of Black folk here. But these struggles must lead to a world of just economic organization and not the exploitation of colored peoples by colored peoples. "Then and only then, can the union of the darker races bring a new and beautiful world, not simply for themselves, but for all men."

1124. June 6, 1936. The rape of Ethiopia throws great doubt as to the wisdom of pacifism. Our common segregation and suffering and resistance have "welded the black people of the United States into a nation within a nation ... and before us lies, whether we will or no, long years and centuries of separation from other human beings; when we must develop our abilities, concentrate our strength, and increase our powers of knowledge and self-defense."

1125. June 13, 1936. Du Bois goes to Europe. "Again President Roosevelt is popular, and with reason. He has done little, but he at least tried." From the work of Cendrars (No. 1122) material is quoted on "African architecture." Our emancipation depends upon what we do; we must be in the forefront in our own battle and must make music for ourselves and write books for ourselves. Only then will they be great.

1126. June 20, 1936. Du Bois offers his "creed for American Negroes today" which has 11 basic components and emphasizes self-organization and self-defense, joining and participating in trade union activity, agitating for significant economic and social reform looking towards socialism, the rejection of war and of violence as means towards healthful social ends. "To this vision of work, organization and service we welcome all men of all colors so long as their subscription to this basic creed is sincere and is proven by their deeds." Du Bois notes that the white press has heaped praise upon him for having said, when interviewed, that "the tactics of the Communist party in America in the past had 'given me a pain in the neck.'" It is too much praise and from the wrong people; the sentence was out of context and the reporters failed to report that Du Bois had also said "that I thought the experiment in Russia was the most promising in the world." He adds that he has had differences and still has differences with the Communist party, but he hopes for success to the efforts at unity of Communists and Socialists and other workers and to the efforts of the CIO.

1127. June 27, 1936. There is among many of us often a kind of *schaden-freude*—a joy in another's ill-fortune; the source of this is explained and Du Bois urges that it stop. A movement for sterilization is growing; watch it, for like everything else in the United States, it will seek us as its victims. The column begins an effort to outline the political history of Black people; it deals with the period of [B.T.] Washington's ascendency 1896–1900.

1128. July 4, 1936. Du Bois notes that now the Black people are significantly divided, North (20 percent) and South (80 percent) and differ in condition and position more than ever before. The political history continues with details concerning the decade prior to the World War with emphasis upon the process of disfranchisement.

1129. July 11, 1936. Du Bois observes the growing militarization of U.S. life, "and the military lobby that works to increase this utterly indefensible temptation to war is not steeped in honesty or even decency." Italy's conquest of Ethiopia has turned attention to Egypt; Egypt's efforts at real independence continue and one day will succeed. Political history continues with further data on developments from 1900–1908.

1130. July 18, 1936. Du Bois quotes from a defense of "Tobacco Road" in a letter by Erskine Caldwell in the New York *Times* (May 10). Political history from 1908–1916 is sketched.

1131. July 25, 1936. A fairly long summary of the career of Martin R. Delany is offered, ending, "his was a magnificent life, and yet how many of us have heard of him?" Political history from 1916–1919 is sketched, with emphasis on the NAACP and the growth of Black political power in such cities as New York, Chicago, and St. Louis.

1132. August 1, 1936. Again, on cooperative economic endeavor and an insistence that its logic is socialism. The outline of political history concentrates on 1919–1920 with special attention to the effort to obtain anti-lynching legislation.

1133. August 8, 1936. Sacrifice and devotion are basic ingredients in successful social effort. Du Bois is astonished at the actions of the new editor of the *American Mercury*, Paul Palmer, in suggesting not only that Du Bois submit an essay on the New Deal period but that it must be "distinctly unfavorable to the administration." This is, presumably, "freedom of the press." Under these circumstances, I prefer to "stop writing," or "get a job in Italy." Political history from 1920–1928 is treated, noting La Follette's effort and the intensely antilabor character of the South.

1134. August 15, 1936. He urges again—as he has done for a decade—the creation of a "Negro Book-of-the-Year Club." In his political history, he treats the years of the depression and the first administration of Roosevelt.

1135. August 22, 1936. There is too much talking and too little real listening and thinking among us. He has recently read *Middletown* (New York: Harcourt Brace 1929) by Robert and Helen Lynd and found it "thoughtful and thorough," but "they left entirely out of account the five percent of colored people" in that city. The political history deals with the year, 1936, as it then faced the Black voter.

1136. August 29, 1936. Contact among human beings is basic to education; it is easier in Europe than in the United States to accomplish this. He notes his conversations with Henry James, Havelock Ellis, H. G. Wells, Ramsay MacDonald, Keir Hardy and, on his latest visit, a long talk with a Belgian scholar, Natal De Cleene. In Belgium he visits its collections of Africana—the best in Europe.

1137. September 5, 1936. Du Bois notes signs of some increasing racism in England and tells of discrimination practiced against Paul Robeson in a London restaurant. Still, it is as nothing compared to the United States. In Europe he has seen the renewed arms race partly because of the failure to stop Mussolini in Ethiopia. There are "plans for wholesale murder. God save the World!"

1138. September 19, 1936. The entry is devoted to the Olympics just concluded in Berlin, while Du Bois was there. He notes the necessity to redistribute income and the absurdity of Landon's appeals as Republican candidate for the Presidency decrying such efforts.

1139. September 26, 1936. Du Bois urges travel in Europe—not of a frantic sort but with visits limited to one or two countries. One learns a great deal. He has dined with Malinowski in England, Westermark in Germany, and Wells in London on this trip.

1140. October 3, 1936. He describes the German Museum of Science and Technology in Munich, containing 70,000 exhibits. "We can do wonderful things and there ought to be left for every man a large amount of leisure time. This is not true, but it is going to be true."

1141. October 10, 1936. Du Bois describes further the Munich museum. He observes the German chauvinism that characterizes its exhibits. He concludes, "if now we are going to have in the future a civilization of art and thought, it must be because we know technique and rearrange it so that the mass of men have sufficient income to use their leisure for new ends."

1142. October 17, 1936. In Germany, attending a music festival; he notes the high cost, which means "for the poor" there is no festival.

1143. October 24, 1936. Victories by Black men in the Olympics were important for us and for opinion in Europe. But we must be represented also "in science, in literature, and in art." The war in Spain is of enormous significance and "there is no working class in the world that is not intimately and definitely interested in the outcome of this battle." The Balkans remain backward and a tinderbox.

1144. October 31, 1936. A little essay on "Opera and the Negro Problem," emphasizing "the poet and musician, the dreamer and the prophet must all be known and consulted by those who seek real education—who wish in truth to know Life."

1145. November 7, 1936. On industrial education in Germany Du Bois sees the use of education "as a means of carrying on and perfecting industry."

1146. November 14, 1936. With what the social sciences have demonstrated in the past generation, it is clear that the so-called race problem is at its heart a socioeconomic question. It is really identical "with the labor problems of the world, and with the whole question of the education, political power, and economic position of the mass of men." And that mass is primarily colored.

1147. November 21, 1936. Continuing the above thought, it does not mean that there are not distinctive questions arising because of color, but it does mean that such questions are basically socioeconomic and historical questions and not mystical ones covered over by phrases about "race." Related to this is maldistribution of income and the rape of colonial peoples.

1148. November 28, 1936. Egypt brings to mind England's methods of indirect rule. In the South, Black farmers must organize collectively and defend such collectivity, or else they cannot survive.

1149. December 5, 1936. Du Bois is now out of Germany and may write freely of what he saw; while he was there his mail was opened. He believes that most Germans stand "back of Adolf Hitler today." Economic conditions—especially unemployment—have been improved. "And yet, in direct and contradictory paradox to all this, Germany is silent, nervous, suppressed. . . . There is a campaign of race prejudice carried on, openly, continuously and determinedly against all non-Nordic races, but specifically against the Jews, which surpasses in vindictive cruelty and public insult anything I have ever seen; and I have seen much." Labor was divided and through this opening "Hitler and Big Industry" entered into full dictatorial power. Socialism thus was prevented and the trade unions were destroyed.

1150. December 12, 1936. Again on Nazi Germany and its tyranny and terror. But its propaganda and activity have convinced many Germans that the system works and racism feeds this idea. Basic to the propaganda is hostility to the Soviet Union and hatred of the Jew.

1151. December 19, 1936. Largely devoted to an excoriation of the anti-Semitism of Hitler's Germany, which, it is held, is not a mere phase as many say. "There has been no tragedy in modern times equal in its awful effects to the fight on the Jew in Germany. It is an attack on civilization, comparable only to such horrors as the Spanish Inquisition and the African slave trade." Julius Streicher's newspaper is "the most shameless, lying advocate of race hate in the world, not excluding Florida. It could not sell a copy without Hitler's consent."

1152. December 26, 1936. Du Bois sees the chief faults and cracks in Hitlerism to be its racism, its demand for colonies, its male supremacy and its ambiguity—according to this column—as to private profit or socialism.

1937

1153. January 2, 1937. A conversation with "a German friend" who offers explanations for and rationalizations of the Hitler regime.

1154. January 9, 1937. While the column appears long after his departure from Europe, it still deals with Germany and Austria; in the former case, "I am bathing myself in music." He attends a Verdi opera—*La Forza del Destino* (*The Power of Fate*)—which deals with the love of Leonore for "a brown mulatto." But in Germany this is changed and all are white and blonde! In Germany a scientist meets him, he dines at his home and his wife is gracious. There is much frank talk—"so frank that he said hesitatingly at last: 'Of course you won't quote us.' To this has science come in the Land of Free Thought and Teaching!" But, where in the United States would a white family have treated him with such openness and courtesy? "At Chicago? At Columbia? At Harvard?"

1155. January 16, 1937. Du Bois briefly mentions crossing Poland on his way to the U.S.S.R. What is new are the great number of building foundations everywhere visible. "Russia says that bread for the million masses is more important than diamond rings for the hundreds." Russia means to show that by releasing the energies and will of the masses it is possible to build a society in which the welfare of those masses is much better than prior to the social change.

1156. January 23, 1937. Impressions of his journey through the U.S.S.R. He observes more electricity than a decade ago and fewer churches; "we have been taught to think in terms of Classes; of Bests and the Smartest. ... Consider the enormous task to which Russia has set herself. She proposes to make a nation where the masses rule .... What American who now rails at the rule of Russian boors, would not have accepted a summons to the Winter Palace with tears of gratitude?"

1157. January 30, 1937. "Russia is a frontier. ... Russia has supplied a surprising amount of idealism, sacrifice and character, in large and apparently increasing numbers of people. ... The only hope of human unity today lies in the common cause, the common interests of the working classes, in Europe, Africa and Asia."

1158. February 6, 1937. U.S.S.R. as a frontier—"perhaps the greatest of the remaining frontiers." It "declares that the majority of mankind can become efficient members of a culture state." Her lack of capital and the world-wide hostility and boycott hurt, but she has tightened her belt and she endures and moves forward.

1159. February 13, 1937. In Manchuria Du Bois meets Yosuke Matsuoka, who was Japan's last delegate to the League of Nations and is now a leading administrator of Japanese rule in Manchuria. As for the latter, Du Bois thinks it exceptional as a form of colonialism devoid of racism.

1160. February 20, 1937. In China; it "is inconceivable ... Never before has a land so affected me"—not even Africa. Its vastness, its teeming millions, its ancient quality are all overwhelming.

1161. February 27, 1937. Shanghai and the power of foreign capital and the terrible differentiation in rich and poor among the Chinese. The vast poverty. "The most disconcerting thing about Asia is the burning hatred of China and Japan [for each other]."

1162. March 6, 1937. "Three things attract white Europe to China: cheap women; cheap child-labor; cheap men."

1163. March 13, 1937. Du Bois describes the shrines of Japan. He reports on the extraordinary hospitality heaped upon him.

1164. March 20, 1937. Theater in Japan; the hospitality shown him was a gesture from one colored people to another and "for this reason, my visit is not to be forgotten."

1165. March 27, 1937. Japan's accomplishments in modernization have been remarkable; but there is danger in it for she is is pursuing the capitalist path in her drive towards greatness. She fears England and this helps drive her toward expansionism. But, "worst of all, this alliance of Japan with fascism sets her down as an enemy of Russia."

1166. April 13, 1937. Hawaii with its beauty and mixture of peoples —"if one could but die and find this paradise forever, endless with youth."

1167. April 10, 1937. The journey has afforded opportunity for perspective. The accomplishments of Paul Williams in architecture and

William Hastie in law—now appointed a federal judge—are cause for rejoicing, though they are individual matters. Central to the United States remain the questions of economics, of jobs and these today mean social planning.

1168. April 17, 1937. Many among us are trying to become part of a system which is doomed. We should be "fighting for universal equality ... not to become white men; not to become yellow men; but to become ourselves and to hold ourselves the equal of any." We have fought for education, and for political rights and we must fight, too, for "economic power" and to "enter the ranks of organized labor."

1169. April 24, 1937. The perspective now is for "the working class white and black in America [to] make one assault upon poverty and race hate." We must concentrate upon obtaining economic power. The millions among us can organize and plan and guarantee our economic survival and we must, as a group, do that.

1170. May 1, 1937. The masses can never raise themselves; there must be "that saving nucleus of a conscious dictatorship of intelligence." The evil in segregation comes from the compulsion "and not from the grouping." The logical end of his thinking now is this, "the American Negro does not wish to be forced into association with Negroes, or segregated by force from contact with the world. But, on the other hand, he recognizes that the voluntary grouping of Negroes in their own organizations, and in the forwarding of their own ideals is their normal and natural method of advance. ... "

1171. May 8, 1937. If we will not cooperate with each other, who will? As of now, our leaders seem "too ashamed of themselves and their people, their past and their present, to dare to stand up alone and show the universe just what they are. ... "

1172. May 15, 1937. We exist as a group and a common group, whatever name we are given and there is no escape and should be no desire for escape. While we have made advances in this country, our caste condition remains and "for many centuries" [Black people] will "be held as an inferior caste with limited rights."

1173. May 22, 1937. Hence, we must face the reality that "we have decades and centuries of work" in combatting racism in this country. We often despair of ourselves or do not believe in ourselves; but "there are some things which men simply have to do." We must fight against our impoverishment as a people; our being insulted as a people; and to assert our full manhood.

1174. May 29, 1937. Where there has been segregation—as in education—it came into being because otherwise there would have been nothing at all for us. In breaking through the racism of the trade union movement to the degree that we are organized as a group, we will be better able to break down the segregation in time.

1175. June 5, 1937. No real labor movement in the United States is possible which does not envisage "a whole Negro-White labor class." Pan-Africanism is an idea that cannot die; "it is a movement to begin a leadership of the exploited among the most exploited, with the idea of its ultimate expansion to the colored laboring class of the world and to the laboring class of all colors throughout the world." The real need is "labor solidarity across the color line."

1176. June 12, 1937. To the degree that we win recognition and human treatment we rejoice and we must "try in every legal way to co-operate with surrounding civilization and integrate ourselves with it." But this does not mean giving up our own group identity; on the contrary, building the strength in ourselves helps break down the walls against us. He comments on splendid economic cooperative efforts going forward in Gary, Indiana.

1177. June 19, 1937. Du Bois notes cooperative economic efforts by Black people right after the Civil War and that he had emphasized this in his book *Black Reconstruction*. There is much economic cooperation in various exodus and migration efforts and also in much of the history of our churches.

1178. June 26, 1937. Our first Black schools were cooperative enterprises. So, too, were our fraternal, beneficial, and insurance societies. He explains the Rochdale consumer cooperative scheme.

1179. July 3, 1937. Du Bois tells the story of the Chesapeake Marine and Dry Dock Company in Baltimore, led by Issac Myers, which was a kind of producers' cooperative; it lasted 12 years and forced white shipbuilding unions to accept Black members.

1180. July 10, 1937. Du Bois refers to many cooperative efforts among Black people in the past, as "a colored railroad in Wilmington, North Carolina, an automobile company in Nashville, Tennessee, and a street railway company in Jacksonville, Fla." He refers to the Coleman Manufacturing Company in Concord, North Carolina, as another example and to other efforts of this type in Chattanooga and in Birmingham.

1181. July 17, 1937. He refers to some traces of the idea of cooperatives in certain of our banking and insurance efforts. Examples are given. He thinks that this is the means by which insurance can be made successful among ourselves.

1182. July 24, 1937. Du Bois refers to his efforts, commencing in 1917 [actually 1914] to encourage cooperative business; one result was the Citizens' Co-Operative Stores in Memphis begun in 1919. He mentions the work of W. C. Matney of West Virginia in connection with cooperative efforts but the state finally forced him to terminate these efforts late in the 1920's.

1183. July 31, 1937. There were efforts at cooperative retailing in Buffalo but the 1929 crash killed them. A. C. Holsey made a similar effort with the Colored Merchants Association, but most of their stores have failed. He tells something of the struggles and growth of cooperatives in England.

1184. August 7, 1937. Du Bois treats the history of cooperation in Belgium, France, Germany, Italy, and some smaller countries, such as Denmark, Switzerland, Iceland, and Norway.

1185. August 14, 1937. Communists tend to insist that cooperatives lull revolutionary activity. But this is not true for efforts at cooperation can educate people in collective conduct and in proper economics. In any case, it can also actually help people in the present. He offers further data on cooperatives in various Balkan countries and in India, China, and Japan.

1186. August 21, 1937. Cooperation is not a palliative as some radicals and Marxists fear; it can serve as an important educational force and it also has worked in many places and assisted thousands of people.

1187. August 28, 1937. There is room and need for the thinker and the dreamer as well as for the activist; if these can be combined in one person that is fine. He reports on the growth of cooperatives in the Northwest of the United States and gives data.

1188. September 4, 1937. An effort to explain the advantages, in small retail trades, of cooperative distribution.

1189. September 11, 1937. Consumers' cooperatives face as a major difficulty the assumption in this country that the purpose of business "is not Service but Wealth." Du Bois insists that cooperation is feasible and that we could do it and do it effectively if we set our minds and hearts to it.

1190. September 18, 1937. He writes on the need for a real change of habits if one is to benefit from vacations with plenty of exercise, reading, and sleeping.

1191. September 25, 1937. The attack of Japan upon China is really an attack by Japan upon Europe which has sought to conquer China and thus inhibit Japan. "It would have been magnificent providence of God if Russia and China could have made common ground for the emancipation of the working classes of the world." But after the death of Sun Yat-sen, this did not happen and China fell under the domination of capitalist and imperialist forces. Description is offered of important efforts at producers' cooperatives going forward in Georgia under the guidance of Jesse B. Blayton, an instructor at Atlanta University.

1192. October 2, 1937. A plea for culture even if it does not mean more income and for good manners and cleanliness which are not signs of philistinism. One does not have to be unclean in order to show he is a radical.

1193. October 9, 1937. To be cultured is to be widely informed; to know and love beauty in art and letters—and to understand the need of a change from capitalism and individualism to a planned society for social betterment. He urges the need to read good books—not simply newspapers or magazines—in order to keep up and to comprehend the world. In the past year he has found worthwhile, John Spivak's *Europe Under the Terror*; John Gunther's *Inside Europe*; Robert Brady's *The Rationalization Movement in Germany*; Robert and Helen Lynd's *Middletown*; Lewis Mumford's *Technics and Civilization*; Freda Utley's *Japan's Feet of Clay*, among others.

1194. October 23, 1937. The way out in Asia is unity between Japan and China, not each slaughtering the other; such an alliance would "save the world for the darker races." Du Bois highly recommends Julian Huxley's *Africa View* and the writings of Cedric Dover, "the great Eurasian author," who is soon to visit the United States. He is troubled with the recent dearth of poetry coming from ourselves, "Poetry is wisdom clothed in beauty: beauty of form, sound, and sheer fitness."

1195. October 30, 1937. Du Bois notes that lately the Baha'i movement has succumbed to racism. He praises very highly Mumford's *Technics and Civilization*; a work that ranks, he suggests, with Marx's *Capital* and Veblen's *Theory of the Leisure Class*.

1196. November 6, 1937. Du Bois thinks that there has been a deterioration in the quality and a lessening in the functioning of faculties in colleges. He praises Emil Ludwig's *The Nile*(London; 1936) and quotes from the poetry of Louis Untermeyer on the exploitation of working people.

1197. November 13, 1937. The second meeting of the National Negro Congress was a good one but it must turn to actual accomplishment and not just meetings. The latter can take the form of careful planning of a viable economic program for our people or it might take the form of becoming like the Indian National Congress—a representative political congress of all of us and then a means of fighting for the programs we want. Du Bois recommends Wyndham's *The Atlantic and Slavery* and summarizes its contents.

1198. November 20, 1937. Du Bois cites examples of significant combatting of racism in the United Automobile Workers Union and in the Amalgamated Clothing Workers of America. In the former he observes the election of William Sneed, the first Black president of an auto local (No. 453 in Chicago), whose membership is 60 percent white. He suggests there is much of value in a book published in 1936 in England, Mair's *Native Policies in Africa*.

1199. November 27, 1937. A record of a conversation with a refugee from Nazi Germany—"he may or may not have been Jewish," who was an editor of the *Frankfurter Zeitung*, once a great paper though today there is no real newspaper in Germany. A discussion was held of the enrichment of the few in Italy and Germany and the inevitability of war fairly soon in Europe.

1200. December 4, 1937. Du Bois summarizes the essay by Benjamin Stolberg, "Minority Jingo," in a recent issue of the *Nation* (October 23, 1937). The point is that out of racial loyalty, Black people tend to overpraise what is really mediocrity. Mr. Stolberg may not know us as well as he thinks but he has a point. Du Bois remembers that he had similar feelings and that a lecture by Franz Boas on African civilization at Atlanta University helped release him from them.

1201. December 11, 1937. There is "a partial basis of truth" in the idea that Black leadership has been and is bourgeois. In my case it is true because of my earlier education, but I have changed through my experiences and studies and see the need and logic of socialism —although in the early period there were the seeds of this thinking, too. "The real and basic question is not whether we shall plan, but how—as capitalists or socialists."

1202. December 18, 1937. Du Bois offers high praise for the character and efforts of Catherine Walker, known to thousands as Madame Walker of beauty products fame. We do not have the sharp class differences that the whites do, and therefore a kind of group cooperative economic effort is still possible for us. This requires understanding and planning and dedication. He suggests that a lesson of the experience of Jews in Germany is the importance of building one's own group solidarity and power, which they did not do in their anxiety to be "good Germans."

1203. December 25, 1937. "A Christmas Parable" on those with and those without talents and what use they do and do not make thereof and the reward or the punishment meted out therefore by the Lord.

1204. January 23, 1938. This is the final column; he wishes, therefore, to make some criticisms and corrections. He had said that Standard Life was the first "old line life insurance company organized by Negroes"; but this is an error since the Mississippi Life Insurance, founded in January, 1913, beat it by two months. He had written that the Mme. C. J. Walker Manufacturing Company had been taken over by white owners; he was wrong and regrets the error. He gives some facts concerning Bermuda, in terms of where Jim Crow practices prevail and where they do not, correcting errors in the past.

THE AMSTERDAM NEWS

(This column was entitled, "As the Crow Flies.")

1939

1205. October 21, 1939. A panoramic view of Black history beginning with the 1911 Universal Races Congress, through the First World War, the post-war reaction, and the depression beginning in 1929 with its devastating impact upon the Afro-American, from which we have not yet recovered.

1206. October 28, 1939. He calls attention to "two excellent books": Horace M. Bond's *Negro Education in Alabama* and E. Franklin Frazier's *The Negro Family in the United States*. He refutes the idea that the British Empire no longer exists. Du Bois pays very warm tribute to his long-time friend, Dr. Owen M. Waller, who has just died. He gives an account of his life as an Episoopal clergymen and physician, as a member of the Niagara Movement, and formerly of the board of the NAACP, but above all, as a splendid gentleman.

1207. November 4, 1939. Du Bois asks whether or not we Black people really believe in democracy, in ourselves, and in service to our people. A brief history of the recurrence of depressions in the United States follows, then a recapitulation of the high points of his recent trip abroad, especially touching on Germany and China.

1208. November 11, 1939. Du Bois suggests that George W. Carver "has one great duty unperformed" and that is to train a coming generation of Black youth in his own field. Highly recommended is the new book on trade unions by Horace Cayton and George S. Mitchell.* He continues from his column of October 28 with a similar overall view of the French empire, seeing it as somewhat less racist and more democratic than the British, but still an empire. He commends increasing activity in terms of educational needs. They are mainly three now: admission to the best facilities available; active voice in the education of our own children; adequate pay and security for our teachers.

1209. November 18, 1939. The tactics of Britain and France have helped make the agreement between Germany and the U.S.S.R.; similar pressures draw Japan towards Germany. John R. Lynch has just died; a brief biography of the Black speaker of the Mississippi House of Representatives and author of a fine book on Reconstruction is offered; "in the end he cannot be forgotten." The present World War is called the Second but if history is examined carefully it is more nearly the Fifteenth.

1210. November 25, 1939. Devoted in large part to India whose opposition to Britain continues and must continue despite the war. Basing himself on the Cayton and Mitchell book on trade unions (No. 1208) Du Bois points to formation of the United Hebrew Trades in the late 19th century as a form of so-called self-segregation whose aim was to break down the anti-Semitism in the general trade union movement.

Black Workers and the New Unions

Similar efforts by us would be helpful. He denies a point made in that book that the upper class Blacks have been "ultra-nationalistic." This is "nonsense" because "among American Negroes the upper classes have always wanted to be white or to be treated as white folk."

1211. December 2, 1939. Again India and the justice of her struggle, led by Gandhi and Nehru. In the course of remarking about so-called young men, he writes, "youth is not a matter of years; it is a question of brains, honesty and tireless work." He commends the work of the W.P.A. and explains the special reasons why such efforts are important for Black people.

1211a. December 9, 1939. Data offered on the mixture of peoples and on educational policies in South Africa. He observes that in trade unions and in politics in the United States there is a growing concentration among ourselves or building our own centers and strength. "Planned racial effort for the salvation of the Negro race—call it segregation or what you will—is the path of the future."

1212. December 16, 1939. Chamberlain of England talks of peace without once mentioning India or Africa. There has been an ominous silence lately from West Africa; a description of Nigeria follows. He notes that Elmer W. Dean of White Plains, New York, has suggested a march in Washington next winter to be called, "We Who Have Been Lynched." He visits the school in Daytona, Florida, founded by Mary Bethune.

1213. December 23, 1939. Noting the absorption of the Baltic states by the U.S.S.R., he is astonished at the denunciation that it has aroused. All had been part of old Russia, all had had reactionary governments serving as a *cordon sanitaire* about the U.S.S.R.; besides, look who is denouncing Russia for "land-grabbing"—England, France, and the United States! He commends President Buell Gallagher of Talladega for his recent remarks on the value and uniqueness of elements in Afro-American culture. He notes that white youth in Atlanta have published a careful study of the realities of discrimination in their own city. The U.S. press is creating "quite a dither" about China, but our interest there is not in her independence; it is, rather, in trying to maintain China's dependence upon the United States.

1214. December 30, 1939. Ex-President Hoover is ranting about "poor little Finland"; did anyone hear him make a sound concerning the rape of Ethiopia? "But after all the Finns are blond." He has decided to start a movement to terminate Christmas; in any case, "Jesus Christ is not usually invited to his birthday celebration." He likes neither Thomas Dewey nor Robert Taft—the leading Republican contenders for presidential nomination; but he admires Mrs. Roosevelt who "insists on thinking in public."

1940

1215. January 6, 1940. Thomas Dewey says we should stop being halfway for creeping socialism and halfway for private enterprise. Du Bois summarizes a few of the many economic activities conducted, financed, or supervised by government; does Dewey mean to end this? Again an ironic note on the sudden concern about "aggression" in terms of Finland from folks silent for generations about aggressions from Ethiopia to Nicaragua.

1216. January 13, 1940. Studies in Harvard are showing the natural sources of variation in skin color; two points should be in the fore: the terrible discrimination against our children's education practiced by this nation, and its colossal expenditures on weapons rather than schools. Tribute is paid to the compassion and courage of Heywood Broun, who has just died.

1217. January 20, 1940. Du Bois thinks that "Gone With the Wind" is not to be compared in viciousness with "Birth of a Nation"; the former is merely "conventional provincialism." Kelly Miller's death brings an evaluation: swift in thought and often brilliant but somewhat cynical and not a hard worker or a scholar. He left no really lasting literary work and had unfortunate ambitions but withal he was a good man and one to be "widely missed." *A World Survey* of land ownership by Margaret Bateman shows the degree of concentrated ownership prevailing in lands such as Germany, Italy, Hungary, and Poland. A summary of Henry George's views is offered.

1218. January 27, 1940. Rushton Coulborn's warning at a meeting in Dallas, Texas, in March, 1939, of the possibilities of fascism in the South is quoted at length. Why is it that Phi Beta Kappa has never allowed the formation of a chapter at any Black college?

1219. February 3, 1940. Again, a call for a Negro Book Club. Du Bois notes that "a number of voices"—he names Patrick Hurley, formerly Secretary of War, and Charles A. Londbergh—are calling for the white nations to stop fighting each other and to gang up in nice little wars against the colored peoples of the world.

1220. February 10, 1940. Du Bois urges votes for W.P.A., C.C.C., and T.V.A. and not Dewey and Taft who opposed such efforts. He argues for birth control. He recalls the history of the American Missionary Association, and the connection therewith of the *Amistad* case and of John Quincy Adams.

1221. February 17, 1940. Du Bois offers the highest praise for Prairie View State College in Texas where modern techniques are taught well, unlike our older industrial schools.

1222. February 24, 1940. A defense of Russia despite the intense attacks upon that country by John Haynes Holmes—"much as I admire the man. ... I never considered the Russians even after the Revolution as supermen. I expected them to stagger on in blood and tears toward their magnificent goal with many a stumble and retreat. I love the victim Radek more than the tyrant Stalin"—but the accomplishments of that revolution and of the peoples of the U.S.S.R. have been enormous and therefore, "I still believe in Russia." He has received a letter from Henry L. Stimson suggesting aid in deterring Japan and pointing in fact to war by the United States against Japan. He will not get my help. The United States cares not a rap for China; it wants to exploit all Asia itself. This does not make Japan right in its wars but it certainly does not make the United States correct in its Asian policies and purposes. He does not remember any letters from Mr. Stimson about Italy and Ethiopia, by the way.

1223. March 2, 1940. The New York *Times* sneers at Earl Browder's critical remarks about what he calls "sham democracies" and says that those shams do not go about killing people without trial. The esteemed *Times* has—again—managed to forget the over 5,000 victims of lynching, the thousands of victims of racist pogroms—"without a single aggressor arrested, much less punished. ... We have a feeling that Earl Browder had a certain amount of truth back of his assertions." Tribute is paid to the quiet but effective leadership of H. L. McCrorey, president of Johnson C. Smith University in North Carolina. A student in California has discovered Du Bois' *Black Reconstruction* (published five years earlier) and has called its data to the attention of a professor who said, "If this is true more people ought to know about it."

1224. March 9, 1940. An attack upon the program of the Republican party opens the column. Du Bois had lunch in Chicago with four young men—Arna Bontemps, Langston Hughes, Allison Davis, and a "new face"—Richard Wright. "One feels a certain sense of relief and confidence in meeting four such sturdy pillars of the day to come." He has been lecturing again to thousands in Kentucky (thinks well of Kentucky State University) and in Chicago, Detroit, Cleveland, and Dayton.

1225. March 16, 1940. Du Bois urges joining the Consumers Union in New York to get the most for your dollar (in addition, Martin Dies has denounced it!). He suggests support for a movement begun by Mercer Cook at Atlanta for donations to send gifts to the Black Africans fighting for France. Du Bois pays tribute to Stanislaus von Estreicher, the Pole whom he knew when they were students at the University of Berlin. He has suffered a martyr's death in a German concentration camp.

1226. March 23, 1940. Du Bois defends the right of men and women to believe in communism and to assert that belief and denounces all who would impede this; in this connection he specifically praises "young Ben Davis." But hailing this right does not mean assenting to the views of the Communists. Du Bois does not; he thinks that their program is not suitable for conditions in the United States and did not work well in the Scottsboro Case and is today impeding the best functioning of the National Negro Congress.

1227. March 30, 1940. The presidential campaign would be a clearcut issue of Finance Monopoly *versus* the New Deal but there are several obstacles: F.D.R. as Wilson's servant participated in Haiti's ravishment; his Secretary of State (Cordell Hull) hates Japan and his Secretary of the Navy (F. L. Knox) "loves Big Business."

1228. April 6, 1940. It is already clear that wealth is buying local and national elections. He objects to the widespread idea of the secrecy of one's income. It should be a matter of public record; if so, it would speed needed reforms.

1229. April 13, 1940. Du Bois writes at length and glowingly of the successes of the "Home Demonstration Program" led by the Prairie View State College in Texas.

1230. April 20, 1940. The W.P.A. was important for Black people and saved many from actual starvation. It should not be scuttled. He quotes with approval the call for the Second Southern Conference for Human Welfare to meet in Chattanooga in mid-April.

1231. April 27, 1940. A singular service of Black people to the nation was their example of humility and of courage; their insistence upon the glaring deficiencies in American society. We folk have been effective gadflies.

1232. May 4, 1940. Du Bois is enthralled by the singing and manner of Marian Anderson, whom he heard again in Atlanta. One note of criticism; at times she seems to slightly caricature certain of our songs. The seating arrangements for her concert bring to his mind the idea that much of the race separation is basically economic—"equality of income precedes today equality of civil and political rights."

1233. May 11, 1940. The record of Jewish effort in Palestine during the past 20 years is one of remarkable achievement. "What the wretched and scourged Jew would have done without Zion in this modern revival of race hatred is inconceivable."

1234. May 18, 1940. Du Bois observes that expositions have turned into commercial enterprises and not sites for education. He recalls the Paris Exposition of 1900 and the one in New York in 1913 and gives details of their plans and execution and hopes for a return of that kind of effort.

1235. May 25, 1940. It is to the great credit of the New Deal that it appointed a substantial number of Afro-American experts to help administer policies especially in areas most effecting Black people. He praises highly and enumerates the policies recently adopted by the Louisiana Colored Teachers Association.

1236. June 1, 1940. Du Bois tells the life story of Malaku Bayen, recently deceased, who was Haile Selassie's personal physician. He studied medicine at Howard University, married an Afro-American woman, and was a strong link in Pan-Africanism. Du Bois notes that Antonio Meucci, the actual inventor of the telephone, died in poverty and obscurity, while the Bell Telephone Company, as the Supreme Court found in 1888, "acquired the patent fraudulently."

1237. June 8, 1940. Du Bois writes again about the problem of improving sales of books among our people. Tribute is paid to the late Robert Moton.

1237a. June 15, 1940. Du Bois deals with expositions as of 1913 and repeats column of May 18, above.

1238. June 22, 1940. Du Bois notes the increasing reality of Pan-Africanism; he pays tribute to Dantes Bellegarde of Haiti, the late Malaku Bayen of Ethiopia and Lester Walton, for years U. S. Minister to Liberia. He hopes this will grow; perhaps the Fifth Pan-African Congress could be held in Haiti in 1942?

1239. June 29, 1940. Du Bois has been at three commencements; at Atlanta University; at Wilberforce University, where he spoke the truth as he saw it—and some liked it and some did not—and at Harvard University, which still retains much of its freedom despite all. He "shook with pleasure the hand of the curiously young President Conant" and remembered the days when William James, Albert Bushnell Hart, and Nathaniel Shaler walked among his other teachers.

1240. July 6, 1940. The greatness of France in her culture and people will not and cannot die. All that was taken from Russia after the First World War is now again part of the U.S.S.R. "If Russia now proves, despite her alliance with Hitler, to be the real salvation of the workers of the world, all is well." There are contradictory reports from India.

1241. July 13, 1940. Du Bois has heard Dorothy Maynor sing at Tuskegee Institute; splendid. It brings to mind that in our time it is not so difficult for our artists—he mentions also Robeson, Anderson, and Hayes—to receive something approaching the recognition their artistry merits. But a generation before them it was not possible and great voices such as those belonging to Sissy Dorsey, Alice Maynor, and Tom Talley went unnoticed in the world at large. The same kind of recognition "is coming in painting and sculpture; more slowly but just as surely in literature; but not yet, alas, in labor."

1242. July 20, 1940. When men are drafted for war that is patriotism; when they are drafted for tasks of peace, "that is interference with Liberty."

1243. July 27, 1940. The career of Hitler—a man of the lower classes with almost no education—shows, despite all its perversity, how absurd are his racist and elitist doctrines. It is likely, if this is now indeed the end of the war, that the United States, "an armed camp," will seek world hegemony.

1244. August 3, 1940. The real campaign issues should be eliminating the poverty afflicting one-third of the nation, curbing monopolies effectively, and eliminating racism. But none of these will actually represent real issues in the campaign.

1245. August 10, 1940. A tribute to the late William Trent Andrews, one of the early Black West Point cadets, whom Du Bois knew at Fisk

University; in terms of training our youth for "defense" why is that defined as training youth to be efficient killers? What kind of defense is this; what are we defending? In the campaign, the Republican effort to make much of the "third term" question is stupid. F.D.R. has faced up to the problem of dealing with poverty and that is more than the Republican party has done.

1246. August 17, 1940. There is among us—for good reason—a high degree of envy and a tendency not to pay proper tribute to our own people. Let us face this fault and set our minds and hands to changing matters.

1247. August 24: Basic to the New Deal was the concept of social security. A common suffering has made of the Afro-American people a unity, a cultural group.

1248. August 31, 1940. He has known two fools: John who did not enjoy youth because he was preparing for life and did not enjoy life because he was preparing for old age. Tom had such a wild time enjoying youth that he never reached old age.

1249. September 7, 1940. "We have no right to assume that the collapse of Europe will automatically free Asia and Africa." Du Bois hails the Second Meeting of the Southern Conference on Human Welfare. "The slow but undoubted advance toward democracy in the South is obvious."

1250. September 14, 1940. "We older ones are quick to condemn the present generation of youth . . . . Let us cultivate a vast patience with the overburdened youth of our day."

1251. September 21, 1940. He has observed a hostility towards Mexico among our people and this is due to the U.S. press; actually the people of Mexico suffered from U.S. aggression and there should be real sympathy between us and their people.

1252. September 28, 1940. Du Bois has enjoyed the film "Pride and Prejudice" because Jane Austen's artistry was great. Yet, it must be remembered that she wrote of only a small fraction of the real England with its workers and its poverty, not to speak of its colonial world that supported the characters in Miss Austen's books.

1253. October 5, 1940. A denunciation of anti-Semitism appears and the fact that the poison is present among Black folk, too. American music is now deeply African and Afro-American. Increasingly, this is becoming true of literature in the United States.

1254. October 12, 1940. Notice of the character of Paul Cravath, son of Erastus Cravath of Fisk University, when Du Bois was there. Paul helped Fisk but somewhat shamefacedly which was characteristic of the second generation post Abolitionists. The contribution of Black people themselves to education, especially in the South, has been ignored but is important, nonetheless. The world is faced with the process terminating traditional capitalism; that is more important than the Battle of Britain.

1255. October 19, 1940. Two men have died recently and both were worthy: Charles Loram, a white South African in a kind of exile in this country, a professor at Yale where he did not forget Black people—at which Yale is adept; James H. Dillard, a white Virginian, whose administration of the Slater and Jeanes Funds "was a miracle of path-breaking accomplishment."

1256. October 26, 1940. David F. Houston, chairman of the Mutual Life Insurance Company of New York—and formerly in Wilson's cabinet—has died. Du Bois knew him in 1891 as a fellow graduate student at Harvard. He was from North Carolina; they met occasionally and each time a new introduction was required. He was distinguished-looking but otherwise undistinguished and thus just the man to hold the presidency of several colleges and to be in Wilson's Cabinet. Black people must conserve themselves as a group and what we need in the world "is the respect of group for group." More and more Africa is becoming a center—again—of the present war.

1257. November 2, 1940. The religion of Black folk has served as a basic rock to which they have clung—the triumph of Good in the end. Its method has influenced all religious practice in the United States and the Salvation Army copied wholesale from our style. Something of the nature and scope of Swahili is explained.

1258. November 9, 1940. Wesley Mitchell, Franz Boas, and others have protested the decision of the government to prosecute Earl Browder on a passport case, the facts of which were known for years; they do so because it violates free speech. They are correct, says Du Bois and I join them.

1259. November 23, 1940. Roosevelt seeks an end to poverty. He has a long way to go and his program is very partial, but he does have that kind of commitment and its achievement is the prime task of this century. No Republican has such a vision.

1260. November 30, 1940. Du Bois hears talk of a political party just of Blacks; this is "arrant nonsense." At lunch an English Lord said that Americans with whom he has been talking have said that Hitler's anti-Semitism is the best thing about him.

1261. December 7, 1940. Du Bois shows in detail how the South dominates the committees in both the House of Representatives and Senate and how this negates political democracy.

1262. December 14, 1940. "Is Japan's seizure of Saigon a threat to Europe, or was England's fortification of Singapore a threat to Asia? Or both?" He returns to Swahili at request of a reader and recommends an article on its prose literature appearing in *Bantu Studies*, published in South Africa.

1263. December 21, 1940. A parody on Christmas with a "revision" of the Gospel. The Baby turns out to be Black.

1264. December 28, 1940. One hundred years ago, in 1841, the rebel slaves of the *Creole* won their freedom and the slaves aboard the *Amistad* rebelled. These kinds of memories should guide our present New Year resolutions. Among others, Du Bois suggests, "I am going to worship Truth and Truth only. ... "and "I will face each sunrise with one prayer: There is no God but Love and Work is his Prophet."

1941

January 4, 1941. (No column in this issue.)

1265. January 11, 1941. An unnamed "high government official" writes him a long letter—here quoted—assuring Du Bois that the draft will be conducted democratically and fairly. Du Bois says he thinks the man is honest but: "I have little faith in the United States Army and none at all in Southern Draft Boards."

1266. January 18, 1941. A nineteen-year-old youngster named Ruth Daniels of Los Angeles has read him and wonders if he loves "the colored race" really as his writings seem to say and "if you ever cursed the fate that bound you to such a race as the Negro?" The answer is long and subtle and objective; it is yes, and especially lately. He never had other than pride in his people and as he has learned more this has grown. He understands the pressures which induce such questions. "Be of good cheer," he writes, "human nature and more especially the human nature of black folk, is worth believing in." When your experience leads you to see this, "you may essay a further and higher step and believe in all folk not because of their race and color but because of their humanity."

1267. January 25, 1941. Du Bois argues against United States participation in the war at present. He notes that the Jews are acting to save themselves as shown in Palestine; and there one has a kind of segregation in the face of reality, but it is a segregation seeking to result in "an unsegregated humanity."

1268. February 1, 1941. A proposed inaugural address for President Roosevelt; he did not say it but should have. It is an affirmation of the horror of war, a demand that those now fighting cease, the establishment of a World League, the creation of an international armed force to maintain peace and a commitment to terminate war as a means of settling disputes.

1269. February 8, 1941. The heart of the so-called race question is in the South. He has always either lived in it or studied it and he thinks he knows it. Again, lately he has taken a trip through Alabama and Mississippi and spent some time in Texas at a meeting with Black and (southern) white professors concentrating on questions of agriculture. He has spoken at Lincoln University in Missouri on its 75th anniversary and is impressed with its spirit. Some Black people in the state are opposed to its existence because it is for Black people only; but whose fault is that? And meanwhile, faced with the fact of a lily-white University of Missouri, the thing to do is make Lincoln in every way superior educationally to the white school.

1270. February 15, 1941. He is dismayed by the growing acceptance among our middle classes of capitalist morality: that making money is the sole object of business, rather than service as a purpose in life.

1271. February 22, 1941. "Why not send Mrs. Bethune now to look England over and ask Winston [Churchill] a few pertinent questions about India and Africa?" He repeats the substance of the letter he sent a Fisk student opposing the United States joining the present war. (No. 287)

1272. March 1, 1941. "A Letter from Africa" projecting a township by and for Africans as a kind of model for the rest of South Africa. No comment by Du Bois.

1273. March 8, 1941. A Jesuit priest and professor of sociology, Father J. E. Coogan, of the University of Detroit, takes Du Bois to task for his treatment of the Catholic church and some of its revered figures in his *Dusk of Dawn*. Du Bois replies in some detail and closes, "I am sorry to offend your convictions by these statements but I am a student of the truth and not a missionary of religion."

1274. March 15, 1941. Modern education has trained only an elite and so is clearly a failure. Modern capitalism is plagued by a world with poverty and hunger and mass unemployment and only war-making brings big profits. Such a system must go. Attention is called to the autobiography of Nehru—now in jail in India.

1275. March 22, 1941. The United States edges closer and closer to entry into war. The 1940 census shows the continued splendid growth of our people; it points to the fact that many more Black women than white women work. Again, an appeal for a Book-of-the-Year Club for Black readers.

1276. March 29, 1941. A letter from the Philippines is quoted concerning conditions of near peonage imposed upon "our Filipino cousins."

1277. April 5, 1941. "Browder is sent to jail not for lying but for being a Communist. We may disagree with his beliefs but it is cowardly evasion to call it crime."

1278. April 12, 1941. It is said that " 'Du Bois is a rabid pro-Nazi!' " What slanderous nonsense. He believes in four things germane to the present world crisis: 1) the need for basic—revolutionary—change in the organization of industry; 2) in production for use, not profit; 3) in planned economic functioning; 4) in the abolition of unemployment. "I do not regard Russia as a scapegoat but rather as the greatest single hope for future industrial democracy, and her neutrality in the present conflict is the best promise for that hope."

1279. April 19, 1941. Du Bois writes, I have been told that only a Catholic can understand that church and that I do not. I am writing, however, of that church's attitude towards us and that I can and do understand. My protestor writes, for example, that there are about 700 priests devoting full or part time to work among Black people. No doubt, but the protestor failed to say how many of them were Black and the answer is *five*. Why? The church trains Irish to shepherd its Irish members, Africans for the Africans, and Asians for the Asians —why in the United States, whites to tend the souls of Black people?

1280. April 26, 1941. The basic enemy of democracy is poverty and it is this which must be conquered. Lengthy quotations to this point are offered from an article published in 1939 by Benjamin C. Marsh.

1281. May 3, 1941. Struggles in Youngstown, Ohio, for the placing of Black teachers in the school system are described.

1282. May 10, 1941. He quotes the call of the First Phylon Institute and emphasizes the need for careful planning by the Afro-American leadership for the economic salvation and advancement of their people.

1283. May 17, 1941. Du Bois notes with great regret the death of Charles E. Russell. He tells of speaking engagements in Springfield, Indianapolis, Detroit, Cleveland, and Chicago. Forums among us are healthy and growing.

1284. May 24, 1941. Du Bois lectured at the University of Minnesota, Macalester College, and at Northwestern University. The education he received made the effort worthwhile.

1285. May 31, 1941. "If Hitler wins, down with the blacks! If the democracies win, the blacks are already down." Du Bois notes the appearance of *Negro Youth*, in its first number and its attack upon the mulatto as distinguished from the Black. This was strong in the West Indies and given its history had some reason but in the United States it has had less force and is utterly divisive. The periodical repeats the "ancient lie that Marcus Garvey's expulsion from America was due to any action of mine. There is ample printed evidence of the support and praise which I gave Garvey for much of his work, and the warnings that I often voiced, which if they had been followed, would have doubtless left him alive today."

1286. June 7, 1941. Du Bois tells the story of Pearl Mason of Philadelphia, a Black woman, who won the lottery for $150,000 and with it paid the city all she had ever received in relief and then with the help of the attorney Raymond P. Alexander has financed the building of a modern apartment building for her people since, as, she said, they had "to get themselves homes where the roof don't leak."

1287. June 14, 1941. "If you want to lose friends and jobs just oppose the war, defend strikes and declare that even communists have rights." Hess' flight to England was a gesture of a kind of idealism that is peculiarly German but its actual meaning is obscure.

1288. June 21, 1941. Du Bois is visiting Cuba and sees it as a colored land with a high degree of real fraternity.

1289. June 28, 1941. Again on Cuba with concentration upon the educational system of Oriente province; he has had a long talk with the superintendent of education in that province, a "colored woman" named Señorita Causse.

July 5, 1941. (No column in this issue)

1290. July 12, 1941. "The Russo-German war compels nearly all of us to rearrange our thoughts and forecasting. ... But Hitler cannot win, simply because no such organization as he has today built up, can command the brains, the loyalty and the manpower which will enable it to conquer the world."

1291. July 19, 1941. Du Bois offers advice to whomever becomes president of Wilberforce University: be president and not subservient to bishops or state officials.

1292. July 26, 1941. "The war between Russia and Germany reorientates all our thinking whether we will or not. ... Now Germany has laid aside all camouflage. She essays to lead Western Europe against Communism. ... The hopes of the modern world rest on the survival of the new conception of politics and industry which Russia represents. ... Neither of them [England and the U.S.] really wishes to fight for the kind of industrial democracy which the best ideals of Russia represent, and which must eventually triumph or modern culture fails."

1293. August 2, 1941. Devoted to typical misrepresentations in economics as taught in most schools and a call for a study of that discipline.

1294. August 9, 1941. Again, an insistence that war upon Japan would not be for democracy but for profit and exploitation and because of racism.

1295. August 16, 1941. Important to remember when vacationing are—plenty of sleep, reading good books and exercise such as brisk walking.

1296. August 23, 1941. Charles Burroughs has died; in his death "we lose one of the great dramatic artists of the Negro race." In all the talk of war, every spot on earth is mentioned—except Africa. Again, an attack upon the envy that infests certain upper circles of Black life.

1297. August 30, 1941. He is dissatisfied with "the Roosevelt-Churchill manifesto" for it is worse than unclear when it comes to racism and colonialism—or, better, never gets to either. "Did not Mr. Churchill and Mr. Roosevelt really mean peace among white folk for the more successful mastery of Asia and Africa?"

1298. September 6, 1941. "It is the deep and prayerful hope of many followers of Christ, that Germany and Russia will in the end kill and ruin each other, while England and America step in and sift the ashes." The request from the United States and Great Britain for a mandate "to rescue the world again," forces this question, "what new assurance, what new promise have we, that these countries will or can do better in 1942, than they did in 1918?"

1299. September 13, 1941. "Again the tragedy of the Negro American soldier festers as it did in the Revolution, the Civil War, the Spanish War and the first World War. The sore will never heal, so long as we fight for a Freedom and Democracy which we dare not practice."

1300. September 20, 1941. Since we have never been exploiters, we may help lead in the New Abolition: the abolition of poverty.

1301. September 27, 1941. Devoted largely to a reader's comments on his *Dusk of Dawn*.

1302. October 4, 1941. There are varying views of the war and the world. " ... I believe that the Russian Revolution in its essence and depth of real meaning was greater than the French Revolution, with more vivid promise of healing the ills of mankind than any movement of our day; and we believe this despite the murder of Trotsky and dozens of great Russians who dared to disagree with Stalin."

1303. October 11, 1941. The Allies' hostility forced the Soviet-Nazi Pact and now that Hitler has attacked the U.S.S.R. it is a matter of expiation for the Allies to support her.

1304. October 18, 1941. Of decisive importance in the education of our youth is the implanting of pride in ourselves. Reiteration of the importance of the social security and federal housing features of the New Deal.

1305. October 25, 1941. Bishop Reverdy Ransom "is a brave man" for daring to expose the corruption in the A.M.E. Church in terms of electing bishops. The struggle in Jamaica for enhanced democracy should receive the support of all of us.

1306. November 1, 1941. A defense of building up good all-Black neighborhoods in face of the existing racism; and the need for the best possible kinds of schools and surroundings for our people.

1307. November 8, 1941. It is well that President Roosevelt has decided that Black men shall train to become officers in nonsegregated officers' schools; but we must be vigilant as to how that decision is in fact implemented.

1308. November 15, 1941. Praise for Mayor La Guardia in New York City. Quotation from the strong statement on racism and Hitlerism made by the Black attorney, Euclid L. Taylor, in addressing the American Legion in Milwaukee.

1309. November 22, 1941. Du Bois faces the question of work as domestic servants which, according to the 1930 census, is how one and a half million Black people make a living. The need to raise its status, its working conditions, and its wage level is very great.

1310. November 29, 1941. In attacking the realities of the British Empire one is not favoring Hitler; one is telling the truth. We Black people must strive to protect our interests; one of those interests is the freedom of Africa, and we should use our political influence in the United States to further that end.

1311. December 6, 1941. A very moving letter from a twenty-one-year old Black woman—one who is dark and meets color prejudice among her own people; the letter is given in full and Du Bois damns such prejudices among us. "Are we going to let the color line enter our own colored world and ruin it?"

1312. December 13, 1941. Du Bois has been in Cuba on the invitation of the American Council of Learned Societies; the column describes meeting people like Jules Romains of France and Count Sforza of Italy, and the sense of common unity in dedication to a world free of racism that was present.

1313. December 20, 1941. His participation in Cuba suggests to him that much of Latin America is thinking in terms of mimicking the white world; this is a disaster.

1314. December 27, 1941. Again a Christmas parable, with a man from Mars trying to understand how Christians are practicing their Christianity.

1942

1315. January 3, 1942. It is not too early to consider Africa when this war ends. Du Bois offers proposals that should guide the planning for that continent's future and its relationship to other continents; the emphasis is upon an end to colonialism and the achievement of real independence and a rational, planned economic order for Africa.

1316. January 10, 1942. A Debit and Credit stock-taking for 1941. Among the former: war; economic discrimination; discrimination in the army; the deaths of Ernest Just, Harry C. Smith and a good social worker, George Arthur. Among the latter: Black aldermen in New York and a Black woman elected to New Haven's governing body; some advances in education and in trade unions; antidiscrimination orders from the President; accomplishments of L. D. Reddick, Paul Robeson, Dorothy Maynor, Marian Anderson. Books by Black scholars of the year of great merit were: Rayford Logan's *The Diplomatic Relations of the United States with Haiti*; Alain Locke's *The Negro in Art*; C. S. Johnson's *Growing up in the Black Belt* and *Statistical Atlas of Southern Counties*. Among white authors Henrietta Buckmaster's *Let My People Go*; Marie Carpenter's *The Treatment of the Negro in American History School Textbooks* and Willa Cather's *Sapphira and the Slave Girl* were notable.

1317. January 17, 1942. A short story, "The Missionaries"—Christians from Africa have come to convert the inhabitants of the United States and do not get very far.

1318. January 24, 1942. "If General MacArthur is fighting as hard in the Philippines as he is in the American newspapers, the Japanese are doomed." "Among the 'yellow bastards' we are not fighting are several hundred million Chinese, Filipino, Malays, and East Indians." A student who befriended him at Harvard, a white youngster named James F. Morton—for years a librarian in New Jersey—has died; he was a radical and a poet and a fine man. He commends Pearl Buck for her stand in defense of India's freedom; and quotes with approval recommendations on education coming from Albert Einstein.

1319. January 31, 1942. Educators from all parts of Georgia met in Atlanta this month; Black educators were not invited; the keynote speech was entitled: "Moral Obligations of Democracy." If the Japanese do not surrender quickly, "why not send Dorothy Thompson over there to talk them to death?" A South American writes him to confirm his suspicions that Latin-American countries, in international meetings, tend to draw a color line. The death of E. H. Webster—a white man—who had taught science for 42 years at Atlanta University, is a blow to all of us. He and his remarkable wife were living proof of the possibilities of real friendship among peoples of different colors.

1320. February 7, 1942. Again a call for a Book Club which would help sustain genuine Afro-American literature, not literature written by Black people for a white audience. Only Black people writing freely and knowing that their own people (as well as others) are reading them will produce a genuine Afro-American literature of true greatness.

1321. February 14, 1942. On the whole, a defense of his position in the First World War; he writes that again we "close ranks" and fight for democracy—for all people of all colors.

1322. February 21, 1942. Of course, the colored peoples of the world want democracy and detest Hitlerism; but how to get real democracy and how to extirpate what is behind Hitlerism—these are the questions.

1323. February 28, 1942. Again on the book club idea and reports of growing support for it. A rather full account of the frame-up and conviction of Festus Coleman in San Francisco; a defense committee headed by Paul Robeson and Augustus Hawkins, Black State Assemblyman, should be supported.

1324. March 7, 1942. The heads of several New York City colleges say they would welcome Black people on the faculties, but they know none qualified. Of course they are lying but what we should now do is flood those officials with applications and records of scholarship. He tells of an analagous case involving himself and President Hayes and his getting a Slater scholarship to study abroad 50 years earlier.

1325. March 14, 1942. (This column is in two parts and its continuation appears in the next week's issue [March 21] under "Guest Editorial"; in addition that issue also contained his regular column. The two-part essay made the following points.) There is need for agreement among us for a three-part program; immediate program, group pressure for longer term objectives; and long term program, century-long planning. An end to racism in the army is immediate, in pay, in unions, in public places; intermediate objectives are to look toward group organization and cooperatives in consumer and producing areas and creation among ourselves of first-rate communities; the long term—perhaps to be achieved in 2042—"the disappearance from the world of all artificial racial distinctions."

1326. March 21, 1942. The basic purpose of this war must be an end to poverty; with that goes the possibility of real freedom. The effort to end poverty was the real meaning of the Bolshevik Revolution and that revolution—despite all its problems and difficulties—held power and nothing the capitalist powers could do has toppled it. That its Revolution has the support of the Soviet peoples is proven today by the magnificent defense against Hitlerism. Britain and the United States still oppose this, but this is the main point of the present century and when one speaks of the liberation of the colored peoples he must also mean industrial transformation.

1327. March 28, 1942. A dinner has been given for Oswald Garrison Villard, who has been and remains a pacifist. Hitler could only be stopped by weapons, Du Bois says, but the idea of pacifism and the commitment to it are splendid; hence, he is delighted that Villard was honored.

1328. April 4, 1942. Lectures to packed halls in Columbia, S. C., on the need after this war to build a world free of poverty; only then can we talk seriously of freedom and democracy. Du Bois tells of an automobile accident with a car packed with soldiers—all white and some drunk. Not a serious accident but for a few moments a nasty and even dangerous atmosphere prevailed.

1329. April 11, 1942. "Social classes are growing among us." He quotes extensively from a study by one of his students of this phenomenon on the campus of an unnamed Black college showing such distinctions and their relationship to color with the richest being lighter and the poorest being darker.

1330. April 18, 1942. Du Bois emphasizes the complexity of the so-called Negro question, pointing to differences marking a small northern town, a large industrial center in the North, in the South and the rural districts of the South. All this must be carefully borne in mind in working on programs.

1331. April 25, 1942. He had remarked once on Dr. Moton's selection of his son-in-law, Frederick D. Patterson, to be his successor in charge of Tuskegee Institute. This has been misconstrued into a criticism; I was not being critical, writes Du Bois, for I believed that Mr. Patterson was the best choice and that Mr. Moton showed courage in selecting him despite the criticism that would follow. An analysis of the four "Tuskegees" follows: the town, the Black citizens living in it, the school, and the hospital. Tuskegee has accomplished a great deal and its hospital and now its training program for Black air cadets are astonishing accomplishments.

1332. May 2, 1942. Du Bois calls attention to the mounting numbers of Black folk in the United States, refuting the widespread prophecy that with emancipation we would die out. But he affirms that there is a tendency for overcrowding in certain cities, especially in New York; the reasons he understands, but not enough planning is being done. "Unless the Negroes of New York take this matter deeply to mind, the result after the war, of unemployment with its resulting crime and sickness, is going to make New York City a terrible center of social disaster."

1333. May 9, 1942. If this war is being fought for the genuine freedom of all humanity, "my gun is on my shoulder." He thinks now that the gains made by Black people as a result of this war will be fairly considerable: greater entry into industry and unions, more officers in the army, a breach in the navy. Two good meetings were held recently in Georgia; one of Black school teachers; they demanded equal pay and showed fine spirit. The other of the Alpha Kappa Alpha Sorority and while it had much socializing of course, as it should, it also showed fine social consciousness.

1334. May 16, 1942. He has lectured at Vassar and at Yale. The former was noteworthy in the past for its racism and snobbishness, but this has been overcome; it now has a few Black women as students and its student body shows great interest in the labor movement. At Yale he has noticed some welcome changes, although not as dramatic as at Vassar. He does not find very great differences among students at such places and at Atlanta University.

1335. May 23, 1942. "In South Africa the whites have gotten to the place where they say that in the last resort they would be willing to arm the blacks against the enemy. Which enemy?" He visits Krum Elbow in New York state, one of Father Divine's establishments. His religion is interracial and it certainly does help people; "of the various religious movements of our day, there is least in this that one may criticize."

1336. May 30, 1942. "The central protagonist for civilization today is Russia; page Lothrop Stoddard!" The chaplain of Ohio State Penitentiary in Columbus asks for books as no fund is provided for this and many of the imprisoned are anxious to read and study. "Of all the barbarities which we visit upon prisoners, I think this is the most devilish and unjustifiable." And "a terribly high percentage" of those jailed are guilty of nothing. "If all this is true in Ohio, think of what is true in Mississippi!"

1337. June 6, 1942. Du Bois offers again some lessons in economics and the creation of value, the source of unemployment, and the nature of profits.

1338. June 13, 1942. Du Bois is not certain about the charges that Harry Bridges endangers democracy but he certainly has been dangerous as far as "those organized monopolies on the Pacific Coast who specialize in slave wages" are concerned.

1339. June 20, 1942. Again some lessons in economics, especially countering the idea that "private property is created by individual effort."

1340. June 27, 1942. He notes the appointment of Allison Davis as an assistant professor at University of Chicago and hails it. The time will come when a Black scholar will have the choice of teaching at Fisk or at Yale and then the decision will not be an easy one, depending upon many factors, not least what the professor wishes to accomplish.

1341. July 4, 1942. There are three phases to education: to master the "tool courses"; to accumulate knowledge; and "learning to earn a living." But, "the object of education is to make the period of knowledge-getting just as long and complete as possible."

1342. July 11, 1942. In Henri Bonnet's postwar plans Africa is not mentioned; in the plan of the World Federation of New York, Malaysia and India go to the United States and Britain, and "Africa is handed out to Europe." "Listen, brethren: Now you are planning for war sure enough." He hails efforts at new educational methods at Hampton Institute; and, "I admire the courage of Charles Wesley who has undertaken the rebuilding of Wilberforce."

1343. July 18, 1942. Plans are omitting the *people* of Africa in building a postwar world. Such a program is "fatal"; Black people will not accept it. The hope of holding "black Africa in perpetual subjection is arrant nonsense and tragic shortsightedness."

1344. July 25, 1942. A visit to the air training center at Tuskegee Institute brings reiteration in very clear terms of a basic idea: "We know the dangers of segregation; we hate it and fight against it. We are segregated; we are going to be segregated for years if not for centuries; and we are going to use that segregation in every possible way to increase our knowledge and power."

1345. August 1, 1942. He is thinking of a book the theme of which would be, "how men act, achieve, fail, because of the possibility vouchsafed them to enjoy the goods and services and opportunities of this world."

1346. August 8, 1942. Du Bois offers samples of the above project and wonders, "how far could humanity actually plan its history and future development in accordance with reason and right?"

1347. August 15, 1942. The attack on Roland Hayes in Rome, Georgia, illustrates the small Southern town where racism is most deeply imbedded. One solution is flight, "but running away never won a battle ... . Even if I can say nothing helpful, I can at least keep my fool mouth shut."

1348. August 22, 1942. "It would be sad if the proposed flag of the United Nations would have to represent India with a jail and Gandhi and Nehru looking out."

1349. August 29, 1942. Differences in income are the most important elements of inequality. They do not result from race differences or from differences in ability. How can this problem be solved?

1350. September 5, 1942. A defense of a college education; it remains an important medium if used well to gain consequential knowledge.

1351. September 12, 1942. The continued racism within the U.S. Navy violates the government's own laws and orders and represents "deliberate official lawlessness."

1352. September 19, 1942. The persistence of poverty is the greatest indictment against modern civilization; its elimination is at the top of any rational plans for the future. September 26, 1942. (No column on this date.)

1353. October 3, 1942. The lack of democracy in Washington, D.C. "makes our war aims clear." Again, the need to end poverty; and poverty does not exist because of the character of the poor but because of the character of society.

1354. October 10, 1942. The economic morality of Black men in business is no better than white people; they fleece their own people without mercy or ethics. "What American Negro business men have got to remember is that a new economic morality is facing the world, and that emancipation from unfair private profit is going to be as great a crusade in the future as emancipation from Negro slavery was in the past."

1355. October 17, 1942. The basic discrimination is not that which touches matters of dining or riding trains; it is rather that which keeps one out of jobs or from promotions or from equal pay. The Fair Employment Practice Committee is positive even though in our society, under present conditions, actual enforcement will be quite spotty.

1356. October 24, 1942. The urge among many of us to "be Americans" has toned down our criticisms of the reality of the United States, but this is wrong and we should speak out in criticism not only of the treatment we receive but of the greed and inhumanity of the social order in general.

1357. October 31, 1942. The point is not to join the United States but rather to transform it; this is a peculiar opportunity for our people because of our history and situation.

1358. November 7, 1942. We need careful study by ourselves of ourselves, including the awful things that we do to ourselves and why and how to end it; for example, this year in Atlanta, Black men have killed 50 other Black men.

1359. November 14, 1942. " ... nothing would help the South more, both black and white, than to have the underpaid and inefficient black peons come out of the white kitchens to keep their own kitchens clean and to let white women learn what it means to build a home." Du Bois returns again to theme of the October 10 column, "we exploit our own people."

1360. November 21, 1942. There are not great differences as to basic demands of our people, whether in the North or South: "they want really to be free and equal."

1361. November 28, 1942. Du Bois details the world-wide growth of the cooperative movement; he indicates its development in the United States and reiterates that it should be widely adopted by Black people.

1362. December 5, 1942. Du Bois notes the speech by Mark Ethridge, general manager of the Louisville, Kentucky, *Courier Journal*, when resigning his chairmanship of the F.E.P.C. and quotes from it: right-minded Southerners who are white want economic and political equality for Black people but will never allow abandonment of "social segregation." What if the latter does in fact vitiate the former?

1363. December 12, 1942. Du Bois develops the realities of the South which show the inanity of the Ethridge position. We Black people will keep on pointing this out, whether Mr. Ethridge likes it or not, writes Du Bois, and we will continue to live under present conditions, too, trying to make that life as little unpleasant as we can.

1364. December 19, 1942. He thinks that certain legislation could be passed soon: anti-lynching, antipoll tax, federal support for education; in addition to the legislative front there are the educational and agitational forms of struggle. All have to be used but with a plan and with rational organizational methods.

1365. December 26, 1942. The bus situation is "critical" in the South. The rules are brutal and the drivers often more brutal. A. Philip Randolph's suggestion for a Congress of Black people to meet simultaneously with the Peace Congress after this war leads him to reminisce about the 1919 Pan-African Congress.

1943

1366. January 2, 1943. The retiring President of the National Association of Manufacturers has announced his undying passion for capitalism and production for profit. But the postwar world will not do well under such a system; one of planning for human welfare must be tried.

1367. January 9, 1943. In no so-called democracy today does one find the workers in control of industry—of their own jobs.

1368. January 16, 1943. The slaughter of Jews in Europe is a fierce condemnation of the entire so-called Christian Western civilization and the fault by no means is confined to Hitler or to Germany. Must we turn to Asia and Africa for the saving of civilization?

1369. January 23, 1943. In commenting upon the recent death of George Washington Carver, Du Bois suggests that it is from such a life that the future leadership of the world ought to come: it was a life dedicated to fact and to science, to helping mankind, to increasing nature's bounty and a life wherein material pleasures and bounties were consciously rejected. A defense of the Black press appears here also, in protest against an article held to be one-sided appearing in the *Saturday Review of Literature*.*

*Warren H. Brown, "A Negro Looks at the Negro Press," *Saturday Review of Literature*, December 19, 1942, Vol. XXV, No. 51, pp. 5–6.

1370. January 30, 1943. "The government of the United States is changing ... The executive power is expanding enormously. ... " A great battle is shaping up along class and ideological lines in terms of the power of monopoly and the imperative need for economic rationality. We Black people must organize among ourselves for our own care and uplift through our churches, our women's organizations, etc. We do not do this enough.

1371. February 6, 1943. The resignation of William H. Hastie as civilian aide in the War Department was dignified and showed that he was not getting the cooperation he required. He is the kind of civil servant among us that we need.

1372. February 13, 1943. The overly critical article on the Black press (no. 1369) written by a young Black journalist for the white press brings to mind the career of William Hannibal Thomas, a Black man whose first little book, *Negro Problems, Land and Education* (1890) was a strong attack upon racism but whose second book *The American Negro: What He Was, What He Is, And What He May Become* was among the most vicious attacks upon Black people ever penned. (No. 66) It got into every library and was quoted by white writers a hundred times and did enormous damage. We are only human and our people have shortcomings. "But this does not justify slander nor spite. It does not excuse deliberate overstatement just because such falsehood will secure its author publicity. It is no pathway to success even in the white press."

1373. February 20, 1943. Meetings between Churchill and Roosevelt do not build confidence in the purposes of this war. They suggest, rather, that "we are facing the wrong way. We must conquer Hitler. We must curb the imperialism of Japan. We must free China and India. We must recognize the right of Russia to organize her industry as she wishes and let the world know about it. But it is not our duty or wish to conquer the world and rule it."

1374. February 27, 1943. He has reached his 75th year (February 23) and offers thoughts on the process of aging. But his emphasis is on the need of the unity of the special insights of the young and the old; how necessary is a combination of both!

1375. March 6, 1943. An authentic literature of our folk needs a readership made up of our folk and publications controlled by us. He repeats the story of his encounter with Paul Palmer of *The American Mercury* and urges Black authors never to sell themselves.

1376. March 13, 1943. Du Bois doubts if a general strike or passive resistance en masse would work in the United States in terms of the needs of Black people. He gives his reasons and thinks that agitation and publicity still remain "our trump cards."

1377. March 20, 1943. He has completed a lecture tour through 19 states and spoken to audiences of approximately 4,500 persons while by radio he has reached scores of thousands. Such trips help refresh him and teach him; he is pleased by the calibre of the audiences and their questions.

1378. March 27, 1943. The growing rebellion of "colored labor" in the world remains a central feature of today's globe.*

1379. April 3, 1943. The thought behind my "talented tenth" idea was service not self-service. Abram Harris thought it meant in life the "privileged tenth" but I think that the leadership which has been developed among us is outstanding and on the whole is committed to service. Instances of the work of William H. Hastie, Theodore Berry (who resigned from the Office of Facts and Figures), and of A. Philip Randolph are given.

1380. April 10, 1943. We are "a nation within a nation"; ... "we American Negroes are the bound colony of the United States just as India is of England." We should organize ourselves and our communities; we are not using the power we possess if we but realized it. This is economic and could be political. Moreover, we should not remain disarmed and permit all the arms to be in the hands of white police and white militia. "For the sake of democracy and world peace the Negro has no business voicelessly to submit to such a situation. He has the right to bear arms, he has the right of self-defense, he is already in the army."

1381. April 17, 1943. Increasing signs of impending explosions from the army camps of the nation are appearing. "When will the F.E.P.C. be revived? When will the soldiers at Fort Huachuca be entrained? When will the Tuskegee flyers be given a job? When will the black fighters of the United States become a real part of the military and naval forces?"

---

*Dr. Du Bois, in a letter dated March 29, 1943, to Julius J. Adams, the managing editor of the newspaper, protested that the column of that date did not contain what he had written; that it was "drivel" and that "it is indefensible to have me apparently sanctioning stuff like this."

1382. April 24, 1943. As to the right of self-defense to which he turned (No. 1380), this meant what it said and did not mean a strategy of mass armed uprising. That would be suicidal for we are but 9 percent of the population and we do not have the arms!

1383. May 1, 1943. The U.S. Government in published reports on insurance and banking gives figures on Black businesses in these efforts. They are summarized here and, again, Du Bois pleads that among us businesses must have before them service to our people in the first place and not profits for a few.

1384. May 8, 1943. Perry Howard has said recently that universal suffrage "is the one and only solution for the ills besetting" us. A generation ago I would have agreed and I was saying substantially the same thing. But today I believe that back of the vote is the question of poverty and of economics; without the elimination of poverty there can be no real democracy. Insofar as the vote helps in this, well and good, but the basic drive must be against poverty if freedom is to be real.

1385. May 15, 1943. As a youngster he had three "great holidays" —Christmas, the cattle show, and the circus. He still loves the last and writes at some length of the Barnum and Bailey show he has visited. He writes appreciatively, too, of Thornton Wilder's "The Skin of Our Teeth."

1386. May 22, 1943. The funds needed for our higher education are immense and philanthropy is more and more drying up. We must increase our own economic and political power so that we can effectively guide the education of our youth.

1387. May 29, 1943. The editorial is devoted to the need to get Black instructors and professors into the "white" universities; a letter from a white undergraduate at the University of Michigan suggests that possibility for Ann Arbor.

1388. June 5, 1943. A column devoted to detailing the work of the Pullman porter and the great qualities of service he has manifested and to hailing the union which was formed of such men. "Too little has been written and known of the Pullman porter. We should know the facts and tell them to our children."

1389. June 12, 1943. Elmer Carter warns against falling for segregation and of course he has a point. But for ten years Mr. Carter edited *Opportunity* and that was and is a Black magazine. He could have done well as an editor of *Harper's* or *The Atlantic* but he was not asked and he was not asked for the same reason that though I was an "assistant instructor" at the University of Pennsylvania, I was never asked to be on its faculty. It is important to remember that there have been generations "of hard-working youth" in the past who "dared to be Negroes in order to be men."

1390. June 19, 1943. The death of George Frazier Miller, a minister in Brooklyn, brings tribute to this militant and courageous man—an early supporter of William Monroe Trotter and of the Niagara Movement. The poll tax struggle brings to the fore the whole question of the "rotten borough" system in the South which must yet be overcome if we are ever to be a political democracy.

1391. June 26, 1943. A balance sheet after one and a half years of war: debits—Jim-Crow army and Waves; discrimination in Southern camps; failure to convict lynchers and peon-masters, failure of F.E.P.C.; racism against Japan; among credits, Roosevelt's visit to Liberia and President Barclay's visit here; increased antiracism of unions, the March-on-Washington Movement; training of Black and white together in officer's schools. ...

1392. July 3, 1943. The death of Albert Bushnell Hart, of Harvard, removes a man who tolerated no discrimination on the grounds of race. The frank and open act of Doxey Wilkerson—one "of our best social [science] students" in leaving Howard University and going to work for the Communist Party is honorable. The series of anti-Negro riots is the result of "organized determined propaganda"—that in Mobile, Alabama, was instigated by the Alabama Dry Dock and Shipbuilding Company. It is documented in reports coming from the N.Y. *Times* and in a detailed study by James E. Jackson, educational director of the Southern Negro Youth Congress in Birmingham.

1393. July 10, 1943. In the recent riots in Detroit, Mobile, and Beaumont, most of those killed were Black people and the police did most of the killing. The riots will recur because they spring out of racism and that continues. What are we as a people doing to protect ourselves and to take care of the families of the victims?

1394. July 17, 1943. In previous riots, the killers and racists were not in hiding and were open; this time they are hiding and clandestine. That means some progress, even with blood.

1395. July 24, 1943. After the pogrom in Detroit one must say, "the real war will be won in Detroit, not in Palermo, Orel, nor Gaudalcanal."

1396. July 31, 1943. Vacation is a time for refreshing the mind as well as the body and often these days the mind more than the body. Some new books are recommended: Waldo Frank, *South American Journey*; Carey McWilliams, *Brothers Under the Skin*; Richard Sterner, *The Negro's Share*; Wood Gray, *The Hidden Civil War*; William Beveridge, *Social Insurance: Report*; Anna Graves, *Benevenuto Cellini Had No Prejudice Against Bronze*; Herbert Agar, *A Time for Greatness*; H. J. Laski, *The Revolution in our Time*.

1397. August 7, 1943. A Brooklynite writes of his visit to the museum and being told by those in charge of the Egyptian collection that Dr. Du Bois is not an authority and that Black African people had no connection with Egyptian history. Du Bois replies in some detail, citing authorities, and noting that even Arnold Toynbee now "admits a 'Negroid element' in Egyptian civilization." Du Bois closes, "never doubt, Egypt was mulatto."

1398. August 14, 1943. "Does America really feel itself capable, mentally and morally, of taking a leading part in the reforming of the postwar world?"

1399. August 21, 1943. For obvious reasons we tend to ignore the existence of criminals among us; their social source is clear. And their victims are overwhelmingly among us. We must face this or it will become worse and we must end it—we, no one else. This should be done by our churches and organizations and also as a result of our battle against its social roots: we must have work at good wages, our illiteracy must be ended; we must have adequate medical care; we must end unemployment.

1400. August 28, 1943. "Get rid of poverty and its brood of crime, sickness and ignorance. But hate and avoid them even as you work to get rid of them, and because you are working to get rid of them."

1401. September 4, 1943. Du Bois notes that the census reports we as a people are now 40 percent urban; a most momentous change. It carries with it increasing discontent and this is healthy. In certain cities we are over a third of the population—Washington, New Orleans, Memphis, Birmingham, Atlanta—but most cannot vote. "Perhaps there is the place where a new fight for the franchise should begin."

1402. September 11, 1943. We have ourselves, as a people, not really practiced democracy; we should begin to do so with real meetings and real congresses with actual popular participation.

1403. September 18, 1943. The systematic destruction of millions of Jews in Nazi-occupied Europe is among the most vast horrors of history. "It is a case of race prejudice on a scale unknown and unconceived of since the Emancipation Proclamation. ... What is happening to Jews may happen to us in the future." The United States and Britain could help rescue the surviving 3,000,000 Jews but "they stand dumb" because of the racism and anti-Semitism in those countries. "Unless it is destroyed, rooted out, absolutely suppressed, modern civilization is doomed."

1404. September 25, 1943. Strange people are now praising Russia! Can the greatness in Italy come forth again—"the real Italy ... the dark beauty of one of the most gifted people on earth."

1405. October 2, 1943. Du Bois reverts to the possibilities of small scale producer's cooperatives as offering one form of useful economic activity for us.

1406. October 9, 1943. The riots are more like wars because never have there been so many of us determined on freedom. Here is a program: Get as much education as possible; let us get work and live sensibly and not competitively; let us express what we think fearlessly; let us beget children and raise them well; and "let us have guts"; show "your creed by deeds." With that we cannot lose.

1407. October 16, 1943. It is the really criminal activity of the "captains of industry that makes communists faster than demagogues like [Martin] Dies can smell them out."

1408. October 23, 1943. A call for us to do more by ourselves and for ourselves.

1409. October 30, 1943. We must take much more interest than we do in the education of our children and parents, and teachers should work together on this. After we end segregation, do we end miseducation?

1410. November 6, 1943. The data—here summarized—show immense deficiencies in the education of Black people; this is at the heart of our difficulties and we must face up to this and plan to overcome it and fight until we do.

1410a. November 13, 1943. (This, presumably by error, reprints the column of April 24, 1943.)

1411. November 20, 1943. England and the U.S. are saying that the U.S.S.R. is moving towards capitalism; don't you believe it. One of our greatest needs is socialized medicine.

1412. November 27, and December 4, 1943. A story in two parts of a Black couple who decide to open a restaurant with "southern-style" cooking in downtown New York. The wife suggests not serving Black people; the husband insists on doing so. The latter decision causes the collapse of a flourishing business. No moral, no real ending—except that is the end.

1413. December 11, 1943. He has had fine meetings at Cooper Union and Columbia University and believes that the community forum —with questions and answers—should be more widely employed. Visiting New York he saw Robeson's "Othello" and doubts "if ever again an actor will dare portray Othello as white." Twenty-five years ago the play thus cast would never have been shown on Broadway.

1414. December 18, 1943. "What should we aim at? Political power to enable us to get what we want." The fight must be against monopoly power.

1415. December 25, 1943. "Social equality" still causes shudders among white people. It is necessary and actually means human dignity and real equality in human intercourse.

1944

1416. January 1, 1944. The loss of Buell Gallagher from Talledega shows that a stand for democracy is one that Alabama is not yet ready to accept. The regressive tax system is denounced and is especially wrong in wartime.

1417. January 8, 1944. "Let Negroes remember one thing: the greatest evil of this evil war, is the attack on the Jewish people. It is the most unforgiveable and unwarranted result of this collapse of civilization. The man or race that condones it, is lost."

1418. January 15, 1944. He recommends Ina C. Brown's *Socioeconomic Approach to Educational Problems,* a volume in a survey of higher education for the Afro-Americans published by the Office of Education. It leads him to reiterate that the basic question confronting us is jobs and income.

1419. January 22, 1944. Du Bois rejoices at news that in Springfield, Massachusetts, Chicago, and Pittsburgh, the school administrations have pledged that there will be courses offered in Negro history. Most people could go to school for 15 years in the United States and never learn anything of that rich history. There is much talk of general affluence, but Du Bois insists that at least 20percent of the population lives in poverty in the midst of the wartime "prosperity."

1420. January 29, 1944. The tobacco workers striking in North Carolina receive $23.53 a week; the president of American Tobacco Company receives over $4,000 a week. The Senate again killed efforts to appropriate federal funds for education. Our children are growing up without an education.

1421. February 5, 1944. Du Bois highly recommends the new book by Nathan Straus on housing and summarizes its contents. (*The Seven Myths of Housing*)

1422. February 12, 1944. Tribute is paid to the pioneering intercultural work for the past 20 years of "a Quaker teacher from south Jersey" named Rachel Davis Du Bois; her book has just been published and is recommended, *Get Together Americans*. The colored majority is embarrassing to such British statesmen as Churchill, Smuts, and Halifax. Praise is accorded the musical work of William Grant Still.

1423. February 19, 1944. Two Scottsboro boys still remain in jail; a committee is working for their release. Du Bois calls favorable attention to an issue of *The Journal of Educational Sociology,* which is devoted to "The Negro in the North During Wartime"; it is edited by L. D. Reddick. He indicates the origins of the Myrdal Study, reports its completion, and finds it to be "the most complete vindication of the American Negro." Again there is some talk of a third party and this time labor—especially the CIO—shows interest. Ida Tarbell has just died; Du Bois mentions the good work done by her and other "muckrakers" as Upton Sinclair and Lincoln Steffens.

1424. February 26, 1944. "The greatest color problem in the world is that of India." Censorship keeps news of India out of the U.S. press; there is no doubt, however, of the revolutionary commitment of that people. Amy Jacques Garvey—Marcus Garvey's widow—has recently written him of the election of the Black Jamaican, Harold Moody, as chairman of the London Missionary Society. A statement by Moody is quoted indicating that he means to place that society at the disposal of the movement to enhance the rights of Africans. Howard Kester—a radical white Southerner—has been placed in charge of the Penn School at St. Helena Island, South Carolina, which has an old history of successful education among the Black population.

1425. March, 1944. The national Y.W.C.A. has recommended an interracial setup for itself. The executive committee of the Southern Conference for Human Welfare has just issued a program calling for the end of poll taxes, the end of Jim Crow in transportation, federal aid *without racism*, for education. Their members are Clark Foreman, Lillian Smith, Paula Snelling, and Tarleton Collier; "God hold their hands." Net profits of U.S. corporations in 1943 came to $8,500,000,000; thus do they "fatten on the world's misery." He notes the forced settlement of 10,000 Japanese-Americans in Southcentral Arizona, and the establishment in Arizona of an organization called Toward Freedom, which urges an end to colonialism.

1426. March 11, 1944. Education is suffering in the war; double sessions and emphasis upon so-called practicality. The war is slowly moving to an end but there is insufficient planning for the peace. He notes that the state department has finally set up a Division of African Affairs; it is headed by Henry S. Villard, a great-grandson of William Lloyd Garrison.

1427. March 18, 1944. When labor is allowed to organize, this is attacked as an assault on "private initiative" but now that the U.S. government has loaned hundreds of millions of dollars to steel and aluminum and chemical corporations to expand, no one speaks of violating "private initiative"; and "watch after the war" when the loans will probably be made into gifts. Lever Brothers are the dominant force in Nigeria; this is basic to the colonial problem everywhere.

1428. March 25, 1944. The case of Louis Buchalter—head of "Murder, Inc."—shows the social origins of crime. It is true with all people including us. It is likely that this war spells the end of Europe's pre-eminence in the world. Probably the U.S.A. and U.S.S.R. will emerge as the leading powers in the postwar world—and China, too.

1429. April 1, 1944. The South Carolina legislature has adopted a resolution pledging adherence to white supremacy. The idea that racism has instinctive roots is false. Dr. T. F. Tsiang has indicated that China must industrialize in the future and that her method will probably be more like the Russian than the American. Du Bois summarizes an essay by Professor Arthur M. Schlesinger [Sr.] in a recent *New Republic* [February 14, 1944] showing that Lincoln's attitude was one of deep hostility to slavery.

1430. April 8, 1944. The first annual report on lending institutions operated by Black people has been released by the Department of Commerce; it was prepared by Martin Lancaster and shows "appreciable progress." Du Bois summarizes a recent book by Leland Stowe* about Asia, especially his findings on the corrupt nature of the Chiang Kai-shek regime.

1431. April 15, 1944. The U.S. Office of Education has urged Southern states to "provide opportunities for higher and professional education for Negroes." The Russians are losing heavily of their youth in defeating Nazi Germany and they alone are doing any real fighting; what effect the air war conducted by the West upon Germany is having is problematical. Du Bois notes that Adam Clayton Powell will undoubtedly be elected to Congress this November; he urges concentration on electing Black representatives also in Pennsylvania and in St. Louis. "Once we get a really vocal group of Negro representatives in Washington, the course of history in this land is going to be altered."

1432. April 22, 1944. The walls of segregation in the South are crumbling; the latest breach was the Supreme Court decision invalidating the White Primary. The formation of the United Negro College Fund was a wise move. The Bourbon attacks on Roosevelt may yet cost him re-election; and the President's dissatisfaction with the Democratic party is growing.

1433. April 29, 1944. When one observes what is being spent on this war, he understands that the lament that "we cannot afford" useful social reforms is a fraud. The National Smelting Company in Cleveland is actually combatting racism in its own plant.

1434. May 6, 1944. A Mr. Doar of Orangeburg, South Carolina, writes in the Columbia *Record* that there are only two ways of dealing with minorities: 1) the Hitler method of extermination; 2) the oldfashioned method of keeping them illiterate. We should choose one or the other! Du Bois announces with praise the symposium on Interracial problems early in June at Western Reserve University. He notes the economic enslavement of Bolivia to the United States.

*Leland Stowe, *They Shall Not Sleep*.

1435. May 13, 1944. Racist demagogy which so often assured political victory in the South is not paying off in that way with the same certainty—examples are cited from Florida and Alabama.

1436. May 20, 1944. Mr. Avery of Montgomery Ward is screaming about "private initiative" but his company hires few Black people and then only in the lowest paying jobs. How about allowing some "private initiative" for us? An Australian professor [A. P. Elkin] has written a fine pamphlet, *Wanted: A Charter for the Native Peoples of the Southwest Pacific*; it proposes greater freedom for these peoples after the war.

1437. May 27, 1944. The accomplishments of Harry Burleigh in music are monumental. The Southern Negro Youth Congress has boldly and wisely formed an Association of Young Writers and Artists. He favors a bill to permit immigration of Indians on same basis as other peoples. Du Bois praises Shirley Graham's *George Washington Carver*. He also praises Eleanor Roosevelt for her courage, not least on the Negro question, as it is called; she is "a woman with guts."

1438. June 3, 1944. Du Bois notes the arrest of a woman who operated a house of prostitution in Washington with eminent clientele and who, though not visually so, announced herself as "colored." She threatened in court to release the names of her customers and that is the last anyone has heard of the arrest! Senator Maybank of South Carolina has been screaming lately about white supremacy; he should look into this little enterprise right in Washington. The death of Felix Eboue —the Black leader of Free France—is a blow to the entire democratic world. He likes the stand of the newly founded Liberal party of New York on the question of racism. Churchill's assumption of British– United States domination of the postwar world is a foolish and dangerous one. Despite Roosevelt's hostility, De Gaulle will rule in postwar France.

1439. June 10, 1944. "The novel, *Strange Fruit* by Lillian Smith is one of the most sincere, trustworthy and fundamental studies of the present day South that has come out of that part of the country." The novel will long outlast "the cheap melodrama" *Gone with the Wind*. Du Bois denounces the forced removal of Japanese-Americans in the West as a most foul example of racism and greed.

1440. June 17, 1944. The treatment of India—and of Gandhi and Nehru—remains a basic test of the nature of this war. Secretary of the Interior Ickes at a dinner honoring Einstein, noted the existence of

racism and anti-Semitism in the United States and praised the U.S.S.R.
for overcoming such poisons since the revolution. Meanwhile in the
U.S.S.R. as the Nazis are driven out, rebuilding begins at once.

1441. July 1, 1944. Du Bois favors Henry Wallace as the Vice-
Presidential candidate in 1944 but reactionary forces seek to sidetrack
him. In a 12,000-word speech on the world after the war, Mr. Churchill
says nothing about India and other colonies.

1442. July 8, 1944. Visiting Tuskegee and its cemetery, where lie the
remains of Booker T. Washington and his wife Margaret Murray—Du
Bois' classmate at Fisk University; others buried there, as George
Washington Carver; he recalls many struggles. A recent issue of the
Nation details the enormous profits made by the Steel Trust during the
war. De Gaulle will and should be the ruler of postwar France despite
United States and British hostility. While the fascist Mosley has been
released from prison in England, political prisoners in England's
colonies in Asia and Africa remain in jail!

1443. July 15, 1944. Salaries of teachers in Atlanta are on the way to
equalization. He calls attention to very low salaries of Black ministers
and urges change. Du Bois hails the work of Sylvia Pankhurst on
behalf of Ethiopia; he calls attention to the recent massive famine in
India.

1444. July 22, 1944. Southern politicians like Eugene Talmadge of
Georgia met in Chicago with the objective of assuring Roosevelt's
defeat in November; it is likely they sealed their own defeat. The
Republican party platform is probably not sincere in its references to
anti-lynching and anti-poll tax legislation for their members voted
against these in Congress. Its approval of F.E.P.C. is important, but
that is, after all, a measure sponsored by F.D.R. In any case we should
make perfectly clear that in any war after this one we will not
participate "without being recognized [at the outset] as full and equal
American citizens." Two English scholars, Margery Perham and John
Carter, are quoted at some length in criticism of British colonial policy.
In March, 1944, Ethiopia formally presented a gift to the U.S.S.R. in
celebration of the magnificent Battle of Stalingrad, a battle which "has
become a symbol: the shield of civilization against fascist barbarism,
against those who call themselves a superior race."

1445. July 29, 1944. Du Bois calls attention to the views of Professor
William F. Ogburn that the government will be playing an increasingly
important role in the economy and that the power of the presidency

will grow. He notes that the Michigan Sociological Society has utterly condemned segregation. He quotes the antiracist remarks of Rev. Ashby Jones of Georgia and adds that "it is astonishing how few Southern white people dare to speak out on the race problem." Du Bois agrees with a recent warning from H. G. Wells against the revival of "so-called religion", filled with cant, that often follows wars.

1446. August 5, 1944. The Left in Holland is now raising anticolonial proposals. The life and work of the Virginia antislavery figure of the 18th century, Robert Pleasants—largely taken from Stephen B. Weeks' *Southern Quakers and Slavery*—are summarized. Harold Laski's *Faith, Reason and Civilization*, whose theme is the disintegration of capitalist society, with the U.S.S.R. playing the role of early Christianity in our own time, has been received very hostilely in the United States. Naturally, says Du Bois, but "sooner or later we Negroes have got to take sides" on capitalism or socialism; "the fight between them is the fight of the remaining twentieth century."

1447. August 12, 1944. Real-estate men are seeking desperately to stop the entry of the federal government into housing; they seek to protect their high profits. We are fighting in Asia to drive the Japanese from areas they have taken; but what will we do with those areas and the peoples in them? "Are we in Asia for profit or for progress?" Norman D. Humphrey is correct in a recent article in *Social Education* [VIII, No. 4, April, 1944] when he points out that the so-called race problem really deals with many socioeconomic problems and not a problem of biology at all. Sir William Beveridge correctly argues the need for a humane redistribution of wealth. De Gaulle has prestige because he said, "no," to Hitler; why Roosevelt and Churchill thought they could dominate him is a riddle.

1448. August 19, 1944. In the campaign of 1944 the real question is, "shall this land be a new realm of private profit and exploitation or a new land of socialized wealth, medicine, and opportunity." The greatest single question is the ending of colonialism, for unless this is done, the world cannot be democratic. "This is the problem to which I propose to devote the remaining years of my life."

1449. August 26, 1944. Though Gandhi has made some concessions to Britain, it is doubtful that these will be accepted. Du Bois notes that many of the leaders of so-called "farmers movements" are really multimillion dollar corporations and he names 11 of them. He notes the low wages paid miners in West Africa and calls for increasing connections among the inhabitants of that region. He reports on a conference of Indian youth living in South Africa.

1450. September 2, 1944. Du Bois calls attention to a recent issue of the *American Sociological Review* [Vol. IX, No. 3, June, 1944] which is devoted to the U.S.S.R. The death of Hendrik Willem Van Loon is a loss for the Netherlands and the world.

1451. September 9, 1944. Du Bois tells of his two-week vacation in August, as part of the Cambridge Gun and Rod Club, founded in 1894; since then most summers he has spent two weeks of fishing and chatting in Maine. Originally there were white and Black men as members, but now "all is in some degree, colored" and occasionally wives participate. He agrees with and publishes the International Bill of Rights, released by the American Jewish Congress.

1452. September 16, 1944. The campaign of 1944 is unreal for the only question revolves around the war and its outcome and the kind of society to build after the peace. Du Bois announces that soon he will be in Haiti.

1453. September 23, 1944. He describes the beauty of Haiti and touches on its extraordinary history. Du Bois reverts to problems of educating our children; problems intensified by the war. Perhaps parents will find it possible to put more time and more thought into helping the education of their children.

1454. September 30, 1944. An indication of the intense problems facing Haiti—especially overcoming impoverishment. But she has a landowning and sturdy peasantry. In education "Mercer Cook and his wife have helped enormously."

October 7, 1944. (No column on this date.)

1455. October 14: Du Bois enjoyed meeting again, in Haiti, Price-Mars, the noted anthropologist; he notes that Gandhi is soon to reach his seventy-five year and hails him as one of the great figures of history. William Phillips, the grandson of Wendell Phillips, has hitherto been a "correct" diplomat; it is said, however, that as U.S. Ambassador to India he has strongly supported the movement there for independence —this, perhaps, is why he is back in Washington now at Britain's request. The rural electrification cooperative efforts are successful and show the possibilities of that form of economic activity.

NEWSLETTER ON INTERCULTURAL RELATIONS

The *Newsletter* was issued under the editorship of Rachel Davis Du Bois, by the Committee of Peace and Service of Friends' General Conference, Philadelphia. It succeeded a publication called *Just Among Friends* of which three numbers had been issued in 1941. Du Bois contributed what was called "An Overview of Intercultural Relations" to at least two issues of this mimeographed *Newsletter*.

1456. Letter 4, November 3, 1942, pp. 3–4. "Cultural differences" are what "make our race problems rather than physical differences." Consideration is given to such cultural differences as characterize Jewish people, the society in the U.S.S.R., and the great revolutionary developments then stirring all Asia.

1457. Letter 5, December 16, 1942, p. 3. Devoted to "India" and her relationship with Britain through a review of Nehru's recently published *Autobiography* (No. 1078) which underlines the West's "basic unwillingness to face the problem of race relations."

THE CHICAGO DEFENDER

(The column was entitled "The Winds of Time")

1945

1458. January 6, 1945. Du Bois thought of the 19th century as having been one of peace and dedicated to progress; he worked in his youth on the assumption that once those having power knew the truth they would respond properly. But I now know that the world of the 19th century was not one of peace but of war and of colonial conquest. He urges the reading of Devere Allen's *The Fight For Peace*. (No. 1091)

1459. January 13, 1945. The passing of Europe was foretold by Whitman (here quoted) but now all may see it. Du Bois writes, that just as I was brought up thinking the 19th century was one of peace so in my economics I was led to believe that the poor were poor because "they were thoughtless and careless." In his youth people spoke freely so far as he can recall but the question of income and wealth and economics was not discussed; presumably every one understood these matters—or did they?

1460. January 20, 1945. Du Bois recalls his youth in the Berkshires; his people were poor but not as poor as the Irish. He worked first putting coal into a stove at a millinery store and received 25cents a week; and then errands and mowing lawns, etc. I was convinced that with hard work one obtained money and that if one was poor, it was his own fault. "It took me nearly fifty years" to re-examine and correct this opinion.

1461. January 27, 1945. He did not think of the question of the inheritance of wealth when a youngster. Why should one be able to inherit vast riches and so start out with enormous advantages over another? The Great Barrington schools were good, he thinks, but hardly taught economics; no doubt this lack in Massachusetts was repeated throughout the United States and perhaps the world; "it explains much muddled thinking today."

1462. February 3, 1945. As a boy he worked for the widow of Mark Hopkins, who built a palace in Great Barrington; his sympathies then were with the bosses, but he tells here of the source of the Hopkins fortune and what became of it and the fact that neither logic, reason, nor social benefit had any connection therewith. Further, that no one really knew the sources or the uses of the fortune and that no effort was made, then or since, in schools to convey this vital information.

1463. February 10, 1945. The argument between the millionaire Jesse Jones and Vice-President Henry Wallace over disposal of war plants is a basic one and its outcome will tell who is to dominate this society as the war moves to a close.

1464. February 17, 1945. Du Bois tells of his experience in real estate; four times he bought property and three times he lost it but the fourth time—with the help of the Federal Housing Authority—he has paid off his mortgage and now owns a home.

1465. February 23, 1945. Carnegie Hall means much to him: he recalls Rabbi Stephen S. Wise before the First World War, introducing him to explain the reality of our oppression; he remembers introducing Theodore Roosevelt at the hall; and hearing Roland Hayes and Marian Anderson—"staged like a fold of velvet"—holding an audience spellbound. But a performance he had just attended was unique: Dean Dixon leading an international "American Youth Orchestra" of every race and color in tribute to the martyrs of the Warsaw Ghetto uprising. The arts of us Black folk "have not only made America; they are an integral part of the 20th Century."

1466. March 3, 1945. Du Bois defends the use of the word, "Negro." He states that through effort and struggle—he mentions Paul L. Dunbar, Charles W. Chesnutt, James W. Johnson—"the word Negro is no longer an epithet. It no longer means slaves or despised people."

1467. March 10, 1945. The article is largely devoted to the reasons for and the actual practices of banks; now they exist to make bankers rich, and they indulge in gambling and speculating to do it. In time they will be conducted socially for the benefit of society and not for bankers.

1468. March 17, 1945. Early in March he attended a briefing by the Secretary of the Treasury and his assistant on the meaning of the Bretton Woods proposals. He listened carefully and then asked where in those proposals were the question of colonies and of cartels. He was told, nowhere. "Here you have the old dichotomy: is the restoration of the world after this war a matter of private profit or public welfare?"

1469. March 24, 1945. He has seen the cathedral in Cologne, the university at Bonn, the museums at Dresden, the complexity of Tokyo, and now all of this is destroyed. What a verdict on civilization! Why? Because of the idea of the worthlessness of the vast majority of mankind; that "kind of insanity" was bound to lead to this barbarism.

1470. March 31, 1945. Again, an insistence on the importance of cooperatives as a means of educating in economics and as an alternative in life to business for private profit.

1471. April 7, 1945. There are several Polands: and basically, there is the Poland of the rich and of the poor. The former have been abettors of fierce racism and anti-Semitism and none more so than Poles in the United States, especially when they have become fairly well off. The same development has occurred with the Irish in the United States. In his own boyhood, he remembers having anti-immigrant feelings, "this of course was a foolish and short-sighted judgment." Only recently, through the C.I.O., have the foreign-born and the Black people begun the process of knowing each other.

1472. April 14, 1945. Do the rich want prosperity? Who then would be their servants and who would do necessarily unpleasant work?

1473. April 21, 1945. The problems raised in the previous column touch us especially, for domestic service is something tens of thousands of us do. There is a need to raise the status of such work and to raise wages paid for such work.

1474. April 28, 1945. With Walter White and Mary McLeod Bethune he is serving as consultant to the U.S. Delegation in San Francisco at the founding of the United Nations. That the Afro-American has been so recognized—even if without any power at this point—marks some advance over earlier practices by the U.S. government. Basic to a real remaking of the world after the war will be an end to colonialism and to the diplomatic and economic policies associated with colonialism.

1475. May 5, 1945. The article is devoted to an estimate of the just-deceased President Roosevelt. It is a high estimate because of three reasons: the New Deal, his record on race relations, and in the war. On the first he did not go very far but he began the process of seeking to curb the worst practices of monopolies and of backing the organization of labor; with the F.E.P.C. and his new diplomacy vis-à-vis Haiti, Liberia and Ethiopia and with his appointment of Black men of real merit—as Robert Weaver and William Hastie—he did more than any predecessor. His joining the U.S.S.R. in war means the recognition of its form of social order and government as a viable one. We are lucky that Garner of Texas was not Vice-President when he died, and unlucky that Henry Wallace did not hold that position. One can only hope that Harry S. Truman will do well in the "tremendous task" in which "he deserves charity and sympathy."

1476. May 12, 1945. The entry is devoted to summary and quotations from the demands of the African National Congress in South Africa; Du Bois notes that its functioning since 1943 was not reported in the U.S. press and that he has just now learned of it. In essence the Congress insists that if fascism is to be wiped out, it must be wiped out everywhere and that the victors in the war "must grant the just claims" of the "non-European peoples to freedom, democracy and human decency."

1477. May 19, 1945. Probably in the drafting of the U.N. charter, Britain and the United States—they are working together—will maintain colonialism, but with the U.S.S.R., changes in France, China looming in the rear, a free India soon to be born, and changes that cannot forever be restrained in Latin America, it is likely that the U.N. will one day turn against colonialism.

1478. May 26, 1945. The article is devoted to an account of Du Bois' efforts after the First World War to bring the question of colonialism to the diplomats at Versailles through the 1919 Pan-Africa Conference. Details of its organization are given. It did not succeed in influencing the deliberations at Versailles and that is one reason for the Second World War and the present need for a United Nations which must not again dismiss this question of colonialism.

1479. June 2, 1945. The bay area in California is among the loveliest spots on earth. Recently the University at Berkeley conferred honorary degrees upon Lord Halifax and Anthony Eden of Britain, Jan Smuts of South Africa, and Mr. Soong of China. It is said that Molotov of the U.S.S.R. was offered the honor but refused it, saying he was not a scientist or a scholar. More persons should follow his example. Du Bois suggests what he would have written of each of these statesmen in awarding them degrees: Halifax and Eden for keeping colonialism; Smuts for "keeping the Negro in his place"; and Soong "for saying nothing." He recalls the occasion of his graduation from Harvard and suggests that there is too great a dependence on university degrees in the United States and in its educational system.

1480. June 9, 1945. Du Bois discusses California and the racism that is rampant in the South and less so in the North. In the area around Los Angeles the restrictive covenant is widespread and applies to Black people, Jews, Orientals, and those of Mexican origin. It is shameful and should be fought very energetically.

1481. June 16, 1945. No clear-cut stand against colonialism emerged in San Francisco but there are many signs—here detailed—that in the future the U.N. will stand in opposition as a body to colonialism.

1482. June 23, 1945. At San Francisco no real coming to grips with racism was discernible. The United States, with its holdings in the Pacific, is now a major colonial power. There are evidences of a ganging up by the leading capitalist powers against the U.S.S.R., "I seem to see outlined a third World War based on the suppression of Asia and the strangling of Russia. Perhaps I am wrong. God knows I hope I am."

1483. June 30, 1945. At San Francisco Du Bois has been talking with Dr. Emanuel Abraham, in charge of education in Ethiopia; he tells of his plans and notes that the second language in Ethiopia is now English and not French. Rumors that Ethiopians keep apart from Afro-Americans are false; they are a restrained people, but this is true in their intercourse with all peoples.

1484. July 7, 1945. Du Bois tells of his visit to the Redwoods of California, after passing Stanford University, "the Hoover monstrosity." He has dinner with the daughter of William James, whom he had known as a child. He recalls his great teachers at Harvard—Royce and Santayana, "but above all James ... that breadth of man who gave my younger years a glimpse of utter truth."

1485. July 14, 1945. Du Bois has dinner at a famed San Francisco restaurant. With him is Helen Hayes—appearing in San Francisco in a play based on the life of Harriet Beecher Stowe; she "is small and pleasant, eager and understanding." At the table, too, was the sister of Nehru, Madame Pandit, while Nehru himself is still in prison.

1486. July 21, 1945. On the 55th reunion of his Harvard class; of 300 graduates, 100 are alive. The consensus was one of dull conformity and conservatism; even reaction. Yet, all were pleasant, though none had any idea of the real changes, challenges, and revolutions that had marked the world in the past half century.

1487. July 28: Since leaving San Francisco, he has toured 19 states, spoken at large and small gatherings, and before college audiences. On the whole Du Bois is encouraged, and especially so, with his Black auditors, who seemed to him alert and militant. There is some change, too, in the sentiment of white Southerners, but it will take time and much courage.

1488. August 4, 1945. Devoted to the problems of Liberia and the efforts of Firestone and the State and Naval Departments to make it into a complete puppet. Lester Walton, as U.S. minister, opposed this and F.D.R. kept him on, but now Truman has accepted his resignation. The column ends with a remark on the great significance of the centenary of Antonio Maceo—the Afro-Cubano hero—celebrated with a splendid meeting at Town Hall in New York City.

1489. August 11, 1945. In Berlin, on July 20, President Truman said the United States expects and wants "not one piece of territory" as a result of the war. But the United States certainly did not behave that way at the founding of the U.N. where it insisted upon retention of its Pacific empire. If Mr. Truman meant what he said at Berlin, "he is in for a fight with reaction and Big Business that will make F.D.R. turn happily in his grave."

1490. August 18, 1945. The Labor victory in England points to the promise and the advance of socialism. Hopefully this will not be stymied in most of Europe again as it was after the First World War.

Will this forward movement occur in the United States? "We have got to work hard for a new organization of industry and a new distribution of wealth. In no other way can real freedom come to the American people."

1491. August 25, 1945. Most of us have been unhappy about the war upon Japan because they are a colored people and because the motives of Britain and the United States are suspect. But insofar as a Japanese exploitative ruling clique was trying to capture all of Asia, we welcome its defeat. We must be on the alert to oppose extended U.S. occupation of Japan, or any effort to repress the people there.

1492. September 1, 1945. Du Bois begins a renewed discussion of Pan-Africanism; he is attempting to hold another congress. He quotes his remarks made approximately 25 years ago in defense of the movement.

1493. September 8, 1945. In a time when there is talk of reconversion, he offers some guide lines for individuals: 1) reading—a good daily paper like the New York *Times* and a good weekly Afro-American newspaper; a good weekly (he mentions the *Nation, New Republic, New Masses*); 2) reading books and owning them, not depending on libraries; 3) education for one's self and children—in mathematics, sciences, psychology; 4) the making of real homes; 5) above all, work, jobs, and wherever possible, work that is challenging and fulfilling even if less lucrative.

1494. September 15, 1945. What have we lost and what have we gained from the war? War itself kills physically and also psychologically and this is a great loss; Japan's defeat and humiliation is a setback for colored peoples; military regimentation may take hold; and we "have seen in this war, to our amazement and distress, a marriage between science and destruction ... such as we had never dreamed of before." On the other hand: the war has forced a restatement of the meaning of "democracy" in terms of the power of the masses; Asia is no longer a mere appendage; China is in the center of history again; the great prestige and endurance of the U.S.S.R.; the clearly impending termination of French and Dutch rule in Southeast Asia; and the great "upheaval in Pan-Africa." In all this, the opportunity for human service of the Afro-American people is great.

1495. September 22, 1945. Du Bois refers to origins of Pan-Africa and its history after the First World War; he notes the impact upon this of the Garvey movement and remarks, " ... while Garvey tended toward commercial and political power, we were trying to stress cultural and economic development."

1496. September 29, 1945. The Board of the NAACP has voted to send Du Bois as a delegate to the Fifth Pan-African Congress; he notes George Padmore's role in this and that he is the nephew of the Sylvester-Williams who called the first congress in 1900.

1497. October 6, 1945. Du Bois does not want segregated education; it is generally bad, but he does not want bad education and at times (as in Harlem) one may have technically nonsegregated schools but precious little education. The point is to get good education for our children.

1498. October 13, 1945. In our opposition to segregated schools we must be careful not to demean the Black teachers and the pupils who often do very well, indeed. He, himself, taught only in all-Black schools, and the same has been true of his daughter. Segregated education is wrong because it provides poor education usually for the poorest people and results in more money being spent for those who have more money!

October 20, 1945. No column.

1499. October 27, 1945. He is disgusted with those who are attacking the play, "Uncle Tom's Cabin," and argues for its positive nature today when properly viewed. Moreover, in the book the hero is not at all what we mean today by the fawning "Uncle Tom." The answer is not censorship of such works, but its production and the production of fine works as "Deep are the Roots" now playing to full houses on Broadway. He recalls Inez Milholland opposing the NAACP campaign to ban "Birth of a Nation," but that play was a complete libel upon a people and was deliberately produced as part of a campaign to re-enslave a people. Let us concentrate on finishing the work to which Harriet Beecher Stowe gave her strength—our freedom—and not waste our energies trying to censor her creation.

1500. November 3, 1945. He recalls the Second Pan-African Congress (in 1921) and notes the roles therein of Walter White, Jessie Fauset, and Rayford Logan. He quotes from the rather fearful—but respectful —reports and editorials in leading European newspapers of that time.

1501. November 10, 1945. He observes that the leading white newspapers print almost nothing about Africa and especially nothing of the great popular stirrings therein. He quotes at length from demands being made by the Black people in South Africa.

1502. November 17, 1945. He has flown to Europe—a miracle—and describes the flight. "One of these mornings we will breakfast in New York, lunch on the moon, and after dinner, shake hands with God." With these means of communication could not the Sixth Pan-African Congress meet in Liberia in 1947? Would Liberia be ready "to venture the imperial powers with a vast world demonstration of the might and unity of the black folk and its final challenge to colonialism?"

1503. November 24, 1945. Du Bois reports on the discussions at the Fifth Pan-African Congress held at Manchester, England. The column is devoted to the remarks of delegates from the West Indies with their documentation of poverty and indignity and their demand for federation and self-government. "One delegate referred to the two 'M. G. 's'—Marcus Garvey and Mahatma Gandhi. It was interesting to see the widow of Marcus Garvey present, making a moving plea for the black women of Jamaica."

1504. December 1, 1945. Du Bois visited H. G. Wells; he is very ill. He describes his home and room and the brief conversation, while Du Bois served both of them tea. "The end of man is always sad. But the shadow which hovers about a great genius is ultimate tragedy."

1505. December 8, 1945. This is his tenth visit to London. He describes in some detail the impact of the war, especially in the working-class areas. The people are hungry and Britain is less cocky than before. The great political question is: will socialism really move forward and will the English socialists understand, finally, that socialism in England requires a change in the actions of London towards Africa and Asia?

1506. December 15, 1945. He has a half-hour talk with Harold Laski, a leader of the victorious English Labour Party and a man he had known since 1923. He really wants a socialist state and is intently antiracist. "Laski said frankly that he felt this kind of oppression because he was a Jew." Laski asked about the Myrdal study in the United States and Du Bois praised it highly. A young Jamaican Black scholar has been appointed lecturer at the London School of Economics; Laski has high hopes for him.

1507. December 22, 1945. Du Bois reports on a press conference held in London after the Pan-African Congress and its questions and answers. An Indian asked if he thought "it possible for the colored peoples of the world to gain their freedom without fighting the whites?"

After the slaughter of two world wars—and one would be hard put differentiating the victor from the vanquished—he hoped so and he certainly planned to labor towards that end, though 50 years ago, "I would have agreed that only force and force to the uttermost would bring the white world to its senses. ... "

1508. December 29, 1945. At this Christmas one may rejoice at the very significant advances on many fronts by Afro-Americans; yet at the basic level for the masses of us and of colored peoples in the world, racism persists. But in this era, "this is a morning when the sunlight is streaming from the East and I mean the East: China and India and Indonesia."

1946

1509. January 5, 1946. He compares the present with 1845; such comparisons can give one strength. On the basis of advances in the past century, "perhaps we have a right to assume that in 2045" second-class citizenship for us will have ended. He hopes it will not mean that we as a people will have disappeared for we have a splendid culture and spirit and this should be preserved and enhanced and will help advance Mankind.

1510. January 12, 1946. "Just what does the Colored and Colonial World say to the atomic bomb?" Will it assure domination by Europe and the United States? Probably not, because in the first place, the white nations do not trust each other, and in the second place, why is it assumed that nations such as China, India, and Japan will not be able to produce the bomb? What can render such disasters needless except "new freedom for colonies; education for all mankind; and the final end of the theft which is property and the slavery of mankind which is poverty?" Moreover, who can be sure, among the so-called white nations, of what the U.S.S.R. will do in terms of this new energy?

1511. January 19, 1946. He believes that emancipation of slaves by Britain represented "a transfer of capital to more profitable fields aided by philanthropy but not caused by philanthropy."

1512. January 26, 1946. The death of Countee Cullen at forty-six years of age evokes an analysis of his artistry, an insistence that only Black people can produce a literature truly mirroring their experience and that, of course, a Black artist is first of all a *Black* artist. But Cullen never really completed the artistic monument of which he was capable perhaps because of our habit of neglecting our creative artists. Thus, "we starved Richard Brown ... we crucified C. H. Turner ... we lost Henry Tanner." Somehow, we as a people, need "a sort of united determined effort" to really preserve, honor, and nurture our creative genius.

1513. February 2, 1946. Strikes are increasing and Black people should take their stand on them. There persists among some of us a hostility towards unions and strikes partly because of some historical justification, but basically, strikes are the weapon of exploited workers and unions are their shield. Now tens of thousands of us are in the unions and more will be; hence, "every American Negro ought to stand back of the strikers, give them their support and sympathy. ... " Mention is made of the importance of Ferdinand Lundberg's, *America's Sixty Families* (New York: Vanguard, 1937).

1514. February 9, 1946. The Tuskegee Center for the treatment of Black children suffering from poliomyelitis is discussed with details about its staff and operation.

1515. February 16, 1946. Du Bois is now writing a book which will attempt to place Africa within the context of world history; it is to be called *The World and Africa*. "The twentieth century spells the end of European domination of the world through the manipulation of the color line."

1516. March 2, 1946. Du Bois envisions a realistic discussion of democracy by the "Big Three": Truman, Attlee, and Stalin. He thinks that in terms of accomplishments in the war and since—taking into account such matters as Greece, India, Alabama, and the unity and endurance in combat shown by the U.S.S.R.—Stalin's contribution might well be the richest. At any rate, with the divisions plaguing the United States, "it is not Communism that we need fear, it is ourselves."

1517. March 9, 1946. The first meeting of the United Nations showed Britain and the United States doing all it could to preserve reactionary regimes, as in Greece, and preserving or extending colonial holdings. The U.S.S.R., alone denounced these activities and the press in the United States quite misrepresented the realities of the United Nations session.

1518. March 16, 1946. Treats the "outmoded" wage fund theory of Ricardo that was still being taught by Frank Taussig when he was a student at Harvard. Explains the theory with its concept of the "natural" level of wages and therefore the "proof" that unions were stupid and strikes criminal. He notes labor's demand for higher wages and its insistence that wartime profits were exorbitant. Du Bois holds that if the classical pattern of economic behavior continues, it will lead to an economic collapse "as disastrous as that in the thirties."

1519. March 23, 1946. The Fulton, Missouri, speech by Winston Churchill—with a smiling President Truman in the background—"was one of the most discouraging occurrences of modern times." Churchill has been wrong on every social question during his life—a determined imperialist, an opponent of women's rights, an opponent of the struggles for national independence, a fanatical opponent of the Russian Revolution—and now he dares to speak of defending "free people," with the British empire reeking of the blood of millions! If his policy is adopted by Britain and the United States, the result will be catastrophe for mankind.

1520. March 30, 1946. After a pogrom, such as had lately occurred in Columbia, Tennessee, there is a pretense at investigation, but there is never any real investigation in terms of the socioeconomic realities because there is never actual punishment of those truly guilty. As for the victimized Black families, is this not a splendid opportunity for organized and nationwide service on the part of the Black church?

1521. April 6, April 13, and April 20, 1946. Together a single essay on the relationship of the exploitation of Africa and the labor of African-derived people to the development of capitalism in the United States; the private monopolization that has ever since the days of slavery continued to characterize the economy; the growing need for rational planning and understanding that "industry must be carried on not for private profit but for public welfare."

1522. April 27, 1946. He has seen "ultimate beauty" in a plane at night overlooking a glistening Los Angeles. And another kind of beauty when speaking at Occidental College and learning of the principles of the group sponsoring his lecture—"Friends of the American Way." Those principles are quoted at length and they constitute a reasoned rejection of racism and an avowal of the justice and propriety of fully fraternal forms of social organization.

1523. May 4, 1946. Black people should be planning carefully for their futures since the aftermath of the war will bring many maladjustments and serious problems, especially economic.

1524. May 11, 1946. He tells of his six visits to Los Angeles since 1913 and the changes in people and city from then until today.

1525. May 18, 1946. "New Day at Lincoln University" in Pennsylvania tells of its administration under its first Black president, Horace Mann Bond. He has a forward looking spirit but with enormous financial problems. Can the alumni help it solve the latter?

1526. May 25, 1946. Du Bois is shocked at the "American Addiction to Alcohol" and this includes those of us who are Afro-Americans. The habit is a bad one; indulgence in wine and light beer is enjoyable, but the hard distilled liquor makes for befuddlement, addiction, and unpleasantness in general.

1527. June 1, 1946. The retirement of Lester Walton after serving from 1935 to 1945 as U.S. Minister to Liberia should not pass without notice. He has been an excellent public servant; " ... there has been built up through Mr. Walton's efforts a condition of cordial relations between his government and the Liberian and a chance for economic progress."

1528. June 8, 1946. The excessive religiosity of the West coast is well-known and often a cause for merriment, but there has also developed a splendid interracial church effort, illustrated in the work of Howard Thurman, co-pastor of a church in San Francisco, and the church of Christian Fellowship in Los Angeles, whose chief pastor is a Black man, formerly of Chicago, Harold M. Kingsley. His two assistants are white and Japanese. Neverthless, as a rule the church in the United States is the most segregated of all institutions which is "the strongest attack upon religion that could be made."

1529. June 15, 1946. Something is being done by a young Black Jamaican woman—who had attended the Manchester, 1945 Pan-African Congress—to assist the 1,000 illegitimate children with Black fathers and white mothers born in England during the war; her name is Anna LaBadie and Du Bois hopes her initiative will really help the babies.

1530. June 22, 1946. The "Demand for Higher Wages" being made by workers and supported by strikes merit the support of Black people; on the whole we are more sympathetic to unions than earlier, and we are now members ourselves in increasing numbers. We should even support the struggles of the railroad union men, though they bar Black workers, but in supporting them, we must call to their attention how they weaken themselves by persisting in racist practices.

1531. June 29, 1946. He thinks that "Summer Schools [are] Devil's Device" for "I would not say that nothing worthwhile was ever done in summer school but I would say from my experience that the amount that is accomplished either in teaching or learning is not worth ruining the tempers and softening the brains of those engaged in this questionable work."

1532. July 6, 1946. The U.S. (Baruch) Plan for atomic energy presented to the United Nations is wrapped in fine phrases but the point of the plan "is that Russia shall not have the power to stop England and America from punishing Russia or anyone else if in their opinion atomic energy is misused."

1533. July 13, 1946. One of his dearest friends, the physician, Thomas Bell, has died; an account of his life is given.

1534. July 20, 1946. Now that the United States and Great Britain control a majority in the United Nations they suddenly reversed themselves and have no use for the veto power, which they insisted upon in San Francisco. But power relationships may well change in the future. The United Nations so far has not been an effective force against colonialism. Meanwhile the growth of socialism proceeds in much of the world.

1535. July 27, 1946. Taking off from a letter by William Kassim in the *Nation* (July 6), Du Bois reiterates the need for planning and action to assure Black people employment in industry; in addition, the development of cooperatives among ourselves should be undertaken.

1536. August 3, 1946. Socialism is growing and the United States and England will not be able to stop it. The United Nations, dominated by those two powers, as of this moment, has done nothing to oppose colonialism; he denounces British plans to divide India in terms of a Moslem and a Hindu state.

1537. August 10, 1946. Cooperative consumer markets would be of great help to all working people but especially to Black workers with their meagre incomes.

1538. August 17, 1946. Secretary of State Byrnes is lecturing communist countries in Eastern Europe about democracy. The South Carolina politician does not understand the term, as I said of him in 1919 when he was attacking me and the *Crisis*.

1539. August 24, 1946. There is no organization or group now able to speak for the colonial peoples of the world; he proposes the formation of such an organization with "the right at least to sit in the Assembly [of the U.N.] and listen to its work and perhaps even to take part in debate."*

1540. August 31, 1946. On "Vacation Talk"; he is off for two weeks in Maine. Vacation is for recreation and should be taken with that in mind. Women working at home especially need vacations and they should be vacations for them in fact, not in words. He ends, "I shall never forget my visit while in Russia to some of the great palaces of the Czars. I remember Tsarkoe Selo where the rulers of Russia used to live in splendor. The great palaces are now given over to laborers for their vacation and I can see no finer compensation for senseless extravagance in the past."

1541. September 7, 1946. He lays out plans for a celebration of the Centennial of Liberia, "if I were master of Liberia"; it is detailed, "but I am not Master of Liberia."

1542. September 14, 1946. "Old Man Paradox"—on being Black and being an American, what to do about both, and how to do whatever should be done. He ends by saying that his thoughts require the use of words that the paper would not publish and the mails would not carry.

September 21, 1946. (Column missing)

1543. September 28, 1946. Glowing tribute is paid to H. G. Wells who has just died; Du Bois knew him well and saw him often, here and in England. He hated war and racism, was a socialist, a prophet, and his *History of the World*—though it almost omits Black people—is nevertheless a good book, "and Wells was a great man."

1544. October 5, 1946. In the elections coming up this November the main questions of our time—labor unions; colonialism; foreign policy; rotten boroughs in the South; lynching; job discrimination—will not be discussed, and the choice between Democrats and Republicans is not a real choice at all. Both agree on capitalism—on greed.

1545. October 12, 1946. From our own vantage point as especially oppressed, we should see more clearly than others in this country that

---

*In early August, the Associated Negro Press sent out the text of Du Bois' letter to a score of Black organizations and to the governments of Ethiopia, Liberia, and Haiti—in his capacity as president of the Pan-African Congress—asking for support to his proposal "seeking a way by which the peoples of Africa may be represented to the United Nations Assembly, at least as observers, if not participants." (It was widely published in the Black press at the time—as the *Atlanta World*, August 4, 1946.)

the old idea of "rugged individualism" and "private initiative" is vicious nonsense; we must work together cooperatively.

1546. October 19, 1946. "Education" is boasted of in the United States, but in reality it is quite poor; even illiteracy is widespread and the ignorance of simplest arithmetic and algebra is appalling. "We spend millions on education and billions on war."

1547. October 26, 1946. He praises and summarizes a book, *The Voice of Labor*, edited by George Padmore, containing the speeches by colonial delegates to the World Trade Unions Congress held in Paris in 1945.

1548. November 2, 1946. Recommends highly as a first-class piece of scholarship the book by Harry Davis of Cleveland *A History of Free Masonry among Negroes in America*; he summarizes its contents.

1549. November 9, 1946. Du Bois sees a deterioration in the manners of young Black people; courtesy is characteristic of Africans and has been of us. It is valuable and we older people should consciously inculcate it in our children.

1550. November 16, 1946. Summarizes the convention of the Southern Negro Youth Congress held in October in Columbia, South Carolina, where he spoke and was honored. He compares it to the meeting of the historic founding of the NAACP in 1909.

1551. November 23, 1946. Du Bois summarizes and quotes from the address he delivered at the above mentioned congress (No. 1550).

1552. November 30, 1946. In "Failure of an Experiment" mention is made that after five years a New York daily newspaper (he means *PM*, but the name is not mentioned) has given up the effort to publish without advertisements. It is symptomatic of the hold advertising has on the press in the United States; on the whole its influence is debasing.

1553. December 7, 1946. He thinks Christmas ought to be abolished, but if readers think otherwise and want gift suggestions, he offers the writings of Shirley Graham—especially her recently published life of Paul Robeson—and the books of her brother, Lorenz, especially his *How God Fix Jonah*.

1554. December 14, 1946. Du Bois reminisces about presidential elections from the time of Cleveland's first term in 1885 to the present with illuminating comments upon William Jennings Bryan and Theodore Roosevelt in particular.

1555. December 21, 1946. The F.D.R. presidency showed Black people that with political power significant laws and results could be achieved. There is little hope now in President Truman, but by concentrating on local elections, we can have an impact.

1556. December 28, 1946. For youth—Black youth in particular—he recommends this creed: to fight to eliminate poverty; to get work that is not demeaning; to get the fullest possible education; to make the most frontal fight against disease; "and in all life equality of sexes."

1947

1557. January 4, 1947. That the A.M.E. church had the capacity and leadership to unfrock two corrupt bishops is a matter for congratulation among the Black people. He, himself, always "venerated" such leaders in the church as the late bishops Daniel Payne and Benjamin Lee.

1558. January 11, 1947. He recently attended the sixth annual dinner of the Nobel Anniversary Committee. He was asked to say a final word; it was, "the emancipation of the black masses of the world is one guarantee of a firm foundation for world peace."

1559. January 18, 1947. All Afro-American people should express their appreciation to Madame Pandit for her successful fight in the U.N. Assembly for a resolution condemning the racism against Indians practiced by the Union of South Africa.

1560. January 25, 1947. The tremendous burdens of the Black mother, wife, and homemaker are discussed, with the point made that the husband "must share housework" and more must be done to get much of the work in the house done outside or done communally.

1561. February 1, 1947. The questioning of the right of Theodore Bilbo to his seat in the Senate is a good move even if it is not successful. The power of the Bourbon south must be challenged even more boldly. Legislation is important, but even more important, is the enhancement of our economic power.

1562. February 8, 1947. Red-baiting and witch-hunting have begun again; they are classical devices "to distract the thought of the people of the United States from the main issues which confront them and the world. ... Stop witch-hunting and Red-baiting by positive effort to attack poverty, ignorance and private monopoly."

1563. February 15, 1947. The proposed federal budget recommends that over half of all monies go to war, while for social welfare, health and security, only 4 percent is suggested and for education and research less than 3 percent. The priorities should be reversed. "Then we could build a nation to which everybody would be proud to belong."

1564. February 22, 1947. We should begin now thinking of the 1948 election and should watch not words but deeds on the part of the two major parties.

1565. March 1, 1947. The platform announced by the Progressive Citizens of America is excellent in general and in its specifics so far as the Afro-American people are concerned. It is detailed. At the same time, it is "most discouraging" to find "a parallel movement of progressives placing its first emphasis upon fighting communism, and classing Russian Communism which saved civilization from Hitler, as one with Fascism."

1566. March 8, 1947. "I am a pacifist"—by which he means he is against war; but not always. He thinks Poland had to resist Hitler, for example, and that Toussant was right to fight. But the experience of India is most impressive.

1567. March 15, 1947. The "greatest industry on earth" increasingly seems to be gambling. "If you want your child to be an honest worker with faith in the efficiency of human effort, for God's sake guard him against gambling."

1568. March 22, 1947. A story of a friend who gambled away $1,500 in one session. Du Bois is appalled and suggests that it would be better if he threw himself out of a window.

1569. March 29, 1947. He has been traveling in the South and does so because he likes the South and because he wants to understand; although he is not living there, he regularly travels through it. He expects the worst from whites and if he gets less, is pleasantly surprised. The Jim-Crow travel is awful; in this sense an automobile, if one can afford it, is a godsend.

1570. April 5: Fine tribute to Mollie Huston Lee, a Black woman, who is spending her time in a dogged fight—with occasional success, as in Raleigh—to establish good public libraries for her people in North Carolina. Here is a model person, "strong, brave, clear-sighted and untiring."

1571. April 12, 1947. A ride in a Greyhound bus in Louisiana has its unpleasant moments but Du Bois keeps seated and the driver finally decides he isn't Black! He is stirred by the growth of the state colleges for Black people in the South such as Virginia State and the College in Durham and Florida State.

1572. April 19, 1947. President Truman's message calling for entry into the war in Greece by the United States—aimed at the U.S.S.R.—is "to my mind the most stupid and dangerous proposal ever made by the leader of a great modern nation." Communism's aims are the aims of all decent people and because someone may sympathize with the Soviet Union certainly does not make him a scoundrel.

1573. April 26, 1947. The free, rich white man and the mess he has made in the past generation is nothing to what he seems to be preparing for the world in the next generation, if the world lets him!

1574. May 3, 1947. The late President Roosevelt understood that the old idea that one could do with his property anything he wished was a bad one, and if continued, would cause ruin.

1575. May 10, 1947. Topping Jackie Robinson in baseball is John Howard of New York—"the first Negro college graduate of Princeton University."

1576. May 17, 1947. A detailed description of the visit to South America made by Dr. Irene Diggs under the auspices of the cultural division of the State Department.

1577. May 24, 1947. Having met the grandson of Charles Turner—a Phi Beta Kappa at the age of 15 at the University of Cincinnati—he recalls the scientific work in the study of insects done by Dr. Turner and how Jim Crow forced him out of proper employment. What our people, and the world is losing in creativity because of racism and poverty! We should have some organization among us with the specific purpose of helping our promising children get the best possible education.

1578. May 31, 1947. He knew Bishop Henry M. Turner "and liked his bluff and hearty ways." It brings to Du Bois' mind the fact that he cannot lie to people who—having met him ten years earlier—are chagrined to discover that he does not remember them. Du Bois laments his "New England penchant for blurting out the truth, especially when it was unpalatable."

1579. June 7, 1947. Details are offered about the governance of Wilberforce University and efforts to improve it.

1580. June 14, 1947. Du Bois is in the South again; especially Little Rock, Arkansas, where teachers are fighting bravely for equal pay and for better schools. The total neglect of handicapped Black children —deaf, etc.—especially incenses and appalls him, but the fight is going on.

1581. June 21, 1947. In Washington a State Department representative was heard complaining that Czechoslovakia was not producing exquisite glassware but rather glass tumblers for everyday use. Du Bois does not agree that this is backward; whom do the expensive objects serve and whom the tumblers? The basis of all significant social reform must lie in the reorganization of the work of the world so that it is rational and aimed at satisfying the greatest needs of the most people.

1582. June 28, 1947. The recurring floods in this country are a reflection on the social priorities within the nation for with sufficient attention and diversion of funds from war, such disasters could be lessened greatly if not eliminated altogether.

1583. July 5, 1947. Most people think of atomic energy in terms of the Bomb; this is like thinking of electricity in terms of the electric chair! The taming of that energy and its use for peace, not war, would be accomplished quickly except for the power of monopoly in the United States.

1584. July 12, 1947. Many people still believe that poverty is necessary or the result of some kind of natural law. This may have been so in the past but in our day "there is no adequate reason why a single human being on earth should not have sufficient food, clothing and shelter for healthy life."

1585. July 19, 1947. At its recent 38th annual convention, the NAACP affirmed these propositions: poverty is unnecessary; colonies are the most impoverished areas of the earth containing most of mankind; socialism is an attack upon poverty; the United Nations is the greatest hope for abolishing colonialism and therefore poverty in the world.*

1586. July 26, 1947. Some persons have questioned my remark (April 25) that library facilities for Black people were inadequate in Atlanta.

---

*An editorial in this issue of the Chicago *Defender*, entitled "Du Bois Still Pioneers," reports his remarks and urges that they be given the "respect and attention" his education and life merit.

The figures are: the total appropriated by the city for library services, $268,215. Of this, $13,886, was for the libraries servicing the Black population—which amounts to 3 percent of the whole!

1587. August 2, 1947. The bland acceptance by President Truman in a recent speech of the morality of profit making business illuminates his profound ignorance of the world today. Data are offered, from an essay by Fritz Sternberg in the *Nation* (June 28, 1947), on the colossal wealth of U.S. monopolies.

1588. August 9, 1947. The Marshall Plan has been much praised, but I think it is essentially a plan to assure U.S. dominance over the European market and economy. Of course, the U.S.S.R. objects.

1589. August 16, 1947. We as a people must develop our own economic plans; this does not mean giving up or lessening our other battles. It means making the others more effective for we must plan together on how we make a living.

1590. August 23, 1947. We know more about stones and trees than people; for instance, we have no exact data on how poor people live and how many are poor. Dr. Oscar Lewis recently has published a careful study of this in one small Mexican city and it is extremely valuable work.*

1591. August 30, 1947. The poor are forgotten because their existence is unpleasant. Generally, the idea is expressed that their poverty is their own fault and that wealth marks merit. It is false and poverty can be and should be overcome; that means social reorganization.

1592. September 6, 1947. "In our thinking of American Negroes, we have got to remember ... that we are not a race, and certainly not a nation" but "there is distinctly an American Negro culture. ... The time will come when a course in American Negro culture will be a central study of students of sociology, not only in Negro colleges but in white colleges and in the universities of the world."

1592. September 13, 1947. Reprints above column.

1593. September 20, 1947. The great prevalence of illiteracy—much more than the figures given in the census—was disclosed during the second World War, as Herbert Aptheker demonstrates in a recent

---

*Oscar Lewis, *Life in a Mexican Village*.

article in the *Journal of Negro History*.* His essay shows, too, that with proper effort illiteracy was overcome by Black and white men with about the same aptitude, completeness, and speed. Discrimination in education is despicable, but "denial of education is worse" and that is the condition facing many of our people.

1594. September 27, 1947. The United States is increasingly unpopular in the world and only the American people do not know this, just as "nobody but Americans believes that the Marshall Plan is philanthropy." Civil liberties are being suppressed, and it is because the truth does not bear honest inspection. "When a man like Henry Wallace points this out, our only answer is to sing the 'Star Spangled Banner.'"

1595. October 4, 1947. In the 19th century we used to emphasize something we called "character"; this is not done now but that quality is important. Among our people there is too much "gossip and envy" and of "dishing dirt ... We should cultivate the will to believe in good because there is good in the world."

1596. October 11, 1947. The Masons in Massachusetts have finally, after inquiry, decided that the Negro Masonry in that state is legitimate. This after 170 years—that is progress!

1597. October 18, 1947. "The most serious rift in the moral fibre" of this country is reflected in "the widespread practice of the buying and selling of opinions and beliefs."

1598. October 25, 1947. Summarized is the account of the Black inventor who lived in Louisiana and in France—Norbert Rillieux, whose work revolutionized sugar refining.

1599. November 1, 1947. Du Bois reverts to the question of the children of Black soldiers and white Englishwomen born during the war; he quotes extensively from a British paper, *Mother and Child*, which reports that no solution has yet been found for the approximately 550 children.

1600. November 8, 1947. Discussion of the Marshall Plan again neglects the colonies, but part of its working assumption is the continued existence of impoverished raw-material producing colonies to be exploited by industrialized, capitalist nations.

---

*The article appeared in *The Journal of Negro Education*, Fall, 1947.

1601. November 15, 1947. In fighting now for colonial freedom, we must bear in mind the economic question, "for there can be no adequate expression of political power on the part of the people who are receiving like the Egyptian peasantry, $17 a year."

1602. November 22, 1947. The "long fight of the Negro to enter the ranks of Union Labor is not finished, but is well begun." Advances have been notable especially during the past decade.

1603. November 29, 1947. Du Bois corrects common misinterpretations about his ideas that have appeared, again, in a current *Ebony* issue. But he is especially incensed that *Ebony* should "think that the only goal for Negro intellectuals is to teach white people. I see no reason to commit suicide because no white university has ever offered me a chair. That is their loss not mine. I have spent a quarter of a century teaching Negro students in Negro schools. I am proud of it."

1604. December 6, 1947. The speculation involved in the acquisition by private investors of oil pipe lines built with federal funds is explained and pointed to as the antisocial essence of capitalism.

1605. December 13, 1947. Again Du Bois has received letters protesting or questioning the term "Negro." Names are but symbols. It is absurd to think that changing our name would solve the problems we confront. " ... In the future the time will come when men will be proud to say that they were descended from Negroes. The change will come in the people, not in the name."

1606. December 20, 1947. He has received a letter from the Grand Mufti of the Western United States—head of persons professing Mohammedanism in the West. He writes of his religion's opposition to racism. Du Bois knows of it but in Mohammedan lands there has been no effective attack upon economic questions. "It is my fervent hope that in Egypt and the Middle East the uplift of the mass of people will be the next step in the development of the Mohammedan world."

1607. December 27, 1947. Robert Taft is a candidate for nomination for the presidency but his stand on FEPC and on education is not sound.

1948

1608. January 3, 1948. Du Bois urges that Black people write Henry Wallace and ask him to stand for president on a third party ticket. The alternative candidates in both parties are worthless.

1609. January 10, 1948. Du Bois calls for support of a coming conference (January 24 to January 25) to be held in New York on "American Policy in China and the Far East." The conference is being called by people who object to U.S. policy of identifying the corrupt and reactionary Chiang Kai-shek with China.

1610. January 17, 1948. The loss of a cane cover and what canes have meant to him since his student days in Germany and what finding it meant to him are described.

1611. January 24, 1948. Du Bois has heard the views of Harold Stassen who is seeking the Republican nomination for president; they ignore us and they defend what he calls "modern" capitalism; they openly threaten the U.S.S.R. and wish that country ill. Black people should shun a man of those opinions.

1612. January 31, 1948. Du Bois sees the "world going socialistic." Because he thinks of "socialism" as government participation in the economy, he calls Franco's Spain and Mussolini's Italy "socialistic" and points to evidences of socialism in the United States, despite claims of "free enterprise."

1613. February 7, 1948. President Truman's recent speeches have had good passages on "race discrimination," but the Democratic party is beholden to the Bourbon South; therefore, words mean little since real action is not forthcoming. The same is true of the Republican party. A man like Wallace is needed; his opposition to universal military training also makes him a superior candidate for our vote.

1614. February 14, 1948. Socialism means "generically, the attempt to regulate the activities of men for the good of the mass of the people, instead of letting government or industry be run for the benefit of certain individuals. ... The real fight, then, is whether industrial organization shall be planned by private persons for their own benefit, or planned by the public through democratic control for the benefit of the state." This apparently amending No. 1612.

1615. February 21, 1948. He urges Black people to vote for Henry Wallace, a brave man who "has stuck his neck out" and faced racism in the South. The other candidates are typical "politicians." Of course, Wallace may not win in 1948, but if his movement gains some support now, its principles may be triumphant by 2048. All significant movements start as those of a minority and must win their way—as did abolitionism or trade unionism.

1616. February 28, 1948. Ed Pauley, of the War Department, has resigned under fire; he is a speculator and a millionaire. What does this mean? It means that he is a successful gambler and that he contributes nothing to the wealth or well-being of mankind.

1617. March 6, 1948. Du Bois has seen Southern white liberals who meant well yield under the great pressures a racist society brings. But it has not been true in the case of the Georgia teacher and poet, Don West, who is now being persecuted because of his honesty and courage. Readers are told how to support him as he now faces trial.

1618. March 13, 1948. Du Bois quotes the work of John Strawroom and of Leo Frobenius who show the more highly developed civilizations in ancient periods of Asia, the Middle East, and of Africa as compared with Europe.

1619. March 20: Again, an appeal for Henry Wallace with a note on how the press will no doubt try to ignore him at first and—this failing—will then smear him.

1620. March 27, 1948. The U.N. Commission on Human Rights, under Eleanor Roosevelt and a subcommission on discrimination with Jonathan Daniels of North Carolina as the United States representative, have managed to kill effective discussion of the NAACP petition to the United Nations denouncing racism in the United States.

1621. April 3, 1948. The U.S.S.R. representative to the subcommission of the United Nations on discrimination made an important proposal in Geneva in December. He would have called for receiving the two petitions* denouncing racism in the United States, the appointment of a United Nations investigating committee to examine matters in colonies, and the adoption of a statement of principle denouncing racism. The proposal, however, was killed.

1622. April 10, 1948. Further details concerning the debates on above.

1623. April 17, 1948. Petitions held in Geneva with the net result that given U.S. opposition, the petitions on racism (and on the status of women) were tabled or ignored. Jonathan Daniels "in a private letter" defends his course, essentially by insisting that the purposes of the

---

*In addition to the NAACP volume, edited by Du Bois, and detailing discrimination in the United States and presented to the United Nations in 1947, a less ambitious petition under the auspices of the National Negro Congress—the text of which was written by the author of this volume—was presented to the United Nations in June, 1946.

Soviet Union were "political". What of that, Du Bois asks; suppose
they were, what does that have to do with the substance of the petitions
and the fact that the United States killed their consideration? Was not
that U.S. act also "political"?

1624. April 24, 1948. Opposition is expressed to universal military
training, which means universal Jim Crow, and to selective service,
which means selective segregation. The history of Black men in the
armed forces is traced from the American Revolution through the
Second World War, showing a persistent pattern of racism and
indignity, which was only partially broken in the last war.

1625. May 8, 1948. A column in praise of San Francisco—more
beautiful than Charleston and New Orleans; the weather is unique, the
color line is least consequential, and the strength of the labor
movement produces a positive political climate.

1626. May 15, 1948. " ... The plight of the Jews throughout the world
has been even harder and more desperate than anything the Negroes
have passed through in modern times. ... They have met with
opposition for thousands of years, not on account of laziness and
inefficiency, but on account of their determined will to survive and to
be spiritually free." Du Bois denounces Britain and the United States
for placing difficulties in the way of those Jews who wish to go to
Palestine.

1627. May 22, 1948. Du Bois believes that the election of E. Franklin
Frazier as president of the American Sociological Society was an event
of great significance; the Afro-American press seems to have largely
ignored it. (The editor adds a note pointing out that the Chicago
Defender had news stories about the event on two occasions.)

In addition to his regular column in the Chicago *Defender*, Du Bois
from time to time also contributed signed articles to the newspaper.
This occurred in 1942 and five times in 1945 as follows.

1628. "We Fight for a Free World: This Or Nothing!" Chicago
Defender, September 26, 1942, Section II, p. 4. A special 40-page
section of this paper,—with essays by President Roosevelt, former
President Hoover, and General MacArthur—and Du Bois—was devoted to the meaning of the Second World War. He held that if
national unity is called for in the United States to affirm American
hegemony in the world, he would have no part of it. He closes, "To
uplift the stricken masses of men of all races and colors from the

morass into which greed for wealth and power has cast them—this is the object of this agony and bloody sweat of war—this or nothing."

1629. May 5, 1945. A description of the opening plenary session of the United Nations Conference on International Organization. "The ceremonies were rather conspicuously American, English; no other tongue was heard, no allusion to their cultures." The 17 representatives, men and women of branches of U.S. services, who were on the platform were all white. The only one who was cheered by ordinary people was Molotov of the U.S.S.R. No evidence of the color line in San Francisco; he meets friends as Rayford Logan, Noble Sissle, and Metz T. Lochard.

1630. May 12, 1945. Again from San Francisco; he is deeply impressed with the necessity "that the oppressed groups of the world get into close understanding with each other for co-operation in action." He flees the official delegation from India since they are "stooges of Britain" but is charmed with Madame Pandit who has no official status at the moment but is more representative of the will towards independence of the Indian millions.

1631. May 19, 1945. Du Bois writes from San Francisco; the NAACP has official status as consultant but this delegation also represents about a score of other national Afro-American organizations such as the March-on-Washington Movement, the National Urban League, etc. Our main work has been to try to impress the U.S. delegation and the delegations from other nations of the significance of overcoming colonialism, if future wars are to be prevented.

1632. May 26, 1945. He calls attention to the remarks of Molotov, who alone of the delegates, stressed the need to overcome racism, to end discrimination against women, and to terminate colonialism. He quotes Marquis Childs who stated that Roosevelt was anxious to bring colonialism to an end and had especially wished to do so in Indo-China; that Stalin had agreed but Churchill's opposition had killed that effort.

1633. November 24, 1945. A front-page story, signed, sent from London, headlined: "GIs Leave Good Impression On England, Du Bois Finds." This refers, of course, to the Black soldiers of whom there were about 500,000 stationed in England, Scotland, Wales, North Ireland, and the Orkney Islands. On the whole, they were more polite than the white Americans, and therefore, tended often to be favored by the British. The British did issue certain racist orders though this was denied. A Black chaplain, named Golding, was removed for opposing the racism of U.S. officials. There were some serious fights between Black and white American soldiers in Manchester in December, 1943. A rape conviction of a Black soldier "on ridiculously inadequate testimony" brought 80,000 signatures from the British for clemency, and Eisenhower did release the man. On the whole, Du Bois thinks the impact of the Black soldier upon the British public was positive.

PEOPLE'S VOICE

(From March, 1947, through February, 1948, Dr. Du Bois contributed a weekly column, entitled "Pan-Africa," to the *People's Voice*, Adam Clayton Powell's paper, issued in New York City. Through the issue dated July 26, 1947, the column was accompanied by a map of Africa with numbers upon it designating the names of countries and colonies.)

1947

1634. March 15, 1947. The British royal family's visit to South Africa is observed and West Africans hope the family kept its eyes open. An unnamed official, returning from the Belgian Congo, reports conditions have not improved from what they were before the war. While the Africans have won a majority in the Legislative Council of the Gold Coast, it is merely advisory; the power is in the hands of the governor and that means London.

1635. March 22, 1947. The People's Party of the Sudan has sent an appeal to the United Nations demanding independence; it is here quoted.

1636. March 29, 1947. Du Bois quotes from the late Raymond L. Buell, who noted that 1947 would make the centenary of Liberia; praise will be in order but long-needed social reforms would be more helpful. Description of the history and geography of Basutoland (in South Africa) is offered. The opening of the Legislative Council of the Gold Coast—the first with an African majority—is observed.

1637. April 5, 1947. The column is largely devoted to a description and history of Uganda with the murderous activities of Lord Frederick Lugard exposed.

1638. April 12, 1947. Evidences of rising African dissatisfaction with colonialism, from Nigeria, the Cameroons, and Northern Rhodesia.

1639. April 19, 1947. Parliament spent six minutes considering a new constitution for Nigeria; the problems of Robert Gardiner, formerly of British West Africa and now working for the United Nations, are detailed. The medical work in Ethiopia of Dr. W. Z. Park and his team is highly evaluated. Notice of the British effort to play off East Indians against African-derived and African peoples in various colonies is described.

1640. April 26, 1947. Du Bois notes that the Allies have not yet decided upon the specific boundaries of Ethiopia and warns about this.

1641. May 3, 1947. The *International Labor Review* (May-June, 1946) devotes considerable space to conditions in the Belgian Congo; during the war the stirring of social unrest increased, and at present, this shows small signs of being abated.

1642. May 10, 1947. A description of the new and very complicated British constitution for Nigeria is offered; the awful conditions in the Union of South Africa have been exposed, again, in a Johannesburg magazine, *Common Sense*, herein copiously quoted.

1643. May 17, 1947. The "great liberal", Count Sforza who is Foreign Minister of Italy, has been demanding the return of her African colonies—so much for liberalism! The history and present status of the Sudan are described. Note is take of the support of the Arab League offered by the Black sultan of Morocco, Sidi Mohammed.

1644. May 24, 1947. Prime Minister Smuts has promised greater authority for the Black majority in South Africa; this is a result of protests from them. However, promises have been made before and never fulfilled. There is a significant and growing consumers' cooperative movement in Jamaica.

1645. May 31, 1947. In November, 1946, Norman Manley, a Jamaican leader, said that all Africa must be united some day and that the same objective is becoming increasingly popular among West Indians. The two movements, he said, were fraternal. A recent edition of *West Africa* describes the attitude of young and old Africans towards white Christian missionaries; it is not complimentary.

1646. June 7, 1947. British and French colonial offices continue their mutual consultation, but they continue to exclude the colonial peoples!

Ethiopia at the Paris conference of foreign ministers (held late in July, 1946) was most impressive through the person of Ato Akilou who pleaded eloquently for justice and security for his nation.

1647. June 14, 1947. Governmental structures in the Barbados and the Bahama Islands need change in a democratic direction. An article in the *Manchester Guardian* (September 6, 1946) by E. S. Sachs, South African Mineworkers' Delegate to the International Labor Organization, exposes the peonage-like conditions imposed upon the Black workers and details the fabulous profits made by the owners.

1648. June 21, 1947. The strike of about a quarter of a million South African goldminers has finally been broken; about 30 workers were killed and "untold hundreds" were seriously injured. Meanwhile, Creech Jones, the British Secretary of State for Colonies, lamented the illusion, widespread in the United States, that Britain was still an imperial power. Details of the life of the Englishman, George Maclean, who died 100 ago, is given, concentrating upon his efforts to recognize the national rights of the Ashanti people in West Africa.

1649. June 28, 1947. The argument of the Ethiopian Emperor for returning Eritrea and Somaliland to Ethiopia is summarized and economic and cultural developments therein are reported.

1650. July 5, 1947. The terribly backward and racist conditions existing in Bermuda are summarized. Plans are going forward among the West Indians themselves for federation and greater autonomy.

1651. July 12, 1947. Kenya's importance to British colonial plans is described. A Pan-African conference of trade unionists was held recently at Dakar. The situation is tense in Jamaica because of high prices and great unemployment.

1652. July 19, 1947. The economic history of Liberia—marked by dependence upon Britain and the United States—is told with an indication that some improvement has occurred under the present administration of President Barclay.

1653. July 26, 1947. Britain is seeking to destroy the very old cooperative producing and marketing system developed by the cocoa producers in the Gold Coast. A history of Madagascar vis-à-vis French domination is provided; it is noted that a rebellion had been in process there for some weeks and that the situation remains unclear.

1654. August 2, 1947. An account of the ancient history of what had become Portuguese Congo is given; Tunisians are demanding freedom from colonialism and the level of struggle is very high.

1655. August 9, 1947. A movement to combine the Windward and Leeward Islands into the Caribbean Federation is well advanced. J. Merle Davis is head of an effort, endowed by the Carnegie Fund, to prepare movies for showing in Africa; the British authorities do not like this.

1656. August 16, 1947. The educational efforts of T. K. Utchay in Nigeria are praised. Improvement in the economic condition of Haiti is reported. The trade union movement in South Africa suffers from the devastating illness of racism, dividing Black and white workers.

1657. August 23, 1947. General Smuts recently offered Black people in South Africa some share in executing policy; Professor Z. K. Matthews, a Black leader, said the point was to change the policy, not share in its execution. A speech by Margery Perham on the BBC criticizing colonial policy is quoted. An article by K. P. Pankhurst in the *New Times and Ethiopian News* insists that only now, as the living standard in the colonial world rises, can that in the metropolitan powers be safely increased; the author adds that from the European standpoint we must not forget the words of Karl Marx, "a nation that oppresses another cannot be free."

1658. August 30, 1947. France seeks to replace her colonial empire with a French union; perhaps it can be done, but meanwhile from Madagascar to Indo-China that empire is in rebellion.

1659. Septemb er 6, 1947. Belgian colonization in the Congo has been most profitable; Du Bois thinks that the U.N. Trusteeship Council "will undoubtedly exercise close supervision" over that colony in the future. Portugal has always considered her empire a part of her soil. However, developments in Angola and Mozambique will increasingly force her to realize that this is fictitous.

1660. September 13, 1947. England seeks to hold a colonial empire in Africa running from the Sudan to Somaliland, but "in each case there is going to be a fight of European Empire with African freedom and autonomy."

1661. September 20, 1947. The price of cocoa in the United States is at an all-time high but while this is raised in the Gold Coast and Nigeria, the increased price brings greater profits to English merchants, not to the producers of the crop.

1662. September 27, 1947. The slaughter of hundreds in Southwest Africa in 1922, organized by Prime Minister Smuts, is recalled because the same area, which is very rich in minerals, is now being ruthlessly exploited.

1663. October 4, 1947. A description is offered of the enslavement of most of the people in South Africa. "Yet this medieval slave-ridden oligarchy is placed in the front ranks of the 'democracies' of the world. It is a situation too tragic to be even ridiculous."

1664. October 11, 1947. A history of Sierra Leone is given and the realities of its repressive present regime are explained; among its "great sons" is Edward Blyden.

1665. October 18, 1947. Du Bois treats the role of Eritrea in history and its relationship to England's plans to thwart the real freedom of Ethiopia.

1666. October 25, 1947. A publication of whites in East Africa quotes a Black African as learning with pleasure of the existence of a Pan-African movement. This reflects the tight censorship in Africa concerning such news; it also reflects the growing penetration of news despite censorship.

1667. November 1, 1947. Du Bois quotes from a pamphlet by Alice Baily, issued by a New York organization, Men of Good Will, which contrasts the ancient history of the Jews with the lack of any real history among Africans. Du Bois corrects such gross ignorance and hopes that the aforementioned organization "will try to base its future publications upon the truth and not upon fairy tales."

1668. November 8, 1947. A delegation from Nigeria and the Cameroons, headed by Dr. Nnambi Azikiwe, has been officially received by the British; it is unusual but is due to the strength of the movement for greater freedom headed by Dr. Azikiwe.

1669. November 15, 1947. Africa's importance is growing; Africans must move ahead to demand unity and freedom.

1670. November 22, 1947. Indication of the sweep of Egyptian history is given and of the decisive influence therein of Black Africa.

1671. November 29, 1947. The background to popular demands for greater autonomy in Kenya is supplied.

1672. December 6, 1947. Berto Pasuka, the 27-year-old Jamaican who heads the Ballet Nègres Société, has been hailed as a master choreographer. The société seeks to advance all forms of creativity among peoples of African descent; its appearance is part of the rise of such peoples to a more significant role in the world.

1673. December 13, 1947. Different points of view are provided in a pamphlet issued in London by the Fabian Colonial Bureau; it is entitled *The Kenya Controversy* and presents four opinions—here summarized.

1674. December 20, 1947. Extracts are published from a report to the Native Laws Commission of Inquiry concerning conditions in South Africa made by the Institute of Race Relations in Johannesburg; it documents, again, the racist, antidemocratic and intensely exploitative situation.

1675. December 27, 1947. In a case of alleged murder, Africans were executed and jailed without final appeal and now it is admitted that British justice failed; of course, it failed in Africa, says Du Bois, and offers specific reasons in this case, involving the family of the chief, Ofori Atta, who had opposed British rule.

1948

1676. January 3, 1948. Kenya reflects some "of the worst results of British penetration"; now the Labour government has revised a provision that would have somewhat advanced popular representation and thus again has betrayed its principles where colonial peoples are involved.

1677. January 10, 1948. The *Newsletter* of the League of Coloured Peoples, in London, quotes Bishop S. W. Lavis of Cape Town, South Africa, as denouncing the "two consciences" that prevail in his country because of racism. Benedetto Croce, the Italian philosopher, remarked that colonialism was wrong, but that he "wanted Italy to have a chance to help in bringing civilizing influences to Africa" and so thought the return of Italy's African colonies would be all right!

1678. January 17, 1948. A brief history of Tanganyika in East Africa is climaxed with the contents of a petition recently presented to the

United Nations on behalf of the 5,000,000 people there who have no rights; this was done by Marius Fortie, a white man, an Italian-born naturalized American, who lived in East Africa from 1901 to 1945.

1679. January 24, 1948. The petition of Marius Fortie, mentioned above, is quoted at length.

1680. January 31, 1948. A declaration of the National Council of Nigeria and the Cameroons, made to the British government, is quoted; it ends, " ... immediate steps be taken now towards self-government for Nigeria and the Cameroons."

1681. February 7, 1948. Du Bois spent an evening with Michael Scott from South Africa—a Christian in the sense that Jesus was a Christian—and an unnamed white woman also from South Africa. The woman told Du Bois of two successful strikes by Black Africans in Johannesburg which involved walking to work rather than paying increased tram fares.

1682. February 14, 1948. A summary of the career and present selfless work of Michael Scott about whom "the white press was persistently silent."

1683. February 21, 1948. The text of the demand for autonomy by Frederick Mahareru, Paramount Chief of the Herero people, presently in exile in Bechuanaland, is published.

1684. February 28, 1948. We Afro-Americans "know comparatively little of the great leaders of Africa, even in our day." One such, Herbert Macaulay, died in May, 1946. He was eighty-one years old when he died; he had been the founder of the Nigerian National Democratic party and president of the National Council of Nigeria and the Cameroons. The "stirring funeral oration" delivered by Nnamdi Azikiwe is quoted.

1685. March 6, 1948. "One of the complaints which Negroes in West Africa have against the British government is the discrimination against them based on color, in the case of appointees to the Civil Service." This is documented in terms of physician appointees.

NEW AFRICA

(Beginning in 1948, Dr. Du Bois became—with Paul Robeson—co-chairman of the Council on African Affairs. For six years thereafter, signed articles, partial texts of speeches and interviews by or with Du Bois appeared in the organ of this council called *New Africa* and later, *Newsletter*.)

1686. "The Riot in South Africa," signed, January, 1949. Du Bois refers to an outbreak between the Indian and Zulu population in and around Durban in the Union of South Africa. [This occurred in mid-January, 1949, and resulted in approximately 100 persons dead and about 1,000 injured, mostly Indian]. Du Bois analyzes its history and sources; he places blame upon oppressive and racist rule of the white minority and calls for effective action by the United Nations and the creation of a democratic society in South Africa.

1687. "Africa Today," signed, February, 1949. He takes off from Armed Forces *Talk*, No. 260, published by the U.S. Army, which emphasizes Africa's commercial possibilities. This has been the traditional concentration of the white world's interest in Africa, and now the United States means to play a major role in the exploitation of that continent. That way lies disaster.

1688. "Ethiopia and Eritrea," signed, March, 1949. The disposition of the former Italian African colonies is on the agenda of the United Nations; Du Bois here discusses the relationship of the above two lands and the needs of Ethiopia if its independence is to be real.

1689. "Colonial Peoples and the Fight for Peace," April, 1949. Extract from an address by Du Bois in Madison Square Garden, before 20,000 people, March 27, 1949, emphasizing the relationship between the elements of the above title; the "dark world is on the move" and that progress "depends first on world peace."

1690. "To Save the World—Save Africa!" May, 1949. Extract from a speech before 2,000 delegates at a conference for World Peace, held in Paris in April. To stop war, tear up its seeds in colonialism by advancing the cause of national liberation in Africa.

1690a. Testimony in part before the House Committee on Foreign Affairs, August 8, 1949, in *New Africa*, September, 1949 opposing a Military Assistance Bill. "Socialism ... is the natural and inevitable end of the modern world and grows out of the industrial revolution. ... To try stopping it by Red-baiting and hysterics is stupid. To turn back the clock by war is a crime." (No. 1827)

1691. "Abolition and the End of Colonialism," signed, November, 1949. The condemnation of Abolitionists was similar in the 19th century in style and content to the condemnation of Communists in our own day. Unrest in the darker world is charged to "outsiders" and "Reds" but it is in fact, of course, due to the desire in that world for human dignity and freedom. The propaganda seeks to maintain "colonial empires" for the benefit of "Bond Street and Wall Street."

1692. "Background and Significance of Seretse Khama Case," signed, April, 1950. Seretse Khama, chief of the Bamanwato in Bechuanaland, educated in England and married to a white English woman, has refused the demand that he vacate his rule. An incident of this nature will yet light up the continent of Africa in flames; it will gain its freedom in this century. The effort to stop it is perhaps the greatest single threat to peace in the world.

1693. "Repression Madness Rules South Africa," signed, May-June, 1950. *New Africa* has been banned from South Africa, Kenya, and the Belgian Congo. It is a high honor and reflects the title of the essay. Within the next 50 years, the Black majority in Africa will "take over this wretched and reactionary section of the world and make it into a new democratic state."

1694. "African Youth at Prague", signed, September, 1950 (mimeographed). In Prague in August he visits the Second Congress of the International Youth Congress. The members are mostly from West Africa—especially Nigeria; he was impressed with the peace-seeking character and noted strong differences of opinion among the delegates on socialism and capitalism.

1695. Text, in part, of a speech at the "Right to Advocate Peace" meeting, Town Hall, New York, September 28, 1951 in *New Africa* (mimeographed), November, 1951. In protest against the effort to imprison Du Bois; Bishop R. R. Wright, Jr., of the A.M.E. Church spoke and demanded that Du Bois, "our symbol, must not be hurt." Du Bois attacks the Cold War; he insists that the U.S. ruling class is basically responsible for it; and that a major source of the war danger lies in the system of colonialism.

1696. "Du Bois Urges Speed-Up of Petition Campaign," *Spotlight* on *Africa* (new title of the Newsletter of the Council on African Affairs), August 21, 1952 (mimeographed); the petition effort is in support of the Campaign of Defiance of Unjust Laws launched in June in South Africa.

1697. "The Last Battle of the West", signed, is part of the text of the keynote address Du Bois delivered at the Conference in Support of

African Liberation, sponsored by the Council on African Affairs, held in New York City, April 24, 1954, *Spotlight on Africa*, May 18, 1954, Vol. XIII, No. 5, pp. 3–4. That "last battle" is the effort to retain Africa as a colonial reserve; an effort that should be and must be resisted not only in terms of political independence but also in terms of a turn towards socialism.

1698. "Pan-Colored," signed, *Spotlight on Africa*, January, 1955. He hails the forthcoming Bandung Conference of the Colored Peoples as an event that will have lasting and decisive influence.

THE CHICAGO GLOBE

(As observed, Du Bois' column, "The Winds of Time," stopped appearing in the Chicago *Defender* in the spring of 1948. One of the editors of that paper and a warm admirer of the Du Bois was Metz T. Lochard. In 1950 he began his own newspaper and persuaded Dr. Du Bois to write a weekly column for it—under his famous title, "As the Crow Flies"—and it began to appear in April, 1950, running until December of that year.)

1699. April 1, 1950. Du Bois notes that this crow has had varying nests in the preceding decades and that "even the gag applied securely in 1948 ... now falls away." The emphasis is on the distinctive character of the Great Depression beginning in 1929 and its devastating impact upon capitalism and colonialism.

1700. April 8, 1950. The drive towards a new war has made the nation "crazy." The death of Harold J. Laski—whom Du Bois knew—is deeply regretted; the publication of P. S. Foner's work on Frederick Douglass is hailed.

1701. April 15, 1950. He comments on the increasingly reactionary character of national trade union leadership and of much of the "recognized" Afro-American leadership. Du Bois expresses doubts about the alleged benevolent motivations of President Truman's foreign policy and warns that another war "will kill the souls of men."

1702. April 22, 1950. He emphasizes—with interesting autobiographical sidelights—the lack of basic training in economics in the high schools and colleges. He insists on the social—collective—source of wealth.

1703. April 29, 1950. He notes the death of the scientist, Dr. Charles Drew, as a result of overwork and overhaste; he pays tribute to the work of George Padmore, "one of the best informed writers on economic subjects in the world," and calls attention to his most recent book, *Africa: Britain's Third Empire*; splendid tribute is paid to the indomitable Carter G. Woodson and his historic, pioneering work in Afro-American history: "no white university ever recognized his work; no white scientific society ever honored him. Perhaps this was his greatest award."

1704. May 6, 1950. The U.S.S.R. is not on the offensive, but rather the defensive in the world today; basic to the difficulties in the United Nations is British and U.S. opposition to the seating of People's Republic of China; the Labour party has attempted some worthwhile efforts in Britain but its fundamental failure has been to really attempt to help free the colonial peoples; the French effort to subjugate the Vietnamese people is evil and those people are bravely and justly resisting, "let us hope they will continue to fight"; an explanation of the source of labor strikes and a defense of them is offered.

1705. May 13, 1950. The charge of "Communists in the State Department" is absurd; of course intelligent people have often sympathized with efforts towards socialism, including aspects of this in the U.S.S.R. and for anyone now to fawn or to lament is shameful. Hainan has been liberated by the forces of People's Republic of China; where will Chiang go when Taiwan is so liberated? A third party is needed, for neither the Democrats nor the Republicans really mean our liberation.

1706. May 20, 1950. The strike of 12,000 elevator men in New York City was well conducted and has succeeded. The secretary of the union, Thomas Young, is a Black man. The worst situation for the French empire is Indo-China, especially Vietnam. Its real leader is Ho Chi-Minh and the independence movement is keeping the French army at bay and may yet triumph. It appears now that British plans to hurt Ethiopia through the device of Eritrea have been defeated. In the question of "the recovery of Europe" lies a desire on the part of the United States to dominate that continent. Disunity in Germany will not be permanent and what kind of social system will prevail there is behind much of the war danger today.

1707. May 27, 1950. Madagascar, conquered by the French, has seen many uprisings and will see more. The effort of dock workers in Belgium to refuse to handle war material is splendid.

1708. June 3, 1950. Truman's speeches are tailored to his audiences and often contradict each other; on the other hand, the speeches of Henry Wallace are thoughtful, consistent, and point a way towards real peace; several of the books by George Padmore are recommended. Highly recommended is the 1948 volume by Rayford W. Logan, *The African Mandates in World Politics.* The U.S. Supreme Court has refused to interfere with the antidemocratic county-unit primary election system of Georgia; "as at present constituted" that court "is probably the worst" in a century.

1709. June 10, 1950. The most important question in the world is peace; the Marshall Plan is not an act of philanthropy but rather a piece of United States economic penetration. Du Bois reports what he feels to have been the defection from a sound antiracist stand by Jonathan Daniels and Frank Graham. He notes with joy increased organizational activity by Indians in the United States and reports the emasculation of the U.N. Commission on Human Rights.

1710. June 17, 1950. The United States is increasingly helping France in its war in Indo-China, but "we have no business in Indo-China. . . . " An award by the National Institute of Arts and Letters to Shirley Graham leads to a brief account of her artistic and literary work. The recent jailing of Dr. Edward K. Barsky, Howard Fast, and others is shameful, as is the impending imprisonment of several Communist leaders. One of the Scottsboro boys—jailed at the age of thirteen—has just been paroled.

1711. June 24, 1950. A group of students from Virginia Union University are to tour Europe and the rumor is that they are to explain how "fine" things are at home. Du Bois hopes this is untrue. Again, a demand for the seating of People's Republic of China in the United Nations if the latter is to work at all. The gang-up of all political parties against Representative Vito Marcantonio to drive him out of Congress is a testament to his excellence. Many people are playing it "smart" today and keeping silent because of the persecution and intimidation, but "one of these days, and it is not so far off" those who kept still when they knew things were wrong will be "execrated and cursed by the majority of mankind."

1712. July 1, 1950. Tribute is paid to the prizewinning Black pianist, Roy Eaton, and to the fine poet, Gwendolyn Brooks. E. Franklin Frazier and Albert Einstein have issued splendid statements attacking racism in higher education. Tribute is paid the late Black governor of

Chad, Felix Eboué. The emergence of India and Indonesia as independent nations heralds the nature of the coming world. Attention is called to *The Book of My Heart* by Waizaro Senedu Gabru, which tells the story of Ethiopia's resistance to Mussolini's invasion.

1713. July 8, 1950. If China were seated in the United Nations, it may be possible to terminate the fighting in Korea quickly. Africa will be making the same kind of history as Asia in terms of major liberation struggles in the near future. The fighting leadership and honesty of Paul Robeson is hailed.

1714. July 15, 1950. His wife of 55 years has been buried in Great Barrington; she had long been ill. He had feared that he might die before she and then she would have been without proper care. Tribute is paid to her "singularly honest character." Their lives together and the loss of the son are described. A paragraph is devoted to the Peekskill, New York, outbreak where fascistic-like mobs attacked people for the "crime" of listening to Paul Robeson sing.

1715. July 22, 1950. The president of Virginia Union University has refused to allow his students to be made tools of the Cold War (No. 1711). The deepest tragedy of the war in Korea is that men still hold to the idea of war as a means of solving social questions; in this instance we know almost nothing of the realities in Korea and there seems no hard evidence at all that the U.S.S.R. is responsible for that war as the press insists.

1716. July 29, 1950. UNESCO has announced that racism is a lie but will racist practices cease? No and that is because of the socioeconomic roots of the poison and the services it performs for the rulers. Youth more and more are asking why. The rule of the few over the many is wrong and will be overcome.

1717. August 5, 1950. War induces a stoppage to thinking, but exactly during war thought is most needed. Korea shows this and resorts to force will settle nothing.

1718. August 12, 1950. The relationship between the Indians of Asia and the Black people in the United States has not been very good. A reason is the tendency of Indian visitors and students here to try to keep away from us and our problems; an illustration is the recent conduct of Madame Pandit, now the Indian ambassador in Washington, where she has adopted that city's Jim Crow pattern.

1719. August 19, 1950. The column is devoted to the Malay states and the fight raging there against British imperialism.

1720. September 2, 1950. The history of Burma and the developing struggle there for full independence are discussed.

1721. September 9: Du Bois' visits in the past to socialist states (the U.S.S.R., Poland, Czechoslovakia) and an insistence that the future moves towards forms of socialism are discussed. In present day socialist societies great advances in education, medicine, employment have been made.

1722. September 23, 1950. War must not bring about an end to one's reasoning in the name of "patriotism"; it is "our bounded duty to stop this fighting in Korea" and to help see to it that Koreans make their own decisions without U.S. "help."

1723. September 30, 1950. In the 1890's, when peace was discussed, what was meant was peace in Europe; today peace means and must mean peace for the world and a peace without poverty.

1724. October 7, 1950. Again, an emphasis on the over-riding necessity for peace and an insistence that it is those driven from power by social revolution and those enriching themselves in the West who want war.

1725. October 21, 1950. He explains that for the first time he has decided to run for public office [U.S. Senator on American Labor Party ticket in New York] because of the urgency of bringing forward the message of peace and civil rights.

1726. October 28, 1950. The hysteria in the United States does not reflect the existence of a true threat to the well-being of our nation; it is rather concocted by those who fear an idea and that idea is socialism. It did not begin with Russia and does not exist because of Russia but came into being and persists because of real human problems, such as poverty in the midst of plenty.

1727. November 4, 1950. The effort to establish a Pax Americana is madness; no nation can conquer today's world; he reiterates the basic character of peace and civil rights and civil liberties in the United States.

1728. November 11, 1950. Du Bois has campaigned not for himself but to advance the cause of peace, equality, and free speech; he may not win in this election but the platform will in time emerge triumphant.

1729. November 25, 1950. The heart of this column and those before it is in the following paragraph: "Social control of production and distribution of wealth is coming as sure as the rolling stars. The whole concept of property is changing and must change. Not even a Harvard school of business can make greed into a science, nor can the unscrupulous ambition of a Secretary of State use atomic energy forever for death instead of life."

1730. December 2, 1950. He demonstrates the manner in which taxes fall most heavily upon those least able to pay it; this, plus tax loopholes, allow the rich to place much of their capital abroad and to reap therefrom—because of colonialism—enormous profits. It is questions of this nature—taxes, colonialism, socialized medicine, an end to racism, better housing, above all, foreign policy and peace, which should form the heart of our political campaigns and education.

FREEDOM

(One of the efforts to fight back against McCarthyism and specifically to make it possible for Paul Robeson's ideas to be heard—if only to a few—was the establishment of a newspaper in Harlem by him and some friends—with Louis E. Burnham as the responsible editor late in 1950. It was called *Freedom* and appeared monthly, with fair regularity, until the latter part of 1954. Dr. Du Bois' writings appeared in this newspaper fairly frequently.)

1731. February, 1951. "John Brown: God's Angry Man," emphasizes the depth of Brown's religious convictions and the social nature thereof; his martyrdom was not in vain for of him one may say with Goethe, "happy man whom death shall find in victory's splendor." (Reprinted in *National Guardian*, February 14, 1951.)

1732. January, 1953: "One Hundred Years in the Struggle for Negro Freedom," rejects idea of Black people constituting a nation as such, but sees more validity to idea of a cultural unity, although "they do not even form a complete cultural unit." At present they are an overwhelmingly poor farming and working-class folk, though there is a mounting development of its own bourgeoisie; "its extreme development must be opposed." Needed are: an end to all Jim-Crow regulations and customs; strong national and state F.E.P.C. laws; increasing Black-white labor unity, especially in the South; universal suffrage and an end to "rotten boroughs"; more equitable distribution of wealth; universal free education "with systematic adult education."

1733. June, 1953. "Africa: Key to War or Peace," examines the degree of penetration of British, French, Italian, Belgian and, above all, U.S. capital into Africa region by region. Resistance to this exists and will increase and here lies a dire threat to the peace of the world.

1734. September, 1953. "Robeson Receives Peace Prize", offered by the U.S.S.R. Text of presentation speech, September 23, 1953, made by Du Bois who notes that the recipient is "without doubt today, as a person, the best known American on earth, to the largest number of human beings."

1735. December, 1953: "Smith Act Seeks to Stop Thinking, Leads to A Fascist Dictatorship," is a large part of the text of the speech delivered in New York City at a mass meeting on December 17, 1953, calling for amnesty for those imprisoned under the Smith Act. In addition to the point made in the title, Du Bois tells of his knowledge of Benjamin Davis' father in Atlanta and of his son, now in jail; of the son's choice of a life of struggle and dedication rather than ease and of his splendid work as a member of the New York City Council. "It is to the disgrace of this country that Ben Davis ever went to jail or that he is kept there now."

1736. April and May, 1954. "Colonialism in Africa Means Color Line in U.S.A.," is somewhat condensed from an address at the Conference for African Freedom held in New York City, April 24, 1954, tracing the history of European intervention in Africa, of the struggle against this, of its meaning for the development of capitalism and imperialism, and of the developing international struggle to end colonialism and to see to it that Africa is for Africans.

1737. August, 1954. "Politician in the Finest Sense," a tribute to the former Congressman Vito Marcantonio, who has just died; he summarizes his career and beliefs, emphasizing that his opposition to punishing people for their thoughts rather than their deeds was among his most worthy—and deeply American—activities.

NATIONAL GUARDIAN

(From 1948 to 1961, Dr. Du Bois contributed somewhat irregularly to the Left weekly, the *National Guardian*, published in New York City; its origins lay in opposition to the Cold War and the repression at home that accompanied it. As such, it was a supporter of the Henry Wallace movement and of subsequent efforts at developing a third party organization. The titles below are the headlines chosen by the *Guardian* editors.)

1738. "Africa Today", November 29, 1948. This is an overall introduction to Africa, emphasizing the idea that it is to be the center of imperialism's efforts to survive in the 20th century.

1739. "Africa for the Europeans!" December 6, 1948. Du Bois demonstrates by quotations from speeches of British figures, ranging from the Earl of Portsmouth to "the outspoken anti-Semite, Sir Oswald Mosley", the plans of the British ruling circles to expand exploitation of Africa. But the African peoples have their own plans.

1740. "Black Africa Fights Back," December 13, 1948. The title is illustrated with data—normally not printed in the leading U.S. papers—concerning strikes, outbreaks, mutinies in Nigeria, the Gold Coast, South Africa, and Sierra Leone.

1741. "Watch Africa; Watchword for Thinking People," January 3, 1949. Censorship of news from Africa prevails; all Western Europe seeks to reinstitute full scale exploitation, but this is being resisted by the Africans and will get the increasing sympathy of other peoples.

1742. "The White Folk Have a Right To Be Ashamed," February 7, 1949. Published during Negro History Week, it is largely a tribute to the efforts of Carter G. Woodson.

1743. "Africa: A 'Natural' for the Plunderers," March 14, 1949. Attention is called to the U.S. Army publication, *Armed Forces*, No. 260, which observes the richness of Africa and comments that it offers a very rich source for raw materials and a good market for finished goods.

1744. " 'None Who Saw Paris Will Ever Forget,' " May 16, 1949. The meeting of 2,000 delegates at a convention for peace was greater than any meeting he has attended; greater than the Universal Races Congress of 1911, the first meeting of the League of Nations Assembly, or the founding meeting of the United Nations. This was because at the

Paris meeting "the colored world was present ... as members of a world movement in full right and with full participation." The demonstrations of the hundreds of thousands and his meetings with those who survived concentration camps are events that are unforgettable as well.

1745. "Moscow Peace Congress," September 26, 1949. The Waldorf Conference in New York tried to alert the United States to the danger of war; the recent Paris meeting "aroused the world; now the Moscow meeting, held in August had, at its center, the knowledge that "it is not enough not to want war; the threat must be actively opposed."

1745a. In the issue dated October 24, 1949, the editors asked various leading figures for their reaction to the recent conviction under the Smith Act of several leaders of the Communist party. Dr. Du Bois was quoted as declaring, in part, "it marks the nadir of our hysteria and determination to throttle free speech and make honest thinking impossible."

1746. "What We Need," March 8, 1950. Du Bois' views as chairman of the Resolutions Committee of the Progressive Party at its newly concluded convention are summarized, "public welfare must replace private profit ... socialized medicine ... abolition of slums ... social security ... consumers co-operation."

1747. " 'No Progress Without Peace,' " October 4, 1950. It is the full text of the statement issued by Du Bois on the opening of the American Labor Party campaign in 1950 (in which he stood as candidate for the U.S. Senate). In addition to the title, the following, italicized in the original, gives its essence, *"What the American Labor Party asserts is that the present plan of* Big *Business to compel the world to adopt our philosophy and our methods by force of arms is not only unreasonable in the light of our failures, but impossible in itself and can only end in disaster."*

1748. " 'No Power Can Stop Us,' " October 11, 1950. A report with partial quotations of a speech in the election campaign made by Du Bois before 3,000 people in Harlem; he was introduced by Paul Robeson. The text shows concentration upon who truly holds power in the United States, how this must be changed, the great issues of peace, and the enhancement of the rights of Black people, which have led him to run for public office for the first time in his life.

1749. "U.S. Needs No More Cowards," October 25, 1950. A large part of the campaign address delivered in Rochester, New York, with emphasis upon the need to reverse the Cold War and internal repression policies of the Truman administration.

1750. "Money Buys American Elections," December 13, 1950. He was astonished to get about 200,000 votes; and he notes that 1,000,000 out of 5,000,000 voters preferred to stay at home. The influence of money was overwhelming; he was able only to scratch the surface in reaching people, yet there were those 200,000 votes. "It was a fine adventure. I enjoyed it."

1751. "The Big Problem: To Get the Truth to the People," January 24, 1951. He deals with the appearances in the past of third party movements; he states such an effort on a mass basis is required now. Because of media monopolization, this will require in our era, "house-to-house, door-to-door canvassing on a scale never before attempted in modern times ... not simply in campaigns but especially between campaigns."

1752. " 'There Must Come a Vast Social Change in the United States,' " July 11, 1951. " ... Either in some way or to some degree, we socialize our economy, restore the New Deal and inaugurate the welfare state, or we descend into military fascism which will kill all dreams of democracy, or the abolition of poverty and ignorance, or of peace instead of war." (Text of a speech delivered on June 30 before 7,000 people in Chicago; it was part of a month tour of the mid-West for the campaign to fight the indictment of Du Bois and four codefendants under the McCormick Act as "unregistered foreign agents." He spoke to tens of thousands in St. Paul, Gary, Oakland, Los Angeles, San Francisco, Tacoma, Portland, Denver, Seattle, Cleveland; press coverage was almost completely absent, except for St. Paul, and Gary.

1753. "A Call to Courage", October 3, 1951. Part of the text of an address delivered on September 28, 1951, at a packed meeting in Town Hall, New York, again in defense of Du Bois and codefendants in a trial to begin in November. "My words are not a counsel of despair, rather a call to new courage and determination to know the truth." Essentially a part of the truth as he saw it was the following idea:

> American exploiters and overlords drove the Chinese peasants straight into the arms of communism. The same thing will happen in Africa, the West Indies, Southeast Asia, and South America,

unless this vast reservoir of world wealth becomes a source of peace and plenty instead of perpetual incentive for greed to wage war.

1754. "The Rise of American Negroes," January 2, 1952. A review of H. Aptheker's *A Documentary History of the Negro People in the United States*; Du Bois refers to the author's past work, especially concerning slave rebellions and highly estimates the present book; he adds, "it will not be reviewed in the commercial press" because of the author's politics.

1755. "The Choice That Confronts America's Negroes," February 13, 1952. Class lines are mounting among the Afro-American population which can disrupt unity; if this is kept to a minimum and if Black people do not mimic the economics of the dominant whites, then a united Black people will find it possible to unite with other oppressed and disadvantaged peoples—including white—and so help "loose for future civilization the vast energy and potentialities of the mass of human beings now held in thrall by poverty, ignorance and disease."

1756. "Come on Out: The Dream Is Ours!" May 1, 1952. A dream of the future when antiwar and antimilitarism forces have emerged triumphant in U.S. politics; how the federal budget might be reallocated in terms of 90 percent for socially useful purposes and perhaps 10 percent for arms. And how this shift in the United States will be part of a world-wide change, with East and West Germany coming to agreement between themselves and with Poland and the U.S.S.R. The conclusion is the title.

1757. "'We Cry Aloud,'" July 10, 1952. Major excerpts from the keynote address by Du Bois at the Progressive party convention held in Chicago, July 4. The opening paragraph is the theme: "The platform of the Progressive Party may be reduced to these planks: Stop the Korean War; Offer Friendship to the Soviet Union and China; Restore and Rebuild the United States."

1758. "The Negro Voter and the 1952 Elections," September 11, 1952. For the Black voter the two parties are identical; on the other hand, his power has been enhanced and so how to use it is an even greater puzzle than in the past. The Progressive candidacy of Vincent Hallinan and Charlotta Bass—a Black woman from California—would be very attractive to Black voters if they learned of it and felt that they could with safety vote for it. Du Bois urges that they do so as an indication of what Black people need and want.

1759. "On a Nation Going Mad," December 4, 1952. Examples of senseless violence and of vindictive persecution are offered. "They are not simply wrong and evil—they are crazy in pattern. ... In the end the nation develops a pattern which is evil; and individuals follow in wild, cruel deeds, which drive them insane. Civilization falls."

1760. "In Defense of Beasts", December 18, 1952. A spoof on the habit of insulting animals in English—such as snaky, dumb as sheep, the jackass and the Democratic party, the elephant and the Republican party, etc.—all of which is insulting to the beasts.

1761. "The Hard-Bit Man in the Loud Shirts," January 22, 1953. Of Truman and his administration: "they distort the Truth and the Right so completely, that the nation last November said in vast despair: 'Anything but Truman—even Eisenhower.'" Included is a two-column table with "Truman" heading one column and "Truth" the other and contrasting Truman's statements with realities as Du Bois sees the latter, especially in relations with the U.S.S.R.

1762. "On the Collection of Honest News," January 29, 1953. From a speech delivered at the City Center of New York, January 16, 1953, for the fourth anniversary of the *National Guardian*; an appeal for maintaining an independent and radical newspaper as important to the intellectual and political health of the country.

1763. "Color Lines," February 12, 1953. He had written that the color line was to be the problem of the 20th century; recent developments in the United Nations show it might have been true. But only the U.S.S.R. and "her sister group of states" vote consistently "non-white" and for this Britain, France, and the United States really ought to be thankful.

1764. "On Stalin," March 16, 1953. Written on the occasion of Stalin's death, Du Bois finds him to have been "a great man; few other men of the 20th century approach his stature." Notable, too, is his attack upon Trotsky and his movement. Stalin's preparation and leadership in the Second World War are especially commended.

1765. "On Cats, Public Manners and Education of Educators," March 23, 1953. A reader notes his omission of cats in his recent piece in defense of animals. He does confess to a certain prejudice and apologizes. Recently he received a letter to address a meeting of educators and accepted. But since others had second thoughts, the invitation was withdrawn. He received a phone call from a worried person who wanted to know if he had received the letter. Yes, he replied; there was a pause on the line and Du Bois then understood and added, "Don't worry. I do not plan to be present."

1766. "The Commonsense Party," April 6, 1953. Du Bois provides planks for such a party with emphasis on antiwar, social welfare, and what are now called ecological demands.

1767. "'The Right to Speak Up Implies the Right to Keep Silent,'" May 4, 1953. An examination of the statement on "Rights and Responsibilities" issued March 30 by the Association of American Universities finds its opening section a quite good defense of universities and withal it is "a brave, forthright statement." But its final section violates and contradicts all that went before because in fact it is a defense of McCarthyism, an attack upon Marxism, socialism, communism, and the Soviet Union. It rationalizes a shameful period when Shostakovich and Picasso have been banned from our shores, and when scores of professors have been fired with hundreds of our best teachers, "thousands of college students driven into hysterical cowardice" while others have been jailed. And then all this is called, "*Gerechtige Gott*—Academic Freedom!"

1768. "On the Right to Express and Hear Unpopular Opinion," May 25, 1953. This right is basic to democracy and he had been brought up believing fervently in the need to read and consider views opposite from his own. It is difficult now to get access to diverse views and every American who believes in democracy should resist such curbing, or else our children later will wonder how we could permit the present witch-hunting to continue.

1769. "Of A Man Born of the People," June 8, 1953. A long and highly favorable review of *Born of the People* by Luis Taruc, then a leader of the Left anticolonial struggle in the Philippines.

1770. "An Epitaph for Senator Taft," August 10, 1953. Robert Taft is one of the 200,000 Americans who die each year of cancer. He was also one of the very few national public figures with a mind that was worth listening to, although almost always Du Bois thought him wrong. His death from cancer highlights the lop-sided priorities of our society that spends billions of dollars for war and pennies for medical research.

1771. "Dr. Du Bois Scans His Crystal Ball," September 21, 1953. He outlines the 1954 campaign; Joseph McCarthy for president and Louis Budenz—now professor of moral philosophy—for vice-president; the Cabinet will be occupied by the leading corporations rather than their representatives, except for the Department of Education and Health —that will be represented by the American Medical Association. The suggested platform is the reverse of the Ten Commandments.

1772. "Third Party or 'Lesser Evil'?" October 19, 1953. Excerpted from his address at the annual dinner of the American Labor party in New York City and a careful argument for the role and service of a third party in U.S. politics.

1773. "1876 and Today," February 18, 1954. The betrayal of Reconstruction is analogous to the betrayal of democracy and hopes for an altered foreign policy today. One led to disaster and the other will, too.

1774. "The Great Tradition in English Literature," March 8, 1954. It is a review of the book by that title; the author, Annette Rubinstein, "has described my well-known authors from the point of view of what they knew and realized of the want and suffering of the mass of men."

1775. "Cannot This Paralyzed Nation Awake?" April 12, 1954. A call for the development of a peace movement in the United States, "shall Gandhi plan our future, or McCarthy?"

1776. "A Third Party—Or Even A Second," May 17, 1954. A real choice in U.S. politics is not now provided but it is desperately needed.

1777. "The School Segregation Decision," May 31, 1954. A history of the fight that finally led to this decision of the Supreme Court. Racism still exists and much must be done even to implement this decision in the area of education. Still, the decision is cause for rejoicing, "many will say complete freedom and equality between black and white Americans is impossible. Perhaps; but I have seen the Impossible happen. It did happen on May 17, 1954."

1777a. (In a story by John T. McManus on the funeral of Vito Marcantonio (August 23, 1954) the eulogy offered by the Doctor is quoted quite fully.)

1778. "Seeds of Destruction", October 25, 1954. A review of the book with that title by Cedric Belfrage, praising it highly for its disclosures concerning Allied policy in the early period of the occupation of Hitler's Germany.

1779. "American Negroes and Africa," February 14, 1955. He tells of the founding, in 1939, under the leadership of Paul Robeson, of the Council on African Affairs which was killed a decade later by the federal government as part of the Cold War. The exploitation of Africa has been intensified but resistance thereto in Africa has grown. The Black press does not cover that story perhaps as part of an understanding that if Afro-Americans acquiesce in the exploitation of Africa, they—or leaders among them—will be given rewards and positions. When Black youth learn of this kind of deal, it is likely that they will protest mightily.

1780. "Ethiopia: State Socialism Under An Emperor," February 21, 1955. A brief history of the country, an indication of the Emperor's use of capital from many foreign countries in an effort to modernize the nation and conjecture on its future.

1781. "Uganda—and the Prisoner of Oxford," March 14, 1955. Of the history of Uganda, recent revolutionary strivings and the arrest of its king and his exile to England.

1782. "British West Africa: 35,000,000 Free?" March 21, 1955. He deals with the history and the current situation in what used to be the Gold Coast region of Africa—the present Ghana and Nigeria.

1783. "The Belgian Congo: Copper Cauldron," March 28, 1955. He discusses the modern history of the land, its economic realities and the current political developments within and without.

1784. "Kenya: The War That Can't Be Won," April 4, 1955. Du Bois tells of Jomo Kenyatta, whom he knows, and of the struggle for independence which he leads—even while in jail. That struggle cannot be suppressed forever.

1785. "Africa: Declaration of Independence Near?", April 18, 1955. An examination of what remains of political and economic imperialism on the continent and a prophecy that this century should witness its termination. Du Bois offers a projected continental declaration of independence.

1786. "What Is Wrong With the United States?", May 9, 1954, (text of address at a meeting called by *National Guardian,* in New York City, April 20). "We did not understand that we were too late for colonial imperialism and had to yield freedom to the colored world or give up our own. We elected to give up our own and to use war to help our effort. The price is too great."

1787. " 'My Beliefs are None of Your Business,' " October 10, 1955. The title is from the text of a letter by Du Bois sent to Frances G. Knight of the U.S. Passport Office upon her refusal to grant him a passport for travel to Europe. The whole correspondence is here printed; Dr. Du Bois did not get his passport at this time.

1788. "The Wealth of the West *vs.* A Chance for Exploited Mankind," November 28, 1955. Partial text of an address delivered in Chicago, on October 28, following the holding of the Geneva meeting of the foreign ministers of France, Great Britain, the United States and the Soviet Union, which, it was hoped, might mark a step forward towards disarmament. The connection between the wealth and the exploitation of the title is explained in detail. The conclusion is: "The wealth, waste and luxury of the United States, Britain, and France must be sternly held in check if the rest of mankind is to have a chance at decency in our time. ... The alternative is war and barbarism. ... "

1789. December 5, 1955, excerpts are printed from the speech by Du Bois at the seventh anniversary dinner of the *National Guardian* held in New York on November 17; this is an appeal for funds in order to keep alive a radical and dissenting press so badly needed at this time in the United States.

1790. "Looking a Gift Horse in the Motor," December 26, 1955. Du Bois comments upon the nature of democracy and the need to seek its restoration, evoked by the announcement that Henry Ford II has appropriated half a billion dollars to assist higher education.

1791. "Let's Restore Democracy to America," January 2, 1956. "Come back home and look at America. ... Set your own house in order before you try to rule the world, or to buy its submission. ... ."

1792. "The Negro in America Today" began a series of five articles on that theme, which appeared in the issues dated: January 16, January 23, January 30, February 13, and March 5, 1956. No fully scientific study has been made on this subject and so reports must be general. Advances in politics, economics, education, and the arts have been made, but the masses remain an oppressed people. An "outstanding fact" about the Negro people today is the intensification of class divisions. In the South bitter battles are shaping up and they will be among the decisive ones for Black people and for the nation. Democracy is not obsolescent; it has not been tried, and especially in the United States, racism has vitiated it as its twin, colonialism, has on a world-wide scale. A result here is the enormously disproportionate power of an oligarchic and racist South; until this is terminated there can be no serious talk of democracy in the United States.

1793. "The Theory of a Third Party," March 26, 1956. The theory is sound and the need is great. We tried in 1948 and the effort was worthwhile, even if Wallace himself broke down in the effort. But with 1956 no effective opposition vote is possible; therefore, he will not vote and in this way express his opposition.

1794. "Cold War Hysteria," June 11, 1956. Du Bois remarks prepared for a debate held at Carnegie Hall in New York on May 27 (participating in addition to Du Bois were: Eugene Dennis, General Secretary, Communist party; Roger Baldwin, International League for the Rights of Man; Norman Thomas, Socialist party leader; A. J. Muste and Charles Lawrence, Fellowship of Reconciliation. America must look within to find the trouble; not in China and not in the Soviet Union. "We must regain our reverence for truth," and our respect for work and "we must revise our whole concept of education and look to our children. ... Education is for building human minds which can reason and love."

1795. "Clean Out the Congress," June 25, 1956. He reiterates the lack of significant choice in the presidential elections and his decision, therefore, not to vote; he adds that there is need for and opportunity of making changes in Congress if a grass root effort begins now.

1796. "The Saga of Nkrumah," July 30, 1956. Du Bois tells of Nkrumah's history, their meeting in 1945, the struggles since to his victory earlier in July in nation-wide elections in Ghana.

1797. "Africa's Choice," October 29, 1956. A review of George Padmore's *Pan-Africanism or Communism? The Coming Struggle for Africa.* On the whole a useful and thoughtful book but he thinks Padmore underestimates the problems of a "rising black bourgeoisie closely associated with foreign investors", suggests an "American Marshall Plan" for Africa, and thinks the Philippines are free. With all this Du Bois disagrees but the book "should be read."

1798. "Reform the U.S. Senate or Lose Your Democracy," November 5, 1956. Du Bois demonstrates how populous industrial states have the same vote in the Senate as Southern states where much of the population is disfranchised and Western states, such as Nevada, where oligarchic domination is especially easy; he shows that this negates elementary concepts of democratic government.

1799. "National Guardianship," December 3, 1956 (address at the eighth anniversary dinner for the newspaper, held in New York on

November 15). This is a time of discouragement but there have been many such times in the past—and many are traced—but the forward progress of humanity is a fact and continues. Whitman is quoted (as he is quite often by Du Bois) to confirm that, *"what we believe in waits latent forever through all the continents ... waiting its time."*

1800. "Negro History Centenaries," January 14, 1957. Du Bois has called to the attention of "several leading men and organizations within the Negro race" that 1957 will usher in "a series of centenaries" of historic import, such as 1857: Dred Scott decision; 1859: death of John Brown; 1863: Emancipation Proclamation, etc.

1801. "Will the Great Gandhi Live Again?" February 11, 1957. In his early youth he thought war brought progress and "that if my people ever gained freedom and equality, it would be by killing white people." Later he turned to a kind of pacifism and then greatly admired Gandhi. And now in Montgomery, Alabama, plain folk who work hard and are led by one "who had read Hegel, knew of Karl Marx" and Gandhi (meaning Martin Luther King, Jr., but not using his name) are seeking a solution through the Gandhian method. The trouble is that they are facing sick people, people who are diseased by racism and such people cannot be persuaded by reason or impressed by moral fortitude. Here is a real dilemma. Du Bois suggests, too, that "it is possible any day that their leader [meaning King] will be killed."

1802. "The Collier's Story," February 25, 1957. He shows the domination of Big Business in the media industry and the decisive role in that industry of the profit motive, for here was a magazine with 4,000,000 readers and it was terminated solely because it was not returning enough dividends.

1803. "Negroes and Socialism," April 29, 1957. "The one hope of American Negroes is Socialism." He had himself once "stressed Negro private business enterprise," then "group economy," and then cooperatives and helped establish 50 of them but they failed "because without the support of the state, it cannot succeed." In the world socialism is spreading and in the United States we should guide our voting by the consideration of trying to bring that system nearer the time of its realization.

1804. "The Present Leadership of American Negroes," May 20, 1957. A review of E. Franklin Frazier's *The Black Bourgeoisie*, Du Bois finds it an honest and severe criticism of its subject with much truth in that criticism, but with a certain exaggeration which Du Bois analyzes. He reverts to the necessity of socialism if Black people are to "survive in the United States as a self-respecting cultural unit, integrating gradually into the nation, but not on terms which imply self-destruction or loss of possible gifts to America."

1805. "Colombo: No Peace Delegate from United States?" June 10, 1957. A meeting is to be held in Ceylon in June attended by delegates from almost every nation in the world. It is a meeting to discuss peace, under the auspices of the World Council of Peace and the absence of an American bespeaks the backwardness of this country.

1806. "James Weldon Johnson," June 24, 1957. A brief résumé and appreciation of the life of this poet, author, teacher, and organizer with some indication of why he left the NAACP. This man must not be forgotten; he has suggested to his widow an appropriate memorial meeting to be held in the fall.

1807. "The Meaning of the Washington Pilgrimage," July 8, 1957. Twenty-seven thousand Black people marched in Washington and performed remarkably, keeping their restraint and showing their determination. The main thing was their main decision—to register and vote and to do this especially in the South. If that can be accomplished, it will help revolutionize this country.

1808. "What is the Meaning of 'All Deliberate Speed'?" November 4, 1957. It refers to the phrase used by the U.S. Supreme Court in 1954 ordering desegregation of education. Little progress has been achieved and much violence has been used. The world watches to see whether or not the United States is a totally depraved country.

1809. "A Vista of Ninety Fruitful Years," February 17, 1958. The occasion is his ninetieth birthday. "I do not apologize for living long ... socialism progresses and will progress. All we can do is to silence and jail its promoters. I believe in socialism. I seek a world where the ideals of communism will triumph—to each according to his need; from each according to his ability. For this I will work as long as I live. And I still live."

1810. "To an American Born Last Christmas Day," March 10, 1958. This is the address delivered before 1,000 people at the Hotel Roosevelt in New York City, March 2, celebrating his ninetieth birthday. Among the speakers preceding Dr. Du Bois were Professor John Hope Franklin, Judge Hubert T. Delany, and Mrs. Paul Robeson. The

"American" being addressed is Du Bois' great-grandson. That which "has been the secret of whatever I have done is the fact that I have been able to earn a living by doing the work which I wanted to do and that work was what the world needed done."

1811. "The Real Reason Behind Robeson's Persecution," April 7, 1958. Occasioned by his sixtieth birthday, an excoriation of those who attack him and a glowing tribute to Robeson as artist and man and symbol of the capacity for greatness in his people.

1812. "The Independocrat at the Dinner Table," July 7, 1958. A discussion with "friend wife" and a few others at dinner; he explains why, once again, he will do his best to develop a third party—"one can never tell when the change will come. ... The nation may awake this fall. It may not. If not, we fail and try again."

1812a. "Dr. Du Bois Is Honored by 600-year-old Charles University in Prague," November 10, 1958. A report of the conferring of a Doctorate in Historical Science, written in Prague by George Wheeler, with quotations from his acceptance speech, stressing the need for peace and socialism.

1813. "The Future for All Africa Lies in Socialism," text of address by Du Bois (read for him by his wife, Shirley Graham Du Bois) at the All-African People's Conference held in Accra, in December, 1958; December 22, 1958. He urges that this be seen, that contrary temptations be avoided, and that a united Africa choose the road towards socialism with that road being one of its own making and form.

1814. "The Vast Miracle of China Today," June 8, 1959. Du Bois reports on a ten-week tour during which he visited most of its great cities, went to schools and factories, lectured at universities, spent four hours with Mao Tse-tung and met twice with Prime Minister Chou En-lai. "I have never seen a nation which so amazed and touched me as China in 1959. ... I have seen the world. But never so vast and glorious a miracle as China."

1815. "Forty-Two Years of the U.S.S.R.," September 7, 1959. A positive appreciation of the transformation in the life of Russia accomplished since 1917.

1816. "Crusader Without Violence," a review of L. D. Reddick's, *Crusader Without Violence: A Biography of Martin Luther King, Jr.,*

November 9, 1959. The book is a good one written by a scholar who knows the man and the subject. Du Bois himself does not find persuasive absolute pacifism and misses any economic or political or social program for action.

1817. "Rediscovery of Africa's Civilization," November 16, 1959. A review of Basil Davidson's *The Lost Cities of Africa*, calling it "excellent" and sustaining "the growing idea that the culture of Africa is peculiar and different from that of Europe and Asia and yet tremendously significant and developed to a high degree."

1818. "The Lie of History as it is Taught Today," July 25, 1960. He treats slavery and the Civil War with the former presented as an idyllic society and the latter an unfortunate accident with which slavery had precious little to do. In fact, there was militancy among the slaves, leadership from Blacks in Abolitionism and in the struggles of the Civil War, while the status of the Afro-American was basic to the war and to the postwar era.

1819. "A Program of Reason, Right and Justice for Today," May 23, 1960. He hails the militancy shown by students in Turkey, Japan, and South Korea—and in the United States, especially the Black sit-inners. Du Bois sees no great distinction in the parties in terms of the presidential contest and therefore calls for concentration on the lower levels. The need for a third party persists. He spells out a foreign and domestic program reversing present course of the nation.

1820. "John Brown's Battle for Kansas," June 6, 1960, a review of Truman Nelson's *The Surveyor*. Described as an extraordinary book in which the author "is trying meticulously to fix what actually took place out there on the borders of civilization where slavery and freedom fought a bloody duel embellished and made possible by the color of men's skins and the stealing of toil."

1821. "On the Vast and Reckless Waste of Human Life," June 20, 1960. This is an address given at a memorial meeting upon the untimely death, at the age of forty-four, of Louis E. Burnham, then of the *National Guardian* staff, one of the founders in the 1930's of the Southern Negro Youth Congress and a remarkably effective and beloved figure in the movement for Black liberation and socialism. Here the Doctor pleads for greater care of one's body and the practice of preventive medicine as well as the changing of society so that provisions for the health of citizens are adequate.

1822. " 'I Never Dreamed I Would See This Miracle,' " September 19, 1960. From Accra where Nkrumah has become the first president of the Republic of Ghana, he writes of Nkrumah in the highest terms; Du Bois also notes domestic opposition, some bureacracy, and the hostility of international cartels but hopes that with care and with the building of socialism and the support of socialist states Nkrumah will be able to succeed. Also stresses Ghana's role as a leader of an effort to unite all Africa against colonialism.

1823. "The World Must Wake Soon To Bar War in Africa," September 26, 1960. Reference is made to the Congo crisis, with the U.N. still apparently backing Lumumba as was Nkrumah and the U.S.S.R. He warns of impending war within South Africa if the racism and superexploitation persist and that may well be the place wherein a new world war begins. He remarks that in discussion with Nkrumah he has asked the Doctor to head an effort at creating an *Encyclopedia Africana.*

1824. "Nigeria Becomes Part of the Modern World," and "What Future Holds for Nigeria," a two-part article, January 16 and January 23, 1961, based on a visit there in December, 1960 (attending the inaugural of Dr. Azikiwe as the first African Governor General of Nigeria) dealing with its history, its anticolonial struggles, and the outlook for the future of this vast country.

1825. "American Negroes and Africa's Rise to Freedom," February 13, 1961. Du Bois traces the relationships between Afro-Americans and Africans, the development of African leaders for their own liberation, and the meaning for Blacks in the United States of the successes so far achieved—and those to come—in Africa.

1826. May 1, 1961, p. 2, contains a letter dated Brooklyn, New York, from Du Bois calling attention to some of the more fantastic developments in U.S. foreign and domestic antics—all very briefly —and suggesting that "there are some aspects in which we are so far ahead of the U.S.S.R. that they hope never to beat us."

1827. "A Logical Program for a Free Congo," May 15, 1961. An examination of the roles of Patrice Lumumba, Moise Tshombe and Joseph Kasavubu, and the presentation of a program that could—Dr. Du Bois suggests—result in a united, free, and forward-looking Congo.

CHAPTER IV

GOVERNMENT PUBLICATIONS
AND PROCEEDINGS

A. Reports for Governmental Bodies

Six studies by Dr. Du Bois were published, between 1898 and 1936, by various departments of the United States government. Five of these were rather long; the last was a brief pamphlet. They were:

1828. *The Negroes of Farmville, Virginia*: A *Social Study*, U.S. Labor Department, *Bulletin*, Vol. III, No. 14, January, 1898 (Washington: Government Printing Office), pp. 1–38. The study has "but the one object of ascertaining, with as near an approach to scientific accuracy as possible, the real condition of the Negro" (p. 1). It commences with a brief history and statistical picture of Prince Edward County, of which Farmville is the county seat. It then presents an overall picture of Farmville and notes that as of August, 1897 about three-fifths of the town's population "were of Negro descent" and that "it is with this part of the population that this study has to do." Dr. Du Bois states that he spent July and August, 1897, in the town; "he lived with the colored people, joined in their social life, and visited their homes" (pp. 6–7). There follow the 21 questions upon which his investigation was based; commentary on certain difficulties involved and then the findings under the following headings: Age, Sex and Birthplace; Conjugal Condition, Births and Deaths; Schools and Illiteracy; Occupations and Wages (done in great detail); Economics of the Family. From page 31 through page 38 a section is entitled, "A Side Light: Israel Hill", which is a community about two miles from Farmville, founded by manumitted slaves of the John Randolph family and then occupied by 123 of their descendants, plus only 1 white family. In the conclusion, Du Bois emphasizes "the growing differentiation of classes among Negroes" and remarks that this is a phenomenon often missed. He thinks the town was typical of "the condition of the Virginia Negro today" but cannot be certain, except "by further study." He also writes that there is in the community of Black people "a peculiar hopefulness" and a belief "that one day black people will have all rights they are now striving for" (p. 38).

1829. *The Negro in the Black Belt: Some Social Sketches, Bulletin of the Department of Labor,* Vol. IV, May, 1899 (Washington: Government Printing Office), pp. 401–417. These sketches "are based mainly on seminary notes made by members of the senior class [named in footnotes of this study] of Atlanta University." They were "born and bred under the conditions which they describe" and therefore "have unusual facilities for firsthand knowledge of a difficult and intricate subject" (p. 401). Small communities of Black people in a rural area within DeKalb County, Georgia studied were in a county seat, Covington, Newton County, Georgia; another county seat, Marion, Perry County, Alabama; "a large town," Marietta in Georgia; and Athens, Georgia. Data covering matters similar to that in the 1898 study are offered; again, note is made of the social stratification that is present. The conclusion suggests that those among the people studied who have managed to acquire some property, marry with care, and provide education for their children point the way "so far as they go, [to] a solution of the Negro problem." "In them," it is added, "lies the hope of the American Negro, and—shall we not say—to a great extent, the hope of the Republic" (p. 417).

1830. *The Negro Landholder of Georgia, Bulletin of the Department of Labor,* Vol. VI, July, 1901. (Washington; Government Printing Office), pp. 647–777. After a brief examination of the policy concerning land for the landless Black folk during and just after the Civil War, the task of the study is placed," ... to make clear the steps by which 470,000 black freedmen and their children have in one of the former slave States gained possession of over a million acres of land in a generation, the value of this land and its situation, the conditions of ownership, and the proper interpretation of these statistics as social phenomena" (p. 649). The precise method employed is explained, the history of Georgia is sketched, the Black population, by counties, for each decade, since the census of 1790 is mapped, the occupations and incomes of Georgia's Black people are presented as of 1900. Then, in great detail, the history and the present condition of landholding by Black people in the state follow together with an account of tenant farming and sharecropping and the role of the merchant. The actual economic condition of Black people in each county is tabulated, from Appleton to Worth, and the text often gives salient bits of history as, for example, the fact that Liberty County "voted solidly against secession" (p. 735) and why.

1831. *The Negro Farmer, Bulletin* VIII, U.S. Bureau of the Census (Washington Government Printing Office, 1904) pp. 69–98. This is a study of all kinds of Black farmers—owners, renters, sharecroppers, etc.—in the United States. It was found: "The Negro farmer conducts 13 percent or about one-eighth of the farms in continental United States, and controls 4.6 percent of the total farm acreage, 5.6 percent of the improved acreage, and 2.4 percent of the farm property. He raises 5.4 percent of the total farm products measured by value and 6.1 percent of the farm products not fed to live stock" (p. 90). "The Negro cultivates one-half of all the cotton farms, more than one-third of all the rice farms, rather less than one-fifth ... of the tobacco farms, and one-seventh of the sugar farms" (p. 92).

1832. *The Negro Farmer*, United States Twelfth Census, *Special Reports: Supplementary Analysis and Derivative Tables* (Washington: Government Printing Office, 1906), pp. 511–579. Page 511 to page 540 are an exact reproduction of the preceding Bulletin No. VIII. A section headed, "Supplementary Analysis" follows, commencing on page 542 and terminating on page 579. It consists of very elaborate tables, for example, Table XLV: "Number and Acreage of Farms Operated by Negroes, Value of Specified Classes of Farm Property, June 1, 1900, with Value of Products of 1899, and Expenditures in 1899 for Labor and Fertilizers, with Averages, by States and Territories." Another offers "Average Expenditures for Farms of Negro and of White Farmers, by States and Territories, 1900." Other tables offer data for Indian and "Mongolian" (meaning Asian) as well as Negro farmers throughout the country.*

1833. *What the Negro Has Done for the United States and Texas,* (Washington: Government Printing Office, 1936), 10 pp. This pamphlet, containing eight pages of text by Du Bois was prepared at the request of the Negro Advisory Committee, chaired by Eugene Kinckle Jones, of the Texas Centennial Commission. As part of the celebration of that Centennial a rather imposing building called the Hall of Negro Life was unveiled. It was, Du Bois wrote, "an attempt to tell in small

---

*It is of some interest that Lenin, in his *Capitalism and Agriculture in the United States,* first published in 1917, pays tribute to the "remarkably detailed descriptions" in the U.S. census reports, "unavailable," he adds "in any other country." He certainly studied the above works of Du Bois and they merit his description. The quotation from Lenin will be found conveniently in Lenin, *On the United States of America* (in English, Moscow, 1967), p. 115.

space the nature of the contribution which the Negro has made to civilization in the United States."

The essay commences by asserting that the United States demonstrates the creative potential of the so-called ordinary people and that the history of Black people shows this; that given greater opportunity that creativity would be enhanced. Black people gave, first of all, labor to the development of the United States, much of it unskilled but a good portion skilled and some of it of the character of genius as in the case of inventors such as Jan Matzeliger and Granville Woods. Black people helped in the exploration of the New World and here Du Bois emphasizes their role in the Southwest. In beauty the Black people's contribution has been notable; this is described in music, literature, and drama. In science the contributions of Carver, Just, Fuller, and Hinton are mentioned.

In a dramatic and dynamic sense "the Negro is the central thread of American history"; how is shown. Emphasis is given to their own activity especially in bringing an end to slavery and in seeking to extend democracy. The spiritual contribution of the Afro-American is elaborated and the particularity of their religion indicated. The special connection of Black people and Texas history is sketched and the role of slavery and its expansion is candidly treated. Special tribute is paid to the leadership in Texas during Reconstruction of J. T. Ruby and after Reconstruction of Norris Wright Cuney. With Texas' population (1936) of over 4,000,000 white people, almost 900,000 Black people, and almost 700,000 people of Mexican and Indian ancestry, and with its enormous size and riches, for its glory, "all that is necessary is justice and freedom and understanding between men."

B. Testimony Before Official Bodies

Four times, from 1901 to 1949, Du Bois testified before committees either appointed in accordance with federal law or committees of the House of Representatives or Senate. That testimony and questions and answers which accompanied or followed it were published as follows.

1834. The Industrial Commission, constituted by Act of Congress, June, 1898, with hearings extending over several years and filling 19 volumes; Du Bois testified before it on February 13, 1901, in hearings on "General and Industrial Education" published as Vol. XV, *Immigration and Education* (Washington, Government Printing Office: 1901) pp. 159–175. He explains that his effort has been to date to give a scientific basis to discussions of the South and the Negro—subjects tossed about as generalities. He then refers to his studies of Farmville, Virginia (No. 1818), and of his current work in studying rural and urban Georgia (No. 1819). Du Bois tells in some details of his investigations in Dougherty County as published thereafter. He describes sharecropping and notes the new importance of the merchant, many of the latter being Jewish who "have no objection at all to calling the negro 'mister,' and they are pleasant to him and never find any particular fault with him unless he is in debt" (p. 163). He describes the homes of the Black people and the form of local government, and the secret societies for social security and the central position of the church. Schools for the white children are "bad" but "better" than those for Black children (p. 174). He thinks the federal government at some point must participate more directly in Southern education.

1835. *Committee on Education, House of Representatives*, 75th Congress, 1st session, *Hearings on Federal Aid for the Support of Public Schools*, in connection with H. R. 5962—"to promote the general welfare through the appropriation of funds to assist the states and territories in providing more effective programs for public education." (Washington, Government Printing Office, 1937). These hearings were held on March 30 to March 31, 1937, and April 1, April 2, April 6, April 8, and April 13, 1937. Du Bois testified on April 2 as chairman of education, Georgia Association of Negro Colleges and High Schools; his testimony appears on pages 284–295. He began, "The task which I have undertaken is that of showing just what the problem of ignorance is in the State of Georgia, especially as it touches 38 percent of the population, who are of Negro descent" (p. 284). Data are then presented in terms of the discrimination manifested in expenditures on schools, teachers' salaries, etc. "From these figures it seems clear that the discrimination between white and colored schools in Georgia is large and growing" (p. 287). The main point of the testimony after establishing the above facts, was to urge that the distribution of the moneys provided in the act not be left to local officials but that strict guidelines, based on equity, should be set by the federal government. This brought the following exchange between Graham A. Barden of North Carolina and the doctor. *Mr. Barden*, "Do you want to pass the buck from the State folks down there that are elected by the people to the folks up here elected by the people?" *Dr. Du Bois*, "I want to pass the buck from the State folks who are elected by some of the people to the Congress who are elected by a larger proportion of the people" (p. 294).

1836. *The Committee on Foreign Relations, United States Senate,* 79th Congress, 1st session, [Revised], hearings on *The Charter of the United Nations,* July 9 to July 13, 1945 (Washington, D. C.: Government Printing Office, 1945); the testimony of Du Bois, given July 11, is printed on pages 391–393. The Chairman, Senator Tom Connally of Texas, asked, "is the Reverend Du Bois here?" With this note of ignorance to encourage him—and making no reference to it—Du Bois began by stating that he was an official of the NAACP and was an associate consultant to the U.S. delegation at San Francisco, but that "I am speaking officially only for myself." He thinks the U.N. charter is a "far step toward peace and justice" but that it requires certain amendments having "to do with colonies." Colonialism has kept the world "in continuous turmoil" for a century and a half and has been at the root of two world wars. "This proposed Charter should, therefore, make clear and unequivocal the straightforward stand of the civilized world for race equality, and the universal application of the democratic way of life, not simply as philanthropy and justice, but to save human civilization from suicide" (p. 392). Specific proposals toward this end are presented. The Chairman, Senator Connally, said. "we thank you very much, Doctor, for a very fine presentation of your views."

1837. *Committee on Foreign Affairs, House of Representatives,* Hearings on Mutual Defense Assistance Act of 1949, 81st Congress, 1st session, (Washington; Government Printing Office, 1949) pp. 261–270. Hearings held July 28, July 29, August 1, August, 2, August 5, and August 8, 1949, Du Bois testified on August 8, as Vice-Chairman, Council on African Affairs and as also representing the American Continental Congress for Peace. The hearings were on appropriations of $1½ billion as a "down payment" "to promote the foreign policy and provide for the defense and general welfare of the United States by furnishing military assistance to foreign nations" in this case the so-called Truman Doctrine to support the military needs of Greece and Turkey and to finance the North Atlantic Treaty Organization. The Doctor opposed this as solidifying the Cold War and making quite possible a Third World War; his language was impassioned. "We who hate niggers and darkies, propose to control a world full of colored people. Will they have no voice in this matter?" (p. 262). He added to Congress, "if you vote this blank check, gentlemen, do not assume that you will decide when and where to fight" (p. 266). The questions asked dealt with the organizational affiliations of the Doctor and whether or not he had ever been to Russia. At the close, the chairman of the committee, John Kee (D., W. Va.) asked if Du Bois was a citizen; when he replied that he was and that his great grandfather was a soldier in the American Revolution, Chairman Kee said—and this closed the Doctor's appearance—"Don't you think you should have a few of your family fight to make our country safe from Russia?" (p. 270). Part of Du Bois' testimony is published in *National Guardian*, August 22, 1949.

C. Memorials to Government Bodies

While resident in Georgia, Du Bois was the author of three jointly signed and separately printed memorials on behalf of Afro-American people presented to the state legislature; these were:

1838. *A Memorial to the Legislature of Georgia on the Hardwick Bill* (n.d., n.p.); written by Du Bois and signed by 24 leading Black men of Georgia, including John Hope and William A. Pledger.* It was presented to the legislature in November, 1899; the Hardwick Bill sought to disfranchise the Black population of the state by various literacy, "understanding," and property devices. This bill was defeated but the same purposes were accomplished later through the constitutional amendment in Georgia as throughout the South—the last state being Oklahoma in 1910. " ... No Nation or State can advance faster than its laboring classes and that whatever hinders, degrades or discourages the Negroes weakens and injures the State."

1839. *A Memorial to the Legislature of Georgia on Negro Common Schools* (n.d., n.p.)signed by eight leading Black men in Georgia, including Du Bois who wrote it and J. W. E. Bowen, John Hope, W. H. Crogman, and H. H. Proctor. The memorial was aimed against passage of a bill introduced into the Georgia Senate on October 30, 1900, which declared that money to support segregated schools in the state shall be "in proportion to the amount of taxes paid by each race"—that is to say, it would have legalized and intensified the discriminatory appropriations already provided by the state for the two school systems. A typical paragraph reads: "Equal opportunity for all men is the spirit of the Age-end, and that people who assert that the unrisen cannot rise and then emphasize the assertion by sitting on them, lead all

*Published in H. Aptheker, ed., *A Documentary History of the Negro People in the United States*, I, pp. 784–786.

fair-minded men to suspect them of insincerity." The Bell Bill was in fact defeated in both 1900 and 1901.

1840. *A Memorial to the Legislature of Georgia on the Proposed Amendment Touching the Distribution of the School Fund*, is a larger four-page pamphlet, issued in Atlanta but undated. It probably was issued early in 1901; certainly somewhat later than the preceding pamphlet. Its wording is similar but far from identical and there is no doubt its chief author was Du Bois, whose name is first among the 14 signers, including again John Hope, J. W. E. Bowen, and W. H. Crogman. It concludes with the following paragraph. "Popular government in the United States is not a failure, but it is having in these days a severe and critical trial. Its success in the future depends upon the ability of great classes of men to rise above prejudice and do strict justice to their fellow-men. And today strict justice in Georgia demands free common school training for every single child of the State."

D. Organizational Leaflets and Pamphlets

In his connection with the Niagara Movement and with the National Association for the Advancement of Colored People, and the Pan-African Movement, Du Bois authored certain separately published leaflets, calls, resolutions, and pamphlets. Included in this category were:

1841. A one page printed leaflet, signed by Du Bois as "Provisional Secretary" headed (Private and Confidential) *The Niagara Movement*. This is not dated but it announces that the "undersigned fifty-nine gentlemen" from 18 states have joined in a call to meet "in the vicinity of Buffalo, New York" during the week beginning July 9, 1905, in order "to inaugurate a permanent national forward movement."

1842. *Constitution and By-Laws of the Niagara Movement* as adopted July 12 to July 13, 1905 is a three-page pamphlet unsigned whose chief author was Du Bois.

1843. *The Niagara Movement: Declaration of Principles: 1905*, is a three-page pamphlet, unsigned, whose chief author was Du Bois.*

---

*Reprinted, in full, H. Aptheker, *op. cit.*, pp. 901–904.

1844. Five *Dollars*, is the heading of a one-page printed leaflet, signed by Du Bois as General Secretary. It is not dated, but its contents indicate that it was issued probably early in 1906. It enumerates the cost of running the Movement and asks that each member pay an annual stipend of $5 which, Du Bois states, will make possible its continuance. A characteristic note is this, "we'll pay our bills or make none. That's the Niagara way."

1844a. There was issued sometime after August 18, 1906, a new printing, in four pages, of *Constitution and By-Laws of the Niagara Movement*, which carried, on page 4, the amendments adopted at the 1906 meeting to the constitution as approved in 1905. These amendments changed the titles of some of the departments and added several departments, including a Pan-African, a Women's, an Art, a Junior, and a department of Economics. It also specifically provided that "properly qualified persons may be admitted to the Niagara Movement without distinction of sex"—though the earlier document had nowhere specified that only males might become members.

1845. *Niagara Address of 1906* was issued separately and was reprinted widely in newspapers and magazines throughout the nation. Here occur the words, "We will not be satisfied to take one jot or tittle less than our full manhood rights. We claim for ourselves every single right that belongs to a freeborn American, political, civil, and social; and until we get these rights we will never cease to protest and assail the ears of America."*

1846. *Third Annual Meeting of the Niagara Movement, August 26 to August 27, 1907, at Parker Memorial Hall, Boston, Massachusetts.* A two-page leaflet, unsigned, but the abstract of the minutes, the report of the public meeting (attended by 800 persons) at Faneuil Hall, and the text of the address to the country were all by Du Bois. The latter urged that no Black person vote for the Roosevelt-Taft group; rather, "vote with the white laboring classes, remembering that the cause of labor is the black man's cause, and the black man's cause is labor's own"—in this moment this could only mean urging a vote for the Socialist party, here not mentioned.

1846a. One of the problems at the Boston meeting in 1907 of Niagara

---

*Reprinted in full in H. Aptheker, ed., *op. cit.*, pp. 907–10.

was to agree upon and to confirm the actual membership from Massachusetts. This was done by balloting and the result was a membership of 91 men and women. This is explained and the names listed on a one-page printed leaflet, signed by Du Bois; the leaflet is not dated but states that the ballots themselves may be examined "at the office of the State Secretary [Clement G. Morgan] on either September 26 or 27th" [1907].

1847. In a off-printed one-page letter dated Atlanta, Georgia, March 14, 1908, signed and addressed to "Dear Colleagues," and ending with "Yours for Freedom," Du Bois summarizes the main work of the Niagara movement for the year 1907. A case contesting railroad Jim Crow was in process, public meetings had been held in Washington, Cleveland, Baltimore, New York, and Minneapolis; a "staunch anti-Taft" campaign was conducted; Mrs. Carrie Clifford of Washington and Mrs. Clement Morgan of Boston have undertaken the work of the Women's department after the death of Mrs. Ida D. Bailey; there is effort to sustain a John Brown Memorial Committee; scholarships for college students are being attempted; and Bishop Alexander Walters has decided to join the movement.

1848. Sometime early in 1909 a one-page leaflet was issued, signed by Du Bois (with a treasurer's comment signed by Mason A. Hawkins). It summarizes briefly the work of 1908 and indicates what may be done in 1909; its salutation is "Yours for Freedom" and it refers to the members as "comrades."

1849. *The Niagara Movement Fifth Annual Meeting* is a one-page printed call, signed by Du Bois. This was for the final meeting, held at Sea Isle City, New Jersey, in August, 1909. The call gives details of time and place and methods of travel as well as of the program. The merging of the Niagara Movement with the newly projected NAACP came about at this time.

D. NAACP

1850. *The Crisis: Prospectus* is a four-page pamphlet published in 1910, sometime prior to November, stating what the magazine will attempt to do, the writers associated with it, and its function as the organ of the NAACP. It is not signed but it is by Du Bois.

1850a. *The Crisis*, a six-page pamphlet, was issued in 1911, sometime prior to June. It repeats much of the above, but adds the names of contributors to early issues, affirms that the magazine "is the organ of no clique or party," that it plans to print 12,000 copies for June, 1911, and appends two pages of "unsolicited testimonials" from people like Mrs. Paul L. Dunbar, Charles W. Chesnutt, Charles Edward Russell, and J. G. Phelps Stokes.

1851. *A Memorandum to the Board of Directors of the National Association for the Advancement of Colored People—on the Objects and Methods of the Organization*, a six-page, signed, but undated pamphlet, published sometime towards the end of 1912 or early (certainly before April) 1913. Of the greatest interest, pointing to most of the features of Du Bois' later demands and campaigns as well as criticisms of the organization. He warns against excessive "concentration of power" and of "the 'color line' which, because of abnormal conditions without, will again and again quite unconsciously obtrude itself within an organization of this sort."

1852. *Memorandum in Support of Proposed Amendment to* H. R. 7951, *Entitled a Bill to Provide for Co-Operative Agricultural Extension Work Between the Agricultural Colleges in the Several States ... and the United States Department of Agriculture*, a sixteen-page pamphlet published by the NAACP, signed by Chapin Brinsmade, as attorney, and Du Bois as director of Publicity and Research for the association, but written in largest part by the latter, including seven pages of statistical tables on the disposition in the past of the Land Grant Fund and income of A & M Colleges, both divided by Black and white institutions. The amendment, called the Jones Amendment for Senator Wesley L. Jones of the state of Washington (who introduced it on February 5, 1914), would have required that the distribution of federal moneys not be racially discriminatory; the Memorandum argues in its favor both in terms of history and justice and need.*

1853. *The Last Word in Caste*, appeared early in 1914, first as the *Fourth* (1914) *Annual Report of the* NAACP (pp. 66–81) and then as a separate sixteen-page pamphlet issued by the association. This summarizes the setbacks in political and educational rights endured by the

---

*On February 6, 1914, Senator J. H. Gallinger of New Hampshire presented a brief communication from the NAACP summarizing the above memorandum; it undoubtedly came from Du Bois; *Congressional Record*, 63rd Congress, 2nd session., 3035. The Jones Amendment was not passed; a much less satisfactory one was and the act became law on May 8, 1914.

Black people during the past decade and warns of new attacks upon their economic rights, including proposals to forbid sale or even renting of land to them—the latter being the inspiration for the title of this essay. (This essay was widely commented upon in the press and in some instances quoted at length, as in the Springfield Massachusetts *Republican*, March 13, 1914.)

1854. *Report of the Department of Publications and Research*, NAACP, *from August, 1910, through November, 1915*, is a four-page pamphlet signed, and dated November 1915. There are six aspects to the work of this department and for each, detailed data are provided: the *Crisis*; Research Work; Lectures (a total in the period of 314 lectures in 31 states, Jamaica, Canada, and England with almost 140,000 auditors); Publications; Other activities (as the Universal Races Congress in England in 1911); Miscellaneous—i.e., a Bureau of Information, soliciting funds, etc. This ends with the suggestion that "an *Encyclopedia Africana*, to be written through the co-operative endeavor of Negro scholars, with the advice and co-operation of scholars of all races" be undertaken now so that it might be out in 1919, the tercentenary of the "permanent landing of the Negro in the United States."

1855. *Completing the Work of the Emancipator*, no author or editor given, published in March, 1916, by the NAACP and being the Sixth Annual Report with 23 pages of text. It follows closely the organizational form of the above mentioned *Memorandum to the Board* dated 1913 and stylistically shows every evidence of being either entirely or very largely the work of Du Bois.

E. Pan-African Congresses

There were several separately printed statements and announcements issuing from the Pan-African Movement which were the work of Du Bois. These include:

1856. *Résolutions* Votées *Par Le Congrès Pan-Africain, Réuni les 19, 20, 21 Fevrier 1919, au Grand-Hotel, Paris. Pour la Protection des Indigenes D'afrique et des Peuples D'Origine Africaine*, a two-page leaflet, in two columns, with French and English text, signed by Blaise Diagne (a deputy from Senegal) as president and Du Bois as secretary. The text is by Du Bois and calls—in terms radical for that period—for a significant enhancement in the well-being and rights of the African peoples. It notes that there were 57 delegates from 15 countries, 12 of the delegates from Africa.

1857. *The Second Pan-African Congress*, a one-page "Bulletin" dated May, 1921 and signed by Diagne and Du Bois and written by the latter; this gives details, including travel plans, for the Congress to be held in late summer and early fall of 1921 with sessions sitting in London, Brussels, and Paris.

1858. *The Second Pan-African Congress*, another "Bulletin", this dated July, 1921 and not signed; it details the projected program of the congress in each of the three cities named above.

On September 26, 1921, Du Bois went to Geneva, on behalf of the Second Pan-African Congress, and delivered a paper to the League of Nations delegates urging the adoption of a colonial mandate system whose purposes would reflect the enhancement of the rights of the inhabitants of the colonies. This was published in French and English, as a six page pamphlet.

1859. *Mandates. Second Pan-African Congress, August-September,* 1921, (Geneva, 1921, Imp. Atar)

1860. *The Pan-African Association: Declared 8 December 1921; Statutes,* a four-page leaflet indicating in the word "Association" that this was to be a permanent and on-going organization with headquarters in Paris (8, Avenue du Maine); its objects, methods, membership terms and forms are described. It is added that the translation from the French is the work of Rayford Logan.

1861. *The Pan-African Congress: Third Biennial Sessions* is a two-page leaflet announcing the holding of this Congress in November in London and Lisbon and giving the program for the London sessions.

CHAPTER V

WRITINGS IN WORKS EDITED BY OTHERS

1862. "Careers Open to College-Bred Negroes," in a pamphlet, *Two Addresses Delivered by Alumni of Fisk University, in Connection with the Anniversary Exercises of Their Alma Mater, June, 1898* (Fisk University, Nashville, [1898], pp. 1–14 (the second essay, "The Fisk Idea," is by the Rev. H. H. Proctor, pp. 15–22). This is devoted to developing "the relation which, in your lives, a liberal education bears to bread-winning." In life there are three "laws": "the law of work, the law of sacrifice, the law of service." Each is illustrated. "The German works for Germany, the Englishman serves England, and it is the duty of the Negro to serve his blood and lineage, and so working, each for each, and all for each, we realize the goal of each for all." He develops idea of college graduates going into industry and developing services to the Black millions: "here is a chance to set a nation working, to make their work more effective, to build and fortify Negro homes, to educate Negro children ... to make the Negro people able to help others even as others have helped us." He emphasizes need for Black professionals, especially physicians, and in this regard one has a life work that women might find most "congenial." He seeks a ministry that "will transform the mysticism of Negro religion into the righteousness of Christianity." Du Bois ends by urging that they "cherish unwavering faith in the blood of your fathers" and that they serve the cause of truth and freedom.

1863. "The Negro in the South and in the North," is Lecture Five in *University Extension Lectures: Syllabus of a Course of Six Lectures on the American Negro* by G. R. Glenn, W. A. Blair, W. H. Page, Kelly Miller, W. E. B. Du Bois, H. B. Frissell (Series J. No. 12, Philadelphia, 1900, American Society for the Extension of University Teaching), pp. 18–21. These lectures were given sometime in the latter part of 1899 or the early part of 1900. Du Bois' lecture notes concentrate upon the complexity of the so-called Negro problem and the great differences

North and South, urban and rural. The latter are traced historically and sociologically. The "real root of the problem" is the need for "the recognition of the Negro manhood." The conclusion, "this problem becomes more pressing today than ever, as we enter into possession of an island empire. Indeed, the race question today is world wide, and the problem of the twentieth century is the problem of the color line." Here, then, would appear to be the first printed usage by Du Bois of that famous line.

1864. "To the Nations of the World," in a *Report of the Pan-African Conference*, held on the 23rd, 24th, and 25th July, 1900, *at Westminster Town Hall, Westminster, S.W.* [London, 1900] (Head Quarters: 61 and 62, Chancery Lane, London, England), pp. 10–12, written by Du Bois as Chairman of the Committee on Address. The pamphlet as a whole consists of 17 pages. In the opening paragraph occur the words, "the problem of the twentieth century is the problem of the colour line, the question as to how far differences of race, which show themselves chiefly in the colour of the skin and the texture of the hair, are going to be made, hereafter, the basis of denying to over half the world the right of sharing to their utmost ability the opportunities and privileges of modern civilisation." The appeal calls upon the Black people of the entire world to "take courage, strive ceaselessly, and fight bravely, that they may prove to the world their incontestible right to be counted among the great brotherhood of mankind."

1865. "The Talented Tenth," in *The Negro Problem: a Series of Articles by Representative American Negroes of Today*, contributions by Booker T. Washington, W. E. Burghardt Du Bois, Paul Laurence Dunbar, Charles W. Chesnutt, and others (New York: James Pott & Company, 1903), pp. 33–75. This seminal essay commences, "the Negro race, like all races, is going to be saved by its exceptional men." "Men we shall have only as we make manhood the object of the work of the schools—intelligence, broad sympathy, knowledge of the world that was and is, and of the relation of men to it. ... On this foundation we may build bread winning, skill of hand and quickness of brain, with never a fear lest the child and man mistake the means of living for the object of life." The character of past leadership is traced down to "the present—a day of cowardice and vacillation, of strident widevoiced wrong and faint hearted compromise; of double-faced dallying with Truth and Right." He shows the need of and the accomplishments of the few institutions of higher learning for Black people. As to education itself, this is his emphasis, "there must be teachers, and teachers of teachers, and to attempt to establish any sort of a system of common and industrial school training, without *first* (and I say *first* advisedly) without *first* providing for the higher training of the very best teachers, is simply throwing your money to the winds." The opening line quoted above is repeated as the conclusion of this essay. This book was printed in September, 1903, which means that it appeared a little after Du Bois' *The Souls of Black Folk*.

1866. "The Negro in America," signed (and dated Atlanta University) in *The Encyclopedia Americana*, edited by Frederick C. Beach, in 16 volumes (New York: Encyclopedia Americana Company, 1904), Vol. XI, (no pagination, the article itself consumes six double-column large sized pages). Filled with population data, tables on economic status, education, prisoners, churches, and degree of "amalgamation of blood" stating that the official figures on the latter phenomenon "are admittedly far below the truth." Notable in its insistence upon resistance by slaves, prominent roles of Black people in the Abolitionist movement and in the Civil War and positive estimate of the Reconstruction era and the contributions made in literature, art, and music.

1867. "Atlanta University," in *From Servitude to Service Being the Old South Lectures on the History and Work of Southern Institutions for the Education of the Negro* (Boston, 1905, American Unitarian Association) Chapter V, pp. 155–197. A fairly detailed history of the institution, including in its beginnings the primary school, the grammar school, the high school, and the college and a treatment of the leading personalities involved. He details the careers of graduates from its college but its theme has these opening lines, "most men in this world are colored. A faith in humanity, therefore ... must, if honest, be primarily a belief in colored men." It closes by calling attention to the historic consequences of Japan's successful challenge to Russia in the war then going on and concludes, "force and fear and repression have hitherto marked our attitude toward darker races. Shall this continue or be replaced by freedom and friendship and opening opportunity? Atlanta University stands for opportunity."*

1868. "The Economic Revolution in the South" and "Religion in the South," being Chapters III and IV of *The Negro in the South: His Economic Progress in Relation to His Moral and Religious Development*

---

*Earl E. Thorpe, in his *Black Historians: A Critique* (New York:Morrow, 1971),p.245,credits Du Bois as the editor of this volume. In responding to a letter, Professor Thorpe stated that he was not able to locate the source on which he based this statement. It is my opinion that Du Bois did not edit this book; no editor is given in it. My guess is that the editor was Edwin D. Mead.

by Booker T. Washington and W. E. Burghardt Du Bois (Philadelphia: George W. Jacobs, 1907) pp. 77–122; 123–222.* The contrast between Washington and Du Bois is especially sharp in this unique book where only the two appear, side by side. In the first essay there appears Du Bois' concept of the need for a "group economy"—something he was to develop in the remaining 56 years of his life; he emphasizes here the need for enfranchisement and projects the coming together of all who labor, whatever their color. Religion in the United States, as practiced by white people, had utterly belied the teachings of Jesus and essentially because the churches refused to consider the Afro-American people as being indeed people—personalities, human beings, made —according to the teaching of their religions—in the image of God Himself.

1869. "Negro Education and Evangelization," signed essay in *The New Schaff-Herzog Religious Encyclopedia*, edited by Samuel M. Jackson (12 volumes, New York: Funk & Wagnalls, 1910), Vol. VIII, pp. 100–108. He traces the early history of education, the differences in the North and South, the work of various benevolent societies and educational agencies with an indication of present status, underlining in the latter case, that the money for such education came in the largest part from Black people themselves. Similarly, in the section on religion, he traces the early history of organized church work, problems in conversion, fears among masters, the split off of the Black churches, and something of their history, numbers, and leading personalities. Very full tables are given with exhaustive data on "Colored Church Organizations in the United States, 1890–1906" and "Colored Church Organizations by States and Territories, 1906." A fairly full bibliography is offered.

1870. "The Negro Race in the United States of America," in G. Spiller, ed., *Papers in Inter-Racial Problems Communicated to the First Universal Races Congress Held at the University of London, July 26-29, 1911* (London: P. S. King & Son, 1911; Boston: World's Peace Foundation; published simultaneosuly in a French-language edition), pp. 348–364.†An encyclopedic overview, heavily statistical, of history, social differentiations, economy, religion, family status, education, with

---

*This book was issued in 1907 in London by Moring, Ltd., and in 1909 under the title, *The American Negro (Southern States)* by T. Fisher Unwin. A reissue of the Jacobs edition, edited and with an introduction by H. Aptheker, was published in 1970 by the Citadel Press (New York).

†A new edition of this book, with an introduction by H. Aptheker, was published in 1970 by the Citadel Press (N.Y.).

a posing of the differences between himself and Booker T. Washington; he concludes, "whether at last the Negro will gain full recognition as a man, or be utterly crushed by prejudice and superior numbers, is the present Negro problem of America."

1870a. "Races of Men," in J.A.Bigham, ed., *Select Discussions of Race Problems* (Atlanta: Atlanta University Publications, No. 20, 1916), pp. 17–24. This is reprinted from Atlanta University Publications No. 11, 1906, edited by Du Bois which is annotated hereafter (No. 1909).

1871. "Foreword," signed and dated New York, August 4, 1922, to Georgia Douglas Johnson, *Bronze: a Book of Verse* (Boston: B. J. Brimmer, Company, 1922) p. 7. He urges reading this book, which "as a revelation of the soul struggle of the women of a race is invaluable."

1872. "Georgia: Invisible Empire State," in Ernest Gruening, ed., *These United States* (2 vols., New York: Boni & Liveright, 1924), Vol. II, pp. 322–345. A lyrical and profound study of a state, its history, its peoples, its torment, and its promise. Especially significant is its analysis of the "New South" idea of Henry Grady and its reception; and of the use of racism to divide the working people of the state. He develops the sources of lynching and terror and the character of the KKK. He ends with the vision and the hope of a coming unity between those who labor—Black and white.

1872a. "The Negro Mind Reaches Out," in Alain Locke, ed., *The New Negro: An Interpretation* (New York: Albert & Charles Boni, 1925),pp. 385–414, is reprinted with some revisions made by Du Bois (mostly additional historical data) from his essay, "Worlds of Color," in *Foreign Affairs*, April, 1925, (Vol. III, No. 3) pp. 423-444.

1873. "Negro Literature," initialled, in *The Encyclopaedia Britannica*, XIII edition (Supplement, or, at times, called Vol. 29); New York: Encyclopedia Britannica, Inc. 1926) pp. 110–111. This is published as the concluding section (V) in a survey of "American Literature." Du Bois affirms that beginning about 1910 there commenced "something that can be called a renaissance." Since then there has appeared "a more careful consideration of the Negro's social problems." He notes developments in what he calls propaganda and in history and science. In history, he calls special attention to the work of Carter G. Woodson and Benjamin Brawley. "The true renaissance has been a matter of spirit" and this has appeared especially among the poets, dramatists, and novelists, many of whom are named, as well as the collectors of

Afro-American music such as J. Rosamond Johnson, T. W. Talley, and J. W. Cotter. "All these things are beginnings rather than fulfillments, but they are significant beginnings. They mean much for the future."

1874. "The Answer of Africa," Chapter 2 of Maurice Maeterlinck, et al. *What is Civilization?* (New York: Duffield Company, 1926) pp. 43–57. Africa has given the world three things, and "they form the essence of African culture: Beginnings, the village unit, and art in sculpture and music." Of the beginnings, perhaps Africa was the home of "the discovery of the use of iron." The village unit "socialized the individual completely," but did not destroy individuality. He analyzes the impact of slave trade and concludes with an examination of "the sense of beauty" which is "the best gift of Africa to the world and the true essence of the black man's soul." Music in particular is discussed.

1875. "Immortality," in Sydney Strong, ed., *We Believe in Immortality* (New York: Coward-McCann, 1929), p. 18. In which, despite the title, Du Bois writes, "My thought on personal immortality is easily explained, I do not know." (The editor was a Congregational clergyman, and the father of Anna Louise Strong.)

1876. "The Negro Citizen," in Charles S. Johnson, ed., *The Negro in American Civilization* (New York: Henry Holt & Colorado, 1930), Chapter XXIX, pp. 461–470. This is the paper Du Bois delivered in December, 1928, in Washington at a National Inter-Racial Conference, mentioned earlier. In the past there was question as to whether or not the Black people could survive without slavery; that is no longer a question. Could he learn? That is no longer a question. The question now is: political power. Can he get it and how, and having it how will he use it? Being deprived of it, vitiates everything in this country; it costs the Black people much and it costs the nation much. Interracial meetings are fine, but they will be really useful when they "attack the main problem, which is and has been the question of political power for the Negro citizens of the United States."

1877. "Helen Keller," in Edna Porter, comp., *Double Blossoms: Helen Keller Anthology* (New York: Lewis Copeland, 1931), p. 64. When a student at Harvard, he visited the Blind Asylum in Roxbury, Massachusetts, and first saw Helen Keller as a child. He remembers her bravery in denouncing racism in her own state of Alabama. " ... This woman who sits in darkness has a spiritual insight clearer than that of many wide-eyed people who stare uncomprehendingly at this prejudiced world."

1878. "Black America," in Fred J. Ringel, ed., *America as Americans See It* (New York: The Literary Guild, 1932), pp. 140–155. (Page 139 has an appreciation of Du Bois—written by Walter White—which concludes that "he stands as one of the chief molders of modern thought regarding the Negro.") Du Bois begins with an outline of history and of present conditions; he sees the present generation as "much sterner and more resourceful" than his fathers. He notes migration plans from that of the American Colonization Society in the early 19th century to that of Garvey, "an impractical fanatic." Political power is growing and probably will continue to do so. Attention is paid to the NAACP. Du Bois notes great contributions in labor and art. He traces the impact of Black people's exploitation on diseases such as racism and excesses such as violence in U.S. life. He emphasizes the positive activity of Afro-American people throughout, including slave uprisings and flight, and the uniqueness of their churches. "So-called Black America is of every conceivable hue and shade and white America is by no means 'lily-white.'"

1878a. "Black America," in Nancy Cunard, ed., *Negro Anthology* (London: Wishart & Company, 1934), pp. 148–152. A shortened version of the above paper; the historical summaries are cut; but otherwise the language of the two papers is identical and there is nothing in the Cunard piece which is not in the Ringel essay.

1879. "A Word," preceding text in Reverdy C. Ransom, *The Negro, The Hope or the Despair of Christianity* (Boston: Ruth Hill, 1935), dated August 29, 1935 and signed. He recalls Bishop Ransom's great speech at the 1906 Harper's Ferry Meeting of the Niagara Movement. Du Bois concludes, "I have little faith that Christianity can settle the race problem, but I have abiding faith in men."

1880. "Washington, Booker Taliaferro," in *Encyclopedia of the Social Sciences*, edited by Edwin R. A. Seligman (15 vols., New York: Macmillan, 1935), Vol. XV, pp. 365–66. " ... He minimized political power and emphasized industrial education." He made Tuskegee into "a large and flourishing institution." He points to failures of the effort and its reasons but concludes on a generous note, "his earnestness, shrewd common sense and statesmanlike finesse in interracial contacts mark his greatness; and Tuskegee Institute stands as his magnificent monument." A brief bibliography is included.

1880a. "The Negro in America," in *The Encyclopedia Americana*, edited by A. H. McDannald (New York: Americana Corp, 1941), Vol.

XX, pp. 47–52; it is somewhat similar in organization to the 1904 essay in this Encyclopedia (No. 1866). It is almost identical—with only some data brought up-to-date—and an occasional verbal change, to essays having same title and same pagination in the 1928 and 1931 editions of this Encyclopedia.

1881. Untitled two-paragraph statement in George Vaughan, ed., *Temples and Towers: A Survey of the World's Moral Outlook* (Boston: Meador Published Co., 1941), pp. 256–257, making the point that a so-called return to religion during calamitous times does not indicate progress but regression in human thinking; Du Bois suggests that he sees now the beginning of an intensified interest in planning and working "for better conditions."

1882. "A Program for the Land-Grant Colleges," in *Proceedings of the Nineteenth Annual Conference of the Presidents of Negro Land Grant Colleges, November 11–13, 1941, Chicago, Illinois* (n. p., n.d.) pp. 42–56. Du Bois delivered this paper on November 11. Four so-called axioms hitherto have dominated conduct in Western civilization, "what is best for the best is best for all"; extending high cultural attainment to the masses will diminish that attainment; science and art are and must be a monopoly of the few; domination of property, of capital, of income is, and should be, and must be, in the hands of a few. All these are now being more and more seriously questioned. He projects an effort which requires careful planning, scientific study, group unity, fighting for equality, for the best possible education, developing the potential of the masses. He sees the need for "tying up the community and the college" and this would come if the latter would participate in developing the kind of planning our people need. Our colleges must face frontally the question of how they can help the people in our communities to earn a good living. The colleges must plan for the future and anticipate the future. "We must have a group to group and person to person knowledge of the condition of the laboring masses, of their oppor-tunities and hindrances." " ... We must aim at a continuous moving picture of ever increasing range and accuracy." With all this going forward at all the colleges "a national planning institute must annually gather up and compare and interpret this great body of fact." Du Bois holds "it is an indictment of the Negro college that the chief studies of the Negro's condition today are not being done by Negroes and Negro colleges." He pictures the work that churches and societies of all sorts could do and again projects the value of consumer and producer cooperatives.

1883. In the *Dictionary of American Biography*, edited by Allen Johnson and Dumas Malone (20 vols., New York: Charles Scribner's Sons, 1943), Du Bois provided accounts as follows:

James DeWolfe (slave-trader, manufacturer, and U.S. Senator from Rhode Island, 1821–1825) in Vol. V, p. 275

Frederick Douglass, in Vol. V, pp. 406–407, noting that he had learned as a slave that resistance paid, that he was a central figure in Abolitionism, had a practicality superior to that of Garrison, and a sense of the realities of slavery that no white Aboltionist could have. He stresses his determination and effectiveness and his wide concern for all human equality, not least the equality of women.

Elijah Johnson, one of the founders of Liberia; he died in 1849; his son Hilary Johnson was President of Liberia, 1884–1892, in Vol. X, pp. 97–98.

Joseph Jenkins Roberts (1809–1876) originally from Virginia, born free, became first president of Liberia serving from 1847 until 1855 and did so "carefully and wisely." He also served as president from 1871 until his death early in 1876; in Vol. XVI, pp. 10–11.

Edward J. Roye (1815–1872), born in Ohio, fifth president of Liberia; overthrown in insurrection, jailed, drowned trying to escape; in Vol. XVI, p. 212.

John Brown Russwurm (1799–1851) was first superintendent of public schools in Liberia; graduate of Bowdoin College in Maine in 1826 —probably the first such graduate of acknowledged African descent. Established earliest Black newspaper, *Freedom's Journal* in New York City in 1827; but abandoned abolitionism and migrated to Liberia in 1829; in Vol. XVI, p. 253.

1884. "My Evolving Program for Negro Freedom," in Rayford W. Logan, ed., *What the Negro Wants* (Chapel Hill: University of North Carolina Press, 1944), pp. 31–70. A very frank and revealing auto-biographical essay, especially illuminating on the period through Harvard and the impact of Germany and of the South upon him. Data on the University of Pennsylvania experience are new and on his first Atlanta years very full. He was naïve to think that the presentation of Truth would be wanted or would be effectual in terms of the realities to which Marx and Freud pointed. He notes efforts to employ him at Tuskegee and why these were unsuccessful. He tells of NAACP Board's lack of interest in Africa. Impact of visits to U.S.S.R.; "Russia was and still is to my mind the most hopeful land in the modern world." But he felt that "the program of the American Communist Party was suicidal." With the depression he became convinced that "mere agitation for 'rights' " was not the real need. He sees three stages in his effort: I, to get the Truth to the white population, hoping they would change reality; II, "United action" of Black and white through propaganda and agitation to force results; III, from about 1928 to the present (i.e., about 1944) organized action and study among ourselves to assure our survival, "*until the cultural development of America and the world is willing to recognize Negro freedom.*" This to be done, not for the race alone, "but for the emancipation of mankind, the realization of democracy and the progress of civilization."

1885. "The Pan-African Movement," (signed, with Du Bois identified here as "International President, Pan-African Congress"), in George Padmore, ed., *Colonial & Coloured Unity: a Programme of Action: History of the Pan-African Congress* (Manchester [1945] Pan-African Service Ltd.), pp. 13–26. A history of the effort for such a movement, commencing with 1900; additional data on the 1919 effort buttressed by long quotations from the contemporary press; and then on subsequent Congresses. Again, quotations and details not available from Du Bois elsewhere. Great detail on the background to the 1945 Congress is given.

In this same publication Du Bois appears two more times, as follows:

1886. "Memorandum to U.N.O.", pp. 8–9, a "resolution calling for adequate representation of the coloured peoples of the world within the United Nations Organization", prepared by Dr. Du Bois, was presented to the U.N. Secretariat by the doctor with the support of 35 organizations of Black people in Africa, the United States, and the West Indies.

1886a. Remarks made by Du Bois at Congress on October 19, 1945, are on page 54. The African peoples "want the right to govern themselves ... and we are saying we have a right to make mistakes ... we must have self-government even if we make mistakes."

1887. "Foreword," to Lorenz Graham, *How God Fix Jonah* (New York: Reynal & Hitchcock, 1946), p. ix. "This is the stuff of which literature is made; and in the lore of the world, the literature of Africa has its place although this is often forgotten."

1888. "John Haynes Holmes, the Community Church and World Brotherhood," in *Dedication Book in Celebration of the New Building of the Community Church of New York, October 17, 1948: 1825–1948* (New York: Community Church Publications, 1948), pp. 36–37. Pays tribute to Holmes as one who helped found the NAACP, who fought racism, who saw the connection between labor's struggles and those of Black people, who refused to join the witch-hunters after the First World War and who sympathized with the aims of the revolution in the Soviet Union.

1889. "A Program of Emancipation for Colonial Peoples," in Merze Tate, ed., *Trust and Non-Self Governing Territories: Papers and Proceedings of the Tenth Annual Conference of the Division of the Graduate School Howard University*, April 8–9, 1947 (Howard University Studies in the Social Sciences, Vol. VI, No. 1, Washington, 1948), pp. 96–104. (Dr. Du Bois' paper closed the final session of this conference; he was introduced by Professor Rayford W. Logan as one whose "voice and pen have never been stilled in this relentless struggle."). Within the developed countries it is clear that private profit must not remain the motive force of production and in the colonial areas, such extraction of profit by alien masters must be terminated. With all this "must go self-rule." The first step needed is the elimination of "segregation, discrimination and class rule based on color and race."

1890. "The Black Man and Albert Schweitzer," in A. A. Roback, ed., *The Albert Schweitzer Jubilee Book* (Cambridge Massachusetts, n. d. [probably 1946 or 1947], Sci-Art Publishers), pp. 121–27. Black people's attitude towards missionaries "is tinged with bitterness" and with good reason; on the other hand, all Black men "revere" people like Mungo Park, David Livingstone, and Albert Schweitzer. There follows an account of Schweitzer's life—in music, in medicine, in religion. But Schweitzer "had no broad grasp of what modern exploitation means . . . if he had, he probably would have tried to heal the souls of white Europe rather than the bodies of black Africa."

1891. "The Nature of Intellectual Freedom," in Daniel S. Gillmor, ed., *Speaking of Peace: an Edited Report of the Cultural and Scientific Conference for World Peace*, New York, *March 25–27, 1949, under the auspices of the National Council of the Arts, Sciences and Professions* (New York: 1949), p. 78. This was the much maligned "Waldorf Conference for Peace" held at the depths of the Cold War; at it Du

Bois made an appeal for intellectual freedom and analyzed its dialectics in terms of the necessities of nature and the aspirations of humanity.

1892. "The Church and the Negro," in Stanley I. Stuber and Thomas C. Clark, eds., *Treasury of the Christian Faith: An Encyclopedic Handbook of the Range and Witness of Christianity* (N.Y., 1949, Association Press), p. 49. A 300-word signed statement noting that established churches in the past stood "on the side of wealth and power" and expecting they will continue to do so in the present and future. When "human brotherhood is a fact" the Churches will claim credit for the achievement but will probably deserve none.

1893. "Preface," signed, to Herbert Aptheker, ed., *A Documentary History of the Negro People in the United States* (New York: The Citadel Press, 1951), p. vii. "Historical scholarship has done all too little of this sort of research. We have the record of kings and gentlemen *ad nauseam* and in stupid detail; but of the common run of human beings, and particularly of the half or wholly submerged working group, the world has saved all too little of authentic record and tried to forget or ignore even the little saved."

1894. "Foreword," signed and dated, August 17, 1952, to Carl Marzani, *We Can be Friends: The Origins of the Cold War* (New York: Topical Books Publishers, 1952), pp. 5–7. A brief biography of the author (an early prisoner of Cold War reaction) and a recommendation of the work as a persuasive exposure of the Washington responsibility for the launching of the Cold War.

1895. "Foreword," to a 1952 edition of Howard Fast's, *Freedom Road*, first issued by Duell, Sloan & Pearce in 1944; new Crown edition of 1969 contains this foreword, pp. v–vi. He commends the book as basically accurate with a "profound" psychological insight and great "literary charm" and illuminating a decisive historical era—that of Reconstruction in the United States.

1896. "An Appreciation," in *Thirty-Five Years of the Soviet State, 1917–1952, The Nineteenth Anniversary of the Establishment of Diplomatic Relations Between the United States and the Soviet Union, 1933–1952* (New York: National Council of American-Soviet Friendship, 1952), pp. 5–10. An account of his early attitude towards Russia and then towards Soviet Russia. Tells of his visits in 1926, 1936, and 1949. "Here is a land which has found itself and believes in its destiny.

... It is a permanent center of human progress." He pays tribute to the leadership of Stalin especially in crushing "at fearful cost the obscene Monster of Berlin."

1897. "A Foreword," signed, to *To Live or to Die: The H-Bomb Versus Mankind, containing public statements by Albert Schweitzer, Albert Einstein ... and others* (New York: New Century Publishers, 1957), pp. 3–4. " ... Immediate disarmament is our only and our imperative problem—not experiments with the Hydrogen-bomb."

1898. "Foreword," to W. Alphaeus Hunton, *Decision in Africa* (New York: International Publishers, 1957), pp. 9–10. Commends the work for its scholarship and its illumination on a subject of which little of value has been published in the United States. The book is "a notable contribution to African freedom."

1899. "The Negro and Socialism," in Helen Alfred, ed., *Toward a Socialist America* (New York: Peace Publications, 1958), pp. 179–91. "In order to let the nation return to normal sanity we must realize that socialism is not a crime nor a conspiracy. ... American Negroes must study socialism, its rise in Europe and Asia, and its peculiar suitability for the emancipation of Africa. ... The Negro church which stops discrimination against bus riders must next see how those riders can earn a decent living and not remain helplessly exploited by those who own busses and make jim-crow laws."

1900. "Whites in Africa After Negro Autonomy," in A. A. Roback, ed., *In Albert Schweitzer's Realm: A Symposium* (Cambridge, Massachusetts, Sci-Art Publishers, 1962), pp. 243–255. He has no love for the " 'white' race" and why should he, considering its record. But there are classes among whites and there are socialist nations among whites. There is reason to believe that all Africa will be socialist in good time and there also is reason to hope that when that happens there will be no vengeance wreaked upon white people. One should honor the work in medicine of Dr. Schweitzer, but even more needed than workers in medicine, are "defenders of manhood." It would be well if people like Dr. Schweitzer would "train Negroes as assistants and helpers ... who can in time carry on and spread his work and see that it is supported by the new African states and does not continue to be dependent on European charity." That would be "fundamental" and not "paternalistic."

CHAPTER VI

WORKS EDITED BY DUBOIS

Conferences on various aspects of life with special emphasis upon the needs of rural Southern Black people had been held in the 1880's and early 1890's at both Tuskegee and Hampton Institutes. Influential people at Atlanta University—especially its president, Horace Bumstead, and a banker-trustee, George Bradford—conceived of their institution as holding conferences concentrating on urban Black people in the South. The first of these was held in 1896 and dealt with *Mortality among Negroes in Cities* and was published that year by Atlanta University Press as publication Number 1. The next year, again in May, another conference was held and its proceedings again were published as Number 2, *Social and Physical Condition* of *Negroes in Cities*.

Du Bois, having then completed his year's work at the University of Pennsylvania, came to Atlanta with the task of extending and deepening the Atlanta University Conferences and serving as Professor of Economics and History. From 1898 through 1913 (Studies Nos. 3–18), Dr. Du Bois edited the proceedings (with Augustus G. Dill as fellow-editor of Numbers 15–18).*

1901. *Some Efforts of American Negroes For Their Own Social Betterment: Report of an Investigation under the direction of Atlanta University; together with the Proceedings of the Third Conference for the Study of the Negro Problems, held at Atlanta University, May 25–26, 1898.* (Atlanta: Atlanta University Press, 1898), 66 pp.. The first 44 pages are written by Du Bois himself; these introduce the purposes of the conference and then present the "Results of the Investigation" into the subject of the conference. The results come from investigations and reports made by graduates of Fisk, Berea, Lincoln (Missouri), Howard, Meharry, Spelman. Data on churches, various secret and beneficial and insurance societies, cooperative business ventures, benevolent and

*All the *Atlanta University Publications* (Nos. 1–20) have been reissued in two volumes with helpful introductions by Ernest Kaiser (New York: Arno Press, 1968, 1969).

charitable institutions are examined and tabulated. Altogether 236 different organizations and associations were described and the point is made of a certain survival of Africanisms (p. 43). Remaining pages present papers by Rev. H. H. Proctor of Atlanta on the functioning of the church; by H. R. Butler, M.D. of Atlanta on various secret and beneficial societies in Atlanta; by Professor J. M. Colson of Virginia Normal and Collegiate Institute in Petersburg on organizations among Afro-Americans in that city; by Helen A. Cook on the work of the Women's League (organized in 1892) in her own city of Washington; by Minnie L. Perry of Atlanta on an orphanage in that city; and by L. M. Hershaw on mortality among Black people in Baltimore, Charleston, Memphis, and Richmond, which continues data he had supplied in the 1897 volume.

1902. *The Negro in Business: Report of a Social Study made under the direction of Atlanta University; together with the Proceedings of the Fourth Conference for the Study of the Negro Problems, held at Atlanta University*, May 30–31, 1899. (Atlanta: Atlanta University Press, 1899) 77 pp. The first 46 pages are by Du Bois. The introduction repeats matter in No. 3, but adds details on relevant courses at the university, gives a listing of publications by himself (without mentioning his name), and names people and institutions who have sent in requests for information to him as Corresponding Secretary of the Atlanta Conferences. This is followed by a 42-page summary of the "Results of the Investigation" in which is explained the scope of the inquiry into business and then descriptive matter plus extensive tables on, for example, "Negro Business Men by States" and "Negro Business Men, According to Occupations", data on capital invested, duration of the businesses, characteristics of localities having significant number of such businesses, and detailed tables on businesses in certain cities, such as Washington, Houston, Richmond, Mobile, Charleston, San Francisco, Cleveland, and elsewhere. Letters from various businessmen giving their biographies are quoted at length and the sources of their savings are tabulated. The proceedings present papers by John Hope on "The Meaning of Business," another on "A Negro Cooperative Foundry" located in Chattanooga, and one on "Negro Business Ventures in Atlanta." A report, by Du Bois himself, on "The Negro Newspaper" appears on pages 72–76 giving historical details of great present value. Du Bois remarks at the end of his study: "A strong, fearless, national newspaper or magazine which the Negroes could feel was their own, with sane views as to work, wealth and culture, could become, in years, a vast power among Negroes."

(It was this conference which formed the basis for the organization by Booker T. Washington, in 1900 of the Negro Businessmen's League.)

1903. *The College-Bred Negro: Report of a Social Study made under the direction of Atlanta University; together with the Proceedings of the Fifth Conference for the Study of the Negro Problems, held at Atlanta University, May 29–30, 1900* (Atlanta: Atlanta University Press, 1900), 115 pp. Pages 3–5 repeat and bring up-to-date the material contained in the same section in the preceding *Report*. On pages 6–9 there is "A Select Bibliography of the American Negro for General Readers" (this, like his listing of Negro newspapers in the earlier report, was issued in pamphlet form by the university). Pages 10–114 are by Du Bois and offer a summary of the "Results of the Investigation." The scope of the inquiry is explained and the text of the 26 questions propounded to 2,600 Black college graduates is reproduced. These asked biographical data; information on work or profession; if a teacher, detailed questions about students, institutions, publications, political activity if any, and such questions as: "Are you hopeful for the future of the Negro in this country? Have you any suggestions?" Almost half (1,252) responded and their responses are summarized and often quoted. In addition, much data with tables are offered concerning colleges for Afro-American people, with requirements for entry and with courses given for each of the four years (including, in many cases, the texts used). There then follow tables concerning "Negroes in Other Colleges" by name and number of such students, coming to a total of 390. Letters from officials of many of these colleges and from others (refusing Black students) are reproduced with a note that "among the women's colleges the color prejudice is much stronger and more unyielding" (p. 34). The summary concludes with Du Bois affirming the success and need of college training and insisting that this in no way denies the need of elementary and/or industrial training; all these "are rather supplementary and mutually helpful in the great end of solving the Negro problem."

1904. *The Negro Common School: Report of a Social Study made under the direction of Atlanta University; together with the Proceedings of the Sixth Conference for the Study of the Negro Problems, Held at Atlanta University, on May 28, 1901* (Atlanta: Atlanta University Press, 1901), 119 pp.. One page simply lists the program of the Sixth conference; another prints the "Resolutions" of the Conference, signed by a committee, headed by Du Bois and pointing out the shocking inadequacy of public school education in the South for Black children and urging increased state and federal aid for such education. The first four pages summarize the sociological work being done at Atlanta University; this is followed by nine pages of "A Select Bibliography of the American Negro for General Readers," divided this time, under headings such as "History," "Present Social Conditions," "Literature of American Negroes," and other bibliographical sources. From page 14 through page 118 is what amounts to a book by Du Bois on the subject at hand. Data were secured from printed school reports of the states; from reports of the Freedmen's Bureau, the U.S. Bureau of Education, and three sets of questions sent to county superintendents, superintendents of a number of city school systems, and to principals of town and city schools for Black children. All this is summarized in a history of education for Black youth in the North and South, tables on current conditions state by state, per capita educational expenditures, data on teachers and extensive quotations from answers to above mentioned questionnaires. The conclusion in italics is:

> The South is still poor, and, worse than that, it is, to a vast degree, ignorant. Race antagonism can only be stopped by intelligence. It is dangerous to wait, it is foolish to hesitate. Let the nation immediately give generous aid to Southern common school education.

1905. *The Negro Artisan: Report of a Social Study made under the direction of Atlanta University; together with the Proceedings of the Seventh Conference for the Study of Negro Problems, held at Atlanta University, on May 27, 1902* (Atlanta: Atlanta University Press, 1902) 192 pp. This commences with a three-page (v–vii) "Bibliography of the Negro Artisan and the Industrial Training of the Negro"; three pages again describe the educational, publishing, and lecture work in sociology by the university; four pages are then given to the program of the Seventh Conference. Of great interest is the publication, in part, of the remarks made at the closing of the conference by Booker T. Washington (pp. 5–7). He has watched "with keen interest and appreciation," he says, the work of the conferences and believes that, "the work that Dr. Du Bois is doing will stand for years as a monument to his ability, wisdom and faithfulness." The study itself commences on page 8; here, again, the scope and method of the inquiry are laid out. A schedule of questions concerning biographical data, trade, trade-union connection, wages, relations to whites, education, etc., were answered by 1,300 "Negro skilled workers" mostly in Georgia. In addition, a schedule of questions was placed in the hands of numerous Afro-

American college graduates and they sent in returns from 32 states and from Canada, Costa Rica and Puerto Rico. Questions especially relevant to trade-union practices and status were sent to every trade union affiliated with the AFL and many others. Ninety-seven replied; 11 refused replies. Somewhat similar questions were sent to central labor bodies in every city and town in the nation; 200 representing 30 states replied. Letters were sent to state federations of labor; most replied. Each of the Black industrial schools were sent pertinent questions; most replied. And in 1889 and 1891 the Chattanooga *Times* "made interesting and exhaustive studies of skilled Negro labor in the South." At the request of Du Bois, that newspaper joined the university in this study and sent a questionnaire about Black workers to "business establishments all over the Southern States." Superintendents of Education in all Southern states were asked questions; most responded; 600 children in public schools in Atlanta were asked about their own work habits and plans for the future. Finally, printed sources on the subject, official and unofficial, were examined. Commencing on page 13 all of this information is presented in summary form, with history, present conditions, present practices, and future hopes. Particularly full data are given for each of various industrial schools that are named; the income and expenditures of such schools are itemized; work of their graduates is tabulated; official data on numbers and kind of Black workers in the nation are itemized; reports from the field are quoted, often giving facts for individual cities such as Charleston, South Carolina, and Danville, Virginia, etc.; From page 153 to page 180 one finds the fullest data available as of that time—and for many decades since—on the relationship of Black people towards trade unions and of the unions towards them, with data on numbers, strikes, etc., and with quotations from letters to Du Bois from trade-union leaders, including Samuel Gompers (p. 177).

1906. *The Negro Church: Report of a Social Study made under the direction of Atlanta University; together with the Proceedings of the Eighth Conference for the Study of Negro Problems, held at Atlanta University, May 26, 1903* (Atlanta: Atlanta University Press, 1903), 212 pp. The summary of the actual proceedings and the program commence on page 202 and include remarks made by Dr. Washington Gladden, president of the American Missionary Association. The preceding pages are written by Du Bois with the exception of a total of about 30 pages which deal with the history of early all-Black churches (by John W. Cromwell), churches in a contemporary black belt county in

Georgia (by W. H. Holloway), in a Florida town (by Annie M. MacLean), in Illinois (by Monroe Work and Du Bois) and in Ohio (by R. R. Wright, Jr.). In the remainder one finds a rather full history of the impact of religion upon the Afro-American and vice versa—including a discussion of Toussaint L'Ouverture and slave rebel leaders in the United States, such as Gabriel, Vesey, and Turner—and an examination of current conditions among the A.M.E., A.M.E.Z., Colored Methodists and leading Protestant denominations, with material also on "children and the church" and "the training of ministers."

1907. *Some Notes on Negro Crime Particularly in Georgia: Report of a Social Study made under the direction of Atlanta University; together with the Proceedings of the Ninth Conference for the Study of the Negro Problems, held at Atlanta University, May 24, 1904* (Atlanta: Atlanta University Press, 1904) 68 pp.

In the preface Du Bois remarks that census reports on this subject "are very inadequate"; therefore, he has relied upon special studies of court returns and prison data in Atlanta and Savannah, reports from mayors and police chiefs and other officers in 37 counties of Georgia, reports from Black and white people in those counties, a study of arrests and of commitments in 20 cities in the United States, 7 reports by the Georgia Prison Commission and answers from 2,000 students to questionnaires. A three-page "Select Bibliography on Negro Crime" is presented. Twenty-four of the pages are by others: Franklin B. Sanborn, H. H. Proctor, M. N. Work, A. G. Coombs, and L. D. Davis. The essence of Du Bois' conclusions as of that date are in the following words:

> ... absolutely impartial courts; the presence of intelligent Negroes on juries when Negroes are tried; the careful defense of ignorance in law and custom; the absolute doing away with every vestige of involuntary servitude except in prisons under absolute state control, and for the reformation of the prisoner; the encouraging of intelligent, ambitious, and independent black men; the granting of the right to cast an untrammelled vote to intelligent and decent Negroes; the unwavering defense of all women who want to be decent against indecent approach, and an effort to increase rather than to kill the self-respect of Negroes, it seems certain that such a policy would make quickly and decidedly for the decrease of Negro criminality in the South and in the land. (p. 59).

1908. *A Select Bibliography of the Negro American; A Compilation made under the direction of Atlanta University; together with the*

Proceedings of the Tenth Conference for the Study of the Negro Problems, held at Atlanta University, on May 30, 1905 (Atlanta: 1905 Atlanta University Press,), 71 pp.. The subject of the 10th Conference was "Methods and Results of Ten Years' Study of the American Negro." Participating, among others, were L. M. Hershaw of Washington, Frances Kellor of New York, Mary W. Ovington of New York, Mrs. Butler Wilson of Boston, and Professor Walter F. Willcox, of the U.S. Census Bureau and of Cornell University. In a preface Du Bois thinks the bibliography is "very imperfect" and suggests it be viewed as a third edition of the efforts in 1900 and 1901. The bibliography covers page 9 through page 71. Despite all the work in this area done in the ensuing 70 years, this remains of value, not only in terms of understanding Du Bois but also in terms of the subject as a whole; especially is this true for the listing of hundreds of magazine articles and pamphlets.

1909. *The Health and Physique of the Negro-American; Report of a Social Study made under the direction of Atlanta University; together with the Proceedings of the Eleventh Conference for the Study of the Negro Problems, held at Atlanta University, on May 29, 1906* (Atlanta: Atlanta University Press 1906), 110 pp. Two sections of this work are not by Du Bois. Section 6 (pp. 53–60) on "Some Psychological Considerations on the Race Problem" is by Professor Herbert A. Miller; and a portion of section 9 dealing with "Mortality in Cities" (pp. 83–91) is by R. R. Wright, Jr. There is a "Bibliography of Negro Health and Physique" (pp. 6–13) including some titles in German and French. There follow sections on "Races of Men," "The Negro Race," "The Negro Brain" (with material contributed by M. N. Work), geographic sources of "The Negro American" and the degree of intermixture with other peoples; "Physical Measurements," "The Increase of the Negro American," data on "The Sick and Defective" and on "Mortality." There are sections of particular interest—based upon the questionnaire methods, including letters to every medical school of record in the country—concerning practices of companies on insurance, data on hospitals for Black people; on medical colleges for Black students; on physicians, dentists and pharmacists, with invaluable quotations from letters to Du Bois by them, as well as officials of medical colleges. Details of the program are on pages 109–110; among those giving papers was Professor Franz Boas.

1910. *Economic Co-Operation Among Negro Americans: Report of a Social Study made by Atlanta University, under the patronage of the*

Carnegie Institution of Washington, D. C., together with the Proceedings of the 12th Conference for the Study of the Negro Problems, held at Atlanta University, May 28, 1907 (Atlanta: Atlanta University Press,) 1907, 184 pp. This book commences with a four-page bibliography and then states its purpose: "How far is there and has there been among Negro Americans a conscious effort at mutual aid in earning a living?" (p. 10). In the answer one is introduced to relevant aspects of African and West Indian history and to conditions in the American colonies. The underground railroad and some aspects of Civil War and Reconstruction history also are examined afresh from the viewpoint of this subject. Efforts at migration without and within the country also are so examined. As for "types of co-operation" the functioning of Black churches, schools, and burial and benevolent societies are studied; much of the data here can be found nowhere else. Secret societies, such as the Masons and the Odd Fellows are also analyzed in detail in terms of their economic functions. Homes and orphanages, hospitals, cemeteries are surveyed. Great attention is given to the history and then current condition of banking institutions established by Black people, while 30 pages are devoted to the fullest survey and history of cooperative businesses for consumers, for production, for transportation yet produced. All this culminates with Du Bois pointing to the significance of what he calls "the group economy"; he remarks, "so far has this gone that today in every city of the United States with a considerable Negro population, the colored group is serving itself with religious ministration, medical care, legal advice, and education of children: to a growing degree with food, houses, books, and newspapers." The data in this regard for Philadelphia as of 1907 are presented.

1911. *The Negro American Family: Report of a Social Study made principally by the college classes of 1909 and 1910 of Atlanta University, under the patronage of the Trustees of the John F. Slater Fund; together with the Proceedings of the 13th Annual Conference for the Study of the Negro Problems, held at Atlanta University, May 26, 1908* (Atlanta: Atlanta University Press) 1908, 156 pp. The program of the conference is on page 5; of special interest is the fact that the concluding speaker was Jane Addams. A "select bibliography" appears on pages 6–8. The scope of the study is an effort to understand the subject's "formation, its home, its economic organization and its daily life." Several pages discuss the family in Black Africa and the impact of slavery upon family. The "present conjugal condition" among the Afro-American people was presented via census and other reports; similar sources were used to present the data on "the size of the family." A section called "sexual morals" dealt largely with data on illegitimacy; here the study emphasized class differentiation as a significant phenomenon in Black life. A long section on "the home" was largely reprinted from the articles on this subject which appeared in *The Southern Workman* and are annotated. There is offered a detailed study of eight homes which was made by Du Bois' students; this is complete down to floor plans of the houses and covers page 68 to page 80. From page 80 through page 96 are presented photographs of various kinds of African and Afro-American homes, showing in the latter, class differentiation. The study treats "The Economics of the Family" and offers data generally of income among Black people—especially in Georgia—and data on "budgets" are presented, in great detail for specific kinds of families. In a section on "The Family Group" Du Bois again emphasizes class differentiation and states that failure to understand this has vitiated much past investigation. Here a section on New York City done by Mary White Ovington (and published in *Charities* magazine, in October, 1906) is reprinted with permission, from pages 132–134. A description of 11 relatively well-off families is detailed enough to include the breakfast menu; this commences on page 134 and terminates on page 148.

1912. *Efforts For Social Betterment among Negro Americans: Report of a Social Study made by Atlanta University under the patronage of the Trustees of the John F. Slater Fund; together with the Proceedings of the 14th Annual Conference for the Study of the Negro Problems, held at Atlanta University on May 24, 1909* (Atlanta: Atlanta University Press,) 1909, 136 pp. On page 4 is published the program of this conference; here the final address was on "The Social Betterment of the Russian Peasant," by I. M. Rubinow, formerly of the Imperial Russian Civil Service and then employed in Washington by the Labor Bureau; Rubinow was a socialist, had corresponded with Lenin and with Du Bois. The preface notes that the subject of this conference was the subject 11 years earlier, in accordance with Du Bois' idea of re-examining subjects every decade to see changes. A two-page bibliography on the topic follows. The fresh data herein came largely on the basis of letters written by Du Bois to leading Afro-American figures throughout the nation. There follow charts and tables on charitable, reform, and other kinds of "uplift" work done by Black people, institutions (especially the church) and organizations—the emphasis is upon what the Black people themselves do, and here women are especially outstanding. The special acts of charity of Black people are detailed by name where the latter is available. The data on women's self-help organizations is a special treasure of otherwise unobtainable information. On page 114 to page 117 appear the names and details concerning about 250 newspapers and magazines then being issued by Black people.

1913. *The College-Bred Negro American: Report of a Social Study made by Atlanta University under the patronage of the Trustees of the John F. Slater Fund; with the Proceedings of the 15th Annual Conference for the Study of the Negro Problems, held at Atlanta University on May 24, 1910* (Atlanta: Atlanta University Press,) 1910, 104 pp. This is the first of these studies which was jointly edited by Du Bois and Augustus G. Dill, at that time an associate professor of sociology at Atlanta and later Business Manager of the *Crisis*. The precise subject of the 15th Conference was "The Higher Education of Negro Americans"; in the program several presidents of Black colleges participated, as did J. H. Dillard, president of the Jeanes Fund. It is noted in the preface that a conference was devoted to this subject in 1900; it is added, "our object is not simply to serve science. We wish not only to make the truth clear but to present it in such shape as will encourage and help social reform." The resolution of the conference states that "there is an increased and pressing demand for college trained Negroes." It calls attention to the need for high schools for Black youngsters in the South and states that each Southern state should have at least one "liberally endowed" college for its Black youth. A three-page bibliography is presented. The method of the study, in addition to normal research, was to send a questionnaire to every "living colored college graduate"; it is here reproduced, and on the basis of replies as well as published data, etc., a picture of the actualities of college-level education for Black people is detailed. There is also a consideration of Northern institutions and their attitudes towards Black students. Certain specific studies were done by people other than the editors: Paul S. Peirce on Black alumni from Iowa colleges (pp. 26–34); Black students and graduates of the University of Kansas, by L. M. Peace (pp. 34–41). There also is a careful report on the experiences of Black physicians, teachers, lawyers, and preachers. A four-page listing of books and pamphlets published by Black college graduates is given (74–78) and a list of the public offices held by them throughout the country is published (p. 78–79). Fascinating sections include "hindrances" and "philosophy of life" both depending heavily upon quotations from letters. The "conclusion" is "that the work of the Negro college and that of the college-bred Negro American have been of inestimable value."

1914. *The Common School and the Negro American: Report of a Social Study made by Atlanta University under the patronage of the Trustees of the John F. Slater Fund; with the Proceedings of the 16th Annual Conference for the Study of the Negro Problems, held at Atlanta University on* May 30, 1911 (Atlanta: Atlanta University Press,) 1911, 140 pp. Again, Professor Dill is a fellow editor. A four-page bibliography appears. Certain historical material repeats the report on the same question made ten years earlier. But the data are based on latest reports of the U.S. Commissioner of Education and of the Superintendents of Education in the Southern states, plus the District of Columbia and Kansas. In addition a letter-questionnaire was sent to dozens of city superintendents of education and to Black teachers throughout the South. Notes that not only are schools, when they exist, very poor, but that there are whole counties in Missouri, Kentucky, Maryland and the Gulf states (Alabama, Louisiana, Mississippi) where no schools at all for Black children exist. Teacher salaries, expenditures on students, cost of buildings and equipment are all detailed and compared with data for whites—this is done state by state. A long section summarizes and quotes from responses to the questionnaires. The study shows a deterioration in education for Black people since disfranchisement.

1915. *The Negro American Artisan: Report of a Social Study made by Atlanta University under the Patronage of the John F. Slater Fund; with the Proceedings of the 17th Annual Conference for the Study of the Negro Problems, held at Atlanta University, May 27, 1912* (Atlanta: Atlanta University Press, 1912) 144 pp. Again jointly edited by Dill and Du Bois. The Proceedings program (p.4) notes that Florence Kelley delivered two papers at this Conference and also gave the concluding address. The preface begins: "There is only one sure basis of social reform and that is Truth—a careful, detailed knowledge of the essential facts of each social problem." There follows an apt summary of Du Bois' main commitment to this point and, in essentials, thereafter. This study goes "over virtually the same ground" as that of 1902. In the resolutions it is insisted that hostility to the labor movement "is a mistake." It adds: "Let black men fight prejudice and exclusion in the labor world and fight it hard; but do not fight the labor movement."

The bibliography of 12 pages is particularly valuable. The text repeats the earlier material (not verbatim) in terms of historical background and then on the basis of printed material and replies to questionnaires and offers a state-by-state study of Black workers, their jobs and income, and their relationship with the trade-union movement.

1916. *Morals and Manners Among Negro Americans: Report of a Social Study made by Atlanta University under the patronage of the Trustees of the John F. Slater Fund; with the Proceedings of the 18th Annual Conference for the Study of the Negro Problems, held at Atlanta University, on May 26, 1913* (Atlanta: Atlanta University Press,) 1913, 138 pp. Again jointly' edited by Dill and Du Bois—the latter now stated, on the title page, to be with the NAACP.

In the program Du Bois (now of New York City) delivers an opening and a closing address. This is the second study of the subject; the first having been made in 1903. In the resolutions, it is affirmed that the Black church has improved in its social dedication and that the women have been outstanding. "no group of women in the world have amid studied insult and race discrimination made so brave a fight for social betterment or accomplished so much of actual, tangible good." A two-page bibliography appears. Perhaps of greatest value in this study is its extensive and very critical examination of the official data regarding crime among Black people (beginning on page 36 and ending on page 50) showing not only the racism of the police and courts but also the role of the white press. Marital conditions and latest data on church organization plus the opinions of many Black people on the functioning of the churches conclude this study.

1917. *Report of the first Conference of Negro Land-Grant Colleges for Coordinating a Program of Cooperative Social Studies (Twenty-Sixth Atlanta University Conference to Study the Negro Problems)*, No. 22, (Atlanta: Atlanta University Publications, 1943), 84 pp. This met at Atlanta University in April, 1943; the first ten pages, by Du Bois, summarize the history of the Atlanta conferences from 1896 to 1943, giving in detail his proposals of 1941 and 1942 which led to the present conference and press comments are quoted. The details of this 1943 conference commence on page 33 and include comments thereon by various scholars, as E. Franklin Frazier, Thomas L. Smith, and others. The work concludes with plans in each of the concerned colleges for their research activities in the following year.

1918. *Encyclopedia of the Negro: Preparatory Volume with Reference Lists and Reports*, by W. E. B. Du Bois and Guy B. Johnson, prepared with the cooperation of E. Irene Diggs, Agnes C. L. Donohugh, Guion Johnson, Rayford W. Logan, and L. D. Reddick, introduction by Anson Phelps Stokes (New York: Phelps-Stokes Fund), 1945, 208 pp. A second, "revised and enlarged" edition was published in 1946, (containing 217 pages). The full history of the idea of this *Encyclopedia* must await later publication; here it may be stated that it dates from no later than 1909 when Du Bois began active work on the idea. In 1931 the Phelps-Stokes Fund began its support of the effort, and after some delay, compounded by the Second World War, the first edition of the book appeared in March, 1945. The senior editor throughout was Dr. Du Bois. Early in the project his associate editor was Professor Robert E. Park of the University of Chicago but after a few years Professor Guy B. Johnson, formerly of the University of North Carolina and Executive Director of the Southern Regional Council, became his associate editor. There is a seven-page essay, signed by Du Bois and Johnson, on "Need of an Encyclopedia of the Negro," which gives some background to such efforts, an indication of relevant work hitherto published and affirms as the purpose of this effort "to use the best scholarship in the world in placing before average intelligent citizens of the world a carefully considered statement concerning the past and present of the Negro race." The second edition has no additional writing by Du Bois but contains new entries and references not in the first edition.

1919. Du Bois was the author of an undated and unsigned printed one-page sheet—probably issued in 1935—headed, "Scope of Proposed Encyclopedia." This was sent to scholars whom Du Bois wished to interest in the project. It described in some detail the kind of effort Du Bois had in mind, suggested that four large volumes (totalling 2,000,000 words) might be sufficient and traced the history of research in this field from the Atlanta University studies of the late 19th century to the efforts of the Department of Records and Research established at Tuskegee Institute in 1908, Monroe Work's *Negro Year* Book, commencing in 1912, and Dr. Woodson's Association for the Study of Negro Life and History, established in 1915. Note was also taken of relevant developments in Africa and in Europe.

1920. *An Appeal to the World: A Statement on the Denial of Human Rights to Minorities in the Case of Citizens of Negro Descent in the United States of America and an Appeal to the United Nations for Redress* (New

York: prepared for the NAACP 1947), 94 pp. Du Bois worked on assembling the material for this appeal to the United Nations for approximately 18 months beginning in 1945. It contains 16 chapters as follows: Introduction by Du Bois; on the legal status of Black people in the United States to 1914 by Earl B. Dickerson; since the First World War by Milton R. Konvitz; the present legal and social status by William R. Ming, Jr.; the patterns of discrimination in basic human rights by Leslie S. Perry; and the United Nations and the rights of minorities, by Rayford W. Logan. Du Bois' introduction (pp. 1–14) is a swift survey of Afro-American history, present population, political disabilities, past efforts at petition by the Afro-American people, an indication of the problems the color line will present to the United Nations in the United States, a description of the NAACP as the spokesman of the Afro-American people in this case. Throughout the introduction is Du Bois' sense of a kind of Afro-American nationality; he constantly refers to the Black people of the United States in comparison with "other smaller nations" or as really "one of the considerable nations of the world," or as constituting "almost a nation within a nation", etc. (pp. 1, 14).

CHAPTER VII

PAMPHLETS AND LEAFLETS BY DU BOIS

(In this section are annotated only those pamphlets and leaflets which were *not* originally published in other forms.)

1921. *The Conservation of Races*, American Negro Academy, *Occasional Papers*, II, (Washington, 1897), 15 pp. The reality of race, but that term defined as "a vast family of human beings, generally of common blood and language, always of common history, tradition, and impulses, who are both voluntarily and involuntarily striving together for the accomplishment of certain more or less vividly conceived ideals of life." He adopts a fairly conventional view (for that time) of the "races" and of their characteristics, but denying, of course, concepts of inferiority. He holds, however, to the need for the integrity of the Black people and sees those in the United States as being "in the van of Pan-Negroism" and therefore "their destiny is not absorption by the white Americans." They must develop their own individuality and "wonderful possibilities of culture." Here first occur the following lines: "What after all, am I? Am I an American or am I a Negro? Can I be both?" Given "a satisfactory adjustment of economic life" two or more different peoples could live together harmoniously under one citizenship. We should seek, therefore, "to conserve our physical powers, our intellectual endowments, our spiritual ideals ... for the accomplishment of the ends we need race organizations ... for positive advance [and] for negative defense." *We* must lead our own liberation and guard our own people and for this we need careful and regular conferring and planning together—a role, he suggests, that the American Negro Academy might fulfill. Showing the date of this effort, it emphasizes, as "the first and greatest step" to the solution of what is "commonly called the Negro Problem," correction of the deficiencies within ourselves—something simultaneously being stressed, then (and later) by Booker T. Washington. But Du Bois does add the need on the part of "the white people in this country" to provide greater impartiality in economic and intellectual matters and "a greater respect for personal liberty and worth, regardless of race."

1922. *A Program For Social Betterment* is a four-page pamphlet issued probably sometime in 1898 in Atlanta; it was an abstract of a paper given by Du Bois before the First Sociological Society of Atlanta. It defines the character of sociology and the subjects properly within its domain; its connection with efforts at social reform is made explicit. A bibliography is included, which mentions the work of Charles Booth in England and the *Hull House Maps and Papers* published in New York in 1895 by T. Y. Crowell & Co. On the last page, Du Bois lists and briefly describes 32 "possible efforts among Atlanta Negroes", including the establishment of day nurseries, circulating libraries, and cooperative businesses.

1923. *Careers Open to Young Negro-Americans* (Atlanta University Negro Conference Tract No. 1 (Atlanta: c. 1900), 4 pp. It lists kinds of work, advantages and disadvantages of each, suggestions for "self-development," and a table divided in two columns for men and women, showing the occupations followed by Afro-American people in 1900.

1924. *The African Development Company* is a printed one-page leaflet dated March 1, 1902, giving its office as Philadelphia. This is a prospectus of a company to develop lands in East Central Africa; the committee behind it is made up of Du Bois as secretary, T. J. Minton (Theophilus J. Minton, a prominent Afro-American businessman of Philadelphia) as chairman, and H. T. Kealing (Hightower T. Kealing, then editor of the A.M.E. *Review*, president of Western University in Kansas after 1910, and formerly a president of Paul Quinn College in his native Texas, as treasurer.)

1925. *Some Notes on the Negroes in New York City: Compiled from the Reports of the United States Census and Other Sources* (Atlanta: Atlanta University Press, 1903, 5 pp.) Data on population, including changes since 1800, with a separate section for Brooklyn; character of the population by age groups, sex, marital status, occupations of men and women, kinds of homes, schools, voters, death-rate, data on arrests, and a calendar of "Historic Events Touching the Negro in New York."

1926. *A Bibliography of Negro Folk Songs*, (Atlanta: Atlanta University Press, 1903 8 pp.) One of the earliest of such efforts, reflecting Du

Bois' keen love for Afro-American music. He had been a manager of the Fisk University chorus when a student and, in 1903, published in his book, *Souls* a magnificent chapter on spirituals.

1927. *Heredity and the Public Schools: A Lecture Delivered under the Auspices of the Principals' Association of the Colored Schools of Washington, D.C. Friday, March 25, 1904* (Washington: R. L. Pendleton, Printer, 1904, 11 pp.). The address is to Afro-American teachers and the question posed, "is the average Negro child capable of essentially the same training and development as the average white child" (p. 4). The answer is, yes, and it is argued with care. The emphasis is that in terms of biological heredity there is no disadvantage for the Black child and in terms of social heredity—what would now be called environment—where that is not at the highest level our duty is to raise that level, and meanwhile, work unceasingly with the children, have confidence in and love for them, and transmit that feeling to them.

1928. *An Attack* is a one-page printed leaflet, dated Atlanta, and signed. It was issued in 1906 in 250 copies and was mailed by Du Bois to many Afro-American leaders. It urges protest against an attack upon the honor of Black women in an article by "a colored minister," named T. Nelson Baker of Pittsfield, Massachusetts, and published in the *Congregationalist* on April 7, 1906. Du Bois' fury shows through; the last line reads, "will you not help defend our best black womanhood?"

1929. *Race Prejudice: An Address delivered at 'The Saturday Discussions' of The Republican Club, New York, March 5, 1910* (New York: The Republican Club, 1910 Document No. 77, 5 pp.) He argues the unwholesome effect of racism upon the politics of the country —strengthening especially the Democratic Party—and upon the economics of the country, for it limits productivity and intensifies unrest. In any case, "*there is in this world no such force as the force of a man determined to rise.*" (p. 8). In view of all these considerations, " ... it is a matter not simply of politics but of the widest and broadest statesmanship, of economic foresight and deepest religious thought to see that race prejudice in the United States is combatted and corrected and lessened."

1930. *The Atlanta University Extension Lectures,* 1910 is a one-page printed leaflet giving the titles of "A course of seven lectures at Atlanta Baptist College" on "The History of the Negro Race" from April 11 to April 20, when an examination was given.

1931. *College-Bred Negro Communities: Address of Professor W. E. B. Du Bois at Brookline, Massachusetts.* Atlanta University Leaflet No. 23, (Atlanta: Atlanta University Press, 1910, 16 pp.) The Black people must teach themselves and help themselves; for this they must have the best possible education, the best possible teachers—*in the first place* —and to get the best possible teachers they must have excellent colleges. This is a main commitment of Atlanta University; it is deserving of the assistance of all who favor democracy and human progress.

1932. *Race Relations in the United States: An Appeal to England and Europe,* signed by Du Bois and 32 other leading Afro-Americans, including Bishop Alexander Walters, William Pickens, William Monroe Trotter, Archibald H. Grimké, dated New York, October 26, 1910 [but actually sent out November 23 after additional signatures were obtained]. This is a reply to Booker T. Washington, who, on a tour in Europe, had given "the impression that the Negro problem in America is in process of satisfactory solution." It isn't and this summarizes reality. It was written by Du Bois.

1933. *The Social Evolution of the Black South: American Negro Monographs* Vol. I, March, 1911, edited by J. H. Cromwell, published by R. L. Pendleton (9 pp., throughout, including cover, Du Bois' name is spelled Burkhardt). This traces "the way in which the more intimate matters of contact of Negroes with themselves and with their neighbors have changed in the evolution of the last half century from slavery to larger freedom" (p. 3). An incisive examination of the slave-plantation "community" is made. As he develops the theme to the present, Du Bois remarks that of all the types abounding "I believe that at the end of the devious way of the compromiser and liar lies moral death," (p. 11). He wants people with the moral courage "to say that *this is wrong* in the South and *that is right,* and *I am fighting for the right*; who will stoop, if necessary, but will let no man ever doubt that they stoop to conquer."

1934. *Disfranchisement* (New York: [1912] National American Woman Suffrage Association, 8 pp. A careful examination of the current arguments against enfranchising women and a reasoned rejection of them all, fundamentally on the grounds of partisanship for democracy. It ends with an emphasis upon democracy if a sane economy is ever to appear. "The passing of the strong monarch in industry as in politics will spell anarchy in many places, but social justice will eventually come. How necessary then to build a state of the broadest democracy to cope with the industrial problem within nations and between nations and races."

1935. *A Half Century of Freedom* (New York: (NAACP,) [1913] 4 pp. This pamphlet is not identical with, but is highly repetitious of, "Forty Years of Freedom," published in *Missionary Review*, June, 1911.

1936. *A Pageant*, signed by Du Bois, a four-page leaflet issued, as internal evidence makes clear, in 1915, probably in November. The "pageant" is *The Star of Ethiopia* which Du Bois wrote in 1911 —originally with the idea of helping raise money for the NAACP. This leaflet explains that the pageant was first performed in 1913 in New York to audiences of approximately 14,000 people. With the showing of "Birth of a Nation," he was determined to have this pageant again shown; it was in Washington and witnessed by 12,000 people (among the patrons were Margaret Wilson, daughter of the President). The A.M.E. Church has asked him to present the pageant in May (1916). "When one considers the traditional attitude of the Negro church hitherto to drama this is a most significant and encouraging sign."

1937. *The Star of Ethiopia: A Pageant: Hollywood Bowl, June 15 and 18, 1925* a printed four-page program of the pageant which details its six "episodes" and names the principal participants; the proceeds went to the Welfare Bureau of the Los Angeles Branch of the NAACP.

1938. *The Amenia Conference: An Historic Negro Gathering*, Troutbeck Leaflets Number Eight, Amenia, New York, 1925, privately printed [in 200 copies] at the Troutbeck Press, 18 pp. This conference occurred at the estate of the Joel Spingarns in upstate New York, August 24 to August 26, 1916; it came at the end of an era (Booker T. Washington had recently died) and marked "the end of the old things and the old thoughts and the old ways of attacking the race problem ... it was the beginning of the new things ... [with] the Negro race more united and more ready to meet the problems of the world ... " (p. 17). Among those participating were Kelly Miller, Leslie Hill, Emmett J. Scott, John Hope, Mary B. Talbert, Charles W. Chesnutt, Addie W. Hunton, Mary Church Terrell, George W. Crawford, and "Inez Milholland, in the glory of her young womanhood dropped by, in this which was destined to be almost the last year of her magnificent life" (p. 13).

1939. *Report of the Debate Conducted by the Chicago Forum: "Shall the Negro Be Encouraged to Seek Cultural Equality?" Affirmative*: W. E.

Burghardt Du Bois ... *Negative*: Lothrop Stoddard ... *March 17, 1929* Fred Atkins Moore, *Director of the Chicago Forum* [Chicago, 1929], 24 pp. This debate was heard by thousands and very widely reported by the Black and white press in the country. Du Bois attacks not only racism but elitism as a whole; shows that Stoddard's ideas also rule out most of the white people from the "Nordic" superman universe. A devastating attack upon the history and conduct of these supermen and upon the cost of that conduct upon the well-being of humanity. The days of rule by these supermen are numbered—why is explained—and this is the final sentence in Du Bois "Closing Statement" (p. 24). "I wonder if the future is not going to show that the civilization of the world is the gift of the Few simply because only the few have a chance to develop; and that when the millions of all people, white and black, yellow and brown, have real opportunity, that civilization in its highest and best form is coming from them and not from the present aristocracy?"

1940. A *Study of the Atlanta University Federal Housing Area*, giving Du Bois as author, assisted by Louise Torrence, Lula Gambrell, William H. Shell, Rynalder D. Rambeau, Edward R. Rodriquez, John E. Bowen, Jr., and other Students of Atlanta University (Atlanta: May, 1934), mimeographed, with a printed schedule, 24 pp. The survey was made at the request of President Rufus E. Clement, of Atlanta University; a planned federal housing project was in the offing. Du Bois prepared a careful questionnaire on the status of families in the area, stores available, and their own desires. Two hundred and forty-one Black and one white family were interviewed, several store owners and 67 vacant houses examined. All the details are here presented.

1941. A *Pageant in Seven Decades*: 1868–1938: *An Address Delivered on the Occasion of his Seventieth Birthday at the University Convocation of Atlanta University, Morehouse College, and Spelman College, February 23, 1938, c.* 1938, Atlanta, 44 pp. This is a succinct and characteristically objective and open summary of his life; he recapitulates his attitude towards Marcus Garvey (p. 35), quotes from his pieces on him in the *Crisis*, and adds, "in his case, as in the case of others, I have repeatedly been accused of enmity and jealousy, which have been so far from my thought that the accusations have been a rather bitter experience." On this occasion, Rayford W. Logan—then a Professor at Atlanta University—made the presentation of the bust of Du Bois (by Alexander Portnoff) to the university, which now graces the main reading room of its library. (The text of this pamphlet ran serially in the Amsterdam *News* for 25 weekly installments, from March 26, 1938 to September 17, 1938.)

1942. *A Colonial conference* is a printed card, signed by Du Bois as head of the Department of Special Research. It was issued early in 1945 (possibly at the end of 1944) and is a call to a conference to be held April 6, 1945 at the 135th Street Branch of the New York Public Library. People from the colonies and close students of them were to be present. This conference was held; resolutions were adopted which went to the United Nations and served as one of the preparatory efforts culminating in the 1947 *Appeal to the World* (No. 1920).

1943. *Behold the Land*, (Birmingham, Alabama, Southern Negro Youth Congress, 1946, Du Bois text on pages 7–15). Text of the address delivered in Columbia, South Carolina, October 20, 1946, at the closing session of the Seventh south-wide conference of the S.N.Y.C. which was attended by 861 young Black and white people. The speech is a prose poem calling upon the youth of the South—especially those who are Black but including those who are white and love justice—to stand and fight, never to yield, and thus to make it possible, if not for our children, then our children's children, to make of the South a land of beauty and reason and brotherhood. (The compiler of this book was present and has never seen an audience so attentive and so deeply moved as this one on this occasion.)*

1944. *I Speak For Peace*, (New York: Peace Information Center, 1950), 4 pp. This is the statement made by Du Bois at a press conference held in Harlem on September 24, 1950, when he announced his candidacy on the American Labor Party ticket for U.S. Senator. "The fundamental problem of our age," he said, and these words were italicized, *"is that in our unprecedented organization of industry, with its marvelous technique and world-wide extent, the vast majority of mankind remain sick, ignorant and starved while a few have more income in goods and services than they can use."*

1945. *Elect the First Negro U.S. Senator From New York*, is a one-page printed letter, signed, and urging registration during October, 1950, so that votes may be cast for him. This is issued by the Harlem Council, A.L.P., whose chairman was Ewart G. Guinier (Professor Guinier is

*A fairly full—but cold—report of this speech and occasion, by George Streator, is in the New York *Times*, October 21, 1946, p. 31.

now head of the Afro-American Studies Department at Harvard University).

1946. *Peace Is Dangerous* (New York: *The National Guardian*, 1951), 15 pp. This is the text of an address delivered on Armistice Day, November 11, 1951, at the Community Church in Boston and is, in the main, an appraisal of the Cold War as stemming from "the desperate American attempt to revive colonial imperialism with the United States in the saddle instead of Britain" (p. 12). It calls for determined resistance to aggression abroad and repression at home and insists that such resistance can succeed.

1947. *What Is Wrong with the United States?* a fourteen-page pamphlet, (New York: American Labor Party, 1952). This is the complete text of the speech delivered in Madison Square Garden, May 13, 1952, when the campaign of that party was launched for local candidates and for Vincent Hallinan and Charlotta Bass for president and vice-president. It is an analysis of why McCarthyism exists and what can be done about it; above all, it affirms that at this time in history there is a vital need for a real alternative in politics and that only a third party offers hope for such an alternative.

1948. *The Story of Benjamin Franklin*, (Vienna: World Peace Council 1956), in French and English editions 39 pp. Issued on the 250th anniversary of his birth, this is a straightforward account of his life, taken mainly—as Du Bois states—from Franklin's own autobiography and the biographies of him by Samuel Morse and, in particular, Carl Van Doren. It stresses his anticolonialism, antislavery, rationalism and scientific efforts, and his hatred of cant and devotion to enhancing human well-being.

1949. *The American Negro and the Darker World* (Brooklyn: New York, National Committee to Defend Negro Leadership, 1957) 5 pp., unnumbered, pamphlet, with introduction by Paul Robeson. Text of a speech delivered in Harlem, April 30, 1957. What linked the darker peoples of the world was "the immensely important fact of economic condition" even more than "the essentially unimportant fact of skin color." A call for studying socialism as that form of society—in varied particulars—which will be the shape of the world. Du Bois comments that, "in the West Indies, Garvey tried to have Negroes share in western exploitation of Africa." But, "white industry stopped him before he could begin."

1950. *Africa in Battle Against Colonialism, Racialism, Inperialism*, (Chicago: Afro-American Heritage Association, 1960) 12 pp., unnumbered pamphlet, with an introduction by Ishmael Flory. This is the text of an address delivered in Chicago in 1958; it sketches the history of colonialism and ends on a note indicating belief that "it will be but a few years before European colonialism supported by American capital will cease to control Africa."

1951. *Socialism Today*, (Chicago: Afro–American Heritage Association, 1960) 8 pp., unnumbered pamphlet, the text of a speech delivered in Chicago, November 11, 1959. He has returned from 11 months in Britain, Holland, France, Czechoslovakia, East Germany, the Soviet Union, and China. Du Bois describes the likenesses and contrasts in capitalist and socialist lands. He emphasizes social planning and welfare in the latter, plus great fear of a world war; notes elimination of church influence in the U.S.S.R. as "one of the greatest forward steps taken by any nation." "Even more astonishing than the Soviet Union," he says, "is China"; he believes that "sooner than any nation today it is likely to achieve complete communism." It refutes theories of racism and elitism. With the assistance of the U.S.S.R., China has been transformed. It is necessary—especially for Black Americans—to study questions of socialism and, if possible, to visit socialist societies.

1952. *The Peoples of Africa and World Peace*, in *Current Documents and Papers on International Problems Relative to World Peace* (Vienna: No. 31, 1960) a seven-page essay, dated New York City, December 27, 1959 and stressing the danger to world peace in the intention of colonialist powers to thwart the movement toward national liberation among the people of Africa.

1953. *Selected Poems*, (Accra: Ghana University Press, 1964), 42 pp. It contains a brief foreword by Kwame Nkrumah written shortly before Du Bois' death and a two-and-a-half-page "exposition" by Shirley Graham Du Bois written after his death (August, 1963). The selections were few and the editing inadequate so it was decided not to distribute this little pamphlet.

CHAPTER VIII

BOOKS BY DUBOIS

(In annotating the books by Dr. Du Bois no effort is made to trace the publishing history of these volumes. Most of his books were translated into several languages at one time or another and many have been issued in several printings, especially *The Souls of Black Folk*. In what follows, however, attention is called to new editions of his books if they contain additional or revised material.)

1954. *The Suppression of the African Slave Trade to the United States of America, 1638–1870; Harvard Historical Studies Number 1* (New York, Longmans, Green, 1896; reissued, New York: The Social Science Press, 1954), 339 pp. The 1954 edition is identical with that of 1896, except that it contains an "Apologia" on pages 327–329. There Du Bois states he was "gratified to realize how hard and honestly I worked on my subject as a young man of twenty-four." He makes certain criticisms from the vantage ground of almost 60 years: the monographic method tends to abstract from the whole flow of history a particular component and in so doing some distortion appears; the work of Freud and of Marx were not mastered or really known at this time. Du Bois offers no further hint on how Freud's thought might have improved this monograph but he does go into some detail as to the significance of large economic and class forces in the history of the African slave trade that he would have considered more fully had he been conscious of Marxism. Had he seen this, he wrote in the Apologia, his presentation would have been less moralistic and idealistic and more concerned with questions of profits and power.

The original work's preface is dated Wilberforce University, March, 1896. In it he made the point that he felt his research into political and legal questions had been full but that "on the other hand, facts and statistics bearing on the economic side of the study have been difficult to find, and my conclusions are consequently liable to modification from this source." He also noted the distortion that inevitably appears in the monographic method of abstraction. Still, he hoped, "that I have succeeded in rendering this monograph a small contribution to the scientific study of slavery and the American Negro." This work may be considered the pioneer effort in such scientific study.

The work contains 199 pages of text, four appendices totalling 115 pages, including a bibliography of 27 pages. After an introductory chapter, the book treats its subject in terms of "the planting colonies"; "the farming colonies" and "the trading colonies." It then treats the period of the American Revolution and the debates in the Constitutional Convention. A chapter is devoted to the impact of the Haitian revolution and other chapters examine the effort at suppression (1807–1825), the international status of the trade (1783–1862), the impact upon it of "the rise of the cotton kingdom" (1820–1850). A chapter entitled "The Final Crisis" deals with the movement in the South to lift the ban upon the international slave trade—one of the first published accounts of that significant effort and not yet superceded.* The final chapter—"The Essentials in the Struggle"—condemns the "cupidity and carelessness" of those controlling power in the United States; its closing words are, " ... we may conclude that it behooves nations as well as men to do things at the very moment when they ought to be done."

1955. *The Philadelphia Negro: A Social Study: Publications of the University of Pennsylvania: Series in Political Economy and Public Law,* No. 14 (Philadelphia, published for the University, Ginn & Co., Boston, selling agents 1899), vii-xx, and 423 pages.† In 1967 a new edition of this book was issued by Shocken Books (New York) with a 40-page introduction by Professor E. Digby Baltzell of the University of Pennsylvania; strangely, this edition omitted Du Bois' own three-page preface to the original book. Otherwise, the reprint is exact.

The empirical, detailed study of urban life, together with its concern about class stratification and its insistence upon the consequence of social environment upon human behavior, make Du Bois' *Philadelphia Negro* an exceptional piece of seminal work in the history of sociology

---

*Despite the publication in 1970 of R. T. Takaki's *A Pro-Slavery Crusade: the Agitation to Reopen the African Slave Trade* (New York: The Free Press)

†Bound with Du Bois' study, as its title page states, was *A Special Report on Domestic Service,* by Isabel Eaton, a fellow of the College Settlements Association in Philadelphia, forming pages 427 through 509 and based on the model provided by Du Bois' work. Isabel Eaton was an early friend of Jane Addams and like her was very active in anti-war and anti-racist movements. She studied at Smith and at Columbia University. She died in Massachusetts at the age of 73 in May, 1931. For a time she was in charge of the Robert Gould Shaw House in Boston; she and the doctor remained friends from the 1890's until her death.

(especially urban sociology). This type of study had been undertaken first, perhaps, by Frederick Engels in his *The Condition of the Working Class in England* (1844) and was pursued beginning approximately 20 years thereafter in Germany and in England—in the latter case, the work of Charles Booth was outstanding. The Booth effort directly influenced Jane Addams, who was in England in the 1880's and who, of course, founded Hull House in Chicago in 1889. Six years thereafter, began the appearance of the *Hull House Papers and Maps*.

It is within this context that one may place *The Philadelphia Negro*, whose preface is dated Atlanta University, June 1, 1899. Professor Samuel McCune Lindsay, then of the University's sociology depart-ment—and influential in having Du Bois undertake this study—states in his "Introduction" (pp. vii–xv) that "this inquiry into the condition of the Negroes of Philadelphia was begun August 1, 1896, and, with two months' intermission in the summer of 1897, was pursued continuously until January 1, 1898." That two months intermission was spent by Du Bois in studying the Afro-American population in Virginia; a reason for this, he states in the preface, was that "large numbers of the Philadelphia Negroes immigrate from Virginia" and so he studied that area "for my own enlightenment."*

In this preface, too, Dr. Du Bois expresses "the general sense of obligation which I feel toward the Negroes of Philadelphia, and especially toward those of the Seventh Ward, for their broad-minded attitude toward an inquiry which was at best a prying into private affairs." Of course, during the period of the study, Dr. Du Bois (and Nina Gomer of Iowa, whom he had just married) lived in that ghetto. He added in that preface—clearly he knew then that the addition was crucial—that he had studied the inhabitants of the Seventh Ward with the assumption "that the Negro problems are problems of human beings"; he pointed out that without these kinds of detailed, sympa-thetic, scientific studies "the labors of philanthropist and statesman must continue to be, to a large extent, barren and unfruitful."

The study itself is an exhaustive examination of every aspect of ghetto life: history, demography, family, migrations, education, oc-cupations, health, organized life (especially the churches), criminals and prisons, pauperism, alcoholism, housing, amusements, class dif-ferentiations, contact between white and Black, extent of voting and political activity; and there is "a final word." Appendices give the schedules (questions) used in the house-to-house inquiry, legislation

---

*The result appeared in the 1898 *Bulletin* of the U.S. Department of Labor, *The Negroes of Farmville, Virginia: A Social Study* (No. 1818).

and petitions and court references to Black people (including "slave tumults") and a five-page bibliography. The final section in this book takes up the then extraordinary idea of "the duty of whites" in connection with the socalled Negro question. Its last paragraph reads:

> A polite and sympathetic attitude toward these striving thousands; a delicate avoidance of that which wounds and embitters them; a generous granting of opportunity to them; a seconding of their efforts, and a desire to reward honest success—all this, added to proper striving on their part, will go far even in our day toward making all men, white and black, realize what the great founder of the city meant, when he named it the City of Brotherly Love.

1956. *The Souls of Black Folk: Essays and Sketches* (Chicago: A. C. McClurg & Co.,1903), 265 pp., and a two-page "Forethought." A new edition, copyrighted by Du Bois in 1953, was published by the Blue Heron Press of New York. This was in the midst of the McCarthy period when the respectable newspapers and publishers would have nothing to do with Du Bois; nor with Howard Fast who established the Blue Heron Press in order to issue books written by himself and other "criminals" of the day, such as Du Bois. The 1953 edition contains 7 substantive changes and about 20 additional minor verbal ones. Beginning in the 1960's, paperback editions of the 1903 edition were published and sold by the hundreds of thousands; they were, however, filled with typographical errors, omissions, and alterations. It is, therefore, important that either the McClurg edition (and there were 24 printings—all identical) or the Blue Heron edition be used.*

This book is one of the classics in the English language; it is noteworthy that, on the whole, contemporary reviewers, Black and white, knew that they had examined a book that appears once in a lifetime. Several of its chapters had been published earlier—in somewhat altered form—in magazines, but its essay "Of Booker T. Washington and Others" (Chapter III) was largely new and historic in bringing before a wide audience the essential distinctions that were to become organizational within a short time, for example, the Niagara Movement (1905) versus the Tuskegee Machine. The book is redolent with Du Bois' pride in and love for his people and the sense that they had a specially ennobling mission to perform for Mankind because of their oppressed condition and their great artistry and dramatic sense. The volume affirms the centrality of the so-called Negro question in

---

*A detailed comparison of the 1903 and 1953 editions and some indication of the failings in recent paperback editions are in this writer's essay in the *Negro History Bulletin*, January, 1970.

terms of U.S. history and society; it reflects a kind of national consciousness that was also marked throughout Du Bois' life and his awareness of the relationship of the position of the Afro-American peoples with the dark peoples of the world and with the new turn of the United States towards imperialism—what he calls in this book, "the recent course of the United States toward weaker and darker peoples in the West Indies, Hawaii, and the Philippines" (p. 52).

Each essay is a gem, but the ones in which he describes the wonderful Josie, the classical study of the spirituals, the loving treatment of Alexander Crummell and the excruciatingly intense essay on the death of the son, Burghardt,* are examples of magnificent prose.

The very title of the book—*Souls of Black Folk*—is important in comprehending its impact; for just as Du Bois in his Philadelphia study felt it important to remark in the preface that he was writing of Black people as *people*, so *Souls* appeared at a time when the idea of the subhumanity (not merely inferiority) of the Afro-American was common. In that sense, the book when read—as, for example, by Washington Gladden, the influential Christian reformer, or by Henry James—had an overwhelming impact; at the same time, its insight, which amounted to genius and its militancy which in its day was extraordinary, moved to the marrow tens of thousands of Black people. It retains that impact for all who are able to read and think and feel.

1957. *John Brown* (Philadelphia: George W. Jacobs & Co., 1909), reprinted in December 1962 by International Publishers (New York) with a new two-page preface and the addition, in the last chapter —"The Legacy of John Brown"—of eight pages (pp. 395–402). In the original preface, Du Bois wrote that with the existence of the several biographies already available "the only excuse for another life of John Brown is an opportunity to lay new emphasis upon the material which they have so carefully collected, and to treat these facts from a different point of view." That he did—and the point of view was from behind the Veil—so eminently appropriate for "the man who of all Americans," as Du Bois wrote, "has perhaps come nearest to touching the real souls of black folk." Writing in 1909, Du Bois held that "the cost of liberty is less than the price of repression, even though that cost be blood." He reaffirmed this idea, with emphasis, in the pages added for

---

*The doctor carried a photograph of his child and a lock of his hair with him to his dying day; Mrs. Du Bois was never quite the same after his passing. The child was carried to Great Barrington to be buried so that he would not lie in Georgia's tainted Jim Crow soil. *The Souls* is dedicated to him, and to the newly born daughter—"To Burghardt and Yolande the lost and the found."

the 1962 edition and pointed to the revolutions in Russia and China as confirming that opinion. Dr. Du Bois once told this writer that of all his books, that on John Brown was his favorite; it was a great joy to him that he lived to see the 1962 edition.

1958. *The Quest of the Silver Fleece: A Novel* (Chicago: A. C. McClurg & Co., 1911), 434 pp. After the great success of *Souls,* its publisher urged the Doctor to put "the problem" into a novel and thus—he suggested —reach a wider audience. The result was this novel but its sale never approached that of *Souls.* The novel remains an interesting effort at a realistic portrayal of the impact of cotton, racism, and peonage upon the nation early in the 20th century, as Upton Sinclair and Frank Norris had done about the same time with meat and wheat. The Black figures—especially the women—are strong and the whites are drawn in varied form—the "car-window expert" (as he had written of Northern white "touring" professors in his *Souls*), the hesitant liberal, the evil Bourbon, the courageous and dedicated white opponent of racism (also a woman). The "note" preceding the text is dated New York City, August 15, 1911; it affirms the effort at honesty. At the end of the book, speaking explicitly to the reader, he asks him not to lay "these words aside for a moment's phantasy, *but lift up thine eyes to the Horror in this land:—the maiming and mocking and murdering of my people, and the prisonment of their souls.*" The book's appearance in 1911 places Du Bois among the significant precursors of the renaissance to break forth in less than a decade.

1959. *The Negro* (volume XCI of the Home University Library of Modern Knowledge, New York: Henry Holt, 1915), 254 pp. The preface to this book is dated New York City, February 1, 1915. Among its inspirers were Franz Boas, Leo Frobenius of Germany, Harry H. Johnston of Great Britain, and the following Africans: Edward Blyden, Majola Agbebi (whom Du Bois had met at the 1900 Pan-African Congress and at the 1911 Universal Races Congress), J. Tengo Jabavu, (whom he also met at the 1911 congress). That congress itself was important for its influence upon certain publishers in England and the United States, which made them at least conscious of Africa's existence. One must note, also, that *The Negro* appears the same year as Woodson's Association for the Study of Negro Life and History is launched; it reflects the general intensification of Black consciousness and militancy which spelled the end of Tuskegee's domination (as the year marks the death of Booker T. Washington).

The book is a pioneering effort at depicting, within one modest volume, the entire scope of Africa's past; bearing this in mind, its scholarship has stood well the test of time.* It places also, within this context, the position of African-derived peoples in the United States, Latin America, and the West Indies and does not fail to show the relationship between the exploitation of Africa and the rise of capitalism and imperialism in Europe and the United States.

In his original preface, Du Bois pointed to limitations of previous research, his own linguistic limitations, especially in terms of African languages, and the brevity of the effort, as precluding the possibility of definitive treatment. Yet, he hoped his effort would "enable the general reader to know as men a sixth or more of the human race"; that it accomplished.

1960. *Darkwater: Voices from within the Veil* (New York: Harcourt, Brace & Co., 1921; copyright, 1920 by Harcourt, Brace and Howe), 276 pp. This consists of poems, essays, sketches previously published in the *Crisis*, the *Independent*, the *Atlantic*, and the *Journal of Race Development* but here very considerably revised, changed, expanded. The book was widely reviewed and sold fairly well; almost all the white reviewers, in the United States and abroad, were astonished at the intensity of feeling, the great militancy, and the hatred for the oppressor manifested in the volume.

The preface—called "postscript"—is dated New York, 1919, but at one point (p. 23) Du Bois writes that he is finishing the book "On my Fiftieth Birthday"—i. e., February 23, 1918. In a chapter called "Of the Ruling of Men" there is reference to the "Russian Soviets" and to the rich who "fly to arms to prevent that greatest experiment in industrial democracy which the world has ever seen." He closes that essay by remarking, "perhaps the finest contribution of current Socialism to the world is neither its light nor its dogma, but the idea back of its one mighty word—Comrade!" This, plus his chapter on "The Damnation of Women," which excoriated the racists for their behavior towards Black women, were grounds enough for Congressman James F. Byrnes of South Carolina to denounce the "Bolshevik agent", Dr. Du Bois!

1961. *The Gift of Black Folk: Negroes in the Making of America* (Boston: Stratford Co., 1924), 349 pp. This book was copyrighted by the Knights of Columbus in 1924 and was written at the request of that organization. It was a volume in the Racial Contribution Series sponsored by the Knights of Columbus. That organization was moved

---

*On this point, see the introductory essay by Professor George Shepperson to the paperback reissue of *The Negro* (New York: Oxford University Press, 1970).

to this effort because of the anti-Catholicism and nativism which reached a high point as part of the reaction and repression of the post-World War period; the upsurge of the KKK was especially unwelcome to organizations such as the Knights of Columbus. All this is made fairly explicit in an essay, "The Racial Contributions to the United States," appearing as an introduction to this volume (pp. 1–28) and written by Edward F. McSweeney, the editor of the series. The book contains a foreword of four pages which is unsigned but which was probably written by Du Bois;* the body of the book then begins on page 33. Its first five chapters treat "Black Explorers," "Black Labor," "Black Soldiers," and the Civil War and Reconstruction periods. The last four chapters are the freshest, especially the sixth, "The Freedom of Womanhood," dealing with the special difficulties and contributions of Black women; the others treat the Black contribution in music, art, and literature while "The Gift of the Spirit" deals with the church and the sense of compassion that permeates an especially oppressed people.

1962. *Dark Princess: A Romance* (New York: Harcourt, Brace & Co., 1928), 311 pp. A novel, mostly set in postwar America about a worldwide conspiracy of the colored peoples—led by an Indian princess—to forcibly overthrow the domination of white people. The conspiracy never reaches the point of actual attempt, but in the course of developing the theme, the reader is introduced to the details of Chicago politics (Du Bois correctly prophesied the election of a Black man to Congress from that city), to upper-class Black life as well as to working-class life, with the latter portrayed with greater sympathy. In his visits to Europe in 1900 and 1911 Du Bois had met people from the colored world who had proposed—for example—a military assault upon Europe via North Africa and through Spain; he had met Asian women whose beauty and insight had made deep impressions; and he had probably read of the conspiracies against the British Empire participated in by Indians in the United States, with several of them sentenced to long prison terms.† In this "romance" he was seeking to let White America have a conception of the depths of discontent in the Black world and the critical need for significant change.

*The contents page lists all the chapters and includes this foreword; the language, however, does not quite have the lilt and fire of most of Du Bois but he sometimes muted this and its content is certainly in keeping with his views at this time. In the paperback reprint of this book, with an introduction by Truman Nelson (New York: Washington Square Press, 1970), this foreword is omitted without explanation.

†*See,* Kalyan Kumar Banerjee, *Indian Freedom Movement: Revolutionaries in America* (Calcutta: Jijnasa, 1969)

1963. *Africa, Its Geography, People And Products*, 64 pp. and *Africa —Its Place in Modern History*, 63 pp. Both published in Girard, Kansas, in 1930 by the Haldeman-Julius Publications, as Little Blue Book No. 1505 and No. 1552. The first book describes the geography of the continent and compares and contrasts it with that of Europe. It describes the various peoples of Africa, their religions and languages. The resources of Africa are named and the history and results of the partition of the continent are conveyed to the reader. Attention is paid to "independent Africa" in the history and description of Abyssinia and of Liberia as well as of "partially independent Africa"—meaning Egypt and the Union of South Africa. Finally, the parts of Africa possessed by Britain (including the mandated areas), Belgium, France, Portugal, Spain, and Italy are treated historically but also with greater attention to their geography.

The second book, on *History*, is somewhat repetitious of The *Negro* but it deals only with Africa and concentrates, as the title indicates, upon the modern period, i.e., the 19th and early 20th centuries. It places Africa within the context of European power politics and shows its close connection with the imperialism of the major powers. A feature of the little book is the attention it pays to evidences of African resistance and initiative.

1964. *Black Reconstruction in America: An Essay Toward a History Of the Part Which Black Folk Played in the Attempt To Reconstruct Democracy In America, 1860–1880*, (N.Y.: Harcourt, Brace & Co., 1935), 746 pp. This is Du Bois' *magnum opus* as he knew and as the world now acknowledges. He was writing on themes related to what became this book since the close of the 19th century; with this book he revolutionized the historical profession in the United States. He acknowledged the earlier significant work by John R. Lynch, Alrutheus A. Taylor, and Carter G. Woodson, as well as Frederic Bancroft, John Eaton, Charles Edward Russell, and Augustus F. Beard, and others, and noted that for a variety of reasons—including the fact that at that time Southern major libraries and archives were closed to Black scholars—there were many documentary sources that he had not examined. Yet, he believed that the story as he told it was substantially true and the work of the following 40 years has amply vindicated him. Essentially, he showed the active role of Black people during and after the Civil War and demonstrated that the conventional "Tragic Era" picture of the Reconstruction period (to cite the title of Claude G.

Bowers' popularization of that picture) was a travesty upon truth stemming out of racism and seeking to rationalize an atrocious *status quo*. The positive and democratic content of the strivings of Southern Black people in the decade after Appomattox is presented in detail, in state after state; the terror, propaganda, chauvinism, violence, and fraud with which those efforts were undone are shown mostly from official documents. The final chapter of this work, "The Propaganda of History," remains a classic condemnation of the chauvinism of dominant U.S. historiography, that is, alas, by no means altogether outdated.

1965. *Black Folk Then And Now: An Essay in The History and Sociology of the Negro Race* (New York: Henry Holt & Co. 1939), 401 pp. In the conclusion to his preface to *The Negro* (1915) Du Bois had written: "Manifestly so short a story must be mainly conclusions and generalizations with but meagre indication of authorities and under-lying arguments. Possibly, if the Public will, a later and larger book may be more satisfactory on these points." This 1939 book is what Du Bois had in mind; as he writes in its preface, (dated Atlanta University, May, 1939) some of the 1915 study was incorporated but, he added, the 1939 effort "for the most part is an entirely new production."

The work contains 16 chapters and an extensive bibliography. The first nine chapters offer a history of Africa and its early civilization, the coming of modern slavery and the slave trade and the movement for the abolition of both. Two chapters treat the Black people in the United States and in Europe contemporaneously, while four chapters treat Africa at that time, especially land-ownership, the working masses, systems of political control and of education. A final chapter, "The Future of World Democracy," deals with little-known uprisings and a major strike in the first third of the 20th century; its concluding lines are:

> The proletariat of the world consists not simply of white European and American workers but overwhelmingly of the dark workers of Asia, Africa, the islands of the sea, and South and Central America. These are the ones who are supporting a superstructure of wealth, luxury, and extravagance. It is the rise of these people that is the rise of the world. The problem of the twentieth century is the problem of the color line.

1966. *Dusk of Dawn: An Essay Toward an Autobiography of a Race Concept* (New York: Harcourt, Brace & Co., 1940), 334 pp.* With the coming of his seventieth year, Du Bois produced several autobiographical essays. In 1938 and 1939, with the encouragement of his friend, Alfred Harcourt, he worked on the above book, copies of which became available early in August, 1940. He conceived of this book, as he says in its "Apology," "to be not so much my autobiography as the autobiography of a concept of race. ... " His *Souls* and *Darkwater*, he remarks, "were written in tears and blood," but this book, while "set down no less determinedly" is nevertheless written "with wider hope in some more benign fluid." Hence, he adds, "I have not hesitated in calling it 'Dusk of Dawn'."

The biographical data are given and his own thoughts and feelings —and what influenced them—are displayed, often in exceptionally beautiful writing. In the period of this book, he embraced a generally socialist outlook but with it went an attitude of opposition to the Communist Party of the United States. The attitude towards the U.S.S.R. remained warm and hopeful; from the time of the Revolution in 1917 until his death, it was never to be less. On the final page occurs a paragraph which is particularly revealing of his temperament and nature:

> Perhaps above all I am proud of a straightforward clearness of reason, in part a gift of the gods, but also to no small degree due to scientific training and inner discipline. By means of this I have met life face to face, I have loved a fight and I have realized that Love is God and Work is His prophet; that His ministers are Age and Death.

1967. *Color and Democracy: Colonies and Peace* (New York: Harcourt, Brace & Co., 1945), 143 pp. The preface of this volume is dated New York, January 1, 1945. Du Bois was now back with the NAACP as Director of Special Research. The premise of the book was that with the world to come after the Second World War, "the majority of the inhabitants of earth, who happen for the most part to be colored, must be regarded as having the right and the capacity to share in human progress and to become co-partners in that democracy which alone can ensure peace among men, by the abolition of poverty, the education of the masses, protection from disease, and the scientific treatment of crime." The thought is developed that "colonies are the slums of the

---

*Pages 34 through 40 are reprinted in William Bentinck-Smith, ed., *The Harvard Book* (Cambridge, Mass.; Harvard University Press, 1953) pp. 226–230.

world" (p. 17) and the slum dwellers are in righteous rebellion. If these slums are not ended, there will be not only these "justifiable revolts" but also "recurring wars of envy and greed because of the present inequitable distribution of gain among civilized nations" (p. 57). Statements from the Western Allies and their propositions—as those issuing from Dumbarton Oaks—show a failure to consider this question of colonialism and the need for liberation; this is fatal, for, "so long as colonial imperialism exists, there can be neither peace on earth nor good will toward men" (p. 103). The U.S.S.R. is hailed for having released the energies of the masses and faced frontally the problem of poverty. "It has not, like most nations, without effort to solve it, declared the insolubility of the problem of the poor, and above all, it has not falsely placed on the poor the blame of their wretched conditions" (p. 116).

1968. *The World And Africa: An Inquiry Into the Part Which Africa Has Played In World History* (New York: Viking Press, 1947), 276 pp. The enlarged edition (New York: International Publishers, 1965), 368 pp. contains the articles on Africa written for the *National Guardian* in the 1950's and annotated earlier (Nos. 1781–1785).

The foreword is dated New York, May, 1946; it refers to the earlier works, *The Negro* and *Black Folk*, but adds that the world has so changed in the decade since the latter had been written that it might be useful to attempt "a history of the world written from the African point of view." In this foreword he offers a brief bibliography of his main sources; they include the works of William Howitt in the 19th century, Robert Briffault, George Padmore, Anna Graves, Eric Williams, Wilson Williams, Rayford Logan, Chapman Cohen, Reginald Coupland, E. D. Moore (particularly), Edwin W. Smith, C. G. Seligmann, A. F. Chamberlain, W. M. Petrie, Alexander Moret, Leo Frobenius, R. S. Rattray, Maurice Delafosse, Leonard Barnes, and Leo Hansberry (who "has been of greatest help to me"). "I have also made bold to repeat the testimony of Karl Marx, whom I regard as the greatest of modern philosophers, and I have not been deterred by the witch-hunting which always follows mention of his name." Appreciation also is expressed to "my assistant, Dr. Irene Diggs."

The book begins with a consideration of the meaning of the just concluded worldwide war; it moves on to an analysis of the impact of European colonialism, especially in Africa, in the past two centuries; of the "rape of Africa" in the four centuries beginning with the mid-15th century; then a consideration of what the Africa thus ravished had been; a history of Egypt, of West Africa, Central Africa, of Asia in Africa to about 1500 *a.d.*, the Black Sudan, and finally, an essay into "the future of the darker races" whose coming liberation is "indispensable to the fertilizing of the universal soil of mankind" (p. 260). The final thought, "there can be no perfect democracy curtailed by color, race, or poverty. But with all we accomplish all, even Peace."

1969. *In Battle For Peace: The Story Of My 83rd Birthday, with comment by Shirley Graham* (New York: Masses & Mainstream Publishers, 1952), 192 pp. There was also a special edition of this book (printed in 200 copies) which contained in addition to the above, the text of the doctor's speech at his 83rd Birthday Dinner held in New York City; and essays by Langston Hughes and Herbert Aptheker. This volume tells the story of the indictment of Du Bois—and four codefendants—as unregistered foreign agents under the McCormick Act, his arraignment and fingerprinting in February, 1951, his trial in November, 1951, and the acquittal. As background the book tells of the Council on African Affairs, various peace congresses of the 1940's, the work of the Peace Information Center, headed by the Doctor, the campaign for signatures to the Stockholm pledge for outlawry of atomic weapons (2,500,000 Americans signed), and his Senatorial campaign in 1950. The role of O. John Rogge as informer, the efforts of the NAACP leadership to spread rumors of his "guilt" as explaining their refusal to assist his defense, the offer by the government of a "deal" and Du Bois' rejection, and the campaign to arouse world opinion—in which the Doctor and Shirley Graham (his wife) took leading roles—make up the substance of this rousing book. Dr. Du Bois' directed acquittal was one of the first successes scored against reaction in the decade of the fearful fifties.

1970. *The Black Flame: A Trilogy*: (New York: Mainstream Publishers), Book One; *The Ordeal of Mansart* (1957), 316 pp., Book Two: *Mansart Builds a School* (1959), 367 pp., Book Three: *Worlds of Color* (1961), 349 pp. These three volumes tell Du Bois' view of what it meant to be a Black man in the United States from 1876 to 1956. Historic figures—many of whom he knew well—appear under their own names, from Booker T. Washington to Franklin Delano Roosevelt, from William Monroe Trotter to Harry Hopkins, from Florence Kelley to Kwame Nkrumah. Actual quotations from speeches, newspapers, books make the three volumes a goldmine of information; all this is ensconced within the life of Manuel Mansart, who in his thinking, is an approximation of Du Bois. In many ways this trilogy tells more of Du Bois—of what Du Bois thought about himself and the world in which he lived—than his more formal autobiographies which were published earlier and which were to be published after his death. These 1,100 pages were written by him in their first draft from 1955 through 1957; that is to say, when he was eighty-seven to eighty-nine years old.

1970a. *Africa: An Essay Toward a History of the Continent of Africa and its Inhabitants* (Moscow, 1961), 357 pp. This was written in 1959; the compiler of this volume has not seen a copy; it was published in Russian.

1971. *An ABC of Color: Selections From Over a Half Century of the Writings of W. E. B. Du Bois* (Berlin: Seven Seas Publishers, 1963) 213 pp; and, (New York: International Publishers, 1969), 215 pp. These editions are identical in text; the Berlin edition has an introduction by Kay Pankey; the New York edition has an introduction by John O. Killens, and a brief index. The International edition's title is slightly different and is more accurate; it reads: "Selections chosen by the author from over a half century of his Writings." It is a fact that Du Bois did the choosing—mostly from the *Crisis*; it may be added that he did this twice for the manuscript was apparently lost in the first mailing and he mailed a second selection to Germany himself from England, while he was on his way, late in 1961, to Ghana. Copies of the finished book actually reached him in Ghana about a month prior to his death in August, 1963.

The volume contains very few selections from his writings in the 1930's, none from the 1940's, but there is a section of approximately 12 pages from the 1950's.

1972. The *Autobiography of W. E. B. Du Bois: A Soliloquy on Viewing my Life from the Last Decade of its First Century* (New York: International Publishers, 1968), 448 pp. The basic draft of the book was written by Du Bois in his ninetieth year—1958–1959; it was revised by him during 1960 and 1961 and taken with him to Ghana. Somewhat shortened versions were published in their respective languages in 1964 and 1965 in the German Democratic Republic, the U.S.S.R., and the People's Republic of China. After the coup in 1966 in Ghana, the original manuscript reached the hands of its editor (the present writer) and it was published two years later in full, and as Du Bois wrote it, with additions by the editor of a biographical, historical, and bibliographical nature in appendices; plus a photographic section. Changes by the editor in the manuscript were solely of a technical nature

—translations, corrections of a date, or the completion of a name and the like. (This is again made explicit—it is stated in the book's preface—because certain people have stated in print that the manuscript had been altered by the editor; these statements were made without inquiry, were totally gratuitous and false.)

This volume is more directly an autobiography than the earlier *Dusk of Dawn*, and while there is necessarily some repetition, it is minor. It is especially full on the period from his rejoining of the NAACP to the completion of his extended journey in 1958–1959, when he spent considerable time in the Soviet Union and in the People's Republic of China.

ADDENDUM

1973. In the paragraph preceding number 1834, it is stated that Dr. Du Bois testified four times before Congressional Committees. After this volume was in galleys, the printed text of his testimony on a fifth occasion was found. The Committee on Industrial Expositions of the United States Senate held hearings in February, 1912 on the proposition by Black people in Georgia to hold in that State an exposition celebrating the 50th anniversary of the emancipation of slaves. The proposal did not come to fruition but one of those testifying for it was Du Bois; he appeared before the Committee on February 2 and presented his ideas for an exhibition which might not only be offered in Georgia but which could then be shown in other parts of the nation. He projected an exhibit which, commencing with Africa, would convey something of the history, sociology, struggles, organizations and present conditions of the Afro-American people. This is printed in *Congressional Record*, April 2, 1912, pp. 4374–75.

1974. Item number 47 records the publication of a piece by Du Bois in the Boston *Courant*; there notice was taken of the fact that Du Bois had stated in his *Autobiography* that his writings frequently appeared in that newspaper—files of which no longer exist. After this volume was in pages another contribution in that newspaper was found. This is entitled "Does Education Pay?". The clipping does not give the date of publication, but accompanying the printed copy is a notation by Du Bois, made at the time and reading: "Delivered before the National Colored League in Boston, March 10, 1891." This essay comes to about 8,500 words and the copy is complete except for one missing page of perhaps 750 words.

The speech itself is of the greatest interest for it shows that as of this very early date, Du Bois was publicly arguing against any special limitation upon the education offered Black people; was insisting that a purely vocational form of education insulted them and that there was nothing more deeply "practical" than the fullest and highest form of education. It is in this speech that there first appears an oft-repeated thought—and phrase—"Never make the mistake of thinking that the object of being a man is to make a carpenter—the object of being a carpenter is to be a man."

1975. In a magazine called *Palms,* published in Guadalajara, Mexico, in a special issue October, 1926 (IV, No. 1) containing poetry by Afro-Americans and edited by Countee Cullen, there were two poems by Du Bois (pp. 18–19). One, of twenty lines, was entitled "The Song of America"; it was reprinted in the N. Y. *Herald Tribune* of October 10, 1926, not, as incorrectly stated earlier in this work (No. 240), in 1928. The second is entitled simply "Poem" and contains three stanzas of four lines each; the theme is that "Truth" is "Death's destruction."

In 1904, the American Economic Association appointed a Special Committee on the Economic Position of the Negro; it consisted of the Cornell Professor and Census chief, Walter F. Willcox, his assistant, H. T. Newcomb, the Harvard Professor, William Z. Ripley, the Mississippi planter, A. H. Stone, and Du Bois. All five men signed a report on "The Economic Position of the American Negro," detailing occupations, income, etc., which was published in American Economic Association, *Publications*, February, 1905, 3rd series, number 1, pp. 216-221.

In May, 1931, a dinner in honor of James Weldon Johnson, on his impending 60th birthday, and his departure from the NAACP to take up teaching duties at Fisk, was given in New York City. On that occasion, Du Bois delivered a brief speech evaluating Johnson's life and personality. Further details and the text of the speech will be found in H. Aptheker, ed., "Du Bois on James Weldon Johnson," in *The Journal of Negro History* (July, 1967), LII, pp. 224-27.

CHAPTER IX

INDEX OF BOOKS NOTED BY DU BOIS

(Note to the user; all references are to the item number in the text.)

Battle, Charles A., *Negroes on the Island of Rhode Island* (Newport; n. p., 1932), 968

Beckwith, Martha W., *Black Roadways* (Chapel Hill: University of North Carolina Press, 1929), 863

Belfrage, Cedric, *Seeds of Destruction* (New York: Cameron & Kahn, 1954), 1778

Bellegarde, Dantés, *Pour Une Haiti Heureusse* (Port-au-Prince: Cheraquit, 1929), 863

————, *L'Occupation Americain D'Haiti, Les Consequences Morales et Economiques* (Port-au-Prince: Cheraquit, 1929), 863

Beveridge, William, *Social Insurance: Report* (London: H. M. Stationery Office, 1942), 1396

Blatchford, Robert, *Not Guilty* (New York: Vanguard, 1927), 772

Boas, Franz, *The Mind of Primitive Man* (New York: Macmillan, 1911), 503

Bolton, Dorothy G. and Harry T. Burleigh, *The Old Songs Hymnal* (New York: Century, 1929), 867

Bond, Horace Mann, *Negro Education in Alabama: A Study in Cotton and Steel* (Washington: Associated Publishers, 1939), 282, 1206

Bontemps, Arna, *God Sends Sunday* (New York: Harcourt, Brace, 1931), 924

————, and Langston Hughes, *Popo and Fifina* (New York: Macmillan, 1932), 968

Botkin, Benjamin A., ed., *Folk-Say: A Regional Miscellany* (Norman: University of Oklahoma Press, 1932), 956

Boudin, Louis, *Socialism and War* (New York: New Review Publishing Assoc., 1915), 578

Bradford, Roark, *This Side of Jordan* (New York: Harper, 1929), 844

Brady, Robert A., *Business as a System of Power* (New York: Columbia University Press, 1943), 1077

————, *The Rationalization Movement in Germany* (Berkeley: University of California Press, 1193)

Bragg, G. F., *Men of Maryland* (Baltimore: published by author, 1914), 548

Braithwaite, W. S., ed., *Anthology of Magazine Verse for 1914* (Boston: published by author, 1914), 548

————, *The Anthology of Magazine Verse for 1925* (Boston: Brimmer, 1925), 738

————, *Anthology of Magazine Verse, 14th edition* (Boston: Brimmer, 1926), 1926), 756

————, *Anthology of Magazine Verse, 15th edition* (Boston: Brimmer, 1927), 797

Brawley, Benjamin, *Short History of the American Negro* (New York: Macmillan, 1913), 523

————, *A Short History of the American Negro* (New York: Macmillan, 1931; 3rd revised edition), 937

Brown, George W., *The Economic History of Liberia* (Washington: Associated Publishers, 1941), 1072

Brown, Hallie Q., *Homespun Heroines* (Xenia, Ohio: privately printed, 1927), 768

Brown, Ina C., *Socio-Economic Approach to Educational Problems* (Washington: U.S. Office of Education, 1942), 1418

Brown, Sterling A., *Southern Road* (New York: Harcourt, Brace, 1932), 949

Bruce, John E., *Short Biographical Sketches: Eminent Negro Men and Women* (Yonkers, N.Y.: Gazette Press, 1910), 486

Buckmaster, Henrietta, *Let My People Go* (New York: Harper, 1941), 1316

Buell, Raymond L., *The Native Problem in Africa* (New York: Macmillan, 2 vols.; 1928), 241, 833

Bullock, Ralph W., *In Spite of Handicaps* (New York: Association Press, 1927), 784

Burton, Charles W., *Living Conditions among Negroes in the Ninth Ward* [of New Haven] (New Haven: New Haven Civic Federation, 1913), 536

Butler, Alpheus, *Make Way for Happiness* (Boston: Christopher, 1932), 968

Byars, J.C., ed., *Black and White* (Washington: Crane Press, 1927), 797

Caillaux, Joseph, *Agadir* (Paris: Michel, 1920), 195

Caliver, Ambrose, comp., *Bibliography on Education of the Negro, 1928-1930* (Washington: U.S. Office of Education, 1931), 946

Carpenter, Marie, *The Treatment of the Negro in American History School Text-Books* (Madison, Wis.: Banta Publishing, 1941), 1316

Carpenter, Niles, *Nationality, Color and Economic Opportunity in Buffalo* (Buffalo: University of Buffalo Studies, Vol. V, No. 4, 1927), 784

Carson, W. J., *The Coming of Industry to the South* (Philadelphia: American Academy of Political and Social Science, 1931), 919

Cather, Willa, *Sapphira and the Slave Girl* (New York: Knopf, 1941), 1316

Cayton, Horace and George S.

Mitchell, *Black Workers and the New Unions* (Chapel Hill: University of North Carolina Press, 1939), 1208

Cendras Blaise, *The African Saga* (New York: Payson & Clarke, 1927), 797, 1122

————, *Little Black Stories for Little White Children* (New York: Payson & Clarke, 1929), 867

Childs, Marquis, *Sweden: The Middle Way* (New Haven: Yale University Press, 1936), 1114

Clarke, Edwin L., *The Art of Straight Thinking* (New York: Appleton, 1929), 863

Cocks, F. Seymour, *E. D. Morel: The Man and His Work* (London: Allen & Unwin, 1921), 196

Committee on Africa, *The War and Peace Aims, The Atlantic Charter and Africa from An American Viewpoint* (New York: Africa Bureau, 1942), 299

Cook, Mercer, *Five French Negro Authors* (Washington: Associated Publishers, 1943), 1087

Cooley, Rossa B., *Homes of the Freed* (New York: New Republic, 1926), 756

Corbett, M. N., *The Harp of Ethiopia* (Nashville: National Baptist Publications Board, 1914), 548

Corkey, Alexander, *The Testing Fire* (New York: H. K. Fly Co., 1912), 507

Cromwell, John W., *The Negro in American History* (Washington: American Negro Academy, 1914), 536

Cromwell, Otelia, Lorenzo D. Turner, Eva B. Dykes, eds., *Readings from Negro Authors for Schools and Colleges with a Bibliography of Negro Literature* (New York: Harcourt, Brace, 1931), 937

the Native Peoples of the South-west (Sydney: Australasian Publishing, 1943), 1436 (pamphlet)

Ellis, George W., *Negro Culture in West Africa* (New York: Neale, 1914), 548

Embree, Edwin R., *Brown America* (New York: Viking, 1931), 931

————, *Indians of the Americas* (Boston: Houghton Mifflin, 1939) 1058

————, et al., *Island India Goes to School* (Chicago: University of Chicago Press, 1934), 1115

Fabian Society, *The Kenya Controversy* (London: the Society, 1949), 1673

Fauset, Arthur Huff, *For Freedom: A Biographical Story of the American Negro*, (Philadelphia: Franklin Publishers, 1928), 821

Fauset, Jessie R., *Plum Bun* (New York: Stokes, 1929), 246, 840

————, *The Chinaberry Tree* (New York: Stokes, 1932), 946

Feldman, Herman, *Racial Factors in American Industry* (New York: Harper, 1931), 919

Ferris, William H., *The African Abroad* (New Haven: Tuttle, Morehouse & Taylor, 1913, 2 vols.), 531

Feuchtwanger, Lion *'Tis Folly To Be Wise* (New York: Messner, 1953), 398

Firbank, Ronald, *Prancing Nigger* (New York: Brentano, 1924), 713

Fishberg, Maurice, *The Jews: A Study of Race and Environment* (New York: Scribner, 1911), 490

Fisher, Rudolph, *The Walls of Jerico* (New York: Knopf, 1928), 824

Fisher, W. A., *Seventy Negro Spirituals* (New York: Ditson, 1926), 1090

Fleming, Walter L., *Freedman's Savings Bank* (Chapel Hill; University of North Carolina Press, 1927), 790

Foner, Philip S., ed., *The Life and Writings of Frederick Douglass* (New York: International Publishers, 1950, Vols. I-II), 372

Forster, E. M., *A Passage to India* (London: Arnold, 1924), 714c

Frank, Waldo, *South American Journey* (New York: Duell, Sloan & Pearce, 1943), 1396

Frazier, E. Franklin, *The Negro Family in Chicago* (Chicago: University of Chicago Press, 1931), 942

————, *The Negro Family in the United States* (Chicago: University of Chicago, 1939), 283, 1206

————, *The Black Bourgeoisie* (Glencoe, Ill.: Free Press, 1957; first published in France in 1955), 1804

George, Henry, *Progress and Poverty* (New York: Doubleday & McClure, 1899, new edition), 657

Georges-Gaulis, Berthe, *La France au Maroc* (Paris: Colin, 1920), 195

Gide, André, *Travels in the Congo* (New York: Knopf, 1929), 863

Gilligan, F. J., *Negro Workers in Free America* (New York: Paulist Press, 1939, pamphlet), 1061

Gordon, Taylor (pseudonym for Muriel Draper), *Born To Be* (New York: Covici-Friede, 1929), 877

Graeber, I. et al., *Jews in a Gentile World* (New York: Macmillan, 1942), 296

Graham, Effie, *The Passin'-On Party* (Chicago: McClurg, 1912), 526

Graham, Lorenz, *How God Fix Jonah* (New York: Reynal & Hitchcock, 1946), 1553

Graham, Marcus, ed., *The Anthology of Revolutionary Poetry* (New York: Active Press, 1929), 863

Graham, Shirley, *George Washington Carver* (New York: Messner, 1941), 1437

————, *Paul Robeson* (New York: Messner, 1946), 1553

Graves, Anna, *Benevenuto Cellini Had No Prejudice Against Bronze,* (Baltimore: Waverly Press, 1943), 1396

Gray, Wood, *The Hidden Civil War* (New York: Viking, 1942), 1396

Green, Elizabeth L., *The Negro in Contemporary American Literature* (Chapel Hill: University of North Carolina Press, 1928), 833

Greene, Lorenzo J., and Carter G. Woodson, *The Negro Wage Earner* (Washington: Associated Publishers, 1931), 251

Gregg, Richard B., *Gandhiji's Satyagraha or Non-Violent Resistance* (Triplicane, Madras: Ganesan, 1930), 894

Grimke, Archibald H., *The Ballotless Victim of One-Party Government* (Washington: American Negro Academy, 1913), 532

————, *The Ultimate Criminal* (Washington: American Negro Academy, 1915, pamphlet), 560

Gruening, Ernest, ed., *These United States* (New York: Boni & Liveright, 1929, 2 vols.), 722

Gulick, S. L., *The American-Japanese Problem* (New York: Scribner, 1914), 548

Gunther, John, *Inside Africa* (New York: Harper, 1955), 420

————, *Inside Europe* (New York: Harper, 1936), 1193

Hammond, L. H., *In Black and White: An Interpretation of Southern Life* (New York: Revel, 1914), 542

Handy, William C., *Blues* (New York: Boni, 1926), 1090

Hankins, Frank H., *The Racial Basis of Civilization* (New York: Knopf, 1928) 812

Harben, W. N., *Mam 'Linda* (New York: Harper, 1907), 469

Hare, Maud Cuney, *Norris Wright Cuney* (New York: Crisis Publishing Company, 1913), 531

Harmon, J. J., A. G. Lindsay and C. G. Woodson, *The Negro as a Business Man* (Washington: Associated Publishers, 1929), 867

Harris, Abram L., *Negro Population in Minneapolis* (Minneapolis: Urban League, 1927), 784

Hart, Albert Bushnell, *Southern South* (New York: Appleton, 1909), 483

Hayes, Arthur Garfield, *Let Freedom Ring* (New York: Boni & Liveright), 812

Helm, MacKinley, *Angel Mo' and Her Son, Roland Hayes* (Boston: Houghton Mifflin, 1942), 1080

Herbst, Alma, *The Negro in the Slaughtering and Meat-Packing Industry* (Boston: Houghton Mifflin, 1932), 968

Herskovits, Melville J., *The Myth of the Negro Past* (New York: Harper, 1941), 290, 294

————, *The American Negro* (New York: Knopf, 1928), 809

Heywood, Chester D., *The Story of the 371st Regiment* (Worcester, Mass.: Commonwealth Press, 1929), 867

Heywood, Du Bose, *Mamba's Daughters* (New York: Doubleday, Doran, 1929), 840

Hibben, Paxton, *Henry Ward Beecher* (New York: Doran, 1927), 794

Hill, J. L., *Negro: National Asset or Liability* (New York: Literary Associates, 1931), 251

Hill, Leslie P., *Toussaint L'Ouverture* (Boston: Christopher, 1928), 812

Hill, T. Arnold, *Report of the West Virginia Bureau of Negro Welfare and Statistics* (Morgantown: The Bureau, 1927), 784

Village, (Urbana: University of Illinois Press, 1947), 1590

Lewis, Roscoe E., ed., *The Negro in Virginia* (New York: Hastings House, 1940), 1068

Lewis, Sinclair, *It Can't Happen Here* (New York: Doubleday, 1935), 1112

Leyburn, James G., *The Haitian People* (New Haven: Yale University Press, 1942), 295

Leys, Norman, *Kenya: A Study of English East Africa* (London: Leonard and Virginia Woolf at Hogarth Press, 1925), 737

Lindbergh, Anne Morrow, *The Wave of the Future* (New York: Harcourt, Brace, 1940), 1067

Linton, Ralph, ed., *Most of the World: The Peoples of Africa, Latin America and the East Today* (New York: Columbia University Press, 1949), 363

Locke, Alain and Montgomery Gregory, eds., *Plays of Negro Life* (New York: Harper, 1927), 790

Locke, Alain, ed., *The New Negro* (New York: Boni & Liveright, 1925), 735

———, *Four Negro Poets* (New York: Simon & Schuster, 1927), 772

———, *The Negro in Art* (Washington: Associates in Negro Folk Education, 1940), 1068, 1316

Logan, Rayford W., *The Diplomatic Relations of the United States with Haiti* (Chapel Hill: University of North Carolina Press, 1941), 1316

———, *The African Mandates in World Politics* (Washington: Public Affairs Press, 1950), 1708

Loggins, Vernon, *The Negro Author: His Development in America* (New York: Columbia University Press, 1931), 937

Lundberg, Ferdinand, *America's*

Sixty Families (New York: Vanguard, 1937), 1513

Lynch, John R., *Facts of Reconstruction* (New York: Neale, 1913), 533

Lynd, Robert S. and Helen M. Lynd, *Middletown* (New York: Harcourt, Brace, 1929), 1135

Lynd, Robert S., *Knowledge For What?* (Princeton: Princeton University Press, 1939), 1058

MacCulloh, John A. ed., *The Mythology of All Races*, in 13 volumes; Du Bois reviewed volume two, containing "Armenian Mythology," by M. H. Amanikian and "African Mythology," by Alice Werner (Boston: Marshall Jones Co., 1925), 229

Manning, Joseph C., *The Fade-Out of Popularism* (New York: T. Hebbons, 1928), 815

Marks, Jeannette, *Thirteen Days* (New York, Boni, 1929), 844

Marot, Helen, *American Labor Unions* (New York: Holt, 1914), 578

Marshall, Harriett G., *The Story of Haiti* (Boston: Christopher, 1930), 886

Maugham, R. C., *The Republic of Liberia* (New York: Scribner, 1920), 195

Mayo, Marion J., *The Mental Capacity of the American Negro* (New York: The Science Press, 1913), 174

Mazyck, Walter, *George Washington and the Negro* (Washington: Associated Publishers, 1932), 946

McAlpin, E. A., ed., *Prize Sermons* (New York: Macmillan, 1932), 974

McCulloch, James E., ed., *The Human Way: Addresses on Race Problems at the Southern Sociological Congress* (Atlanta: published by the congress, 1913), 535

————, *The American Race Problem* (New York: Crowell, 1927), 777

Rice, Madeline R., *American Catholic Church in the Slavery Controversy* (New York: Columbia University Press, 1944), 307

Riley, B. F., *The White Man's Burden* (Birmingham: privately printed, 1911), 503

Roberts, J. T., *Character Sketch of the Late J. Claudius May* (London: Wesley Church, 1912), 526

Robertson, William J., *The Changing South* (New York: Boni & Liveright, 1928), 800

Robeson, Eslanda, *Biography of Paul Robeson* (New York: Harper, 1930), 891

Rogers, J. A., *From 'Superman' to Man* (New York: Lenox, 1924), 713

————, *World's Greatest Men of African Descent* (New York: published by author, 1931), 946

Royce, Josiah, *Race Questions and Other American Problems* (New York: Macmillan, 1908), 578

Rubinstein, Annette, *The Great Tradition* (New York: Citadel, 1954), 1764

Russell, Charles E., *Story of Wendell Phillips* (Chicago: Kerr, 1914), 548

————, *Blaine of Maine* (New York: Cosmopolitan Book, 1931), 957

————, *Bare Hands and Stone Walls* (New York: Scribner, 1933), 1010

Sachs, E., *The Choice Before Us* (New York: Philosophical Library, 1952), 396

Sale, John B., *The Tree Named John* (Chapel Hill: University of North Carolina Press, 1929), 863

Samuelson, R. C., *Long, Long Ago* (Durban, South Africa: 1929), 877

Scarborough, Dorothy, *On the Trail of Negro Folk Songs* (Cambridge: Harvard University Press, 1925), 226

Schmalhausen, Samuel, *Humanizing Education* (New York: New Education, 1927), 772

Scott, O. A., *Home Buyer's Guide and Calculator* (Kansas City, Mo.: privately published, 1927), 777

Schuyler, George S., *Slaves Today* (New York: Brewer, Warren & Putnam, 1931), 937

————, *Black No More* (New York: Macauley, 1931), 908

Seabrook, William C., *The Magic Island* (New York: Harcourt, Brace, 1929), 844

Sharp, Evelyn, *The African Child* (London: Longmans, 1931), 255, 961

Siegfried, André, *America Comes of Age* (New York: Harcourt, Brace, 1927), 765

Simon, Kathleen, *Slavery* (London: Hodden & Stoughton, 1929), 877

Sinclair, William, *The Aftermath of Slavery* (Boston: Small, Maynard, 1905), 129

Skaggs, William H., *The Southern Oligarchy* (New York: Devin-Adair, 1924), 714c

Smith, Lillian, *Strange Fruit* (New York: Reynal & Hitchcok, 1944), 1439

Smith, William B., *The Color Line* (New York: McClure, Phillips, 1905), 117

Southern Commission on Study of Lynching, *The Mob Murder of S. S. Mincey* (Atlanta: by the Commission, 1932), 961

Spencer, Samuel R., Jr., *Booker T. Washington and the Negro's Place in American Life* (Boston: Little, Brown, 1955), 421

Spengler, Oswald, *The Hour of Decision* (New York: Knopf, 1933), 1085

CHAPTER X

INDEX OF PROPER NAMES

(Note to the user: all references are to the item number in the text.)

898, 916, 919, 922, 936, 959, 979,
987, 989, 1005, 1014, 1046, 1061,
1066, 1081, 1108, 1133, 1148,
1218, 1249, 1261, 1269, 1330,
1359, 1363, 1390, 1432, 1435,
1439, 1480, 1544, 1561, 1569,
1613, 1617, 1792, 1834, 1838,
1863, 1884, 1901, 1904, 1905,
1913, 1914, 1933, 1943, 1964
South Africa, 336, 396, 457, 462,
481, 483, 487, 509, 525, 666, 670,
781, 795, 806, 830, 892, 956,
1007, 1059, 1064, 1069, 1070,
1088, 1211a, 1272, 1335, 1449,
1501, 1559, 1634, 1642, 1644,
1648, 1656, 1657, 1663, 1674,
1686, 1693, 1696, 1714, 1823
South America 523, 636, 769, 780,
806, 831, 896, 931, 1070, 1075,
1576, 1753, 1965
South Atlantic Quarterly 538
South Carolina 486, 489, 541, 550,
714a, 722, 791, 873, 915, 1072
South Carolina legislature 1429
South Korea 1819
South Today 1083
Southern Commission on Lynching
912, 936, 961
Southern Conference for Human
Welfare 1059, 1061, 1071, 1230,
1249, 1425
Southern Education Board 534
Southern Historical Association 1071
Southern Negro Youth Congress
333a, 1392, 1437, 1550, 1551,
1821, 1943
Southern News Almanac 1061
Southern Sociological Congress
524, 535, 537
Southern Sociological Society 285
Southern Workman 53, 58, 62, 72-78,
768, 1911
Southwest Africa 1662
Southwestern Christian Advocate
567, 633
Soviet Russia Today 325, 342, 356,
362, 366
Soviet-Nazi Pact 1303

Spain 704, 710, 850, 913, 933,
1143, 1612, 1963
Spanish-American War 850, 1299
Spanish Inquisition 1151
Spargo, John 158, 464
Spaulding, Charles C. 550
Spelman College 86, 848
Spelman Messinger 86
Spencer, Samuel R. 421
Spengler, Otto 918, 1085
Spero, Sterling 251, 942
Spiller, G. 1870
Spingarn, Arthur B. 951, 1122
Spingarn, Joel E. 496, 523, 581, 594,
840, 905, 909, 914, 1000, 1057,
1938
Spingarn Award 552, 568, 692, 948
Spivak, John 1193
Spotlight on Africa 1696-1698
Springfield, Massachusetts 551,
1419
Springfield, Missouri 579, 645
Springfield, Ohio 694
Springfield (Mass.) *Daily Republi-
can* 104, 141a, 170a, 460, 1853
Springfield (Ohio) *Sun* 103
Staatszeitung Herold 272
Stafford, A. F. 534
Stalin, Joseph 423, 1222, 1302,
1516, 1632, 1764
Stalingrad, Battle of 1444
Standard Life Insurance Company 556,
720
Stanford, Kentucky 490
Stanford University 1484
"Star of Ethiopia" 224, 565,
1936, 1937
Starks, George S. 830
Starr, Frederick 534, 1072
Starr, Pony 496
Stassen, Harold 1611
Steffens, Lincoln 1423
Stein, Gertrude 486
Steiner, Jesse F. 790
Stephenson, Gilbert T. 538
Stephenson, John 318a
Sterling-Towner Education Bill
663, 668, 673, 694, 703, 717, 721

CHAPTER XI

SUBJECT INDEX

(Note to the user: all references are to the item number in the text.)